THE HALAKHAH
AN ENCYCLOPAEDIA
OF THE LAW OF JUDAISM

VOLUME III

THE BRILL REFERENCE LIBRARY
OF
ANCIENT JUDAISM

Founding Editor

JACOB NEUSNER

Editors

ALAN J. AVERY-PECK
WILLIAM SCOTT GREEN
GÜNTER STEMBERGER
ITHAMAR GRUENWALD
JOSÉ FAUR

VOLUME 1/III

THE HALAKHAH

AN ENCYCLOPAEDIA OF THE LAW OF JUDAISM

VOLUME III

WITHIN ISRAEL'S SOCIAL ORDER

BY

JACOB NEUSNER

BRILL
LEIDEN · BOSTON · KÖLN
2000

This book is printed on acid-free paper.

Library of Congress Cataloging-in-Publication Data

Neusner, Jacob, 1932–
　　The Halakhah : an encyclopaedia of the law of Judaism / by Jacob Neusner.
　　　　p.　cm. — (The Brill reference library of ancient Judaism, ISSN 1566-1237 ; vol. 1/1–)
　　Includes bibliographical references and index.
　　Contents: v. 1. Between Israel and God.
　　ISBN 9004116176 (set : cloth : alk. paper) — ISBN 9004116117 (v. 1 : cloth : alk. paper) — ISBN 9004116125 (v. 2 : alk. paper) — ISBN 9004116113 (v. 3 : alk. paper) — ISBN 9004116141 (v. 4 : alk. paper) — ISBN 9004116168 (v. 5 : alk. paper)
　　1. Jewish law—Encyclopedias.　2. Judaism—Customs and practices—Encyclopedias.　3. Mishnah—Criticism, interpretation, etc.　4. Tosefta—Criticism, interpretation, etc.　I. Title.　II. Series
BM520.4.N48　　2000
296.1'8'03—dc21
　　　　　　　　　　　　　　　　　　　　　　　　　　00–039826
　　　　　　　　　　　　　　　　　　　　　　　　　　　　CIP

Die Deutsche Bibliothek - CIP-Einheitsaufnahme

Neusner, Jacob:
The halakhah : an encyclopaedia of the law of Judaism / by Jacob Neusner. – Leiden ; Boston ; Köln : Brill
　(The Brill reference library of ancient Judaism ; Vol. 1)
　ISBN 90–04–11617–6

Vol. 3. Within Israel's social order. – 2000
　ISBN 90–04–11613–3

　　　　　　　　　　ISSN　1566-1237
　　　　　　　　　　ISBN　90 04 11613 3 (*Vol. III*)
　　　　　　　　　　ISBN　90 04 11617 6 (*Set*)

© *Copyright 2000 by Koninklijke Brill NV, Leiden, The Netherlands*

All rights reserved. No part of this publication may be reproduced, translated, stored in a retrieval system, or transmitted in any form or by any means, electronic, mechanical, photocopying, recording or otherwise, without prior written permission from the publisher.

Authorization to photocopy items for internal or personal use is granted by Brill provided that the appropriate fees are paid directly to The Copyright Clearance Center, 222 Rosewood Drive, Suite 910 Danvers 01923, USA. Fees are subject to change.

PRINTED IN THE NETHERLANDS

CONTENTS

Preface xi
Contents of Volumes I–II, IV–V xix

CIVIL SOCIETY. REPAIRING DAMAGE TO, PRESERVING THE PERFECTION OF, THE SOCIAL ORDER

1. TRACTATE BABA QAMMA 1
   I. *An Outline of the Halakhah of Baba Qamma* 1
      i. Damage by Chattels 2
         A. The Fundamental Rules of Assessing Damages When the Cause is One's Property, Animate or Inanimate 2
         B. Damages Done by Chattels in the Public Domain 7
         C. Damages Done by the Ox 9
         D. Damages Done by the Pit 19
         E. Damages Done by the Crop-Destroying Beast 21
         F. Damages Done by Fire 22
      ii. Damages Done by Persons 23
         A. Penalties for the Theft of an Ox or a Sheep 23
         B. Penalties for Abuse of the Land 27
         C. Penalties for Assault 28
         D. Penalties for Damages Done by Persons to Property; Restoring What Is Stolen 34
   II. *Analysis: The Problematics of the Topic, Baba Qamma* 44

2. TRACTATE BABA MESIA 52
   I. *An Outline of the Halakhah of Baba Mesia* 52
      i. The Disposition of Other Peoples' Possessions 52
         A. Conflicting Claims on Lost Objects 52
         B. Returning an Object to the Original Owner 54
         C. Rules of Bailment 61

ii. Commercial Transactions	64
A. Overcharge and Misrepresentation	64
B. Usury	67
iii. Hiring Workers. Rentals and Bailments	75
A. The Mutual Obligations of Worker and Employer	75
B. Rentals	77
C. Bailments: The Special Case of Depositing Materials with Craftsmen	79
D. The Mutual Obligations of Worker and Employer	80
E. Bailments	83
iv. Real Estate	87
A. Prologue	87
B. Landlord-Tenant Relationships	88
C. The Landlord's Relationships with a Tenant-Farmer or a Sharecropper	90
D. Paying Laborers Promptly. Taking a Pledge	95
E. Joint Holders of a Common Property	98
II. *Analysis: The Problematics of the Topic, Baba Mesia*	100
3. TRACTATE BABA BATRA	110
I. *An Outline of the Halakhah of Baba Batra*	110
i. Real Estate (continued)	110
A. Joint Holders of a Common Property [continuing Baba Mesia VI.E]	110
B. Not Infringing upon the Property Rights of Others	117
C. Establishing Title to a Field through Usucaption	120
D. Transferring Real Estate and Movables through Sale	125
ii. Licit Commercial Transactions	131
A. Conditions of Irrevocable Transfer of Goods	131
B. Unstated Stipulations in Commercial Transactions	133
iii. Inheritances and Wills. Other Commercial and Legal Documents	138
A. Inheritance	138

B. The Preparation and Confirmation of Commercial Documents, e.g., Writs of Debt 150
C. Concluding Miscellany 153
II. *Analysis: The Problematics of the Topic, Baba Batra* 155
III. *Interpretation: Religious Principles of Baba Qamma, Baba Mesia, and Baba Batra* 158

PROTECTING THE COMMONWEALTH: IDOLATERS, SINNERS AND CRIMINALS AND THE COURTS

4. TRACTATE SANHEDRIN 173
   I. *An Outline of the Halakhah of Sanhedrin* 173
      i. The Court-System 174
         A. Various Kinds of Courts and their Jurisdiction 174
         B. The Heads of the Israelite Nation and the Court-System 177
         C. The Procedures of the Court-System: Property Cases 179
         D. The Procedures of the Court-System: Capital Cases 183
      ii. The Death Penalty 190
         A. Stoning 190
         B. The Four Modes of Execution that Lie in the Power of the Court and How They Are Administered 192
         C. Stoning 192
         D. Burning or Decapitation 199
         E. Strangulation 201
         F. Extra-Judicial Punishment 202
         G. Death At the Hands of Heaven: Denial of Eternal life 203
   II. *Analysis: The Problematics of the Topic, Sanhedrin* 206

5. TRACTATE MAKKOT 210
   I. *An Outline of the Halakhah of Makkot* 210
      i. Penalties for Perjury 211

ii. The Penalty of Exile (Banishment)	214
A. Those Who are Sent into Exile	214
B. The Cities of Exile	216
iii. The Penalty of Flogging	218
A. Those Who Are Flogged	218
B. The Conduct of the Flogging	224
II. *Analysis: The Problematics of the Topic, Makkot*	226
III. *Interpretation: Religious Principles of Sanhedrin-Makkot*	227
6. Tractate Shebuot	235
I. *An Outline of the Halakhah of Shebuot*	235
i. The Uncleanness of the Cult and its Holy Things and the Guilt-Offering	237
A. General Introduction	237
B. Uncleanness and the Cult	237
ii. Oaths	239
A. Oaths in General	239
B. The Rash Oath, the Vain Oath	240
C. The Oath of Testimony	242
D. The Oath of Bailment	247
E. The Oath Imposed by Judges	249
F. Oaths and Bailments	258
II. *Analysis: The Problematics of the Topic, Shebuot*	260
III. *Interpretation: Religious Principles of Shebuot*	264

PROTECTING THE COMMONWEALTH:
SINNERS AND CRIMINALS

7. Tractate Keritot	272
I. *An Outline of the Halakhah of Keritot*	272
i. The Sin-Offering	273
A. Classes of Transgressions that are Subject to Extirpation or the Sin-Offering	273
B. The Sin-Offering	276
ii. Multiple Sin-Offerings	278
A. The Single Sin-Offering and Multiple Sins	278
B. The Offering of Variable Value	280
iii. The Suspensive Guilt-Offering	281
A. Cases of Doubt in which the Suspensive Guilt-Offering is Required	281

B. When the Animal Designated for the Suspensive Guilt Offering May Not be Required	285
II. *Analysis: The Problematics of the Topic, Keritot*	289
III. *Interpretation: Religious Principles of Keritot*	291

PROTECTING THE COMMONWEALTH: THE COURTS

8. TRACTATE HORAYOT	300
I. *An Outline of the Halakhah of Horayot*	300
i. The Offering Brought Because of an Erroneous Decision by a Court	302
ii. The Offering Brought by the High Priest Who Has Unwittingly Done What is Contrary to the Commandments of the Torah. The Ruler	305
iii. The Individual. The Anointed Priest. The Community	307
II. *Analysis: The Problematics of the Topic, Horayot*	311
III. *Interpretation: Religious Principles of Horayot*	313

PROTECTING THE COMMONWEALTH: IDOLATERS

9. TRACTATE ABODAH ZARAH	321
I. *An Outline of the Halakhah of Abodah Zarah*	321
i. Commercial Relationships with Gentiles	323
A. Festivals and Fairs	323
B. Objects Prohibited Even in Commerce	326
C. Objects Prohibited For Use but Permitted in Commerce	330
ii. Idols	332
A. General Principles	332
B. The Asherah	333
C. The Merkolis	335
D. Nullifying an Idol	336
iii. Libation Wine	338
II. *Analysis: The Problematics of the Topic, Abodah Zarah*	344
III. *Interpretation: Religious Principles of Abodah Zarah*	348

INDEXES	361

PREFACE

> I will dwell among the people of Israel and will be their God. And they shall know that I am the Lord their God who brought them forth out of the land of Egypt that I might dwell among them; I am the Lord their God.
>
> Ex. 29:38–46

The Halakhah sets forth the norms for a society worthy of God's presence, the laws of the sanctification of the social order that God himself has revealed to Israel at Sinai in the Torah. That broadly recognized conception requires amplification: what is the Halakhah, and how does the Halakhah make it possible to achieve the goal of sanctification? What exactly does the Halakhah set forth to realize the conviction that if one follows its many carefully-crafted regulations for the many dimensions of life, God will dwell among Israel? Here we take up the specificities of the law in quest of the modes of realizing the divine imperative.

Besides the instructions of the Torah, particularly the Pentateuch, what, exactly, do I mean by "the Halakhah"? I refer to the formulation of the normative law of Judaism in its initial statement, set forth in the Mishnah (ca. 200 C.E.), in the Tosefta (ca. 300 C.E.), the Yerushalmi (ca. 400 C.E.) or the Bavli (ca. 600 C.E.). The four Halakhic documents of late antiquity, a law code, a supplement, and two commentaries to the law and its code and supplement, all together form the statement of the norms of behavior, realizing the norms of belief, set forth in the formative age of Judaism. These documents are held to record the originally-orally-formulated and orally-transmitted tradition given by God to Moses at Sinai along with the written-out part of the Torah. The Halakhah makes its statement in a continuous and harmonious form, each document establishing close ties to its predecessors,[1] so in this account, I focus not upon differentiating from one another the documentary media of the Halakhah and their

---

[1] With the qualification that the Bavli is not continuous with the Yerushalmi, but, along with the Yerushalmi, appeals to the Mishnah, Tosefta, and corpus of formally-formulated rules assigned to the same authorities but not included in the Mishnah and Tosefta called *Baraitot*. I have spent nearly twenty years differentiating

traits but upon synthesizing the single, unitary message of the Halakhah.[2]

The Halakhah takes over the rules of Scripture and transforms them into a cogent construction, a structure and a system, that is orderly, coherent, and purposive. In that way the Halakhah translates the narrative of the Written Torah into an account of the history and destiny of God's stake in humanity: the children of Abraham and Sarah and their continuators who at Sinai by reason of the Torah became Israel. For the Oral Torah, resting as it does upon deep foundations in the Written Torah, God created nature as the setting for his encounter with humanity. But with the sin of Man, the loss of Eden, and the advent of death began the long quest for the regeneration of Man. In the unfolding of generations, ten from Adam to Noah, ten from Noah to Abraham and thence to Sinai, it was only Israel that presented itself for the encounter. But then Israel too showed itself Man. For on the other side of Sinai came the celebration of the Golden Calf. Then God provided for Israel, surrogate of humanity, the commandments as a medium of sanctification for the reconciliation with God and renewal of Eden, the triumph over the grave. Freed of sin through offerings that signified obedience to God's will, by reason of repentance and atonement, signifying man's acceptance of God's will over his own, which to begin with had brought about the fall from Eden, man might meet God,

---

one document from another and in other studies on comparative hermeneutics continue to do so. But the Halakhah is set forth by all documents as unitary, harmonious, and consistent throughout — that forms the generative hermeneutics of all Halakhic discourse — and any account of Judaism that is other than narrowly historical must accommodate that fundamental principle of presentation. Hence the way taken here: I relate the Halakhah whole and complete, document by document, in a continuous, unfolding statement. As I shall explain, the shift from one type face to another accommodates the requirements of the documentary reading of Rabbinic Judaism for the present purpose.

[2] My commentary to the several media of the Halakhah and the Aggadah takes the form of annotated translations, with special interest in questions of form and structure. The several series, in many volumes, are as follows: *The Tosefta. Translated from the Hebrew.* N.Y., 1977–1985: Ktav; *The Talmud of the Land of Israel. An Academic Commentary to the Second, Third, and Fourth Divisions.* Atlanta, 1998: Scholars Press for *USF Academic Commentary Series*; and *The Talmud of Babylonia. An Academic Commentary.* Atlanta, 1994–6: Scholars Press for *USF Academic Commentary Series*. The translations of the Talmuds are my second go-around in each case, providing a commentary in semiotic form in to each Talmud. I have done the same for the Midrash-compilations of formative Judaism in *The Components of the Rabbinic Documents: From the Whole to the Parts.* Atlanta, 1997–8: Scholars Press for USF Academic Commentary Series.

the two in mutual and reciprocal commitment. Where Israel atoned for sin and presented itself as ready for the meeting, there God and Israel would found their Eden. The Halakhah then serves as the medium of sanctification of Israel in the here-and-now, in preparation for the salvation of Israel and its restoration to Eden.[3]

This account of the Halakhah is encyclopedic, in that it covers, rubric by rubric, all of the native category-formations that organize the diverse laws into a systematic and coherent structure. I introduce each category-formation with attention to its definition and foundations, if any, in Scripture. I then summarize the Halakhah of the Mishnah-Tosefta-Yerushalmi-Bavli, identifying what is fresh and well-focused in the two Talmuds. I then identify the problematics of the law, the questions that the framers bring to bear upon the topic and the data they have in hand. Finally, in each category-formation, I provide a religious commentary to the Halakhah of the Oral Torah, the first complete, encompassing one of its type ever undertaken. That commentary addresses to the law questions of religious logic: how the modes of thought concerning the facts of the Torah revealed at Sinai produce a coherent statement. Specifically, the commentary asks the topical program of the Halakhah and the detailed articulation thereof to signal the sages' plan for holy Israel's social structure and system. This structure and working system they produced in response to a very specific set of questions concerning God in relationship to the world: one and only God engaged in creating a perfect world-order based on justice.

A full Introduction to the entire project is set forth in Volume I. Let me briefly explain how this work is organized in its entirety. Volumes I and II address Israel in relationship to God. Volume III explains how holy Israel will restore and then maintain that society that comes into being when the Torah is realized by the kingdom of priests and the holy people. In Volumes IV and V of this study, we take up the life of the Israelite household in the encounter with God. So we move from regulating relationships between Israel and God to establishing stable and equitable relationships among Israelites and finally to nurturing in the household itself a realm of sanctification: Israel at home in space and time with God. It is the Halakhah,

---

[3] That statement summarizes my *Theology of the Halakhah* (in press), and the basis for that statement is contained in this encyclopedic account of each of the native category-formations of the Halakhah.

and not the Aggadah, that sets forth all of these interior lines of order: the norms of the kingdom of priests and the holy people.

Each encyclopaedia entry, or chapter, follows the same outline, as the table of contents signals. I define the category-formation, summarize the principal components of the Halakhah, document by document, then identify the problematics of the Halakhah, and finally I propose what I conceive to be the systemic statement that the Halakhah makes through that particular category-formation. We can work our way back from [1] the topic to [2] the problematic to [3] the deeper statement of a religious character that sages wished to make through a given topic — here and not there, to say this and not to say that — we can claim to define the structure and system that sages composed and empowered through their exposition of the Halakhah. My account of matters therefore moves from

[1] description of the law, to
[2] the analysis of the problematics (where pertinent) that governs, and onward to
[3] the interpretation of the religious convictions and conceptions that imparted energy to the enterprise throughout.

Sages made choices, just as those writing in the name of Moses in setting forth the Pentateuchal laws did things in one way rather than in some other: supplied for this topic, information of that sort, rather than some other; set forth in this context and sequence, and not in that. Since, here too, sages could have asked another range of questions altogether, we have at each topic to ask, for this topic, why this particular problematics? And the ultimate answer links the Halakhah in particular to the religious structure and system that animate the Halakhah in general.

I find the cogency of the Halakhah in its statement of religion, which I conceive to cohere in three dimensions, already adumbrated:

[1] Israel's public life with God, thus relationships between Israel and God, Volumes One and Two,
[2] in a holy community founded on the principles of justice that governed God's creation of the world, thus relationships among Israelites, Volume Three,
[3] a society comprised of Israel's dwelling places, the households, viewed as counterparts to God's dwelling place in the Temple

in Jerusalem, thus relationships within the interiority of Israel's households (the "tents, tabernacles" of Balaam's blessing). Volumes Four and Five.

Now let us dwell on the work at hand, to discern the interior lines of order and composition and proportion that form of the Halakhah the cogent system sages have always insisted it is. As always, we commence by examining the data that reveal the governing category-formation: how, precisely, does the Halakhah organize and systematize the Torah's facts and rules of ordinary life?

In the presentation of the Halakhah by topics but in the documentary sequence, Mishnah, Tosefta, Yerushalmi, Bavli, I use **bold face type for the Mishnah,** regular type for the Tosefta, *italics for the Yerushalmi,* and LOWER CASE CAPS FOR THE BAVLI. I include in my outline of the topical representation only what is absolutely necessary for an account of the principal points that the Halakhah makes about a given topic. For the Tosefta, Yerushalmi, and Bavli, this involves only new details about the topic that carry forward the exposition, not that clarify received law in one way or another. Since I have already outlined both Talmuds and brought the two outlines into juxtaposition for the divisions of the Mishnah that are covered by both, no purpose would be served by citing more than details of a topic first occurring in the continuator-writings. My main goal is to demonstrate the seamless character of the Halakhah, to show how the Halakhic structure — topics, problematics — emerges nearly whole and complete in the Mishnah, to be refined and amplified and complemented later on, but never to be vastly reconstructed as to its generative categories.

I have made no effort to impose upon the sources "gender-neutral" language, which would violate their character, imputing an originally-exclusionary intent that is in fact rarely present. When sages wish to use "Adam" or "he" to refer only to men, they signal that intent in a loud and clear fashion.[4] In any event, in Rabbinic literature,

---

[4] That — as everyone knows — an implicit male bias pervades the whole forms a trivial banality. We accomplish no worthwhile intellectual mission by judging the second century by the standards of the twentieth, let alone the twentieth by the standards of the second.

"man/Adam/he" ordinarily stands for male and female, that is, "all of humanity," as "he" and "mankind" in much contemporary usage and in the whole of historical usage of the English and American languages are deemed to encompass both genders. In these pages that usage governs throughout, and "he-or-she" and its persnickety variations and circumlocutions do not occur.

For the sake of clarity throughout, it is necessary to explain that, in conformity to the usage in the authoritative sources under discussion here, when I refer to "Israel" I mean, the holy Israel of which the Torah, written and oral, speaks, that is, a theological formulation, the social entity created within, and by, the theology of the Torah and defined solely in its terms. Sometimes in the Halakhic sources by "Israel" sages mean, individual Israelite, and I follow suit. I do not confuse "Israel" in the holy books with the Land of Israel, the State of Israel, the Jewish People defined as a secular or ethnic entity, or any of the other reference-points of the same word that today serve in common discourse. Prior research of mine has shown how the word "Israel" finds definition in the documents of the Oral Torah. The results are utilized here.[5]

All the translations from the documents of the Oral Torah are my own. Of some of the documents, I was the first translator, for example, Sifra, Sifré to Numbers, Tosefta, and the Talmud of the Land of Israel. Of others, I was the second, for instance, the Mishnah, Sifré to Deuteronomy, the Rabbah-Midrashim, and the Talmud of Babylonia. It was necessary to redo the work of others in my form-analytical translations, because I was the first (and to date remain the only) person to conduct systematic form-analysis, spilling over into form-history, of the entire literature. The consequent reference system, imposed consistently throughout these translations, is the first ever carried out systematically and uniformly for the entire corpus. Each item signals not only location in a given document but the formal role, within the construction of that document, of a given unit of thought.

I have treated certain Hebrew words, Aggadah, Halakhah, and the like, as naturalized to the American language and therefore I have not italicized them as words of a foreign language.

---

[5] *Judaism and its Social Metaphors. Israel in the History of Jewish Thought.* N.Y., 1988: Cambridge University Press, and *The Theology of the Oral Torah.*

Thanks to go the University of South Florida for the Distinguished Research Professorship that sustains my research, and to Bard College for valued support and research assistance as well. I doubt that any academic scholar in any field of the humanities enjoys a more suitable setting for academic research than I do in my association with that University and that College and their respective Departments of Religious Studies.

It gives me special pleasure to publish this *Encyclopaedia* at Brill, and in the new series that Brill has asked me to organize and edit with my colleague Professor Alan J. Avery-Peck. I have worked with Brill, off and on, for nearly four decades. In 1962 Brill published my first book and many subsequent ones, and over time I have organized and edited a number of monograph series for the firm. The director for my first twenty years with Brill was Dr. F.C. Wieder, Jr., since gone on to his eternal reward and still missed by those fortunate enough to work with him. From his time and in his tradition I have found in Brill's editors understanding, respect, and support. In Elisabeth Venekamp and Julian Deahl I encounter the newest generation and find it fully worthy of the tradition of scholarly integrity and dignity embodied in Frits Wieder.

JACOB NEUSNER

Research Professor of Religion and Theology
Bard College
Annandale-on-Hudson, NY

CONTENTS VOLUMES I–II, IV–V

VOLUME I
BETWEEN ISRAEL AND GOD:
PART A.
FAITH, THANKSGIVING, ENLANDISEMENT POSSESSION AND PARTNERSHIP

Preface	xvii
Introduction	1

FAITH, THANKSGIVING

1. TRACTATE BERAKHOT	47
I. *An Outline of the Topic, Berakhot*	47
i. The Declaration of the Creed [the *Shemaʿ*]	48
A. Reciting the Shemaʿ, Evening and Morning	48
B. The Attitude And the Manner in Which One Recites the Shemaʿ: To Carry Out One's Obligation to Do So	49
C. Those Exempt from the Obligation to Recite the Shemaʿ and certain other obligatory Prayers	50
ii. Reciting The Prayer	52
A. Reciting The Prayer, Morning and Evening	52
B. The Correct Attitude for Reciting The Prayer	53
C. Inclusion of Prayers for Special Occasions in the Recitation of The Prayer	53
D. Inclusion of Votive Prayers in the Recitation of The Prayer. Errors in the Recitation of The Prayer	54
iii. Blessings Recited on the Occasion of Enjoying the Benefits of Creation	54
A. The Requirement to Recite Blessings	54
B. Appropriate Blessings for Various Edibles	55

      iv. Communal Meals and their Protocol 57
         A. Establishing the Communal Character of a
            Meal. Private and Public Gatherings and the
            Recitation of Blessings 57
         B. Declaring a Quorum for the Recitation of
            Grace: Special Problems 58
         C. Special Problems Debated by the Houses of
            Shammai and Hillel in Regard to the
            Protocol of Blessings at Table. The Normative
            Law 60
      v. Blessings on Exceptional Occasions 61
         A. Blessings For Evil as Much as For Good 61
         B. Blessings in Commemoration of Miracles or
            Other Exceptional Events 61
         C. Prayers and Protocol in Connection With
            Entering a Given Location. A Town, the
            Temple in Jerusalem 64
  II. *Analysis: The Problematics of the Topic, Berakhot* 64
 III. *Interpretation: Religious Principles of Berakhot* 65

ENLANDISEMENT

2. Tractate Kilayim 71
   I. *Enlandisement* 71
  II. *An Outline of the Halakhah of Kilayim* 72
      i. Raising Together Diverse Species of Plants 72
         A. Plants That Are or Are Not Classified as
            Diverse Kinds 72
         B. Grafting 73
         C. Sowing Together or in Adjacent Spaces
            Diverse Species of Crops 74
         D. Sowing Crops in a Vineyard 76
     ii. Mating Animals of Different Species 81
         A. Prohibition of Hybridization 81
         B. Prohibition of Yoking Diverse Species of
            Beasts 81
    iii. Mingling Wool and Linen Fibers 82
         A. The Prohibition 82
         B. Application of the Prohibition 83

III. *Analysis: The Problematics of the Topic, Kilayim* 84
IV. *Interpretation: Religious Principles of Kilayim* 86

3. TRACTATE SHEBIʿIT 91
   I. *An Outline of the Halakhah of Shebiʿit* 91
      i. According Sabbath-Rest to the Land:
         Ceasing Work 92
         A. Ceasing in the Sixth Year Work that Benefits
            the Crop in the Seventh Year: Orchards,
            Grain Fields 92
         B. Ceasing in the Sixth Year Work that Benefits
            the Crop in the Seventh Year, and Labor that
            is Permitted Because the Effects of the Work
            Pertain Mainly to the Sixth Year 93
         C. Ceasing in the Sixth Year Work that Benefits
            the Crop in the Seventh Year: Interstitial
            Cases. The Result of the Work may Pertain
            to Either the Sixth or the Seventh Year 94
      ii. The Prohibition against Working the Land in the
          Seventh Year 95
          A. Appearing to Cultivate the Land 95
          B. Actually Cultivating the Land 97
      iii. Special Problems in Connection with the
           Prohibition against Working the Land in the
           Seventh Year 99
           A. Produce that Grows Over Two or More
              Calendar Years 99
           B. Assisting Others in Harvesting Crops or
              Processing Produce during the Seventh Year 100
           C. Application of the Seventh Year Laws to
              Diverse Regions within the Land of Israel 101
      iv. Restrictions on the Use of Produce that Grows
          in the Seventh Year 103
          A. Species of Produce that Are Deemed
             Sanctified, therefore Prohibited for Common
             Use, during the Seventh Year 103
          B. Restrictions upon Using Seventh Year
             Produce 105
          C. Not Hoarding Seventh Year Produce: The
             Law of Removal 108

v. Remission of Debts by the Advent of the Seventh Year	111
A. What Types of Debts are Cancelled	111
B. The Prozbul	112
C. Repaying Debts Remitted by the Advent of the Seventh Year	112
II. *Analysis: The Problematics of the Topic, Shebiʿit*	114
III. *Interpretation: Religious Principles of Shebiʿit*	118
4. TRACTATE ʿORLAH	126
I. *An Outline of the Halakhah of ʿOrlah*	126
i. Definition of Terms	126
A. What is a Fruit-Tree?	126
B. Reckoning the Three Years from the Moment of Planting	127
ii. Mixtures of Forbidden and Permitted Produce	128
A. What Happens When Forbidden and Permitted Produce is Mixed Together, without Particular Reference to ʿOrlah-Fruit	128
B. Neutralizing Forbidden Produce Mixed with Permitted Produce	129
C. Mixtures of Forbidden and Permitted Leaven in Dough, Seasonings, Oil	130
D. Complex Mixtures (Three Components)	130
iii. The Prohibition against the Use of ʿOrlah-Fruit	131
A. Forbidden Dye and Weaving	131
B. Fire Made from Coals from ʿOrlah-Fruit	131
C. Mixtures of Items made from ʿOrlah-Fruit	132
II. *Analysis: The Problematics of the Topic, ʿOrlah*	133
III. *Interpretation: Religious Principles of ʿOrlah*	135

POSSESSION AND PARTNERSHIP

5. TRACTATE MAʿASEROT	142
I. *An Outline of the Halakhah of Maʿaserot*	142
i. Conditions Under which Produce Becomes Subject to the Law of Tithing	144
A. General Conditions	144
B. Specific Conditions	144

ii. Procedures by which Harvested Produce is
Rendered Liable to the Removal of Tithes 146
  A. Processing and Storage of Untithed Produce 146
  B. Acquisition of Another's Untithed Produce
     in Four Modes: Gifts 148
  C. Acquisition of Another's Untithed Produce in
     Four Modes: Purchases 150
  D. Acquisition of Another's Untithed Produce in
     Four Modes: Barter 151
  E. Acquisition of Another's Untithed Produce
     in Four Modes: Lost Produce Found by
     Another 154
iii. Bringing Produce from the Field into the
Courtyard or Home and So Rendering the
Produce Liable for Tithing 156
iv. Preparing of Untithed Produce for Use in a
Meal and So Rendering the Produce Liable for
Tithing 158
v. Incomplete Procedures, Unmet Conditions:
Produce not Subject to Tithing 161
  A. Produce that is Edible but is Normally not
     Deemed Food 161
  B. Produce that is Taken from the Field Prior
     to the Harvest of the Crop 161
  C. Produce that is Sold or Purchased while Still
     Inedible 163
  D. Produce that is Insufficiently Processed, or
     Produce the Processing of which is in Doubt,
     and So is not Liable to Tithing 165
  E. Produce not Grown in the Land or Produce
     that is not Food 165
II. *Analysis: The Problematics of Ma'aserot* 166
III. *Interpretation: Religious Principles of Ma'aserot* 171

6. TRACTATE TERUMOT 177
   I. *An Outline of the Halakhah of Terumot* 177
      i. How Heave-Offering is Designated and Separated   179
         A. Improper Ways of Separating
            Heave-Offering, which Yield Heave-Offering
            that is not Valid 179

	B. Improper Ways of Separating Heave-Offering that Nonetheless Yield Valid Heave-Offering	187
	C. Heave-Offering Separated from One Kind of Produce to Fulfill the Obligation of Produce of a Different Kind	194
	D. Cases of Doubt on Whether or not Heave-Offering has been Validly Separated	197
ii.	The Rite of Separating Heave-Offering	199
	A. The Oral Designation	199
	B. The Percentage of a Batch of Produce that is to be Designated and Separated as Heave-Offering	202
	C. When the Rite of Separating Heave-Offering Takes Place	206
iii.	The Proper Handling of Heave-Offering that has been Separated but not Yet Given to the Priest	208
	A. Heave-Offering that is Mixed with Unconsecrated Produce and How it is Neutralized	208
	B. Rules Regarding the Batch in which Heave-Offering was Neutralized and the Produce Taken to Replace the Heave-Offering	211
	C. Heave-Offering that is Eaten by a Non-Priest: Unintentional Consumption. Payment of the Principal and Added Fifth	218
	D. Heave-Offering that is Eaten by a Non-Priest: Intentional Consumption. Payment of the Principal but not the Added Fifth	223
	E. Cases of Doubt Concerning the Non-Priest's Liability for Eating Heave-Offering	223
	F. The Cultic Contamination of Heave-Offering	227
	G. Heave-Offering that is Planted as Seed	232
	H. Heave-Offering that is Cooked or Otherwise Prepared with Unconsecrated Produce	235
iv.	The Preparation and Use of Heave-Offering by the Priest	241
	A. Proper Preparation of Produce in the Status of Heave-Offering	241

	B. Refuse from Produce in the Status of Heave-Offering	243
	C. Heave-Offering that is not Fit as Human Food but has Some Other Use	246
II.	*Analysis: The Problematics of the Topic, Terumot*	250
III.	*Interpretation: Religious Principles of Terumot*	256

7. TRACTATE HALLAH 261
    I. *An Outline of the Halakhah of Hallah* 261
        i. Definition of Dough that is Liable to Dough-Offering 263
            A. Definition of Bread: Kinds of Grain that Yield Baked Goods, Kinds of Dough 263
            B. Cases of Doubt 267
        ii. The Process of Separating Dough-Offering 267
            A. Separating the Offering Properly and Improperly 267
            B. Cases in which a Circumstance that May Cause Exemption Comes into Effect, before or after the Dough Becomes Liable 269
        iii. Mixtures 272
            A. Mixtures of Liable and Exempt Dough 272
            B. Mixtures of Two Batches of Exempt Dough 274
        iv. Liability to Dough-Offering Outside of the Land of Israel 277
    II. *Analysis: The Problematics of Hallah* 280
    III. *Interpretation: Religious Principles of Hallah* 283

8. TRACTATE MA'ASER SHENI 289
    I. *An Outline of the Halakhah of Ma'aser Sheni* 289
        i. Improper Disposition of Second Tithe 292
            A. Improper Use of Consecrated Food 292
            B. Improper Use of Consecrated Coins 294
        ii. Proper Disposition of Second Tithe 297
            A. Proper Use of Consecrated Food 297
            B. Proper Transference of the Status of Second Tithe to and from Coins: Coins to Coins 300
            C. Proper Transference of the Status of Second Tithe to and from Coins: From Coins to Produce 303

        D. Proper Transference of the Status of Second Tithe to and from Coins: From Produce to Coins After Produce Has Been in Jerusalem 306
        E. Proper Transference of the Status of Second Tithe to and from Coins: From Produce to Coins Before Produce Has Been in Jerusalem 311
        F. Produce and Coins the Status of which is in Doubt 321
   iii. Produce of a Planting's Fourth Year, Which is in the Status of Second Tithe 325
   iv. The Law of Removal 328
  II. *Analysis: The Problematics of the Topic, Ma'aser Sheni* 331
  III. *Interpretation: Religious Principles of Ma'aser Sheni* 338

9. TRACTATE BIKKURIM 344
  I. *An Outline of the Halakhah of Bikkurim* 344
   i. Those Who Present Firstfruits and Make the Declaration; Those Who Present but Do Not Recite the Declaration; Those who Do Not Present Firstfruits at all 347
        A. Those Who Do Not Present Firstfruits 347
        B. Those Who Present Firstfruits but Do Not Recite the Declaration 348
        C. Those Who Present Firstfruits and Recite the Declaration 350
   ii. Comparisons: Firstfruits and Other Agricultural Gifts and Tithes 351
        A. Comparison of the Laws of Firstfruits, Heave-Offering, and Second Tithe 351
        B. Ways in which a Heave-Offering of the Tithe is Like Firstfruits and Heave-Offering 353
   iii. The Disposition of Firstfruits 354
        A. Designating Produce as Firstfruits 354
        B. Bringing Firstfruits to the Priest 354
        C. Firstfruits when in the Custody of the Priests 357
  II. *Analysis: The Problematics of the Topic, Bikkurim* 358
  III. *Interpretation: Religious Principles of Bikkurim* 359

CONTENTS VOLUMES I–II, IV–V

10. TRACTATE PE'AH 365
    I. *An Outline of the Halakhah of Pe'ah* 365
       i. Pe'ah: The Poor Offering Set Aside When the
          Farmer Begins to Harvest His Entire Field 368
          A. Basic Definition: Amount, Location, Types of
             Produce 368
          B. Definition: The Area of Land Defined as a
             Field from which a Single Portion of Pe'ah
             Must be Designated 372
          C. Distributing Pe'ah to the Poor 378
          D. When Produce Becomes Subject to the
             Laws of Gleanings, Forgotten Sheaves, and
             Pe'ah 380
       ii. Gleanings: The Poor Offering Separated When
           the Householder Cuts Individual Stalks 382
           A. Definition 382
           B. Distribution 385
           C. The Collection of Poor-Offerings in
              General 385
           D. Poor-Offerings Gathered by Poor
              Field-Owners 386
       iii. Forgotten Sheaves: The Offering Separated
            after the Farmer Has Completed the Reaping
            of the Field, When He Binds the Grain into
            Sheaves 387
            A. Definition 387
            B. Ambiguous Cases: Sheaves that the
               Householder Leaves Behind, Yet Does not
               Forget, with the Result that They are
               Exempt from the Law of the Forgotten
               Sheaf 391
            C. Types of Produce Intentionally Left in the
               Field 394
            D. Olive Trees with Distinctive Features and
               How the Laws of the Forgotten Sheaf
               Pertain 395
       iv. Separated Grapes and Defective Clusters:
           Offerings Set Aside while the Householder
           Harvests the Vineyard 397
           A. Separated Grapes 397

	B. Defective Clusters	397
	C. Poor-Offerings in General: Their Status after the Harvest Has Been Completed but before the Processing at the Threshing Floor has Gotten Underway	400
	v. Poor-man's Tithe: The Offering Separated at the Threshing Floor	400
	A. The Poorman's Claims Regarding Poor-Offerings and Poorman's Tithe	400
	B. Definition: The Proper Amount of Food to Give to Each Poor Person as Poorman's Tithe	401
	C. Types of Charity Given throughout the Year from One Harvest to the Next	404
	vi. Defining Who Is Poor	405
	II. *Analysis: The Problematics of the Topic, Pe'ah*	407
	III. *Interpretation: Religious Principles of Pe'ah*	413
11.	TRACTATE DEMA'I	419
	I. *An Outline of the Halakhah of Dema'i*	419
	i. Items that May or May not Be Subject to Tithing as Dema'i; the Handling and Use of Dema'i Produce	421
	ii. Commercial and Commensal Relations between Those Who Are Trustworthy in the Matter of Tithing and Those Who Are Not	427
	A. The Trustworthy Person [Haber] and the Untrustworthy Person ['Am Ha'ares]: Definitions	427
	B. Situations in which One Tithes Produce Left in his Possession	433
	C. Situations in which Those Who Ordinarily Are Not Deemed Trustworthy as to Tithing Are Believed; Credibility	441
	iii. Details of the Tithing Procedure: Tithes Must Not Be Separated for Produce Liable to Tithing from Produce that is Exempt	443
	iv. Responsibility: To What Extent Must One Take Responsibility for Tithing the Portion Given to Another Person	451

A. Shared Ownership	451
B. Tithing Produce that is Liable to Tithing from Produce that is Exempt; Mixtures	459
II. *Analysis: The Problematics of the Topic, Dema'i*	466
III. *Interpretation: Religious Principles of Dema'i*	470

12. TRACTATE SHEQALIM 477
   I. *An Outline of the Halakhah of Sheqalim* 477
      i. Collecting the Sheqel 478
         A. The Imposition of the Obligation to Pay 478
         B. Transporting the Sheqel. Sacrilege 482
      ii. The Use of the Sheqel for Offerings for the Altar 485
         A. Taking Up Sheqels for the Public Offerings 485
         B. Disposition of the Sheqel-Funds for Various Offerings 487
      iii. The Temple Administration and Procedures 491
         A. The Administration 491
         B. Procedures for the Sale of Drink-Offerings 492
         C. Collecting Other Funds in the Temple 493
         D. Disposing of Coins and Objects Found in the Temple and in Jerusalem 497
         E. Miscellany 499
   II. *Analysis: The Problematics of the Topic, Sheqalim* 502
   III. *Interpretation: Religious Principles of Sheqalim* 507

13. TRACTATE ʿARAKHIN 511
   I. *An Outline of the Halakhah of ʿArakhin* 511
      i. Valuations and Vows for the Benefit of the Temple 512
         A. Basic Rules 512
         B. Special Rules 514
         C. Ability to Pay in Assessing Vows 516
         D. The Difference between Pledging a Valuation and Vowing the Worth, or Price, of Someone or Something 519
         E. Collecting Valuations 522

ii. The Dedication and Redemption of a Field That Has Been Received as an Inheritance 526
iii. The Devoted Thing [Herem] 531
iv. The Sale and Redemption of a Field That Has Been Received as an Inheritance and of a Dwelling Place in a Walled City 534
II. *Analysis: The Problematics of the Topic ʿArakhin* 540
III. *Interpretation: Religious Principles of ʿArakhin* 544

14. TRACTATE TAʿANIT 551
I. *An Outline of the Halakhah of Taʿanit* 551
i. Fasts Called in order to Bring Rain 552
A. The Sequence of Fasts for Rain 552
B. The Liturgy of the Community for a Fast Day 555
C. Other Rules about Public Fasts 559
D. Other Uses of the Shofar as an Alarm 560
ii. The Delegation [Maʿamad]: Israelite Participation in the Cult. Various Special Occasions 563
A. The Delegation 563
B. Mourning Days for Public Calamity 567
II. *Analysis: The Problematics of the Topic Taʿanit* 569
III. *Interpretation: Religious Principles of Taʿanit* 572

INDEXES 577

VOLUME II

BETWEEN ISRAEL AND GOD

PART B

TRANSCENDENT TRANSACTIONS: WHERE HEAVEN AND EARTH INTERSECT

Preface xi

1. TRACTATE ZEBAHIM 1
I. *An Outline of the Halakhah of Zebahim* 1
i. Improper Intention and Invalidating the Act of Sacrifice 5

            ii. The Rules of Sacrifice of Beasts and Fowl 33
                A. Beasts 33
                B. Fowl 39
           iii. The Rules of the Altar 48
                A. Disposing of Sacrificial Portions or Blood
                   that Derive from Diverse Sacrifices and
                   Have Been Confused 48
                B. The Altar Sanctifies What Is Appropriate
                   to It, but Not What Is Not Appropriate
                   to It 58
                C. Precedence in Use of the Altar 62
                D. Blood of a Sin-Offering that Spurts onto
                   a Garment 66
                E. The Division among the Eligible Priests
                   of the Meat and Hides of Sacrificial
                   Animals 69
           iv. The Proper Location of the Altar and the Act of
               Sacrifice Performed Thereon 74
      II. *Analysis: The Problematics of the Topic, Zebahim* 87
     III. *Interpretation: Religious Principles of Zebahim* 100

2. TRACTATE MENAHOT 115
      I. *An Outline of the Halakhah of Menahot* 115
            i. Reprise of the Principles of Zebahim on
               Improper Intention and the Invalidation of
               Meal-Offerings 117
                A. Reprise of Zebahim 117
                B. Other Rules of Invalidation of
                   Meal-Offerings 130
           ii. The Proper Preparation of Meal-Offerings 148
                A. General Rules 148
                B. The Meal-Offering that Accompanies the
                   Thank-Offering 155
                C. Sources of Flour, Oil, and Wine Used for
                   the Meal-Offering 161
                D. Measuring the Materials Used for the
                   Offering 166
          iii. Special Meal-Offerings 172
                A. The 'Omer 172
                B. The Two Loaves of Pentecost and the
                   Show-Bread 177

	iv. Vows in Connection with Meal-Offerings	182
II.	*Analysis: The Problematics of the Topic, Menahot*	193
III.	*Interpretation: Religious Principles of Menahot*	201

3. TRACTATES TAMID AND YOMA 207
   - I. *An Outline of the Halakhah of Tamid* 207
     - i. The Priests Arise in the Morning and Clear the Altar of Ashes ... 208
       - A. The Priests in the Morning 208
       - B. Clearing the Altar 209
     - ii. Selecting the Lamb for the Daily Burnt-Offering 210
     - iii. Clearing the Ashes from the Inner Altar 211
     - iv. Slaughtering the Lamb 212
     - v. Blessing the Congregation, Placing the Limbs on the Altar .. 214
       - A. Prayer: A Blessing, the Ten Commandments, and a Blessing . 214
       - B. Carrying the Limbs to the Altar 214
     - vi. Clearing the Ashes and Disposing of Them 215
     - vii. Conclusion of the Rite. Tossing the Limbs on the Altar ... 216
   - II. *An Outline of the Halakhah of Yoma* 217
     - i. The Conduct of the Temple Rite on the Day of Atonement 221
       - A. Preparing the High Priest for the Day of Atonement 221
       - B. Clearing the Ashes from the Altar 225
       - C. The Daily Whole Offering on the Day of Atonement 226
       - D. The High Priest's Personal Offering for the Day of Atonement ... 229
       - E. The Two Goats and Other Offerings on the Day of Atonement ... 231
       - F. The Scape-Goat and its Rule 242
       - G. The Rite Concludes with Reading from the Torah and with Prayer ... 246
     - ii. The Laws of the Day of Atonement 248
       - A. Not Eating, Not Drinking 248
       - B. Repentance and Atonement 251
   - III. *Analysis: The Problematics of the Topic, Yoma* 254

	IV. *Interpretation: Religious Principles of the Topic, Yoma*	....	255
	V. *How the Halakhah of Yoma Reached Judaism*	....	256
4.	TRACTATE HAGIGAH	....	268
	I. *An Outline of the Halakhah of Hagigah*	....	268
	i. The Appearance-Offering, Festal-Offering, and Peace-Offering of Rejoicing	....	270
	A. Liability, Cost	....	270
	B. The Festal Offering and the Sabbath	....	276
	ii. The Rules of Cultic Uncleanness as They Affect Ordinary Folk and Holy Things	....	279
	A. Gradations of Strictness of Rules of Uncleanness	....	279
	B. Holy Things and the Festival	....	285
	II. *Analysis: The Problematics of the Topic, Hagigah*	....	287
	III. *Interpretation: Religious Principles of Hagigah*	....	290
5.	TRACTATE BEKHOROT	....	295
	I. *An Outline of the Halakhah of Bekhorot*	....	295
	i. The Firstborn of Animals. General Rules	....	298
	A. The Firstborn of an Ass	....	298
	B. The First-born of a Cow	....	302
	C. The Resolution of Matters of Doubt	....	306
	D. Not Shearing the Firstling	....	308
	E. The Requirement to Tend the Firstling before Handing It Over to the Priest	....	309
	ii. Slaughtering a Firstling by Reason of Blemishes	....	310
	A. Examining a Firstling to See Whether or Not It Is Blemished	....	310
	B. Further Rules of Slaughtering the Firstling	....	313
	C. Blemishes in Animals	....	316
	D. Blemishes in Priests	....	320
	iii. The Firstborn of Man	....	323
	iv. Tithe of Cattle	....	330
	II. *Analysis: The Problematics of the Topic, Bekhorot*	....	335
	III. *Interpretation: Religious Principles of Bekhorot*	....	339
6.	TRACTATE MEʿILAH	....	342
	I. *An Outline of the Halakhah of Meʿilah*	....	342

i. Sacrilege Committed against Sacrifices in
   Particular 343
   A. When the Laws of Sacrilege Apply to an
      Offering 343
   B. Stages in the Status of an Offering:
      The Point at Which the Laws of Sacrilege
      Apply to Various Offerings 346
   C. Cultic Property That is Not Subject to
      Sacrilege but that also Is Not to be Used for
      Non-Cultic Purposes 348
ii. Sacrilege of Temple Property in General 354
   A. Sacrilege Has Been Committed Only When
      the Value of a Perutah of Temple Property
      Has Been Used for Secular Purposes 354
   B. Sacrilege Is Defined by the One Who Does
      It or by the Thing to which It Is Done 357
   C. Sacrilege Effects the Secularization of Sacred
      Property 358
   D. Agency in Effecting an Act of Sacrilege 360
II. *Analysis: The Problematics of the Topic, Meʿilah* 363
III. *Interpretation: Religious Principles of Meʿilah* 366

7. TRACTATE TEMURAH 370
   I. *An Outline of the Halakhah of Temurah* 370
      i. The Rules of Substitution: Who May Do So,
         and to What 371
         A. Liability to the Law of Substitution 371
         B. Exemptions from the Law of Substitution 374
         C. The Individual's Offerings are Subject to the
            Law of Substitution, Those of the Community
            are Not 376
      ii. The Status of the Offspring of Substitutes 380
         A. Diverse Sacrifices, their Substitutes and
            Offspring 380
         B. The Supererogatory Sin-Offering 384
      iii. The Language Used in Effecting an Act of
           Substitution 386
      iv. Formal Appendix 390
   II. *Analysis: The Problematics of the Topic, Temurah* 395
   III. *Interpretation: Religious Principles of Temurah* 400

8. TRACTATE MEGILLAH 407
   I. *An Outline of the Halakhah of Megillah* 407
      i. The Laws of Declaiming the Scroll of Esther 411
      ii. The Laws of Synagogue Property and Liturgy 417
         A. The Disposition of Synagogue Property 417
         B. Rules for Reading Scriptures in Synagogue Worship 419
         C. The Lections 421
   II. *Analysis: The Problematics of the Topic, Megillah* 428
   III. *Interpretation: Religious Principles of Megillah* 431

9. TRACTATE ROSH HASHANAH 438
   I. *An Outline of the Halakhah of Rosh Hashanah* 438
      i. The Designation of the New Month through the Year 440
         A. The Four New Years 440
         B. The New Moon: Receiving Testimony of the Appearance of the New Moon and Announcing the New Month 443
      ii. The Shofar 449
         A. The Halakhah of the Shofar 449
         B. The Liturgy of the New Year 452
         C. Sounding the Shofar in the Synagogue Liturgy 455
   II. *Analysis: The Problematics of the Topic, Rosh Hashanah* 457
   III. *Interpretation: Religious Principles of Rosh Hashanah* 461

INDEXES 467

VOLUME IV

INSIDE THE WALLS OF THE ISRAELITE HOUSEHOLD

PART A

AT THE MEETING OF TIME AND SPACE SANCTIFICATION IN THE HERE AND NOW: THE TABLE AND THE BED SANCTIFICATION AND THE MARITAL BOND THE DESACRALIZATION OF THE HOUSEHOLD: THE BED

Preface xv

AT THE MEETING OF TIME AND SPACE

1. TRACTATE SHABBAT 1
   I. *An Outline of the Halakhah of Shabbat* 1
      i. Dimensions: Space, Time and the Sabbath 2
         A. Space 2
         B. Time 4
      ii. Preparing for the Sabbath: Light, Food, Clothing 5
         A. The Sabbath Lamp 5
         B. Food for the Sabbath 7
         C. Ornaments for Animals, Clothing for Persons 10
      iii. Prohibited Acts of Labor on the Sabbath: Not Transporting Objects from One Domain to Another 14
         A. The Generative Categories of Prohibited Acts of Labor 14
         B. Domains and the Prohibition of Transporting Objects from One Domain to Another 16
         C. The Prohibition of Carrying on the Sabbath Across the Lines of Domains 19
         D. Throwing Objects from One Domain to Another 21
      iv. Prohibited Acts of Labor 24
         A. What Constitutes a Whole Act of Labor 24

	B. Healing on the Sabbath	30
	C. Knot-Tying, Clothing and Beds	31
v.	Actions that are Permitted on the Sabbath	32
	A. Saving Objects from a Fire on the Sabbath	32
	B. Handling Objects on the Sabbath in Private Domain	34
	C. Circumcision on the Sabbath	37
	D. Preparing Food for Man and Beast	39
	E. Seemly and Unseemly Behavior on the Sabbath	42
II. *Analysis: The Problematics of the Topic, Shabbat*		45
2. TRACTATE ERUBIN		60
I. *An Outline of the Halakhah of Erubin*		60
i.	The Delineation of a Limited Domain	63
	A. Forming an Alley-Way into a Single Domain	63
	B. Forming an Area Occupied by a Caravan into a Single Domain for the Sabbath	65
	C. A Well in Public Domain	67
ii.	The 'Erub and the Sabbath-Limit of a Town	68
	A. The 'Erub: A Symbolic Meal for Establishing Joint Ownership of a Courtyard or for Establishing Symbolic Residence for Purposes of Travel on the Sabbath	68
	B. The 'Erub and Violating the Sabbath-Limit	70
	C. Defining the Sabbath-Limit of a Town	73
iii.	The 'Erub and Commingling Ownership of a Courtyard or an Alleyway	78
	A. The 'Erub and the Courtyard	78
	B. Areas that May Be Deemed Either Distinct from One Another or as a Commingled Domain so that the Residents Have the Choice of Preparing a Joint 'Erub or Two Separate Ones	82
	C. The Shittuf and the Alleyway	86
	D. Neglecting the 'Erub for a Courtyard	88
	E. An 'Erub for More than One Courtyard	89
	F. The 'Erub and the Area of Roofs	91
iv.	Public Domain in General	92

II. *Analysis: The Problematics of the Topic, Erubin* 97
III. *Interpretation: Religious Principles of Shabbat and Erubin* 104

3. TRACTATE PESAHIM 118
   I. *An Outline of the Halakhah of Pesahim* 118
      i. Preparation for Passover 120
         A. Removal of Leaven 120
         B. Grains Suitable for Unleavened Bread, Herbs Suitable for the Bitter Herbs 123
         C. Removal and Avoidance of What is Fermented 125
         D. Other Requirements for the Fourteenth of Nisan 127
      ii. The Passover-Offering: Slaying and Eating It 128
         A. General Rules on Slaughtering the Lamb Designated as the Passover-Offering 128
         B. The Special Problems of the Sabbath 132
         C. Roasting and Eating the Passover-Offering 134
         D. Uncleanness and the Passover-Offering 135
         E. Not Breaking the Bone of the Passover-Offering 137
         F. Eating the Offering in a Group Other Than the Natural Family 138
         G. Dealing with Unclean and Other Persons In Whose Behalf the Passover is Not to be Slaughtered 142
         H. The Second Passover 144
         I. The Animal Designated for a Passover that is Lost, or For Which a Substitute is Designated 146
      iii. The Passover Seder 151
   II. *Analysis: The Problematics of the Topic, Pesahim* 152
   III. *Interpretation: Religious Principles of Pesahim* 154

4. TRACTATE SUKKAH 163
   I. *An Outline of the Halakhah of Sukkah* 163
      i. The Appurtenances of the Festival of Sukkot: The Sukkah, the Lulab 164

      A. The Sukkah and its Roofing 164
      B. The Obligation to Dwell in the
         Sukkah 168
      C. The Lulab and the Etrog 168
   ii. The Rites and Offerings of the Festival 170
      A. The Festival Rites Carried Out on Various
         Days of the Festival 170
      B. The Offerings 174
  II. *Analysis: The Problematics of the Topic, Sukkah* 176
  III. *Interpretation: Religious Principles of Sukkah* 180

5. TRACTATE MO'ED QATAN 185
  I. *An Outline of the Halakhah of Mo'ed Qatan* 185
   i. Labor on the Intermediate Days of the
     Festival 187
      A. In the Fields 187
      B. Miscellanies 188
      C. Cases of Emergency and Loss 189
   ii. Commerce 189
   iii. Burial of the Dead, Mourning on the
      Intermediate Days of a Festival 192
  II. *Analysis: The Problematics of the Topic, Mo'ed Qatan* 194
  III. *Interpretation: Religious Principles of Mo'ed Qatan* 195

6. TRACTATE BESAH 199
  I. *An Outline of the Halakhah of Besah* 199
   i. Preparing Food on the Festival Day 199
      A. Cases and their Implications 199
      B. Designating Food before the Festival for Use
         on the Festival 204
      C. Doing Actions Connected with Preparing
         Food on a Festival Day in a Different
         Manner from on Ordinary Days. Other
         Restrictions 206
      D. The Status of a Person's Possessions in
         Respect to the Sabbath Limit 209
  II. *Analysis: The Problematics of the Topic, Besah* 212
  III. *Interpretation: Religious Principles of Besah* 214

SANCTIFICATION IN THE HERE AND NOW:
THE TABLE AND THE BED

7. Tractate Hullin 220
   I. *An Outline of the Halakhah of Hullin* 220
      i. Rules of Slaughtering Unconsecrated Animals for
         Use at Home or in the Temple 222
         A. General Rules of Slaughter 222
         B. Specific Regulations. *Terefah*-Rules 228
         C. Slaughter and Illicit Sacrifice 230
         D. *Terefah* and Valid Carcasses 232
         E. The Affect of Valid Slaughter on the Parts
            of a Beast's Body, e.g., on the Foetus 236
      ii. Other Rules Governing the Preparation of Food,
         Principally for Use at Home 238
         A. Not Slaughtering "It and Its Young"
            (Lev. 22:28) 238
         B. The Requirement to Cover Up the Blood
            (Lev. 17:13–14) 240
         C. The Prohibition of the Sciatic Nerve
            (Gen. 32:32) 242
         D. The Separation of Milk and Meat (Ex. 23:19,
            34:26, Dt. 12:21) 245
         E. Connection for the Purposes of Contracting
            Uncleanness 247
         F. The Gifts to the Priest Taken from a Beast
            Slaughtered for Secular Purposes:
            The Shoulder, Two Cheeks, and Maw
            (Dt. 18:3) 248
         G. The Gift to the Priest of the First Fleece of a
            Sheep (Dt. 18:4) 251
         H. Letting the Dam Go from the Nest When
            Taking the Young (Dt. 22:6–7) 253
  II. *Analysis: The Problematics of the Topic, Hullin* 255
 III. *Interpretation: Religious Principles of Hullin* 260

8. Tractate Qiddushin 270
   I. *An Outline of the Halakhah of Qiddushin* 270
      i. Betrothals 272
         A. Rules of Acquisition of Persons and
            Property 272

B. Procedures of Betrothal: Agency, Value, Stipulations	276
C. Impaired Betrothal	279
D. Stipulations	281
E. Cases of Doubt	283
ii. Castes for the Purposes of Marriage	285
A. The Status of the Offspring of Impaired Marriages	285
B. Castes and Marriage Between Castes	286
C. Cases of Doubt	287
II. *Analysis: The Problematics of the Topic, Qiddushin*	288
III. *Interpretation: Religious Principles of Qiddushin*	291
9. TRACTATE KETUBOT	299
I. *An Outline of the Halakhah of Ketubot*	299
i. Foundation of the Household: The Material Rights of the Parties to the Marital Union [1] The Wife	301
A. The Marriage Contract of the Virgin	301
B. Conflicting Claims for the Marriage-Contract of a Virgin	303
C. The Rules of Evidence in Connection with the Validation of the Marriage-Contract	305
ii. The Formation of the Marriage: The Material Rights of the Parties to the Marital Union [2] The Father and the Husband	308
A. The Fine that Is Paid to the Father for Rape or Seduction (Dt. 21:22)	308
B. The Father	311
C. The Father and the Husband	311
D. The Husband	313
iii. The Duration of the Marriage. The Reciprocal Responsibilities and Rights of the Husband and Wife	315
A. The Wife's Duties to the Husband	315
B. The Husband's Obligations to the Wife	317
C. The Dowry	318
D. The Marital Rights and Duties of the Wife	321
E. Property Rights of the Wife	324
iv. Cessation of the Marriage: The Collection of the Marriage-Contract	326

　　　　A. Imposing an Oath in Connection with
　　　　　 Collecting the Marriage-Settlement 326
　　　　B. Multiple Claims on an Estate, Including the
　　　　　 Wives' for their Marriage-Settlement 330
　　　　C. Support for the Widow 332
　　　　D. Rights to, And Collection of, a Marriage
　　　　　 Contract: Special Cases 334
　　　　E. Two Case-Books 337
　　II. *Analysis: The Problematics of the Topic, Ketubot* 339
　　III. *Interpretation: Religious Principles of Ketubot* 342

SANCTIFICATION AND THE MARITAL BOND

10. TRACTATE NEDARIM 351
　　I. *An Outline of the Halakhah of Nedarim* 351
　　　　i. The Language of Vows 354
　　　　　 A. Euphemisms 354
　　　　　 B. Language of No Effect 357
　　　　　 C. Language of Limited Effect 358
　　　　ii. The Binding Effects of Vows 360
　　　　　 A. Vows Not to Derive Benefit 360
　　　　　 B. Vows Not to Eat Certain Food 364
　　　　　 C. Vows Not to Use Certain Objects 367
　　　　　 D. The Temporal Limitation in Vows 368
　　　　iii. The Absolution of Vows 370
　　　　　 A. Grounds for the Absolution of Vows 370
　　　　　 B. The Annulment of the Vows of a
　　　　　　　Daughter 373
　　　　　 C. The Annulment of the Vows of a Wife 374
　　　　　 D. The Husband's Power to Annul the Wife's
　　　　　　　Vows. Special Rules 375
　　　　　 E. Vows of a Woman that Are Not Subject to
　　　　　　　Abrogation 377
　　II. *Analysis: The Problematics of the Topic, Nedarim* 379
　　III. *Interpretation: Religious Principles of Nedarim:*
　　　　A Preliminary Observation 382

11. TRACTATE NAZIR 384
　　I. *An Outline of the Halakhah of Nazir* 384
　　　　i. The Special Vow of the Nazirite 386

	A. The Language of the Vow to be a Nazirite	386
	B. Stipulations and the Nazirite Vow	389
	C. The Duration of the Vow	392
	D. Annulling the Vow	393
ii.	The Special Offerings of the Nazirite	396
	A. Designation and Disposition of the Nazirite's Offerings	396
iii.	Restrictions on the Nazirite	400
	A. The Grape	400
	B. Cutting Hair	402
	C. Corpse-Uncleanness	404
	D. Doubts in the Case of a Nazirite	405
II. *Analysis: The Problematics of the Topic, Nazir*		410
III. *Interpretation: Religious Principles of Nedarim-Nazir*		414

12. TRACTATE SOTAH 426
    I. *An Outline of the Halakhah of Sotah* 426
        i. Invoking the Ordeal 429
        ii. Narrative of the Ordeal 429
        iii. Rules of the Ordeal 436
            A. Exemptions and Applicability 436
            B. Testimony and Exemptions from the Ordeal 439
        iv. Rites Conducted in Hebrew 440
            A. A Catalogue 440
            B. The Anointed for Battle and the Draft-Exemptions 444
            C. The Rite of the Heifer 448
    II. *Analysis: The Problematics of the Topic, Sotah* 451
    III. *Interpretation: Religious Principles of Sotah* 454

THE DESACRALIZATION OF THE HOUSEHOLD: THE BED

13. TRACTATE GITTIN 468
    I. *An Outline of the Halakhah of Gittin* 468
        i. The Writ of Divorce 471
            A. Transmitting the Writ of Divorce 471
            B. The Writ of Divorce and the Writ of Emancipation of Slaves 475
            C. Preparing a Writ of Divorce 476

ii.	Rules of Agency and Writs of Divorce	479
iii.	Rulings Pertinent to the Writ of Divorce Made for Good Order of the World, and Other Rulings in the Same Classification	480
iv.	The Slave	484
v.	The Wife's Receipt of the Writ of Divorce	485
vi.	The Husband's Instructions on the Preparation & Delivery of the Writ	487
	A. Instructing Agents to Prepare the Writ	487
	B. The Conditional Writ of Divorce	488
vii.	The Impaired Writ of Divorce	492
	A. The Writ of Divorce that is Subject to Doubt	492
	B. The Writ of Divorce that is Subject to Flaws or Imperfections	493
	C. An Invalidating Restriction in a Writ of Divorce	495
	D. Confusing Writs of Divorce	496
II.	*Analysis: The Problematics of the Topic, Gittin*	498
III.	*Interpretation: Religious Principles of Gittin*	502

14. TRACTATE YEBAMOT 509
   I. *An Outline of the Halakhah of Yebamot* 509
      i. When the Levirate Connection Does Not Pertain 512
         A. Women Who Are Near of Kin to their Deceased, Childless Husband's Brother but Cannot Enter into Levirate Marriage with the Deceased Childless Husband's Brother 512
         B. Surviving Brothers Eligible for Levirate Marriage: When the Levirate Connection is Null. Cases of Confusion 519
      ii. The Interstitial Case: The Flawed Levirate Connection and the Rite of Removing the Shoe 523
         A. Brothers Married to Sisters 523
         B. When the Levirate Connection is Subject to Doubt: Flawed Betrothal or Divorce 527

	C. When a Brother Bespeaks the Levirate Widow but Dies before Consummating the Relationship	528
	D. When the Brothers Act in Error	528
	E. When the Levirate Connection is Effected in Error	529
iii.	The Consequence of the Levirate Marriage	531
	A. Property Relationships	531
	B. Personal Relationships	531
	C. Inheritance	532
	D. Further Marriages	532
	E. Sequences of Levirate Transactions	536
	F. Sexual Relations in the Levirate Marriage	538
iv.	Marriages that Violate the Restrictions of the Torah. The Consequences for the Priesthood as to the Consumption of Priestly Rations	539
	A. A Widow Wed to a High Priest, a Divorcee to an Ordinary Priest	539
	B. Other Considerations Involved in Consuming Priestly Rations. Uncleanness	544
	C. Prohibited Marriages	546
	D. Consequences of Violating the Prohibitions against Marriage	550
v.	Marriages that Are Subject to Doubt by Reason of the Status of the Parties Thereto	553
	A. The Marital Bond of a Boy Nine Years and One Day Old	553
	B. Special Cases: The Rapist, the Convert	555
	C. The Confusion of Offspring	555
vi.	The Rite of Removing the Shoe	559
vii.	Exercising the Right of Refusal. The Minor and Levirate Marriage	562
	A. The Rite of Refusal	562
	B. The Minor and Levirate Marriage	563
viii.	The Marriage of the Deaf-Mute and the Person of Sound Senses	567

ix. Ascertaining whether the Husband Has Actually Died 569
    A. When the Husband is Missing 569
    B. Testimony that the Husband Has Died 569
II. *Analysis: The Problematics of the Topic, Yebamot* 573
III. *Interpretation: Religious Principles of Yebamot* 577

INDEXES 587

VOLUME V

INSIDE THE WALLS OF THE ISRAELITE HOUSEHOLD

PART B

THE DESACRALIZATION OF THE HOUSEHOLD: THE TABLE FOCI, SOURCES, AND DISSEMINATION OF UNCLEANNESS. PURIFICATION FROM THE POLLUTION OF DEATH

Preface xv

THE DESACRALIZATION OF THE HOUSEHOLD: THE TABLE. FOCI OF UNCLEANNESS

1. TRACTATE KELIM 1
  I. *The Halakhah of Uncleanness and Sanctification: General Considerations* 1
  II. *An Outline of the Halakhah of Kelim* 9
    i. Proem for Purities: Hierarchies of Uncleanness and Corresponding Hierarchies of Sanctification 12
      A. The Hierarchy of Sources of Uncleanness: From Least to Most Virulent 12
      B. The Hierarchy of Sources of Uncleanness: Those that Pertain to Man 14
      C. The Hierarchy of Loci of Sanctification: From Least to Most Holy 15

ii. Susceptibility to Uncleanness of Clay Utensils 17
   A. Wood, Leather, Bone, Glass, and Clay
      (Earthenware) 17
   B. Damage That Renders Clay Utensils
      Useless and Therefore Insusceptible to
      Uncleanness 19
   C. The Point, in the Process of Manufacturing
      Clay Utensils, at which the Utensils Become
      Susceptible to Uncleanness; and, When Broken
      Down, the Point at which They Cease to Be
      Susceptible to Uncleanness: Ovens 23
   D. The Insusceptibility to Uncleanness of the
      Insides of Tightly-Sealed Clay Utensils 36
iii. Susceptibility to Uncleanness of Metal Utensils 40
   A. When Objects Made of Metal Become
      Susceptible, and When They Lose
      Susceptibility 40
   B. Specific Metal Objects and their Status 41
   C. The Point, When a Metal Object Is Broken
      Down, at which the Object Ceases to be
      Susceptible to Uncleanness 49
   D. Further Metal Objects and their Status 50
iv. Utensils of Wood, Leather, Bone, and Glass 52
   A. When Objects Made of Wood, Leather, Bone,
      and Glass Become Susceptible, and When
      They Lose Susceptibility 52
   B. Specific Objects Made of Wood, Leather,
      Bone, and Glass and their Status 52
   C. The Point, in the Process of Manufacturing
      Utensils of Wood, at which the Utensils
      Become Susceptible to Uncleanness; and,
      When Broken Down, the Point at which They
      Cease to Be Susceptible to Uncleanness 54
   D. The Point, in the Process of Manufacturing
      Utensils of Leather, at which the Utensils
      Become Susceptible to Uncleanness; and,
      When Broken Down, the Point at which They
      Cease to Be Susceptible to Uncleanness 55
   E. The Status as to Uncleanness of Specific
      Leather Objects 56

v. The Measure of Breakage that Renders an Object Useless, No Longer Fit to Serve as a Receptacle, and therefore Insusceptible to Uncleanness. General Rules 58
   A. Specific Objects and the Measure of a Whole That Renders Them No Longer Serviceable as a Receptacle 58
   B. Taking the Measure of Specified Objects to Assess their Status 62

vi. The Effect of Dismantling an Object upon the Status, as to Uncleanness, of Said Object 62
   A. A Bed 62
   B. Leather Objects 68
   C. Wooden Objects 68

vii. Variables: Susceptibility of Objects in One Form to One Type of Uncleanness, and in a Different Form to Another Type of Uncleanness. Corpse-Uncleanness, Affecting Receptacles, as against Midras-Uncleanness, Affecting What Is Used for Sitting and Lying [Lev. 15] 71
   A. The Basic Distinction, Based on the Function that a Utensil Serves, between Corpse- and Midras-Uncleanness. Cases 71
   B. Differentiating Primary from Secondary Components of a Utensil 72
   C. Tables and Chairs 73
   D. The Contents of a Utensil and its Function and Form 76
   E. Midras Uncleanness in its Own Terms 76
   F. Midras-Uncleanness, Corpse Uncleanness, Insusceptibility to Uncleanness: A Systematic Repertoire 77

viii. Differentiating the Insides from the Outsides of Utensils for the Purpose of Assessing Uncleanness ... 79

ix. The Principles of the Uncleanness of Utensils Systematically Instantiated in the Analysis of the Status of Leather Objects: Intentionality and Deed, Receptacles and Chairs 81

x. The Principles of the Uncleanness of Utensils Systematically Instantiated in the Analysis of the Status of Cloth Objects 84

xi. Connection	90
xii. Objects Made of Glass	92
III. *Analysis: The Problematics of the Topic, Kelim*	93
IV. *Interpretation: Religious Principles of Kelim*	103

2. TRACTATE UQSIN ... 119
   I. *An Outline of the Halakhah of Uqsin* ... 119
      i. Food: Handles, Husks ... 122
         A. Susceptibility to Uncleanness ... 122
         B. Joining Together ... 123
      ii. Food: Connection ... 124
      iii. Food: Preparation to Bring about Susceptibility to Uncleanness ... 127
   II. *Analysis: The Problematics of the Topic, Uqsin* ... 129
   III. *Interpretation: Religious Principles of Uqsin* ... 132

3. TRACTATE OHALOT ... 135
   I. *An Outline of the Halakhah of Ohalot* ... 135
      i. Corpse-Uncleanness, its Affects on Man and Utensils ... 137
         A. The Matter of Removes ... 137
         B. The Comparison of the Susceptibility of Man and Utensils to Corpse- and Other Uncleanness ... 138
         C. Defining the Corpse that Conveys Corpse-Uncleanness ... 138
         D. Defining Corpse-Matter that Does Not Convey Corpse-Uncleanness through Overshadowing, but only through Contact and Carrying ... 141
         E. Defining Corpse-Matter that Does Not Convey Uncleanness at All ... 141
         F. Corpse-Matter that Is Divided; Corpse-Matter that is Joined Together, to Form the Requisite Volume to Convey Uncleanness ... 142
      ii. The Opening of a Handbreadth Squared Affords Passage to Uncleanness or Interposes against the Transmission of Uncleanness ... 144
         A. Effecting Contamination and Affording Protection ... 144
         B. The Utensil and the Tent: Effecting Contamination and Affording Protection ... 146

	C. Man, Utensils, and the Tent	148
	D. Corpse-Matter in a Wall	149
iii.	Defining the Tent: Its Sides, its Apertures, the Materials of which it is Constructed	152
	A. The Sloping Sides of the Tent	152
	B. The Apertures	153
	C. The Materials of Which the Tent Is Constructed	153
	D. The Utensil and the Tent, Illustrated by the Hive and the Tent	156
	E. The Hatchway of the Tent	161
iv.	Dividing the Tent or House; Dividing Utensils. Interposition	164
	A. Dividing the Household and its Appurtenances	164
	B. Walling off the Flow of Corpse-Uncleanness in Various Circumstances	166
	C. Holes in the Walls of Tents and Utensils and the Passage of Corpse-Uncleanness, and Diminishing the Dimensions of the Hole to Impede the Flow of Corpse-Uncleanness	168
	D. Wall-Projections and the Flow of Corpse-Uncleanness	170
	E. Other Media of Interposition	171
	F. Dividing the House/Room by Filling It with Dirt and Stone	172
	G. The Moving Tent	174
v.	Graveyards and Contaminated Dirt	175
II.	*Analysis: The Problematics of the Topic, Ohalot*	181
III.	*Interpretation: Religious Principles of Ohalot*	189

SOURCES OF UNCLEANNESS, DISSEMINATION OF UNCLEANNESS

4.	TRACTATE TOHOROT	195
I.	*An Outline of the Halakhah of Tohorot*	195
i.	Principles of Uncleanness of Food: Meat. Fathers and Offspring of Uncleanness. The Matter of Removes	196

ii. Susceptibility to Uncleanness of Holy Things, Heave-Offering, and Unconsecrated Food	198
iii. Doubt in Matters of Uncleanness	203
iv. The *Haber* and the 'Am Ha'ares	217
v. Concluding Miscellanies and Reprise. Uncleanness of Foods, Liquids, Connection	222
II. *Analysis: The Problematics of the Topic, Tohorot*	228
III. *Interpretation: Religious Principles of Tohorot*	239

5. TRACTATE MAKHSHIRIN 252
   I. *An Outline of the Halakhah of Makhshirin* 252
i. Intention: Divisible or Indivisible	255
ii. Water Capable of Imparting Susceptibility Mixed with Water Incapable of Imparting Susceptibility	257
iii. Absorption of Water	259
iv. Water Used for One Purpose: Its Status as to a Secondary Purpose	260
v. The Stream as a Connector	266
vi. The Insusceptibility of Liquids that are Not Used Intentionally	266
vii. The Liquids that Have the Power to Impart Susceptibility to Uncleanness	268
II. *Analysis: The Problematics of the Topic, Makhshirin*	268
III. *Interpretation: Religious Principles of Makhshirin*	272

ANIMATE SOURCES OF UNCLEANNESS

6. TRACTATE ZABIM 275
   I. *An Outline of the Halakhah of Zabim* 275
i. Becoming Unclean as a Zab	281
ii. Transferring the Uncleanness of the Zab. Pressure	284
iii. Transferring the Uncleanness of the Zab. Generalizations	288
II. *Analysis: The Problematics of the Topic, Zabim*	292

7. TRACTATE NIDDAH 300
   I. *An Outline of the Halakhah of Niddah* 300
      i. Retroactive Contamination 301

ii. Unclean Excretions ... 306
- A. Unclean Blood ... 306
- B. The Status of Abortions as to Uncleanness ... 307
- C. Samaritan, Sadducee, and Gentile Women ... 310
- D. Status of Blood Produced in Labor ... 310
- E. Status of Blood Produced in the Zibah-Period ... 311
- F. Status of Blood Produced in a Caesarian Section ... 312
- G. Point at which Unclean Fluid Imparts Uncleanness ... 312

iii. Rules Applicable at Various Ages ... 312

iv. Doubts in Connection with Unclean Excretions ... 315
- A. Bloodstains and Other Matters Subject to Doubt ... 315
- B. Blood of Menstruating Women, Flesh of a Corpse ... 317
- C. Doubts about Things, Bloodstains ... 317
- D. Bloodstains [Doubtfully-Unclean Blood] of Israelites, Gentiles, and Samaritans ... 318
- E. Doubts about Bloodstains and Drops of Blood ... 318
- F. The Fixed Period ... 322

v. Concluding Miscellanies ... 323
- A. Girl Married before Puberty: Status of Blood ... 323
- B. Doubts about Cleanness Failure to Examine ... 324
- C. Uncleanness of the Zab, the Menstruating Women ... 325
- D. Status of a Woman in the Period of Purifying after Childbirth ... 326
- E. She Who Produces Blood on the Eleventh Day of the Zibah-Period ... 327

II. *Analysis: The Problematics of the Topic, Niddah* ... 327
III. *Interpretation: Religious Principles of Zabim and Niddah* ... 333

8. TRACTATE NEGAIM ... 345
I. *An Outline of the Halakhah of Negaim* ... 345
i. Generalizations ... 349
- A. The Colors of Plagues ... 349
- B. Variations in Skin-Tone, Examining Plagues ... 351

ii. Types of Nega'im: The Bright Spot Boil, Burning, Scalls, Bald Spots 353
iii. The Bright Spot 354
    A. Tokens of Uncleanness in the Bright Spot 354
    B. Miscellanies on White Hair 355
    C. Fifteen Problems Involving the Bright Spot 355
    D. Doubts in Matters of Plagues Resolved in Favor of Cleanness 357
    E. The Relationship of Quick Flesh and Spreading 359
    F. Places on the Human Body that are Not Susceptible to Uncleanness [1] Because of the Appearance of a Bright Spot Containing Quick Flesh or [2] Because of the Appearance of a Bright Spot and [3] Bright Spots that are Not Susceptible to Uncleanness, No Matter Where They Occur 359
    G. Removing the Symptoms of Uncleanness 361
    H. When the Spot Breaks Forth Over the Entire Body 362
iv. The Boil and the Burning 365
v. Scalls 365
vi. Bald-Spots on Forehead and Temples 368
vii. Garments 369
viii. Houses 373
ix. Process of Purification of the Person Afflicted with a Nega' 380
II. *Analysis: The Problematics of the Topic, Negaim* 385
III. *Interpretation: Religious Principles of Negaim* 389

9. TRACTATE TEBUL YOM 401
I. *An Outline of the Halakhah of Tebul Yom* 401
    i. Connection in the Case of the Tebul Yom 403
        A. The Governing Principle 403
        B. Liquids and Connection in the Case of the Tebul Yom 404
        C. Solids and Connection in the Case of the Tebul Yom 407
    ii. The Uncleanness of the Tebul Yom 408

II. *Analysis: The Problematics of the Topic, Tebul Yom* 410
III. *Interpretation: Religious Principles of Tebul Yom* 413

10. TRACTATE YADAYIM 418
   I. *An Outline of the Halakhah of Yadayim* 418
      i. Washing Hands. A Repertoire of Rules 420
      ii. Washing Hands. The Status and Condition of the Water. First and Second Pourings of Water 422
      iii. The Status of Uncleanness Imputed to Hands 426
      iv. The Uncleanness of Sacred Scriptures 426
   II. *Analysis: The Problematics of the Topic, Yadayim* 428
   III. *Interpretation: Religious Principles of Yadayim* 430

PURIFICATION FROM THE POLLUTION OF DEATH

11. TRACTATE PARAH 434
    I. *An Outline of the Halakhah of Parah* 434
       i. The Red Cow Defined 436
       ii. The Conduct of the Rite. A Narrative 439
       iii. The Conduct of the Rite. Laws 443
       iv. Utensils Used in the Rite 446
       v. Mixing the Ash and Water 450
       vi. Drawing the Water for Mixing with the Ashes 451
       vii. The Kind of Water that is Used for the Rite 458
       viii. Uncleanness and the Purification Rite 461
       ix. The Rules for Sprinkling Purification-Water 466
    II. *Analysis: The Problematics of the Topic, Parah* 471
    III. *Interpretation: Religious Principles of Parah* 476

12. TRACTATE MIQVAOT 482
    I. An Outline of the Halakhah of Miqvaot 482
       i. Six Grades of Gatherings of Water 483
    II. Resolving Doubts about Immersion and Immersion-Pools 486

III. Diverse Volume and Mixtures of Water of
    Immersion-Pools 490
IV. The Union of Pools to form the Requisite Volume
    of Water 496
V. Water and Wine, Water and Mud, Water in
    Various Locales 499
VI. Using the Immersion Pool. The Matter of
    Interposition 502
II. *Analysis: The Problematics of the Topic, Miqvaot* 508
III. *Interpretation: Religious Principles of Miqvaot* 512

INDEXES 517

1.

TRACTATE BABA QAMMA

I. An Outline of the Halakhah of Baba Qamma

As I said in the Introduction to this project, the goal of the system of civil law is the recovery of the just order that characterized Israel upon entry into the Land. The law aims at the preservation of the established wholeness, balance, proportion, and stability of the social economy realized at that moment. This idea is powerfully expressed in the organization of the three tractates that comprise the civil law, which treat first abnormal and then normal transactions. The framers deal with damages done by chattels and by human beings, thefts and other sorts of malfeasance against the persons and the property of others. The civil law in both aspects pays closest attention to how the property and person of the injured party so far as possible are restored to their prior condition, that is, the state of normality disrupted by the damage done to property or injury done to a person. So attention to torts focuses upon penalties paid by the malefactor to the victim, rather than upon penalties inflicted by the court on the malefactor for what he has done.

When speaking of damages, the halakhah, initially stated by the Mishnah in the terms of injury and misappropriation, takes as its principal concern the restoration of the fortune of victims of assault or robbery. In its account of damages inflicted by chattel and persons, the native category defined by tractate Baba Qamma incorporates facts supplied by Scripture but frames the topic in its own way. That way makes itself manifest only when we consider the three Babas together as a single coherent statement, an approach postponed until Chapter Three. To state the character of the halakhah of the Oral Torah in the present category, it suffices simply to note that what Scripture presents episodically, the halakhah portrays systematically.

i. *Damage by Chattels*

A. *The Fundamental Rules of Assessing Damages when the Cause is One's Property, Animate or Inanimate*

M. 1:1 [There are] four generative causes of damages: (1) ox [Ex. 21:35–36], (2) pit [Ex. 21:33], (3) crop-destroying beast [Ex. 22:4], and (4) conflagration [Ex. 22:5]. What they have in common is that they customarily do damage and taking care of them is your responsibility. And when one [of them] has caused damage, the [owner] of that which causes the damage is liable to pay compensation for damage out of the best of his land [Ex. 22:4].

M. 1:1 IV.2/5B: For what definitive purpose did Scripture find it necessary to make explicit reference to each such classification? [1] Horn: to make the distinction between the beast deemed harmless and that one that is an attested danger. [2] Tooth and foot: to exempt the owner from damage that was done within these classifications in public domain. [3] Pit: to exempt the owner from damage done to inanimate objects; [4] Man: to impose upon him the four additional classifications of compensation to be paid for damage done by a human being to another human being. [5] Fire: to make one immune for damage done to objects that were hidden away [and not known by the person who kindled the fire] by a fire one has kindled.

T. 6:29 A strict rule applies to an ox which does not apply to a pit, and a strict rule applies to a pit which does not apply to an ox. For [the owner of] an ox is liable to pay ransom and liable for the thirty *selas* to be paid in the case of killing a slave. And when [the ox's] court-process has been completed, it is prohibited for the owner to gain benefit from it. And it is assumed usually to walk along and to do damage which is not the case with a pit. A more strict aspect of the pit is that the pit is always deemed to be an attested danger, which is not the case with an ox.

T. 6:30 A more strict rule applies to an ox which does not apply to fire and a strict rule applies to fire which does not apply to an ox. For [the owner of] an ox is liable to pay ransom and liable for the thirty *selas* to be paid in the case of killing a slave. And when [the ox's] court-process has been completed, it is prohibited for the owner to gain benefit from it. And if one has handed it over [to the guardianship of] a deaf-mute, idiot, or minor, he remains liable, which is not the case with fire A more strict aspect of fire is that fire is always deemed to be an attested danger, which is not the case with an ox.

T. 6:31 A strict rule applies to a pit which does not apply to fire, and to fire which does not apply to a pit. For in the case of a pit, [if] one has handed it over [to the guardianship] of a deaf-mute, idiot, or minor, he remains liable, which is not the case with fire. A more strict aspect of fire is that fire is assumed to go along and to do damage."

M. 1:2 In the case of anything of which I am liable to take care, I am deemed to render possible whatever damage it may do. [If] I am deemed to have rendered possible part of the damage it may do, I am liable for compensation as if [I have] made possible all of the damage it may do. (1) Property which is not subject to the law of Sacrilege, (2) property belonging to members of the covenant [Israelites], (3) property that is held in ownership, and that is located in any place other than in the domain which is in the ownership of the one who has caused the damage, or in the domain which is shared by the one who suffers injury and the one who causes injury — when one has caused damage [under any of the aforelisted circumstances] [the owner of] that one which has caused the damage is liable to pay compensation for damage out of the best of his land.

B. 1:2 I:1/9B: IN THE CASE OF ANYTHING OF WHICH I AM LIABLE TO TAKE CARE, I AM DEEMED TO RENDER POSSIBLE WHATEVER DAMAGE IT MAY DO. HOW SO? IN THE CASE OF AN OX OR A PIT THAT ONE HAS HANDED OVER TO A DEAF-MUTE, AN INSANE PERSON, OR A MINOR, WHICH DID DAMAGE, ONE IS LIABLE TO PAY COMPENSATION, WHICH IS NOT THE CASE WITH FIRE.

M. 1:2 II.1/10A: [IF] I AM DEEMED TO HAVE RENDERED POSSIBLE PART OF THE DAMAGE IT MAY DO, I AM LIABLE FOR COMPENSATION AS IF [I HAVE] MADE POSSIBLE ALL OF THE DAMAGE IT MAY DO: HOW SO? HE WHO DIGS A PIT NINE CUBITS DEEP, AND SOMEONE ELSE COMES ALONG AND FINISHES IT TO TEN — THE LATTER IS LIABLE [HAVING COMPLETED THE PIT SO THAT IT CAN KILL SOMEONE].

M. 1:3 Assessment [of the compensation for an injury to be paid] is in terms of ready cash [but is paid in kind — that is,] in what is worth money, before a court, on the basis of evidence given by witnesses who are freemen and members of the covenant. Women fall into the category of [parties to suits concerning] damages. And the one who suffers damages and the one who causes damages [may share] in the compensation.

M. 1:4 [There are] five [deemed] harmless, and five [deemed] attested dangers. A domesticated beast is not regarded as an attested danger in regard to butting, (2) pushing, (3) biting, (4) lying down, or (5) kicking. (1) A tooth is deemed an attested danger in regard to eating what is suitable for [eating]. (2) The leg is deemed an attested danger in regard to breaking something as it walks along. (3) And an ox which is an attested danger [so far as goring is concerned]; (4) and an ox which causes damage in the domain of the one who is injured; and (5) man. If that which is deemed harmless [causes damage], [the owner] pays half of the value of the damage which has been caused, [with liability limited to the value of the] carcass [of the beast

which has caused the damage]. But [if that which is] an attested danger [causes damage], [the owner] pays the whole of the value of the damage which has been caused from the best property [he may own, and his liability is by no means limited to the value of the animal which has done the damage].

B. 1:4A–J I.1/16A: [THERE ARE] FIVE [DEEMED] HARMLESS, BUT IF THEY ARE SUBJECTED TO A WARNING, THEN ALL FIVE OF THEM ARE THEN CLASSIFIED AS ATTESTED DANGERS. AND THE TOOTH AND FOOT ARE HELD TO BE ATTESTED DANGERS TO BEGIN WITH. AND THIS IS THE WAY IN WHICH THE OX IS AN ATTESTED DANGER. THERE ARE, MOREOVER, OTHER CLASSIFICATIONS OF THOSE THAT ARE ATTESTED DANGER IN THE SAME CATEGORY AS THESE: (1) A WOLF, (2) LION, (3) BEAR, (4) LEOPARD, (5) PANTHER, AND (6) A SERPENT — LO, THESE ARE ATTESTED DANGERS.

M. 2:1 A beast is an attested danger to go along in the normal way and to break [something]. [But if] it was kicking, or if pebbles were scattered from under its feet and it [thereby] broke utensils — [the owner] pays half of the value of the damages [caused by his ox]. [If] it stepped on a utensil and broke it, and [the utensil] fell on another utensil and broke it, for the first [the owner] pays the full value of the damage. But for the second he pays half of the value of the damage. Fowl are an attested danger to go along in the normal way and to break [something].

T. 2:1 Fowl which were scratching at dough or at pieces of fruit, or which pecked — [the owner] pays half-damages. [If] they scratched dirt onto dough or onto pieces of fruit, [the owner] pays full damages. [If] they were pecking at the rope of a well-bucket, and [in consequence it was weakened and] fell and broke, [the owner] pays full damages. [If] it fell and broke and furthermore broke another utensil [alongside], for the first, [the owner] pays full damages, and for the second, [he pays] half-damages. Fowl which went down into a vegetable patch and broke the young shoots and chopped off the leaves [of the plants] — [the owner] pays full damages.

M. 2:2 An ox is an attested danger to eat fruit and vegetables. [If, however,] it ate [a piece of] clothing or utensils, [the owner] pays half of the value of the damage it has caused. Under what circumstances? [When this takes place] in the domain of the injured party. But [if it takes place] in the public domain, he is exempt. But if it [the ox] derived benefit [from damage done in public domain], [the owner] pays for the value of what [his ox] has enjoyed. How does he pay for the benefit of what [his ox] has enjoyed? [If] it ate something in the midst of the marketplace, he pays for the value of what it has enjoyed. [If it ate] from the sides of the marketplace, he pays for the value of the damage that [the ox] has caused. [If he ate] from [what is located at] the doorway of a store, the owner pays for the value of what it has enjoyed. [If it ate] from [what is located]

inside the store, the owner pays for the value of the damages that it has caused.

T. 1:6 A beast which on its own entered private domain and did damage with its foreleg, hind-leg, or horn, with the yoke which is on it, the saddlebag which is on it, the pack which is on its back, or with the wagon which it is pulling — [the owner] pays the full value of the damage which has been done. He who causes damage in neutral domain [neither public nor private] pays the full value of the damage which has been done.

T. 1:7 A beast which was going along in its usual way in public domain and fell into a garden and derived benefit [by eating the vegetables there] pays for the value of the benefit it has derived [If it has eaten things growing] on the sides of the road or located in a store, it pays the value of the damage which it has caused How [do we assess damages in a case in which] it pays the value of what it has eaten? They make an estimate of how much a man is willing to pay to feed his beast in the amount of what it has eaten, in food he does not regularly feed to the beast. Therefore if it ate grain which is suitable [for feeding] to it, lo, this one is exempt. [If it] chewed and ate, one pays the value of the damage which it has caused.

T. 1:8 A beast which ate food which is not suitable for it, or drank liquid which is not suitable for it, and so too, a wild beast which ate food which is not suitable for it, [which] tore [meat] off of a beast and ate the flesh — an ass which ate lupines — a cow which ate barley — a pig which ate pieces of meat — a dog which licked up oil — [the owners of these animals] pay the full value of the damages [their beasts have caused].

M. 2:3 The dog or the goat which jumped from the top of the roof and broke utensils — [the owner] pays the full value of the damage [they have caused], because they are attested dangers. The dog which took a cake [to which a cinder adhered] and went to standing grain, ate the cake, and set the stack on fire — for the cake the owner pays full damages, but for the standing grain he pays only for half of the damages [his dog has caused].

T. 2:1 A dog or a goat which fell and did damage — lo [their owners] are exempt. [But if] they jumped down and did damage, lo, [their owners] are liable [M. B.Q. 2:3A]. But a man who jumped, whether from above or from below, and did damage, lo, this one is liable. [If] he fell onto his fellow and did damage — [if] the one below [did damage] to the one above, the one above is liable. [If] the one above [did damage] to the one below, the one below is exempt from liability. If he said to him, "Catch me!" then both of them are responsible for the safety of one another [and share liability for damages].

B. 2:3 I.2/21B: A DOG OR A GOAT THAT JUMPED — IF IT WAS FROM BELOW TO ABOVE, THE OWNER IS EXEMPT. IF IT WAS FROM ABOVE TO BELOW, THE OWNER IS LIABLE. [IN THE FORMER CASE, THIS WOULD BE UNUSUAL, AND THE OWNER DOES NOT HAVE TO PAY FULL DAMAGES, BUT ONLY HALF-DAMAGES IN THE CLASSIFICATION OF HORN.] IN THE CASE OF MEN OR CHICKENS,

WHETHER THEY JUMPED FROM BELOW TO ABOVE OR ABOVE TO BELOW, THEY ARE LIABLE [SINCE MEN AND CHICKENS JUMP A LOT].

M. 2:4 How does he pay for the benefit of what [his ox] has enjoyed? [If] it ate something in the midst of the marketplace, he pays for the value of what it has enjoyed. [If it ate] from the sides of the marketplace, he pays for the value of the damage that [the ox] has caused. [If he ate] from [what is located at] the doorway of a store, the owner pays for the value of what it has enjoyed. [If it ate] from [what is located] inside the store, the owner pays for the value of the damages that it has caused.

M. 2:5 An ox which causes damage in the domain of the one who is injured — how so? [If] it gored, pushed, bit, lay down, or kicked, in the public domain, [the owner] pays half of the value of the damages [the ox has caused]. [If it did so] in the domain of the injured party, the owner pays half of the value.

M. 2:6 Man is perpetually an attested danger whether [what is done is done] inadvertently or deliberately, whether man is awake or asleep. [If] he blinded the eye of his fellow or broke his utensils, he pays the full value of the damage he has caused.

T. 2:2 Under no circumstances is an ox declared an attested danger unless people give testimony in the presence of the owner and of the court. [If] they gave testimony in the presence of the owner but not in the presence of the court, in the presence of the court but not in the presence of the owner, it is not declared to be an attested danger — unless people gave testimony in the presence of the owner and the court. [If] they gave testimony before two on the first occasion, before two on the second occasion, and before two on the third occasion, lo, these constitute three distinct acts of giving testimony. But they constitute a single act of testimony so far as an accusation of conspiracy [against the witnesses] is concerned. [If] the first set [of witnesses] turns out to be perjured, lo, [the witnesses as to] the other two occasions [on which the ox allegedly misbehaved] are exempt from paying compensation [along with the conspirators].

T. 2:3 [If] the second set of witnesses turns out to be perjured, lo, [the witnesses as to] one occasion [namely, the third] are exempt from paying compensation [along with the conspirators]. [If] all three sets of witnesses turn out to be perjured, [the owner] is exempt [from paying compensation for damage done by his ox], but they are liable.

B. 2:4 I.4/24A: AN OX IS NOT DECLARED AN ATTESTED DANGER UNLESS THE WITNESSES GIVE TESTIMONY AGAINST HIM BEFORE THE OWNER AND BEFORE THE COURT. IF THEY GAVE THEIR TESTIMONY AGAINST THE OX BEFORE THE COURT BUT NOT BEFORE THE OWNER, OR BEFORE THE OWNER BUT NOT BEFORE THE COURT, THE OX IS NOT DECLARED AN ATTESTED DANGER. THAT CAN ONLY BE IF THE TESTIMONY IS GIVEN AGAINST THE OX BOTH BEFORE THE COURT AND BEFORE THE OWNER. IF TESTIMONY WAS GIVEN AGAINST IT BY TWO ON THE FIRST DAY, TWO ON THE SECOND, AND TWO ON THE THIRD, LO, THERE ARE IN HAND THREE ACTS OF TESTIMONY, WHICH FORM A SINGLE

ACT OF TESTIMONY FOR THE PURPOSES OF DECLARING THE WITNESSES A CONSPIRACY [SHOULD THAT BE THE FACT]. IF, THEREFORE, THE FIRST OF THE THREE PAIRS OF WITNESSES IS FOUND TO FORM A CONSPIRACY, LO, ONLY TWO ACTS OF TESTIMONY THAT ARE VALID REMAIN, WITH THE RESULT THAT THE OX IS EXEMPT FROM THE STATUS OF AN ATTESTED DANGER, AND THE WITNESSES ARE EXEMPT FROM PENALTY. IF THE SECOND GROUP IS LIKEWISE FOUND TO BE A CONSPIRACY, LO, ONLY A SINGLE ACT OF TESTIMONY IS IN HAND [OF THE REQUIRED THREE], WITH THE RESULT THAT THE OX IS EXEMPT FROM THE DEFINED STATUS AND THEY ARE EXEMPT FROM PENALTY. IF THE THIRD OF THE THREE SETS IS FOUND A CONSPIRACY, THEN ALL THREE SETS OF WITNESSES ARE LIABLE TO THE PENALTY, AND IN THIS CASE SCRIPTURE DECLARES, "THEN YOU SHALL TO DO HIM AS HE HAD THOUGHT TO HAVE DONE TO HIS BROTHER" (DEUT. 19:19).

B. *Damages Done by Chattels in the Public Domain*

M. 3:1 He who leaves a jug in the public domain, and someone else came along and stumbled on it and broke it — [the one who broke it] is exempt. And if [the one who broke it] was injured by it, the owner of the jug is liable [to pay damages for] his injury. [If] his jug was broken in the public domain, and someone slipped on the water, or was hurt by the shards, he is liable.

Y. 3:1 I.2 *An ox which mounted its fellow, and the owner of the one beneath came along and pulled his beast out from underneath: if before it had mounted, he pulled it out, and the ox fell down and died, the one who did so [and saved his property] is exempt. If he pushed it off and it fell and died, he is liable. [That is, the owner pulled his ox away before the other ox mounted up; he in no way bears responsibility for the death of the other ox, nor can he be accused of saving his own capital at the expense of the other party's. Clearly, then, there is a distinction to be drawn between saving one's property at the expense of someone else when the damage already has been done, and doing so when it has not yet been done. If the damage has been done, one may not necessarily injure one's fellow . . . If the damage has not been done, one may save himself at the cost of his fellow so that he will not suffer any damage at all.]*

M. 3:2 He who pours water out into the public domain, and someone else was injured on it, is liable [to pay compensation for] his injury. He who put away thorns or glass, and he who makes his fence out of thorns, and a fence which fell into the public way — and others were injured by them — he is liable [to pay compensation for] their injury.

T. 2:5 He who places thorns and pebbles on his wall, [which extends] into the public domain, and someone else came along and was injured by them, lo, this one is exempt. [If the walls] fell down, and someone else came along and was injured by them, lo, this person is liable [M. B.Q. 3:2D–H]. [If] he built them in the normal way, he is exempt, unless they gave him time [to clear them out]. [If] they gave him time, and they fell down during that time, he is exempt. [If they fell] after that time, he is liable. How much is the time [they must give the man]? J. No less than thirty days.

T. 2:6 He who stored away thorns and glass in the wall of his fellow, and the owner of the wall came along and tore it down, and someone else came along and was injured by them, lo, this one [nonetheless] is liable.

M. 3:3 He who brings out his straw and stubble into the public domain to turn them into manure and someone else was injured on them — he is liable [to pay compensation for] his injury. But whoever grabs them first effects possession of them.

T. 2:4 [If] one's jug or jar broke in public domain, and someone else came along and was injured by them, lo, this person is liable. [If] he left his stone or burden in the public way, [and] they said to him, "Clear them out," [and] he said to them, "I don't want them," whoever grabs them first acquires possession of them. [If] someone else came along and was injured by them, lo, this person [nonetheless] is liable. [If] his walls fell into the public domain, and they said to him, "Clean them out," and he said to them, "I don't want them," — whoever grabs [the stones of the walls] first acquires possession of them. [If] someone else came along and was injured by them, lo, this person is liable [cf. M. B.Q. 3:3A–F].

T. 2:8 He who heaps up cattle dung to acquire possession of it in the public domain, and someone else came along and was injured by it — lo, this person is liable. And [to others the dung] is prohibited under the laws of robbery [vs. M. B.Q. 3:3].

M. 3:4 Two pot sellers who were going along, one after another, and the first of them stumbled and fell down, and the second stumbled over the first — the first one is liable [to pay compensation for] the injuries of the second.

T. 2:9 Ass-drivers going after one another — the first of them stumbled and fell down, and his fellow came along and stumbled on him and fell down — even if they are a hundred — all of them are exempt [from having to pay damages]. An ox which pushed its fellow, and its fellow pushed its fellow — the first pays [compensation] to the second, and the second to the third. But if it was on account of the first one that they all fell down, the first one pays for all of them. Five people who sat down on a bench, which broke — all of them are liable to pay [compensation for the bench]. But if it was on account of the last one [alone] that it broke, the last one must pay damages for all of them.

T. 2:10 Asses, the legs of one of which were infirm — they are not permitted [e.g., in a narrow passage] to set him aside [and pass him]. [If] one of [the asses] was loaded and one of them was mounted, they set aside the one which was loaded in favor of the one which was mounted. [If] one of them was mounted and one of them was unburdened, they set aside the one which is unburdened in favor of the one which is mounted. [If] both of them were carrying burdens, both of them were mounted, or both of them were unburdened, they make a compromise-agreement among themselves. And so is the rule governing two boats which were coming toward one another, one of them unloaded, and one of them loaded — they set aside the one which is unloaded in favor of the one which is bearing a burden. [If] both of them were unloaded or both of them were carrying cargo, they make a compromise between themselves.

B. 3:4 I.1/31A: POTTERS OR GLASS CARRIERS WHO WERE WALKING INDIAN FILE, THE FIRST OF THEM STUMBLED AND FELL, AND THE SECOND STUMBLED ON THE FIRST, THE THIRD ON THE SECOND — THE FIRST IS LIABLE FOR THE DAMAGES SUFFERED BY THE SECOND, THE SECOND IS LIABLE FOR THE DAMAGES SUFFERED BY THE THIRD, BUT IF IT WAS ON ACCOUNT ONLY OF THE FIRST ONE THAT THEY FELL DOWN, THEN THE FIRST ONE IS LIABLE FOR THE DAMAGES SUFFERED BY ALL OF THEM. BUT IF EACH OF THEM GAVE A WARNING TO THE OTHERS, THEN ALL OF THEM ARE EXEMPT FROM HAVING TO PAY COMPENSATION.

M. 3:5 This one comes along with his jar, and that one comes along with his beam — [if] the jar of this one was broken by the beam of that one, [the owner of the beam] is exempt, for this one has every right to walk along [in the street], and that one has every right to walk along [in the same street].

M. 3:6 Two who were going along in the public domain, one was running, the other ambling, or both of them running, and they injured one another, both of them are exempt.

M. 3:7 He who chops wood in private property, and [the chips] injured someone in public domain, in public domain, and [the chips] injured someone in private property, in private property, and [the chips] injured someone in someone else's private property — he is liable.

B. 3:7 I.7/33A: A WORKER WHO HAS COME TO COLLECT HIS WAGES FROM THE HOUSEHOLD, AND THE OX OF THE HOUSEHOLDER GORED HIM, OR THE DOG OF THE HOUSEHOLDER BIT HIM, AND HE DIED — THE HOUSEHOLDER IS EXEMPT [FROM HAVING TO PAY RANSOM].

C. *Damages Done by the Ox*

M. 3:8 Two oxen [generally deemed] harmless which injured one another — [the owner] pays half-damages for the excess [of the value of the injury done by the less injured to the more injured ox]. [If] both of them were attested dangers, [the owner] pays full damages for the excess [of the injury done by the less injured to the more injured ox]. [If] one was deemed harmless and one an attested danger, [if] it was an ox which was an attested danger [which injured] an ox deemed harmless, [the owner] pays full damages for the excess. [If] it was the ox deemed harmless [which injured] the one which was an attested danger, [the owner] pays half — damages for the excess. [If it was a case of] a man who injured an ox which was an attested danger, or an ox which was an attested danger which injured a man, one pays full damages for the excess [of the injury done by the one to the other].

3:1 An ox, which was an attested danger as to use of its horn [e.g., in goring] but harmless as to use of its tooth, which inflicted injury both with this and with that — [as to the injury inflicted by that on account of which it was deemed] harmless, [the owner] pays half-damages, limited to the value of its own carcass. [And as to the injury inflicted by that on account of which it was deemed] an attested danger, [the owner] pays full damages, out of the best of his real property. [If] there is no real property of suitable quality, [as to the injury caused by that on account of which it was deemed] harmless, [the owner] pays half-damages limited to the value of its own carcass. [And as to the injury inflicted by that on account of which it was deemed] an attested danger, let [the owner] lay out funds and seek property of suitable quality.

T. 3:2 A governing principle did they state in connection with damages: [if] one has killed another's ox, torn his garment, or cut down his shoots, [the injured party] may not say to him, "Take the carcass and give me a cow, ". . . the rags and give me a cloak," "Take the broken shoots and give me whole plants." But they make an estimate of the value [of the damaged] items as to their worth before they were damaged and as to their worth now that they have been damaged. And in accord with that calculation do they pay compensation.

M. 3:9 Two oxen [generally deemed] harmless which injured one another — [the owner] pays half-damages for the excess [of the value of the injury done by the less injured to the more injured ox]. [If] both of them were attested dangers, [the owner] pays full damages for the excess [of the injury done by the less injured to the more injured ox]. [If] one was deemed harmless and one an attested danger, [if] it was an ox which was an attested danger [which injured] an ox deemed harmless, [the owner] pays full damages for the excess. [If] it was the ox deemed harmless [which injured] the one which was an attested danger, [the owner] pays half-damages for the excess. And so is the rule for two men who injured one another: they pay full damages for the excess [of the injury done by the less injured to the more injured man]. [If it was a case of] a man who injured an ox which was an attested danger, or an ox which was an attested danger which injured a man, one pays full damages for the excess [of the injury done by the one to the other]. [If it was] a man [who injured] an ox deemed harmless, or an ox deemed harmless [which injured] a man — [if it was] the man [who injured] the ox deemed harmless, he pays full damages for the excess. [If it was] the ox deemed harmless [which injured] the man, one pays half-damages for the excess. An ox [deemed harmless] worth a maneh [a hundred zuz] which gored

an ox worth two hundred [zuz], and the carcass [of the latter] is worth nothing — [the owner of the ox which is gored and worthless] takes the ox [worth a maneh, which did the goring].

T. 3:5 How does one pay half damages for the excess [of the value of the injury done by the less injured to the more injured one]. An ox which is worth a maneh [a hundred zuz] which gored an ox worth two hundred zuz — they both lost fifty zuz in value — [but] the latter [of the two oxen which gored one another] lost [better: gained] in value another three golden denars [in addition] [the owner of] the latter pays [the owner of] the former a half a golden denar. An ox worth two hundred zuz which gored an ox worth two hundred zuz and did fifty zuz damage — the animal which had been gored gained in value, so that it was worth four hundred zuz — but if [the former ox] had not done injury to it, it would have been worth eight hundred zuz — now, if before the case came to court, the gored ox gained in value, the owner has a claim only for the value of the ox as it stood at the time of its being injured. And if it was after the case came to court that it diminished in value, the owner has a claim only for the value of the ox as it stood at the time the case came to court.

B. 3:9A–C I.9/34A: AN OX WORTH TWO HUNDRED ZUZ THAT GORED AN OX WORTH TWO HUNDRED ZUZ, AND DID TO THE BEAST DAMAGES WORTH FIFTY ZUZ, BUT THEN THE INJURED OX INCREASED IN VALUE AND WAS WORTH FOUR HUNDRED ZUZ, SINCE ONE MAY CLAIM THAT, IF IT HAD NOT BEEN INJURED, IT WOULD HAVE BEEN WORTH EIGHT HUNDRED ZUZ, THE RESPONSIBLE PARTY HAS TO PAY DAMAGES IN ACCORD WITH THE STATE OF AFFAIRS AT THE TIME OF THE INJURY. IF THE VALUE OF THE INJURED BEAST DEPRECIATED, THE ASSESSMENT IS MADE IN ACCORD WITH THE STATE OF AFFAIRS AT THE TIME OF THE VALUATION IN COURT. IF THE OX THAT DID THE DAMAGE GAINED IN VALUE, COMPENSATION IS STILL ASSESSED IN ACCORD WITH THE STATE OF AFFAIRS AT THE TIME OF THE INJURY. IF IT LOST IN VALUE, THE ASSESSMENT IS MADE IN ACCORD WITH THE STATE OF AFFAIRS AT THE TIME OF THE VALUATION IN COURT.

M. 3:10 There is (1) he who is liable for the deed of his ox and exempt on account of his own deed, exempt for the deed of his ox and liable on account of his own deed. His ox which inflicted embarrassment — [the owner] is exempt. But he who inflicted embarrassment is liable. His ox which blinded the eye of his slave or knocked out his tooth — [the owner] is exempt. But he who blinded the eye of his slave or knocked out his tooth is liable. His ox which injured his father or his mother — [the owner] is liable. But he who injured his father and his mother is exempt. His ox which set fire to a shock of grain on the Sabbath — [the owner] is liable. But he who set fire to a shock of grain on the Sabbath is exempt because he is subject to liability for his life.

T. 3:4 There is one who is liable for damages caused by himself and for damages caused by his ox or his ass, exempt both for damages caused by himself and for damages caused by his ox or his ass [cf. M. B.Q. 3:10A]. How is one liable for damages caused by himself and for damages caused by his ox or his ass? [If] he is responsible for causing damage in private domain, he is liable, [and] his ox or his ass is liable. [If] he caused injury unintentionally, he is liable, [and] his ox or his ass is liable. [If] he set fire to the standing grain of his fellow on the Day of Atonement, he is liable, and his ox or his ass is liable. How is he exempt for damages caused by himself and for damages caused by his ox or his ass? [If] he is responsible for causing damage in public domain [through the normal manner of walking of his ox or his ass, he is exempt, [and] his ox or his ass is exempt. [If] he [through his beast] killed someone inadvertently, he is exempt, [and] his ox or his ass is exempt. [If] he did damage to property belonging to the sanctuary, to a proselyte, or a freed slave, he is exempt, and his ox or his ass is exempt. And he is exempt for injuries caused by his boy-slave or his girl-slave.

M. 3:11 An ox which was running after another ox, and [that latter ox] was injured — this one claims, "Your ox did the injury," and that one claims, "Not so, but it was hit by a stone" — he who wants to exact [compensation] from his fellow bears the burden of proof. If two [oxen] were running after one [ox] — this one says, "Your ox did the damage," and that one says, "Your ox did the damage" — both of them are exempt. [But] if both of them belonged to the same man, both of them [oxen] are liable [to pay compensation]. [If] one of them was big and one little — the one whose ox has suffered an injury says, "The big one did the damage," but the one who is responsible for the damage says, "Not so, but the little one did the damage" — one of them was deemed harmless, and one was an attested danger — the one whose ox has suffered an injury says, "The one which was the attested danger has done the damage," but the one who is responsible for the damage says, "Not so, but the one which had been deemed harmless did the damage, — he who wants to exact [compensation] from his fellow bears the burden of proof.

T. 3:6 An ox which was running after its fellow, [and] the one which was being pursued turned around and clobbered [the partner] — [if] others clobbered the pursuer — lo, these are liable. [If] the pursuing ox was injured by the one which was being pursued, [the latter] is exempt. [If] the one which was being pursued was injured by the pursuer, [the owner of the latter] is liable. An ox which mounted its fellow, and the owner of the one beneath came along and pulled [his beast] out [from underneath] — or if [the ox] pulled itself off, and fell and died — [the owner of the ox underneath] is exempt. [If] he pushed him and he fell and died, [the owner of the ox underneath] is liable. An ox which was grazing, and another ox went out after it, and the one which was grazing was found dead — even if this one has been gored, and that one is an attested danger as to goring, or this one died of a bite, and that one was an attested danger as to biting, [the owner of the surviving ox] is exempt.

T. 3:7 Two oxen who were grazing, and two other oxen went out after them, and these which were known [to be grazing] were found dead — it is a matter of doubt whether these killed them, or whether death came from some other source and they died — lo, [the owners of] these are exempt. If it is a matter of certainty that they killed them, lo, [the owners of] these [oxen] pay compensation, in accord with the value of the smaller of the two, not in accord with the value of the larger of the two; in the assumption that the one which was deemed harmless did the killing, not in the assumption that the one which was an attested danger did the killing. If it is a matter of certainty that the black [oxen] did the killing of the white ones, [if] there was there one large one and one small one, one which was deemed harmless and one which was an attested danger, lo, these pay compensation for the large ox and for the small one — for the large ox from the carcass of the small one, and for the small ox from the carcass of the large one; for the large ox from the value of the one which had been deemed harmless, and for the small ox from the value of the one which had been an attested danger. [If] the oxen which had been injured belonged to two people, and the oxen which had done the damages belonged to one person, [if it is then] a matter of doubt that those oxen had killed them, or that death had come from some other source and they died, lo, these [owners of the accused oxen] are exempt. If it is a matter of certainty that they had killed them, lo, these pay compensation — in accord with the value of the small one, and not in accord with the value of the large one; in accord with the rules governing the one which had been deemed harmless, and not in accord with the rules governing an attested danger. If it is a matter of certainty that the black ones had killed the white ones, if there were there one which was large and one which was small, one which was deemed harmless and one which was an attested danger, lo, these pay compensation for the large one and for the small one — for the large one from the [value of the] smaller [of the two oxen which had done the killing], and for the smaller one from the larger one; for the large ox from the value of the one which had been deemed harmless, and for the small ox from the value of the one which had been an attested danger. And the owners of those oxen which had been injured divide the compensation between them — this one takes a sum in accord with the value of his ox, and that one takes a sum in accord with the value of his ox.

M. 4:2 An ox which is an attested danger as to its own species, but not an attested danger as to what is not its own species — [or] an attested danger as to man, and not an attested danger as to beast, [or] an attested danger to small [beasts] but not an attested danger as to large ones — for that for which it is an attested danger, [the owner] pays full damages, and for that for which it is not an attested danger, he pays half — damages.

B. 4:2 I.2–3/37A: IF THE OX SEES ANOTHER OX AND GORES IT, ANOTHER AND DOES NOT GORE IT, ANOTHER AND GORES IT, ANOTHER AND DOES NOT GORE IT, ANOTHER AND GORES IT, ANOTHER AND DOES NOT GORE IT, IT IS DEEMED

AN OX THAT IS AN ATTESTED DANGER ALTERNATELY TO GORE OTHER OXEN. IF THE OX SEES ANOTHER OX AND GORES IT, AN ASS AND DOES NOT GORE IT, A HORSE AND GORES IT, A CAMEL AND DOES NOT GORE IT, A MULE AND GORES IT, A WILD ASS AND DOES NOT GORE IT, IT IS DEEMED AN OX THAT IS AN ATTESTED DANGER ALTERNATELY TO GORE OTHER SPECIES.

M. 4:3 An ox of an Israelite which gored an ox belonging to the sanctuary or an ox belonging to the sanctuary which gored an ox belonging to an Israelite [M. 1:21 — the owner] is exempt, since it is said, "The ox belonging to his neighbor" (Ex. 21:35) — and not an ox belonging to the sanctuary. An ox belonging to an Israelite which gored an ox belonging to a gentile — [the Israelite owner] is exempt. And one of a gentile which gored one of an Israelite — whether it is harmless or an attested danger, [the gentile owner] pays full damages.

T. 4:1 An ox, half of which belongs to an Israelite and half of which belongs to the sanctuary, which inflicted injury upon an ox which belongs to an Israelite — [if it is] an attested danger, [the owner] pays full damages. [And if it is] deemed harmless, [the owner] pays half-damages. [An ox] belonging to the sanctuary, whether it is deemed harmless or whether it is an attested danger, is exempt. [If] it is injured by another [ox], belonging to an Israelite, [the owner] is liable. [And if it is injured by one] belonging to the sanctuary, it is exempt. An ox which belongs to the sanctuary [by reason of dedication on the part of the original owner] — [the original] owner is liable to replace it if it is lost. And the owner receives damages paid if it is injured. And the owner pays damages owing if it injures [another ox]. An ox, half of which belongs to an Israelite and half of which belongs to a gentile which injured one belonging to an Israelite — [if it is] an attested danger, [the owners] pay full damages. [If it is] deemed harmless, [the owners] pay half-damages. But one belonging to a gentile, whether it is deemed harmless or whether it is an attested danger — [the owner] pays full damages.

T. 4:2 An ox belonging to a gentile which injured an ox belonging to another gentile, his fellow, even though they accepted upon themselves the authority of the laws of Israel — [the owner] pays full damages. For the distinction between an ox deemed harmless and one which is an attested danger does not apply in the case of damages done in regard to a gentile.

T. 4:3 An ox belonging to an Israelite which gored an ox belonging to a Samaritan, and an ox belonging to a Samaritan which gored an ox belonging to an Israelite — [the owner of] one which is an attested danger pays full damages, and [the owner of] one which is deemed harmless pays half-damages.

M. 4:4 An ox of a person of sound senses which gored an ox belonging to a deaf-mute, an idiot, or a minor — [the owner] is liable. But one of a deaf-mute, idiot, or minor which gored an ox belonging to a person of sound senses — [the owner] is exempt. [As to] the ox of a deaf-mute, idiot, or minor, the court

appoints a guardian for them, and they bring testimony against [the ox, to have it declared an attested danger] to the guardian.

B. 4:4 I:9/40A: IF SOMEONE BORROWED AN OX ASSUMING THAT IT WAS HARMLESS BUT IT TURNED OUT AN ATTESTED DANGER, THE OWNER WOULD HAVE TO PAY HALF-DAMAGES, AND THE ONE WHO BORROWED IT WOULD PAY HALF-DAMAGES. IF THE BEAST WAS DECLARED AN ATTESTED DANGER WHILE IN THE HOUSEHOLD OF THE BORROWER AND HE RETURNED IT TO THE OWNER, THE OWNER WOULD THEN HAVE TO PAY HALF-DAMAGE AND THE OWNER WOULD BE EXEMPT FROM ANY PAYMENT WHATSOEVER.

M. 4:5 An ox which gored a man, who died — [if it was] an attested danger, [the owner] pays a ransom price [of the value of the deceased]. But [if it was deemed] harmless, he is exempt from paying the ransom price. And in this case and in that case, [the oxen] are liable to the death penalty. And so is the rule [if it killed] a little boy or girl [son, daughter: Ex. 21:31]. [If] it gored a boy slave or a girl slave, [the owner] pays thirty selas [Ex. 21:32], whether [the slave] was worth a maneh or a single denar.

T. 4:6 There is [the beast] which is liable to a ransom-payment and liable to death, liable to the death penalty but exempt from the ransom-payment, liable to the ransom-payment but exempt from the death-penalty, exempt from the death-penalty and exempt from the ransom-payment [delete: and exempt from the death-penalty]. An ox deemed an attested danger which killed someone — [the owner] is liable to the ransom-payment, and [the ox] is liable to be put to death. An ox deemed harmless which killed somebody, an ox belonging to a deaf-mute or an idiot which killed, and [an ox which] killed a proselyte or a freed slave — [the ox] is liable to the death penalty but [the owner] is exempt from the ransom-payment [which is omitted, since there are no heirs].

T. 4:7 How does one estimate the compensation to be paid? They estimate the value of the one who has been injured [and is now deceased]: how much he is worth. In accord with that [estimate] the owner pays compensation.

T. 4:8 In any case in which one is liable for damages done to a free man, he is liable for damages done to a slave, whether this is in regard to the ransom-payment or the death-penalty. In any case in which one is exempt from liability to damages done to a free man, he is exempt from liability for damages done to a slave, whether this is in regard to the ransom-payment or the death penalty. [If an ox] killed a Hebrew slave, [the owner] pays all his ransom money. [If an ox killed] a slave belonging to two partners, [the owner] pays it to both of them. [If half of the man] was slave, and half free, [the owner] pays it proportionately: half of the ransom goes to the estate, and half of thirty *selas* goes to the owner.

M. 4:6 An ox which was rubbing itself against a wall, and [the wall] fell on a man, [if] it had intended to kill (1) another beast, but killed a man, (2) a gentile but killed an Israelite, (3) an untimely birth but killed a viable infant — [the ox] is exempt [from death by stoning].

B. 4:6 I.2/44B: There is the beast that is liable to a ransom payment and liable to death, liable to the death penalty but exempt from the ransom payment, liable to the ransom payment but exempt from the death penalty, exempt from the death penalty and exempt from the ransom payment. How so? An ox deemed an attested danger that intentionally killed someone — the owner is liable to the ransom payment and the ox is liable to be put to death. An ox deemed an attested danger that unintentionally killed somebody — the owner is liable to the ransom, but the ox is not liable to the death penalty. An ox deemed harmless that unintentionally killed somebody, the owner is exempt, and the ox is exempt, from any penalty. [Tosefta's version: An ox belonging to a deaf-mute or an idiot that killed, and an ox that killed a proselyte or a freed slave — the ox is liable to the death penalty, but the owner is exempt from the ransom payment, there being no heirs. An ox that was rubbing itself against a wall and the wall fell on a man, if it had intended to kill another beast but killed a man, a gentile but killed an Israelite, an untimely birth but killed a viable infant, the owner is liable to the ransom payment, but the beast is exempt from the death penalty.]

M. 4:7 (1) An ox belonging to a woman, (2) an ox belonging to orphans, (3) an ox belonging to a guardian, (4) an ox of the wilderness, (5) an ox belonging to the sanctuary, (6) an ox belonging to a proselyte who died lacking heirs — lo, these [oxen] are liable to the death penalty.

M. 4:8 An ox which goes forth to be stoned, and which the owner [then] declared to be sanctified is not deemed to have been sanctified. [If] one has slaughtered it, its meat is prohibited [Ex. 21:28]. But if before the court process had been completed the owner declared it sanctified, it is deemed sanctified. And [if] one had slaughtered it, its meat is permitted.

T. 4:9 That ox which is accused of manslaughter at the testimony of a single witness, or which is accused of having committed bestiality or having been a victim of bestiality on the evidence of a single witness is invalid for use on the altar. And is exempt from the death-penalty. And it is available for the benefit [of the owner]. And an ox which is accused of manslaughter at the testimony of two witnesses, or of having committed bestiality or having been a victim of bestiality on the evidence of two witnesses is invalid for use on the altar. It is liable to the death-penalty. And it is prohibited from use for the benefit [of the owner]. And [that ox which has] committed manslaughter, whether it belongs to him [who has been killed] or to someone else, whether the manslaughter takes place before it has been consecrated or after it has been consecrated [M. B.Q. 4:8], whether [the manslaughter was] inadvertent, deliberate, under constraint, or by choice, is prohibited for use on the altar. An animal which commits bestiality or upon which bestiality is committed, whether it belongs to him [who has done the deed] or to someone else, whether this takes place before it has been consecrated or after it has been consecrated, [whether the act of bestiality] was inadvertent or deliberate — is invalid for use on the altar. [If the act] was done under constraint, it is valid [for use on the altar]. [If it was done] willingly, it is invalid [for use on the altar].

T. 5:1 An ox which had been deemed harmless which inflicted injury — [if] before it came to court, the owner declared it consecrated, it is consecrated. [If] he slaughtered it, sold it, or gave it away as a gift, what he has done is valid. [If] after it came to court, the owner declared it consecrated, it is not deemed consecrated. [If] he slaughtered it or sold it or gave it away as a gift, what he has done is not valid. For he has to pay compensation from the corpus of the animal itself [which therefore must be kept available, once the court has made its decision, for use for compensation].

T. 5:2 An ox which had been deemed an attested danger which inflicted injury, whether before or after it has come to court — [if] the owner declared it consecrated, it is deemed consecrated. [If] the owner slaughtered it, sold it, or gave it away, what he had done is deemed valid. For [the owner] pays damages from the choicest real estate [no matter the condition of the corpus of the beast].

B. 4:8, 4:9A–F I.1/44A–45A: AN OX THAT KILLED SOMEONE — IF THE OWNER SOLD IT BEFORE THE COURT DECREE WAS ISSUED, IT IS DEEMED TO HAVE BEEN VALIDLY SOLD. IF THE OWNER SANCTIFIED IT TO THE TEMPLE, IT IS VALIDLY SANCTIFIED. IF HE SLAUGHTERED IT, ITS MEAT IS PERMITTED. IF THE BAILEE RETURNED IT TO THE HOUSEHOLD OF THE OWNER, IT IS VALIDLY RETURNED [AND THE BAILEE HAS NO FURTHER OBLIGATION]. IF AFTER THE COURT DECREE WAS ISSUED, THE OWNER SOLD IT, IT IS DEEMED NOT TO HAVE BEEN VALIDLY SOLD. IF THE OWNER SANCTIFIED IT TO THE TEMPLE, IT IS NOT VALIDLY SANCTIFIED. IF HE SLAUGHTERED IT, ITS MEAT IS NOT PERMITTED. IF THE BAILEE RETURNED IT TO THE HOUSEHOLD OF THE OWNER, IT IS NOT VALIDLY RETURNED.

M. 4:9 [If] one had handed it over to an unpaid bailee, or to a borrower, to a paid bailee, or to a renter, they take the place [and assume the liabilities] of the owner. [For an ox deemed an] attested danger [one of these] pays full damages, and [for one] deemed harmless [he] pays half-damages.

T. 5:3 An ox which had been harmless which inflicted injury, and afterward it killed someone, [or] it killed someone, and afterward it inflicted injury — [the owner] is exempt. An ox which was an attested danger which inflicted injury and afterward killed [someone] — [the owner] bears liability. [If] it killed someone and afterward inflicted injury, [if] this was before its court-process was completed, [the owner] is liable. [If this was] after its court-process was completed, [the owner] is exempt.

T. 5:4 An unpaid bailee, a borrower, a paid bailee, or a renter [of an ox], in the domain of any of whom the ox has inflicted injury — [any of the afore-named, responsible for] an ox deemed an attested danger pays full damages, and one deemed harmless pays half-damages [M. B.Q.

4:9A–F]. [If] one had borrowed it in the assumption that it was harmless and it turned out to be an attested danger, [however], the owner pays half-damages, and the borrower is exempt. [If a] warning [attesting the animal as dangerous] was made in the presence of the borrower, and afterward [the borrower] gave it back to the owner, the owner pays half-damages, and the borrower pays half-damages. [If] it committed manslaughter in his domain, and afterward he handed it back to the owner, if before the court-process concerning it was complete, he had handed it back to the owner, he is exempt. [If] after the court-process concerning it was complete, he had handed it back to the owner, he is liable.

T. 5:5 A cow which committed manslaughter and afterward gave birth, [if] before its court-process was completed, it gave birth, its offspring are permitted. [If] after its court-process was completed, it gave birth, its offspring are prohibited. [If] they were confused with others, and the others yet with others, all of them are prohibited from being so used as to derive benefit. What should they do with them? They keep them in a stockade until they perish.

M. 5:1 An ox [deemed harmless] which gored a cow [which died] and her newly born calf was found [dead] beside her — and it is not known whether, before it gored her, she gave birth, or after it gored her, she gave birth — [the owner of the ox] pays half-damages for the cow, and quarter-damages for the offspring. And so too, a cow [deemed harmless] which gored an ox, and her newly born young was found beside her, and it is not known whether before she gored, she gave birth, or after she gored, she gave birth — [the owner of the cow] pays half-damages from the corpus of the cow, and a quarter-damages from the corpus of the offspring.

M. 5:2 (1) The potter who brought his pots into the courtyard of the householder without permission, and the beast of the householder broke them — [the householder] is exempt. (2) And if [the beast] was injured on them, the owner of the pots is liable. (3) If [however], he brought them in with permission, the owner of the courtyard is liable, (1) [If] he brought his produce into the courtyard of the householder without permission, and the beast of the householder ate them up, [the householder] is exempt. (2) And if [the beast] was injured by them, the owner of the produce is liable. (3) But if he brought them in with permission, the owner of the courtyard is liable.

M. 5:3 (1) [If] he brought his ox into the courtyard of a householder without permission, and the ox of the householder gored it, or the dog of the householder bit it, [the householder] is exempt. (2) [If] that [ox] gored the ox of the householder, [the owner] is liable. [If] it fell into his well and polluted its water, [the owner of the ox] is liable. [If] his father or son was in [the well and was killed], [the owner of the ox] pays ransom

money. **(3) But if he brought it in with permission, the owner of the courtyard is liable.**

T. 5:13 There is that [owner] who pays the ransom, and [the ox] is not stoned, there is that ox which is stoned, and the [owner] does not pay ransom. He who digs a pit with permission and an ox fell in on him and killed him — [the owner of the ox] pays the ransom, but [the ox] is not stoned. [If] he went into the courtyard of a householder without permission, and the ox of the householder gored him, or the dog of the householder bit him, and he died — [the animal] is stoned, but [the owner] does not pay the ransom.

T. 6:2 He who digs a pit in his own domain, and an ox fell on him and killed him — [the owner of the ox] is liable to pay the ransom-money. And if the ox was injured [in the pit], the owner of the pit is exempt.

T. 6:3 He who digs a pit in public domain and an ox fell on him and killed him — [the owner of the ox] is exempt from having to pay the ransom money. And [if] the ox is injured in the pit, the owner of the pit is liable.

M. 5:4 An ox which was intending [to gore] its fellow, but hit a woman, and her offspring came forth [as a miscarriage] — [the owner of the ox] is exempt from paying compensation for the offspring. And a man who was intending [to hit] his fellow but hit a woman, and her offspring came forth, pays compensation for the offspring.

D. *Damages Done by the Pit*

M. 5:5 He who digs a pit in private domain and opens it into public domain, or in public domain and opens it into private domain, or in private domain and opens it into private domain belonging to someone else, is liable [for damage done by the pit]. He who digs a pit in public domain, and an ox or an ass fell into it and died, is liable. It is all the same whether one digs a pit, a trench, cavern, ditches, or channels: he is liable.

T. 6:4 [If] he dug a pit in public domain with its opening into private domain, even if it belonged to the public, he is liable, until he gives over [the pit] to the public. What is the sort of pit concerning which the Torah spoke? [If] one dug a pit in private property and opened it into private property. [If] he has the right to open [a pit] in public domain, and he opened it in public domain, [if] he has no right to dig and no right to open [a pit] in private domain, and he opened it in public domain, [if] he has the right to dig it but has no right to open it, but he has the right to do so in public domain, [if he has the right] to enter there in public domain, and he opened it in private domain — even if it is public property, he is exempt.

T. 6:5. [If] he dug a pit [cistern] and opened it up and handed it over to the public, he is exempt.

T. 6:6 [If] one has dug a hole in the proper way and covered it up in the proper way, and made a fence around it in the proper way, ten handbreadths high, and handed it over to a sick person or to an old person who is intelligent, he is exempt [having done his duty for the protection of the well].

T. 6:7 [If] he has dug [a hole] not in the proper way, and covered it up not in the proper way, or [if] he handed it over to a deaf-mute, idiot, or minor, who lack intelligence, he is liable.

T. 6:9 If one has dug ten handbreadths, and someone else came along and put in plaster and cemented it, the one who came along at the end is liable. [If] one person has dug ten handbreadths, another dug twenty, another dug a hundred, and another dug two hundred, all of them are liable.

T. 6:12 And what is the measure of a pit so as to cause injury? Any depth at all. And to cause death? Ten handbreadths.

M. 5:6 A pit belonging to two partners — one of them passed by it and did not cover it, and the second one also did not cover it, the second one is liable. [If] the first one covered it up, and the second one came along and found it uncovered and did not cover it up. the second one is liable. [If] he covered it up in a proper way, and an ox or an ass fell into it and died, he is exempt. [If] he did not cover it up in the proper way and an ox or an ass fell into it and died, he is liable. [If] it fell forward [not into the pit] because of the sound of the digging, [the owner of the pit] is liable. [If] it fell backward [not into the pit] because of the sound of the digging, [the owner of the pit] is exempt. [If] an ox carrying its trappings fell into it and they were broken, an ass and its trappings and they were split, [the owner of the pit] is liable for the beast but exempt for the trappings. [If] an ox belonging to a deaf-mute, an idiot, or a minor fell into it, [the owner] is liable. [If] a little boy or girl, a slave boy or a slave girl [fell into it], he is exempt [from paying a ransom].

T. 6:10 A pit belonging to two people, one covers it, and one uncovers it — the one who uncovers it is liable. [If] he covered it up and it became uncovered, while he was standing there and saw it uncovered but did not cover it up, lo, this one is liable. [If] he covered it up and went along, even though it became uncovered later on, he is exempt.

M. 5:7 All the same are an ox and all other beasts so far as (1) falling into a pit, (2) keeping apart from Mount Sinai [Ex. 19:12], (3) a double indemnity [Ex. 22:7], (4) the returning of that which is lost [Dt. 22:3, Ex. 23:4] (5), unloading [Ex. 23:5], (6) muzzling [Dt. 25:4], (7) hybridization [Lev. 19:19, Dt. 22:10], and the (8) Sabbath [Ex. 20:10, Dt. 5:14]. And so too are wild beasts and fowl subject to the same laws. If so, why is an ox or an ass specified? But Scripture spoken in terms of prevailing conditions.

T. 6:18 All the same are an ox, an ass, and all other beasts, wild animals, and fowl, as to the payment of damages: the owner of an attested danger pays full damages, and of one deemed harmless pays half-damages. All the same are an ox, an ass, and all other domesticated beasts, wild beasts, and fowl, as to bestiality and as to hybridization.

E. *Damages Done by the Crop-Destroying Beast*

M. 6:1 He who brings a flock into a fold and shut the gate before it as required, but [the flock] got out and did damage, is exempt. [If] he did not shut the gate before it as required, and [the flock] got out and did damage, he is liable. [If the fence] was broken down by night, or thugs broke it down, and [the flock] got out and did damage, he is exempt. [If] the thugs took [the flock] out, [and the flock did damage], the thugs are liable.

T. 6:19 [If] he shut the gate as is required [M. B.Q. 6:1A], tied up [the beasts] as is required, made for [the flock] a fence ten handbreadths high, or handed it over to a sick person or an old person of sound senses, [the owner of the flock] is exempt [from liability to damages done by the flock]. [If] he shut the gate not as is required, tied up the gate not as is required, made for [the flock] a fence less than ten handbreadths high, or handed it over to a deaf-mute, an idiot, or a minor, he is liable [to pay compensation for damages done by the flock]. What is the definition of doing so in a way not such as is required? Any situation in which [the corral-fence] cannot stand up to the wind.

M. 6:2 [If] he left it in the sun, [or if] he handed it over to a deaf-mute, idiot, or minor, and [the flock] got out and did damage, he is liable. [If] he handed it over to a shepherd, the shepherd takes the place of the owner [as to liability]. [If the flock] [accidentally] fell into a vegetable patch and derived benefit [from the produce], [the owner must] pay compensation [only] for the value of the benefit [derived by the flock]. [If the flock] went down in the normal way and did damage, [the owner must] pay compensation for the [actual] damage which [the flock] inflicted.

T. 6:20 A shepherd who hands over his flock to another shepherd — the first is liable, and the second is exempt. He who hands over his flock to a shepherd, even if it is one who is lame, or even sick, or even if there are under his oversight as many as three hundred sheep, is exempt [cf. M. B.Q. 6:2E]. [If] he handed it over to a deaf-mute, an idiot, or a minor, he is liable. [If he handed it over to] a slave or a woman, he is exempt. And they pay compensation after an interval. How [does a woman or a slave pay compensation after an interval]? They call a court into session to deal with their case. They write a writ of debt against them. [If] the woman is divorced or the slave freed, they are then liable to pay compensation.

M. 6:3 He who stacks sheaves in the field of his fellow without permission, and the beast of the owner of the field ate them up, [the owner of the field] is exempt. And [if] it was injured

by them, the owner of the sheaves is liable. But if he had put his sheaves there with permission, the owner of the field is liable.

T. 6:25 [If one] went into the shop of a carpenter without permission [and] a chip flew and hit him in the face, [the carpenter] is exempt [from liability for damages]. If he went in with permission, the owner of the shop is liable [cf. M. B.Q. 6:3]

T. 6:26 [If] one went into the shop of a smith without permission, [and] sparks flew and did damage to him, [the smith] is exempt. If he went in with permission, the owner of the shop is liable [cf. M. B.Q. 6:3].

6:27 A worker who went into the courtyard of a householder without permission, even though he has the right to go in and to collect their [the workers'] salary, if the ox of the householder gored him, or if his dog bit him, [the householder] is exempt. But if [the householder] said to him, "Come in," the householder is liable [cf. M. B.Q. 6:3].

F. *Damages Done by Fire*

M. 6:4 He who causes a fire to break out through the action of a deaf-mute, idiot, or minor, is exempt from punishment under the laws of man, but liable to punishment under the laws of heaven. [If] he did so through the action of a person of sound senses, the person of sound senses is liable. [If] one person brought the flame, then another person brought the wood, the one who brings the wood is liable. [If] one person brought the wood and the other person then brought the flame, the one who brought the flame is liable. [If] a third party came along and fanned the fire, the one who fanned the flame is liable. [If] the wind fanned the flame, all of them are exempt. He who causes a fire to break out, which consumed wood, stones, or dirt, is liable.

T. 6:23 [If the fire] crossed a stream, a fence, or rivulet, any of which is eight cubits wide, he is exempt [cf. M. B.Q. 6:4].

T. 6:16 He who frightens his fellow to death is exempt from punishment by the laws of man, and his case is handed to Heaven. [If] he shouted into his ear and deafened him, he is exempt. [If] he seized him and shouted into his ear and deafened him, he is liable. He who frightens the ox of his fellow to death is exempt from punishment by the laws of man, and his case is handed over to Heaven.

T. 6:17 [If] one force-fed [the ox of his fellow] with asafoetida, creeperberries, a poisonous ointment, or chicken shit, he is exempt from punishment under the laws of man, and his case is handed over to Heaven. He who performs an extraneous act of labor while preparing purificationwater or a cow for purification belonging to his fellow [thus spoiling what has been done] is exempt from punishment by the laws of man, and his case is handed over to Heaven. A court-official who administered a blow by the decision of a court and did injury is exempt from punishment by the laws of man, and his case is handed over to Heaven. He who chops up the foetus in the belly of a woman by the decision of a court and did damage is exempt from punishment by the laws of man, and his case is handed over to Heaven. A seasoned physician who administered a remedy by a decision of a court and did damage is exempt from punishment by the laws of man, and his case is handed over to Heaven.

6:6 A spark which flew out from under the hammer and did damage — [the smith] is liable. A camel which was carrying flax and passed by in the public way, and the flax it was carrying got poked into a store and caught fire from the lamp of the storekeeper and set fire to the building — the owner of the camel is liable.

ii. *Damages Done by Persons*

A. *Penalties for the Theft of an Ox or a Sheep*

M. 7:1 More encompassing is the rule covering payment of twofold restitution than the rule covering payment of fourfold or fivefold restitution. For the rule covering twofold restitution applies to something whether animate or inanimate. But the rule covering fourfold or fivefold restitution applies only to an ox or a sheep alone, since it says, "If a man shall steal an ox or a sheep and kill it, or sell it, he shall pay five oxen for an ox and four sheep for a sheep" (Ex. 22:1 [21:37]). The one who steals from a thief does not pay twofold restitution. And the one who slaughters or sells what is stolen does not pay fourfold or fivefold restitution.

T. 7:14 If one stole and gave the ox and sheep to someone else, who slaughtered it, or stole and gave it to someone else, who sold it, or stole and traded an ox, or stole and consecrated the ox or sheep, or stole and gave the ox or sheep to someone else as a gift, or stole and gave the ox or sheep to someone as a loan, or stole and paid with the ox or sheep a debt that he owed, or stole and sent the ox or sheep to his father-in-law's house as a gift, he must pay the fourfold or fivefold indemnity.

T. 7:15 He who steals [an ox or a sheep which was] mutilated, lame, or blind, he who steals [an ox or a sheep] belonging to partners pays fourfold or fivefold restitution. Partners who stole [an ox or a sheep] pay twofold restitution, but are exempt from having to pay threefold restitution in addition].

T. 7:17 He who steals a pregnant cow and slaughtered or sold it pays fourfold or fivefold restitution. [If he stole] a pregnant cow, which then gave birth, and afterward he slaughtered its offspring, he pays twofold restitution, but is exempt from having to pay an additional threefold restitution. He who steals a pregnant cow, which gave birth, and afterward which he slaughtered, or a goat and which he milked and afterward slaughtered — or a fat cow and it lost weight — he pays twofold restitution of the value of the beast as at the time it was stolen, and fourfold or fivefold restitution for the beast as at the time it was slaughtered or sold. [If] it was scrawny and it got fat, he pays twofold restitution and fourfold or fivefold restitution of the beast [assessed] as at the time it was stolen.

M. 7:2 [If] one stole [an ox or a sheep] on the evidence of two witnesses, and [was convicted of having] slaughtered or sold on the basis of their testimony, or on the basis of the testimony of two other witnesses, he pays fourfold or fivefold restitution. (1) [If] he stole or sold [an ox or a sheep] on the Sabbath, (2) stole and sold [an ox or a sheep] for idolatrous purposes, (3) stole and slaughtered [an ox or a sheep] on the Day of Atonement, (4) stole [an ox or a sheep] belonging to his father and slaughtered or sold it, and afterward his father died, (5) stole and slaughtered, and afterward consecrated [an ox or a sheep], he pays fourfold or fivefold restitution. (1) [If] he stole and slaughtered [an ox or a sheep] for use in healing or for food for dogs, (2) he who [steals and] slaughters [an ox or a sheep] which turns out to be terefah, (3) he who slaughters unconsecrated beasts in the Temple courtyard — he pays fourfold or fivefold restitution.

M. 7:3 [If] one stole [an ox or a sheep] on the evidence of two witnesses, and [was convicted of having] slaughtered or sold [it] on the basis of their testimony, and they turned out to be false witnesses, they pay full restitution. [If] he stole on the evidence of two witnesses, and [was convicted of having] slaughtered or sold it on the basis of the testimony of two other witnesses, [and] these and those turn out to be false witnesses, the first pair of witnesses pays twofold restitution, and the second pair of witnesses pays threefold restitution. [If] the latter pair of witnesses turn out to be false witnesses, he pays twofold restitution, and they pay threefold restitution. [If] one of the latter pair of witnesses turns out to be false, the evidence of the second one is null. [If] one of the first pair of witnesses turns out to be false, the entire testimony is null. For if there is no culpable act of stealing, there is no culpable act of slaughtering or selling.

T. 7:22 [If] two give testimony against a man that he has stolen, and two testify against him that he has slaughtered or sold [the animal], if the two [who testified] concerning his having slaughtered or sold the animal turn out to be perjurers, then he pays twofold restitution, and they pay threefold restitution [M. B.Q. 7:3I]. [If] they turned out to be perjurers for both matters, they are liable for both this [form of restitution] as well as that [M. B.Q. 7:3A–D].

T. 7:23 If two give testimony against a man that he has stolen, and two testify against him that he has slaughtered or sold [the animal], and the two [who testified] concerning his having stolen the animal turn out to be perjurers [M. B.Q. 7:3], he pays twofold damages, and they pay threefold damages.

T. 7:24 "Give me back my ox!" And that one said, "I have only the money [paid for it]" — "Give me the money!" "I have only the beast [I purchased with that money]" — "Give me fourfold or fivefold compensation!" And that one said, "I have only enough for a single ox" — if it was worth, in fact, the value of all [fivefold restitution], they make an estimate of its value [and it is paid over as acceptable restitution].

T. 8:1 He who steals a soul from among his brethren, the children of Israel — it is all the same if the thief is a man, a woman, a proselyte, a freed slave — it is all the same if it is a man, woman, proselyte, or freed slave whom they have stolen — lo, these [who do so] are liable. [If] one has sold him, whether to his father, brother, or any one of his relatives, he is liable. [If] he stole him but did not sell him, or [if] he sold him and he is standing there in the market [not yet taken away], he is exempt. He who steals slaves is exempt. [If] two give testimony against a thief that he has stolen, and two give testimony against him that he has sold [a sheep or ox], and they are found to be perjurers in connection with the theft, he and they are exempt [M. B.Q. 7:3K–L]. [If] they turn out to be perjured as to the sale, he is exempt, and they are exempt. [If] they turn out to be perjurers for both this and that [both the stealing and the selling], in such a case as this does [Scripture] say, "Then you shall do to him as he had meant to do to his brother" (Deut. 19:19).

M. 7:4 [If] one stole [an ox or a sheep] [and was so accused] on the evidence of two witnesses and [was accused of having] slaughtered or sold [the ox or sheep] on the basis of only one, or on the basis of the evidence of his own [confession], he pays twofold restitution and does not pay fourfold or fivefold restitution. (1) [If] he stole and slaughtered on the Sabbath, (2) stole and slaughtered for idolatrous purposes, (3) stole from his father's [herd of oxen or sheep] and then his father died and afterward he slaughtered or sold [the beast], (4) stole and then consecrated [the animal] and afterward slaughtered or sold it, he pays twofold restitution and does not pay fourfold or fivefold restitution.

B. 7:4 I.4/75B IF TWO WITNESSES GAVE TESTIMONY THAT HE HAD STOLEN, AND THERE WERE TWO OTHERS WHO GAVE TESTIMONY THAT HE HAD SLAUGHTERED AND SOLD THE MEAT, IF THE WITNESSES AS TO THE THEFT WERE PROVEN TO BE A CONSPIRACY OF PERJURERS, THEN TESTIMONY PART OF WHICH HAS BEEN NULLIFIED IS WHOLLY NULL. IF THE WITNESSES TO THE SLAUGHTER WERE PROVED TO BE A CONSPIRACY OF PERJURERS, THEN HE HAS TO PAY THE DOUBLE INDEMNITY, AND THEY HAVE TO PAY THE INDEMNITY OF THREE TIMES THE VALUE OF THE BEAST.

M. 7:5 (1) [If] one sold [all] but one hundredth part of [a stolen ox or sheep], (2) or if [the thief already] owned a share of it,

(3) he who slaughters [an ox or a sheep] and it turns out to be made into carrion by his own hand, (4) he who pierces [the windpipe], (5) and he who tears out [its gullet] pays two fold restitution and does not pay four fold or five fold restitution. [If] (1) he stole it in the owner's domain but slaughtered or sold it outside of his domain, or (2) [if] he stole it outside of his domain and slaughtered or sold it in his domain, or (3) if he stole and slaughtered or sold it outside of his domain, he pays fourfold or fivefold restitution, But if he stole and slaughtered or sold it [wholly] in his domain, he is exempt.

M. 7:6 [If the thief] was dragging [a sheep or ox] out [of the owner's domain], but it died in the domain of the owner, he is exempt. [If] he lifted it up or removed it from the domain of the owner and then it died, he is liable. [If] he handed it over for (1) the firstborn offering at the birth of his son, or (2) to a creditor, to (3) an unpaid bailee, or (4) to a borrower, or (5) to a paid bailee, or (6) to a renter, and [one of these] was dragging it away, and it died in the domain of the owner, he is exempt. [If] he raised it up or removed it from the domain of the owner and then it died, he is liable.

T. 7:20 [If] he handed over [an ox or a sheep which he had stolen] for the redemption of his firstborn son, or to his creditor, or to a woman for payment of her marriage-settlement, he has done nothing of effect. [If, however,] he raised it up and then handed it over for the redemption of his firstborn son, or to his creditor, or to a woman for payment of her marriage-settlement, what he has done is entirely valid.

T. 8:2 "Where is my ox, which you stole?" And the other said to him, "You sold it to me," or, "You gave it to me as a gift!" "Your father sold it to me!" or, "Your father gave it to me as a gift!" and witnesses bear testimony against him that he stole it [and] slaughtered or sold it — he pays fourfold or fivefold restitution. But if he confessed to the matter before witnesses gave testimony against him, he pays only the principal. [If he did so] after the witnesses gave testimony against him, he pays fourfold or fivefold restitution.

T. 8:3 "Where is my ox, which you stole?" He said to him, "I found it wandering around and I slaughtered it!" "It came to me of its own accord, and I slaughtered it" "It came to me of its own accord and I slaughtered it!" "It was standing around in the market and I slaughtered it!" [the plaintiff then says], "I impose an oath upon you to that effect," and he says, "Amen" — and then witnesses come along and testify against him that he had stolen and slaughtered or sold [the sheep or the ox] — he pays fourfold or fivefold restitution. But if he confessed to the matter, whether this is after the witnesses came upon the scene or even before the witnesses came upon the scene, he pays only the principal.

T. 8:4 "Where is my ox, which I left under your guardianship?" He said to him, "I don't know what in the world you're talking about!" or if he said to him, "It disappeared," and then witnesses came along and testified against him that he had eaten it — he pays only the principal. And if he confessed to the accusation, whether this was after the witnesses came along or before the witnesses came along, he pays only the principal.

T. 8:5 "Where is my ox, which you stole?" [if] he said to him, "You sold it to me!" or, "You gave it to me as a gift!" "Your father sold it to me!" Your father gave it to me as a gift!" [and the plaintiff responds], "I impose an oath upon you," [and the defendant said,] "Amen" — and then witnesses come along and testify against him that he had stolen and slaughtered or sold [the sheep or the ox], he pays fourfold or fivefold restitution. But if he had confessed to the matter after the taking of the oath, if this was before the witnesses came along, he pays the principal and an added fifth, as well as a guilt-offering. Now if this was after the witnesses came along, he pays fourfold or fivefold restitution.

T. 8:6 "Where is my ox, which you stole?" He said to him, "I found it wandering around and I slaughtered it!" "On its own it came to me and I slaughtered it!" "I impose an oath upon you [that you are telling the truth]," and he said, "Amen" — then witnesses come along and give testimony against him that in fact he had stolen and slaughtered or sold it — he pays fourfold or fivefold restitution. [If] he confessed after the taking of an oath, whether this is after the witnesses had come along or before the witnesses had come along, he has to pay the principal, an added fifth, and a guilt-offering.

T. 8:7 "Where is my ox, which I left under your guardianship?" He said to him, "I haven't got the slightest idea what you're talking about!" or if he said to him, "It got lost," "I impose an oath on you," and he said, "Amen," then witnesses come along and give testimony against him that he had in fact eaten it — he pays only the principal. [If] he confessed after the taking of the oath, whether this was before the witnesses came along or after the witnesses came along, he pays the principal, the added fifth, and a guilt-offering.

T. 8:8 "Where is my ox?" He said to him, "It was stolen." "I impose an oath on you!" And he said, "Amen." Then witnesses come along and give testimony concerning him that he had stolen it — he pays twofold restitution.

B. *Penalties for Abuse of the Land*

M. 7:7 They do not rear small cattle in the Land of Israel, but they do rear them in Syria and in the wastelands which are in the Land of Israel. They do not rear chickens in Jerusalem, on account of the Holy Things, nor do priests [rear chickens] anywhere in the Land of Israel, because of the [necessity to preserve] the cleanness [of heave offering and certain other foods which are handed over to the priests]. They do not rear pigs

anywhere. **A person should not rear a dog, unless it is kept tied up by a chain. They do not set traps for pigeons, unless they are thirty ris from a settlement.**

T. 8:17 Just as they do not raise small domesticated cattle, so they do not raise small wild beasts.

B. 7:7 I.1/79B THEY DO NOT REAR SMALL CATTLE IN THE LAND OF ISRAEL, BUT THEY DO REAR THEM IN WOODLANDS IN THE LAND OF ISRAEL, AND IN SYRIA, EVEN IN INHABITED AREAS, AND ONE NEED NOT SAY OUTSIDE OF THE LAND OF ISRAEL ALTOGETHER. THEY DO NOT REAR SMALL CATTLE IN THE LAND OF ISRAEL, BUT THEY DO REAR THEM IN THE WILDERNESS OF JUDAH AND IN THE WILDERNESS AT THE BORDER OF AKKO. AND EVEN THOUGH SAGES HAVE SAID, "THEY DO NOT RAISE SMALL CATTLE," THEY MAY IN ANY EVENT RAISE LARGE CATTLE, FOR A DECREE MAY NOT BE ISSUED FOR THE COMMUNITY THAT THE MAJORITY OF THE COMMUNITY CAN CARRY IT OUT. IN THE CASE OF SMALL CATTLE, IT IS POSSIBLE TO IMPORT THEM FROM ABROAD; IN THE CASE OF LARGE CATTLE, IT IS NOT POSSIBLE TO IMPORT THEM FROM ABROAD. AND EVEN THOUGH SAGES HAVE SAID, "THEY DO NOT REAR SMALL CATTLE," ONE MAY NONETHELESS HOLD ON TO THEM FOR THIRTY DAYS PRIOR TO A FESTIVAL, OR FOR THIRTY DAYS PRIOR TO THE CELEBRATION OF A WEDDING OF ONE OF HIS SONS. BUT HE MAY NOT HOLD ON TO AN ANIMAL BOUGHT FOR THIRTY DAYS, IF THE THIRTY DAYS EXPIRE AFTER THE FESTIVAL. BUT A BUTCHER MAY PURCHASE AND SLAUGHTER, PURCHASE AND HOLD A BEAST, SO LONG AS HE DOES NOT HOLD ON FOR MORE THAN THIRTY DAYS TO AN ANIMAL THAT HE HAS BOUGHT.

B. 7:7 I.16/80B–81A THERE WERE TEN STIPULATIONS THAT JOSHUA MADE WHEN THE ISRAELITES ENTERED THE LAND: [1] THAT CATTLE MAY BE ALLOWED TO PASTURE IN FORESTS; [2] THAT WOOD MAY BE GATHERED FREELY IN PRIVATE FIELDS; [3] THAT GRASS MAY BE GATHERED FREELY IN PRIVATE PROPERTY, EXCEPT FOR A FIELD WHERE FENUGREC IS GROWING; [4] THAT SHOOTS MAY BE CUT OFF FREELY IN ANY PLACE, EXCEPT FOR STUMPS OF OLIVE TREES; [5] THAT A SPRING EMERGING EVEN TO BEGIN WITH MAY BE USED BY TOWNSFOLK; [6] THAT IT IS PERMITTED TO FISH AT AN ANGLE IN THE SEA OF TIBERIAS, SO LONG AS NO SAIL IS SPREAD OUT, SINCE THIS WOULD DETAIN THE BOATS; [7] THAT IT IS PERMITTED TO TAKE A CRAP AT THE BACK OF ANY FENCE, EVEN IN A FIELD FULL OF SAFFRON; [8] THAT IT IS PERMITTED TO USE PATHS IN PRIVATE FIELDS UNTIL THE TIME THAT THE SECOND RAINS ARE ANTICIPATED; [9] THAT IT IS PERMITTED TO TURN ASIDE TO PRIVATE PATHS TO AVOID ROAD PEGS; [10] THAT SOMEONE WHO IS LOST IN VINEYARDS IS PERMITTED TO CUT THROUGH GOING UP OR CUT THROUGH GOING DOWN; [11] THAT A DEAD BODY THAT SOMEONE FINDS NEGLECTED AND SUBJECT TO IMMEDIATE BURIAL ACQUIRES THE SPOT ON WHICH IT IS FOUND.

C. *Penalties for Assault*

M. 8:1 He who injures his fellow is liable to [compensate] him on five counts: (1) injury, (2) pain, (3) medical costs, (4) loss of

income [lit.: loss of time], and (5) indignity For injury: How so? [If] one has blinded his eye, cut off his hand, broken his leg, they regard him as a slave up for sale in the market and make an estimate of how much he was worth beforehand [when whole], and how much he is now worth. Pain: [If] he burned him with a spit or a nail, and even on his fingernail, a place in which [the injury] does not leave a lasting wound, they assess how much a man in his status is willing to take to suffer pain of that sort. Medical costs: [If] he hit him, he is liable to provide for his medical care. [If] sores arise on him, if [they are] on account of the blow, he is liable; [but if] they are not on account of the blow, he is exempt. [If] the wound got better and opened up again, got better and opened up again, he remains liable to provide for his medical care. [If the wound] properly healed, he is no longer liable to provide medical care for him. Loss of income: They regard him [in estimating income] as if he is a keeper of a cucumber field, for [the defendant] already has paid off the value of his hand or his leg. Indignity: All [is assessed] in accord with the status of the one who inflicts the indignity and the one who suffers the indignity. He who inflicts indignity on one who is naked, he who inflicts indignity on one who is blind, or he who inflicts indignity on one who is asleep is liable. But one who is sleeping who inflicted indignity is exempt [on that count]. [If] he fell from the roof and did injury and also inflicted indignity, he is liable for the injury [he has inflicted] but exempt from the indignity. One is liable on the count of indignity only if he intended [to inflict indignity].

T. 9:1 There are thirteen generative causes [categories] of damages: ox, pit, destroying beast, conflagration [M. B.Q. 1:1A], unpaid bailee, borrower, paid bailee, renter, injury, pain, medical costs, loss of income, indignity [M. B.Q. 8:1B]. [If] one has inflicted on another person all five [kinds of damage], he pays him for all five. [If he inflicted] only four kinds, he pays him for four. [If he inflicted] only three kinds, he pays him for three. [If he inflicted] only two kinds, he pays him for two. [If he inflicted] only one kind, he pays him for one.

Y. 8:1 I:1 *How so? [If] he hit him on his hand and cut it off, he pays all five kinds of compensation: for injury, pain, medical costs, loss of income, and indignity. [If] he hit him on his hand and it swelled up, he pays him four: pain, medical costs, loss of income, and indignity. [If] he hit him on his head and it swelled up, he pays him three: pain, medical costs, and loss of income. [If] he hit him on a part of the body which is not visible, he pays him two: pain and medical costs. In the case of hitting his book which is in his hand, he pays him only compensation for the humiliation.*

T. 9:2 For injury: How so? [If] he hit him and cut off his hand, hit him and cut off his leg [M. B.Q. 8:1D], they do not regard him as if he makes a sela a day, or as if he makes a maneh a day. But they regard him as if he is a cripple who serves as a watchman for a cucumber-field. And if you say that this smites the rule of justice, the rule of justice indeed has not been smitten. For in any event they pay off the value of the hand or the value of the leg [M. B.Q. 8:1P].

T. 9:3 But [if] he hit him and his hand dried up [and withered], or he hit him and his leg dried up, they do regard him as if he makes a sela a day, and they pay him compensation of a sela a day, or they do regard him as if he makes a maneh a day and pay him off a maneh a day. And they pay him all the compensation for damages. And all of them do they estimate and pay off forthwith. Therefore if he continues to fail, even for five years he has a claim only on the [original] estimate they made for him. How long do they continue to pay him off? Until he returns to health.

T. 9:4 If ulcers grew up on the body because of the wound, and the wound broke open again, he still has to heal him and pay for loss of time, but if it was not because of the wound, he does not have to pay for the healing or the loss of time.

T. 9:5 He who hit his fellow — [if] they formed a prognosis that he would die, they again assess that he would live. [If they formed a prognosis] that he would live, they do not again assess that he would die. [If] they assessed that he would die, then the defendant is liable to the death penalty but exempt from having to pay monetary compensation. [If] they made an estimate as to the monetary compensation, the defendant is liable to pay monetary compensation and exempt from the death penalty. [If] they assessed that he would die, and he got better, they make an estimate of the monetary compensation to be paid a second time. From what point does he pay him off? From the point at which he hit him.

T. 9:6 [If] they assessed that he would live and he died, [the defendant] pays compensation for injury, pain, medical costs, loss of income, and indignity, to the estate of the deceased. [If] they assessed that he would die and he got somewhat better and then got somewhat worse and finally died, they make an estimate of the matter. If on account of the original injury he died, he is liable. [If this] was not the case, lo, this one is exempt.

B. 8:1 V.2/86A IF ONE CUT OFF THE OTHER'S HAND, HE PAYS HIM THE VALUE OF HIS HAND, AND, AS TO LOSS OF TIME FROM WORK, THEY REGARD HIM AS THOUGH HE WERE A WATCHMEN OF A CUCUMBER FIELD. IF HE CUT OFF HIS LEG, HE PAYS HIM FOR THE DEPRECIATION TO HIS WORTH CAUSED BY THE LOSS OF THE LEG, AND, AS TO LOSS OF TIME FROM WORK, THEY REGARD HIM AS THEY HE WERE A DOORKEEPER. IF HE PUT OUT HIS EYE, HE PAYS HIM FOR THE DEPRECIATION OF HIS VALUE BECAUSE OF THE LOSS OF THE EYE, AND AS TO THE LOSS OF TIME FROM WORK, HE IS REGARDED AS IF HE WERE PUSHING THE GRINDING WHEEL IN A MILL. BUT IF HE MADE THE OTHER PARTY DEAF, HE PAYS THE ENTIRE VALUE OF THE PERSON, PURE AND SIMPLE [SINCE HE IS WORTH NOTHING].

T. 9:12 He who inflicts indignity on his fellow when he is naked, lo, he is liable. But it is not the same thing to inflict indignity upon him when he is naked as it is to inflict indignity on him when he is clothed. If he inflicted indignity on him when he was in the bathhouse, lo, this one is liable. But it is not the same thing to inflict indignity upon him when he is in the bathhouse as it is to inflict indignity on him when he is in the market. [And it is not the same thing to receive an indignity from an honored person as it is to receive an indignity from a worthless person. And the indignity inflicted upon a great person who is humiliated is not equivalent to the indignity inflicted upon an unimportant person who is humiliated, or the child of important parents who is subjected to an indignity to the child of unimportant parents who is subjected to an indignity.]

M. 8:2 This rule is more strict in the case of man than in the case of an ox. For a man pays compensation for injury, pain, medical costs, loss of income, and indignity; and he pays compensation for the offspring [Ex. 21:22]. But [the owner of] an ox pays compensation only for the injury. And he is exempt from liability to pay compensation for the offspring.

M. 8:3 He who hits his father or his mother but did not make a wound on them, or he who injures his fellow on the Day of Atonement is liable on all counts. He who injures a Hebrew slave is liable on all counts, except for loss of time when he belongs to him [who did the damage]. He who injures a Canaanite slave belonging to other people is liable on all counts.

M. 8:4 A deaf-mute, idiot, and minor — meeting up with them is a bad thing. He who injures them is liable. But they who injure other people are exempt. A slave and a woman — meeting up with them is a bad thing He who injures them is liable. And they who injure other people are exempt. But they pay compensation after an interval: [if] the woman is divorced, the slave freed, they become liable to pay compensation.

T. 9:8 He who injures his adult sons or daughters is liable under all counts. If he injured a Hebrew boy-slave or girl-slave belonging to other people, they collect from him. And [as to what he owes] his daughter, he pays her off immediately. [As to what he owes] his son, he sets it aside for him [in trust]. [If he injured] his minor sons or daughters, he is exempt on all counts. He who injures his minor daughter — the compensation for her injury belongs to her, and for all other forms of compensation lo, he is exempt.

T. 9:9 [If] others injured her, compensation for her injury belongs to her. And as to the rest of the compensation, he sets it aside for her [in trust]. And if she dies, he inherits her estate.

T. 9:10 He who injures his minor son is liable on all counts. [If he injured] his Canaanite boy-slave or girl-slave, he is liable on all counts, but exempt on the count of compensation for the loss of time, for compensation for loss of time in any event belongs to him [the owner] [M. B.Q. 8:3D-E]. [If] he beat them more than is appropriate, he is liable.

T. 9:11 A father who hits his son, and a teacher who smites his disciple, who smote and did damage — lo, these are exempt. [If] they beat them more than is appropriate, lo, these are liable. A court-officer who administered a blow at the behest of the court and did injury is exempt. [If] he beat the criminal more than is appropriate, lo, this one is liable. A qualified physician who administered a remedy at the behest of a court and did damage is exempt. [If] he did more damage than was appropriate for this case, lo, this one is liable.

T. 9:13 He who inflicts injury on a deaf-mute, idiot, or minor, is liable on four counts, but exempt on the count of indignity, because they are not subject to indignity.

T. 9:14 He who inflicts injury upon his wife — whether he injured her or whether others injured her — they collect [damages] from him. With the compensation, a field is purchased, and he enjoys the usufruct thereof.

Y. 8:4 I:1 *[With reference to Ex. 21:26–27: "When a man strikes the eye of his slave, . . . and destroys it, he shall let the slave go free for his eye's sake. If he knocks out the tooth of his slave, . . . he shall let the slave go free for the tooth's sake."] Witnesses who stated, "We testify concerning Mr. So-and-so, that he has blinded both eyes of his slave simultaneously," "he has knocked out two of his teeth simultaneously," — the master pays nothing to the slave at all [but sends him forth free]. [If they testified that he had done so] one after another, the slave goes forth to freedom on account of the first, and the master pays him compensation for the loss of the second. The witnesses who testified, "We give evidence that Mr. So-and-so blinded the eye of his slave and afterward he knocked out his tooth," and so the master says, and who turned out to be perjurers — they pay compensation to the slave. [If they said,] ". . . he knocked out his tooth and afterward he blinded his eye," And so the slave says, and they turned out to be perjurers, they pay to the master. [If they said,] "He blinded both of them at once," or "He knocked out both of them at once," and others came and said, "Not so, but it was two of them in succession," and they turned out to be perjurers — they pay to the slave. [If they said,] "He blinded both of them one after the other, or knocked out both of them one after the other," and others came along and said, "Not so, but he did both of them at once," and they turned out to be perjurers — they pay to the master. He blinded the eye of his slave, and lo, he is yet subject to him and working for him — and they turn out to be perjurer, they pay both the value of the slave and of the blinding to the master [= T. Mak. 1:4–5].*

M. 8:5 He who hits his father or his mother and did make a wound on them, and he who injures his fellow on the Sabbath is exempt on all counts, for he is put on trial for his life. And he who injures a Canaanite slave belonging to himself is exempt on all counts.

T. 9:17 [If someone] killed him and killed his beast simultaneously, killed him and cut off his hand simultaneously, killed him and blinded his eye simultaneously, [the killer] is exempt [from having to pay monetary compensation], since it is said, "when men strive together and hurt a woman with child so that there is a miscarriage] and yet no harm follows, the one who hurt her shall be fined" (Ex. 21:22) if there is harm, then there is no penalty. But if [the defendant] killed his beast and then killed him, cut off his hand and then killed him, blinded his eye and killed him, he is liable, since it is said, "He shall make restitution" (Ex. 22:5). This is the governing principle: Anyone who is subject to both the death penalty and civil damages simultaneously is exempt. [But if he is subject to] the death penalty and afterward to civil damages, or to civil damages and afterward to the death penalty, lo, this person is liable [for both].

T. 9:19 He who steals the purse of his fellow and took it out [of his domain] on the Sabbath, lo, this person is liable, for he already had become obligated on account of the theft of the wallet before it had gone forth. If he was dragging it along and so removed it from the domain of the other, he is exempt [since he did not make acquisition of the purse before he had also and simultaneously violated the Sabbath].

T. 9:21 He who does injury to his Hebrew boy-slave or girl-slave, when they are by themselves [so there are no witnesses] — lo, these are subjected to an oath and collect [damages]. He who does injury to his Canaanite boy-slave or girl-slave, when they are by themselves — is exempt [from paying damages], for [compensation for injury] is a fine, [and a fine is not imposed upon the confession of the defendant alone].

T. 9:22 He who hits his slave — [and then] sold him to someone else, and [the slave] died — is exempt, since it says, "And he died under his hand" (Ex. 21:20) — [meaning that one is punished only] when the act of hitting the slave and the death of the slave take place while the slave is in the master's domain. A slave who inflicted injury upon himself goes forth to freedom and pays off his master. And a woman who inflicted injury on her husband does not lose any of the value of her marriage settlement on that account And just as she cannot sell off her marriage-settlement while she is subject to him, so she cannot lose a penny of the value of her marriage-settlement while she is subject to him [cf. M. B.Q. 8:4G–H].

T. 9:28 He who injures his fellow, and the one who did the injury died — the heirs must pay compensation. [If] the one who was injured died, [the defendant] pays the estate of the one who was injured. Whether there is a claim or not, this one would take an oath and collect [what was coming to him].

M. 8:6 He who boxes the ear of his fellow pays him a sela. [If] he smacked him, he pays him two hundred zuz. [If] it is with the back of his hand, he pays him four hundred zuz. [If] he (1) tore at his ear, (2) pulled his hair, (3) spit, and the spit hit him, (4) pulled off his cloak, (5) pulled apart the hairdo of a woman in the marketplace, he pays four hundred zuz.

M. 8:7 Even though [the defendant] pays off [the plaintiff], he is not forgiven until he seeks [forgiveness] from [the plaintiff]. He who says, "Blind my eye," "Cut off my hand," "Break my leg" — [the one who does so] is liable. [If he added,] "... on condition of being exempt," [the one who does so] is liable [anyhow]. "Tear my cloak," "Break my jar," [the one who does so] is liable. [If he added,] "... on condition of being exempt," [the

one who does so] is exempt. "Do it to Mr. So-and-so, on condition of being exempt," he [who does so] is liable, whether this is to his person or to his property.

T. 9:32 He who says, "Blind my eye, which is doing me harm," "Chop off my hand, which is doing me harm," — he is exempt [cf. M. B.Q. 8:7E–I].

T. 9:33 [If] gentiles forced a person and he took away the possessions of his fellow in his very presence, he is exempt. [But if on his own volition] he took them and handed them out, lo, this person is liable [cf. M. B.Q. 8:7N–O].

B. 8:7 I.1/92A ALL OF THESE SUMS THAT ARE SPECIFIED REPRESENT THE MONETARY COMPENSATION FOR HUMILIATION, BUT AS TO THE ANGUISH, EVEN IF THE OFFENDER BROUGHT ALL OF THE FINEST RAMS IN THE WORLD, THE MAN IS NOT FORGIVEN UNTIL HE ASKS FORGIVENESS FROM HIM, AS IT IS SAID, "NOW RESTORE THE MAN'S WIFE . . . AND HE WILL PRAY FOR YOU" (GEN. 20:7).

D. *Penalties for Damages Done by Persons to Property;*
Restoring What is Stolen

M. 9:1 [If] he stole a pregnant cow and it gave birth, a ewe heavy with wool [needing shearing], and he sheared it — he pays the value of a cow which is about to give birth, or of a ewe which is about to be sheared. [If] he stole a cow, and it got pregnant while with him and gave birth, a ewe, and it became heavy [with wool] while with him, and he sheared, he pays [compensation in accord with the value of the cow or ewe] at the time of the theft. This is the governing principle: all robbers pay compensation [in accord with the value of the stolen object] at the time of the theft.

T. 10:1 He who steals a cow and it became pregnant while in his domain, and did so a second, a third, and even a fourth and fifth time and so too, he who steals a ewe, and it grows a full crop of wool while in his domain, even four or five times, a goat, and he milks it, even four or five times — he pays compensation [in accord with the value of the stolen beast] at the time of the theft.

T. 10:2 [If] he stole wool and bleached it, thread and he bleached it, flax and he washed it, stones and he smoothed them down, he pays compensation [in accord with their value] at the time of the theft [M. B.Q. 9:1A–C].

M. 9:2 [If] he stole a beast and it got old, slaves and they got old, he pays [compensation for them in accord with their value] at the time of the theft. [If] he stole (1) a coin and it got cracked, (2) pieces of fruit and they turned rotten, (3) wine and it turned into vinegar, he pays [compensation for them in accord with their value] at the time of the theft. [If he stole] (1) a coin, and it was declared invalid, (2) heave offering, and it became unclean, (3) leaven, and the festival of Passover passed [making it no longer available for Israelite use], (4) a beast, and a transgression was committed upon it, or (5) [a beast] which was invalidated for use on the altar, or (6) which was going forth to be stoned, [the robber] says to him, "Here is what is yours right in front of you!"

T. 10:4 This is the governing principle: Anything which is stolen, which is available, and [the thief] in no way has changed it from its original condition — [the thief may] say to him, "Lo, there is your property before you." But if he changed it in some way from its original condition, he pays [compensation in accord with the value] at the time of the robbery. The thief under all circumstances pays compensation in accord with the value at the time of the theft.

T. 10:7 He who goes down into the ruin which belongs to his fellow and builds it up without permission — they make an estimate [of the matter], and his hand is underneath. He who goes down with permission — they make an estimate [of the matter], and his hand is now on top. How is it that his hand is on the top? If the increase in value is greater than the outlay, he pays him off the increase in value. If the outlay is greater than the increase in value, he pays him what he has laid out.

B. 9:2 IV.1/98A AN OX THAT KILLED SOMEONE — IF THE OWNER SOLD IT BEFORE THE COURT DECREE WAS ISSUED, IT IS DEEMED TO HAVE BEEN VALIDLY SOLD. IF THE OWNER SANCTIFIED IT TO THE TEMPLE, IT IS VALIDLY SANCTIFIED. IF HE SLAUGHTERED IT, ITS MEAT IS PERMITTED. IF THE BAILEE RETURNED IT TO THE HOUSEHOLD OF THE OWNER, IT IS VALIDLY RETURNED [AND THE BAILEE HAS NO FURTHER OBLIGATION]. IF AFTER THE COURT DECREE WAS ISSUED, THE OWNER SOLD IT, IT IS DEEMED NOT TO HAVE BEEN VALIDLY SOLD. IF THE OWNER SANCTIFIED IT TO THE TEMPLE, IT IS NOT VALIDLY SANCTIFIED. IF HE SLAUGHTERED IT, ITS MEAT IS NOT PERMITTED. IF THE BAILEE RETURNED IT TO THE HOUSEHOLD OF THE OWNER, IT IS NOT VALIDLY RETURNED.

M. 9:3 [If] one gave [something] to craftsmen to repair, and they spoiled [the object], they are liable to pay compensation. [If] he gave to a joiner a box, chest, or cupboard to repair, and he spoiled it, he is liable to pay compensation. A builder who took upon himself to destroy a wall, and who smashed the rocks or did damage is liable to pay compensation. [If] he was tearing down the wall on one side, and it fell down on the other side, he is exempt. But if it is because of the blow [which he gave it], he is liable.

T. 10:8 A carpenter who drove a nail into a box, chest, or cupboard, and it broke [M. B.Q. 9:3B], is liable to pay compensation, because he is tantamount to a paid bailee. [If] one handed [wood] over to a joiner to make a chair for him, and he made a bench, a bench, and he made a chair, the hand of the owner is on top. If he gave [wood] to a carpenter to make him a nice chair, and he made him an ugly one, a nice bench, and he made him an ugly one [M. B.Q. 9:3A], the hand of the owner is on top.

9:4 He who hands over wool to a dyer, and the [dye in the] cauldron burned it, [the dyer] pays the value of the wool. [If] he dyed it in a bad color, if [the wool] increased in value more than the outlay [of the dyer], [the owner of the wool] pays him the money he has laid out in the process of dyeing. But if the outlay of the dyer is greater than the increase in value of the wool, [the owner] pays him back only the value of the improvement.

T. 10:9 He who brings wheat to be ground, and [the miller] did not moisten it, but made it into coarse bran or second-rate flour, or flour to a baker, and he made it into crumbly bread, or meat to a butcher, and he burned it, he is liable to pay damages, because he is in the status *of* a paid bailee.

T. 10:10 He who hands over his beast to a butcher, and it is made into carrion [by the butcher's error], [if he was] a professional, he is exempt. [If he was] an ordinary person, he is liable. [If] he was a paid bailee, one way or the other, he is liable. He who shows a denar to a moneychanger and it turns out to be bad is liable to pay [a good denar], because he is in the status of one who is a paid bailee.

M. 9:5 He who stole something from his fellow worth only a perutah, and took an oath to him [that he had stolen nothing, but then wants to make restitution], must take it to him, even all the way to Media. He should not give it to his son or his agent, but he may hand it over to an agent appointed by a court. And if [the victim] died, [the robber] restores [the object] to his estate.

M. 9:6 [If the thief] paid him back the principal but did not pay the added fifth, [if the victim] forgave him the value of the principal but did not forgive him the value of the added fifth, [if] he forgave him for this and for that, except for something less a perutah out of the principal, he need not take it back to him. [If] he [the thief] gave him back the added fifth and did not hand over the principal. [If the victim] forgave him the added fifth but did not forgive him the principal, forgave him for this and for that, except for an amount of the principal that added up to a perutah, then he has to go after him [to make restitution, wherever he may be].

M. 9:7 [If] he paid him back the principal but swore [falsely] to him about the added fifth [and then confessed], lo, this one pays back an added fifth for the added fifth, [and so is the rule] until the value of the principal [of the added fifth] becomes less than a perutah in value. And so [is the rule] in the case of a bailment. If this one pays back the principal, an added fifth, and a guilt offering. [If one said], "Where is my bailment?" he said to him, "It got lost." "I impose an oath on you!" and he said, "Amen," then witnesses come along and give testimony against him that he had eaten it up — he pays back the principal. [If] he had confessed on his own, he pays back the principal, the added fifth, and a guilt offering.

M. 9:8 "Where is my bailment?" He said to him, "It was stolen." "I impose an oath on you!" And he said, "Amen," — Then witnesses come along and testify against him that he stole it, he pays twofold restitution. [If] he had confessed on his own, he pays the principal, an added fifth, and a guilt offering.

M. 9:9 He who steals from his father and takes an oath to him, and then [the father] dies — lo, this one pays back the principal and an added fifth to his [father's other] sons or brothers [and brings the guilt offering]. But if he does not want to do so or does not have what to pay back, he takes out a loan, and the creditors come along and collect what is owing.

M. 9:10 He who says to his son, "Qonam! You will not derive benefit from anything that is mine!" — if the father died, the son may inherit him. [But if he had specified that the vow applied] in life and after death, if the father died, the son may not inherit him. And he must return [what he has of the father's] to his sons or to his brothers. And if he does not have that to repay, he takes out a loan, and the creditors come along and collect what is owing.

M. 9:11 He who steals from a proselyte and takes a [false] oath to him, and then [the proselyte] dies — lo, this person pays the principal and added fifth to the priests, and the guilt offering to the altar. [If the thief] was bringing up the money and the guilt offering and he died, the money is to be given to his [the thief's] sons. And the guilt offering is set out to pasture until it suffers a disfiguring blemish, then it is sold, and the money received for it falls to the chest for the purchase of a freewill offering.

M. 9:12 If he [who had stolen from a proselyte] had paid over the money to the men of the priestly watch on duty, and then [the thief] died, the heirs cannot retrieve the funds from their possession. [If] he gave the money to the priestly watch of Jehoiarib [which is prior], and the guilt offering to the priestly watch of Jedaiah [which is later], he has carried out his obligation. If he gave] the guilt offering to the priestly watch of Jehoiarib and the money to the priestly watch of Jedaiah, if the guilt offering is yet available, the family of Jedaiah should offer it And if not, he should go and bring another guilt offering. For he who brings back what he had stolen before he brought his guilt offering has fulfilled his obligation. But if he brought his guilt offering before he brought back what he had stolen, he has not fulfilled his obligation. [If] he handed over the principal but did not hand over the added fifth, the added fifth does not stand in the way [of offering the guilt offering and so completing his obligation].

T. 10:14–15 He who robs the public is liable to restore [what he has stolen] to the public. A more strict rule applies to robbing the public than to robbing an individual. For he who robs from an individual can appease him and restore to him what he has stolen. But he who robs from the public cannot appease all of them and restore to them what he has stolen. He who robs from a gentile is liable to restore to the gentile [what he has stolen]. A more strict rule applies to robbing from a gentile than to robbing from an Israelite, because of the profanation of the Divine Name [involved in robbing from a gentile].

M. 10:1 He who steals [food] and feeds [what he stole] to his children, or left it to them — they are exempt from making restitution. But if it was something which is subject to a mortgage, [that is, real estate], they are liable to make restitution. They do not change money from the chest of the excise collectors or from the fund of the tax farmers. And they do not take from them contributions to charity. But one may take [from them contributions for charity] when the funds are] from [the collector's] own home or from the marketplace.

T. 5:25 An Israelite who lends money to his fellow on interest and then repented is liable to return [to him the interest he has collected]. [If] he died and left [the money] to his children, the children do not have to return [the money he collected at interest]. And in such a case it is said, "[Though he heap up silver like dust, and pile up clothing like clay;] he may pile it up, but they just will wear it, and the innocent will divide the silver" (Job 27:17). But if their father had left them a cow, a field, a cloak or any sort of object for which he bore responsibility [for replacement, should the object be lost], they are liable to return such an object, for the honor of their father.

T. 10:20 If one has stolen and exchanged stolen and consecrated [the object], stolen and given the object as a gift, stolen and placed the object out on loan, stolen and paid a debt, stolen and sent gifts to the house of his father-in-law — lo, this one is liable. But the one who receives the object from him is exempt.

T. B.M. 2:25–6 If the father died and left money gained on interest to his children, even if the heirs know that it was money paid as interest, the children do not have to return the money collected as interest. [But if the father had left them a cow, field, cloak, or any sort of object for which he bore responsibility for replacement, should the object be lost, they are liable to return such an object for the honor of their father].

Y. 10:1 II.4 He who robs and feeds his minor children [cf. M. 10:1A], his Canaanite boy-slave or girl-slave — they are exempt from paying restitution. [Yerushalmi's version: He who robs and feeds his children, whether adult or minor, they are exempt from having to pay restitution. If he left it to them, whether adult or minor, they are liable to do so. Sumkhos says, "The elders are liable, the minors are exempt."] [If] he left them something which is subject to a mortgage, they are liable to make resti-

tution. But if they said, "We do not know what reckoning father made with you [at the hour of his death]," they are exempt from liability to make restitution.

B. 10:1A–C I.1/111B IF ONE STOLE SOMETHING [SUCH AS AN ANIMAL], AND, BEFORE THE OWNER HAD DESPAIRED OF GETTING IT BACK [AT WHICH POINT THE THIEF ACQUIRES TITLE TO THE OBJECT], SOMEONE ELSE CAME ALONG AND ATE UP WHAT HE STOLE, THE OWNER HAS THE CHOICE OF COLLECTING THE PAYMENT FROM THE ONE OR THE OTHER.

M. 10:2 [If] excise collectors took one's ass and gave him another ass, [if) thugs took his garment and gave him another garment, lo, these are his, because the original owners have given up hope of getting them back. He who saves something from a river, from a raid, or from thugs, if the owner has given up hope of getting them back, lo, these belong to him. And so a swarm of bees: If the owner had given up hope of getting it back, lo, this belongs to him. And one may walk through the field of his fellow to get back his swarm of bees. But if he did damage, he pays compensation for the damage which he did. But he may not cut off a branch of his tree [to retrieve the swarm, even] on condition that he pay damages for it.

T. 10:23 A thief who took from this one and gave to that one — what he has given he has given, and what he has taken he has taken. A robber who took from this one and gave to that one — what he has given he has given, and what he has taken he has taken [cf. M. B.Q. 10:2A–C]. The Jordan [river] which took [a piece of ground] from this one and [by changing its course] gave it to that one — what it has taken it has taken, and what it has given, it has given.

T. 10:24 [If] the river swept away wood, stones, and beams, from this one, and gave them to that one, if the owner has given up hope of recovering [what he has lost], lo, these belong to him [on whose property they were deposited] [M. B.Q. 10:2E–F]. If the owner continued to go looking for them, or if they were in some other place, lo, these remain [the possession] of the owner.

T. 10:27 At what point does a man acquire possession of a swarm of bees? Once it enters his own enclosed yard. Lo, this one, whose swarm of bees has gone down into the garden of his fellow, but the owner of the garden will not let him go in, so that he will not break down the greens of his vegetables — lo, this one goes down against the will of the other, and saves his swarm of bees [M. B.Q. 10:2J]. But if he did damage, he pays compensation for the damage which he did.

M. 10:3 He who recognizes his utensils or his books in someone else's possession, and a report of theft had gone forth in the town — the purchaser takes an oath to him specifying how much he had paid and takes [the price in compensation from the original owner, and gives back the property] — And if not, [the original owner] has not got the power [to get his property back]. For I say, "[The original owner] sold them to someone else, and this one [lawfully] bought them from that other person."

M. 10:4 This one is coming along with his jar of wine, and that one is coming along with his jug of honey — the jug of honey cracked — and this one poured out his wine and saved the honey in his jar, he has a claim only for his wages. And if he said, "I'll save yours if you pay me back for mine," [the owner of the honey] is liable to pay him back. [If] the river swept away his ass and the ass of his fellow, his being worth a maneh and his fellow's worth two hundred [zuz] [twice as much], [if] he then left his own and saved that of his fellow, he has a claim only for his wages. But if he said, "I'll save yours, if you pay me back for mine," [the owner of the better ass] is liable to pay him back.

T. 10:26 [If] this one unloaded his pieces of wood and saved the flax of his fellow, [the latter] pays him his wages, calculated as the value of returning a lost object. If he had said to him, "... on condition that he [I] may collect the value of mine [which I shall lose] out of yours," he is liable to pay it to him.

T. 10:28 Two who were in the wilderness, and in the hand of one of them was a jar of water, while in the hand of the other was a jar of honey, [if] the jar of water cracked, it is a condition imposed upon the court that this one should pour out his honey and save the water of his fellow. And when he reaches a settled area, he pays him back the value of his honey. For water preserves life in the wilderness, and honey does not preserve life in the wilderness.

T. B.M. 7:13 A caravan that was passing through the wilderness, and a band of thugs fell on it and seized it for ransom — they make a reckoning in accord with the property loss and not in accord with the number of people. But if they sent out a pathfinder before them, they also make a reckoning of the number of people. But in any event they do not vary from the accepted practice governing those who travel in caravans.

T. B.M. 11:25 The ass drivers have the right to declare, "Whoever loses an ass will be given another ass." But if the loss is caused by negligence, they would not have to meet that stipulation, and if it was not on account of negligence, he is given another ass. And if he said, "Give me the money and I'll watch out for it as a paid bailee," they do not listen to him.

T. B.M. 7:14 A boat that was coming along in the sea and got hit by a storm, so they had to toss some cargo overboard — they make a reckoning in accord with the property loss and not in accord with the number of people. But in any event they do not vary from the accepted practice of sailors.

T. B.M. 11:26 And the sailors have the right to declare, "Whoever loses a ship — we'll provide him with another ship." If it was lost through flagrant neglect, they do not have to provide him with another ship. If it was lost not through flagrant neglect, they do have to provide him with another ship. But if he set sail for a place to which people do not prudently set sail, they do not have to provide him with another ship if he loses his on the perilous voyage.

M. 10:5 He who stole a field from his fellow, and bandits seized it from him — if it is a blow [from which the whole] district [suffered], he may say to him, "Lo, there is yours before you." But if it is because [of the deeds] of the thief [in particular], he is liable to replace it for him with another field. [If] a river swept it away, he may say to him, "Lo, there is yours before you."

Y. 10:5 If he left his own to save that of his fellow, but his fellow's property emerged on its own [without the help of the other], the fellow does not owe him a thing. But if he left his own property to save that of his fellow, and his own property emerged on its own, what is the law governing his claim, "I had given up hope of saving my property," [and since it therefore was lost to me, you owe me compensation for it]? [The stipulated payment must be given].

M. 10:6 He who (1) stole something from his fellow, or (2) borrowed something from him, or (3) with whom the latter deposited something, in a settled area — may not return it to him in the wilderness. [If it was] on the stipulation that he was going to go forth to the wilderness, he may return it to him in the wilderness.

T. 10:32 [If] one handed over to another a house as a pledge [for a loan], or a field as a pledge, and he saw a brush-fire coming toward his property, and he said to him, "Come and save these, which I owe you," if the other accepted, [the former] is exempt. And if not, he is liable [cf. M. B.Q. 10:6D–E].

M. 10:7 He who says to his fellow, "I have stolen from you . . .," "You have lent something to me . . . 'You have deposited something with me . . .,' 'and I don't know whether or not I returned [the object] to you'" is liable to pay him restitution. But if he said to him, "I don't know whether I stole something from you," ". . . whether you lent me something," ". . . whether you deposited something with me," he is exempt from paying restitution.

M. 10:8 He who steals a lamb from a flock and [unbeknownst to the owner] returned it, and it died or was stolen again, is liable to make it up. [If] the owner did not know either that it had been stolen or that it had been returned, and he counted up the flock and it was complete, then [the thief] is exempt.

T. 10:33 He who steals a lamb from the flock and returned it to the flock, and afterward the entire flock was stolen, if he had informed the owner, or they had counted [the sheep], he is exempt. And if not, he is liable [M. B.Q. 10:8]. He who steals a jug from a cellar and returned it to the cellar, and afterward all the jugs in the cellar were stolen, if he had informed the owner [that he had returned the jug], he is exempt. And if not, he is liable.

T. 10:35 He who steals a *sela* from a purse and put it back into the purse, and afterward the entire purse was stolen, if he had informed the owner, he is exempt. And if not, he is liable.

T. 10:36 He who steals the purse of his fellow and returned it to him while he was asleep, and he woke up, and lo, his purse is in his hand, if [the victim] recognizes it as his, [the other] is exempt. And if not, he is liable. He who steals a *sela* without the knowledge of the owner that it has been stolen, and then [to return it] included it into the reckoning [of what he owed the owner], has fulfilled his obligation.

T. 10:39 Thieves who snuck in by stealth and then did repent — all of them are liable to restore what they have stolen. [If] only one of them repented, he is liable to restore only his share [of the theft] alone. [If] he had been taking out what was in the house and placing it before the others, then he is liable to make restitution of all that had been stolen.

T. 11:1 They do not accept bailments from women, slaves, or minors. [If] one has accepted a bailment from a woman, he must return it to the woman. [If the woman] died, he must return it to her husband. [If] he accepted a bailment from a slave, he must return it to the slave. [If the slave] died, he must return it to his master. [If] he accepted a bailment from a minor, he sets up a trust for him. [If] he died, he returns it to his father. And in all of these cases, [if] they said at the moment of death, "Let my bailment be given to so-and-so, to whom they belong," let that which has been spelled out be done in accord with the stipulation thereby given.

T. 11:2 A son who does business with what belongs to his father, and so too a slave who does business with what belongs to his master, lo, [the goods] are deemed to belong to the father, [or] lo, they are deemed to belong to the master. If they said at the moment of death [however], "Let such-and-such an object be given to So-and-so, to whom they belong," let that which has been spelled out be done in accord with the stipulation thereby given.

M. 10:9 They do not purchase from herdsmen wool, milk, or kids, or from watchmen of an orchard wood or fruit. But they purchase clothing of wool from women in Judah, flax clothing in Galilee, and calves in Sharon. And in all cases in which [the sellers] say to hide them away, it is prohibited [to make such a purchase]. They purchase eggs and chickens in every locale.

T. 11:9 They do not purchase from shepherds either goats or shearings, or bits of wool. But they purchase from them [garments] which have been sewn. For the ones which have been sewn belong to them. And they purchase from them milk and cheese in the wilderness, but not in settled country In any place at all they purchase from them four or five sheep, four or five bundles of fleece. but not two sheep or two bundles of fleece.

T. 11:11 They do not purchase from a weaver either "thorns," remnants of wool, threads of the bobbin, or remnants of the coil. But they purchase from them a checkered web, spun wool, warp, or woof (woven stuff).

T. 11:12 They do not purchase from a dyer either test-pieces, samples, or wool which has been pulled out. But they purchase from him dyed wool, spun wool, warp, or woof. And they do not buy flocking from the fuller, because they do not belong to him. In a place in which they are usually his, lo, these are assumed to be his land may be purchased from him].

B. 10:9 III.1/119A THEY PURCHASE FROM HOUSEWIVES CLOTHING OF WOOL IN JUDEA AND OF FLAX IN GALILEE, BUT NOT WINE NOR OIL NOR FLOUR; NOR DO THEY MAKE PURCHASES FROM SLAVES OR CHILDREN. BUT IN ALL CASES IN WHICH THEY SAID TO HIDE THE GOODS AWAY, IT IS FORBIDDEN TO DO SO. CHARITY COLLECTORS ACCEPT FROM THEM SOME SMALL THING FOR THE PHILANTHROPIC FUND, BUT NOT A LARGE EXPENSIVE GIFT. THEY DO NOT PURCHASE FROM WORKERS AT THE OLIVE PRESS A SMALL AMOUNT OF OIL OR A SMALL QUANTITY OF OLIVES, BUT THEY PURCHASE FROM THEM OIL BY MEASURE AND OLIVES BY MEASURE.

M. 10:10 Shreds of wool which the laundryman pulls out — lo, these belong to him. And those which the wool comber pulls out — lo, they belong to the householder. The laundryman pulls out three threads, and they are his. But more than this — lo, they belong to the householder. If they were black [threads] on a white [surface], he takes all, and they are his. A tailor who left over a thread sufficient for sewing, or a piece of cloth three by three fingerbreadths — lo, these belong to the householder. What the carpenter takes off the plane — lo, these are his. But [what he takes off] with a hatchet belongs to the householder. And if he was working in the household of the householder, even the sawdust belongs to the householder.

T. 11:13 They purchase flocking from laundrymen, because they belong to him. And he should not comb the garment along its warp but along its woof. And he should not place in the garment more than three fuller's hooks [for stretching the garment], and the two upper threads — lo, these are his.

T. 11:16 He who hands over hides to a tanner — the scrapings and the bits pulled up — lo, they belong to the householder. And what comes out with the rinse-water — lo, these belong to him.

T. 11:17 A tailor who left over a thread shorter than the length of a hem, or a piece of cloth three by three fingerbreadths — and he who hands over hides to a tanner — all of them, [when working] in the house of the householder — lo, they belong to the householder.

T. 11:18 Stone-cutters, vine-trimmers, shrub-trimmers, and weed-cutters, when the householder is supervising them, are subject to prohibition on account of thievery. He who hires a worker to trim shrubs with him, or to cut vines — in a locality where it is customary for them to belong to him, lo, they are his. And in a locality where it is customary for them to belong to the householder, lo, they belong to the householder. And they do not vary from the local custom.

II. Analysis: The Problematics of the Topic, Baba Qamma

While it is fair to say that Baba Qamma takes as is task the exposition of how the victim of assault or robbery is to be returned to his prior condition, the thug or thief not gaining, it is not particularly interesting to say so. That is for three reasons.

First, the same governing consideration — preserving the status quo in a world of perfect order — characterizes many of the native categories of the halakhah. Most of them turn out to provide occasions for realizing the same goal of restoration and stasis. So while true, that statement of the problematics does not pertain in particular to Baba Qamma and explains little about that corpus of halakhah in particular. More seriously, it does not help us identify the hermeneutics that sustains the exegetics of the halakhic statement on the assigned topic. We should find it difficult to build a bridge to the systematic exposition and exegesis of the law from the general problem of how to restore the status quo and preserve it.

Second and concomitantly, that thesis on the topical problematics does not permit us to predict how a given sub-topic will be treated, or, indeed, even to anticipate the division of the topic into sub-topics. It is, once more, much too general to help. To explain what I mean, I point to the topic, Shebi'it, the Sabbatical year Simply stating the topic, we are able to predict the subdivisions thereof. For Shebi'it it is [1] ceasing work at the advent of the seventh year, [2] prohibited work during the seventh year, [3] restrictions on the use of the produce of the seventh year, [4] remission of debts. The logic of the topic dictates the character and even the order of the first three sub-topics. And that is how the topic is expounded by the Oral Torah, following the structure imposed by the Mishnah-tractate upon the Tosefta and Yerushalmi. Not only so, but the generative problematic emerges. For once we know that we are going to discuss the (known) topic, the Sabbatical year, with the further facts, supplied by the Written Torah, that agricultural labor ceases, then we have solid reason to predict the unfolding of a systematic inquiry into the process of shutting down labor, the prohibition of labor during the designated span of time, and the disposition of what grows on its own, without human intervention, in that period. Even changing the order would introduce confusion. As to the fourth topic, Scripture has dictated its facts, and the halakhah added thereto by the Oral Torah simply amplifies the same facts and refines them. It follows that inherent in the topic is the logic that dictates what sages are going to want to know about the topic, on the one side, and the order in which they will set forth their knowledge, on the other. But by the same criterion — the logical necessities inherent in the stated topic and their consequences for the orderly division and articulation of the facts sages select for exposition — no equivalent answer emerges here. For how are we to make sense of the exposition of the topic, damages inflicted by chattel and persons? The subject treated in the present category does not contain within itself an explanation for why damages done by chattels takes priority over damages done by persons, as though the former contains information necessary for understanding the latter. Any other order would work just as well. But knowing the general theme does not even tell us what topics will, or will not, present themselves for analysis.

Third, if we adopt as our theory of the generative problematics the concern to restore order and attain stasis, we cannot explain how specific cases identify the problems that concern them. The opening propositions, which attain a high level of abstraction and generalization, take as their problem the organization of received data, the comparison and contrast of species of a single genus. They do not undertake to propose and demonstrate propositions, formulating new facts out of received givens, such as we see is the case in Shebi'it (among numerous tractates). Indeed, it is the speciation of the components of the genus, causes of damages, that defines the problematics of Mishnah-, Tosefta-, and Bavli-tractate Chapter One. Taking as our criterion for a valid problematics the capacity to predict the division of the topic into sub-topics (or to explain, after the fact, why the topic is treated as it is), we have to reject the proposed theory of the problematics of the topic. It is not only too general. It proves implausible, because it does not even account for the data at hand.

If we work back from the portrait of the halakhah in the Mishnah to the concerns that shape that portrait, we could move from the particular to the general. In all four halakhic categories dealt with there, the Mishnah's exposition of its topic yields a clear picture of the generative problematics discerned by sages in that particular topic. We could even specify why a given topic served as an ideal medium for exploring a given range of questions that yield concrete cases of abstract conceptions, why sages could make the statement that they wished to make only, or particularly well, through said topic. Now using as our exemplary case Shebiʿit, we recall that time and again the law wanted to know how intentionality, encompassing human will and perception, affected the concrete and material working of the law of the Sabbatical year. These define the governing variable, the source of unclarity and confusion; these, too, define the medium for clarification and sorting out disorder. The problematics of the halakhah generates small-scale inquiries into large-bore principles. As is my way, I try to work from the little to the large. In Shebiʿit, for example, the cases yielded a recurrent question, the question exposed an inherent problematics. But here I find it difficult to answer the question, what statement do sages wish to make through their analysis of the law of Baba Qamma, and why does this particular category of halakhah serve as the chosen medium for making that statement?

For to the question, are we able to ask the cases of Baba Qamma to exemplify a recurrent and deeper question treated in them *in nuce*? the answer is negative. Neither the order of the topics nor the character of the problems worked out in connection therewith provides a positive response. Ox, pit, crop-destroying beast, fire — why that order and not pit, fire, ox, crop-destroying beast? When it comes to damages done by persons, what logic inherent in the topic tells me that consideration of penalties for the theft of an ox or a sheep comes prior to assessing damages for assault? And, further, we move from the remarkably specific to the very general, treating the theft of an ox or a sheep as a category equivalent in exegetical challenge to penalties for assault. So the order of analysis is not cumulative and tells us nothing of an inner, governing logic. When it comes to identify recurrent questions brought to bear upon diverse data, the picture changes only a little. The framers of the halakhah clearly intend an orderly exposition, which accounts for the character, e.g., of Chapter One and Chapter Eight. In both expositions they clarify by classifying, then comparing and contrasting the taxa. The exercise in the former case exemplifies sages' power of hierarchical classification, the skill with which the manipulate the principles of natural history, so far as comparison and contrast of categories is made to yield new insight. But that banality about a generative interest in hierarchical classification of types of damages and torts serves no better than the consequential observation concerning a paramount interest that the halakhah in general aims at restoration and stabilization of the social order.

Consider, rather, what question common to a range of sub-topics precipitates inquiry of a uniform character among those diverse sub-topics? By way of experiment, let us simply review a sequence of topical sentences of the several sub-divisions of the halakhah and see whether we can identify a type of question that recurs, now dividing the sub-divisions between injury and misappropriation. This we do so as to ask whether a uniform program of analysis or exegesis governs:

Injury

1. There are four generative causes of damages.
2. A beast is an attested danger to go along in the normal way and to break something. But if it was kicking, or if pebbles were scattered from under its feet and it thereby broke utensils — the owner pays half of the value of the damages caused by his ox.
3. He who leaves a jug in the public domain, and someone else came along and stumbled on it and broke it — the one who broke it is exempt. He who pours water out into the public domain, and someone else was injured on it, is liable to pay compensation for his injury.
4. Two oxen generally deemed harmless which injured one another — the owner pays half-damages for the excess of the value of the injury done by the less injured to the more injured ox.
5. He who digs a pit in private domain and opens it into public domain, or in public domain and opens it into private domain, or in private domain and opens it into private domain belonging to someone else, is liable for damage done by the pit.
6. He who brings a flock into a fold and shut the gate before it as required, but the flock got out and did damage, is exempt. If he did not shut the gate before it as required, and the flock got out and did damage, he is liable.
7. He who causes a fire to break out through the action of a deaf-mute, idiot, or minor, is exempt from punishment under the laws of man, but liable to punishment under the laws of heaven. If he did so through the action of a person of sound senses, the person of sound senses is liable.

Misappropriation

8. More encompassing is the rule covering payment of twofold restitution than the rule covering payment of fourfold or fivefold restitution. For the rule covering twofold restitution applies to something whether animate or inanimate. But the rule covering fourfold or fivefold restitution applies only to an ox or a sheep alone
9. He who injures his fellow is liable to compensate him on five counts: (1) injury, (2) pain, (3) medical costs, (4) loss of income [lit.: loss of time], and (5) indignity
10. He who steals wood and made it into utensils, wool and made it

> into clothing, pays compensation in accord with the value of the wood or wool at the time of the theft.

What do we not find here? Issues common elsewhere, such as intentionality, on the one side, potentiality vs. actuality, on the other, never occur when we deal with the matters at hand. So far as intentionality or human perception serves as a criterion of classification in Kilayim and Shebi'it, we find no counterpart at all. Clearly, Nos. 1–7 in treating injury all work on assessing culpability and assigning responsibility. If a question recurs, it concerns how we sort out that mishap against which we can take precautions from what cannot ordinarily be foreseen and prevented. But a variety of givens predominate, and those givens involve facts, not principles of general intelligibility such as might pertain in other halakhic categories altogether; the givens seem remarkably particular to their context. And the facts on the face of matters scarcely can be said to inhere in the topic at hand. Nos. 8–10 in addressing misappropriation want to know how we assess damages and pay for them. Here too, responsibility to restore the status quo defines the recurrent question.

Then, to return to our basic problem, what, exactly, concerning Nos. 1–7, do the framers of the problems that are solved want to know, and why do they want to know it? If the topic itself does not supply compelling answers to those questions, and the characteristics of the on-going analysis yield no uniformities, what is left as source for sages' exegetical program? Absent traits of the topic on the one side, and a prevailing logical problematics (e.g., the taxonomic power of intentionality) on the other, only one other source of explanation serves to explain the exegetical program of the sages at hand, and that is Scripture. Sages located their exegetical problem in Scripture's rules on the chosen categories — there alone. What we shall now see is that the halakhah categorized as Baba Qamma — the halakhah of injury and misappropriation — systematizes facts supplied by Scripture, identifying the general principles and utilizing those general principles as the basis for the orderly recapitulation of the established facts, now in an improved formulation. Not only so, but that work of secondary amplification of facts of Scripture encompasses nearly the entire tractate; I see little in the halakhah that aims at more than to articulate what is implicit in facts set forth by the Written Torah. No halakhic problematic deriving from the Oral Torah dictates the course of the presentation of the topic.

TRACTATE BABA QAMMA 49

To show that that is the case, let me return to the repertoire of topics given just now ask these specific questions and answer them. I ask the question required by the rough reprise given above, and I answer by a systematic demonstration that the halakhah finds in the Written Torah not only its facts but also such a generative problematics as pertains.

1. How do sages know that there are four generative causes of damages [covering Nos. 1, 3, 5, 6, 7]?

> Ox (No. 1): *"When one man's ox hurts another's, so that it dies, then they shall sell the live ox and divide the price of it; and the dead beast also they shall divide. Or if it is known that the ox has been accustomed to gore in the past, and its owner has not kept it in, he shall pay ox for ox, and the dead beast shall be his"* (Ex. 21:35–6)
>
> Pit (No. 5): *"When a man leaves a pit open or when a man digs up a pit and does not cover it, and an ox or an ass falls into it, the owner of the pit shall make it good; he shall give money to its owner and the dead beast shall be his"* (Ex. 21:33)
>
> Crop-destroying beast (No. 6): *"When a man causes a field or vineyard to be grazed over or lets his beast loose and it feeds in another man's field, he shall make restitution from the beast in his own field and in his own vineyard"* (Ex. 22:5)
>
> Fire (No. 7): *"When fire breaks out and catches in thorns so that the stacked grain or the standing grain or the field is consumed, he that kindled the fire shall make full restitution"* (Ex. 22:6)

The secondary amplification of these generative causes, so elegantly carried forward by the Tosefta's and Bavli's exegesis of the Mishnah's statement, leaves no doubt that, within the prevailing hermeneutics of the native category at hand, the sole task is to articulate the givens of Scripture. That fact becomes more blatant at the next stage.

2. Where do sages learn the distinction between a beast that is deemed harmless and one that is an attested danger [covering Nos. 2, 4, inclusive of [1] half-damages paid in the case of the goring of the former, full damages of the latter; and [2] of selling an ox and dividing the proceeds?

> *When one man's ox hurts another's, so that it dies, then they shall sell the live ox and divide the price of it; and the dead beast also they shall divide. Or if it is known that the ox has been accustomed to gore in the past, and its owner has not kept it in, he shall pay ox for ox, and the dead beast shall be his* (Ex. 21:35–6).
>
> *When an ox gores a man or woman to death, the ox shall be stoned and its flesh shall not be eaten; but the owner of the ox shall be clear. But if the ox has been accustomed to grow in the past, and its owner has been warned but has not kept it in, and it kills a man or a woman, the ox shall be stoned, and the owner also shall be put to death. If a ransom is laid on him, then he shall give for the redemption*

of his life whatever is laid upon him. If it gores a man's son or daughter, he shall be dealt with according to this same rule. If the ox gores a slave, male or female, the owner shall give to their master thirty shekels of silver, and the ox shall be stoned (Ex. 21:28–32).

The entire program of the specified chapters of the Mishnah's presentation of the halakhah derives from Scripture; the exegesis of the implications of the facts, the invention of illustrative problems for solution, and the specification of theorems for demonstration — all depend upon the factual postulates supplied by Scripture.

3. Whence the distinction between the rule covering payment of twofold restitution than the rule covering payment of fourfold or fivefold restitution (No. 7)?

If a man steals an ox or a sheep and kills it or sells it, he shall pay five oxen for an ox and four sheep for a sheep. He shall make restitution; if he has nothing, then he shall be sold for his theft. If the stolen beast is found alive in his possession, whether it is an ox or an ass or a sheep, he shall pay double (Ex. 22:1–3).

If a man delivers to his neighbor money or goods to keep and it is stolen out of the man's house, then if the thief is found, he shall pay double (Ex. 22:7).

The specified chapter does nothing more than take up Scripture's distinctions and explore their implications.

4. How do we know that one compensates a person whom he has injured (No. 9)?

When men quarrel and one strikes the other with a stone or with his fist and the man does not die but keeps his bed, then if the man rises again and walks abroad with his staff, he that struck him shall be clear; only he shall pay for the loss of his time and shall have him thoroughly healed (Ex. 21:18–19).

When men strive together and hurt a woman with child so that there is a miscarriage and yet no harm follows, the one who hurt her shall be fined, according as the woman's husband shall lay upon him; and he shall pay as the judges determine. If any harm follows, then you shall give life for life, eye for eye, tooth for tooth, hand for hand, foot for foot, burn for burn, wound for wound, stripe for stripe (Ex. 21:22–25).

Sages derive the laws of misappropriation and torts from Scripture, the categories being defined out of the passage at hand.

5. What is the basis for requiring compensation for what one has stolen (No. 10)?

If any one sins and commits a breach of faith against the Lord by deceiving his neighbor in a matter of deposit or security or through robbery, or if he has oppressed his neighbor or has found what was lost and lied about it, swearing falsely, in any of all the things that men do and sin therein, when one has sinned and become guilty, he shall restore what he took by robbery or what he got by oppression or the deposit that was committed to him or the lost thing that he found or anything about which he has sworn falsely; he shall restore it in full (Lev. 5:20–24).

Here again, it is not the topic and its inherent logic but Scripture that has dictated the character of the halakhah, within the obvious proviso that, both Scripture's and the Oral Torah's halakhah concur on the justice of restoring stolen property as a principle of the ordering of society. The upshot is that we may account by reference to the Written Torah's laws for nearly the entire exegetical program brought by sages to the halakhic topic of Baba Qamma. Sages chose as their question — the problematic they discerned in the topic at hand — how to organize and systematize Scripture's facts.

Given these facts, what have sages contributed to their elucidation? They clarified details and worked out the secondary and tertiary implications thereof. They spelled out the full range of responsibility ("In the case of anything of which I am liable to take care, I am deemed to render possible whatever damage it may do. [If] I am deemed to have rendered possible part of the damage it may do, I am liable for compensation as if [I have] made possible all of the damage it may do"). They defined the specifics required for applying Scripture's general rules ("a tooth is deemed an attested danger in regard to eating what is suitable for eating"). In the manner of geometry, they showed how, within a given set of postulates, a range of problems was to be solved to yield a proof of a set of theorems. In other words, they did everything but the main thing, which in the case of other native categories is, make a powerful, consequential statement of their own. And yet, the native category delineated by Baba Qamma (along with the other two Babas) takes the primary position in the curriculum of the classical academies where the halakhah is studied. So the native speakers of the halakhah have made known their statement and set down their judgment. Only when all three Babas have been set forth will that judgment emerge in all its gravity.

2.

TRACTATE BABA MESIA

I. An Outline of the Halakhah of Baba Mesia

Continuing the topical program of Baba Qamma, the present tractate takes up where the former left off. Baba Qamma concludes with analysis of the halakhah of restoring what has been stolen; Baba Mesia starts with restoring what has been lost. Then it shifts to a new topic, the halakhah governing transactions of an equitable character between buyer and seller, then, employer and employee. In the former case the halakhah focuses on the counterpart to theft, which is overcharging and usury. In the latter, we proceed to an account of what each party owes the other. We conclude with attention to real estate, specifically, relationships of partners in a given house (a condominium, in our terms), relationships between tenant and landlord or tenant-farmer and householder.

i. *The Disposition of Other Peoples' Possessions*

A. *Conflicting Claims on Lost Objects*

M. 1:1 Two lay hold of a cloak — this one says, "I found it!" — and that one says, "I found it!" — this one says, "It's all mine!" — and that one says, "It's all mine!" — this one takes an oath that he possesses no less a share of it than half, and that one takes an oath that he possesses no less a share of it than half, and they divide it up. This one says, "It's all mine!" — and that one says, "Half of it is mine!" the one who says, "It's all mine!" takes an oath that he possesses no less of a share of it than three parts, and the one who says, "Half of it is mine!," takes an oath that he possesses no less a share of it than a fourth part. This one then takes three shares, and that one takes the fourth.

T. 1:1 Two lay hold of a cloak — This one takes the part of the cloak which is held [by him], and that one takes the part of the cloak which is held [by him]. Under what circumstances? When both of them are holding on to it. But if it was in the hand of one of them, he who wishes to remove property from the hand of his fellow bears the burden of proof.

T. 1:2 This one says, "It's all mine!" And that one says, "A third of it is mine! The one who says, "It's all mine!" takes an oath that he has no less of a share of it than five parts And the one who says, "A third of it is mine!" takes an oath that he has no less of a share of it than a sixth [part]. The governing principle of the matter [is this]: One is subjected to an oath only up to one-half of his claimed share alone.

Y. 1:2 I.1 *A woman who was riding along on a beast, with two men leading it, [and she comes to court and claims,] "These are my slaves, and the ass and its burden belong to me," while this one says, "This is my wife, and the other man is my slave, and the ass and its burden are mine," and the other party claims, "This is my wife, and the other man is my slave, and the ass and its burden are mine" — she requires a writ of divorce from each of the men, and she must also declare both of them free men. And both of them issue writs of emancipation to one another. And as to the ass and its burden, all three of them lay an equal claim [and divide it up].*

M. 1:2 **Two were riding on a beast, or one was riding and one was leading it — this one says, "It's all mine!" — and that one says, "It's all mine!" — this one takes an oath that he possesses no less a share of it than half, and that one takes an oath that he possesses no less a share of it than half. And they divide it. But when they concede [that they found it together] or have witnesses to prove it, they divide [the beast's value] without taking an oath.**

M. 1:3 **[If] one was riding on a beast and saw a lost object, and said to his fellow, "Give it to me," [but the other] took it and said, "I take possession of it" — [the latter] has acquired possession of it. If after he gave it over [to the one riding on the beast], he said, "I acquired possession of it first," he has said nothing whatsoever.**

M. 1:4 **[If] he saw a lost object and fell on it, and someone else came along and grabbed it, this one who grabbed it has acquired possession of it. [If] he saw [people] running after a lost object — after (1) a deer with a broken leg, (2) pigeons which could not fly, and he said, "My field has effected possession for me," it has effected possession for him. [If] (1) the deer was running along normally, or (2) [if] the pigeons were flying, and he said, "My field has effected possession for me," he has said nothing whatsoever.**

Y. 1:4 = T. 1:4 *He who says, "Let my house effect possession for me of any lost object which falls into it today" has said nothing whatsoever. But if any sort of lost object should turn up for him, his words are confirmed.*

B. *Returning an Object to the Original Owner*

M. 1:5 (1) Things which are found by his minor son or daughter, (2) things which are found by his Canaanite slave boy or slave girl, (3) things found by his wife — lo, they belong to him. (1) Things found by his adult son or daughter, (2) things found by his Hebrew slave boy or slave girl, (3) things found by his wife whom he has divorced, even though he has not yet paid off her marriage settlement — lo, they belong to them. [If] one found bonds of indebtedness, he should not return them. For a court will exact payment on the strength of them.

M. 1:7 [If] he found (1) writs of divorce for women, (2) writs of emancipation for slaves, (3) wills, (4) deeds of gift, or (5) receipts for the payment of marriage settlements, lo, he should not return them. For I maintain that they were written out, but [then] the one [who is answerable] for them changed his mind and decided not to hand them over.

Y. 1:7 I.2 A bond on the strength of which one has taken out a loan, but which indicates also that the loan has been paid, one may not return [to write out a second loan] so that the lender may collect with it, because of thereby weakening the hold of purchasers [of the encumbered property, since the creditor, who has been paid, may use the bond to extract from purchasers of the debtor's property land which they have bought, claiming that it was indentured, as proved by the bond].

M. 1:8 [If] one found (1) documents of evaluation, (2) letters of alimony, (3) deeds of *halisah* rites or (4) of the exercise of the right of refusal, (5) deeds of arbitration, or any document which is prepared in a court, lo, this one should return [them]. [If] he found them [wrapped up] (1) in a satchel or (2) a case, (3) a bundle of documents, or (4) a package of documents, lo, this one should return [them]. How many are in a package of documents? Three tied together. [If] he found a document among those belonging to him, and he does not know what it is, let it lie there until Elijah comes. If [however] there were postscripts [notes of cancellation] along with them, let him act in accord with what is written in the postscripts.

T. 1:6 [If] one found a writ of divorce of a woman [M. B.M. 1:7A], when the husband admits its validity, he should return it to the wife. If he does not [concede it], he should not return it either to this party or to that party.

T. 1:7 [If one found] a receipt [in payment for the marriage-settlement] [M. B.M. 1:7A], when the woman admits its validity, he should return it to the husband. And if not, he should not return it either to this party or to that party. [If one found] a writ of emancipation [of a slave] [M. B.M. 1:7A], when the master admits its validity, he should return it to the [former] slave. And if not, he should not return it either to this party or to that party. [If he found] a writ of seizure, when the borrower admits its validity, he should return it to the lender. And if not, he should not return it either to this party or to that party.

T. 1:8 [If he found] wills [M. B.M. 1:7A], or deeds of gift [M. B.M. 1:7A], when the donor concedes [the validity of the document], he should return it to the recipient of the gift. And if not, he should not return it either to this party or to that party. [If he found] writs of purchase or sale, deeds of share-cropping or receipts for a beast — lo, this one should not return it either to this party or to that party.

T. 1:9 [If one found] court decrees or prosbols, lo, he should return them to him in whose name they are written, whether he found them in the market-place or whether he found them among the documents of his father [M. B.M. 1:8A–B]. The governing principle of the matter is this: If there were postscripts along with them, let him act in accord with what is written in the postscripts [M. B.M. 1:8].

T. 1:10 The confession of a party to a case is equivalent to a hundred witnesses. Under what circumstances? In a situation in which one has laid claim against him, and he has conceded it. But if he confessed on his own, he can retract. For the mouth which prohibited is the mouth which can permit. The confession of a party to a case is equivalent to a hundred witnesses. But a depository is more credible than either one. This one says, "Thus and so," and that one says, "Thus and so," and the depository says, "Thus and so," — the depository is more credible than either of the others. Under what circumstances? When the third party produces [a document] in his possession. But if the third party does not produce [a document] in his possession, lo, he is equivalent to anybody else.

T. 1:11 The seller is believed to state, "To this one did I make my sale." Under what circumstances? When the sale is made by him. But if the sale is not made by him, lo, he is equivalent to anybody else.

T. 1:12 A judge is believed to state, "This one did I declare innocent, and that one did I declare guilty." Under what circumstances? When the case is yet before him. But if the case is no longer before him, lo, he is equivalent to anybody else.

T. 1:14 What is a package of documents? Three tied together [M. B.M. 1:8G]. What is a bundle of documents [M. B.M. 1:8D]? Any which is tied up around the outside with a thread or a strap or something else. What is a satchel [M. B.M. 1:8C/I]? This is a small wallet.

M. 2:1 Which lost items belong to the finder [finders-keepers], and which ones is he [who found them] liable to proclaim [in the lost-and-found]? These lost items are his [the finder's]: "[if] he found (1) pieces of fruit scattered about, (2) coins scattered about, (3) small sheaves in the public domain, (4) cakes of figs, (5) bakers' loaves, (6) strings of fish, (7) pieces of meat, (8) wool shearings [as they come] from the country [of origin], (9) stalks of flax, or (10) tongues of purple — lo, these are his," the words of R. Meir. And R. Judah says, "Anything which has an unusual trait is he liable to proclaim. How so? [If] he found a fig cake with a potsherd inside it, a loaf with coins in it."

M. 2:2 And which ones is he liable to proclaim? [If] he found (1) pieces of fruit in a utensil or a utensil as is, (2) coins in a purse or a purse as is, (3) piles of fruit, (4) piles of coins, (5) three

coins, one on top of the other, (6) small sheaves in private domain, (7) homemade loaves, (8) wool shearings as they come from the craftsman's shop, (9) jars of wine, or (10) jars of oil — lo, these is he liable to proclaim.

T. 2:3 [If] one found pieces of meat, pieces of fish, or fish which had been stuck together, he is liable to make proclamation. [If he found] strings of meat, strings of fish, jars of wine, oil, grain, figs, or olives, he is not liable to make proclamation [cf. M. B.M 2:1–2].

T. 2:4 [If] one has written something on a shard and put it on the mouth of a jar, on paper and put it on the mouth of a circle of dried figs, he is liable to make proclamation [cf. M. B.M. 2:1D–F].

T. 2:5 [If] one has found small sheaves in the public domain, he is not liable to make proclamation. [If] he found stacks of grain, whether in private domain or in public domain, he is liable to make proclamation.

T. 2:6 [If] he found pieces of fruit arranged in piles, he is liable to make proclamation. [If he found them] scattered about, he is not liable to make proclamation [cf. M. B.M. 2:1C, 2:2B]. [If] part of them are arranged in piles and part of them are scattered about, he is liable to make proclamation.

T. 2:7 [If] one has found coins arranged in little towers, he is liable to make proclamation. If he found them scattered about, he is not liable to make proclamation. [If] part of them were in little towers, and part of them were not in little towers, he is liable to make proclamation. And how many coins in a pile add up to a tower? Three coins one on top of the other.

T. 2:8 [If] one found a utensil, with pieces of fruit in front of it [M. B.M. 2:2B], a purse, with coins in front of it [M. B.M. 2:2B], he is liable to make proclamation [cf. M. B.M. 2:4]. [If] part of them were in the utensil and part of them were on the ground, part of them were in the purse and part of them were on the ground, he is liable to make proclamation.

T. 2:9 [If] one found something which has no distinguishing mark alongside something which does have a distinguishing mark [M. B.M. 2:1 D, 2:5], he is liable to make proclamation. [If] the owner of the object with the distinguishing mark came along and took that which clearly belonged to him, this person also will have made acquisition of the [similar] object which does not have a distinguishing mark.

T. 2:10 He who finds a *sela*, and his fellow [who claims it] says, "[The one I lost] is new" — "It is of the reign of Nero" — "It is of the kingdom of such-and-such" — he has said nothing at all. For a distinguishing mark does not apply to a coin. And not only so, but even if the person's [own] name is written right on the coin, lo, it [nonetheless] belongs to the one who finds it.

M. 2:3 [If] behind a fence or a hedge one found pigeons tied together, or on paths in fields, lo, this one should not touch them. [If] he found a utensil in a dung heap, if it is covered up, he should not touch it. If it is uncovered, he takes it but

must proclaim [that he has found it]. [If] he found it in a pile of debris or in an old wall, lo, these belong to him. [If] he found it in a new wall, if it is located from its midpoint and outward, it is his. If it is located from its midpoint and inward, it belongs to the householder. If he had rented [the house] to others, even [if he found it] in the house, lo, these are his.

Y. 2:4 I.2 = T. 2:11–12 [If] one found an object on a dung-heap, he is liable to make proclamation. For it is usual for a dung-heap to be cleared away [T. B.M. 2:11]. [If] one found an object in a pile or in an old wall, lo, these things which he finds are his [M. 2:3G]. For he can say to [any claimant], "They come from the time of the Amorites" [T. B.M. 2:12].

Y. 2:4 I.3 = T. 2:13 [If] he found [an object] between the boards [at the threshold of the doorway to the house], [if the object was located] from the door-jamb and outward, it belongs to [the finder]. If it was located from the door-jamb and inward, it belongs to the householder. [If] one found an object in a hole or new wall, if the object was located from the mid-point and outward, it belongs to [the finder]. [If the object was located] from the mid-point and inward [toward the inside of the house], it belongs to the householder (M. 2:3H–J). [If the wall or hole] was open wholly outward, even if the object was located from the mid-point toward the inside of the house, it belongs to the finder. [If the wall or hole] was open wholly inward, even if the object was located from the mid-point toward the outside of the house, it belongs to the householder [T. B.M. 2:13]. If he had rented the house to others, even if he found it in the house, lo, these are his [M. 2:4K–M].

M. 2:4 [If] he found [utensils] in a store, lo, these are his. [If a utensil was located] between the counter and the storekeeper, it belongs to the storekeeper. [If he found them] in front of the money changer, lo, they are his. [If he found them] between the stool [of the money changer] and the money changer, lo, these belong to the money changer. He who purchases produce from his fellow, or sent produce to his fellow, [if] he found coins among the produce, lo, these are his. If there they were bound together, he takes [the money] but proclaims [that he has found it].

T. 2:14 [If] one found an object in a house, if guests have left something over before him, lo, they are his. And if not, lo, they belong to the householder. [If] he found an object in a store, [if they are located] up to the place in which people usually enter, lo these belong to [the finder]. [If they are] farther in that that, lo, they belong to the storekeeper [M. B.M. 2:4A–B].

T. 2:15 He who purchases a beast from his fellow and found on it something worth a *perutah*, he is liable to make proclamation [informing the seller of what he has found]. And he who finds something worth a perutah is liable to make proclamation. If it is worth less than a perutah, he is not liable to make proclamation, since it is said, "[You shall not see your brother's ox or his sheep go astray, and withhold your help from them; you shall take them back to your brother . . . And so you shall do with his ass, and so you shall do with his garment, so you shall do with any lost thing of your brother's, which he loses and you field you may not withhold your help" (Deut. 22:1–3). Just as a garment is distinguished [cf. M. B.M. 2:5] in that it is worth a perutah, in which case one is liable to make proclamation, so for anything which is worth a perutah one is liable to make proclamation. But for something worth less than a perutah, one is not liable to make proclamation.

M. 2:5 Also a garment was covered among all of these things [which one must proclaim, listed at Dt. 22:1-3: "You shall not see your brother's ox or his sheep go astray and withhold your help from them; you shall take them back to your brother. And if he is not hear you or if you do not know him, you shall bring it home to your house, and it shall be with you until your brother seeks it; then you shall restore it to him; and so you shall do with his ass; so you shall do with his garment; so you shall do with any lost thing of your brother's which he loses and you find; you may not withhold your help"]. [So] why was it singled out? To use it for an analogy, to tell you: Just as a garment exhibits distinctive traits, in that it has special marks of identification, and it has someone to claim it, so for everything which has special marks and which has someone to claim one is liable to make proclamation.

M. 2:6 And for how long is one liable to make proclamation [of having found a lost object]? Until his neighbors are informed about it or until three festivals [have gone by]. And for seven days after the final festival, so that one may have three days to go home and three days to come back and one day on which to proclaim [that he has lost the object].

M. 2:7 [If a claimant] has described what he has lost but not specified its special marks, one should not give it to him. And as to a [known] deceiver, even though he has specified its special marks, one should not give it to him, as it is said, "Until your brother seeks concerning it (Dt. 22:2) — until you will examine your brother to find out whether or not he is deceiver. Any sort of thing which is able to perform labor and which eats [is to be kept by the finder and is to] perform labor and [in exchange is allowed to] eat. And something which does not perform labor but which [nonetheless has to be] fed is to be sold, as it is said, "You will return it to him" (Dt. 22:2). Pay attention to how to return it to him!

B. 2:7E–K AS TO CHICKENS AND LARGE BEASTS, ONE TAKES CARE OF THEM FOR TWELVE MONTHS. FROM THAT POINT ONWARD, ONE TURNS THEM INTO MONEY AND LAYS IT ASIDE. AS TO CALVES AND FOALS, ONE TENDS THEM FOR THIRTY DAYS. FROM THAT POINT ONWARD, ONE TURNS THEM INTO MONEY AND LAYS IT ASIDE. AS TO GEESE AND COCKS AND ANYTHING THAT TAKES A MORE WORK THAN THEIR REWARD, ONE TAKES CARE OF THEM FOR THREE DAYS. FROM THAT POINT ONWARD, ONE TURNS THEM INTO MONEY AND LAYS IT ASIDE.

M. 2:8 [If] he found scrolls, he reads in them once every thirty days. If he does not know how to read, he [at least] unrolls them. But he should not [commence to] learn [a subject] in them to begin with, nor should someone else read alongside him. [If] he found a piece of clothing, he should shake it out once every thirty days, and spread it out as needed — but not to show off. Of utensils of silver and of copper one makes use — for their own good but not to wear them out. Utensils of gold and of glass he should not touch until Elijah comes. [If] he found a sack or large basket or anything which he would not usually pick up, lo, this one does not [have to lower himself and] pick it up.

M. 2:9 What is lost property? [If] one found an ass or a cow grazing by the way, this is not lost property. [If he found] an ass with its trappings upset, a cow running in the vineyards, lo, this is lost property. [If] one returned it and it ran away, returned it and it ran away, even four or five times, he is liable [to continue to] return it, since it is said, "You shall surely bring them back [to your brother]" (Dt. 22:1). [If] he lost [work] time [to the value of] a *sela*, he may not say to him, "Give me a *sela*." But he pays him a salary [for his lost time] calculated at the rate paid to an unemployed worker. If there is a court there, he may stipulate before the court [for compensation for lost time]. If there is no court there, before whom may he make such a stipulation? His own [welfare] takes precedence.

T. 2:18 A. He who finds a lost object, if it is of sufficient value for him to return it to the owner so that [the owner will enjoy the benefit of the value] at least to a *perutah* and also [so that he will] collect his finder's-fee from it, he should get involved with the matter. But if not, he may leave it where it is.

T. 2:19 What is lost property [M. B.M. 2:9A]? [If] one found a spade in the parade-ground or a cloak on the parade-ground, or a cow feeding in a field of grain, lo, this is a lost object [cf. M. B.M. 2:9D–F]. [If one found] a cloak lying on the side of a fence, a jar lying on the side of a fence, an ass feeding in high grass, this is not a lost object [cf. M. B.M. 2:9A–C]. But if one found them in such conditions for three successive days, lo, this is a lost object.

T. 2:21 [If] one found scrolls, he reads in them once every thirty days [M. B.M. 2:8A]. But one should not read the weekly lection and go over it again. Nor should one read in them and translate into Aramaic. And three people should not read in a single volume. And one should not open up a scroll for more than three columns.

T. 2:22 As to copper ones: one may use them for hot liquids but not in the fire, because it wears them out. As to utensils of silver, one may make use of them for cold but not for hot liquids, because hot liquids blacken them. Of shovels and axes one makes use with something soft, but not something hard, because that damages them. As to utensils of gold or glass, one is not to touch them until Elijah comes. And just as you specify these rules with regard to a lost object, so these rules apply with regard to a bailment.

M. 2:10 [If he found it loose] in a stable, he is not liable [to return] it. [If he found it] in the public domain, he is liable to take care of it. And if it was a graveyard, [and if he was a priest or a Nazirite] he should not contract corpse uncleanness on its account. If his father said to him, "Contract corpse uncleanness," or if [under normal circumstances] he said to him, "Don't return it," he should not obey him. [If] he unloaded it and loaded it up again, unloaded it and loaded it up again, even four or five times, he is liable [to continue to do so], for it is written, "You will surely help with him" (Ex. 23:5). [If] he went and sat down, and said, "Since the religious duty is yours, if you want to unload it, go unload it," the other is exempt [from doing a thing]. For it is written, "With him." If the owner was old or sick, he is liable. It is a religious duty enjoined by the Torah to unload the beast, but not to load it up.

T. 2:23 He who finds the beast of his fellow is liable to take care of it until he brings it into his domain. [If] he brought it into a place in which some one will see it, [he is no longer liable to take care of it] [cf. M. B.M. 2:10A–B]. [If] one did not take care of it and it was stolen or lost, he is liable to replace it. And he is under all circumstances liable to replace it until he will bring it into [the owner's] domain. [If] he brought it into his garden or his ruin and it was stolen or lost, he is exempt.

T. 2:24 [If] he found an ass loaded [e.g., on the Sabbath] with coals or with prohibited items, they do not require him to touch them. This is the governing principle: Whoever labors in his own behalf — lo, this one is obligated to [help] him. And whoever does not labor in his own behalf — he is not obligated to [help] him [M. B.M. 2:10K–L]. [If] his ass was falling down, he helps him unload it, even a hundred times [M. B.M. 2:10G–J]. He is permitted to lighten the load and to collect a salary for it.

T. 2:25 They do not require him to stand around and put back the load, unload and load [the ass], since it is said, "If you meet your enemy's ox or his ass going astray, you shall bring it back to him. If you see the ass of one who hates you lying under its burden, you shall refrain from leaving him with it, you shall help him lift it up (Ex. 23:34–5). One might think that he is liable to do so two or three times only. Scripture says, If you meet. One might say that this is the case even within four cubits [that is, actually meeting him] only. Scripture says, If you see. Sages have given as a measure for this one-seventh of a *mil*, that is, a *ris*.

M. 2:11 [If one has to choose between seeking] what he has lost and what his father has lost, his own takes precedence. [If he has to choose between seeking] what he has lost and what his master has lost, his own takes precedence. [If he has to choose between seeking] what his father has lost and what his master has lost, that of his master takes precedence. For his father brought him into this world. But his master, who has taught him wisdom, will bring him into the life of the world to come. But if his father is a sage, that of his father takes precedence. [If] his father and his master were carrying heavy burdens, he removes that of his master, and afterward removes that of his father. [If] his father and his master were taken captive, he ransoms his master, and afterward he ransoms his father. But if his father is a sage, he ransoms his father, and afterward he ransoms his master.

T. 2:31 [If one has to choose between seeking] what his father has lost and what his mother has lost, seeking what his father has lost takes precedence over seeking what his mother has lost. Under what circumstances? When she is living with [his father] ... But when she is not living [with his father] ... both of them are equivalent.

T. 2:32 [If one has to choose between seeking] what the husband has lost and what the wife has lost ... seeking what the husband has lost takes precedence over seeking what the wife has lost.

T. 2:33 Gentiles and shepherds of small cattle and those who raise them do not make a difference one way or the other [in figuring out whose lost object to seek first] ... *Minim*, apostates, and renegades are regarded as subordinate and in no way can be regarded as taking priority.

C. *Rules of Bailment*

M. 3:1 He who deposits with his fellow a beast or utensils, and they were stolen or lost, [if the bailee] made restitution and was unwilling to take an oath — (for they have said, "An unpaid bailee takes an oath and thereby carries out his obligation without paying compensation for the loss of the bailment") — [if then] the thief was found, [the thief] pays twofold restitution. [If] he had slaughtered or sold the beast, he pays fourfold or fivefold restitution. To whom does he pay restitution? To him with whom the bailment was left. [If the bailee] took an oath and did not want to pay compensation, [if] the thief was found, he pays twofold restitution. [If he slaughtered or sold the beast, he pays fourfold or fivefold restitution. To whom does he pay restitution? To the owner of the bailment.

T. 3:1 One who borrows has no right to lend out, and one who hires has no right to rent out, and one who borrows has no right to rent out, and one who hires has no right to lend out, And the one with whom these things are left as a bailment has no right to leave them as a bailment with someone else, unless the householder [who owns the objects] has given him permission to do so.

T. 3:3 He who deposited a cow as a bailment with his fellow, and it was stolen, and [the bailee] said, "lo, I shall pay you compensation for it, rather than taking an oath," and afterward the thief was found — [the thief] pays twofold restitution or fourfold or fivefold restitution to the second party [M. B.M. 3:1].

T. 3:4 He who sells a cow to his fellow, and it was stolen — this one says, "It was stolen while in your domain [and the loss is yours]," and that one says, "It was stolen in your domain" — let them divide [the loss].

M. 3:2 He who rents a cow from his fellow, and then lent it to someone else, and it died of natural causes — let the one who rented it take an oath that it died of natural causes, and the one who borrowed it then pays compensation to the one who rented it out.

T. 3:1 One who borrows has no right to lend out, and one who rents has no right to rent out, and one who borrows has no right to rent out, and one who rents has no right to lend out. And the one with whom these things are left as a bailment has no right to leave them as a bailment with someone else, unless the householder [who owns the objects] has given him permission to do so.

M. 3:3 [If] one said to two people, "I stole a *maneh* [a hundred *zuz*] from one of you and I do not know from which one of you it was." "The father of one of you deposited a *maneh* with me, and I do not know the father of which one of you it was," [he] pays off a *maneh* to this one and a *maneh* to that one, for he has admitted it on his own.

M. 3:4 Two who deposited something with one person, this one leaving a *maneh*, and that one leaving two hundred [*zuz*] — this one says, "Mine is the deposit of two hundred [*zuz*]," and that one says, "Mine is the deposit of two hundred [*zuz*]" — he pays off a *maneh* to this one, and a *maneh* to that one, and the rest is left until Elijah comes.

M. 3:5 And so is the rule for two utensils, one worth a *maneh*, and one worth a thousand *zuz* — this one says, "The better one is mine," and that one says, "The better one is mine" — he gives the smaller one to one of them. And from the [funds received from the sale of] the larger one, he gives the cost of a smaller one to the other party. And the rest of the money [received for the sale of the larger one] is left until Elijah comes.

M. 3:6 He who deposits produce with his fellow even if it is going to go to waste — [the fellow] should not touch it.

M. 3:7 He who deposits produce with his fellow — lo, this one [with whom the bailment is left, when returning it,] may exact [from the owner the following] deductions [due to natural depletion of the produce]: (1) for wheat and rice, nine *qabs* and a half for a *kor*; (2) for barley and durra, nine *qabs* to a *kor*; (3) for spelt and linseed, three *seahs* to a *kor* All is relative to the quantity, all is relative to the time [it is left].

T. 3:8 He who deposits produce with his fellow and they rotted — wine and it turned sour, oil and it stank, puts them up for sale in court. He sells them to a third party, but does not buy them for himself."

T. 3:9 Similarly: Charity-supervisors who did not find poor folk among whom to distribute the beans [they have collected for the poor] sell it to others. But they do not sell it to themselves. Charity-supervisors change money for others, and do not change money for themselves.

M. 3:8 He exacts [a reduction] of a sixth for wine. He exacts [reduction] of three logs of oil per hundred — a *log* and a half for the sediment, and a *log* and a half for absorption [into the walls of the clay jars]. If it was refined oil, he may not exact a reduction for the sediment. If the jars were old, he may not exact a reduction for absorption.

M. 3:9 He who deposits a jar with his fellow, and the owner did not specify a place for it, and [someone] moved it and it was broken — if in the midst of his handling it, it was broken, [and if he moved it to make use of it] for his own needs, he is liable. [If he moved it] for its needs, he is exempt. If after he had put it down, it was broken, whether he had moved it for his own needs or for its needs, he is exempt. [If] the owner specified a place for it, and [someone] moved it and it was broken — whether it was in the midst of his handling it or whether it was after he had put it down, [if he had moved it] for his own needs, he is liable.

M. 3:10 He who deposits coins with his fellow — [if the latter] (1) wrapped them up and threw them over his shoulder, (2) gave them over to his minor son or daughter, or (3) locked them up in an inadequate way, he is liable [to make them up if they are lost], because he did not take care of them the way people usually take care [of things]. But if he did take care of them the way people usually take care of things, he is exempt.

Y. 3:7 I.2 *Under what circumstances have they ruled: An unpaid bailee takes an oath [that he has not violated his trust] and quits? When he has carried out his guardianship in an adequate way, as people generally take care of bailments. If he locked up the goods in an adequate way, tied up a beast in an adequate way, put coins in his pouch, bound them in his kerchief, and put them before him, or if he put them in a chest, box, or cupboard — if the money was stolen or lost. He is liable to take an oath and is exempt from having to make restitution. And if there are witnesses available that he has done things properly, even from an oath is he exempt. If he locked up the goods in an inadequate way, tied up a beast in an inadequate way, tossed the coins over his shoulder, or put them up on the roof of his house, and the bailments were stolen, he is liable to make restitution. If he put them in a place in which he was accustomed to put his own possessions, if it was suitable for taking care of a bailment, he is exempt. And if not, he is liable.*

M. 3:11 He who deposits coins with a money changer — if they are wrapped up, [the money changer] should not make use of them. Therefore if they got lost, he is not liable to make them up [as an unpaid bailee (M. 2:7)]. [If they were] loose, he may make use of them. Therefore if they got lost, he is liable to make them up. [He who deposits coins] with a householder, whether they are wrapped up or whether they are loose — [the householder] should not make use of them. Therefore if they got lost, he is not liable to make them up.

M. 3:12 He who makes improper use of a bailment — restores the bailment as it was at the moment at which he took it out [to use it for his own purposes]. He who expresses [in the presence of witnesses] the intention of making use of a bailment is liable [for damages incurred] only when he will actually make use of the bailment, since it is said, "If he has not put his hand to his neighbor's property" (Ex. 22:7). [If] he tipped over the jug and took a quarter-*log* of liquid from it, and it broke — he pays only the value of the quarter-*log* he has actually removed. But if he raised it up [so making acquisition of it], and took a quarter-*log* of liquid from it and it broke, he pays the value of the whole jug.

ii. *Commercial Transactions*

A. *Overcharge and Misrepresentation*

M. 4:1 (1) Gold acquires silver, but silver does not acquire gold. (2) Copper acquires silver, but silver does not acquire copper. (3) Bad coins acquire good coins, but good coins do not acquire bad coins. (4) A coin lacking a mint mark acquires a minted coin, but a minted coin does not acquire a coin lacking a mint mark. (5) Movable goods acquire coins, but coins do not acquire movable goods. This is the governing principle: All sorts of movable objects effect acquisition of one another.

T. 3:13 Gold acquires silver [M. B.M. 4:1A] — how so? [If] one handed over a golden denar for twenty-five pieces of silver, lo, this one has made acquisition [of the silver] no matter where it is. But if he handed over twenty-five pieces of silver for a single golden denar, lo, this one has made acquisition only at the moment at which he actually will draw [into his own possession the pieces of silver which he is buying]. Copper acquires silver [M. B.M. 4:1B] — how so? [If] one has handed over thirty issars [of copper] for a silver denar, lo, this one has acquisition [of the silver] no matter where it is. But if he handed over to him a silver denar for thirty issars of copper, lo, this one has made acquisition only at the moment at which he actually will draw [into his own possession the pieces of copper which he is buying].

T. 3:14 A coin lacking a mint mark acquires a minted coin [M. B.M. 4:1D]. The governing principle is this: Whatever is acquired [as a commodity] effects acquisition. A cloak effects acquisition for a golden denar.

M. 4:2 How so? [If the buyer] had drawn produce into his possession but not yet paid over the coins, he [nonetheless] cannot retract. [If] he had paid over the coins but had not yet drawn the produce into his possession, he has the power to retract. Truly have they said: He who exacted punishment from the men of the Generation of the Flood and the Generation of the Dispersion is destined to exact punishment from him who does not keep his word.

M. 4:3 Fraud [overreaching] is an overcharge of four pieces of silver out of twenty-four pieces of silver to the sela — one-sixth of the purchase price. For how long is it permitted to retract [in the case of fraud]? So long as it takes to show [the article] to a merchant or a relative.

M. 4:4 All the same are the buyer and the seller: both are subject to the law of fraud. Just as fraud applies to an ordinary person, so it applies to a merchant. He who has been subjected [to fraud] — his hand is on top. If] he wanted, he says to him, "Return my money." [Or, if he wanted, he says to him,] "Give me back the amount of the fraud."

T. 3:16 He who has been subjected to fraud — his hand is on top. How so? [If] one sold to him a shirt worth five for six — the hand of the purchaser is on top. [If] he wants, he says to him, "Give me my selas [back]." [If] he wants, he says to him, "Here's your money, and give me my shirt" [cf. M. B.M. 4:4D-F]. But if he had said to him, "Sell me a shirt worth six for five," the hand of the seller is on top. [If] he wants, he says to him, "Give me a sela." And [if] he wants, he says to him, "Here's your shirt, and give me my money."

M. 4:6 How long is it permitted to return [a defective sela]? In large towns, for the length of time it takes to show to a money changer. And in villages, up to the eve of the Sabbath. If [the one who gave it] recognizes it, even after twelve months he is to accept it from him. But [if the one who gave the coin refuses to take it back], he has no valid claim against the other except resentment. He may give it for produce in the status of second tithe, [for easy transportation to Jerusalem], and need not scruple, for it is only churlishness [to refuse a slightly depreciated coin].

M. 4:7 Defrauding [through overreaching] involves [an overcharge of] four pieces of silver [for what one has bought for a sela] [= one sixth over true value]. And a claim [involving a court-imposed oath] must be [for a claim of at least] two silver [ma'ahs]. An admission must be for at least what is worth a perutah. There are five [kinds of rules involving] that which is worth a perutah: (1) An admission must be for at least what is worth a perutah. (2) A woman is betrothed for that which is worth a perutah. (3) He who derives use to the value of a perutah from that which belongs to the sanctuary has committed sacrilege. (4) He who finds that which is worth a perutah is liable to make proclamation. (5) He who steals from his fellow something to the value of a perutah and takes [a false] oath to the contrary [and then confesses his crime] must bring it after him, even to Media.

M. 4:8 There are five instances in which an added fifth applies: (1) He who eats (1) heave offering, (2) heave offering of tithe, (3) heave offering of tithe taken from doubtfully tithed produce, (4) dough offering, and (5) first fruits, [when he makes restitution] adds a fifth [to the value of the principal]. (2) He who redeems [pays coins to bring to Jerusalem in place of] produce deriving from a fourth-year planting or from his second tithe adds a fifth. (3) He who redeems that which he has consecrated adds a fifth. (4) He who derives benefit to the extent of a perutah from that which has been consecrated [when he makes restitution] adds a fifth. (5) He who steals from his fellow that which is worth a perutah and takes a [false] oath to him [when he wishes to confess and effect restitution] adds a fifth.

M. 4:9 These are matters which are not subject to a claim of fraud [on account of overcharge]: (1) slaves, (2) bills of indebtedness [which are discounted and sold], (3) real estate, and (4) that which has been consecrated. They are not subject to twofold restitution, nor [in the case of a consecrated ox or sheep] to fourfold or fivefold restitution. An unpaid bailee is not required to take an oath [on their account, that he has not inflicted damage]. And a paid bailee does not have to pay compensation [on their account, if they are stolen or lost].

M. 4:10 Just as a claim of fraud applies to buying and selling so a claim of fraud applies to spoken words. One may not say to [a storekeeper], "How much is this object?" knowing that he does not want to buy it. If there was a penitent, one may not say to him, "Remember what you used to do!" If he was a child of proselytes, one may not say to him, "Remember what your folks used to do!" For it is said, "And a proselyte you shall not wrong nor oppress" (Ex. 22:20).

M. 4:11 They do not commingle one sort of produce with another sort of produce, even new and new [produce, plucked in the same growing season], and it goes without saying, new with old. To be sure, in the case of wine they have permitted commingling strong with weak, because it improves it. They do not commingle the lees of wine with wine. But one may hand over [to a purchaser] the lees [of the wine he is buying]. He whose wine got mixed with water may not sell it in a store, unless he informs [the purchaser], nor to a merchant, even though he informs him. For [the latter buys it] only to deceive others thereby. In a place in which it is the custom to put water in wine, one may dilute it.

B. 4:11–12C I.1/60A [WITH REFERENCE TO THE STATEMENT, THEY DO NOT COMMINGLE ONE SORT OF PRODUCE WITH ANOTHER SORT OF PRODUCE, EVEN

NEW AND NEW PRODUCE, PLUCKED IN THE SAME GROWING SEASON, AND IT GOES WITHOUT SAYING, NEW WITH OLD], IT IS NOT NECESSARY TO SAY THAT WHEN THE NEW PRODUCE IS AT FOUR SEAHS PER SELA WHILE THE OLD IS PRICED AT THREE, THEY MAY NOT BE COMMINGLED. BUT EVEN IF THE NEW IS AT THREE AND THE OLD IS AT FOUR, THEY MAY NOT BE COMMINGLED, BECAUSE [THE HIGHER PRICE OF THE NEW GRAIN IS THAT] ONE WISHES TO AGE THEM.

M. 4:12 A merchant purchases grain from five threshing floors and puts it [all] into one storage-bin, [wine] from five wine-presses and puts it into a single storage-jar — on condition that he not intend to commingle [wine of diverse quality for the purpose of fraud].

B. *Usury*

M. 5:1 What is interest, and what is increase [which is tantamount to taking interest]? What is interest? He who lends a sela [which is four denars] for [a return of] five denars, two seahs of wheat for [a return of] three — because he bites [off too much]. And what is increase? He who increases [profits] [in commerce] in kind. How so? [If] one purchases from another wheat at a price of a golden denar [25 denars] for a kor, which [was then] the prevailing price, and [then wheat] went up to thirty denars. [If] he said to him, "Give me my wheat, for I want to sell it and buy wine with the proceeds" — [and] he said to him, "lo, your wheat is reckoned against me for thirty denars, and lo, you have [a you have [a claim of] wine on me" — but he has no wine.

T. 4:1 He who sells produce to his fellow in the assumption that he has [produce to sell], and it turns out that he has none, has not got the power to nullify the right of this one [who has purchased the produce, and the seller has to go into the market and buy what he has promised to deliver] [cf. M. B.M. 5:1K–L].

T. 4:2 They increase the rent-charge but not the purchase-price since it is said, "If you lend money to any of my people with you who is poor, [you shall not be to him as a creditor, and you shall not exact interest from him"] (Ex. 22:25) — Just as a loan is distinctive, in that it is not that which you give to the other party which you take back from him so these are excluded, for that which you give to the other party is precisely that which you take back from him.

B. 5:1 III.1/63A LO, IF ONE WAS OWED A MANEH BY HIS NEIGHBOR AND WENT AND STOOD AT HIS GRANARY AND SAID, "PAY ME BACK MY MONEY, SINCE I WANT TO PURCHASE WHEAT WITH IT," AND THE DEBTOR SAID, "I HAVE WHEAT, WHICH I WILL HAND OVER TO YOU, SO GO AND CHARGE ME WITH IT AGAINST MY DEBT AT THE CURRENT PRICE," AND THEN THE TIME CAME TO SELL THE WHEAT [AND THAT WAS ORDINARILY WHEN THE WHEAT HAD

GAINED IN VALUE], AND HE SAID TO HIM, "GIVE ME THE WHEAT [WHICH HAD NOT YET BEEN PAID] SO I CAN GO AND SELL IT AND BUY WINE WITH THE PROCEEDS," AND THE OTHER SAID, "I HAVE WINE, GO AND ASSESS IT FOR ME AT THE MARKET PRICE," AND THE TIME CAME FOR SELLING WINE CAME, AND HE SAID TO HIM, "GIVE ME MY WINE, FOR I WANT TO SELL IT AND BUY OIL FOR IT," AND THE OTHER REPLIED, "I HAVE OIL TO GIVE YOU, GO AND CHARGE IT FOR ME AT THE CURRENT PRICE" — IN ALL OF THESE CASES, IF HE HAS THE COMMODITIES IN HAND, IT IS A PERMITTED TRANSACTION, AND IF NOT, IT IS A FORBIDDEN ONE.

M. 5:2 He who lends money to his fellow should not live in his courtyard for free. Nor should he rent [a place] from him for less [than the prevailing rate], for that is [tantamount to] usury. One may effect an increase in the rent charge [not paid in advance], but not the purchase price [not paid in advance]. How so? [If] one rented his courtyard to him and said to him, "If you pay me now [in advance], lo, it's yours for ten selas a year, "but if [you pay me] by the month, it's a sela a month" — it is permitted. [But if] he sold his field to him and said to him, "If you pay me the entire sum now, lo, it's yours for a thousand zuz. But if you pay me at the time of the harvest, it's twelve maneh [1,200 zuz]" — it is forbidden.

T. 4:3 There are practices which are both usurious and not usurious. One purchases the [right to collect the] loans of his fellow at a discount, and his writs of indebtedness [owed to him by others] at a discount. There are matters which are not regarded as usurious, but are nonetheless prohibited because of the possibility of deception for the practice of usury. How so? [If] he said to him, "Lend me a *maneh*," [and the other] said to him, "I don't have a *maneh*, but take twenty *seahs* of grain," even though the other went and purchased twenty-four — this does not constitute usury. But such a practice is prohibited because of the possibility of deception for the practice of usury.

T. 4:4 He who sells his field to his fellow and said to him, [that he does so] on condition that he should be a share-cropper in it, or that he should be a partner in it or "... that the tithes should be mine," or "... that when you sell it, you sell it to me for this same price," or "... whenever I want, I'll pay the stipulated price and take the field back" — it is permitted.

T. 4:5 [If] one owed money to another party and rented to him a house for a *denar* a month, when it was worth a *sela* a month — it is prohibited. [If the debtor rented it] from him for a *denar* a month and it was worth a *sela* a month, it is permitted.

T. 4:6 [If] one gave him a pledge of a house or gave him a pledge of a field, and said to him, "When you sell them, sell them to me for the value of the money you herewith lend to me" — it is prohibited. But if he said to him, "You will sell it to me for its true value," it is permitted.

M. 5:3 [If] one sold him a field, and [the other] paid him part of the price, and [the vendor] said to him, "Whenever you want,

bring me the rest of the money, and [then] take yours [the field]" — it is forbidden. [If] one lent him money on the security of his field and said to him, "If you do not pay me by this date three years hence, lo, it is mine" — lo, it is his.

T. 4:7 A. [If] one was bringing a cargo from one place to another, and he said to him, "Hand it over to me, and I shall hand it over to her just as you hand it over to me in such and such a place," in a case in which he does this accepting responsibility to replace the cargo if it is lost, the [debtor] who hands it over is permitted to do so. But [debtor] one who receives it from him is prohibited to do so.

T. 4:8 [If] one was bringing produce from a place in which it was expensive to a place in which it was cheap, and one said to him, "Hand them over to me, and I'll put them up [for sale] for you in the place in which they are expensive, in accord with the lower price, out of produce which I have" — if he has [produce] in that place, it is permitted. But if he does not have, it is prohibited. But ass-drivers accept produce from a householder and put it up for sale in a place in which it is expensive, paying the cheaper price [to the householder], and they do not have to scruple [by reason of violating the prohibition against price-gouging.]

T. 4:9 A. If ass-drivers and workers were insistent in the market [awaiting payment], and he said to the money-changer, "Give me copper coins for this *denar*, *so* that I can provide for these, and I'll pay you a *denar* and a *tressis* from money which I have [at home] in my pouch" — if he actually has it in the pouch, it is permitted to do so. And if not, it is prohibited.

T. 4:10 A. "What I am going to inherit from father is sold to you," or, "What is going to come up in my trap is sold to you" — he has said nothing whatsoever. "What I am going to inherit from father today is sold to you," And, "What is coming up in my trap today is sold to you" — his statement is confirmed.

M. 5:4 They set up a storekeeper for half the profit, or give him money to purchase merchandise [for sale] at [the return of the capital plus] half the profit, only if one [in addition] pays him a wage as a worker. They set the hens [of another person to hatch one's own eggs] in exchange for half the profit, and assess [and commission another person to rear] calves or foals for half the profit, only if one pays him a salary for his labor and his upkeep. But [without fixed assessment] they accept calves or foals [for rearing] for half the profits, and they raise them until they are a third grown — and as to an ass, until it can carry [a burden], [at which point profits are shared].

M. 5:5 They assess [and put out for rearing] a cow, an ass, or anything which works for its keep, for half the profits. In a locale in which they are accustomed to divide up the offspring forthwith, they divide it forthwith. In a place in which they are accustomed to raise the offspring, they raise. One may pay increased rent [in exchange for a loan for the improvement of]

one's field, and one need not scruple by reason of interest.

T. 4:12 He who sets up his fellow as a storekeeper for half the profit — if [the latter] was a craftsman, he should not practice his craft. For he cannot be keeping the store when he is practicing his craft. But if he was a full partner with him in the store, it is permitted.

T. 4:13 He who sets up his fellow as a storekeeper for half the profit — the latter should not buy and sell other things [than are covered by the agreement to run the store]. And if he bought and sold [other things], the profit goes into the common pot.

T. 4:14 He who hands over money to his fellow to buy produce with them for half the profit — lo, this one reckons with him a wage for time lost. And what is a wage for time lost? It is to cover the time in which he does the purchasing and the time in which he does the selling. [If] one person does the purchasing, and both do the selling, he makes a reckoning with him for the time for doing the selling. [If] one person does the selling, and both do the purchasing, he makes a reckoning with him for the time spent doing the purchasing. [If] one does the purchasing and one does the selling, two do the purchasing and two do the selling, even if the time spent in the one instance is greater than that spent in the other, that is of no account. But if one said to him, "The rent for the building counts, but the wage for time lost is on your account only," "... for a third of the profits you are a partner with me, and that third counts against you for the time lost," it is permitted.

T. 4:15 He who hands over money to his fellow to buy produce with [the money] for half the profit may not say to him, "lo, this is counted against your account." [If the arrangement was] for a half, a third, or a fourth [of the profits], lo, this one makes a reckoning with him for the cost of renting a building and for the price of time lost from that time onward. If he said to him, "Let the cost of the transportation [of the goods] cover the cost of the upper room," it is permitted.

T. 4:16 He who hands over money to his fellow to buy produce for half the profits and said to him, "Near [a small share] for loss and far [a large share] for profit" — it is permitted in regard to usury. And this is the practice of truly righteous men. [If he said,] "Near for profit and far for loss," it is prohibited by reason of usury. And this is the practice of truly wicked men. "Near for one thing and for the other," "Far for one thing and for the other," it is permitted in regard to usury. And that is the practice of everybody.

T. 4:17 He who hands over money to his fellow to buy produce for half the profits — and said to him, "Here is a *maneh* [for your share]," and he is not able to give a detailed accounting — it is prohibited. If he saw that produce had gone up in price and said to him, "Here is a *maneh*," and he is able to give a detailed accounting — it is permitted.

T. 4:18 He who hands over money to his fellow to buy produce for half the profits — and one of them wanted to leave the profits where they are [and to continue the agreement for future commercial transactions] — his fellow has the right to stop him [and to insist on keeping the terms of the original agreement alone].

T. 4:19 He who hands over money to his fellow to buy produce for half the profits — [the purchasing agent of the partnership] should not buy with his money wheat and with his fellow's money barley, but he should buy either wheat with all the money available to him, or barley with all the money available to him, so that the money belonging to each of them should be treated as a single sum in partnership.

T. 4:20 He who hands over money to his fellow to buy produce for half the profits — [with instructions] to buy wheat, and he bought barley, barley and he bought wheat — the hand [of the one who did the buying] is underneath. If the price went down, the loss is assigned to him. But if the price went up, the gain is assigned to the common fund [to be divided equally].

T. 4:21 He who hands over money to his fellow to buy produce for half the profits — the one who does the purchasing has the right to buy anything he wants, except that he is not to buy spelt or wood with the money. He who hands over money to his fellow to buy produce for half the profits — the one who does the purchasing has the right to buy that same kind [both with his own money and with the common funds] and when he sells, he does not have to sell the entire amount all at once, but [the grain purchased with] this fund by itself and [the grain purchased with] that fund by itself.

T. 4:22 He who hands over money to his fellow to buy produce for half the profits, and in the end [the latter] said to him, "I didn't buy a thing" — the former has no stronger claim on him than a mere complaint. But if there are witnesses [to the fact that] the latter had actually bought and sold, they exact [the proceeds and the return of capital] from him by force.

T. 4:23 [If] one owed [to another] money and came to buy from him in produce at the threshing floor, and he said to him, "Go and calculate the amount for me following the prevailing market price, "and I'll provide it for you over the next twelve months" — lo, this is usury. And this is not equivalent to an *issar* which just happens to come to him. But if he came to him and said to him, "Lend me a *kor* of wheat, and I'll pay you back in accord with the price prevailing at the time at which you sell it," it is permitted [and is not deemed to smack of usury].

T. 4:24 A. A woman rents out to her girl-friend a chick to set on eggs for a fee of two chicks a year, and she need not scruple [by reason of usury].

T. 5:4 They do not assess [and do not put out for rearing] either goats or ewes or any sort of beast which does not work for its keep [cf. M. B.M. 5:5A].

M. 5:6 They do not accept from an Israelite a flock on "iron terms" [that the one who tends the flock shares the proceeds of the flock but restores the full value of the flock as it was when it was handed over to him, so that the other is "near to profit and far from loss"], because this is interest. But they do accept a flock on "iron terms" from gentiles. And they borrow from them and lend to them on terms of interest. And so is

the rule for the resident alien. An Israelite may lend out the capital of a gentile on the say-so of the gentile, but not on the say-so of an Israelite. [If the gentile had borrowed money from an Israelite, one may not lend it out on interest with the Israelite's knowledge and consent.]

Y. 5:5 I.1 = T. 5:14 *Now what is the meaning of an "iron sheep" contract? [If there were a hundred sheep, and he said to him, "Lo, they are counted against your account for a hundred golden denars, and the offspring and the shearing belong to you, and if they die, you are liable to make them up to me, and you must pay over to me a sela for each and every one at the end" — it is prohibited.*

T. 5:5 He who assesses [and takes over the care of] a beast from his fellow does not tend it less than twelve months. If he worked it throughout the dry season and wants to sell it off in the rainy season, [the investor] has the power to stop him — unless he has it [and feeds it too] throughout the rainy season as well.

T. 5:6 He who assesses [and takes over the rearing of] a beast from his fellow — [if the beast] died through willful negligence, he pays its entire value. [If it did] not [die] through willful negligence, he pays half. For thus does he state in writing to him, "If it dies through willful negligence, I shall pay its entire value. [If it dies] not through willful negligence, I shall pay half."

T. 5:7 A man borrows money from his wife and children on usurious terms. But thereby he teaches them to practice usury. An Israelite is not permitted to borrow a sheqel and to lend out a sela. But a gentile is permitted to borrow a sheqel and to lend out a sela.

T. 5:16 A. An Israelite who borrowed money from a gentile and wants to pay it back to him — [if] his fellow came upon him and said to him, "Give it to me, and I'll hand it over for you just as you would hand it over to him" — it is prohibited. But if he made this request from the gentile, it is permitted.

T. 5:17 A. A gentile who borrowed money from an Israelite and wants to pay it back to him — [If] another Israelite came upon him and said to him, "Give them to me just as you would have given them to him" — it is permitted. But if he made this request from the Israelite, it is prohibited.

T. 5:18 An Israelite who said to a gentile, "Here's your salary. Now go and lend out my money on interest" — it is prohibited. And a gentile who said to an Israelite, "Here's your salary. Now go and lend out my money on interest" — it is permitted [cf. M. B.M. 5:6F]. But it truly is prohibited for appearance's sake.

T. 5:25 He who lends money to his fellow on interest and then repented is liable to return [to him the interest he has collected]. [If] he died and left [the money] to his children, the children do not have to return [the money he collected as interest]. And in such a case it is said, "[Though he heap up silver like dust and pile up clothing like clay, he may pile it up, but the just will wear it, and the innocent will divide the silver" (Job. 27:16–17).

T. 5:26 But if their father had left them a cow, a field, a cloak, or any sort of object for which he bore responsibility [for replacement, should the object be lost], they are liable to return such an object, for the honor of their father.

M. 5:7 They do not strike a bargain for the price of produce before the market price is announced. [Once] the market price is announced, they strike a bargain, for even though this one does not have [the produce for delivery], another one will have it [so this is not trading in futures]. [If] one was the first among the reapers [of a given crop], he may strike a bargain with him for (1) grain [already] stacked [on the threshing floor], or for (2) a basket of grapes, or for (3) a vat of olives, or for (4) the clay balls of a potter, or for (5) lime as soon as the limestone has sunk in the kiln.

T. 6:1 They do not strike a bargain for the price of produce before the market price is announced [M. B.M. 5:7A]. Even if the produce of the past year is available for four, they do not strike a bargain for the produce of the coming year for four, until the market price is announced for both the new and the old produce. [If] the market price is announced for other [sorts of produce], even though [the seller] does not have [that sort of produce], it is permitted to come to an agreement with him [M. B.M. 5:7C]. Under what circumstances? When [the seller] is able to find produce for purchase at the price. But if the produce was yet being harvested and going at four, but he is able to find [produce] to purchase only at three, he does not strike a bargain, until the price is announced covering both purchaser and seller.

T. 6:4 They strike a price for milk and fleece only after they are produced. [If] he began to milk [the goat], it is permitted to make a deal. [If] he began to shear the sheep, it is permitted to make a deal.

T. 6:5 They do not strike a price for chicks, young poultry, fish at Tiberias, or bundles of straw. But they strike a price for eggs, birds, fish at all other locations [but Tiberias], and bundles of wood. This is the governing principle: In the case of anything which has a 'season,' they strike a price concerning that thing in accord with its price when it is in season [M. B.M. 5:7M]. And in the case of anything which has no season, they strike a price concerning that thing anytime that one wants.

T. 6:6 [If] there were before him a hundred sheep, and he said to him, "lo, the fleece of these [sheep] are made over to you for a hundred *denars* of gold" — it is permitted. [If he said] "For such and such per litra of fleece," it is prohibited. But if he has it in hand, it is permitted to shear the sheep and to hand it over to him. If there were before him a hundred *kor* of wheat, and he said to him, "lo, this standing grain is made over to you for a hundred golden *denars*" — it is permitted. [If he said,] "It is sold to you for such and such," it is prohibited. But if he has it in hand, it is permitted to cut it and hand it over to him.

M. 5:8 A man may lend his tenant farmers wheat [to be repaid in] wheat, [if] it is for seed, but not [if it is] for food. [If one

lent the wheat when the price was] high and [wheat] became cheap, [or if he lent the wheat when the price was] cheap and [wheat] became expensive, he would collect from them at the cheapest price, not because that is what the law requires, but because he wished to impose a strict rule upon himself.

T. 6:8 A man may lend his tenant farmers wheat [to be repaid in] wheat, [if] it is for seed. Under what circumstances? That is when the tenant has not yet gone down to work his field. But if he has gone down to his field, lo, he is equivalent to any other person [and it is prohibited].

T. 6:9 A man may strike a bargain with his tenant-farmers for seed [M. B.M. 5:8A]. But as to expenses, lo, this is prohibited. And not only so, but even if he planted and the field yielded for a *seah* of seed two *seahs* of grain, he should not make a payment in the middle of the growing season in his field, unless he converts the [grain] into money for him.

M. 5:9 A man should not say to his fellow, "Lend me a kor of wheat, and I'll pay you back at [a kor of wheat] at threshing time." But he says to him, "Lend it to me until my son comes [bringing me wheat]", or, "... until I find the key."

T. 6:10 [If] he made a deal with him for wheat and handed over to him barley, or for barley and handed over to him wheat — it is prohibited. He may not say to him, "He is a *maneh* for you, so go and buy it for yourself from the market." But he purchases it and hands it over to him. A man may say to his fellow, "Lend me a jar of wine until my son comes," or, "... until I open the keg" [cf. M. B.M. 5:9B–C]. If he had a jug in his keg, and the keg was opened, and [the jug] fell and broke, even though he is liable to make it up — it is permitted. To what is the matter comparable? To one who gives money to his fellow to give him produce at the threshing season, and the money was stolen or lost — he is liable to make them up. If it proved to be too little or too much [for the required purchase], he is liable to make it up to him.

T. 6:11 If one purchased from him *logs*, half-logs, quarter-and eighth-*logs*, he is permitted to say to him, "Pay now for less," and he does not have to scruple that he is violating the laws against usury.

T. 6:12 Similarly: He who makes a purchase from his fellow on condition that he pay him between that point and the next twelve months has the right to say to him, "Pay me forthwith at a lower price," and he does not have to scruple that he is violating the laws against usury.

T. 6:13 He who [upon being paid in advance] sells wine or oil to his fellow all year long is liable to provide it for him just as he would charge at retail. And he should not sell the jar at three different prices. And if it was going down and up, he sells the rest at whichever price he wants.

M. 5:10 A man [may] say to his fellow, "Weed with me, and I'll weed with you," "Hoe with me, and I'll hoe with you." But he [may] not say to him, "Weed with me, and I'll hoe with you," "Hoe with me, and I'll weed with you." All the days of the dry season are deemed equivalent to one another. All the days of the rainy season are deemed equivalent to one another. One

should not say to him, "Plough with me in the dry season, and I'll plough with you in the rainy season."

M. 5:11 These [who participate in a loan on interest] violate a negative commandment: (1) the lender, (2) borrower, (3) guarantor, and (4) witnesses. (1) They violate the negative commandment, "You will not give [him] your money upon usury" (Lev. 25:37). (2) And [they violate the negative command], "You will not take usury from him" (Lev. 25:36). (3) And [they violate the negative command], "You shall not be a creditor to him" (Ex. 22:25). (4) And [they violate the negative command], "Nor shall you lay upon him usury" (Ex. 22:25). (5) And they violate the negative command, "You shall not put a stumbling block before the blind, but you shall fear your God. I am the Lord" (Lev. 19:14).

iii. *Hiring Workers. Rentals and Bailments*

A. *The Mutual Obligations of Worker and Employer*

M. 6:1 He who hires craftsmen, and one party deceived the other — one has no claim on the other party except a complaint [which is not subject to legal recourse]. [If] one hired an ass driver or wagon driver to bring porters and pipes for a bride or a corpse, or workers to take his flax out of the steep, or anything which goes to waste [if there is a delay], and [the workers] went back on their word — in a situation in which there is no one else [available for hire], he hires others at their expense, or he deceives them [by promising to pay more and then not paying up more than his originally stipulated commitment].

T. 7:1 He who hires workmen — whether they deceived the householder [and did not provide the promised work] — they have no claim on one another except a complaint [which is not subject to legal recourse] [M. B.M. 6:1C]. Under what circumstances? When the workers did not show up. But [if] he hired ass-drivers and they came, but he did not find them, or [if] he went and hired workers and they came and found the field when it was wet [and not suitable for ploughing], he pays them wages in full. But one who actually does the work is not equivalent to one who sits and does nothing. And one who comes bearing a burden is not equivalent to one who comes empty-handed. Under what circumstances? In a case in which they did not begin [the work]. But if they had actually begun the work, lo, they make an estimate for him [of how much work actually had been done]. How so? [If] one undertook for the householder to cut down his standing grain for two selas, [and] had cut down half of it and left half of it, [or if he undertook] to weave a cloak for two selas, and [had woven] half of it and had left half of it — lo, these make an estimate for him. How so? If what he had made was worth six denars, they hand over to him a sela [four denars], or he completes his work. And if it was worth a sela, they hand over to him a sela. Under what circumstances? In the case of something which does not go to waste. But in the case of something which goes to waste [if there is a delay] [M. B.M. 6:1F], he hires others at their expense, or deceives them [by promising to pay more and then not pay up more than his originally stipulated commitment]. How so? He says to [the worker], "I agreed to pay you a sela. lo, I'm going to give you two." He goes and hires workers from another location, then comes and takes the money from this party and hands it over to that party. Under what circumstances? In a situation in which he comes to an agreement with him while he cannot find others to hire. But if he saw ass-drivers coming along, [the worker] says to him, "Go and hire one of these for yourself." And he has no claim on the other party except a complaint.

T. 7:2 He who hires a boat, and it unloaded his goods in the middle of the wharf — he has no claim against it except a complaint.

T. 7:3 He who hires a worker who suffers a bereavement, or who suffers heat-prostration — lo, they make an estimate for him [of the work already done]. How do they make an estimate for him? If he had been hired for a month, they pay him off in accord with his salary [proportionate to the part of the month he has worked]. [If he had been hired by the job] as a contractor, they pay him off in proportion to the part of the job he has completed. He who hires a worker to bring something from one place to another, and he went but [because he did not find what he had been sent for], he did not bring back [what he was supposed to], he [nonetheless] pays off his full salary.

T. 7:4 He who hires a worker to bring reeds and poles to a vineyard, and he went but did not bring them [as above] — he pays off his salary in full.

M. 6:2 He who hires craftsmen and they retracted — their hand is on the bottom. If the householder retracts, his hand is on the bottom. Whoever changes [the original terms of the agreement] — his hand is on the bottom. And whoever retracts — his hand is on the bottom.

T. 7:6 [If] he hired him to pull weeds and he finished the field to which he may not say to him, "Come along and hoe two vines." If he hired him to hoe and he finished the field to which he had been he may not say to him, "Come along and pull the weeds around two If he finished ploughing by noon-time, he may not say to him, "Come and pull the weeds in another field." For the worker may say to him, "Provide me with work in your property, or pay me my wage for the work I already have done." [If] he finished pulling weeds by noon-time, he may not say to him, "Come and pull the weeds in another field." For the worker may say to him, "Provide me with work in your property, or pay me my wage for the work I already have done." And so too, he who completed his ploughing by noon-time may not say to him, "lo, I am going to plough in the field of Mr. So-and-so." [If] he finished his weeding by noon-time, he may not say to him, "lo, I'm going to pull weeds with you in such-and-such a field." But if he had stipulated with him in advance in such wise, lo, this is permitted. The householder has the right to change the terms of work by assigning an easier form of labor, but not by assigning a more exacting form of labor. How so? [If] he hired him to pull weeds, and he completed the work in the field *to* which he was assigned, he may say to him, [only] with his permission, "Come and hoe around two vines." [If] he hired him to hoe and he completed the work in the field to which he had been assigned, he may say to him whether he likes it or not, "Come and pull the weeds around two vines."

T. 7:7 A. He who hires workers to work in his property, and they made a mistake and did their work in the property of someone else — he pays them their full wages and goes and collects from the householder [in whose property the work was done] [the value of] what he has done for him. [If] he showed them his property, and they went and worked in the property of his fellow, he does not have to give them a thing. But they go and collect from the [other] householder [in whose property the work was done] [the value of] what they have done for him.

B. 6:1–2 I.13 77B AND WHOEVER RETRACTS — HOW SO? LO, IF ONE SOLD HIS FIELD TO HIS FELLOW FOR A THOUSAND ZUZ AND THE OTHER PAID A DEPOSIT OF TWO HUNDRED ZUZ, IF THE SELLER RETRACTS, THE PURCHASER'S HAND IS ON THE TOP. IF HE WANTED, HE MAY SAY TO HIM, "GIVE ME MY MONEY BACK OR GIVE ME THE LAND UP TO THE VALUE OF MY MONEY." AND FROM WHAT PART OF THE LAND DOES HE COLLECT IT? FROM THE BEST QUALITY LAND. BUT WHEN THE PURCHASER IS THE ONE WHO RETRACTS, THE HAND OF THE SELLER IS ON TOP. IF HE WANTS, HE MAY SAY TO HIM, "HERE IS YOUR MONEY BACK." IF HE WANTS, HE MAY SAY TO HIM, "HERE IS THE LAND TO THE VALUE OF YOUR MONEY." AND FROM WHAT PART OF THE LAND DOES HE COLLECT IT? FROM THE WORST QUALITY LAND.

B. *Rentals*

M. 6:3 He who rents out an ass to drive it through hill country but drove it through a valley, to drive it through a valley but drove it through the hill country, even though this route is ten mils and that route is ten mils, and [the ass] died — [the one who rented it is] liable. He who rents out an ass to drive it through hill country, but he drove it through a valley. if it slipped, is exempt. But if it suffered heat prostration, he is liable. [If he hired it out] to drive it through a valley, but he drove it through hill country, if it slipped, he is liable. And if it suffered heat prostration, he is exempt. But if it was on account of the elevation, he is liable. He who rents out an ass, and it went blind or was seized for royal service — [the one who provided it has the right to] say to [the one who rented

it], "Here's yours right before you" [and he need not replace it for the stated period]. [If] it died or broke a leg, [the one who provided it out] is liable to provide him with another ass.

M. 6:4 He who hires a cow to plough in the hill country but ploughed in the valley, if the plough-share was broken, is exempt. [If he hired the cow to plough] in the valley and ploughed in the hill country, if the plough-share was broken, he is liable. [If he hired a cow to] thresh pulse and he threshed grain, [if the cow slipped and fell], he is exempt. [If he hired it] to thresh grain and he threshed pulse, [if the cow slipped and fell], he is liable, because pulse is slippery.

M. 6:5 He who hired an ass to carry wheat on it and he carried barley on it is liable. [If he hired it to carry] wheat and carried straw on it, he is liable, since the [greater] bulk is hard to carry. [If he hired it] to carry a letekh of wheat and it carried a letekh of barley, he is exempt. But if he added to its burden, he is liable.

T. 7:9 He who rents out a beast to his fellow should not change the beast [which he has rented out]. [If] he rented him an ass, he should not seat him on a mule. [If he rented him] a mule, he should not seat him on a horse. [If he rented him] a horse, he should not seat him in a carriage.

T. 7:10 He who hires an ass to carry a *letekh* [fifteen *seahs*] of wheat, [cf. M. B.M. 6:5F], and he brought sixteen of barley — is exempt [for damage to the ass]. [If] he added to its burden, he is liable. And how much does he add to its burden so as to be liable? He who hires an ass to give a man a ride should not give a woman a ride. [If he hired it] to give a woman a ride, it gives her a ride [without regard to] whether she is pregnant or nursing.

T. 7:11 He who hires an ass for the householder to ride loads on it [also] his chair, provisions, and all his articles. [If it was to be] more than this, the ass-driver stops him. An ass-driver loads on it barley, straw, and provisions, until it reaches lodging. [If it was to be] more than this, the householder stops him.

T. 7.12 He who hires an ass and loaded it up with prohibited merchandise, so that the tax-collectors or excise-officers seized them — [the one who hired the ass] is liable. If he [who hired the ass] informed [the renter] that there was a tax-collector on the road, he is exempt.

Y. 6:4 I.2 = T. 7:13 *A caravan which was passing through the wilderness, and a band of brigands fell on it and seized [a ransom] — they make a reckoning in accord with the property loss, and they do not make a reckoning in accord with the number of people. But if they had sent out a pathfinder before them, they also make a reckoning of the number of people. But in any event they do not vary from the accepted practice governing those who travel in caravans.*

Y. 6:4 I.3 = T. 7:14 *A boat which was coming along in the sea and a storm hit it, so that they had to unload some of the cargo — they make a reckoning in accord with the property loss, and they do not make a reckoning in accord with the number of people. But in any event they do not vary from the accepted practice of sailors.*

But he who rents out to his fellow a boat or a wagon — they reckon the cost in accord both with the burden and with the number of people to be carried. But they do not reckon the cost in accord with [one's property's capacity to pay].

Y. 6:4 I.3 = T. 8:25–26 A caravan which was traveling along in the wilderness, and a troop of brigands attacked it, and one of them went ant saved [the property] — what he saved, he has saved for the common fund [of all participants]. But if he made a stipulation with them in a court, what he has saved he has saved for his own possession. Ass-drivers who were going along the way, and a band of thugs attacked them, and one of them went and saved [the property] — what he has saved, he has saved for the common fund [of all participants]. But if they had given him domain, what he has saved he has saved for his own possession. Partners whom tax farmers forgave part of their taxes — what they have remitted falls to the common fund shared by both parties. But if [the tax collectors] declared, "It is for Mr. So-and-so that we have remitted the taxes," then what they have remitted falls to the advantage of [Mr. So-and-so]. As to tax farmers and tax collectors, doing penitence is difficult. They return [what they can to those whom they] recognize. And of the rest [of the taxes they propose to hand back], they make use for the public good.

C. *Bailments: The Special Case of Depositing Materials with Craftsmen*

M. 6:6 All craftsmen are in the status of paid bailees [responsible for both negligence and theft]. But any of them who said, "Take what is yours and pay me off [because the job is done]" [enters the status of] an unpaid bailee [responsible for negligence but not theft]. [If one person said to another], "You keep watch for me, and I'll keep watch for you," [both are] in the status of a paid bailee. "Keep watch for me," and the other said to him, "Leave it down before me," [the latter] is [in the status of] unpaid bailee.

T. 7:15 A weaver who left a thread on the side of a garment and it caught fire is liable to pay compensation, because he is in the status of a paid bailee [M. B.M. 6:6A]. [If] the debris [of a falling building] fell on it before it was completely manufactured, he is liable [to pay compensation]. [If] it was after the work was completed, if the craftsman had informed the owner [that it was ready to be picked up], [the craftsman] is exempt. And if not, he is liable [cf. M. B.M. 6:6B].

T. 7:16 [If] he said to him, "I told you [to make] a shirt," and [the craftsman] said, "You told me [to make] a cloak," it is the householder's job to bring proof.

T. 7:17 [If the householder] said, "I told you [I'd pay] a *sela*," [and the craftsman] said, "You told me two," so long as the goods are in the hand of the craftsman, it is the householder's job to bring proof [of the agreed price]. [If the goods] are in the householder's possession, during the interval, the craftsman has to bring proof. After the interval, the weaver takes an oath [that the agreed price was as he claimed] and collects [what is owing to him].

T. 7:18 He who hands over utensils to the craftsman to do work [on them] for him, and the work was completed, before he has received his wages, lo, he is in the status of a paid bailee. Once he has received his wages, lo, he is in the status of an unpaid bailee. Under what circumstances? When [the craftsman] has laid claim upon the householder and said to him, "Come and take what's yours." But if he did not lay claim on him and did not say to him, "Come and take what's yours," even though he already has received his wages, lo, he remains in the status of a paid bailee.

T. 7:19 He who says to his fellow, "Lend to me, and I'll lend to you" — "Keep watch for me, and I'll keep watch for you," — "Lend to me, and I'll keep watch for you," — lo, these are in the status of an unpaid bailee [cf. M. B.M. 6:6C–F]. And they are not in the status of a paid bailee.

T. 8:1 He who hires a worker to watch his cow for him, [or] to watch his child for him does not pay him a salary for the Sabbath. Therefore [the watchman] does not bear responsibility [to make up any loss which takes place] on the Sabbath. But if he was hired by the week, by the month, by the year, or by the septennate, he does pay him a salary covering the Sabbath. Therefore [the watchman] does bear responsibility to [make up any loss] on the Sabbath. [The watchman] may not say to him, "Pay me my salary for the Sabbath." But he says to him, "Pay me my salary for a ten-day period."

M. 6:7 [If one made] a loan and took a pledge, he is in the status [as to care of the pledge] of a paid bailee.

M. 6:8 [The bailee] who moves a jar from one place to another and broke it, whether he is an unpaid bailee or a paid bailee, must take an oath [that the jar was broken by accident and not through his willful negligence, and so he is exempt from having to make it up].

D. *The Mutual Obligations of Worker and Employer*

M. 7:1 He who hires [day] workers and told them to start work early or to stay late — in a place in which they are accustomed not to start work early or not to stay late, he has no right to force them to do so. In a place in which they are accustomed to provide a meal, he must provide a meal. [In a place in which they are accustomed] to make do with a sweet, he provides it. Everything accords with the practice of the province.

M. 7:2 And these [have the right to] eat [the produce on which they work] by [right accorded to them in] the Torah: he who works on what is as yet unplucked [may eat from the produce] at the end of the time of processing; [and he who works] on plucked produce [may eat from the produce] before processing is done; [in both instances solely] in regard to what grows from the ground. But these do not [have the right to] eat [the pro-

duce on which they labor] by [right accorded to them in] the Torah: he who works on what is as yet unplucked, before the end of the time of processing; [and he who works] on plucked produce after the processing is done, [in both instances solely] in regard to what does not grow from the ground.

T. 8:2 A worker has no right to do his own work by night and to hire himself out by day, to plough with his cow by night and to hire it out in the morning. Nor may he deprive himself of food and starve himself in order to give his food to his children, on account of the robbery of his labor, which belongs to the householder [who hires him].

T. 8:3 Workers have the right to eat their bread with brine, so that they will [have the thirst to] eat a great many grapes. And the householder has the right to make them drink wine, so that they will not eat a great many grapes.

T. 8:4 A householder has the right to starve and torment his cow, so that it will eat a great deal when it is threshing. And one who hired a cow has the right to feed it a bundle of sheaves, so that it will not eat a great deal when it is threshing.

T. 8:5 An ass and a camel may eat from the burden which is on their backs as they go along, on condition that [the beasts' owner] not take [the fodder in the burden, which he is paid to carry] by hand and feed it to them.

B. 7:2 I.13/89B WORKERS WHO WERE WORKING AT PICKING FIGS, HARVESTING DATES, VINTAGING GRAPES, OR GATHERING OLIVES, MAY NIBBLE AS THEY GO ALONG AND ARE EXEMPT FROM HAVING TO DESIGNATE TITHES, FOR THE TORAH HAS ENDOWED THEM WITH THE RIGHT TO DO SO. BUT AS TO EATING THESE THINGS WITH THEIR BREAD, THEY ARE NOT TO EAT THEM UNLESS THEY HAVE GOTTEN PERMISSION FROM THE HOUSEHOLDER, AND THEY SHOULD NOT DRIP THEM IN SALT AND EAT THEM. BUT SALTING THE PRODUCE IS IN THE SAME CATEGORY AS EATING GRAPES AND SOMETHING ELSE. HE WHO HIRES A WORKER TO HOE AND COVER UP THE ROOTS OF OLIVE TREES — THE WORKER MAY NOT EAT [SINCE THIS IS NOT WORK THAT COMPLETES THE PROCESSING]. IF HE HIRED HIM TO VINTAGE GRAPES, PLUCK OLIVES, OR GATHER FRUIT, HE MAY NIBBLE AND IS EXEMPT FROM THE OBLIGATION TO DESIGNATE TITHES, FOR THE TORAH HAS ENDOWED HIM WITH THE RIGHT TO DO SO. IF HE STIPULATED THAT HE MAY EAT, HE MAY EAT THEM SINGLY, BUT NOT TWO AT A TIME [SINCE TWO TOGETHER COUNT AS A STORE AND ARE SUBJECT TO TITHES; SINCE HE HAS STIPULATED HE MAY EAT, IT IS PART OF HIS PAYMENT AND IS SOMETHING THAT IS BOUGHT, AND HE MAY NOT EAT THE STORES WITHOUT TITHING]. AND HE MAY DIP THEM IN SALT AND EAT.

M. 7:3 [If] one was working with his hands but not with his feet, with his feet but not with his hands, even [carrying] with his shoulder, lo, he [has the right to] eat [the produce on which he is working].

M. 7:4 [If the laborer] was working on figs, he [has] not [got the right to] eat grapes. [If he was working] on grapes, he [has] not [got the right to] eat figs. But [he does have the right to]

refrain [from eating] until he gets to the best produce and then [to exercise his right to] eat. And in all instances they have said [that he may eat from the produce on which he is laboring] only in the time of work. But on grounds of restoring lost property to the owner, they have said [in addition]: Workers [have the right to] eat as they go from furrow to furrow [even though they do not then work], and when they are coming back from the press [so saving time for the employer]; and in the case of an ass [nibbling on straw in its load], when it is being unloaded.

Y. 7:5 = T. 8:7 Anything the like of which has not yet reached the time for obligation [to tithing], but some other sort of prohibition affects it — [if the householder] hired [the worker] without making explanations [as to the prohibited status of the food in which he would be laboring], he has to redeem [the produce] and allow the worker to eat it, [or] tithe [the produce] and [so] allow the worker to eat it. But if he made an agreement with him [that he would forego his right to eat while he worked in the field], lo, this one is not to eat anything at all. Anything the like of which has reached the time for obligation to tithing, but some other sort of permitted aspect affects it — [if the householder] hired [the worker] without making explanations [as to the status of the food in which he would be laboring], lo, this [worker] is not to eat [at all]. But if [the householder] made an agreement with him [the worker] that he would provide food], lo, this one has the right to eat.

T. 8:8 A worker may eat a grape-cluster before he begins to work — a grape-cluster, even to the value of a *denar*, cucumbers even to the value of a *denar* dried figs even to the value of a *trisit*.

T. 8:9 He who [has the right to] eat [of the produce on which he is working] by [specification of the law of the] Torah should not pare figs, nor should he suck out grapes. One who works with his whole body [e.g., as a porter] has the right to eat whenever he wants.

M. 7:5 A worker [has the right to] eat cucumbers, even to a denar's worth, or dates, even to a denar's worth. But they instruct the man not to be a glutton and thereby slam the door in his own face [to future employment].

T. 8:6 [If] one was guarding four or five cucumber-patches, he should not fill his belly from one of them. But he eats a bit from each and every one, in proportion [cf. M. B.M. 7:5].

T. 8:11 An Israelite who treads out grain with the cow of a gentile is subject to transgressing the rule against muzzling the ox. And a gentile who treads out grain with the cow of an Israelite is not subject to transgressing the rule against muzzling the ox. [If the ox] is treading out grain in the status of heave-offering or second tithe, [the owner] is subject to transgressing the rule against muzzling the ox. What should he do? He brings a basket and hangs it on the neck of the beast, and puts into the basket some produce of that kind [which it is treading, so that he does not violate the law against muzzling the ox, and the ox will not consume produce in a state of consecration].

T. 8:12 He who muzzles a cow should not give it less than six *qabs* [of fodder], and in the case of an ass, three *qabs*. He who actually muzzles the cow, and he who pairs heterogeneous animals [which is not to be done in ploughing] is exempt [from liability]. You have none who is liable except the one who actually leads or drives [the muzzled ox while it is ploughing] alone.

M. 7:6 A man makes a deal [with the householder not to exercise his right to eat produce on which he is working] in behalf of himself, his adult son, or daughter, in behalf of his adult manservant or woman-servant, in behalf of his wife, because [they can exercise] sound judgment [and keep the terms of the agreement]. But he may not make a deal in behalf of his minor son or daughter, in behalf of his minor boy servant or girl servant, or in behalf of his beast, because [they can] not [exercise] sound judgment [and keep the terms of the agreement].

M. 7:7 He who hires workers to work in his fourth-year plantings [the produce of which is to be eaten not at random but only in Jerusalem or to be redeemed for money to be brought up to Jerusalem (Lev. 19:24)] lo, these do not [have the right to] eat. If [in advance] he did not inform them [of the character of the produce and the prohibitions affecting it], he [has to] redeem the produce and [permit them to] eat [of it]. [If] his fig cakes split up, his jars [of wine] burst open [while yet untithed, and workers are hired to repress the figs and rebottle the wine], lo, these do not [have the right to] eat [them]. If he did not inform them [that the produce on which they would be working was untithed and therefore not available for their random consumption], he has to tithe [the produce] and [allow them to] eat [of it].

M. 7:8 Those who keep watch over produce [have the right to] eat [it] by the laws of the province, but not by [what is commanded in] the Torah.

E. *Bailments*

M. 7:8 There are four classes of bailees: (1) an unpaid bailee, (2) a borrower, (3) a paid bailee, (4) and a lessee. (1) [In the case of damage to the bailment], an unpaid bailee takes an oath in all [cases of loss or damage and bears no liability whatsoever] [M. 3:1]. (2) [In the case of damage to the bailment], the borrower pays in all circumstances [of damages to a bailment]. (3, 4) [In the case of damage to the bailment], the paid bailee and the lessee take an oath [that they have not been negligent] concerning [a beast which has suffered] a broken bone, or which has been driven away, or which has died [Ex. 22:9]. But they pay compensation for the one which was lost or stolen.

T. 8:13 Under what circumstances did they rule, An unpaid bailee takes an oath in all [cases of loss or damage and bears no liability] [M. B.M. 7:8H] and goes forth? In a case in which he carried out his duty as a bailee in the way which people generally serve as bailees. [If] he locked up as was appropriate, tied up as was appropriate, put [the thing] in his girdle and put it before him in his wallet, with its mouth upward, or put it in a chest, box or cupboard and locked it up, and it was lost, lo, this one takes an oath and goes forth. And if there are witnesses that he did matters as he claims, he is exempt [even] from having to take an oath.

T. 8:14 [If] he locked up not as was appropriate, tied up not as was appropriate, put the thing in his girdle and threw it behind him in his wallet, with its mouth downward, put it at the mouth of his wallet, or put [an animal] up on his roof, and it was stolen or lost, he is liable. If he put it into the same place in which he put his own, if it is a place appropriate for safekeeping, he is exempt. And if not, he is liable.

M. 7:9 A single wolf does not count as an unavoidable accident. Two wolves are regarded as an unavoidable accident. Two dogs do not count as an unavoidable accident. A thug — lo, he counts as an unavoidable accident. (1) A lion, (2) wolf, (3) leopard, (4) panther, or (5) snake — lo, these count as an unavoidable accident. Under what circumstances? When they come along on their own. But if he took [the sheep] to a place in which there were bands of wild animals or thugs, these do not constitute unavoidable accidents.

T. 8:18 A shepherd who left his flock and went into town, and thugs came and took the flock — they make an assessment of the case as if he had been there. If he would have been able to save [the flock, had he been present], he is liable. And if not, he is exempt.

M. 7:10 [If a beast] died of natural causes, lo, this counts as an unavoidable accident. [If] one caused it distress and it died [e.g., of cold or hunger], this does not count as an unavoidable accident. [If] it went up to the top of a crag and fell down, lo, this is an unavoidable accident. [If] he brought it up to the top of a crag and it fell down and died, it is not an unavoidable accident. An unpaid bailee may stipulate that he is exempt from [having to take] an oath, and a borrower, that he is exempt from having to pay compensation, and a paid bailee and a hirer, that they are exempt from [having to take] an oath or from having to pay compensation.

T. 8:19 A. An unpaid bailee may stipulate that he is in the status of a borrower [cf. M. B.M. 7:10F]. And a borrower may stipulate that he is in the status of an unpaid bailee [cf. M. B.M. 7:10G]. And a borrower may stipulate that he is in the status of a paid bailee or a hirer. And a paid bailee and a hirer may stipulate that they are in the status of a borrower [M. B.M. 7:10H].

M. 7:11 Whoever exacts a stipulation contrary to what is written in the Torah — his stipulation is null. And any stipulation which

requires an antecedent action — that stipulation is null. But any condition which can be carried out in the end and is stipulated as a condition in the beginning — that stipulation is valid.

M. 8:1 He who borrows a cow, and (1) borrowed [the service] of its owner with it, or (2) hired its owner with it — [or] (1) borrowed [the service] of the owner, or (2) hired him, and afterward borrowed the cow [too], and [the cow] died — [the borrower] is exempt, since it is said, "If the owner is with it, he shall not pay compensation" (Ex. 22:14). But [if] he borrowed the cow, and afterward (1) borrowed [the service] of the owner, or (2) hired him, and [the cow] died, [the borrower] is liable, since it is said, "If the owner is not with it, he shall certainly pay compensation" (Ex. 22:13).

B. 8:1 I.7/95B = T. 8:20 IF HE HAD BORROWED THE COW AND BORROWED THE SERVICE OF THE OWNER, HIRED THE COW AND HIRED THE SERVICE OF ITS OWNER, BORROWED THE COW AND HIRED THE SERVICE OF ITS OWNER, HIRED THE COW AND BORROWED THE SERVICE OF ITS OWN, AND THE COW DIED OR SUFFERED A BROKEN LEG, EVEN THOUGH THE OWNER IS AVAILABLE AND PLOUGHING IN SOME OTHER PLACE, THE ONE WHO BORROWED OR HIRED THE COW IS EXEMPT.

B. 8:1 I.8/95B = T. 8:21 IF HE BORROWED THE COW AND AFTERWARD BORROWED THE OWNER, HIRED THE COW AND AFTERWARD HIRED THE OWNER, BORROWED THE COW AND AFTERWARD HIRED THE SERVICE OF THE OWNER, HIRED THE COW AND AFTERWARD BORROWED THE SERVICE OF THE OWNER, AND THE COW DIED OR SUFFERED A BROKEN LEG, EVEN THOUGH THE OWNER IS AVAILABLE AND PLOUGHING WITH THAT ANIMAL, THE BORROWER IS LIABLE SINCE IT IS SAID, "IF THE OWNER IS NOT WITH IT, HE SHALL CERTAINLY PAY COMPENSATION" (Ex. 22:13).

M. 8:2 He who borrows a cow — [if] he borrowed it for half a day and hired it for half a day, [or] borrowed it for one day and hired it for the next day, [or] borrowed one [cow] and hired another — and [the cow] died — the lender says, (1) "The borrowed one died" — (2) "On the day [C] on which it was borrowed, it died" (3) "At the time that it was borrowed, it died," — and the [borrower] says, "I don't know" — [the borrower] is liable. The hirer [lessee] says, (1) "The hired one died," (2) "On the day on which it was hired, it died," (3) "at the time that it was hired, it died" and the other party says, "I don't know" — [the hirer] is exempt. [If] this party claims that the borrowed one [died], and that party claims that the hired one [died], the one who rents it is to take an oath that the rented one died. [If] this one says, "I don't know," and that one says, "I don't know," then let them divide [the loss].

T. 8:22 "lo, it is on loan to you today, if you will watch it for me tomorrow," "lo, it is on loan to you today, if you will watch its mate for me tomorrow," "lo, its mate is on loan to you today, if you will guard it for me tomorrow," "lo, it is on loan to you up to noon, if you will guard it for me from noon and thereafter," "lo, it is on loan to you up to noon, if you will guard its mate for me from noon onward," "lo, its mate is on loan to you up to noon, if you will guard it for me from noon onward," "lo, it is on loan to you from noon onward, if you will guard its mate for me up to noon" — lo, [the parties who make such agreements] are not in the status of unpaid bailees, but are only in the status of paid bailees. Whether one has borrowed it today and hired it for tomorrow, or hired it for today and borrowed it for tomorrow, or if there were two, one which was borrowed and one which was hired — this one says, "I don't know" — and that one says, "I don't know" — let them divide up [the loss] [M. B.M. 8:2S–T]. [If] this one says it was borrowed, and that one says it was hired [M. B.M. 8:2P–Q], — he who lays claim against his fellow has to bring proof [in support of his claim]."

M. 8:3 He who borrowed a cow, and [the one who lent it out] sent it along with his son, slave, or messenger, or with the son, slave, or messenger of the borrower — and it died — [the borrower) is exempt. If the borrower had said to him, "Send it with my son," ". . . my slave," ". . . my messenger," or ". . . with your son," ". . . with your slave," ". . . with your messenger," or if the lender had said to him, "lo, I'm sending it to you with my son," "my . . . slave," "My . . . messenger" or ". . . with your son," ". . . your slave," ". . . your messenger," and the borrower said, "Send it along," and he did send it along, but it died, [the borrower] is liable. And so is the rule as to returning the beast.

Y. 8:3 I.1 *[The borrower said to the cow owner,] "Lend me your cow for ten days, and you be lent to me yourself for the first five days," [if then the cow] died in the latter period, it is deemed to have died while subject to the indenture of the former period, [and the borrower is exempt from paying compensation, in line with M. 8:1]. [If he said], "Lend me your cow for after ten days [during which ten-day period, the cow owner himself had been lent to the borrower], and the old lady [who owned the cow] said to him, "It is [a weak cow, and it is] as if it is already dead," [then if the cow should die, it is deemed to have died while subject] to the indenture of the latter period, [so that even if the owner was already employed with the borrower before the cow came on the scene, the borrower is responsible to pay compensation for the deceased cow]. [We do not maintain in this case that the cow was with the owner.] [If the borrower had said,] "Lend me your cow, and I shall be lent to you," "Lend me your cow, and come and work with me," "Lend me your spade, and come and weed with me," "Lend me your dish, and come and eat with me," if one had borrowed it from the superintendent of the well, from the steward, or from the town clerk [of the householder], and it died, it is as if the owner was with the cow [and the borrower need not pay]. [These are agents of the owner.]*

iv. *Real Estate*

A. *Prologue*

M. 8:4 He who exchanges a cow for an ass, and [the cow] produced offspring, and so, too: he who sells his girl slave and she gave birth — this one says, "It was before I made the sale," and that one says, "It was after I made the purchase" — let them divide the proceeds. [If] he had two slaves, one big and one little, or two fields, one big and one little — the purchaser says, "I bought the big one," and the other one says, "I don't know" — [the purchaser] has acquired the big [slave]. The seller says, "I sold the little one," and the other one says, "I don't know" — [the latter] has a claim only on the little one, This one says, "The big one," and that one says, "The little one" — let the seller take an oath that it was the little one which he had sold. This one says, "I don't know" and that one says, "I don't know" — let them divide up [the difference].

T. 8:23 He who sells a cow to his fellow and it turns out to be pregnant and gives birth — this one says, "It was while in my domain that it gave birth" and the other one remains silent — [the former] has acquired possession [of the calf]. [If] the other one claims, "It was while in my domain that she gave birth," and this one remains silent — [the former] has acquired possession [of the calf] [M. B.M. 8:4L–N]. [If] this one says, "I don't know," and that one says, "I don't know," let them divide up [the proceeds] [M. B.M. 8:4A–F].

T. 8:24 And so too: He who sells a girl-slave to his fellow, and she turns out to be pregnant and gave birth — this one says, "It was in my domain that she gave birth," and the other remains silent — [the former] has acquired possession [of the baby]. [If] this one claims, "It was in my domain that she gave birth," and the other remains silent, he has acquired possession [of the baby]. [If] this one says, "I don't know," and that one says, "I don't know," let them divide [the proceeds of the sale of the slave-child].

T. 8:25 A caravan which was traveling along in the wilderness, and a troop of brigands attacked it, and one of them went and saved [the property] — what he saved, he has saved for the common fund [of all participants]. But if he made a stipulation with them in a court, what he has saved he has saved for his own advantage. Ass-drivers who were going along the way, and a band of thugs attacked them, and one of them went and saved [the property] — what he has saved, he has saved for the common fund [of all participants]. But if they had given him domain, what he has saved he has saved for his own advantage. Partners who were forgiven part of their taxes by the tax-collectors — what they have been remitted falls to the common fund shared by both parties. But if [the tax-collectors] declared, "It is for Mr. So-and-so that we have remitted the taxes," then what they have remitted falls to the advantage of Mr. So-and-so.

M. 8:5 He who sells olive trees for firewood and [before they had been chopped down], they produced fruit which yielded less than a quarter-[log] of olive oil to a seah — lo, this belongs to the owner of the olive trees [not to the owner of the land, who sold only the trees, not the ground]. [If] they produced a quarter-[log] of oil for a seah, this one says, "My olive trees made it," and that one says, "My ground made it" — let them divide it up. [If] the river overflowed one's olive trees and set them down in the field of his fellow [where they bore fruit], this one says, "My olive trees made it," and that one says, "My ground made it" Let them divide it up.

B. *Landlord-Tenant Relationships*

M. 8:6 He who rents a house to his fellow [without a lease] — in the rainy season, from the Festival to Passover. he has not got the right to evict him. And in the dry season, [he may evict him if he gives] thirty days' [notice]. And in the case of large towns, all the same are the dry season and the rainy season, [he must give notice of] twelve months. And in the case of stores, all the same are small towns and large cities, [he must give notice of] twelve months.

T. 8.27 He who rents a store from his fellow [has the right to remain there without eviction] for no less than twelve months. Under what circumstances? When the completion of the twelve months coincides with the end of the Festival [of Tabernacles]. But if the completion of the twelve months coincides with the end of Passover, they give him three festivals, so that he may collect what is owing to him. Now when they said, "Thirty days," or when they said, "Twelve months," it is not that the tenant may dwell there for [only] thirty days, and not that the tenant should dwell there for [only] twelve months But he has to give him notice thirty days in advance, or give him notice twelve months in advance. And just as the landlord has not got the right to evict prior to notice, so the tenant has not got the right to move out prior to notice. So far as a wine-press is concerned, [there may not be eviction] throughout the time of the vintage. So far as an olive-press is concerned, [there may not be an eviction] throughout the season of the olive-pressing. And as to a pottery, there may not be a notice of less than twelve months.

M. 8:7 He who rents out a house to his fellow — he who rents it out is liable [to provide] (1) a door, (2) bolt, and (3) lock, and anything which is made by a craftsman. But as to anything which is not made by a craftsman, the one who rents the house makes it [for himself]. Shit [left in a rented courtyard by cattle belonging to a third party] is assigned to the householder. The

renter has a claim only on the refuse of an oven or stove alone.

T. 8:29 He who rents a store from his fellow has a say concerning the place in which the oven is to be located But he does not have a say concerning the place in which the stove is to be located. If he hired a courtyard from him, he does not have a say concerning the place in which the oven is to be located or concerning the place in which the stove is to be located. But he sets up the oven in a place which is suitable to it, and the stove in a place which is suitable to it. The ashes which come out of the oven — whatever he collects, lo, it belongs to him [M. B.M. 8:7G] That [manure] which is in the cattle-shed and in the courtyard — lo, it belongs to the owner of the courtyard [M. B.M. 8:7F].

T. 8:30 He who rents out a house to his fellow, and the house was smitten with a *nega'* says to him, "lo, there is what is yours before you." [If] he consecrated [the house to the Temple], he who dwells in it pays the rental fee to the Temple. He who hires a house from his fellow — the latter provides for him millstones turned by an ass, but not millstones turned by hand. He may not make a place to store wine in it, because it lays a burden on the walls. And he may not raise chickens in it, because they peck at the walls. And he should not prepare in it a fixed mortar, because it shakes the walls. And he may not make it into a stall for cattle or into a storage-house for grain.

T. 8:31 He who rents out a house to his fellow for twelve golden *denars* a year — lo, this one pays them out throughout the year. [If he rented the house] up to Adar, and the year was intercalated [receiving a second Adar] — this one says, "It was up to the first Adar," and that one says, "It was up to the second Adar inclusive of the second Adar," they divide the difference between them [M. B.M. 8:8G–I]. [If he had rented the house] to the end of Adar, it is to the end of the second Adar. [If] the year was intercalated [receiving a second Adar] this one says, "It was up to the end of the first Adar," and that one says, "It was up to the end of the second Adar," they divide the difference between them.

B. 8:7 I.1–2/101B HE WHO RENTS OUT A HOUSE TO HIS FELLOW — HE WHO RENTS IT OUT IS LIABLE TO PROVIDE DOORS, MAKE WINDOWS, STRENGTHEN THE CEILING, AND SUPPLY SUPPORTS FOR THE JOISTS. THE TENANT HAS TO PROVIDE THE LADDER TO GET UP TO THE LOFT, TO MAKE THE PARAPET, FIX A GUTTER SPOUT, AND PLASTER THE ROOF. HE WHO RENTS A HOUSE TO HIS FELLOW — IT IS THE OBLIGATION OF THE TENANT TO PROVIDE A MEZUZAH. BUT WHEN HE LEAVES, HE MAY NOT TAKE IT IN HAND AND LEAVE. BUT IF IT IS LEASED FROM A GENTILE, HE MUST TAKE IT WITH HIM WHEN HE LEAVES.

M. 8:8 He who rents out a house to his fellow for a year — [if] the year was intercalated [and received an extra month of Adar], it is intercalated to the advantage of the tenant. [If] he rented it to him by the month, [if] the year was intercalated, it is intercalated to the advantage of the landlord.

M. 8:9 He who rents out a house to his fellow, and [the house] fell down, is liable to provide him with [another] house. [If] it was a small house, he may not make it large. [If] it was a

large house, he may not make it small. [If] it was a single-family dwelling, he may not make it a duplex. [If] it was a duplex, he may not make it a single-family dwelling. He may not provide fewer windows [than had been in the house which fell down] nor more windows, with the concurrence of both parties.

T. 8:32 He who rents out a house to his fellow and [the house] fell down is liable to provide him with another house [M. B.M. 8:9A–C]. [If] it had had a roof of cedar, he may not roof it with sycamore, of sycamore, he may not roof it with cedar.

T. 8:33 [If] it had had windows, [the householder] has not got the right not to open windows for him. [If] it had had no windows, the householder has the right to open windows [in the new house] [cf. M. B.M. 8:9H–I]. Under what circumstances? When the tenant had rented the house from him for a very long time. But if the tenant had rented the house from him for a brief period, [the landlord] has the right to say to him, "There is yours right in front of you!"

C. *The Landlord's Relationships with a Tenant-Farmer or a Sharecropper*

M. 9:1 He who leases a field from his fellow [as tenant farmer or sharecropper], in a place in which they are accustomed to cut [the crops], he must cut them. [If the custom is] to uproot [the crops], he must uproot them. [If the custom is] to plough after [reaping and so to turn the soil], he must plough. All is in accord with the prevailing custom of the province. Just as they split up the grain, so they split up the straw and stubble. Just as they split up the wine, so they split up the [dead] branches and reed props. And both [parties to the agreement] must provide reed props.

T. 9:1 He who leases a field from his fellow, and in it was grain to harvest, grapes to cut, olives to gather — lo, they make an estimate for him [of the value of what is in the field]. [If in the field was] grain already harvested, grapes already cut, olives already gathered they do not make an estimate [of their value] for him. [If] he left the field and gave up possession of it, and there was in it grain to harvest, grapes to cut, olives to gather, lo , they make an estimate for him [of the value of what has not yet been gathered]. How do they make an estimate for him? [If] he was a hired hand, they pay him off [in the estimated value] in proportion to his salary. [If he was] a share-cropper, they pay him off in proportion to his share.

T. 9:2 He who rents an irrigated field from his fellow [takes it] for no less than twelve months. [If it is] a field which relies upon rainfall, he gathers his harvest and goes his way.

T. 9:3 "An irrigated field I rent from you," "An orchard-field I rent from you" — [if] the water-source goes dry, or the trees are cut down, [the landlord] is liable to supply him with another water-source or another tree. [If he had said to him,] "This irrigated field I rent from you," "This orchard-field I rent from you" and the water-source went dry, or the trees were cut down, [the tenant] may deduct [the damages] from the rental [M. B.M. 9:2H–J].

T. 9:4 He who leases a field from his fellow, and there were trees in the field — in a place in which people are accustomed to rent out trees along with a field, lo, they are deemed to belong to the lessee. [And in a place in which people are accustomed to rent out trees] by themselves, lo, they belong to the lessor.

T. 9:6 He who leases a field of vegetables from his fellow and there was in it a row of vegetables of some other sort [than the field as a whole], lo, it belongs to the purchaser. If it was in a place which was separated by itself, lo, it belongs to the seller.

Y. 9:1 I.1 If it was a place in which they are accustomed to cut [the crops], and he pulled them up [instead], the landowner may say to him, "You laid it bare, but I want it to be cut down, with a stubble left to hold the soil]." If it was customary to pull up the crop, and the tenant cut it instead, they say to him, "You go out with the manure. [I want a clean field, free of stubble.]"

B. 9:1 I.1/103B IN A LOCALITY IN WHICH PEOPLE ARE ACCUSTOMED TO CUT OFF THE CROPS, ONE HAS NOT GOT THE RIGHT TO UPROOT THEM; TO UPROOT THEM, ONE HAS NOT GOT THE RIGHT TO CUT THEM OFF, AND EITHER PARTY MAY PREVENT THE OTHER [FROM DIVERGING FROM THE USUAL PRACTICE].

M. 9:2 He who leases a field from his fellow, which is an irrigated field, or an orchard field — [if] the water source went dry, or the trees were cut down, [the tenant] may not deduct [the damages] from the rental. If he had said to him, "Lease me this irrigated field," or ". . . this orchard field," and the water source went dry, or the trees were cut down, [the tenant] may deduct [the damages] from the rental.

M. 9:3 He who [as a sharecropper] leases a field from his fellow and then lets it lie fallow — they make an estimate of how much [the field] is suitable to produce, [and the tenant] pays [that amount] to [the landlord]. For thus does he write to him [in the writ of occupancy or lease], "If I let the field lie fallow and do not work it, I shall make it up to you at its highest rate of yield."

T. 9:7 He who leases a field from his fellow should not plough one year and sow it another year. But he ploughs half of it and sows half of it, so that [the lessor] may have a source from which to collect [an income] [cf. M. B.M. 9:3].

T. 9:8 He who leases a field from his fellow and he would plough one year and sow another year — [the lessor] should not say to him at the time of the harvest, "Give me my rent for two years." But [the lessee] pays him the rent each year by itself.

T. 9:9 He who estimated [the value] of the standing grain of his fellow at ten *kors* of wheat, and it produced more or less [than the estimate] —

they pay him what he estimated [the yield of the field to be].

T. 9:10 He who leases a field from his fellow, in a place in which people are accustomed to put beans among the barley, may put beans among the barley. [In a place in which they are accustomed to plant] twice as much barley as wheat, they put in twice as much barley as wheat, and anything which is received for storage.

M. 9:4 He who leases a field from his fellow and did not want to weed it, and said [to the landlord], "What difference does it make to you? I'm going to give you the rental anyhow!" — they pay no attention to [his claim]. For the [landlord] has the right to say to him, "Tomorrow you're going to leave this field, and it's going to give me nothing but weeds!"

M. 9:5 He who leases a field from his fellow, and it did not produce [a crop], if there was in it [nonetheless sufficient growth] to produce a heap [of grain], [the lessee] is liable to tend it.

T. 9:13 He who leases a field from his fellow, and it did not produce a crop]. if there was in it [nonetheless, sufficient growth] to produce a heap of grain], he is liable to tend it [M. B.M. 9:5A–D]. For thus he writes in the lease: "I shall plough, sow, weed, cut, and make a pile [of grain] before you, and you will then come and take half of the grain and straw. And for my work and expenses I shall take half." And just as in the case of a field which is planted with seed, if there was in it sufficient growth to produce a heap of grain, one is liable to tend it, and if not, he is not liable to tend it, so in the case of an orchard-field, if there was in it sufficient produce to cover his expenses, he is liable to tend it. And if not, he is not liable to tend it.

T. 9:14 He who leases a field from his fellow harvests the crop, makes it into sheaves, and winnows. The measurers, the diggers, the bailiffs, and the town-clerks come and collect [their fees] from the common [stack of wheat, before the division of the crop between landlord and tenant]. The superintendent of the well, bath master, scribe, and the freight-ship captain, when they come as legal agents of the householder, collect their fee on the authority of the householder. When they come as legal agents of the tenant, they collect their fee on the authority of the tenant. And they do not vary from the accepted practice of the province.

T. 9:15 He who leases a field from his fellow and died — [the landlord] may not say to his sons, "Give me what your father has consumed." And so they may not say to him, "Give us what father has produced." But they make an estimate [of what is owing to each party] and pay it.

T. 9:16 He who leases a field from his fellow, [if] he sowed it in the first year and the seed did not sprout, they force him to sow it a second year. [If] he sowed it a second year and the seed did not sprout, they do not force him to sow it a third year [cf. M. B.M. 9:5]. He who sells garden-seed to his fellow, in the case of seed which cannot be consumed, if he sowed it, and it did not sprout, he is liable to make it up. In the case of seed which can also be eaten, if he sowed it, and it did not sprout, he is not liable to make it up. But if he had made a stipulation with him to begin with that it was purchased for seed, he is liable to make it up. What does he have to pay over to him? The cost of the seed. And some say, "The entire expense of the farmer's outlay in planting the seed."

M. 9:6 He who leases a field from his fellow, and locusts ate it up, or it was blighted — if it is a disaster affecting the entire province, he may deduct [the damages] from his rental. If it is not a disaster affecting the entire province, he may not deduct it from his rental.

M. 9:7 He who leases a field from his fellow [in return] for ten kors of wheat a year, [if the field was] smitten [and produced poor-quality grain], [the tenant] pays him off [from produce grown] in [the field]. [If] the grain which it produced was of good quality, he [has] not [got the right to] say to him, "lo, I'm going to buy [you grain] in the marketplace." But he pays him off [with produce grown] in [the field].

T. 9:17 He who leases a field from his fellow to plant trees in it — lo, this [lessor] takes upon himself responsibility for ten failures out of a hundred trees planted [and has no claim on the lessee]. [If there is] more than this, they assign to the lessee all [the loss].

M. 9:8 He who leases a field from his fellow to sow barley in it may not sow it with wheat. [If he leased it to sow] wheat, he may sow it with barley. [If he leased it to sow] grain he may not sow it with pulse, [to sow] pulse, he may sow it with grain.

T. 9:18 He who leases a field from his fellow to plant trees in it — in a place in which they are accustomed to plant four [trees to a grove], he plants on four [to a grove], five, [he plants] five; six; seven, seven. And they do not vary from the accepted practice of the province. He who leases a field from his fellow to plant trees in it — how long is he liable to tend it? In the case of sprouts, until they become available for secular use [after four years].

T. 9:19 He who leases a vineyard from his field is liable to tend it until he produces wine: olives — until he makes a pile of them; flax — until he makes them into stalks. He then splits up the crop and pays off [the landlord]. This party brings his share to market in the city, and that party brings his share to market in the city.

T. 9:20 He who leases a field of figs from his fellow — in a place in which they are accustomed to pack [the figs], [the tenant is expected to] pack them. [If they are accustomed to turn them into] dried figs, he makes them into dried figs. [If they are accustomed to make them into] pressed figs, he makes them into pressed figs. And they do not vary from the accepted practice of the province.

T. 9:21 He who leases a field of vegetables from his fellow — in a place in which they are accustomed to sell the vegetables in the market, he sells them in the market. [In a place in which they are accustomed to sell the vegetables] in the field, he sells them in the field. And they do not vary from the accepted practice of the province.

T. 9:22 He who sharecrops a field of olives from his fellow, even if he rented it from him only for the purpose of raising olives, [the lessor] may not say to him, "You have no claim on what is in it except in the case of olives alone." But whatever produce the field yields — lo, these are his.

T. 9:23 He who sharecrops a field of his fellow for planting has no claim on what is produced by trees therein. Under what circumstances? When he had said to him, "I shall plant seeds in this field. I shall share the crop of this field." But if [the owner] had said to him, "Share the crop of this field, plant seeds in this field, and work this field," all the produce which the field yields — lo, they are his.

T. 9:26 He who sharecrops a field for his fellow should not plough half of it and plant half of it, nor should he plant two different species in it. He who sharecrops two fields ploughs one of them and plants one of them, and he plants two different species. He who sharecrops a town for his fellow ploughs half of it and plants half of it, and plants many different species in it.

T. 9:27 He who sharecrops a field of grain for his fellow may not say to him, "I'm not coming until the grain is gone from it." And he has not got the right to sow it two times.

T. 9:32 He who leases a field from his fellow to sow barley in it [M. B.M. 9:8A–B] may not sow it with fenugrec, [If he leased it to sow] fenugrec, he may not sow it with cucumbers. [If he leased it to sow] cucumbers, he may not sow it with fenugrec, nor may he sow it with barley. [If he leased it to sow] woad, he should not sow it with flax. [If he leased it to sow] flax, he may not sow it with woad. He who leases a field from his fellow to sow it with wheat may not sow it with barley [cf. M. B.M. 9:8F]. [If he leased it to sow] barley, he may not sow flax. [... [If he leased it to sow] flax, he may not sow barley. [If he leased it to sow] barley, he may not sow wheat. [If he leased it to sow] wheat, he may not sow flax. [If he leased it to sow] flax, he may not sow wheat.

M. 9:9 He who leases a field from his fellow for a period of only a few years may not sow it with flax. And he has no [right] to [cut] beams from a sycamore. [If] he leased it from him for seven years, in the first year he may sow it with flax. And he has every right to cut beams from a sycamore.

T. 9:24 He who sharecrops a field for his fellow, and he was ploughing it one year and planting it another year and [the landlord] laid claim on him [for payment] in the year of the ploughing, and said to him, "Give me my share of the crop" — they pay no attention to him. But he is expected to wait until the harvest time comes.

T. 9:25 He who sharecrops a field of his fellow should not plough in it one year after another or plant seed in it one year after another. [If] he sharecropped it on his behalf for a considerable period of time, he may plough it one year after another and plant seed in it one year after another [cf. M. B.M. 9:9].

T. 9:28 He who sharecrops an orchard-field of his fellow may not say to him, "I'm not coming 'until the fruit is gone from it." And he has not got the right to consume the produce two times.

T. 9:29 He who sharecrops a field of his fellow — [if] he ploughed it but did not sow it, he pays him his rent. And even so, they make an estimate [of what he has contributed], since one who leaves it for him all ploughed is not the same as one who leaves it for him with the stubble.

T. 9:30 He who sharecropped a field of his friend for fodder, and he took the gleanings — all the produce which it yields — lo, these are his. [If] he hired it for planting but took the fodder, he may not say to him, "lo, I'm going to wait until all of that species has gone from it." All the produce which it yields, lo, they are his.

T. 9:31 He who leases a field from his fellow for a period of only a few years has no right to cut beams from a sycamore [M. B.M. 9:9A–B, D]. Therefore the rods and reeds are his. [If] he leased it from him for seven years [M. B.M. 9:9E], in a place in which they are accustomed to plant flax, even [if he leased the field] for five years, in the second year he may plant flax in it.

M. 9:10 He who leases a field from his fellow for one septennate at the rate of seven hundred zuz — the Seventh Year counts [in the] number [of years]. [If] he leased it from him for seven years at the rate of seven hundred zuz, the Seventh Year does not count [in the] number [of years].

T. 9:33 He who leased a field from his fellow and the lessee went and leased it to someone else — the householder has the power to say to him, "I have no business with anyone else but you." [If] the householder went and leased it to someone else the lessor has the right to say to him, "I have no business with anyone else but you." [If] the householder went and sold the field, they make a reckoning with the householder. In proportion to how the second sharecropper derived benefit from the field, so he pays to the first. [If] the householder went and declared the field consecrated, it is not deemed consecrated until it reverts to his domain. But whatever benefit the householder derived from it [while the sharecropper was farming it] — lo, it is deemed consecrated. [If] the lessee went and consecrated it, lo, this is deemed consecrated until it leaves his domain. And it yields a rent to the owner and a rent to the sanctuary.

D. *Paying Laborers Promptly. Taking a Pledge*

M. 9:11 (1) A day worker collects his wage any time of the night. (2) And a night worker collects his wage any time of the day. (3) A worker by the hour collects his wage any time of the night or day. A worker hired by the week, a worker hired by the month, a worker hired by the year, a worker hired by the septennate — [if] he completed [his period of labor] by day, collects

any time that day. [If] he completed his period of labor by night, he collects his wage any time during the rest of that night and the following day.

T. 10:2 A. A worker hired by the hour by day collects his wage any time of the day. A worker hired by the hour by day and by night collects his wage any time of the night and all the following day [cf. M. B.M. 9:11C].

M. 9:12 All the same are a fee to be paid to a human being, a fee to be paid for use of a beast, and a fee to be paid for the rental of utensils: [each is] subject to the rule, "In his day you shall give him his fee" (Dt. 24:15). [Each is] subject to the rule, "The wages of a hired worker will not abide with you at night until the morning" (Lev. 19:13). Under what circumstances? When [the worker] has laid claim [on his wages]. [If] he did not lay claim [on his wages], [the employer] does not transgress [the biblical requirement]. [If the employer] gave him a draft on a storekeeper or money changer, [the employer] does not transgress [the biblical requirement]. An employee — [if he claimed his salary] within the stated time takes an oath [that he has not been paid] and collects his salary. [If] the stated time has passed [and he did not collect his salary], he does not take an oath and collect his salary. But if there are witnesses that he had [in fact] laid claim [for his salary], lo, this one takes an oath and collects his salary. A resident alien is subject to the rule, "In his day you shall give him his fee" (Dt. 24:15) [since Dt. 24:14 refers to the alien]. But he is not subject to the rule, "The wages of a hired worker will not abide with you all night until morning."

T. 10:5 [If the employer gave him a draft on a storekeeper or money-changer [M. B.M. 9:12G], they are subject to transgressing on his account [the rule against keeping back wages, if they do not pay up]. But he does not transgress [the biblical requirement]. And if he stipulated with him at the outset in this regard [in that the wages would be deposited as specified], then even they are not subject to transgressing [the biblical law] on his account. And if he told someone to pay him, this one and that one are not liable to transgressing the law on his account.

T. 10:6 An employee [if he claimed his salary] within the stated time takes an oath [that he has not been paid] and collects his salary. [If] the stated time had passed, and he did not collect his salary, he does not take an oath and collect his salary. If there are witnesses that he had in fact laid claim for his salary within the stated time, even after the stated time, lo, this one takes an oath and collects his salary [M. B.M. 9:12I–O]... Under what circumstances? When the employer says to him, "I've already paid you your salary," while he claims, "You never paid me." But if [the worker] says, "You hired me," and the employer says, "I never employed you," [if] the employer says, "I promised you a sela," and [the worker] says, "You promised me two," then he who lays claim against his fellow bears the burden of proof.

T. 10:7 He who hands over utensils to a craftsman to fix for him and the work was done, even if [the item] is yet with him for three days, does not transgress on his account [for not picking up the work and paying for it when it was done] [cf. M. B.M. 9:12E–F]. But if he gave it back to him at noon, once the sun has set the householder [who has not paid for the work] has transgressed on his account.

M. 9:13 He who lends money to his fellow should exact a pledge from him only in court, And [the agent of the court] should not go into his house to take his pledge, as it is said, "You will stand outside" (Dt. 24:11). [If the borrower] had two utensils, [the lender] takes one and leaves one. And he returns [his] pillow by night, and plough by day. But if [the debtor] died, [the creditor] does not return [the objects] to the estate. From a widow, whether poor or rich, they do not take a pledge, since it is said, "You will not take a widow's garment as a pledge" (Dt. 24:17). He who seizes millstones transgresses a negative commandment, and is liable on the count of taking two distinct utensils, since it is said, "He shall not take the mill and the upper millstone as a pledge" (Dt. 24:6). And not concerning a mill and the upper millstone alone did they speak, but concerning any utensil with which they prepare food, as it is said, "For he seizes a man's life as a pledge" (Dt. 24:6).

T. 10:1 He who lends money to his fellow without specification — [the loan is for] no less than thirty days. But in a province in which it is customary for a loan to be for less time or more time [the local custom applies]. Therefore they do not vary from the accepted practice of the province [cf. M. B.M. 9:13G–H].

T. 10:8 He who lends money to his fellow has no right to exact a pledge from him. And if he has exacted a pledge from him, he has to give it back. And he thereby transgresses on every count which applies. An agent of a court who comes to collect a pledge stands outside, and [the residents] bring out for him the pledge, since it says, "When you make your neighbor a loan of any sort, you shall not go into his house to fetch his pledge, you shall stand outside, and the man to whom you make the loan [shall bring the pledge out to you" (Deut. 24:10–11) [cf. M. B.M. 9:13A–C].

T. 10:9 [If] he exacted two utensils as pledges one which the debtor needs and one which the debtor does not need, this one which he needs does he take and return to him. And that one which he does not need he takes but does not return to him [night by night]. But if he returns it to him [one night], he continues to return it to him. But if he returns it to him, why does he take it in the first place? Rabbi says, "I say, lest the Sabbatical Year come and release the debt. or lest the debtor die and the movables remain in the possession of the heirs [who then may not pay up]."

T. 10:11 If one has taken as a pledge a pair of scissors belonging to a barber, or a yoke for cows, he is liable on account of this part of the rule by itself and on account of that part of it by itself, [since it is said, "You shall not take the lower millstone and the upper millstone as a pledge" (Dt. 24:6). Just as a mill and an upper millstone are distinctive in that they constitute two distinct utensils that do work as one, and one is liable on account of this part by itself and on account of that part by itself, so he who exacts as a pledge two utensils that do work as one is liable on account of this part by itself and on account of that part by itself].

Y. 9:12 I.4 At night one exacts as a pledge a garment worn by day, and by day, a garment worn by night. And by day one returns a garment worn by day, and by night one returns a garment worn by night. A pillow and a blanket which one generally uses as a cover by night one exacts as a pledge by day and returns by night. A spade and a plough which one generally works by day one exacts as a pledge by night and returns by day.

E. *Joint Holders of a Common Property*

M. 10:1 A house and an upper story belonging to two people that fell down — the two of them divide the wood, stone, and mortar. And they take account of which stones are more likely to have been broken [and assign them to the likely owner of them]. If one of them recognized some of the stones belonging to him, he takes them, but they count as part of his share in the reckoning.

T. 11:1 A house and an upper story belonging to two people which fell down — [the two of them divide the wood, the stone, and the mortar. Under what circumstances? When both [the lower story and the upper story] were equivalent [in size]. But if one of them was large and the other small, this [owner] takes a share [in the wood, stone, and mortar] in accord with his [proportion of the whole], and that [owner] takes a share in accord with his [proportion of the whole]. And they regard [the stones of the upper story] as though they were the more likely to have been broken.

Y. 10:1 I.1 If the house tumbled inward like a furnace, the constituents of the upstairs room are those which are more likely to have been broken [and are assigned to the owner of the upper story]. [If] the house tumbled outward, the constituents of the downstairs part of the house are those which are more likely to have been broken [and are assigned to the owner of the downstairs].

M. 10:2 A house and an upper story belonging to two people — [if the floor of] the upper room was broken, and the householder does not want to repair it, lo, the owner of the upper story goes down and lives downstairs, until [the other] will repair the upper story for him.

Y. 10:2 I.1 If the place on which the oven stood broke through [and the householder, living below, does not want to repair it], the tenant may move downstairs. If the place of the double-stove broke through, the tenant may do likewise.

M. 10:3 A house and an upper story belonging to two people which fell down — [if] the resident of the upper story told the

householder [of the lower story] to rebuild, but he does not want to rebuild, lo, the resident of the upper story rebuilds the lower story and lives there, until the other party compensates him for what he has spent.

B. 10:3 I.2/117B IF THE OWNER OF THE LOWER STORY [OF THE CONDOMINIUM] WANTS TO CHANGE THE BUILDING MATERIALS IN THE HOUSE, FROM HEWN TO UNHEWN STONES, HE IS PERMITTED TO DO SO; IF HE WANTS TO CHANGE FROM UNHEWN TO HEWN STONES, HE IS FORBIDDEN [LITERALLY: THEY LISTEN TO HIM, THEY DO NOT LISTEN TO HIM, AND SO THROUGHOUT]; IF HE WANTS TO CHANGE FROM WHOLE BRICKS TO HALF BRICKS, HE IS PERMITTED, FROM HALF TO WHOLE, HE IS FORBIDDEN; IF HE WANTS TO MAKE A CEILING OF CEDAR, HE IS PERMITTED, OF SYCAMORE, HE IS FORBIDDEN; IF HE WANTS TO CUT DOWN ON THE NUMBER OF WINDOWS, HE IS PERMITTED, TO INCREASE THEM, HE IS FORBIDDEN; IF HE WANTS TO ELEVATE THE STORY, HE IS FORBIDDEN, TO CUT IT DOWN IN HEIGHT, HE IS PERMITTED. [IF HE WISHES TO MAKE AN ALTERATION THAT STRENGTHENS THE LOWER STORY AND ADS TO ITS WEIGHT, SO THAT IT CAN BETTER BEAR THE BURDEN OF THE UPPER STORY, HE IS PERMITTED. BUT HE MAY NOT WEAKEN IT.] IF THE OWNER OF THE UPPER STORY WANTS TO CHANGE FROM UNHEWN TO HEWN STONES, HE IS PERMITTED, FROM HEWN TO UNHEWN, HE IS FORBIDDEN; TO HALF-BRICKS, HE IS FORBIDDEN, TO WHOLE BRICKS, HE IS PERMITTED; IF HE WANTS TO MAKE A CEILING WITH CEDARS, HE IS FORBIDDEN, WITH SYCAMORES, HE IS PERMITTED; IF HE WANTS TO INCREASE THE NUMBER OF WINDOWS, HE IS PERMITTED; TO DIMINISH THEM, HE IS NOT PERMITTED; TO ELEVATE THE UPPER STORY, HE IS NOT PERMITTED, TO CUT IT DOWN, HE IS PERMITTED. [HE MAY WEAKEN THE UPPER PORTION, LESSENING THE BURDEN ON THE LOWER, BUT MAY NOT STRENGTHEN IT AND SO INCREASE THE WEIGHT ON THE LOWER PORTION.]

M. 10:4 And so too: An olive press which is built into a rock, and a garden is on top of it [on its roof, above], and [the roof] was broken — lo, the owner of the garden [has the right to] go down and sow the area below, until the other party will rebuild vaulting for his olive press. The wall or the tree which fell down into public domain and inflicted injury — [the owner] is exempt from having to pay compensation. [If] they gave him time to cut down the tree or to tear down the wall, and they fell down during that interval, [the owner] is exempt. [If they fell down] after that time, [the owner] is liable.

T. 11:6 A. A person may bring dirt and pile it up at the door of his house in the public way to knead it into mortar. [But if it is] to keep it there, lo, this is prohibited. And if another party came along and was injured by it, lo, this person is liable. And he should not knead the mortar on one side and build on the other side. But he should knead on the side at which he builds.

T. 11:7 [If] the wall fell down because of earthquakes or because of heavy rains, if it had been properly built, [the owner] is exempt [for damage it may do]. But if not, he is liable [cf. M. B.M. 10:4F–G].

M. 10:5 He whose wall was near the garden of his fellow, and it

was damaged [and fell down] — and [the owner of the garden] said to him, "Clear out your stones" but the other said to him, "They're yours!" — they pay no attention to [the latter]. [But if] after the other party had accepted [the ownership of the stones] upon himself, [the original owner of the wall] said to him, "Here's what you laid out! Now I'll take mine!" — they do not pay attention to [the former]. He who hires a worker to work with him in chopped straw and stubble, and [the worker] said to him, "Pay me my wage," and [the employer] said to him, "Take what you've made for your wage!" — they do not pay attention to [the employer]. But [if,] after [the worker] had accepted [the proposition), [the employer] said to him, "Here's your salary, and now I'll take mine!" — they do not pay attention to [the employer]. He who brings out his manure to the public domain — while one party pitches it out, the other party must be bringing it in to manure his field. They do not soak clay in the public domain, and they do not make bricks. And they knead clay in the public way, but not bricks. He who builds in the public way — while one party brings stones, the builder must make use of them. And if one has inflicted injury, he must pay for the damages he has caused in building. And if one has inflicted injury, he must pay for the damages he has caused.

T. 11:8 A person may take out his manure and pile it up at the door of his house in the public way — [if this is] to take it out to manure with it. [But if it was] to keep it there, lo, this prohibited. If another party came along and was injured by it, [the owner] is liable.

II. ANALYSIS: THE PROBLEMATICS OF THE TOPIC, BABA MESIA

Now that we have reviewed the topical program, and the order in which topics are set forth, we begin with the paired questions, first, has Scripture defined what sages wish to know about the topics at hand? and second, if not, then how do sages know what they want to know about said topics? To answer these questions, we rapidly review the main points of our outline. I indicate Scripture's contribution at each pertinent point. The exposition of the topic commences *in medias res*, being continuous with the foregoing. It furthermore is carried forward without interruption into the following tractate. But each of the sub-topics — the divisions of the law — covered in Baba Mesia possesses its own point of interest. Reviewing the topics and the questions sages raise in expounding them reveals the character of the problematics that governs sages' account of what, about the subject at hand, sages find urgent.

A. Disposition of Property Not Held by the Rightful Owner But Lost, Subject to Conflicting Claims, or Deposited with a Bailee
  1. Conflict over property: the character of the oath that resolves the matter, which responds to the nature of the claim of the competing parties. That depends, further, on what portion of the property a claimant alleges is his. The will of each party enters into the transaction, therefore, embodied as it is in the extent of each party's claim.
  2. Restoring an object to the original owner: several issues are pursued. The first is, the right of the householder over what his dependents acquire; the second, the likely disposition of diverse documents; the third, the attitude of the original owner toward the objects that have been found, specifically, has he given up hope of recovering the object, in which case, through despair, he has relinquished ownership of the object? Or can he reasonably hope to regain the object, in which case he retains ownership? The condition of the objects that are found testifies to the imputed attitude of the original owner. The subsidiary problems do not change the picture. The main point is that persons capable of exercising independent will acquire in their own, not in the householder's behalf, whatever they find. The further point is that the right of ownership depends upon an act of will. Stated negatively through the principle that despair marks relinquishing ownership, the principle of the primacy of intentionality governs.

Scripture is explicit that one must restore property owned by another person, when it states the following:

> *You shall not see your brother's ox or his sheep go astray and withhold your help from them; you shall take them back to your brother. And if he is not near you, or if you do not know him, you shall bring it home to your house and it shall be with you until your brother seeks it; then you shall restore it to him. And so you shall do with his ass, so you shall do with his garment, so you shall do with any lost thing of your brother's, which he loses and you find; you may not withhold your help. You shall not see your brother's ass or his ox fallen down by the way and withhold your help from them; you shall help him to lift them up again* (Dt. 22:1–4).

The requirement of Scripture does not account for the governing consideration, relinquishing ownership through imputed despair of recovering the object.

  3. The responsibilities of a bailee: if the bailee accepted full responsibility for the object, he also receives restitution from a thief; a bailee should not lay hands on the bailment, but does not have to make up losses due to natural causes in the bailment; if the bailee disposes of the bailment for his own convenience, he is liable for damages, but if it is for the convenience of the bailment, he is not; if he takes proper precautions, he is not liable, but if not, he is. Here again, the outcome of the transaction is mediated by the extent to which a bailee

is willing to assume responsibility, encompassing compensation, for the bailment. And, again, the attitude of the bailee in disposing of the bailment — for his own convenience, for the service of the bailment — affects the judgment of the case. In all three areas of law, therefore, intentionality enters in and assessing the effects of an act of will forms the main criterion for deciding the types of cases dealt with her.

That the bailee is responsible to take an oath and not required to make restitution if he has not committed negligence is indicated in the following:

> *For every breach of trust, whether it is for an ox, for ass, for sheep, for clothing, or for any kind of lost thing, of which one says, "This is it," the case of both parties shall come before the God; he who God shall condemn shall pay double to his neighbor. If a man delivers to his neighbor an ass of an ox or a sheep or any beast to keep, and it dies or is hurt or is driven away, without anyone seeing it, an oath by the Lord shall be between them both to see whether he has not put his hand to his neighbor's property; and the owner shall accept the oath and he shall not make restitution. But if it is stolen from him, he shall make restitution to its owner. If it is torn by beasts, let him bring it as evidence; he shall not make restitution for what has been torn. If a man borrows anything of his neighbor and it is hurt or dies, the owner not being with it, he shall make full restitution. If the owner was with it, he shall not make restitution; if it was hired, it came for its hire* (Ex. 7:15ff.).

The distinctions among types of bailee and the rules set forth in the halakhah systematize the laws of Scripture.

B. Corollaries of Distributive Economics: Commoditization of Specie; True Value and Price-fixing; Prohibition of Usury

1. The Basis of a Commercial Transaction: it is not the transfer of coins, deemed a mere commodity, that effects a commercial transaction between an informed seller and a willing buyer, but the transfer of goods. The act of acquisition is effected through a symbolic exchange of things of value, not of specie. Even though the buyer willingly parts with the money, and the seller with the goods, the transaction is null until the one effects physical possession with the consent of the other. So an agreed-upon exchange by itself plays no role in determining the ownership of the goods.

2. True Value: Objects (but not slaves, commercial paper, or real estate) have a true, or intrinsic, value, as distinct from a market value. What an informed seller and a willing buyer agree as the price of an object is measured against the true value of the object, and if too great a divergence — more than a sixth — from that true value marks an exchange, fraud results; it may be fraud committed by buyer, if too little is paid, or by seller, if too much. Adulterating commodities involves fraud — giving the impression of value that does not, in fact, inhere. Here intentionality in the form of agreement is null; an objec-

tive, autonomous true value intervenes. The market-transaction, based upon the will of an informed seller and a willing buyer, gives way to the consideration of intrinsic value.

3. USURY: Concomitantly, taking interest is forbidden in transactions among Israelites; it involves payment for waiting for the return of funds that have been borrowed, or paying a higher price for the volume of a commodity that has been borrowed at a lower price, or trading in naked futures. One may lend wheat to be repaid in wheat only if it is for seed, not if it is for food. Variation in price based on supply cannot enter into transactions of lending commodities. Exchanges of labor must be exact, e.g., weeding for weeding, hoeing for hoeing, not weeding for hoeing. Usury in kind, e.g., advantages accorded to the lender of an other than monetary character, is also forbidden. Speculation in commodities or trading in futures is forbidden. Factoring, by contrast, is permitted, if both parties — the capitalist and the proprietor — share in the risk and profit. Israelites may not enter into a factoring arrangement by which the proprietor takes all the risk, the capitalist being guaranteed return of his capital no matter what happens. As above, even though the borrower is willing to pay interest and the lender to accept it, or arrangements of factoring on other than equal terms are freely entered into, the transaction is null. Will alone does not suffice; the intrinsic character of the transaction, violating as it does the law of the Torah by arranging for "payment for waiting" for the return of funds, overrides the attitude of the parties to the transaction.

Scripture explicitly prohibits usury:

And if your brother becomes poor and cannot maintain himself with you, you shall maintain him as a stranger and a sojourner he shall live with you. Take no interest from him or increase, but fear your God; that your brother may live beside you. You shall not lend him your money at interest, nor give him your food for profit (Lev. 25:35–27).

You shall not lend upon interest to your brother, interest on money, interest on food, interest on anything that is lent for interest. To a foreigner you may lend upon interest, but to your brother you shall not lend upon interest, that the Lord your God may bless you in all that you undertake in the land that you are entering to take possession of it (Dt. 23:20–21).

But I do not see here the consideration that is important for sages, that is, the intrusion upon private agreements of an implacable prohibition against all sorts of "payment for waiting."

4. PRICE-FIXING: The market price is set, then bargains can be made. The price is set by current, not past, production. Price-fixing based on speculation, not on market supply in hand, is forbidden. Exactly what has been said pertains here as well. Even though the willing buyer and informed seller have come to an agreement, their act of

will is null; the objective market-price, agreed upon when the crops are in hand and not before, overrides their act of will.

C. MUTUAL OBLIGATIONS IN LABOR, RENTAL, BAILMENT

1. EMPLOYER-EMPLOYEE: Each party is responsible to the other to make up loss caused by failure to carry out an agreement. Whoever changes the original terms of an agreement is liable to make up the loss. The prevailing rules of the labor market govern and may not be changed by private agreement. Workers are permitted by right to eat produce on which they are working. The act of will on the part of one party cannot set aside the agreement entered into by freely-undertaken acts of will of the two parties. But, self-evidently, if both parties concur, the original terms of the agreement are set aside.

One detail of the foregoing derives from Scripture:

When you do into your neighbor's vineyard, you may eat your fill of grapes, as many as you wish, but you shall not put any in your vessel. When you go into your neighbor's standing grain, you may pluck the ears with your hand, but you shall not put a sickle to your neighbor's standing grain (Dt. 23:25–26).

This is taken to pertain to workers, as indicated.

2. RENTALS: One who changes the original terms of a rental agreement is liable to make up the loss or pay damages consequent upon the change. But if there is an unavoidable obstacle, the lessor is not obligated to the lessee. Here, *force majeure* overrides the original agreement, since the unavoidable obstacle does not come about through an act of poor faith on the part of one or the other party.

3. BAILMENTS: In transactions with craftsmen, craftsmen who receive materials from householders are in the status of paid bailees, responsible for negligence and theft. Once the job is done and the craftsman informs the householder, the craftsman is in the status of an unpaid bailee. We differentiate among four classes of bailees, by the criterion of compensation. One who is not paid bears only limited liability. One who is paid, who borrows, or who leases, bears greater liability to compensate the bailer for damages. Differentiation between damage done through negligence and damage that cannot have been prevented accommodates a range of cases. What has already been said pertains here.

D. REAL ESTATE

1. CONFLICTING CLAIMS OF LANDLORD AND TENANT: If one sells trees but not ground, then unanticipated fruit in modest volume belongs to the purchaser of the trees. Where the volume is substantial, the produce is divided. The landlord may not evict the tenant without notice. The landlord makes an implicit contract to provide those components of a building that a craftsman makes, but the rentee provides what is not ordinarily made by a craftsman. The lessor must provide a replacement for a house that collapses, and it must be equivalent to the one originally leased. We impute to the act of agreement of both parties

the prevailing customs of the area, e.g., if a building ordinary includes certain appurtenances, then the agreement between landlord and tenant is assumed to encompass those appurtenances. An act of will on the part of the one or the other is null in the face of the legitimate expectations that both parties bring to the transaction.
2. CONFLICTING CLAIMS OF LANDLORD AND TENANT-FARMER: The lessee must follow prevailing practice, farming the leased land as is customary, and returning the land in suitable condition. The lessee may not change the conditions of the lease in any way. The lessor must supply what is ordinarily included in the lease. The lessor is liable for damages that affect everyone. What has just been said applies here too.
3. PAYING DAY-LABORERS PROMPTLY: Wages and fees must be paid at the end of the work-period, e.g., at the end of the day for a day-laborer, at the end of the night for a night-worker. The scriptural rules on not holding on to a pledge are recapitulated. But if the worker agrees to some other arrangement, the scriptural requirement may be set aside. His act of will, involving relinquishing established rights, is valid. Here the act of will on the part of the worker overrides the protections that the Torah has provided for all workers.

Promptly paying workers is explicit in Scripture:

You shall not oppress your neighbor or rob him. The wages of a hired servant shall not remain with you all night until the morning (Lev. 9:13).

You shall not oppress a hired servant who is poor and needy, whether he is one of your brethren or one of the sojourners who are in your land, within your towns; you shall give him his hire on the day he earns it; before the sun goes down, for he is poor and sets his heart upon it; lest he cry against you to the Lord and it be sin in you (Dt. 24:14–15).

If you lend money to any of my people with you who is poor, you shall not be to him as a creditor, and you shall not exact interest from him. If you take your neighbor's garment in pledge, you shall restore it to him before the sun goes down, for that is his only covering; it is his mantle for his body; in what else shall he sleep? And if he cries to me, I will hear, for I am compassionate (Ex. 22:25–27).

When you make your neighbor a loan of any sort, you shall not go into his house to fetch his pledge. You shall stand outside, and the man to whom you make the loan shall bring the pledge out to you. And if he is a poor man, you shall not sleep in his pledge; when the sun goes down, you shall restore to him the pledge that he may sleep in his cloak and bless you, and it shall be righteousness to you before the Lord your God (Dt. 24:10–13).

You shall not take a widow's garment in pledge (Dt. 24:17–18).

No man shall take a mill or an upper millstone in pledge, for he would be taking a life in pledge (Dt. 24:6).

Scripture has supplied the facts but not adumbrated the governing problematics, so far as I can discern. The same is so in connection with restoring the pledge.

4. JOINT-HOLDERS OF A COMMON PROPERTY: Both parties are equally liable to repair damages suffered in common. If one property-holder depends upon the other, the latter must carry out his obligation, even in the property the latter himself holds.

Our reprise completed, we may now answer the questions raised at the outset.

First, Scripture has supplied important facts, but on the strength of Scripture we could never have predicted the order, let alone the topical program, of the halakhah's presentation of Baba Mesia. In some aspects, the halakhah simply clarifies and refines the Written Torah's laws. But in most, even where Scripture defines the topic and dictates the substance of the law, the halakhah concerns itself with issues that Scripture does not introduce, and that do not inhere in Scripture's own halakhah. So Scripture has not defined either the topical program nor framed what sages wish to know about the topics that they do treat.

That is because sages work with their own set of questions, and, in the present case, those questions derive from a set of considerations in no way inherent in the halakhic topic but beautifully exposed by that topic. Sages found in the topic at hand a remarkably appropriate arena for the exposition of a problem of fundamental concern to them. Specifically, the entire exposition turns out to form an exercise on the interplay between intentionality and value, with specific attention to where the attitude of participants to a transaction governs, where it is dismissed as null, and where it takes a subordinate position in an exchange. These three readings of the role of the will of the parties to a transaction — [1] paramount, [2] excluded, and [3] subordinated but effective — form the expository program that animates the presentation of the topic of Baba Mesia. And, we notice, the layout of the topics permits the law to organize itself around the three possible outcomes for an act of will or intentionality: decisive, null, and mixed, that is, +, −, +/− — a strikingly logical sequence, entirely characteristic of the Mishnah's exposition of variables where topics yield an equivalent range of possibilities, positive, negative, mixed. (Baba Batra will show us yet another approach to the same matter: when one's idiosyncratic intentionality is null.)

When it comes to resolving conflicting claims, we focus upon the attitudes of the participants to the conflict. First, we want conflicting parties to resolve conflict in a manner that is not only equitable but also that is *deemed* by all parties to be equitable. Second, in assessing rights of ownership, we take account of the attitude of the original owner, who gives up his title when he despairs of regaining his property. Third, in assessing liability of a bailee, we assign restitution in proportion to the responsibility that the bailee has accepted. In all three instances, therefore, the variables of the law respond to the attitudes of the participants in a transaction, to acts of will that determine the outcome of untoward consequences.

When we deal with market-transactions, we treat as subordinate or dismiss outright as irrelevant the attitude of the players — informed seller, willing buyer. Rather, we impose the criterion of a fixed or true value. That overrides the agreement of the parties to the transaction. And the law goes out of its way to underscore that in the face of the fixed and true value that inheres in a transaction, the willingness of the parties to ignore true value is simply nullified. A borrower may willingly pay usury — in the innocent form of a warm greeting for instance or a gesture of friendship — but the transaction is illegal. Even though a purchaser is willing to pay a premium for an object, his attitude does not affect the value of the object. One may be willing to pay a premium for the use of capital, but such a premium is deemed not a return on capital but usury and is illegal. All transactions must conform to a measure of exact exchange of true value, and that extends to exchanges of labor. Indeed, unearned value may take the form of not only special concessions but even a polite or obsequious greeting and so is outlawed. It follows that prices will be fixed — in terms of market-conditions affecting what is immediately available — and private agreements cannot upset the public arrangements.

But private agreements can be taken into account in other exchanges. In transactions involving labor, rentals, and bailment, the attitude of the participants to an agreement fixes the terms of the agreement, which then cannot be unilaterally revised. Labor — like slaves, bonds, and other documents — has no true value in the way in which grain does; each party bargains in good faith without the constraints governing usury. But then the transaction involving such and such a wage for so and so a span of labor, once agreed upon by both parties, is binding. Here the initial agreement governs, each party having acceded willingly, and the attitude or intention of one party cannot then dictate changes not accepted by the other. In the matter of bailments, liability responds to the level of responsibility imposed by variable compensation of the bailee; he is assumed to be willing to take greater precautions and accept more substantial liability in response to greater compensation.

What about what is not articulated but only assumed? Here too, we impose upon the parties an imputed attitude, that is, we assume that all parties accept the prevailing norms and make those norms their own. In resolving conflicts in real estate, certain implicit agreements are assumed. Prevailing attitudes or expectations are imputed to the parties, custom then defining what we assume the players to have accepted.

It follows that the halakhah of Baba Mesia both sets forth information about the topics at hand and also works out a theoretical concern through the presentation of those topics. That concern focuses upon the attitude of parties to a conflict or transaction. To what extent does the intentionality of attitude of a participant in an exchange govern, and to what extent do immutable rules override the will of the individual?

[1] In certain situations of conflict, we take full account of the attitude of all parties. When two persons claim ownership of the same object, either because both have grabbed it at the same moment or because one has lost what the other has found, or because one has accepted responsibility in proportion to the other's inveiglement (good will, a fee, and so on), then intentionality reigns supreme. That is to say, we settle the conflict by a weighing or a matching of wills. The Torah requires fairness, and, no other considerations' intervening, all parties have a say on what is equitable.

[2] But the willingness of two persons, e.g., a buyer and seller, to come to an agreement is set aside by other considerations. The will cannot overcome the law of the Torah. The Torah prohibits usury, which involves the concept of distributive economics that inherent in an exchange is a set valuation, which the participants may not set aside. A theory of static wealth comes into play when we maintain that true value inheres in things. God's will overrides man's, and what God does not want, man cannot legitimate merely by an act of will, even in an exchange involving mutual consent. Intentionality or attitude — willingness to evaluate at a higher or lower value than the intrinsic one — no longer enter into the disposition of a transaction. God's will outweighs man's will, hence intentionality plays no part in settling these transactions.

[3] Established custom modifies intentionality, in that people are assumed to conform to a common norm. In exchanges not of conflict

nor of fixed value but of service, attitude or intentionality is subordinated to expectations that are broadly accepted. Intentionality plays its part, but idiosyncrasy does not, and we do not impute to an individual an intention or expectation that diverges from the norm. The parties may willingly enter a valid agreement to exchange service — work, rental of property, and the like — but their agreement cannot violate fixed procedures, any more than a buyer and seller may ignore true value. Custom in intangible relationships matches inherent worth in tangible ones.

What emerges from the presentation of Baba Mesia, therefore, is a coherent exercise on the three dimensions of will or intentionality: where man's will defines the norm, where God's will overrides man's will, and where custom and the social norm enter into the assessment of man's will and turn out to exclude unarticulated idiosyncrasy. We shall now see that Baba Batra works on yet another aspect of intentionality, cases in which intentionality is simply irrelevant to transactions of a certain order. Then we eliminate all consideration of individual preference or will. That completes the picture.

3.

TRACTATE BABA BATRA

I. An Outline of the Halakhah of Baba Batra

Baba Batra begins in the middle of Baba Mesia's concluding topical unit, the rules governing joint holders of a property. It proceeds to further licit real estate transactions: not infringing the property rights of others, establishing title through usucaption, transferring real estate and movables through sale. The next major section turns to licit commercial transactions and unstated stipulations in commercial transactions. The final unit turns to inheritances and wills and other commercial documents.

i. *Real Estate (continued)*

A. *Joint Holders of a Common Property [continuing Baba Mesia VI.E]*

M. 1:1 Joint holders to a courtyard who wanted to make a partition in the courtyard build the wall in the middle. In a place in which they are accustomed to build it of (1) unshaped stones, (2) hewn stones, (3) half-bricks, or (4) whole bricks, they build it [of that sort of material]. All accords with the custom of the province. [If they make it] of (1) unhewn stones, this one contributes [a space of] three handbreadths [of his share of the courtyard], and that one supplies [a space of] three handbreadths. [If they build it] of (2) hewn stones, this one supplies two handbreadths and a half [of space], and that one supplies two handbreadths and a half [of space]. [If they build it] of (3) half-bricks, this one supplies two handbreadths [of space], and that one supplies two handbreadths [of space]. [If they build it out of] (4) whole bricks, this one supplies a handbreadth and a half, and that one supplies a handbreadth and a half. Therefore, if the wall should fall down, the location [on which it had stood] and the stones belong to both parties.

M. 1:2 And so is the rule in the case of a garden: in a place in which it is customary to build a fence, they require [a recalcitrant owner] to do so. But in a valley, in a place in which it is not customary to build a fence, they do not require him to do so. But if he wants, he may withdraw inside his own portion [of the property] and build it. And he places the facing of the wall outside of [the fence] [on the side of the neighbor, indicating his ownership]. Therefore, if the wall should fall down, the location [on which it had stood] and the stones are his. If they had made it with the consent of both parties, they build the wall in the middle. They place the facing of the wall on this side and on that side. Therefore, if the fence should fall down, the location [on which it had stood] and the stones belong to both parties.

T. B.M. 11:10 They do not divide gateways unless there is sufficient for a share for this one and sufficient for a share for that one. [If] one of them said to his fellow, "You take the smaller share and give me my share," that statement is null.

T. B.M. 11:11 The doorways of a courtyard — the large ones belonging to one party, and the small ones belonging to the other party — the large ones are assigned only four cubits. And the small ones are assigned four cubits for each one. [If] one takes a large door, and one takes two small doorways — this one who takes the large door has a claim on only four cubits. And to that one who takes the two small doorways do they assign four cubits for each one. [If] there was a door there ten cubits wide, [the owner] takes four cubits space opposite it and four cubits space in the courtyard. [If it was] less than this, they give it its full measure opposite it, and they assign to him an area for bringing or taking out [his goods] to the extent of four cubits in the courtyard.

T. B.M. 11:12 Manure which is found in the courtyard is divided in proportion to the doorways. And that which is found in a colonnade belongs to everybody. A door which opens onto a porch is assigned only four cubits. The porch itself has four cubits [in the courtyard below]. [Even if] five doors (which) open out onto a porch — to the porch is assigned in the courtyard only four cubits alone.

Y. 1:3 [I:1 In the case of a garden [vegetable patch], whether it is a place in which it is customary to build a fence [cf. M. 1:2B], or whether it is a place in which it is not customary to build a fence, they force [a recalcitrant owner to build a fence if the partner so desires]. But as to a valley, in a place in which it is customary to build a fence, they force [the recalcitrant partner to build a fence], while in a place in which it is not customary to build a fence, they do not force [him to participate in the project].

M. 1:3 He whose [land] surrounds that of his fellow on three sides, and who made a fence on the first, second, and third sides — they do not require [the other party to share in the expense of building the walls].

M. 1:4 The wall of a courtyard which fell down — they require [each partner in the courtyard] to [help] build it up to a height of four cubits. [Each one is] assumed to have given, until one brings proof that the other has not contributed to the cost. [If the fence was built] four cubits and higher, they do not require [a joint holder in the courtyard to contribute to the expenses]. [If the one who did not contribute] built another wall near [the restored one] [planning to roof over the intervening space], even though he did not [actually] put a roof on it, they assign him [his share in the cost of the] whole [other wall]. [He is now] assumed not to have contributed to the cost, until he brings proof that he has contributed to the cost.

T. B.M. 11:4 [If] the ruined building of one party stood alongside the vegetable patch of his fellow and [the latter] went and built a fence [for his] patch, they assign to [the owner of the ruined building his share in] the cost fully in accord with the manner in which [the gardener] has built up the wall. If the ruin was alongside the courtyard of his fellow, even though the owner of the ruin, when he went to rebuild his house, did not put the beam on that side of the building, they assign the owner of the ruin his share in the outlay for the wall when he rebuilds his house. If the building of one party was above the courtyard of his fellow, the owner of the upper building may not say to the owner of the lower, when they build a wall between their houses, "Lo, I am going to provide plaster with him only from the level of my courtyard and above it." But he supplies plaster with him from below to above the entire height of the common wall. If the building lay wholly above the roof of another one, the owner of the higher building in no way is obligated to share in the costs of a wall between his building and the one below.

T. B.M. 11:22 The people who live in a common courtyard have the power to force one another to build for the courtyard a roof ten handbreadths high [cf. M. B.B. 1:4]. [If] one is assumed to have given, they accept his claim not to lay the beam [on his wall]. [If] he is assumed not to have given, they do not accept his claim to lay the beam [on his wall].

B. 1:4 II.12 7A HE WHO SAYS TO HIS FELLOW, "I AM SELLING YOU A BET KOR," EVEN THOUGH THE FIELD CAN HOLD ONLY A LETEKH, IT IS A VALID SALE, BECAUSE HE HAS SOLD HIM ONLY A PLACE USING ITS GENERIC NAME; THAT IS SO, ON THE CONDITION THAT IT IS CALLED A KOR FIELD. "I AM SELLING YOU A VINEYARD," EVEN IF IT CONTAINS NO VINES, IT IS A VALID SALE, BECAUSE HE HAS SOLD HIM ONLY A PLACE USING ITS GENERIC NAME; THAT IS SO, ON THE CONDITION THAT IT IS CALLED A VINEYARD FIELD. "I AM SELLING YOU AN ORCHARD," EVEN IF IT CONTAINS NO POMEGRANATES, IT IS A VALID SALE, BECAUSE HE HAS SOLD HIM ONLY A PLACE USING ITS GENERIC NAME; THAT IS SO, ON THE CONDITION THAT IT IS CALLED AN ORCHARD FIELD.

M. 1:5 They force [a joint holder in the courtyard to contribute to] the building of a gatehouse and a door for the courtyard. They force [each joint holder to contribute to] the building of a wall, gates, and a bolt for the town. How long must one be in a town to be deemed equivalent to all other townsfolk? Twelve months. [If] one has purchased a permanent residence, lo, he is equivalent to all the other townsfolk forthwith.

T. B.M. 11:17 He who has a dwelling in another courtyard — the others who dwell in that courtyard may require him to share with them in the costs of making a door, bolt, and lock for the courtyard. But as to any other requirements of the courtyard, they are not able to impose upon him the requirement to share in the cost. But if he would dwell with them in that same courtyard, they do have the power to impose upon him a share [of the cost] of all which is required for the common upkeep of the courtyard.

T. B.M. 11:18 People who live in a common courtyard may force one another to share in the cost of making a sidepost and crossbeam for an alleyway [for a commingling of the property for carrying on the Sabbath]. People who share a common valley have the power to force one another to share in the cost of making a trench and a rut.

T. B.M. 11:23 The townspeople have the power to require one another to build a synagogue, and to buy a scroll of the Torah and prophets. And the townspeople have the power to stipulate concerning prices, measures, and wages of workers. They have the power to define their stipulations. They have the power to say, "Whoever will be seen with so-and-so will have to pay such-and-so [a fine]." And, "whoever will be seen with the ruling power will have to pay such-and-such [a fine]." And, "whoever lets his cow pasture in the crops [of others] will have to pay such-and-such." They have the power to define their stipulation.

T. B.M. 11:24 The wool-weavers and dyers have the power to say, "Any order which comes to town — all of us will share in it."

T. B.M. 11:25 The bakers have the right to make an agreement on weights and measures among themselves. The ass-drivers have the right to declare, "Whose-so-ever ass dies — we shall provide another ass for him." [If] the ass died through flagrant neglect, they do not have to provide the owner with another ass. [If] the ass died not through flagrant neglect, they do have to provide him with another ass. And if he said, "Give me the money, and I shall buy it for myself," they pay no attention to him. But they purchase an ass for him and give it to him.

T. B.M. 11:26 The ship-masters have the right to declare, "Whosoever's ship is lost — we shall provide him with another ship." [If] it was lost through flagrant neglect, they do not have to provide him with another ship. [If it was lost] not through flagrant neglect, they do have to provide him with another ship. But if he set sail for a place to which people do not [prudently] set sail, they do not have to provide him with another ship [if he loses his on the perilous voyage].

T. B.M. 11:27 He who was a bath attendant for the community or a barber for the community, or a baker for the community, and he is the only one of his profession there, and the time of the festival came, and he wants to go to his home — [the other residents of the community] have the power to stop him, unless he sets up for someone else in his place. But if he had made a stipulation in court with them, or if they had done wrong to him, he has the right to do so.

T. B.M. 11:28 He who plants a tree for the community — one [has the right to] gather the produce and eat it, or to gather the produce and take it into his home. But he should not gather the produce and turn it into dried fruit, or gather the produce and turn it into pressed fruit. For to begin with he planted it only on that condition, for travelers to gather and eat the produce. And it is prohibited for [a traveler] to bring in the produce into his home.

T. B.M. 11:29 He who digs a cistern for the community — one may fill his bucket and drink the water, fill his bucket and bring it home. But he should not fill his bucket and provide water in the market place, or fill his bucket and sell water in the market place.

T. B.M. 11:30 Wool-dealers and dyers draw water for drinking, and they do not draw water for commercial purposes. And bakers and tavern-keepers do not draw water for commercial purposes. The measurers, diggers, and bailiffs draw water for drinking and do not draw water for use. But they pickle pickles in the shop, and they rinse bundles of vegetables for travelers. One draws water and drinks it. But he is prohibited from bringing it home. If workers were working with him, he should not draw water and provide them with it. But each one goes and drinks on his own.

T. B.M. 11:31 He who makes a cave of water for public use — one washes his hands, face, and feet. [If] his feet were dirty with mud or excrement, it is prohibited. In the case of a cistern or a trench, one way or the other, it is prohibited.

T. B.M. 11:32 He who goes into a bathhouse — they warm the cold water for him, or cool the warm water. He shampoos his hair in niter or in urine even though he makes a mess for those who come after him. For it was on this stipulation that Joshua caused the Israelites to inherit the land.

T. B.M. 11:33 A spring belonging to the townsfolk — [when there are waiting to draw water] they and others [outsiders], they come before others. [When there are] others and their cattle, the others take some first, before their cattle.

T. B.M. 11:34 [When there are] their cattle and the cattle of others, their cattle come before the cattle of others.

T. B.M. 11:35 [When there are] others and their own laundry [to be done], [the needs of] the others come before the doing of their laundry.
When there is] their laundry and the laundry of others to be done, their laundry comes before the laundry of others.

T. B.M. 11:37 [When there are] the cattle of others and their [own] laundry [in line for water], the cattle of others comes before their laundry. [If] their irrigation-ditches and the cattle of others [are to draw water], their irrigation ditches come before the watering of the cattle of others. And all of them are taken into account at the end.

M. 1:6 They do not divide up a courtyard unless there will remain [an area of] four cubits [by four cubits] for this one, and four cubits [by four cubits] for that one; nor [do they divide up] a

field, unless there will remain nine qabs' space of ground for this one, and nine qabs' space for that one. Nor [do they divide up] a vegetable patch unless there will be a half-qab of space for this one and a half-qab of space for that one. Nor [do they divide up] (1) a banquet hall, (2) watchtower, (3) dovecote, (4) cloak; (5) bathhouse, or (6) olive press, unless there will be sufficient space for this one and sufficient space for that one [to make some reasonable use of his share]. This is the operative principle: Whatever may be divided and [retain] its original designation do they divide. But if not, they do not divide [such an object]. Under what circumstances? When both parties do not concur. But if both parties concur, even if the measurements are less than specified, they divide [the area]. But as to Sacred Scriptures, even though both parties concur, they do not divide them.

T. B.M. 11:10 They do not divide gateways unless there is sufficient for a share for this one and sufficient for a share for that one. [If] one of them said to his fellow, "You take the smaller share and give me my share," they accept that statement.

B. 1:6 I.5/11B A GATEHOUSE, A COVERED AREA OPEN AT THE SIDES, AND A BALCONY [REACHED BY A LADDER OR STAIR FROM THE COURTYARD] ARE ASSIGNED FOUR CUBITS. IF THERE WERE FIVE ROOMS OPENING ONTO THE BALCONY, HOWEVER, THEY ARE ASSIGNED ONLY THE FOUR CUBITS [AMONG ALL FIVE OF THEM].

T. B.M. 11:11 The doorways of a courtyard — the large ones belonging to one party, and the small ones belonging to the other party — the large ones are assigned only four cubits. And the small ones are assigned four cubits for each one. [If] one takes a large door, and one takes two small doorways — this one who takes the large door has a claim on only four cubits. And to that one who takes the two small doorways do they assign four cubits for each one. [If] there was a door there ten cubits wide, [the owner] takes four cubits space opposite it and four cubits space in the courtyard. [If it was] less than this, they give it its full measure opposite it, and they assign to him an area for bringing in and taking out [his goods] to the extent of four cubits in the courtyard.

T. B.M. 11:12 Manure which is found in the courtyard is divided in proportion to the doorways. And that which is found in a colonnade belongs to everybody. A door which opens onto a porch is assigned only four cubits. The porch itself has four cubits [in the courtyard below]. [Even if] five doors (which) open out onto a porch — to the porch is assigned in the courtyard only four cubits alone.

T. B.M. 11:13 He who has a colonnade inside his house — when it is enclosed, they assign him space for bringing in and taking out objects in the amount of four cubits in the courtyard. [if it is] not enclosed, Lo, it is equivalent to the rest of the entire courtyard.

T. B.M. 11:14 A Tyrian ladder is assigned four cubits. An Egyptian one is not assigned four cubits. But if it was fixed permanently with a nail, it is assigned four cubits. The wing of a building, cistern, and upper story do not have a claim on four cubits.

T. B.M. 11:15 The area around a cistern is assigned four cubits. The cistern nearest the water-channel is filled first. But if one second down the line went and filled his first, lo, this one is rewarded for his promptness. [If] one has brought a house inside his own house, or a garden inside his own garden, he has a claim on the common courtyard only of four cubits alone. He who purchases a house inside the house of his fellow, or a garden inside the garden of his fellow, has on the common courtyard a claim of only four cubits alone. He may not open up an entry into the courtyard of the joint holders. But he may open up into his own [area]. He who has an opening onto a courtyard — the others who share the courtyard may not force him to turn it into a door for the courtyard. For he has the power to say to them, "I want to go in to my own door with my own bundle."

T. B.M. 11:17 He who has a dwelling in another courtyard — the others who dwell in that courtyard may require him to share with them in the costs of making a door, bolt, and lock for the courtyard. But as to any other requirements of the courtyard, they are not able to impose upon him the requirement to share in the cost. But if he would dwell with them in that same courtyard they do have the power to impose upon him a share [of the cost] of all which is required for the common upkeep of the courtyard.

T. B.M. 11:18 People who live in a common courtyard may force one another to share in the cost of making a sidepost and crossbeam for an alleyway [for a commingling of the property for carrying on the Sabbath]. People who share a common valley have the power to force one another to share in the cost of making a trench and a rut.

T. B.M. 11:20 Five courtyards which make use of a single gutter, and the gutter was destroyed — all of them make use of the area which serves the first and the first makes use of that area by itself; and the rest use the area of the second, and the second uses that area by itself. The third of all of them uses its own area by itself and uses the area serving all of them. If it was made for doing laundry, they do not stop him from [doing laundry]. [If it was made] for rain, they do not stop him from using it for laundry.

T. B.M. 11:21 [If] five vegetable-gardens make use of a single water-channel, and the water-channel broke — all of them pay the cost of repairing it, with the one at the head of the channel. But the one at the head may pay the cost of fixing it by himself [for his own use only], and all the rest of them pay the cost of repairing it with the second [party]. But the second may repair it by himself. The one at the very bottom of all of them repairs it for his own use, but he also shares in the costs of repairing it with all of the others.

B. *Not Infringing upon the Property Rights of Others*

M. 2:1 One may not dig (1) a cistern near the cistern of his fellow, nor (2) a ditch, (3) cave, (4) water channel, or (5) laundry pool, unless one set it three handbreadths away from the wall of his fellow, and plastered it with plaster [to retain the water]. They set (1) olive refuse, (2) manure, (3) salt, (4) lime, or (5) stones three handbreadths from the wall of one's fellow, and plaster it with plaster. They set (1) seeds, (2) a plough, and (3) urine three handbreadths from a wall. And they set (1) a hand mill three handbreadths from the lower millstone, which is four from the upper millstone; and (2) the oven so that the wall is three handbreadths from the belly of the oven, or four from the rim.

T. 1:2 They set back a pool, laundry-pond, and vegetables from the wall of one's fellow by three handbreadths and plasters with plaster. And they set back seeds, a plough, and urine three handbreadths back from a wall [M. B.B. 2:1G].

T. 1:3 They set a hand-mill three handbreadths from the lower mill-stone, which is four from the upper mill-stone [M. B.B. 2:1H]. In the case of one turned by an ass, [one sets it] three handbreadths from the cone [lower mill-stone], which is four from the hopper.

M. 2:2 A person should not set up an oven in a room, unless there is a space of four cubits above it. [If] he was setting it up in the upper story, there has to be a layer of plaster under it three handbreadths thick, and in the case of a stove, a handbreadth thick. And if it did damage, [the owner of the oven] has to pay for the damage.

M. 2:3 A person should not open a bake shop or a dyer's shop under the granary of his fellow, nor a cattle stall. To be sure, in the case of wine they permitted doing so, but not [building] a cattle stall [under the wine cellar]. As to a shop in the courtyard, a person may object and tell [the shopkeeper], "I cannot sleep because of the noise of people coming in and the noise of people going out." One may [however] make utensils [and] go out and sell them in the market. Truly one has not got the power to object and to say, "I cannot sleep because of the noise of the hammer, the noise of the millstones, or the noise of the children."

T. B.M. 11:16 People who live in the same alleyway may force one another not to set up among them a tailor-shop or a tannery or any sort of craftsman's shop. But they are not able to prevent a neighbor from doing so.

T. 1:4 A man should not urinate against the wall of his fellow unless he kept [the urine] three handbreadths away from bricks, and a handbreadth away from stones. And in the case of what is cold, lo, this is permitted. To be sure, in the case of wine, they permitted doing so, but not a cattle stall [M. B.B. 2:3C–D]. And even though he limits him, it is only to improve its [the property's] value. If the [bake or dyer's] shop or cattle-stall was there before the storehouse [M. B.B. 2:3A], one has not got the power to stop him and to say, "I cannot sleep because of the noise of the hammer or because of the bad smell or because of the noise of the children" [M. B.B. 2:3H]. As to one's neighbor [however], they may not force him [to desist from annoying practices]. [If] one has a store in the public domain, and he wants to open a door for it into the courtyard [in which he lives], the joint-holders [of the courtyard] have the power to stop him, because he increases traffic for them. [If] he has a house in the courtyard as one of the joint-holders, and he wants to divide it up and to teach children in it, [the joint-holders of the courtyard] have the power to stop him, because he increases traffic for them. [If] he owns a roof in the public domain and he wants to build on it an upper story to open out into the courtyard, [the other joint-holders] have the power to stop him, because he increases traffic for them. What should he do instead? He makes a staircase and opens it up into his own house.

Y. 2:3 I.3 *It was taught: But [if he wanted to rent the store or the stall] to his neighbor, once he has accepted the agreement, he has not got the power to retract. [That is, once one such shop is accepted by the others in the court, they cannot object to someone else's running the same sort of shop.]*

M. 2:4 He whose wall was near the wall of his fellow may not build another wall next to it, unless he sets it four cubits back. [And if he builds a wall opposite his fellow's] windows, whether it is higher, lower, or opposite them, [he must set it back by] four cubits.

T. 1:5 They set a wall four cubits away from windows, above [and] on the sides, so that one will not see in; below, so that one will not peek in; and opposite, so that it will not cast a shadow [on the windows] [cf. M. B.B. 2:4].

M. 2:5 They set [one's] ladder four cubits away from the dovecote [of one's neighbor], so that the marten will not jump in [to the dovecote]. And [they set back] a wall from [one's neighbor's] roof gutter by four cubits, so that [the neighbor] will be able to set up his ladder [to clean out his gutter]. They set up a dovecote fifty cubits away from a town. And one should not set up a dovecote in his own domain, unless he has fifty cubits of space in every direction. But if he had bought it [and it was built in that place], even if it was only a quarter-qab of space, lo, he retains his established right.

T. 1:6 They set up a ladder four cubits away from the dovecote of one's neighbor, so that he will be able to set up his ladder; and a wall four cubits from one's neighbor's roof gutter, so that he should have place for plastering [the gutter]. [M. B.B. 2:5A–D].

T. 1:7 They set up a dovecote fifty cubits away from a town [M. B.B. 2:5E]. He who purchases a dovecote from his fellow, and it fell down — even if it is in a quarter-qab of space, Lo, one builds it up in its place [M. B.B. 2:5J].

M. 2:6 A fallen pigeon which is found within fifty cubits — lo, it belongs to the owner of the dovecote. [If it is found] outside of a fifty-cubit range, lo, it belongs to the one who finds it. [If] it was found between two dovecotes, [If it was] nearer to this one, it belongs to him, and [if it was] nearer to the other one, it belongs to him, and [if it was] exactly in between, the two of them divide it up.

T. 1:7 A fallen pigeon which is found between two dovecotes [M. B.B. 2:6E], if it is fifty cubits from this one and fifty cubits from that one, Lo, it belongs to the one who finds it [M. B.B. 2:6D].

M. 2:7 They keep a tree twenty-five cubits from a town, and in the case of a carob or a sycamore, fifty cubits. If the town was there first, one cuts down the tree and pays no compensation. And if the tree came first, one cuts down the tree but pays compensation. [If it is a matter of] doubt whether this came first or that came first, one cuts down the tree and pays no compensation.

M. 2:8 They set a permanent threshing floor fifty cubits from a town. A person should not build a permanent threshing floor on his own property, unless he owns fifty cubits of space in all directions. And he sets it some distance away from the crops of his fellow and from his ploughed land, so that it will not cause damage.

M. 2:9 They put carrion, graves, and tanneries at least fifty cubits away from a town. They make a tannery only at the east side of a town.

M. 2:10 They set up a pool for steeping flax away from a vegetable patch, leeks away from onions, and a mustard plant away from bees.

M. 2:11 They set up a tree twenty-five cubits away from a cistern, and in the case of a carob and a sycamore tree, fifty cubits, whether higher [than the cistern] or on the same level. If the cistern was there first, one cuts down the tree and pays the value. If the tree was there first, one may not cut down the tree. [If it is a matter of] doubt whether this was there first or that was there first, one may not cut it down.

M. 2:12 A person may not plant a tree near his fellow's field, unless he set it four cubits away from [the other's field]. All the same are vines or any other tree. [If] there was a fence in between, this one plants near the wall on one side, and that one plants near the wall on the other side. [If] the roots of one's [tree] extended into the domain of the other, one may cut them away down to three handbreadths, so that they will not hinder the plough. [If] one was digging a cistern, ditch, or cave, he may cut off the roots as far as he digs down, and the wood is his.

T. 1:13 A person may not plant a tree near his fellow's field unless he set it four cubits away from [the field] [M. B.B. 2:12A–B]. But if he wants, he may make a partition or wall.

M. 2:13 A tree which stretches over into the field of one's fellow — one cuts it away [to a height measured] as far as one reaches by an ox goad held over the plough, and, in the case of a carob and a sycamore, according to the measure of the plumb line [right at the boundary]. In the case of an irrigated field, [he may cut away] any sort of tree by the measure of the plumb line [right at the boundary].

M. 2:14 [In the case of] a tree which extends into the public domain, one cuts [the branches] so that a camel may pass underneath with its rider.

C. *Establishing Title to a Field through Usucaption*

M. 3:1 [Title by] usucaption of (1) houses, (2) cisterns, (3) trenches, (4) caves, (5) dovecotes, (6) bathhouses, (7) olive presses, (8) irrigated fields, (9) slaves, and anything which continually produces a yield — title by usucaption applying to them is three years, from day to day [that is, three full years]. A field which relies on rain — [title by] usucaption for it is three years, not from day to day.

M. 3:2 There are three regions so far as securing title through usucaption [is concerned]: Judah, Transjordan, and Galilee. [If] one was located in Judea, and [someone else] took possession of his property in Galilee, [or] was in Galilee, and someone took possession [of his property] in Judea, it is not an effective act of securing title through usucaption unless [the owner] is with [the squatter in the same province].

M. 3:3 Any act of usucaption [along] with which [there] is no claim [on the property being utilized] is no act of securing title through usucaption. How so? [If] he said to him, "What are you doing on my property," and the other party answered him, "But no one ever said a thing to me!" — This is no act of securing title through usucaption. [If he answered,] "For you sold it to me," "You gave it to me as a gift," "Your father sold it to me," "Your father gave it to me as a gift" — Lo, this is a valid act of securing title through usucaption. He who holds possession because of an inheritance [from the previous owner] requires no further claim [in his own behalf]. (1) Craftsmen, partners, sharecroppers, and trustees are not able to secure title through usucaption. (2) A husband has no claim of usucaption in his wife's property, (3) nor does a wife have a claim of usucaption in her husband's property, (4) nor a father in his son's property, (5) nor a son in his father's property. Under what circumstances? In the case of one who effects possession through usucaption. But in the case of one who gives a gift, or of brothers who divide an estate, and of one who seizes the property of a proselyte, [if] one has locked up, walled in, or broken down in any measure at all — lo, this constitutes securing a claim through usucaption.

T. 2:2 He who purchases a field from another purchaser — even though the original purchaser says, "It is stolen by me," he has not got the power to destroy the right of this one. He who enjoys the usufruct of a field by reason of a deed, and it turns out that his deed is invalid — Lo, this does not constitute valid securing of title through usucaption.

T. 2:3 He who enjoys the usufruct of a field in the assumption that it belongs to him, and [someone else] produced a writ against him that he had sold it to him, or that he had given it to him as a gift — let the writ be confirmed through its signatories [cf. M. B.B. 3:3F]. If he claimed, "I wrote this document, but I did not receive the money," "It is a fraudulent writ which is in your possession" — everything follows usucaption.

T. 2:4 He who enjoys the usufruct of a field for six years, and [the other party] complained against him for the first three years [of his usucaption] — and at the end, the holder of the field said to him, "But you yourself sold it to me," "You yourself gave it to me as a gift" — [M. B.B. 3:3F] if it is by reason of his original complaint, he has not secured title through usucaption. For any claim, part of which is nullified, is deemed to be wholly nullified.

T. 2:5 Under what circumstances have they ruled, "A share-cropper is given an oath when he is not subject to a claim"? So long as he is a sharecropper. When a share-cropper leaves his status as share-cropper of this field, lo, he is like anybody else. A guardian — when a guardian leaves his status as guardian, he is like anybody else. A son who took his share in his father's estate [cf. M. B.B. 3:3M] — a woman who was divorced [cf. M. B.B. 3:3K] — Lo, they are like everybody else. Those who accept bailments, shepherds, and a hired hand are not able to effect title through usucaption [of the field on which they work or for which they bear responsibility].

T. 2:6 Craftsmen are not able to effect title through usucaption [M. B.B. 3:3I]. How so? [If] one saw his utensils at a laundry-man's shop, or his slave at a crafts-man's shop, [if the laundryman or the craftsman] said to him, "You sold them to me," or, "You gave them to me as a gift" [cf. M. B.B. 3:3F], it is not a valid claim of title through usucaption. [If he said], "You told me to sell them," or, "You told me to give them away as a gift," lo, this constitutes a valid claim of effecting title through usucaption.

T. 2:11 One who seizes the property of a proselyte, and has locked up, walled in, or broken down in any measure at all — lo, this constitutes securing a claim through usucaption [M. B.B. 3:3S–U]. [If] one party has locked up, and another party has walled in, lo, this constitutes securing a claim through usucaption. [If] two people have locked up or walled in, lo, this constitutes securing a claim through usucaption. [If the proselyte] had ten fields, once one has secured a title through usucaption to one of them, he has secured a title through usucaption to all of them. [If the proselyte had] ten slaves, even though one has secured title through usucaption to one of them, he has not secured title through usucaption to all of them. [If he had] utensils and slaves, [if] one has made acquisition of the utensils, he has not made acquisition of the slaves. [If he has made acquisition] of the slaves, he has not made acquisition of the utensils. [If he had] utensils and real estate, [if] one has made acquisition of the utensils, he has not made acquisition of the real estate. [If he has] made acquisition of the real estate, he has not made acquisition of the utensils. [If he had] slaves and real estate, [if] one has made acquisition of the slaves, he has made acquisition of the real estate. [If he has made acquisition of] the real estate, he has not made acquisition of the slaves.

T. 2:12 [If] one has purchased from another party ten fields, as soon as he has acquired title through usucaption to one of them, he has acquired title through usucaption to all of them. [If] he leased from him ten fields, as soon as he has acquired title through usucaption to one of them, he has acquired title through usucaption to all of them. [If he acquired] ten slaves, even though he has acquired title through usucaption to one of them, he has not acquired title through usucaption to all of them [If] he purchased part and rented part and acquired title [of part] through usucaption, whether this involves the portion which is acquired through purchase or the portion which is acquired through rental, lo, this constitutes a valid act of securing title through usucaption.

T. 2:13 A. Movable property is acquired along with real estate through an exchange of money, a document, and usucaption. How so? [If] one said to him, "The courtyard and everything which is in it do I sell to you," once [the purchaser] has written the document, [the seller] has received the money, and [the purchaser] has effected usucaption of one of [the objects in the courtyard], he has acquired title through usucaption to all of them. [If one has] a place for setting up an oven or a double-stove in a courtyard, these are not a valid mode of securing title through usucaption [M. B.B. 3:5B]. [If] one has a beam [setting] on them in any measure at all, Lo, this constitutes a valid act of securing title through usucaption. [Merely keeping] chickens in a courtyard is not a valid mode of securing title through usucaption. [If] one made a roof for them ten handbreadths high, Lo, this is a valid means of securing title through usucaption. A gutter-spout does not [impart title through] usucaption, but the place on which it discharges is subject to securing of title through usucaption [M. B.B. 3:6A]. [Having] a doorway in a courtyard, even though one has stopped it up — this is a valid means of securing title through usucaption. [If] one has broken down the sideposts, this is not a valid means of securing title through usucaption.

M. 3:4 [If] two were testifying for another party that he has enjoyed the usufruct of the property for three years, and they turn out to be false witnesses, they must pay to [the original

owner] full restitution (Deut. 19:19). [If] two witnesses [testify] concerning the first year, two concerning the second, and two concerning the third — They divide up [the costs of restitution] among themselves. Three brothers, and another party joins together with [each of] them — lo, these constitute three distinct acts of testimony, and they count as a single act of witness when the evidence is proved false.

T. 2:7 [Title by] usucaption is secured in three years [of usufruct]. [If] the father effected usucaption for one year and the son for two years, the father for two years and the son for one year, lo, this constitutes a valid act of securing title by usucaption. [If] the father [effected usucaption] for one year, the son for one year, and a purchaser [from the father and son] for one year, Lo, this constitutes a valid act of securing title by usucaption.

T. 2:8 [If a squatter] held the property in usucaption in the presence of the father [the original owner] for one year and in the presence of the son for two years, the father for two years and the son for one year, Lo, this constitutes a valid act of securing title by usucaption. [If one held the property in usucaption in the presence of] the father for one year, the son for one year, and a purchaser for one year, Lo, this constitutes a valid act of securing title by usucaption.

T. 2:9 [If] one held a field in usucaption in the presence of two for one year, in the presence of two in the second year, and in the presence of two in the third year, Lo, these constitute three distinct acts of testimony, and they count as a single act of witness when the evidence is proved false [M. B.B. 3:4G–H]. [If] the testimony of the first group proved false, lo, one has in his possession [valid evidence about] two years. [If] the second group proved false, lo, he has in his possession [valid evidence about] one year. [If] the third group proved false, he has nothing whatever in hand. [If] the first group and the last group are the same, and they turn out to be false witnesses, [if] the testimony which turned out to be false concerned the first year, he has nothing at all in hand. [If it concerned] the second [year] lo, he has [valid evidence about] one year in hand. [If it concerned] the third [year], lo, he has [valid evidence about] two years in hand.

M. 3:5 What are [usages] that are effective in the securing of title through usucaption, and what are [usages] that are not effective in the securing of title through usucaption? [If] one put (1) cattle in a courtyard, (2) an oven, (3) double stove, (4) millstone, (5) raised chickens, or (6) put his manure, in a courtyard — this is not an effective mode of securing title through usucaption. But [If] (1) he made a partition for his beast ten handbreadths high, and so, too, (2) for an oven; so, too, (3) for a double stove; so, too, (4) for a millstone — [If] (5) he brought his chickens into the house, or (6) made a place for his manure three handbreadths deep or three handbreadths high — Lo, this is an effective mode of securing title through usucaption.

M. 3:6 The right to place a gutter spout does not [impart title through] usucaption [so that the spout still may be moved], but the place on which it discharges does impart title through usucaption [so that the place must be left for its present purpose]. A gutter does [impart title through] usucaption. An Egyptian ladder does not [impart title through] usucaption, but a Tyrian ladder does [impart title through] usucaption. An Egyptian window does not [impart title through] usucaption, but a Tyrian window does [impart title through] usucaption. What is an Egyptian window? Any through which the head of a human being cannot squeeze. A projection [if it extends] a handbreadth [or more] does [impart title through] usucaption, and concomitantly,] one has the power to protest [its being made]. [If it projects] less than a handbreadth, it is not subject to [imparting title through] usucaption, and one has not got the power to protest [its being made].

M. 3:7 A person should not open his windows into the courtyard of which he is one of the jointholders. [If] he purchased a house in another courtyard [which adjoins the one in which he is living], he may not make an opening into the courtyard of which he is one of the jointholders. [If] he built an upper story on his house, he should not make an opening for it into a courtyard of which he is one of the jointholders. But if he wanted, he may build a [new] room inside of his house, or he builds an upper story on top of his house, and he makes an opening for it into his house. One should not open up in a courtyard of which he is one of the jointholders a doorway opposite the doorway [of another resident], or a window opposite [another's] window. [If] it was small, he should not enlarge it. [If it was] a single one, he should not make it into two. But he may open into the public domain a doorway opposite [another's] doorway [in the public domain], or a window opposite [another's] window [in the public domain]. If it was small, he may enlarge it. If it was a single one, he may make it into two.

T. 2:15 [If] one has built a bathhouse next door to the bathhouse of his fellow, or a store next to the store of his fellow, [the owner of the bathhouse or store next door] cannot prevent him [from doing so], saying to him, "You have brought ruin on me." For the former may say to him, "Just as you do on your property, so I [have every right to] do on mine." [If] one's rain-water was pouring off the roof of his fellow, and the latter went and stopped it up, one has the right to prevent him from doing so, unless he knows in which direction he is going to lead it down. [If] the public way or a stream passed through one's field, and one went and fenced off [the road or the stream] — [so that now] people cross the field of his fellow, the latter has not got the power to stop him, and to say to him, "You have brought ruin on me." For the other party may say to him, "Just as I do on my property, so you have every right to do on yours."

T. 2:16 [If] one owns a cistern in the courtyard of his fellow and lo, the owner of the courtyard wants to dig another cistern for his own use, one has the power to stop him. But he may not make it into a well for the public, or into an immersion pool for the public. And he may not draw water and water [his beasts], [or] draw water and sell it. But he may draw water and water his cattle in the market place, draw water and sell it in the market place.

M. 3:8 They do not hollow out a space under the public domain — cisterns, ditches, or caves. [if it is so strong that] a wagon can go over it carrying stones. They do not extend projections and balconies over the public domain. But if one wanted, he brings in [his wall] into his own property and then projects [a balcony]. [If] one has purchased a courtyard, and in it are projections and balconies, lo, this one retains his right [to keep them as they are].

T. 2:17 [If] one has bought a courtyard and in it were projections and balconies and they fell down, lo, this person has the right to rebuild them in their original locations [cf. M. B.B. 3:8G]. He may not paint, plaster, or stucco them. [If] he bought a house which was painted, plastered, or stuccoed, lo, he retains the right to keep them that way [cf. M. B.B. 3:8E–G]. A man may plaster his entire house with plaster, but he leaves a small bit unplastered, as a memorial to Jerusalem. A woman puts on all her makeup but leaves off some small thing, as a memorial to Jerusalem.

D. *Transferring Real Estate and Movables through Sale*

M. 4:1 He who sells a house has not sold (1) the extension, even though [the extension] opens into [the house], (2) the room behind [the house], or (3) the roof, if it has a parapet ten handbreadths high.

M. 4:2 Nor [has he sold] (4) the cistern, or (5) the cellar, even though he wrote him [in the deed], "The depth and height." [If the seller] sold [the cistern or cellar] to someone else, he has to buy a right-of-way for himself."

M. 4:3 He who sells a house has sold the door but not the key. He has sold a permanent mortar but not a movable one. He has sold the convex millstone but not the concave millstone, nor the oven or the double stove. When he said to him [in the deed], "It and everything which is in it" — lo, all of them are sold.

T. 3:1 A. He who sells a house has sold the door [M. B.B. 4:3A], the bolt, lock, and hollowed-out-mortar. But he has not sold the oven, double-stove, millstones, or permanent mortar [cf. M. B.B. 4:3B–D]. If he said to him, "And what is in it I sell to you," lo, all of them are sold. And even though he said to him, "And everything which is in it I sell to you," he has not sold the cistern, ditch, extensions, cellars, or caves which are in it [M. B.B. 4:1A, 4:2A–B]. If so, why is it written [in the deed of sale], "The depth and the height" [M. B.B. 4:2B]? That if he wanted to raise up [and sell what is higher up], he has the right to raise up; if he wanted to lower [and sell what is in the ground], he has the right to lower. Whatever is not sold in the house is sold [in a sale] of the courtyard. He who sells the courtyard has sold only the open space of the courtyard [M. B.B. 4:4F]. He who sells the courtyard has sold the houses on the inside and the houses on the outside [cf. M. B.B. 4:4A], but he has not sold the hangings, curtains, or bathhouses which are inside of it. But if they were constructed for use in the courtyard, lo, all of them are sold. A resting place which is made for use with the courtyard is sold. [If it is made] for use by the public, it is not sold. Stores which open up inward are sold with it. Those which open up outward are not sold with it. Those which open up both inward and outward — lo, they are sold with it.

M. 4:4 He who sells a courtyard has sold the houses, cisterns, trenches, and caves, but not the movables. If he said to him, "It and everything which is in it," lo, all of them are sold. One way or the other, he has not sold him the bathhouse or the olive press which are in it.

M. 4:5 He who sells an olive press has sold the vat, grindstone, and posts. But he has not sold the pressing boards, wheel, or beam. If he said, "It and everything which is in it," all of them are sold.

T. 3:2 He who sells an olive press has sold the moulds, tanks, press-beams, and lower millstones. But he has not sold the sacks, packing bags, or upper millstones. But if he had said to him, "It and everything which is in it I sell to you," lo, all of them are sold. But even though he has said to him, "It and everything which is in it," he has not sold to him the cistern, ditch, extensions, cellars, or caves which are in it. But if he said to him, "It and everything which is in it I sell to you," Lo, all of them are sold [cf. M. B.B. 4:5].

M. 4:6 He who sells a bathhouse has not sold the boards, benches, or hangings. If he said, "It and everything which is in it," lo, all of them are sold. One way or the other, he has not sold the water jugs or woodsheds.

T. 3:3 He who sells a bathhouse has sold the inner rooms, outer rooms, kettle-room, towel-room, and dressing-room. But he has not sold the kettles, the towels, or the cupboards which are in it. But if he said to him, "It and everything which is in it I sell to you," lo, all of them are sold. And even though he said to him, "It and everything which is in it I sell to you," he has not sold to him the water-channels from which [the bathhouse] derives [water] in the dry season or the rainy season, and also not the wood-shed [cf. M. B.B. 4:6D]. But if he had said to him, "The bathhouse and everything which is needed for using it do I sell to you," all of them are sold.

M. 4:7 He who sells a town has sold the houses, cisterns, ditches, caves, bathhouses, dovecotes, olive presses, and irrigated fields but not the movables If he said to him, "It and everything which is in it," even though there are cattle and slaves in it, lo, all of them are sold.

M. 4:8 He who sells a field has sold (1) the stones which are needed for it, (2) the canes in the vineyard which are needed for it, and (3) the crop which is yet unplucked up from the ground; He also has sold]: (4) a partition of reeds which covers less than a quarter-qab of space of ground, (5) the watchman's house which is not fastened down with mortar, (6) the carob which was not grafted, and (7) the young sycamores.

T. 3:4 He who sells a field has not sold the wine-press or the watchman's hut [M. B.B. 4:8B], even though it is a vineyard. He sells him [along with the field] all the trees therein except for a carob which was grafted and cropped sycamores [M. B.B. 4:9D6–7].

M. 4:9 But he has not sold (1) the stones which are not needed for it, (2) the canes in the vineyard which are not needed for it, (3) the crop which has already been plucked up from the ground. If he had said to him, "It and everything which is in it," lo, all of them are sold. One way or the other, he has not sold to him (4) a partition of reeds which covers a quarter-qab of space of ground, (5) a watchman's house which is fastened down with mortar, (6) a carob which was grafted, and (7) cropped sycamores. (8) A cistern, (9) winepress, or (10) dovecote, whether they are lying waste or in use. Under what circumstances? In the case of one who sells [the aforelisted properties]. But in the case of one who gives these things as a gift, he [willingly] hands over all of them [in a liberal spirit]. Brothers who divided [an estate] — Once they have acquired possession of a field, they have acquired possession of all of them [and no longer may retract] — He who lays hold [through usucaption, seeking title] of the property of a deceased proselyte [lacking Israelite heirs], once he has acquired possession of a field, has acquired possession of all of them. He who declares a field sanctified has declared all of them sanctified.

T. 3:5A. Whatever is not sold in a field is sold in a town. He who sells a town — The town-clerk is not sold along with it. But if he had said to him, "It and everything which is in it I sell you," all of them are sold. And even though he had said to him, "It and everything which is in it I sell to you," he has not sold him the outlying parts or suburbs, or the thickets which are set apart by themselves, or the vivarium for wild beasts, fowl, and fish.

T. 3:6 He who sells a vineyard has sold the reeds, poles, and sycamore beams which are in it. But he has not sold the wood, stones, or joists, whether used for its furrow or for its fence, or the refuse, or the sycamore beams which are in it. [If] he sold him all the trees except for "half of a carob which is grafted, which is in such and such a place," and "half of a cropped sycamore, which is in such and such a place," all the rest of the carobs are not sold, and all the rest of the cropped [sycamores] are not sold.

T. 3:7 Brothers who divided what belongs to them in some other location, even if they are in Judah and the property is in Galilee, they are in Galilee and the property is in Judah, once one of them has acquired possession of [the properties, wherever they are located], all of them have acquired possession [cf. M. B.B. 4:9Q–R]. If he was with him in the same province, once he has accepted upon himself [the ownership of the property], lo, this one has acquired possession.

M. 5:1 He who sells a ship has sold (1) the mast, (2) sail, and (3) anchor, and whatever steers it. But he has not sold (1) the slaves, (2) packing bags, or (3) lading. And if [the seller] had said to [the buyer] "It and everything which is in it," lo, all of them are sold. (1) [If] he sold the wagon, he has not sold the mules. (2) [If] he sold the mules, he has not sold the wagon. (3) [If] he sold the yoke, he has not sold the oxen. (4) [If] he sold the oxen, he has not sold the yoke. The price proves nothing.

T. 4:1 He who sells a ship has sold the wooden implements and the water-tank on it. But he has not sold the deck-cabins, the anchor [vs. M. B.B. 5:1A3], the yard, or the lighter. [If] he has sold the yoke, he has sold the cow. [If] he has sold the cow, he has sold the yoke. [If] he has sold the wagon, he has sold the cow. [If] he has sold the cow, he has not sold the wagon. If he has (not) sold the yoke, he has not sold the oxen. If he has sold the oxen, he has not sold the yoke.

M. 5:2 He who sells an ass has not sold its trappings.

T. 4:3 He who sells a slave-girl to his fellow has sold the clothing which is on her, even if there are a hundred pieces. But he has not sold the silks, rings, nose-rings, or necklace around her neck. But if he said to him, "A slave-girl and everything which is on her do I sell to you," even though she is wearing clothing worth a hundred maneh lo, all of them are sold.

T. 4:4 "A pregnant slave-girl I sell to you," A pregnant cow I sell to you" — he has sold the offspring. "A nursing slave-girl I sell to you" — he has not sold the offspring.

T. 4:5 He who sells a slave-girl to his fellow, stipulating that there are blemishes on her, and he said to him, "She is sick," "She is an idiot," "She is epileptic," "She is dull," and there is on her yet another blemish and he inserted it [when listing the other] blemishes — Lo, this is a purchase made in error. [If] he specified that blemish and did not specify any other blemish along with it, this is not a purchase made in error.

T. 4:6 He who sells a cow to his fellow stipulating that there are blemishes on it, and he said to him, "She is a borer," "She is a biter," "She is a butter," "She is prone to lie down," if there was some other blemish on it and he inserted it [in listing the other] blemishes, Lo, this is a purchase made in error. But if he told him about that blemish and did not refer to any other blemish, this is not a purchase made in error.

T. 4:7 He who sells his boy-slave to his fellow, and [the slave] turns out to be a thief or swindler, or if he joined a band of thugs or was under sentence of the government, Lo, this is a purchase made in error. [If he sold him] a book of deer-hide, and it turned out to be of parchment, or if there is some sort of error in it between one page and another, Lo, this is not sold.

M. 5:3 (1) He who sells an ass has sold the foal. (2) [If] he sold the cow, he has not sold its offspring. (3) [If] he sold a dung heap, he has sold the dung on it. (4) [If] he sold a cistern, he has sold its water. (5) [If] he sold a beehive, he has sold the bees. (6) [If] he has sold the dovecote, he has sold the pigeons. (1) He who purchases "the fruit of a dovecote" from his fellow lets go the first pair that are hatched. (2) [If he bought] "the fruit of a beehive," he takes three swarms, and then [the seller] makes the rest sterile. [If he bought] honeycombs, he leaves two honeycombs (4) [If he bought] olive trees to cut down, he leaves two shoots.

T. 4:7 [If] one has sold a dovecote, he has sold the pigeons [M. B.B. 5:3F]. [If] he has sold the pigeons, he has sold the dovecote. [If] he has sold the beehive, he has sold the bees [M. B.B. 5:3E]. [If] he has sold the bees, he has sold the beehive. [If] he sold honeycombs, he has not got the right to sterilize all of them at once. But he leaves the two outside honeycombs, and the remainder are available for his use [cf. M. B.B. 5:3H]. And if there are available only those, he has not got the right to touch them. [If he purchased] olive-trees to cut down, he has not got the right to uproot all of them at once. But he leaves two shoots with their root and takes the rest [M. B.B. 5:3J]. But in the case of cedar trees and palm trees he uproots them and takes what he wants. In the case of vine-shoots and reeds, he takes the shrubs.

M. 5:4 He who buys two trees in his fellow's field, (1) lo, this party has not bought the ground [on which they are growing]. (2) [If] they grew up, [the landowner] may not trim them. (3) What sprouts from the stem belongs to [the purchaser], [but what sprouts] from the roots belongs to the owner of the land. (4) And if [the trees] died, [the owner of the trees] has no [claim on the] land. (1) [If] he bought three, he has [also] bought the ground [on which they are growing]. (2) [If] they grew up, [the landowner] may trim them. (3) And what sprouts both from the stem and from the roots belongs to [the purchaser]. (4) And if they died, he has a claim on the land.

T. 4:9 He who buys a single tree in the property of his fellow — Lo, this one has not bought the ground. As to all the ground which is under it and outside it as much as is required for the gatherer and his basket — neither this one nor that one has the right to sow. [If] he bought two trees, he has bought the ground [vs. M. B.B. 5:4A–B]. If he bought the tree which is between them, [he has bought] whatever is round about, as much as is required for the gatherer and his basket, and the owner of the field has the right to lop off branches [cf. M. B.B. 5:4I].

T. 4:11 And how near to one another must they be? So that an ox may pass between them with its utensils. And how far may they be from one another? Ten in a planting of a se'ah's field. [If there are] fewer than this or more than this, or if he purchased them in sequence [and not all at once], or if he bought all three of them simultaneously, he has purchased neither the ground nor the tree which is between them.

T. 4:12 He who declares three trees in a planting of ten to a seah to be sanctified has sanctified the ground, but not the tree which is between them. And when he redeems them [from the ownership of the Temple by paying their value], he redeems an area suitable for sowing a homer of barley-seed for fifty silver sheqels. [If] it is less than this or more than this, or if he sanctified them one after the other, or if he sanctified all three of them simultaneously, he has not sanctified the ground or the tree which is between them. And not only so, but even if he went and sanctified the field, when he goes to redeem it, he redeems the tree by itself and the field by itself.

T. 4:13 Two who planted a vineyard — this one keeps distant by two cubits and plants his crop, and that one keeps distant by two cubits and plants his crop. [If] the vineyard was cut down or dried out, the land belongs to both of them. Two who divided up a field, and one of them went and planted his crop — he sets his crop four cubits back [from the ground of the other] and plants it. [If] the vineyard was cut down or dried up, the ground belongs to the owner of the vineyard. Two who planted a vineyard, and one of them went and cut down his share — he [has to] leave a space of four cubits and then he may sow his seed. [If] the vineyard was cut down or dried up, the ground belongs to the owner of the field.

T. 4:14 Two who divided [a field] — one takes a vineyard, and the other takes a "white field" [one planted with grain] — they give him four cubits at the side of the "white field." For it was on that condition that the owner of the vineyard accepted the arrangement. [If] the vineyard was cut down or dried up, the ground belongs to the owner of the vineyard.

M. 5:5 (1) He who sells the head [in the case of] large cattle has not sold the feet. (2) [If] he sold the feet, he has not sold the head. (3) [If] he sold the lungs, he has not sold the liver. (4) [If] he sold the liver, he has not sold the lungs. But in the case of a small beast, (1) [if] he has sold the head, he has sold the feet. (2) [If] he has sold the feet, he has not sold the head. (3) [If] he has sold the lungs, he has sold the liver. [If] he has sold the liver, he has not sold the lungs.

T. 4:8 He who sells the head [of a beast which has been slaughtered] has not sold the cheek. If the butcher was a priest, lo, this is sold. He who sells the head in the case of a large beast has not sold the feet. In a place in which they are accustomed to be sold, lo, these are sold.

ii. *Licit Commercial Transactions*

A. *Conditions of Irrevocable Transfer of Goods*

M. 5:6 There are four rules in the case of those who sell: [If] one has sold good wheat and it turns out to be bad, the purchaser has the power to retract. [If one has sold] bad wheat and it turns out to be good, the seller has the power to retract. [If he has claimed to sell] bad wheat, and it turns out to be bad, [or if he claimed to sell] good wheat and it turns out to be good, neither one of them has the power to retract. [If one sold it as] (1) dark-colored, and it turns out to be white, white, and it turned out to be dark, (2) olive wood, and it turned out to be sycamore [wood], sycamore wood, and it turned out to be olive wood, (3) wine, and it turned out to be vinegar, vinegar, and it turned out to be wine, both parties have the power to retract.

T. 5:1 There are four rules in the case of those who sell [M. B.B. 5:6A]. Under what circumstances? In the case of [the use of] a measure which does not belong to either one of them. But in the case of a measure which belonged to one of them, as soon as the first party [has made acquisition], he has acquired [the item in the sale, and there can be no retraction]. Under what circumstances? [When the transaction takes place] in the public domain, or in a courtyard which does not belong to either one of them. But if the transaction takes place in the domain of the purchaser once he has accepted [the deal], lo, this one has made acquisition. [And if it took place] in the domain of the seller, [unless the purchaser] will lift up [the object] or unless he will remove it from the domain of the owner, [the transaction is not final]. [If it was] in the domain of this party with whom the objects for sale had been left as a bailment, the sale is not complete until he will agree or until he will rent him the place in which the bailment is located].

M. 5:7 He who sells produce to his fellow — [If the buyer] drew it but did not measure it, he has acquired possession of it. [If] he measured it but did not draw it [to himself], he has not acquired possession. If he was smart, he will rent the place [in which the produce is located]. He who purchases flax from his fellow — lo, this one has not acquired possession until he will move it from one place to another. But if it was attached to the ground and he has plucked any small quantity of it, he has acquired possession.

T. 5:2 Under what circumstances have they ruled, "Movables are acquired through [being] drawn [to the purchaser]" [cf. M. B.B. 5:7B–C]? [When the transaction takes place] in the domain of the owner, or in a courtyard which does not belong to either one of them. [But if it takes place] in the domain of the purchaser, once he has accepted [the deal], lo, this one has made acquisition. [And if it takes place] in the domain of the seller, [the deal is not consummated] until the purchaser will raise up the object or will remove it from the domain of the owner. [If it takes place] in the domain of this one with whom the objects are left as a bailment, the transaction is not complete until [the bailee] accepts the deal, or until he rents [to the purchaser] the place in which the bailment is located [cf. M. B.B. 5:7D].

M. 5:8 He who sells wine or oil to his fellow, and [the price] rose or fell, if this took place before the measure had been filled up, [the price advantage goes] to the seller. [If this took place] after the measure had been filled up, [the price advantage goes] to the purchaser. And if there was a middleman between them, [and] the jar was broken, it is broken [to the disadvantage of] the middleman. [After emptying the measure], [the seller] is liable to let three drops drip [further into the utensil of the buyer]. [If thereafter] he turned the measure over and drained it, lo [what is drained off] goes to the seller. But the shopkeeper is not liable to let three more drops drip.

M. 5:9 He who sends his child to the storekeeper with a pondion in his hand, and [the storekeeper] measured out for him an issar's worth of oil [half a pondion] and give him an issar [in change], and [the child] broke the flask or lost the issar [of change] — the storekeeper is liable [to make it up].

M. 5:10 A wholesaler must clean off his measures once every thirty days, and a householder once every twelve months. The storekeeper (1) cleans off his measures twice a week, (2) polishes his weights once a week, and (3) cleans his scales after each and every weighing.

M. 5:11 And [a shopkeeper] is liable to let the scales go down by a handbreadth [to the buyer's advantage]. [If] he was measuring out for him exactly, he has to give him an overweight — One part in ten for liquid measure, one part in twenty for dry measure. In a place in which they are accustomed to measure with small measures, one must not measure with large measures; With large ones, one must not measure with small; [In a place in which it is customary] to smooth down [what is in the measure], one should not heap it up; To heap it up, one should not smooth it down.

T. 5:4 He who sells wine by the vessel — all the overflow — lo, it belongs to the seller. And he who sells at retail in the market — the liquids which are on the outer parts of the funnel — lo, they belong to the purchaser. And one should not pour [wine] from the jar, but he drains [wine] through a strainer. And olive oil which congealed — they do not dilute it.

T. 5:5 A storekeeper has not got the right to make the liquid bubble in the measure, or to make it bound, or to turn it on its side. And he may not make the scales long on one side and short on the other side. And he may not make the strike thick on one side and thin on the other side.

T. 5:6 Nor should [a shopkeeper] mix water in wine, juice of glacium in oil, juice of wild strawberries in honey, meal in honey, vinegar in oil, gum in myrrh, sand in beams, vine-leaves in aromatic leaves, ass-milk in resin, red paint in brine or coriander in pepper.

T. 5:7 A storekeeper dries off his measures for oil once a week, and those for wine, once sediment forms. And he should not put his weights or measures into salt, because that diminishes them. As it is said, "For all who do such things, all who act dishonestly, are an abomination to the Lord your God" (Deut. 25:16).

T. 5:8 [If] one was selling to his fellow logs, half-logs, quarter-logs, and eight-logs, when he comes to reckon up with him, he should not say to him, "Fill the measure up for me," "Forgive me this qortob [morsel]," for the reliability of measures depends only on the people who use them. And the omnipresent has profaned his name on their account.

T. 5:9 One should not make his weights out of tin, lead, cassiterum, or metal, but only out of glass. [If] one wanted to buy ten liters, he should not say to him, "Weigh out for me each one and push the scale down for each one by itself," [cf. M. B.B. 5:11D]. But he weighs all of them out for him at once. [If] he wanted to buy from him three quarters of a liter, he weighs out for him a liter and removes a quarter-liter from it. [If] he wanted to buy a half-liter, he weighs out a liter for him and removes a half-liter from it. [If] he wanted to buy a quarter-liter, he weighs out for him a quarter-liter. [If] he wanted a triple qab, he weighs out for him a se'ah and removes from it a triple-qab. [If] he wanted from him four qabs, he measures out for him a se'ah's volume and removes from it four qabs. [If] he wanted from him two qabs, he hands over to him two qabs.

T. 5:10 A person should not make a short-weight or an excess-weight in his house, because with it he may deceive others. In any place do they make a triple-qab and a half-triple-qab, a qab and a half-qab, a quarter-qab and a half-quarter-qab, a tomen, a half-tomen; and in liquid-measure: a hin, a half-hin, a third-hin, a quarter-hin, a log, a half-log, a quarter-log, an eighth-log, and a half-eighth, and an eighth of an eighth — this is a qartob.

T. 5:11 A perutah of which they have spoken is one out of eight perutot to an issar; an issar is one twenty-fourth of a denar.

B. *Unstated Stipulations in Commercial Transactions 6:1–7:4*

M. 6:1 He who sells produce [consisting of grain] to his fellow [not specifying whether it is for food or for seed], and they did not sprout, and even if it was flax seed, he is not liable to make it up.

M. 6:2 He who sells produce to his fellow — lo, [the buyer] must agree to receive a quarter-qab of spoiled produce per seah. (1) [If he bought] figs, he must agree to accept ten maggoty ones per hundred. (2) [If he bought] a cellar of wine, he must agree

to accept ten sour jars per hundred. (3) [If he bought] jars in Sharon, he must agree to accept ten faulty ones per hundred.

T. 6:2 A. He who sells produce to his fellow — lo, [the buyer] must agree to receive a quarter-qab of spoiled produce per se'ah [M. B.B. 6:2A–B]. [If he sold] barley, [the buyer] must agree to receive a quarter-qab of pulse per se'ah. [If he sold] cucumbers, [the buyer] must agree to receive ten bitter ones per hundred.

T. 6:3 For a hundred jars he must agree to receive ten faulty ones, made tight by a lining of sulphur or pitch [cf. M. B.B. 6:2E]. [If there are] more than that, in all instances he returns the rest to him and gets his money back.

T. 6:4 He who purchases jars [of wine] from his fellow and they turn out to be faulty and break — [the seller] is liable to pay him back the cost of the jars, but not the cost of the wine.

T. 6:6 He who sells a cellar [of wine] to his fellow without further specification — in this case they have said, He must agree to accept ten sour jars per hundred [M. B.B. 6:20].

B. 6:2 I.1 94A HE WHO SELLS PRODUCE TO HIS FELLOW — IN THE CASE OF WHEAT, THE BUYER MUST ACCEPT A QUARTER-QAB OF PULSE FOR EACH SEAH; IN THE CASE OF BARLEY, HE HAS TO ACCEPT A QUARTER-QAB OF CHAFF PER SEAH; IN THE CASE OF LENTILS, HE MUST ACCEPT A QUARTER-QAB OF SANDY MATTER PER SEAH.

M. 6:3 He who sells wine to his fellow that went sour, is not liable to make it up. But if it was known that his wine would turn sour, lo, this is deemed a purchase made in error [and null]. And if he had said to him, "I'm selling you spiced wine," he is liable to guarantee it [and make it up if it goes sour] up to Pentecost. [If he said it is] old [wine, it must be] last year's. [If he said it is] vintage old [it must be] from the year before last.

T. 6:5 He who sells wine to his fellow without further specification is liable to make it up [if it goes sour] up to Passover. [If it is] spiced [wine], he is liable to make it up [if it goes sour] until Pentecost [M. B.B. 6:3D]. If he said it was] vintage wine, he is liable to make it up, [if it goes sour] up to the Festival [M. B.B. 6:3F].

T. 6:7 "A jug of wine I sell you" — he must give him good wine. "A jug of this wine I sell you" — he gives him wine which is acceptable in a store. "This jug I am selling to you" — even if it is vinegar, it belongs to [the purchaser, who cannot retract].

T. 6:9 "A hundred jugs of wine I am selling to you" — he hands over to him wine as good as the average wine which is sold in that shop. "These hundred jugs I am selling to you" — even if it is vinegar, it belongs to [the purchaser, who cannot retract].

T. 6:11 [If] rain falls on the wine-presses, if it is a public calamity, he does not have to inform him [that the wine is watered down]. If it is not a public calamity, he does have to inform him.

T. 6:12 [If] he purchased from him logs, half-logs, quarter-logs, or eighth-logs [of the aforesaid] wine, he should not give it as drink to ass-drivers, workers or anyone who has a claim on him for nourishment unless he so informed them.

T. 6:13 [If] he was going to a house of mourning or a house of rejoicing, and he had in hand a flagon of wine which was shaking about he should not fill it up with water, because he deceives him. But if there was an assembly in the town, it is permitted.

T. 6:15 A person should not send to his fellow a jar of water, and put oil on at the mouth of it, because of the danger [involved in doing so].

T. 6:16 He who purchases utensils to send to the house of his father-in-law, and who said, "If they are accepted by him, lo, I'll pay you what they cost, and if not, lo, I'll pay you such-and-so," if they were taken from him when he was on his way, he is liable. [If it was when he was] on his way back, he is exempt, because he now is in the status of a paid bailee.

T. 6:18 "An orchard I am selling you" — even if there is not a single tree in it, it belongs [to the purchaser], for he sold it to him only by its name. "A vineyard I am selling to you" — even if there is not a single vine in it, it belongs [to the purchaser], for he sold it to him only by its name. "A kor of ground I am selling to you," — whether it is twenty or forty sea's [in size], it belongs [to the purchaser], for he referred to it only by its name.

T. 6:19 "A kor of ground surrounded by a fence I am selling to you" — whether it is twenty or forty sea's in size. it belongs [to the purchaser], for he has [a right] only to the area surrounded by the fence.

T. 6:20 They do not collect from indentured property [a debt incurred] for consummation of produce, for the good order of the world. How so? [If] he purchased a field from him and consumed its produce, and lo, [the field] leaves his possession — [the original owner] collects the principal [the cost of the field] from indentured property, but for the produce of the field [which he had eaten] he collects only from unindentured property.

T. 6:21 And they do not collect from indentured property [a debt incurred] for the improvement of real estate and for the support of a wife and daughters, for the good order of the world. How so? [If] he purchased a field from him, and he paid for improvements, and lo, it is leaving his possession — [the owner of the field] collects from indentured property But the cost for the improvement of the real estate he collects only from an unindentured property. Under what circumstances? When the purchase on the part of this one came before the investment for the improvement of the field on the part of the other one. But if the investment for the improvement of the field of this one came before the sale on the part of that one, both this one and that one collect only from unindentured property. If this one says, "My investment for improvement came first," and that one says, "My sale came first" — he who lays claim against his fellow bears the burden of proof

M. 6:4 (1) He who wants to build a cattle shed builds it four cubits

by six. (2) [If he wants to build] a small house, it is six by eight. (3) [If he wants to build] a large house, it is eight by ten. (4) [If he wants to build] a hall, it is ten by ten. The height is [the sum of] half its length and half its breadth. Proof of the matter is the sanctuary [1 Kgs. 6:17: $40 \times 20 \times 30$].

M. 6:5 He who has a cistern behind his fellow's house goes in when people usually go in and goes out when people usually go out. And he may not bring his cattle in and water them from his cistern. But he draws water and waters them outside. This party makes himself a lock, and that party makes himself a lock.

M. 6:6 He who has a vegetable patch behind the vegetable patch of his fellow goes in when people usually go in and goes out when people usually go out. And he does not bring in merchants. And he may not go in to it through another field. And [the owner of] the outer [patch] sows seeds on the pathway. [If others] have given him a path on the side with the knowledge and consent of both parties, he goes in whenever he wants and goes out whenever he wants and brings merchants in with him. But he may not go in through another field. And neither one of them has the right to sow seed [on the path].

B. 6:6 I.1 99B "LAND THE WIDTH OF A CUBIT FOR AN IRRIGATION CANAL I AM SELLING TO YOU" — HE HAS TO ASSIGN TO HIM IN ADDITION TO THE CUBIT FOR THE CANAL TWO CUBITS OF LAND IN THE FIELD ITSELF, ONE ON EITHER SIDE OF THE CANAL, FOR THE BANKS. "GROUND THE WIDTH OF ONE CUBIT I AM SELLING TO YOU FOR A POND" — HE MUST ASSIGN TO HIM ONE CUBIT OF GROUND IN THE COURTYARD ITSELF, HALF ON EITHER SIDE OF THE BOND, FOR THE BANKS.

M. 6:7 He who had a public way passing through his field, and who took it away and gave [the public another path] along the side, what he has given he has given. But what is his does not pass to him. (1) A private way is four cubits wide. (2) A public way is sixteen cubits wide. (3) An imperial road is without limit. (4) A path to the grave is without limit.

M. 6:8 He who sells a piece of property to his fellow for making a [family] grave — And so, he who receives [a piece of property] from his fellow for making a [family] grave — [The contractor] makes the central space of the vault four cubits by six, and he opens in it eight niches, three on one side, three on the other side, and two at the end. And the niches are to be four cubits long, seven cubits high, and six cubits broad.

T. 6:22 A. These and those which they spoke: the height of a vault is to be four cubits [M. B.B. 6:8C], and the height of the niches is to be seven handbreadths, and a handbreadth for [an opening of] a handbreadth.

M. 7:1 He who says to his fellow, "I am selling you a kor's area of arable land — [if] there were there crevices ten handbreadths deep, or rocks ten handbreadths high, they are not measured with [the area]. [If they were] less than [the stated measurements], They are measured with [the area]. And if he said to him, "Approximately a kor's area of arable land [I am selling to you]," even if there were there crevices more than ten handbreadths deep, or rocks more than ten handbreadths high, lo, they are measured with [the area].

T. 6:24 "I am selling you a centenar [large court]" — lo, this one provides him with one twelve by twelve cubits [cf. M. B.B. 6:4]. Whether he said to him, "I'm selling you a kor of ground" [M B.B. 7:1A], or whether he said to him, "I'm selling you approximately a kor of ground" [M. B.B. 7:1G], Lo, this one [the purchaser] has to accept [responsibility to provide ground for] a ditch and a small ditch and the area occupied by a wall between his land and that of his fellow [cf. M. B.B. 7:4G].

M. 7:2 [If he said to him,] "A kor's area of arable land I am selling to you, as measured by a rope," [if he gave him] any less, [the purchaser] may deduct [the difference]. [If he gave him] any more, [the purchaser] must return [cash or additional land]. If he said, "Whether less or more," even if he gave him a quarter-qab's space less for a seah's area, or a quarter qab's space more for a seah's area, it belongs to [the purchaser]. [If it was more] than this, let him make a reckoning. What does he pay back to him? Cash. But if he wanted, he gives him back land. And why have they said, "He pays back cash"? To improve the claim of the seller, for if he left in a field [of a kor's space] nine qabs of space, or in a vegetable patch, an area of a half-qab — [the buyer] will pay him back in land [and not money]. And not only the quarter-qab of area alone does he return, but all the extra land.

T. 6:25 [He who says to his fellow], "A kor's area of ground I am selling to you, whether less or more," even if he gave him a quarter-qab's space less for a se'ah's area, or a quarter-qab's space more for a se'ah's area [M. B.B. 7:2D–E], If he which are seven and a half qabs, it belongs to [the purchaser]. [If] it was less than this, they return to this one [the excess]. What does he return to him? Cash [M. B.B. 7:2H–I] — just as he purchased it from him [in cash]. But if he wanted, he returns to him real estate.

M. 7:3 [If he said, "I will sell you a kor's area of ground as measured] by its marks and boundaries," and the difference [between the space thus measured and a kor] was less than a sixth, it belongs to [the purchaser] [= the sale is confirmed]. [If it was] more than a sixth, the purchaser deducts [the difference from the price].

T. 6:26 A. [If he said to him,] "I will sell you a kor's area of ground as measured by its marks and boundaries" [M. B.B. 7:3E], even if he provided a sixth too little or a sixth too much, it is equivalent [to an error produced by] a judge's [appraisal, in error], [and the land] belongs to [the purchaser]. [If the purchaser] received less than this or more than this, they make restitution to one another. What does he give back? Cash, just as he purchased it from him [in cash]. But if he wanted, he gives him back real estate [cf. M. B.B. 7:2H].

M. 7:4 He who says to his fellow, "Half a field I am selling to you" — they divide [the field] between them [into portions of equal value], and [the purchaser] takes a half of his field. [If he said], "The half of it in the south I am selling to you," they divide between them [the field into portions of equal value], and [the purchaser] takes the half at the south. And [the seller] accepts [responsibility for providing ground for] the place in which the fence is to be located, and for large and small ditches. How large is a large ditch? Six handbreadths. And a small ditch? Three.

T. 6:27 He who says to his fellow, "Half a field I am selling to you" [M. B.B. 7:4A]. "A letekh's area I am selling to you," they divide his field between them into portions of equal value, and the purchaser takes half of his field [M. B.B. 7:4B–C], a letekh's area going to this one. [If] he had said [to one party], "Half of the field, a letekh's area, I am selling to you," and to that party he had said, "A half of the field, a letekh's area I am selling to you," they divide his field between them into portions of equal value. This one takes half of his field, and that one takes half of his field.

T. 6:28 [If] he had said to this one, "[Half of the field] in the north [I am selling to you]," and to that one he had said, "[Half of the field] in the south [I am selling to you]," they divide his field between them into portions of equal value. This one takes the northern part, and that one takes the southern part. [If he said], "A letekh's area on the north side I am selling to you," he hands over to him a letekh's area on the northern side. [If he had said,] "An area sufficient for sowing a handful of seed," [he hands over to him] an area sufficient for sowing a handful of seed.

iii. *Inheritances and Wills. Other Commercial and Legal Documents*

A. *Inheritance*

M. 8:1 There are those who inherit and bequeath, there are those who inherit but do not bequeath, bequeath but do not inherit, do not inherit and do not bequeath. These inherit and bequeath: the father as to the sons, the sons as to the father; and brothers from the same father [but a different mother], [as to one another] inherit from and bequeath [to one another]. The man as to his mother, the man as to his wife, and the sons of sisters inherit from, but do not bequeath [to, one another]. The woman as to her sons, the woman as to her husband, and the brothers of the mother bequeath to, but do not inherit [from one another]. Brothers from the same mother do not inherit from, and do not bequeath [to one another].

T. 7:1 Whoever is closer [in relationship] than his fellow takes precedence over his fellow. And an inheritance goes on upward, even to Reuben [that is, the ultimate progenitor of the tribe]. And brothers so far as one another are concerned, sisters so far as one another are concerned, brothers so far as the sisters are concerned, and sisters so far as the brothers are concerned, both inherit and bequeath [M. B.B. 8:1B–C]. A *mamzer* causes his relatives to inherit. A gentile and a slave who had intercourse with an Israelite girl, even though thereafter the gentile went and converted, the slave went and was emancipated — his estate is in the status of the estate of a proselyte, or his estate is in the status of a freed slave. So whoever acquired possession of them first gains title to them.

M. 8:2 The order of [the passing of an] inheritance is thus: "If a man dies and had no son, then you shall cause his inheritance to pass to his daughter" (Num. 27:8) — the son takes precedence over the daughter, and all the offspring of the son take precedence over the daughter. The daughter takes precedence over [surviving] brothers. The offspring of the daughter take precedence over the brothers. The [decedent's] brothers take precedence over the father's brothers. The offspring of the brothers take precedence over the father's brothers. This is the governing principle: Whoever takes precedence in inheritance — his offspring [also] take precedence. The father takes precedence over all [the father's] offspring [if none is a direct offspring of the deceased].

M. 8:4 All the same are the son and the daughter as to matters of inheritance, except that the son takes a double portion in the estate of the father [Dt. 21:17]. [The son] does not take a double portion in the estate of the mother. The daughters are supported by the father's estate and are not supported by the mother's estate.

T. 7:10 And just as the son takes precedence over the daughter in the estate of the father, so the son takes precedence over the daughter in the estate of the mother.

M. 8:5 He who says, "So-and-so, my firstborn son, is not to receive a double portion," "So-and-so, my son, is not to inherit along with his brothers," has said absolutely nothing. For he has made a stipulation contrary to what is written in the Torah. He who divides his estate among his sons by a verbal [donation], [and] gave a larger portion to one and a smaller portion to another, or treated the firstborn as equivalent to all the others — his statement is valid. But if he had said, "By reason of an inheritance [the aforestated arrangements are made]," he has said nothing whatsoever. [If] he had written, whether at the beginning, middle, or end, [that these things are handed over] as a gift, his statement is valid. He who says, "Mr. So-and-so will inherit me," in a case in which he has a daughter, "My daughter will inherit me," in a case in which he has a son, has said nothing whatsoever. For he has made a stipulation contrary to what is written in the Torah. He who writes over his property to others and left out his sons — what he has done is done. But sages are not pleased with him.

T. 7:4 The firstborn does not take a double portion in the increase which accrues to the estate after the death of the father.

T. 7:6 How does the firstborn not take a double portion? [If] he inherited writs of indebtedness, he takes a double portion. [If] claims of collection went forth against him [as his father's heir], he pays out a double portion. But if he said, "I don't want to take, and I don't want to pay out [a double portion]," he has every right to do so.

T. 7:7 How does [the firstborn] not take a double portion in what is going to accrue to the father's estate as he does in what is already possessed by the father's estate? [If] the father of his father dies in the lifetime of his father, he takes a double portion in the estate of his father, but he does not take a double portion in the estate of the father of his father. But if his father was firstborn, he takes a double portion in the estate of the father of his father.

T. 7:11 He who says, "Let my sons divide my estate equally," and there was a firstborn there, if [the brothers] had acquired possession of the estate of their father while he was yet alive, [the firstborn] does not take a double portion. And if not, he takes a double portion.

T. 7:12 He who says, "Give two hundred *denars* to So-and-so my firstborn son, with what is coming to him," he takes the [money] and [also] takes a double portion as his right as a firstborn. And his hand is on top. [If] he wants, he takes [what the father has specified]. And [if] he wants, he takes the double portion [in the estate].

T. 7:13 He who says, "Give such-and-such a field to So-and-so my wife with what is coming to her" — she takes [the field] and also collects her marriage-settlement. And her hand is on top. [If] she wants, she takes the field. [If] she wants, she collects her marriage-settlement.

T. 7:14 He who says, "Give two hundred to Mr. So-and-so, my creditor" — he collects the money and [also] collects the debt owing to him. [If he had said,] "For his debt," he has a right only to collect the money owing to him.

T. 7:15 [If] he had a field, and it had been made a surety for the wife for the settlement of her marriage-contract and for a creditor for a settlement of what was owing to him, if he then said, "Give such-and-such a field to my wife, So-and-so, in payment for her marriage-contract, and to Mr. So-and-so, my creditor, in payment for what is owing to him," what is owing to them has been received. And their hand is on top.

T. 7:16 He who says, "Give a portion to Mr. So-and-so in my estate — "let him inherit with my sons in the position of the firstborn," he does not take a double portion. He who says, "Let Mr. So-and-so inherit me," has said nothing whatsoever. If he said, "Give my property to So-and-so, his statement is carried out.

T. 7:17 [If] one used the language of *inheritance* below, and a *gift* above, *inheritance* above and a *gift* below, *inheritance* on this side and on that side, and a *gift* in the middle, since he has simply mentioned the matter of a gift, his statement is confirmed [M. B.B. 8:5J].

T. 8:1 He who writes over his property to someone else, and included were slaves, even though the other party said, "I don't want them," Lo, these eat heave-offering [if the donee was a priest].

T. 8:2 He who writes over his property to ten people, whether [only] one of them has made acquisition, or whether all of them have made acquisition, they all are deemed to have acquired [the property]. [If] he wrote [over the property] and deposited [the deed of gift] for them in the archives, the archives have made acquisition for them.

T. 8:3 He who sends forth ten slaves as freemen, whether [only] one of them has gone forth or all of them have gone forth [to freedom] — all of them are deemed free. [If] he wrote [a writ of emancipation] and deposited it for them in the archives, the archives have made acquisition [of the writ for them, and they are deemed to have been emancipated].

T. 8:4 He who says, "Give my property to So-and-so, and if he dies, to So-and-so, and if he dies, to So-and-so" — the first enjoys the usufruct. And if he dies, it is to be handed on to the second. And if he dies, it is handed over to the third party. [If] the second one died before the first, the first enjoys the usufruct, and if he died, [the usufruct] is to go back to the heirs of the donor.

M. 8:6 He who says, "This is my son," is believed. [If he said], "This is my brother," he is not believed, and [the latter] shares with him in his portion [of the father's estate] — [If the brother whose status is in doubt] died, the property is to go back to its original source. [If] he received property from some other source, his brothers are to inherit with him. He who died, and a will was found tied to his thigh — lo, this is nothing whatsoever. [If he had delivered it and] granted possession through it to another person, whether this is one of his heirs or not one of his heirs, his statement is confirmed.

T. 7:2 A midwife is believed to say, "This one came out first." Under what circumstances? When there is no contesting opinion. But if there is a contesting opinion, she is not believed.

T. 7:3 [If] people took for granted concerning someone that he was a firstborn, and at the time of the gift, [the father] said, "He is not the firstborn," [the father] is not believed. [If] people took for granted concerning someone that he was not the firstborn, and at the time of the gift, [the father] said, "He is the firstborn," he is believed. [If] people took for granted concerning someone that he was his son, and at the time of his death, the [putative father] said, "He is not my son," he is not believed. [If] people took for granted concerning someone that he was not his son, and at the time of [the man's] death, he said, "He is my son," he is believed [M. B.B. 8:6A]. [If] people took for granted concerning someone that he was his son, and at the time of his death, he said, "He is [my] brother," he is believed [cf. M. B.B. 8:6B]. [If] people took for granted concerning someone that he was his brother, and at the time of his death, he said, "He is my slave," he is not believed. [If] people took for granted concerning someone that he was his slave, and at the time of his death, he said, "He is my son," he is believed. [If] he was standing among tax-collectors and said, "He is my son," and then he went and said, "He is my slave," he is believed. [If] he said, "He is my slave," and then he went and said, "He is my son," he is not believed.

T. 8:5 Two who were coming from overseas — even though their trading, eating and drinking were done in partnership, [if] one of them died, his fellow does not inherit him. But if he had conducted affairs in this way because of their being brothers, [the survivor] does inherit.

T. 8:6 He who went overseas with his son — and [the son] came home, and with him was a brother [born to the father, who had died overseas] — and [the son] said, "This is my brother, who was born to me overseas" — and [the son who had come home] had five brothers, and before them was an estate of five *kors* of land — they do not give [to the other brother, born overseas] any portion whatsoever [M. B.B. 8:6B]. But the son [from overseas] gives him a sixth out of his share [M. B.B. 8:6C]. [If then the brother born abroad] died, [the brother who had given him a share] takes what [the decedent] had given to him [M. B.B. 8:6D], and the rest [of the decedent's estate] they bring and divide among [all surviving brothers] [M. B.B. 8:6E].

T. 8:7 He who went overseas, he and his father — and the son died, or the father died — under all circumstances the property is assumed to belong to the elder [the father, and not the son, so that the father's other sons inherit].

T. 8:8 He who was writing a will, and was afraid of the heirs — [the scribe and witnesses] go into visit him like ordinary visitors and hear what he has to say inside. Then they go out and write the will outside.

T. 8:9 A healthy person who wrote a will — a dying man who wrote his property as a gift — even though he gave possession after the gift, he has done nothing at all. But he who writes over his property in the name of his fellow, and he gave him possession after the gift, his statement is confirmed [M. B.B. 8:6H–J].

T. 8:10 He who writes a will can retract. He who writes a deed of gift cannot retract. What is a will? "Let this be confirmed: If I die, let my estate be given to So-and-so." And what is a deed of gift? "As of this date let my property be given to So-and-so."

T. 8:11 He who writes a will, before he gives possession, whether it is he or another party — he can retract. Once he has given possession, whether it is he or another party — he cannot retract.

T. 8:12 Guardians [of the estate of minors] before they have made acquisition of the estate of minors, can retract. Once they have made acquisition of the estate of minors, they cannot retract. 8:13 A. A guardian whom the father of the orphans has appointed is to be subjected to an oath [that he has not misappropriated the property of the minor], [if] a court appointed him, he is not required to take an oath.

T. 8:14 Guardians set aside heave-offering and tithes out of the property of orphans. They sell houses, fields, vineyards, cattle, boy-slaves, girl-slaves, to provide maintenance for the orphans, [or] to build a *Sukkah*, acquire a *lulab*, show-fringes, and otherwise to make it possible to carry out any and all commandments stated in the Torah, to purchase a scroll of the Torah or prophets, [or] any matter which is written in the Torah. But they do not contribute to funds for the redemption of captives on their account, and they do not contribute to charity in the synagogue, [or provide for] any matter, the fixed amount of which is not set forth in the Torah. They have not got the right to emancipate slaves, but they may sell them to others, and the others emancipate them.

T. 8:15 [The guardians of estates of minors] do not sell land at a distance to buy land nearby, land of poor quality to buy land of good quality. They do not go to court to the disadvantage or to the advantage [of the trust], to collect or to disburse in behalf of the orphans, unless they get permission from the court.

T. 8:16 [The guardians of an estate of minors] sell slaves to buy real estate with the proceeds, but they do not sell real estate to buy slaves with the proceeds.

T. 8:17 A court does not appoint women and slaves as guardians to begin with. But if their father had named them while he was alive, they do appoint them guardians.

T. 8:18A. [If] one has written in a document, "I have money and utensils in the possession of Mr. So-and-so," the witnesses have the right to sign [the document]. But [the claimant] cannot collect until he brings proof [of his claim].

M. 8:7 He who writes over his property to his son [to take effect] after his death — the father cannot sell the property, because it is written over to the son, and the son cannot sell the property, because it is [yet] in the domain of the father. [If] the father sold [it], the property is sold until he dies. [If] the son sold the property, the purchaser has no right whatever in the property until the father dies. The father harvests the crops and gives the usufruct to anyone whom he wants. And whatever he left already harvested — lo, it belongs to his heirs. [If] he left adult and minor sons, the adults may not take care of themselves [from the estate] at the expense of the minor sons, nor may the minor sons support themselves [out of the estate] at the expense of the adult sons. But they divide the estate equally. If the adult sons got married [at the expense of the estate], the minor sons [in due course] may marry [at the expense of the estate]. But if the minor sons said, "Lo, we are going to get

married just as you did [while father was still alive]" — they pay no heed to them. But what the father gave to them he has given.

B. 8:7 III.9/138A A DYING MAN WHO SAID, "GIVE TWO HUNDRED ZUZ TO MR. SO-AND-SO, AND THREE HUNDRED TO MR. SUCH-AND-SUCH, AND FOUR HUNDRED TO MR. SO-AND-SUCH," THEY DO NOT SAY, "THE FIRST NAMED PARTY IN THE DEED TAKES PRECEDENCE." THEREFORE, IF A BOND IS PRODUCED AGAINST THE DONOR AFTER HE DIED, THE CLAIMANT CAN COLLECT FROM ALL OF THOSE NAMED. BUT IF HE SAID, 'GIVE TWO HUNDRED ZUZ TO MR. SO-AND-SO, AND THEN THREE HUNDRED TO MR. SUCH-AND-SUCH, AND THEN FOUR HUNDRED TO MR. SO-AND-SUCH,' THEY DO SAY, 'THE FIRST NAMED PARTY IN THE DEED TAKES PRECEDENCE.' THEREFORE, IF A BOND IS PRODUCED AGAINST THE DONOR AFTER HE DIED, THE CLAIMANT CAN COLLECT FIRST FROM THE LAST ONE NAMED; IF HE HASN'T GOT WITH WHAT TO PAY, HE COLLECTS FROM THE ONE BEFORE HIM; IF HE DOESN'T HAVE WITH WHAT TO PAY, HE COLLECTS FROM THE ONE BEFORE HIM.

B. 8:7 III.10/138A A DYING MAN WHO SAID, "GIVE TWO HUNDRED ZUZ TO MR. SO-AND-SO, MY FIRSTBORN SON, AS IS FITTING FOR HIM," HE COLLECTS THEM AND ALSO COLLECTS THE DOUBLE PORTION OF HIS BIRTHRIGHT. IF HE SAID, ". . . AS HIS BIRTHRIGHT," HE GETS FIRST CHOICE. IF HE WANTED, HE COLLECTS THEM, BUT IF HE PREFERS, HE COLLECTS HIS BIRTHRIGHT. AND A DYING MAN WHO SAID, "GIVE TWO HUNDRED ZUZ TO MRS. SO-AND-SO, MY WIFE, AS IS FITTING FOR HER," SHE COLLECTS THAT MONEY BUT ALSO COLLECTS THE FULL SETTLEMENT OF HER MARRIAGE-CONTRACT. IF HE SAID, ". . . AS HER MARRIAGE-SETTLEMENT," SHE GETS FIRST CHOICE. IF SHE WANTED, SHE COLLECTS THEM, BUT IF SHE PREFERS, SHE COLLECTS THE FULL SETTLEMENT OF HER MARRIAGE-CONTRACT.

B. 8:7 III.11/138B A DYING MAN WHO SAID, "GIVE TWO HUNDRED ZUZ TO MR. SO-AND-SO, MY CREDITOR, AS IS FITTING FOR HIM," HE COLLECTS THE MONEY AND ALSO COLLECTS THE DEBT THAT IS OWING TO HIM. IF HE SAID, ". . . MY CREDITOR," HE COLLECTS THE MONEY AND ALSO COLLECTS THE DEBT THAT IS OWING TO HIM. IF HE SAID, ". . . IN PAYMENT OF THE DEBT THAT IS OWING TO HIM," HE COLLECTS THE MONEY IN PAYMENT OF HIS DEBT.

M. 8:8 [If] he left adult and minor daughters, the adults may not take care of themselves [from the estate] at the expense of the minor daughters, nor may the minors support themselves [from the estate] at the expense of the adult daughters. But they divide the estate equally. If the adult daughters got married [at the expense of the estate], the minor daughters may get married [at the expense of the estate] — And if the minor daughters said, "Lo, we are going to get married just as you got married [while father was still alive]," they pay no heed to them. This rule is more strict in regard to daughters than to sons. For the daughters are supported at the disadvantage of the sons [M. 9:1], but they are not supported at the disadvantage of [other] daughters.

T. 8:18 [If the decedent] had left adult and minor sons [M. B.B. 8:7J] and they continued to enjoy support without complaint, the minors should not say to the adults, "Lo, we are going to be supported [at the expense of the estate] in the way in which you were supported when father was alive [and you were minors]." [If] the adults had been married during the lifetime of the father the minors should not say, "Lo, we are going to be married [at the expense of the estate] in the way in which you were married." And not only so, but even if the father [in his lifetime] had left [to the adults] slave-boys and slave-girls, silver and gold utensils, lo, they are theirs [cf. M. B.B. 8:7F].

T. 8:19 [If] he [the decedent] left adult and minor daughters, [M. B.B. 8:8A], and they continued to enjoy support without complaint, the minors should not say to the adults, "Lo, we are going to be supported [at the expense of the estate] in the way in which you were supported [when father was alive, and you were minors]." [If] the adults had been married [during the lifetime of the father], the minors should not say, "Lo, we are going to be married [at the expense of the estate] in the way in which you were married." And not only so, but even if their father [in his lifetime] had left [to the adults] slave-boys and slave-girls, gold and silver utensils lo, they are theirs [cf. M. B.B. 8:8].

M. 9:1 He who died and left sons and daughters — when the estate is large, the sons inherit, and the daughters are supported [by the estate]. [If] the estate is small, the daughters are supported, and sons go begging at [people's] doors.

T. 9:2 He who sells a field belonging to his fellow in the presence of his fellow has done nothing whatsoever. [If, however, the owner] wrote, "I shall confirm what he does after him," his words are confirmed. The son who does business with his father's capital, even though the documents and deeds go out in his name — lo, they belong to his father. But if he said, "What I inherited from the estate of the father of my mother are [the goods in which I am dealing]," let him bring evidence explicitly in accord with his explanation of it. A woman who did business with her husband's capital, even though the documents and deeds go out in her name — lo, they belong to her husband. And if she said, "What I inherited from the estate of my father are [the goods in which I am dealing]," or, "... from the estate of the father of my mother," let her bring evidence explicitly in accord with her explanation of it.

M. 9:2 [If] he left sons and daughters and one whose sexual traits were not clearly defined, when the estate is large, the males push him over onto the females, [If] the estate is small, the females push him over onto the males. He who says, "If my wife bears a male, he will get a maneh," — [if] she bore a male, he gets a maneh. [If he said, "If she bears] a female, [she will get] two hundred [zuz]," [if] she bore a female, she gets two hundred [zuz]. [If he said, "If she bears] a male, [he will get] a maneh, if [she bears] a female, [she will get] two hundred [zuz]," if she bore a male and a female, the male gets a maneh, and the female [gets] two hundred [zuz]. [If] she bore a child whose sexual traits were not clearly defined, he gets

nothing. If he said, "Whatever my wife bears will get [a maneh]," lo, this one gets [a maneh]. And if there is no heir but that [child lacking defined sexual traits], he inherits the entire estate.

T. 9:3 Two women who gave birth to two males in hiding, and [the women] went and gave birth to two males in hiding both of them go to the first [husband's estate] and take a portion of a male. [Then they go] to the second [husband's estate] and take a portion of a male. [If the women produced] a male and a female, [then another] male and female, both of them go to the first [husband's estate] and take the portion owing to a male. [Then they go] to the second [husband's estate] and take the portion owing to a female.

T. 9:5 He who says, "He who informs me that my wife has given birth to a male gets two hundred, [or if she gave birth] to a female, he gets a *maneh*" — [if] she gave birth to a male, [the messenger] gets two hundred. [If she gave birth to] a female, he gets a *maneh*. [If she gave birth to] a male and a female, the messenger gets only a *maneh*.

M. 9:3 [If] he left adult and minor sons — [if] the adults improved the value of the estate, the increase in value is in the middle [shared by all heirs]. If they had said, "See what father has left us. Lo, we are going to work it and [from that] we shall enjoy the usufruct," the increase in value is theirs. And so in the case of a woman who improved the value of the estate — the increase in value is in the middle. If she had said, "See what my husband has left me! Lo, I am going to work and enjoy the usufruct," the increase in value is hers.

T. 10:2 The woman who inherited [property] and went and improved the value of the property, [and she claims], "I brought them to a condition of abundance," may not say, "Give me the value of the increase in worth of the property which I have brought about." And not only so, but [only] if there is property which is real estate does she collect her marriage-settlement. But if not, she does not collect her marriage-settlement.

T. 10:3 Brothers to whom their father left property, and one of them had sons, and his sons went and improved the value of the property, and they brought them to a state of abundance — [their father] may not say, "Give me the value of the increase in the worth of the property which my sons have brought about," and so too, they should not say to him, "Give us the usufruct which your sons have enjoyed." But the usufruct which they have enjoyed they have enjoyed from the common holding, and the increased value which they have brought about goes to the common holding.

M. 9:4 Brothers who were jointholders [in an inherited estate], one of whom fell into public office — [the charge or benefit] fell to the common fund. [If] he became ill and was healed, the healing is at his own expense. Brothers, some of whom made a present as groomsmen [at their father's expense] while their father was alive, [and after the father's death] the groomsmen's gift returned to them, it has returned to the common

fund. For the groomsmen's gift [is deemed a loan and] is recoverable in court. But he who sends his fellow jugs of wine and oil [in his father's lifetime] — they are not recoverable in court, because they count as a charitable deed.

T. 10:4 Brothers, one of whom took two hundred zuz and went off to study Torah or to study a craft — he may not say, "If I had been available, I should have derived support from the common fund." But they may say to him, "If you had been available, you would have derived support from the common fund. Now that you are deriving support [from another source], derive support from your own resources."

T. 10:5 Brothers, one of whom was appointed charity-collector or commissioner — if it was on account of his ownership of property that he fell into this office, [the profits of the office] fall into the common fund. But if it was on his own account that he fell [into office], the profits of the office fall to himself [M. B.B. 9:4A–B].

T. 10:7 [If] they married wives, and [the wives] brought them fields, this one takes that one which is his, and that one takes that one which is his. But if the cost of upkeep is from the common fund, they put the fields into the common fund and divide up [the return]. [If] the wives had brought them utensils, this one takes that which he recognizes as his, and that one takes that which he recognizes as his. And the remainder do they bring to the common fund and divide up. [If] they had made clothing for their wives and children, lo, these belong to them. [If] they had made clothing for themselves, they bring them to the common fund and divide them up. [If] the father had sent a grooms-man's gift, when it returns, it returns in due and proper time. [If the grooms-man's gift] was sent to the father, when it is collected, it is collected from the common fund [M. B.B. 9:4G].

T. 10:8 The grooms-man's gift is not subject to the prohibition against usury. Five rules have been stated in connection with the grooms-man's gift. It is not subject to the prohibition against usury. And it goes back at the proper time. And it is collected from the common fund. And the Sabbatical year does not release it [as a debt]. And the firstborn does not get a double-portion [in that regard].

T. 10:9 [If] one had served as a groomsman for him in public and he wants to serve for him in secret — he has the right to say to him, "Just as you did it for me in public, so I shall do the same for you in public." [If] he had acted as groomsman for him in the case of a virgin, and he wants him to do the same for him in the case of a widow he has the right to say to him, "In the case of a virgin I am willing to do it for you, just as you did it for me with a virgin." [If] he had served as groomsman in the case of two wives, and he wants him to do the same for him in the case of one wife he has the right to say to him, "When you marry yet another woman, I'll bring you [a gift for both occasions]."

M. 9:5 He who sends gifts to his father-in-law's household — [if] he sent gifts worth a hundred manehs and he there ate a wedding feast of even a denar — [if he divorced his wife], [the

gifts] are not recoverable. [If he did not eat a wedding feast at all], lo, they are recoverable. [If the husband] had sent many gifts, which were to be returned with her to her husband's house, lo, they are recoverable. [If he had sent] few gifts, which she was to use in her father's house, they are not recoverable.

T. 10:10 He who sends gifts to his father-in-law's household [M. B.B. 9:5A] — and [the gifts] were consumed in connection with the celebration for the birth of a son or for some other purpose, what [the members of the father-in-law's household] have consumed, they have consumed. He who sends gifts to his father-in-law's household — things which are usually used in the father-in-law's household, [the bride] does not have to bring back with her. But things which usually are not used in the father-in-law's household, [the bride] does have to bring along with her. [If] she died, those things which she would usually have used in her lifetime, the father-in-law does not have to return. And those things which she usually would not have used in her lifetime, the father-in-law does have to return [cf. M. B.B. 9:5E–F].

M. 9:6 A dying man who wrote over all his property to others [as a gift] but left himself a piece of land of any size whatever — his gift is valid. [If] he did not leave himself a piece of land of any size whatever, his gift is not valid. [If] he did not write [in the deed of gift], "... who lies dying," [and if, after recovery, he wishes to reclaim his property], [so] he says he had been dying, and [the recipients] say, "He had been healthy" — he who lays claim against his fellow bears the burden of proof.

T. 9:6 He who says, "Hand over two hundred denars to Mr. So-and-so, three hundred to Mr. Such-and-such, and five hundred to Mr. So-and-so," they do not say, "Whoever is named first in the document has acquired [what is owing to him, without regard to whether there is enough left to pay off the other creditors]. But all of them divide things up equally. [If] the marriage-settlement of his wife and a debt owing to a creditor were laid in claim against them, all of them pay up equally. But if he had said, "Give two hundred *denars* to So-and-so, and afterward, three hundred to Such-and-such, and afterward, five hundred to So-and-so" — whoever comes first in the document has acquired [what is owing to him, without regard to whether there is enough left to pay off the other creditors]. [If] the marriage-settlement of his wife and a debt owing to a creditor then were laid in claim against them, they collect from the last named. [If] he does not have it, they collect from the one before him. [If] he does not have it, they collect from the one before him.

T. 9:7 He who says, "I have two hundred *denars* in the possession of Mr. So-and-so, and three hundred in possession of Mr. Such-and-such, and five hundred in the possession of Mr. So-and-so and Mr. Such and such," let him collect the two hundred. [If] the marriage-contract of his wife and a debt owing to a creditor laid claim against them, he may collect it, even though all of them have not come together. But if he said, "And afterward, let Mr. So-and-so collect two hundred *denars*," if all of them had come together let him collect. And if not, he collects only in proportion.

T. 9:8 He who says, "Hand over two hundred *denars* to Mr. So-and-so, and three hundred to Mr. Such-and-such, and five hundred to Mr. So-and-so," and he inherited the remainder of his property, [if] a claim went forth against them for the settlement of the wife's marriage-contract and a debt owing to a creditor, let it be collected from this one who inherited his property.

T. 9:9 He who says, "Hand over two hundred *denars* to the residents of my town" — they do not go to court before the judges of that town, and they do not bring evidence [in his behalf] from residents of that town. [If he said], "To the poor of my town," they do go to court before the judges of that town, and they do bring proof from residents of that town.

T. 9:10 He who says, "Give my property to Mr. So-and-so and Mr. Such-and-such, my slaves" — they have not made acquisition of the property, nor have they acquired themselves as free men. [If he said, "Give] half of my property to Mr. So-and-so my slave, and half of my property to Mr. Such-and-such, my slave," they have made acquisition of the property. And they have acquired themselves as free men.

T. 9:11A. He who says, "All my property is given over to Mr. So-and-so, my slave, and the rest to a second party" — the second party has acquired possession of the first [party to be named, namely, the slave].

T. 9:12A. He who says, 'I gave such-and-such a field to Mr. So-and-so," "I gave it to him," "It is given to him," "Let it be his," "Lo, it is his" — has said nothing whatsoever.

T. 9:13 "Let Mr. So-and-so take part of my possessions," "Let Mr. So-and-so acquire some of my possessions," "Let Mr. So-and-so take a share of my possessions," "Let Mr. So-and-so take possession of my property," — Lo, this is a valid gift.

T. 9:14 He who says, "I made Mr. So-and-so, my slave, a free man," "I made him a free man," "I am making him a free man," and, "Lo, he is a free man."

T. 10:1 He who says, "Such and such a field is for So-and-so," and the latter says, "He never gave it to him [me]," [the latter] has said nothing whatsoever. For it is possible that he effected acquisition in behalf of [the donee] through the means of another party. And if he said, "I wrote out a document and I received the money," and the other party says, "I did not receive it from him," the admission of a litigant is equivalent to a hundred witnesses He who says, "I made Mr. So-and-so, my slave, a free man," and [the slave] says, "He never made me a free man," [the latter] has said nothing whatsoever. For it is possible that he effected acquisition in behalf of [the slave] through the means of another party. But if he said, "I wrote out a document and I gave it to him," and [the slave] says, "I never got it from him," the admission of a litigant is equivalent to a hundred witnesses.

M. 9:8 [If] the house fell on him and on his father, or on him and on those whom he inherits, and he was liable for the settlement of his wife's marriage contract and for payment of a debt — the heirs of the father claim, "The son died first, and afterward the father died," — the creditors claim, "The father died first, and then the son" — the property remains in its former status [in the hands of those who inherit the father].

M. 9:9 [If] the house fell on him and on his wife, the heirs of the husband say, "The wife died first, and afterward the husband died" — the heirs of the wife say, "The husband died first, and afterward the wife died" — the property remains in its former status. The [money for the] marriage settlement remains in the hands of the heirs of the husband. [But] the property which goes into the marriage with her and goes out of the marriage with her [at the value at which it was assessed to begin with] is assigned to the possession of the heirs of the father [of the wife].

B. *The Preparation and Confirmation of Commercial Documents, e.g., Writs of Debt 10:1–6*

M. 10:1 An unfolded document [has] the signatures within [at the bottom of a single page of writing]. And one which is folded has the signatures behind [each fold]. An unfolded document, on which its witnesses signed at the back, or a folded document, on which its witnesses signed on the inside — both of them are invalid.

M. 10:2 An unfolded document — its witnesses are two. And a folded one — its witnesses are three. An unfolded one in which there is a single witness, and a folded one in which there are two witnesses — both of them are invalid. [If] there was written in a bond of indebtedness, "A hundred zuz, which are twenty selas," [the creditor] has a claim on only twenty selas [even though a hundred zuz are twenty-five selas]. [If it is written,] "A hundred zuz which are thirty selas," he has a claim only on a maneh [a hundred zuz], [since a hundred zuz are twenty-five selas]. "Silver zuzim which are . . .," and the rest was blotted out — there is a claim for no less than two. "Silver selas which are . . .," and the rest was blotted out — there is a claim of no less than two. "Darics which are . . .," and the rest was blotted out — there is a claim for no less than two. [If] written at the top is, "a maneh," and at the bottom, "two hundred zuz," or at the top, "two hundred [zuz]," and at the bottom, "maneh" — all follows what is written at the bottom. If so, why do they write the upper figure at all? So that if one letter from the lower figure is blotted out, one may learn [infer] from the upper figure.

T. 11:2 The body of a writ [of indebtedness is as follows]: "On such-and-such a day, in such-and-such a week, in such-and-such a month, in such-and-such a year, in the reign of So-and-so . . ." [If] one did not insert the name of the day, his hand is on the bottom for that entire week. [If] one did not insert the name of the week, his hand is on the bottom for that entire (week) [month]. [If] one did not insert the year, his hand is on the bottom that entire reign. [If] one wrote in it, "Gold," he pays him off in gold. [If] one wrote in it, golden denars, he pays him off with two golden denars [cf. M. B.B. 10:2H–K]. "In denars, [worth] gold" — one pays him off with two denars of silver. In denars and gold" — one pays him off in denars of silver "In denars, [worth] silver" — One pays him off in two denars of gold. "In denars and silver" — one pays him off in two denars of gold and a denar of silver. "Gold which you owe me" — [the claim is for] no less than a denar of gold. "Silver which you owe me" — the claim is for no less than a silver denar. "Gold denars which are full," — and the rest is blotted out — [there is a claim for] no less than a gold denar. "Darics" — one pays him whatever a daric is worth. Similarly: he who is in trade with his fellow in the market and said to him, "The gold which you owe me" — [there is a claim for] no less than a golden denar. [If] he said to him, "A daric," he pays him whatever a daric is worth.

11:3 A. He who produces a writ of indebtedness of Babylonia collects on the strength of it in Babylonian money. [If he produced] a writ of indebtedness of the Land of Israel collects on the strength of it in money of the Land of Israel. [If] written in it was "money" without further specification, he may collect in the coinage of any place which he wants, which is not the rule covering the payment of the marriage-settlement of a woman.

T. 11:4 Whether it is written in it, "Mr. So-and-so has borrowed from Mr. Such-and-such," or whether it is written in it, "I, Mr. So-and-so, son of Mr. So-and-so, have borrowed from Mr. So-and-so" — so long as the witnesses have signed their names below, it is valid. Under all circumstances what is written below is understood from what is written above [M. B.B. 10:2P], in the case of a folded writ, from a single sign, and not from two signs — whether Hanan or Hanani, whether 'Anan or 'Anani, on the strength of a single mark they confirm it, and on the strength of two marks they do not confirm it. And what is the language of confirmation? "I, So-and-so, have borrowed from So-and-so," or, "I, So-and-so, son of So-and-so, have borrowed from him." [If] it is tied up above, with the witnesses below, it is valid.

M. 10:3 They write out a writ of divorce for a man, even though his wife is not with him. And a quittance for the wife, even though her husband is not with her, on condition that [the scribe] knows them. And the husband pays the fee. They write a writ of indebtedness for the borrower, even though the lender is not with him, but they do not write a writ for the lender, unless the borrower is with him. The borrower pays the scribe's

fee. They write a writ of sale to the seller, even though the buyer is not with him. But they do not write a writ of sale for the purchaser, unless the seller is with him. And the purchaser pays the scribe's fee.

M. 10:4 They write the documents of betrothal and marriage only with the knowledge and consent of both parties. And the husband pays the scribe's fee. They write documents of tenancy and sharecropping only with the knowledge and consent of both parties. And the tenant pays the scribe's fee. They write documents of arbitration or any document drawn up before a court only with the knowledge and consent of both litigants. And both litigants pay the scribe's fee.

T. 11:5 They write out a writ of divorce for a man [M. B.B. 10:3A], without the knowledge and consent of a woman. But they write it only with the knowledge and consent of the man. They write a quittance for a woman without the knowledge and consent of the husband, but they write it only with the knowledge and consent of the woman. They write a writ of emancipation without the knowledge and consent of the slave. But they write it only with the knowledge and consent of the master. They write a writ of seizure without the knowledge and consent of the creditor. But they write it only with the knowledge and consent of the borrower.

T. 11:6 [They write] wills, deeds, and deeds of gift without the knowledge and consent of the donor. But they write them only with the knowledge and consent of the recipient.

T. 11:7 Court decrees and prosbuls [do they write] without the knowledge and consent of either party.

T. 11:8 They switch the language of documents from Hebrew to Greek and from Greek to Hebrew, and they confirm such a document.

M. 10:6 He whose writ of indebtedness was blotted out — witnesses give testimony about it, and he comes to a court, and they draw up this confirmation: "Mr. So-and-so, son of So-and-so-his — bond of indebtedness was blotted out on such-and-such a day, and Mr. So-and-so and Mr. Such-and-such are his witnesses."

T. 11:9 [If] a document was blotted out or rotted, one brings it to court. And the court provides him with a confirmation. [If] the document was torn or lost, he brings the witnesses who had signed it to court, and the court provides him with a confirmation. What is the confirmation provided by the court? "In session before us, Mr. So-and-so, son of So-and-so, produced before us his document, which was torn, and we examined the testimony of the witnesses [of the document], and it turned out to be exact" [cf. M. B.B. 10:6A–D]. He may collect with such a document and does not have to produce proof. But if he does not gain a confirmation in court, he may collect only if he produces proof [of the loan].

T. 11:10 A. A document which has an erasure or an interlinear insertion in the body of its text is invalid. [If it is] not in the body [of its text], it is valid. And if one restored it below, even if it is in the body of its text, it is valid. A document, the witnesses of which signed only after an interval [between the completion of the writing of the text of the document and the signing by the witnesses] sufficient for a greeting is invalid. For they signed only [as witnesses] to the greeting. [If, to deal with this situation, the scribe] added [to the document] one or two matters of the substance of the document, it is valid. [If] the scribe wrote it on one side, and the witnesses signed on the other side, it is invalid. [If, to deal with this situation, the scribe] added [to the document, on the other side] one or two matters of the substance of the document, it is valid. [If] the witnesses signed two or three lines below the body of the text, it is invalid. [If they signed] closer than this [to the body of the text], it is valid.

T. 11:11 A document on which five witnesses signed, and the first three turned out to be relatives or [otherwise] invalid for testimony — the testimony is to be confirmed on the strength of the signatures of the final two. [If the scribe] wrote it in five languages, and five witnesses signed it in five languages — it is valid. [If] it was torn, it remains valid. [If] it was torn to pieces, it is invalid. [If] it was torn with a tear such as is made by a court, it is invalid. [If] it was eaten by moths or rotted or was worm-eaten like a sieve, it is valid. [If] it was erased or faded, with the faint outline what was written on it yet visible, if one is able to read it, it is valid. And if not, it is invalid.

C. *Concluding Miscellany*

M. 10:7 Two brothers — one poor, one rich — and their father left them a bathhouse and an olive press — [if the father] had built them to rent them out — the rent is held in common. [If] he made them for his own use, lo, the rich one says to the poor one, "You buy slaves, and let them bathe in the bath house." Or: "You buy olives, and come and prepare them in the olive press." Two who were in the same town — The name of one was Joseph b. Simeon, and the name of the other was Joseph b. Simeon, they cannot produce a writ of indebtedness against one another, nor can a third party produce a writ of indebtedness against either one of them. [If] among the documents of one of them is found a writ of Joseph b. Simeon which has been paid off, the writs of both of them are deemed to have been paid off. What should they do? Let them write down the names of the third generation And if all three [generations'] names are alike, let them write a description. And if the descriptions are alike, let them write, "Priest." He who says to his son, "There is a bond of indebtedness among my documents which has been paid, and I do not know which one of them it is" — all of his bonds are deemed to have been paid off. [If] two were found applying to a single [debtor], the larger one is deemed to have been paid, and the smaller one is not deemed to have been paid. He who lends money to his fellow on the strength of a guarantor may not collect from the guarantor. But if he had said, "[Lo, I lend to you] on condition that I may collect from whichever party I wish," he may then collect from the guarantor.

M. 10:8 He who lends money to his fellow on the security of a bond of indebtedness collects what is owing to him from mortgaged property. (1) [But if he had lent to him on the security of] witnesses, he collects only from unindentured property. (2) [If] he produced against him [the debtor's] note of hand [as evidence] that he owes him [money], he collects from unindentured property. (3) He who signs as guarantor below the [signature of] bonds of indebtedness — [the creditor] collects [only] from unindentured property.

T. 11:13 He who says, "Make Tabi, my slave, a free man," and there were two Tabis — they do not make inquiry into the intent of the language of an ordinary person, saying, "This one he loved, and this one he did not love." But both of them go forth to freedom. They then collect from both of them the value of one of them. He who says, "Hand over two hundred denars to Joseph b. Simeon," and there were there two Joseph b. Simeons — they do not make inquiry into the intent of the language of an ordinary person, saying, "This one he loved, and this one he did not love." But both of them divide the money equally. [If] against them [there then] came a claim for the marriage-contract of a wife and for the payment of a debt owing to a creditor, both of them pay off [a share] equally. [If] one of them produced a document against his fellow that he owes him money, the other should not say, "It is mine, and I lost it." But whoever has the document in hand collects [what is owing on it]. If among the documents of one of them is found a writ of Joseph b. Simeon which has been paid off, the writs of both of them are deemed to have been paid off [M. B.B. 10:7M]. And when he collects [a debt], he collects only with the knowledge and consent of the debtor.

T. 11:14 He who says to his son, "There is a bond of indebtedness among my documents which has been paid, and I do not know which one of them" — all of the bonds are deemed to have been paid off [M. B.B. 10:7R]. And when he collects, he collects only with the knowledge and consent of the creditor.

T. 11:15 He who lends money to his fellow on the strength of a guarantor may not collect from the guarantor. But if he had said, "[Lo, I lend to you], on condition that I may collect from whichever party I wish," he may then collect from the guarantor [M. B.B. 10:7U–V]. He who lends money to his fellow on the strength of two guarantors may not collect from either one of them. But if he had said, ["Lo, I lend to you] on condition that I may collect from one of them, he may collect from one of the [guarantors of the loan]. A writ of indebtedness produced by a guarantor — one may not collect it. But if the creditor had written [on the writ], "I have been paid off by you [for the debt owed by Mr. So-and-so]," then [the guarantor] may collect [what is owing on the strength of that document].

II. Analysis: The Problematics of the Topic, Baba Batra

Once more we want to know how Scripture has shaped the topical program, now that of Baba Batra. A review of the main points answers that question.

A. RIGHTS OF JOINT HOLDERS OF A COMMON PROPERTY
1. PARTITIONING PROPERTY: Apart from the equal contribution of each party to the property that the law requires, the main concern is to affirm the prevailing custom of the region. A secondary concern is that if a person benefits from a project, he must pay his share of the project. A tertiary concern of the law is, what is done for the community must be generally available (as with the produce of the seventh year) and not used in a selfish manner.
2. NOT INFRINGING ON THE PROPERTY RIGHTS OF OTHERS: One may not utilize his own property in such a way as to damage the rights of the other. One has a right to expect others to respect his property rights and to enforce those rights. The same pertains to the rights of the community as a whole.

B. ESTABLISHING TITLE TO PROPERTY
1. ESTABLISHING TITLE THROUGH USUCAPTION: Three years of utilization of a property establishes the presumptive right of ownership to the property, provided there is an explicit claim to that effect, accompanied by successful demonstration of a claim should it be opposed.
2. TRANSFERRING REAL ESTATE AND MOVABLES THROUGH SALE: WHAT IS INCLUDED IN THE TRANSACTION? It is taken for granted that what is essential to that which is sold is included in the transaction, but what is not essential and is not explicitly included is not covered by the sale, e.g., a permanent mortar but not a movable one. But if the language is used, "It and everything which is in it," lo, all of them are sold. The same goes for a cistern, the water goes with.

C. CONDITIONS OF IRREVOCABLE TRANSFER OF GOODS
1. BOTH PARTIES TO A TRANSACTION HAVE THE RIGHT TO A FAIR DEAL. If one has sold good wheat and it turns out to be bad, the purchaser has the power to retract. If one has sold bad wheat and it turns out to be good, the seller has the power to retract. If he has claimed to sell bad wheat, and it turns out to be bad, or if he claimed to sell good wheat and it turns out to be good, neither one of them has the power to retract.

2. UNSTATED STIPULATIONS GOVERN IN ACCORD WITH REASONABLE EXPECTATIONS. The buyer assumes some of what he buys will be rotten. Customary usage governs.

The requirement of the halakhah that measures be kept clean and accurate is explicit in Scripture:

> *You shall do no wrong in judgment, in measures of length or weight or quantity. You shall have just balances, just weights, a just ephah, and a just hin: I am the Lord your God who brought you out of the land of Egypt* (Lev. 19:35–36).

Dt. 25:13ff. goes over the same matter.

D. INHERITANCES, WILLS, AND OTHER LEGAL DOCUMENTS

1. RULES OF INHERITANCE: There are those who inherit and bequeath, there are those who inherit but do not bequeath, bequeath but do not inherit, do not inherit and do not bequeath. These inherit and bequeath: the father as to the sons, the sons as to the father; and brothers from the same father but a different mother, as to one another inherit from and bequeath to one another. The man as to his mother, the man as to his wife, and the sons of sisters inherit from, but do not bequeath to, one another. The woman as to her sons, the woman as to her husband, and the brothers of the mother bequeath to, but do not inherit from one another. Brothers from the same mother do not inherit from, and do not bequeath to one another. One may not stipulate an inheritance that violates the laws of the Torah, but he may divide his property by donation. He who died and left sons and daughters — when the estate is large, the sons inherit, and the daughters are supported [by the estate]. [If] the estate is small, the daughters are supported, and sons go begging at [people's] doors.

The right of the daughter to inherit is explicit, so too that inheritances pass through the male, not the female line, as stated in the Mishnah's rule, cited just above:

> *If a man dies and has no son, then you shall cause his inheritance to pass to his daughter. And if he has no daughter, then you shall give his inheritance to his brothers. And if he has no brothers, then you shall give his inheritance to his father's brothers. And if his father has no brothers, then you shall give his inheritance to his kinsman that is next to him of his family, and he shall possess it* (Num. 27:8–11).

Scripture, like the halakhah of the Oral Torah, wants inheritances to remain in the male line.

2. TESTIMONY AS TO RELATIONS: One may not give unsubstantiated testimony as to a relationship in such wise as to affect someone else's property rights.

3. JOINT MANAGEMENT OF AN ESTATE: [If] he left adult and minor sons — [if] the adults improved the value of the estate, the increase in value is in the middle [shared by all heirs]. If they had said, "See what father has left us. Lo, we are going to work it and [from that] we shall enjoy the usufruct," the increase in value is theirs. If brothers who jointly hold an estate incur public duties, the estate is charged.
4. GIFTS IN CONTEMPLATION OF DEATH: A gift in contemplation of death may be retracted. A dying man who wrote over all his property to others [as a gift] but left himself a piece of land of any size whatever — his gift is valid. [If] he did not leave himself a piece of land of any size whatever, his gift is not valid.
5. PREPARING COMMERCIAL DOCUMENTS, E.G., WRITS OF DEBT, BONDS AND THE LIKE: If one has the power to issue such a document, it may be prepared in the absence of the other; but if both parties must concur, then both parties must be present when the document is prepared.

While Baba Batra encompasses a few facts of Scripture, it pursues its own program. The main points are these. [1] Joint holders of a common property enjoy equal rights and equal responsibilities. [2] Title passes through usucaption, properly established. [3] Title covers what is integral to that which is sold, not what is peripheral (encompassing C/2, reasonable expectations). [4] Inheritances pass through the male line. If I had to identify the center of it all, it would be at C/1: both parties have a right to a fair deal, and neither may emerge with more than he entered the transaction. Here, once more, Scripture has made its contribution of facts, but the contribution proves paltry. The real question is, whence have sages derived their program, the source of the questions, in respect to the topics that they treat, that they deem urgent?

The fact that the division of the halakhah continues the foregoing supplies the answer. Baba Mesia flows uninterruptedly into Baba Batra, and, it follows, the issue of whether and how intentionality plays a role requires attention. But why cut off the discussion of a topic, such as is done in the break from Baba Mesia Chapter Ten to Baba Batra Chapter One? If not topical, the break then must derive from some other consideration. Since, we noted, the concluding third of Baba Mesia takes up situations in which intentionality may or may not enter into the adjudication of a case, it becomes relevant to take note that in the opening unit of Baba Batra, intentionality plays no role at all. That is to say, joint holders enjoy certain rights in common, and how they personally wish to arrange matters has no bearing. Custom overrides intentionality; the right of the community overrides even agreements among individuals; the rights of the other must be respected. If we wish to make the point that certain considerations override intentionality, there is, moreover, no more effective way of making such a statement than to say, even where the owner of a property has not abandoned the hope of recovering the property — even when despair has not nullified his title — he may still lose the property. His neglect of his rights speaks for itself and overrides his intentionality toward the property; actions here set aside attitude. That comes about when the owner neglects the property, so, by his action, indicates disinterest in the property.

And, finally, the private intention of the purchaser is null, if common usage is violated. The buyer may say that he assumed the sale of property encompassed various movables, that claim is null. People conform to customary usage, including language, and cannot invent their own conditions of sale. The law does not take account of private intentionality. That same matter carries us forward to C/1–2, unstated stipulations govern when all parties share the same general view; so far as nullifying a transaction, the reasonable expectations of each party are taken into account in accord with a common law. When it comes to inheritances, there is a way for one's intentionality to prevail, and that is through an act of donation (gift); but when it comes to transferring property through the right of inheritance, then the Torah's law takes over, and personal intentionality — which we should have placed at the very center of dividing an estate — is null. So, seen from this perspective, the entire set of rules forms a sustained essay on where and how intentionality gives way before established procedures and usages.

III. INTERPRETATION: RELIGIOUS PRINCIPLES OF BABA QAMMA, BABA MESIA, AND BABA BATRA

The halakhah of the Oral Torah here addresses the interior lines of structure and order as these encompass Israelites' relationships with one another, Israel's inner order in its own terms. What issues precipitate the deep reflection of the sages when they contemplate issues of the social order of the holy community? The answer to that question provides the interpretation of the halakhah seen as a statement of religious conviction, not merely social utility.

Most of the halakhah that the Oral Torah sets forth on Israel's civil society makes its appearance in the Babas. Here is where restorationist theology makes its deepest impact upon the halakhah, with its stress on preserving the status quo, securing for all parties to a transaction a proper exchange so that value remains constant, designing and sustaining a social order aimed at an equitable structure and secured by ancient custom. The purpose of the halakhah that we have examined is simply stated. The first half of the tractates, which, as we shall see in just a moment, break in the middle of Baba Mesia, focuses upon repairing damage that is done to the social order, the second half, upon preserving the balance and perfection of that same social order. Israel on its own, in its interior relationships, is governed by halakhah that establishes and maintains stasis, which signifies perfection, all things in their place, all persons possessing appropriate value in property, security in person. That goal the halakhah accomplishes, as is clear, by righting imbalances and preserving them.

That dual purpose explains why the three tractates form a single, unfolding and coherent statement, half (Baba Qamma's ten chapters and the first five chapters of Baba Mesia) devoted to repairing damages done to the political economy of society by chattel and persons, the other half (the second five chapters of Baba Mesia and Baba Batra's ten chapters)[1] to maintaining the perfection of equitable relationships. To interpret that statement, we have to stand back and see the three tractates whole. Then the several dimensions of discourse will emerge. When we survey the entire construction of the three Babas, what we see is a simple set of eight units. They move from abnormal to normal events, I–IV, then V–VIII. The whole begins with damages done by chattels or by persons, thefts and other sorts of conversion of the property of others, with special attention to how we restore to a state of normality the property and person of the injured party. Numbers I–IV runs through the whole of Baba Qamma and half way through Baba Mesia, to M. B.M. 5:11. The second half of the three tractates then shifts to normal transactions,

---

[1] The division into chapters is integral to the presentation of the tractates, as shown by the formal traits that define a given chapter and separate it from others, fore and aft. So form-analysis has shown. If the printers had not imposed the divisions by chapters, we should still know how to divide the several tractates and the halakhah they set forth, since where a topic changes, the form shifts as well. This is now a well-established fact. It accounts for the analysis given in the text, which on formal-analytical bases treats the division into tractates and chapters as integral to the document and not imposed at some later point by copyists or printers.

not those involving torts and damages: labor relationships, rentals and bailments, real estate transactions, inheritances and estates, units V–VIII. Then the whole produces two complementary constructions, first abnormal or illicit, then normal or licit transactions. That is shown by the correspondence of unit IV, illicit commercial transactions (overcharge and usury) and unit VII, licit commercial transactions, the legal transfer of goods, unstipulated conditions and how they are enforced. This plan furthermore explains why we treat bailments twice, at III.C, damages to bailments, and then at V.C, E, responsibilities of the bailee. The former fits into the larger structure of law on the restoration of the balance of the social order (here, the value possessed by parties to the transaction at the outset, equitably distributed at the end), the latter, that on the preservation of the same order. Here, in brief is the picture of the whole:

I. *ILLICIT TRANSACTIONS; RESTORING ORDER*
  Baba Qamma
    i. Damage by Chattels 1:1–6:6
    ii. Damages Done by Persons 7:1–10:10
  Baba Mesia
    iii. The Disposition of Other Peoples' Possessions; Bailments 1:1–3:12
    iv. Illicit Commercial Transactions. Overcharge, misrepresentation, usury 4:1–5:11
II. *LICIT TRANSACTIONS; PRESERVING ORDER*
    v. Hiring Workers. Rentals and Bailments 6:1–8:3
  Baba Mesia, Baba Batra
    vi. Real Estate B.M. 8:4–10:6, B.B. 1:1–5:5
  Baba Batra
    vii. Licit Commercial Transactions 5:6–7:4
    viii. Inheritances and Wills. Other Commercial and Legal Documents 8:1–10-8

The whole of Baba Qamma takes up the results of wicked intentionality, an act of will that takes the form of malice, on the one side, or flagrant neglect of one's duties, on the other. The rules of Baba Mesia address the situations in which intentionality plays a role, is excluded as irrelevant, and may or may not enter into the adjudication of a situation of conflict. And, as we have seen, the topics treated in Baba Batra in common take account of the idiosyncrasy of intentionality and exclude private interest from intervening in customary arrangements.

So we may say that the entire repertoire of topics lays itself out as a huge essay on the role of man's intentionality — his will, his private plans — in the ordering of Israel's inner life. All topics grouped by me as illicit transactions involve righting the wrongs done by people on their own account. When free will is taken into account, encompassing negligence and malice, the social order requires forceful intervention to right the balance upset by individual aggression. Some licit transactions permit individual intentionality to register, specifically, those freely entered into and fairly balanced among contracting parties. And some licit transactions leave no space for the will of the participants and their idiosyncratic plans. Considerations of fairness take over and exclude any engagement with the private and the personal. So Israel's social order takes account of intentionality, especially controlling for the damage that ill will brings about.

The first fifteen chapters then treat intentionality as a critical factor in assessing damages, negligence representing a chapter therein. But normal licit transactions are carried forward in accord with those rules of balance, proportion, and coherence that yield a society that is stable and enduring, fair and trustworthy. In the second fifteen chapters, intentionality forms only one consideration in the process of preserving the status, as to value, of parties to transactions and exchanges; it may make all the difference, no difference, some difference; it may not enter into consideration at all. That underscores the judgment of the halakhah that, when it comes to righting wrongs against chattels and persons, the malefactor has acted willfully and has therefore to be penalized in an equitable manner. By his act of will, he has diminished the property or person of the victim; he must then restore the property or person to its prior value, so far as this is possible, and may not benefit from what he has done.

On what basis does the halakhah undertake the initiatives that it takes? The question is a specific one: does the halakhah of the Oral Torah set forth in the Babas take as its principal task the exegesis of Scripture's laws? So far I have shown that what Scripture presents episodically, the halakhah portrays systematically. That is certainly so in Baba Qamma. But the purpose of the tractates in no way comes to realization in the articulation of the law of Scripture on the topics at hand. That is proved by the simple fact that most of Baba Mesia and Baba Batra pursues problems to which Scripture in no way devotes itself. So where Scripture provides halakhah, the Oral Torah faithfully attends to that halakhah; but the Oral Torah in no way limits itself to Scripture's repertoire of topics. More to the point, the Oral Torah organizes the halakhah systematically, but in accord with its own system and its problematics, not in accord with the system — the order, the program — of the Written Torah. We have, therefore, to look elsewhere for the religious program that animates the halakhah of the Babas.

For that purpose, our mind naturally turns to the results of our reading of the Aggadic formulation of matters, specifically, the formation of a theological structure to spell out the meaning of the generative conviction that the one and only God created the world in justice. That structure further found its dynamism in the dialectics of God's justice and the world's manifest imperfections. The tension between divine justice and man's fate, the claim of a perfect creation and the palpable failure of world order to realize stasis and perfection, come to resolution in the story of humanity beginning with Eden, losing Eden, attaining regeneration through the Torah, and recovering Eden. From Eden man through an act of arrogant will sinned and was expelled. But through the Torah, given to Israel defined by the Torah as God's people, God repaired the condition of man. In the realization of the Torah, man through Israel will return to Eden, the world to its intended, and original, perfection. The halakhah before us takes as its task the work of defining how, in full realization in the here and now, Israel's interior relationships may conform to the principles of perfection embodied in Eden in the beginning, and in the Land of Israel at the end. Stability, stasis, equity in exchange and restoration of what is inequitable — these mark perfection of the social order that the halakhah proposes to bring about in Israel's inner existence.

Now that general account of matters brings us to the halakhah of the Babas. Specifically, we have to ask, what has the restorationist reworking of the civil order into a state of perfection and stasis to do with Israel's interior bonds and relationships? How, specifically, does the formation of a civil order of stable, proportionate relationships in accord with principles of justice bring about Israel's right relationship with God? Asking the question in this way dictates the answer. The opening unit — Baba Qamma and the first half of Baba Mesia — takes the more difficult labor of restoring the perfection of the social order, the closing unit, the rest of Baba Mesia and Baba Batra, the easier one of maintaining it.

How do sages accomplish their statement in the matter of restoring order and value? Through their exposition of Scripture's laws of injury and misappropriation and through their formulation of their own, much more elaborate topical program for the civil order and the resolution of conflict at home, sages expose the rationality and order that inheres in the episodic rules of Scripture. Since, in their intellectual context, consistency, immutability, coherence mark perfection, sages affirm that in its details the Torah's design for dealing with conflict within holy Israel promises to perfect Israel's workaday world in the model set forth at Sinai. The Written Torah makes clear God's intense interest in the justice and equity of the Israelites' ordinary transactions among themselves. They are to form the kingdom of priests and the holy people. Their conduct with one another — the Written Torah's civil law insists in every line — shapes God's judgment of them and therefore dictates their fate. So sages here demonstrate what a man can do actively to participate in the perfection of the social order through the results of his own and his chattels' conduct. Here the consideration of man's free will proves paramount: what man by an act of will has upset, man by an act of will must restore.

Let us then turn to the topical program of the Babas, working our way from start to finish. The general observation concerning the restorationist theology that, I maintain, governs throughout emerges in the halakhah of Baba Qamma — injury and misappropriation. That comes about when we ask, what, as signified by the halakhah of Baba Qamma, does the halakhah ask a man to do in relationship to the exemplary social order under construction within Israel? When we look at the details of the law we have reviewed in Chapter One, the question dictates its own answer, and the restorationist motive takes center-stage.

Specifically, in accord with the halakhah of Baba Qamma man undertakes to assume responsibility for what he does, always in just proportion to causation. Within Israel's social order what God wants a man to do is take responsibility for his own actions, for the results of what he or his chattel has done — no more, no less. And that pervasive point of insistence transforms our view of the halakhic category before us. True, it forms an exercise in restoration and stasis of the just society. But in the details of the law is worked out a chapter of theological anthropology, an answer to the question, what, in the formation of the just society, can a man do? And the answer is, a man can and must take responsibility for not only what he does but also — and especially — what he brings about, the things he may not do but does cause to happen. Viewed in this way, the laws of Baba Qamma form a massive essay upon the interplay of causation and responsibility: what one can have prevented but through negligence (in varying measure depending on context) has allowed to take place, he is deemed in that same measure to have caused. And for that, he is held in that same measure to make amends. And therein, as I shall point out presently, lies a profoundly religious statement within the framework of the Torah, the oral part here realizing in immediate terms along the lines of wholly interior-Israelite dimensions the message of the written part.

Responsibility begins in right attitude. Man must form the intentionality of taking responsibility for his actions; this he must do by an act of will. That is why the whole of Baba Qamma plays itself out as an exercise in the definition of the valid intentionality in transactions involving damage and conflict. Where one has diminished another, he must willingly take responsibility for his deed of omission or commission (as the tractate unfolds). The message of the halakhah on man's taking responsibility cannot be missed in the ringing opening words of the Mishnah-tractate. I underline the full statement of the matter that links causality and responsibility: "What they have in common is that they customarily do damage and taking care of them is your responsibility. And when one of them has caused damage, the [owner] of that which causes the damage is liable to pay compensation... *In the case of anything of which I am liable to take care, I am deemed to render possible whatever damage it may do*. If I am deemed to have rendered possible part of the damage it may do, I am liable for compensation as if [I have] made possible all of the damage it may do." That remarkably eloquent, decisive formulation contains the entire message of Baba Qamma and the first half of Baba Mesia.

It follows that man in all of his dignity is portrayed through the halakhah of Baba Qamma as possessed [1] of free will to assume responsibility, on the one side, and [2] of the power to take action in consequence of responsibility, on the other. And that principle assumes religious status in two steps. First, in the words of the Written Torah God himself has framed the laws that link causation and responsibility — negligence and culpability, for instance. In the very portrayal of the holy society that Israel at Sinai is commanded to realize, God's stake in man's framing of the social order is made explicit. And consequently, second, Israel in the workaday transactions of one person with another acts out in this-worldly terms its governing principle of transactions with Heaven. The one in palpable terms shows the character of the other in intangible ways.

Does the halakhah of injury and misappropriation focus upon the link of causation and responsibility? In nearly every line of the halakhic category we have reviewed here in Chapter One. The cited language shows that the halakhah states in so many words man's responsibility for the consequences of his actions, insisting upon God's stake in the transaction by systematically working out Scripture's rules and even stating their general principle. What follows? A catalogue that encompasses nearly the entire detailed program of the halakhah.

Consider the topical program of the halakhah, and see how, start to finish, the details define a statement concerning the data of the category at hand. Here in yet another reprise is the repertoire: how compensation is to be paid; the variation in compensation by reason of Scripture's distinctions, e.g., between cases of mere accident and those of culpable negligence (attested dangers), where people should have known to take care; man's responsibility for the public interest and the general welfare of the public domain; variables in liability for oneself and one's chattels; attenuated forms of responsibility ("He who causes a fire to break out through the action of a deaf-mute, idiot, or minor, is exempt from punishment under the laws of man, but liable to punishment under the laws of heaven"); penalties for causing damages done in the three dimensions of social concern: damages done to the Land (public property, encompassing ecological considerations), damages done to persons, and damages done to private property.

And the statement that is made, and that can best be made in connection with the topics of injury and misappropriate, emerges in sages' sorting out of details and nuances of responsibility and consequent liability for compensation. If someone set out to teach through a concrete example the variation of responsibility by reason of variables of what is willful and foreseeable and preventable, how better to deliver the message than by distinguishing between what is (formerly) deemed harmless and what is (formerly) an attested danger? Once the Torah makes that distinction, the message emerges: we are responsible for all damages that we could have foreseen, but our responsibility is mitigated when the damages cannot have been foreseen, prevented, let alone wanted. And, further, responsibility is to be accepted, damages compensated — the whole in a forthright transaction among honorable men.

If we could then summarize the details of the law in a few general principles, what should we say? The halakhah holds that we are responsible for what we do and what we cause, but we are not responsible (or not responsible in the same degree) for what we cannot control. So the law asks, how does our action or lack of action relate to the consequence of what we do or not do? If we do not know that an act has caused a result, we cannot hold responsible the person who has done the act for the consequences he has brought about. The law works out these gradations between total culpability or blame, by reason of one's forming the efficient cause without mitigating considerations, and total absolution from culpability and blame, by reason of one's bearing no responsibility whatsoever for what has happened:

[1] responsibility for all damages done, because the event that has caused loss and damage is voluntary and foreseeable, not the result of overwhelming external force; preventable; brought about by willful action; the result of culpable knowledge; deliberate choice, not mere negligence;

[2] responsibility for the greater part of the damages that are done, because the damage is foreseeable; not the result of overwhelming external force; preventable; thus in the event the ignorance is classified as culpable; but not voluntary;

[3] responsibility for the lesser part of the damages that are done, because the damage is foreseeable; but the result of overwhelming external force and not preventable, thus: involuntary, but the result of culpable ignorance and negligence;

[4] no responsibility at all, the event being involuntary, the result of overwhelming external force, not foreseeable, hence, inculpable ignorance; e.g., pure chance.

We therefore identify in the working out of the halakhah three operative criteria — points of differentiation in the analysis of events and the actions that produce them, which form a cubic grid, with, in theory, nine gradations of blame and responsibility and consequent culpability:

[1] an event produced by an action that is voluntary vs. involuntary;
[2] an event that is foreseeable vs. not foreseeable, or an action the consequences of which are foreseeable vs. not;

[3] an event that is preventable vs. not preventable; or an action that is necessary and therefore blameless, or one that is not.

Thus we may construct a grid of three layers or dimensions, one grid formed of considerations of what is voluntary vs. involuntary, the second, of what is foreseeable vs. not foreseeable, the third, of what is preventable vs. not preventable, lines. That permits us to identify an efficient cause that is voluntary, foreseeable, and preventable; voluntary, foreseeable, and not preventable; involuntary, foreseeable, and preventable; involuntary, not foreseeable, and not preventable; and so on.

I dwell on this matter of responsibility because for Baba Qamma it forms the leitmotif of the halakhah, the hermeneutical crux, the exegetical provocation for the analysis of particular problems. Now this elaborate program of thought that is embodied in the exquisite details of the halakhah leads us to ask, what, exactly, is at stake in the linkage of causation and responsibility? The religious dimension of the matter emerges when we explain why the halakhah makes the statement that it does. That statement, set forth in a few words, holds that in a society ordered by God's justice — as Israelite society is supposed to be — man will acknowledge his responsibility and bear the consequences of his actions. The negative here makes all the difference. What will Israelite man not do? He will not deny or dissimulate. He will not blame others but take no blame himself. When he has upset the social order by diminishing the other and aggrandizing the self, he will restore the balance he has upset. Confronted with the result of his own negligence or worse, man cannot shift the burden of blame or avoid responsibility for the consequences of what he has caused. And the entire arrangement for restoring the social balance and preserving the social order builds upon that principle. The social order then forms an exercise in man's accepting responsibility for what he does. What, in Israelite context, marks that statement as critical to the religious world of the Torah?

To answer that question, we revert to the initial point at which the world order of justice was disrupted by an act of man. And when we take up that moment of flaw and imperfection, we must examine whether and how the consideration of accepting responsibility for the damage one has done enters in. In this context, then, we turn to beginnings. So we have to recall how the theology set forth mainly in the aggadic documents dwells upon the story of Adam's fall from Eden by reason of rebellion against God's word.

For the theology of the sages of the Oral Torah, the fall is recapitulated in the setting of Israel's loss of the Land for rebellion against the Torah. Israel's return to the Land marks the opportunity to correct the errors of Eden. The halakhah of the Oral Torah spells out how this is to be done. Those general considerations govern here.

To see how that is so, we have to recall that in the setting of the halakhah of Shebi'it, the halakhah for its part — both as set forth in the Written Torah and as elaborated in the Oral Torah — demonstrates what it means to live in the Eden that is the Land through faithful obedience, by an act of free will, to the Torah. Israel relates to God in one way above all, and that is, by exercising in ways that show love for God and acceptance of God's dominion the power of free will that God has given man.

What has the matter of taking responsibility for what one has caused pertain, so that the halakhah before us turns out to realize in its terms the challenge of the fall and Israel's response to the restoration: do right what then went wrong, correct the error of Eden. That time and again turns out to form the religious statement of the halakhah, just as we noted in connection with the halakhah of 'Orlah. Now to the point: the story of man's disobedience in Eden (Gen. 3:11–13) tells why man's accepting responsibility for what he causes forms the center of the halakhah of damages and misappropriation. Here is the original version of man's denial of responsibility:

God: *Did you eat of the tree from which I had forbidden you to eat?*
Man: *The woman you put at my side — she gave me of the tree and I ate*
God: *What is this you have done?*
Woman: *The serpent duped me and I ate.*

At the center of the story of the human condition after Eden is man's and woman's denial of responsibility for the deed each did, and, implicitly, rejection of responsibility for the consequent loss of Eden that is coming. At the heart of the halakhah of damages and misappropriation is the opposite: Israelite man's explicit acceptance of responsibility for what he causes. Why so? Because if Israel wants to show God that it is regenerate, how better to do so than act out in cases of damages and injury the requirement to bear responsibility for what one does and causes to happen (Adam, Eve, respectively)? Here in its everyday conduct of the inner affairs of the community, Israel shows how, unlike Adam and Eve, through the instruction of the Torah, Israel has learned what it means to take responsibility for injury and damage to others.

Within Israel's workaday life, in the very practicalities of conflict and its resolution aimed at restoring and preserving the perfection of the status quo, is conducted an on-going exercise. It is one of making explicit one's responsibility for what one has caused, then apportioning damages in proportion to one's negligence or malfeasance. What is voluntary, foreseeable, and preventable imposes maximum liability for restoration. Man cannot blame his ox, nor in the public way impose upon bypassers the responsibility to accommodate the obstacles he has set up. The premise of the exercise is that Israel's inner affairs, the transactions between and among Israelites, in the most practical terms, are conducted as a test of whether regenerate man — Israelite man — can bear responsibility for his own actions, now viewed in the broadest context of causation, and, if so, what it means to match levels of compensation to degrees of responsibility. No excuses ("the woman you put at my side," "the snake duped me") exculpate when one has caused damage, because Israelite man assumes the burden of his actions and takes responsibility so far as possible to restore the world to its original condition, before, in the here and now, some deed or act of negligence of his has disrupted it. I can think of no more direct response to "the woman ... the snake ..." than the language, "In the case of anything of which I am liable to take care, I am deemed to render possible whatever damage it may do."

In the myriad of individual transactions for which the law provides, Israel shows it has learned the lesson of Eden and applied that lesson to the social order of the Land. Why in the interiorities of relationships at home? Because it is not among strangers but within the community that workaday actions matter most. In intimacy, responsibility registers. In Eden it was before God that man was ashamed, and, in Israel, it is with one's fellow Israelite that man shows he has learned the lesson of Adam's denial. That is what is at stake in those eloquent, implacable words, which Adam should have said but Israel now does say: In the case of anything of which I am liable to take care, I am deemed to render possible whatever damage it may do. And, in the language of the Mishnah itself: Man is perpetually an attested danger whether what is done is done inadvertently or deliberately, whether man is awake or asleep. If he blinded the eye of his fellow or broke his utensils, he pays the full value of the damage he has caused. Would that Adam had said of himself to God what Israel affirms day by day and, as we see in the spinning out of the halakhah, in every way as well.

So much for the first of the Babas. The second and third gates complete the picture. Here the issue is sustaining the social order, as we have seen. Here too attitude and intentionality come into play, but in a different way from before. Sin, crime, torts and damages — these carry forward bad attitudes; differentiating types and degrees of intentionality when addressing how the social order is disrupted yields nothing of interest. By contrast, in treating ordinary exchanges and transactions, the halakhah turns out to form an essay on when intentionality matters and when it does not.

How is this the case? When it comes to restoring the perfection of society, specifically, where do we take account of intentionality and where not? Intentionality or attitude matters in situations of conflict. Then the attitude of both parties makes all the difference, since to resolve conflicting claims, we have in the end to conciliate all parties to a common outcome; there, intentionality or attitude forms the critical medium for restoring and sustaining balance and order. Parties to an exchange are now responsible to one another, and they must intend the outcome to be a proportionate and equal exchange of value. Both parties must accept the outcome, that is, form at the end the same attitude toward the transaction. A claim of ownership ends in an act of despair. Responsibility is proportionate to the attitude of the bailee, that is, to the degree of accountability that he has accepted to begin with. So much for the uses of intentionality in the restoration and maintenance of the social order.

But then where do we dismiss as null all considerations of intentionality or attitude, even when parties to an exchange concur? In market transactions, by contrast, true value overrides the attitude of the players, who cannot agree to an exchange that in objective terms is deemed null. Even where all parties agree, the Torah too must approve. And, we noted, we impute to all parties the same attitude and deny the pertinence of idiosyncratic or private meanings. Broadly-held expectations govern, whether those of custom or of the written Torah's own law. In these two ways — the Torah's law, which is not relative to the will of man, and established custom, which defines the norm for man — intentionality possesses no power, because it serves no purpose in restoring or sustaining the balances of a well-ordered society.

So the thirty chapters, breaking into two halves at the end of the first fifteen, in the middle of the second tractate, through the exposition of the law set forth a massive exercise in the applied reason and practical logic of the abstract categories, responsibility and intentionality. What message emerges when we move from the illicit to the licit, the abnormal to the normal? The transactions that all together form the ordinary life of inner Israel, Israel on its own, yield two matching propositions. First, when it comes to acts that disrupt the social order, man is responsible for what he does. But, second, when we turn to transactions that sustain the ordinary relationships within Israel, man's proper intentionality takes over. Then man's will forms only one element in a complex transaction. Where wills clash, compromise takes over. Where the Torah imposes its own rule, intentionality is null. Publicly-accepted custom and procedure take the paramount position. In cases of negligence or malfeasance, man takes responsibility for what he has done — so much for the first half of the Babas.

And that brings us to the everyday conduct of affairs in ordinary Israelite society, as in the world of perfect order and stasis of Eden at the outset and the Land of Israel at the end? Social order restored, the status quo as to value regained, what forces hold the whole together? Where responsibility prevails, man's own will and intentionality, God's will in the Torah, and the customary arrangements of a stable, just society — all these variables come into play and are to be sorted out. That is why, while single message addresses the abnormal and the illicit, the realm of torts and damages: take responsibility to attain Eden, a much more complex message states the requirements of maintaining matters. That message responds to the realities of the ideal society that the halakhah makes possible.

Specifically, Israel in its interior arrangements is to hold in the balance [1] personal will, [2] the Torah's law, and [3] the long-standing customary requirements of enduring order. In the Babas, as this survey of the halakhah has shown, these distinct and interrelated forces — man's will, God's law, and accepted public practice — are far from abstractions. In the interplay of individual will, God's absolute law, and ancient, enduring custom, Eden endures in the realization of Israel in the here and now. No wonder the great teacher, Samuel, took the view, "There is no difference between the world to come and the days of the messiah, except the end of the subjugation of the exilic communities of Israel" (B. 11:12 I.24/91B).

That is to say, in context, the Messiah will restore Israel to the Land (one of his two principal missions, raising the dead beyond the other), the Torah to the government of Israel in the Land. Then, for all eternity marked by "the world to come," Eden once recovered will endure forever.

But Eden is an occasion, a situation, a mode of organization, as much as a location. In the statement of the halakhah Eden is a condition that prevails in the here and now of inheritances and wills, real estate and market transactions, a circumstance that comes about in the compromise of conflict and through the fair and just arrangements brought about among the householder and laboring craftsman and farm worker. With the proper intentionality, in full responsibility, maintaining the ancient order and arrangements of the Torah, Israel in the Land will realize Eden — this time around forever.

4.

TRACTATE SANHEDRIN

I. An Outline of the Halakhah of Sanhedrin

The halakhah set forth in the tractate of Sanhedrin — Mishnah, Tosefta, Yerushalmi, Bavli — deals with the organization of the Israelite government and courts and punishments administered thereby. The court system is set forth in the Mishnah's statement of matters at M. 1:1–5:5, the death-penalty at 6:1–11:6, and extra-judicial penalties at 9:5–6, 10:1–6. The penalties other than capital are set forth in tractate Makkot, covering perjury (with variable penalties), banishment, and flogging. While Scripture supplies many facts, the Oral Torah organizes and lays matters out in its own way. Where the Written Torah does not provide information that sages deem logical and necessary, they make things up for themselves. Where verses of Scripture play a role in the halakhic statement of matters, they are cited in context. The details of the organization of the court system do not derive from the Written Torah, nor are the specificities of the death penalty supplied there. The contribution of the Written Torah is therefore episodic. Dt. 16:18–20 specifies appointing judges, Dt. 17:8–13 provides for an appellate system, "If any case arises requiring a decision between one kind of homicide and another, one kind of legal right and another, or one kind of assault and another, any case within your towns that is too difficult for you, then you shall arise and go up to the place that the Lord your God will choose...." The death penalty for murder is specified at Num. 35:30, on the testimony of two or three witnesses, Dt. 17:6–7. The comparison of the high priest and the king at M. San. 2:1ff., rests on Lev. 21:10–12 for the high priest and Dt. 17:14–20 for the king. The death penalty involving hanging the body on a tree until night but burial the same day is at Dt. 21:22–23; the stubborn and rebellious son at Dt. 21:18–21. The city that is wiped out because of idolatry is treated at Dt. 13:12–18. The upshot is that at specific topics, Scripture, cited here and there, contributes facts, but the shape and program of the tractate as a whole is not to be predicted on the basis of the Written Torah.

i. *The Court System*

A. *Various Kinds of Courts and their Jurisdiction*

M. 1:1 (1) Property cases [are decided] by three [judges]; (2) those concerning theft and damages, before three; (3) [cases involving] compensation for full-damages, half-damages [Ex. 21:35], twofold restitution [Ex. 22:3], fourfold and fivefold restitution [Ex. 21:37], by three; (4) cases involving him who rapes [Deut. 32:28–29], him who seduces [Ex. 22:15–16].

T. 1:2 Just as judgment is done before three judges, so arbitration is reached by three judges. Once the court process has been completed, one has not got the right to arbitrate.

M. 1:2 (5) [Cases involving the penalty of] flogging [Deut. 25:2–3] are before three. (6) [The decision to] intercalate the month is before three.

T. 2:2 On account of three signs do they intercalate the year, because of the [premature state of] the grain, because of the condition of the produce of the tree, and because of the lateness of the spring equinox. On account of two of these they will intercalate the year, but on account of only one of them, they will not intercalate the year. But if they declared the year to be intercalated, lo, this is deemed intercalated. If the premature state of the grain was one of them, they would rejoice.

T. 2:3 On account of [evidence of conditions in] three regions do they intercalate the year: Judea, Trans-Jordan, and Galilee. On account of evidence produced in two of them they intercalate the year, but on account of evidence deriving from only one of them they do not intercalate the year. But if they declared the year to be intercalated, lo, this is deemed intercalated.

T. 2:4 A. They do not intercalate the year because [the season of the] kids, lambs, or pigeons has not yet come. But in the case of all of them, they regard it as a support [for intercalating] the year. But if they declared the year to be intercalated [on their basis], lo, this is deemed intercalated.

T. 2:8 They do not intercalate the year by less than a month or by more than a month. And if they intercalated it [by less or by more than a month], it is not deemed to have been intercalated. And they do not intercalate a year in advance. And if they did intercalate a year in advance, it is not deemed intercalated. And they do not intercalate one year after another [successively].

T. 2:12 They intercalate the year only when it needs it. They intercalate it because of the roads, because of the ovens, and because of the residents of the Exilic Communities, who have not been able to go forth from their homes. But they do not intercalate the year because of cold, snow, or the Exiles who already have made the ascent [for the pilgrimage]. But all of those factors do they treat as additional reason [for intercalating] the year. And if they intercalated the year [on these counts], lo, it is deemed intercalated.

B. 1:1–6 VIII. 14 They do not intercalate the year either in the case of the Seventh Year or in the case of the year after the Seventh Year. When are they accustomed to intercalate the year? In the year before the Seventh Year.

M. 1:3 (9) The rite of removal of the shoe [breaking the levirate bond] (Deut. 25:7–9) and the exercise of the right of refusal are done before three judges. (10) [The evaluation of] fruit of fourth-year plantings [which is to be redeemed [(Lev. 19:23–25)] and of second tithe (Deut. 14:22–26) whose value is not known is done before three judges. (11) Assessment of the value, [for purposes of redemption,] of things which have been consecrated is done before three judges. (12) [Property pledged as security for] vows of valuation, in the case of movables, is evaluated by three [judges]. And [evaluation of property pledged as security for vows for valuation] in the case of real estate is done by nine and a priest. And so for [the valuation-vow covering] men.

T. 1:2 Movables which have been consecrated, the fruit of fourth year plantings [which is to be redeemed], and the evaluation of second tithe whose value is not known [M. San. 1:3D] are redeemed in accord with the judgment of [assessment of the value by] three purchasers, and not in accord with the opinion of three who are not [serious] purchasers.

M. 1:4 (1) Cases involving the death penalty are judged before twenty-three judges. (2) The beast who commits or is subjected to an act of sexual relations with a human being is judged by twenty-three, since it is said, "And you will kill the woman and the beast" (Lev. 20:16). And it says, "And the beast you will slay" (Lev. 20:15). (3) An ox which is to be stoned is judged by twenty-three, since it is said, "And the ox will be stoned, and also its master will be put to death" (Ex. 21:29). Just as [the case of the master], leading to the death-penalty, [is adjudged], so is the [case of] the ox, [leading to] the death-penalty. The wolf, lion, bear, panther, leopard, and snake a capital case affecting them is judged by twenty-three.

T. 3:1 A. An ox which caused death — all the same [is the law for] an ox which caused death and any other sort of domestic or wild beast or fowl which caused death — their [trial for the penalty of] death is [before] twenty-three judges].

T. 3:2 An ox which is to be stoned is judged by twenty-three judges [M. San. 1:4E], since it is said, "And the ox will be stoned, and also its master will be put to death" (Ex. 21:29). Just as [the case of the master], leading to the death-penalty is adjudged], so is the case of the ox, leading to] the death-penalty [M. San. 1:4F–G]. Just as the death penalty meted out to the master is by stoning, by being pushed down, and before twenty-three judges, so the death penalty meted out to the ox is by stoning, by being pushed down, and before twenty-three judges.

M. 1:5 (1) They judge a tribe, a false prophet [Deut. 18:20], and a high priest, only on the instructions of a court of seventy-one members. (2) They bring forth [the army] to wage a war fought by choice only on the instructions of a court of seventy-one. (3) They make additions to the city [of Jerusalem] and to the courtyards [of the Temple] only on the instructions of a court of seventy-one. (4) They set up sanhedrins for the tribes only on the instructions of a court of seventy-one. (5) They declare a city to be "an apostate City" [Deut. 13:12ff.] only on the instructions of a court of seventy-one. And they do not declare a city to be "an Apostate city" on the frontier, [nor do they declare] three [in one locale] to be apostate cities, but they do so in the case of one or two.

T. 3:4 They burn the red cow, break the neck of the heifer, and declare an old man to be rebellious, only at the decision of a court [of seventy-one members]. And they prepare a bullock brought by reason of an unwitting sin of the community and appoint a king and a high priest only at the decision of a court of seventy-one members. How do they effect [an alteration in the city and in the courtyard of the Temple] [M. San. 1:5C]? The court comes forth, with two thank-offerings behind them. The inner one [nearest the court] is eaten, and the outer one is burned. But [if] any detail of this was not done, he who enters that area is not liable on that account. The two thank-offerings of which they spoke include their bread-offering but not their meat-offering.

M. 1:6 The great Sanhedrin was [made up] of seventy-one members, and the small one was twenty-three. And how do we know that the great Sanhedrin was to have seventy-one members? Since it is said, "Gather to me seventy men of the elders of Israel" (Num. 11:16). Since Moses was in addition to them, [lo, there were seventy one.] And how do we know that a small one is twenty-three? Since it is said, "The congregation shall judge, and the congregation shall deliver" (Num. 35:24, 25) — one congregation judges, and one congregation saves — thus there are twenty. And how do we know that a congregation is ten? Since it is said, "how long shall I bear with this evil congregation [of the ten spies]" (Num. 14:27) — excluding Joshua and Caleb. And how do we know that we should add three more? From the implication of that which is said, "You shall not follow after the many to do evil" (Ex: 23:20), I derive the inference that I should be with them to do good. If so, why is it said, "After the many to do evil"? Your verdict of acquittal is not equivalent to your verdict of guilt. Your verdict of acquittal may be on the vote of a majority of one, but your vote for

guilt must be by a majority of two. Since there cannot be a court of an even number of members [twenty-two], they add yet another — thus twenty-three. And how many residents must there be in a town so that it may be suitable for a Sanhedrin? One hundred-twenty.

B. *The Heads of the Israelite Nation and the Court-System*

M. 2:1 A high priest judges, and [others] judge him; gives testimony, and [others] give testimony about him; performs the rite of removing the shoe [Deut. 25:7–9], and [others] perform the rite of removing the shoe with his wife. [Others] enter levirate marriage with his wife, but he does not enter into levirate marriage, because he is prohibited to marry a widow. [If] he suffers a death [in his family], he does not follow the bier. And when he gives comfort to others the accepted practice is for all the people to pass one after another, and the appointed [prefect of the priests] stands between him and the people. And when he receives consolation from others, all the people say to him, "Let us be your atonement." And he says to them, "May you be blessed by Heaven." And when they provide him with the funeral meal, all the people sit on the ground, while he sits on a stool.

T. 4:1 A. A high priest who committed homicide — [if he did so] deliberately, he is executed; [if he did so], inadvertently, he goes into exile to the cities of refuge [Num. 35:9ff]. [If] he transgressed a positive or negative commandment or indeed any of the commandments, lo, he is treated like an ordinary person in every respect. He does not perform the rite of removing the shoe [Deut. 25:7–9], and others do not perform the rite of removing the shoe with his wife [vs. M. San. 2:1C]. He does not enter into levirate marriage, and [others] do not enter into levirate marriage with his wife [cf. M. San. 2:1C–E]. [When] he stands in the line [to receive comfort as a mourner], the prefect of the priests is at his right hand, and the head of the father's houses [the priestly courses] at his left hand. And all the people say to him, "Let us be your atonement." And he says to them, "May you be blessed by Heaven" [M. San. [And when] he stands in the line to give comfort to others, the prefect of the priests and the [high] priest who has now passed out of his position of grandeur are at his right hand, and the mourner is at his left. [People may] not watch him while he is getting a haircut, [or while he is nude] or in the bath-house [M. San. 2:5B], since it is said, "And he who is high priest among his brothers" (Lev. 21:10) — that his brethren should treat him with grandeur. But if he wanted to permit others to wash with him, the right is his.

M. 2:2 The king does not judge, and [others] do not judge him; does not give testimony, and [others] do not give testimony about him; does not perform the rite of removing the shoe, and

others do not perform the rite of removing the shoe with his wife; does not enter into levirate marriage, nor [do his brother] enter levirate marriage with his wife. [Others] do not marry his widow.

T. 4:2 An Israelite king does not stand in line to receive comfort [in the time of bereavement], nor does he stand in line to give comfort to others. And he does not go to provide a funeral meal for others. But others come to him to give him a funeral meal [M. San. 2:3F]. And if he transgressed a positive or a negative commandment or indeed any of the commandments, lo, he is treated like an ordinary person in every respect. He does not perform the rite of removing the shoe, and others do not perform the rite of removing the shoe with his wife, he does not enter into levirate marriage, nor] do his brothers enter into levirate marriage with his wife [M. San. 2:2C–D]. And [others] do not marry his widow IM. San. 2:3G], as it is said, So they were shut up to the day of their death, living in widowhood (2 Sam. 20:3). And he has the right to choose wives for himself from any source he wants, whether daughters of priests, Levites, or Israelites. And they do not ride on his horse, sit on his throne, handle his crown or scepter or any of his regalia [M. San. 2:5].

M. 2:3 [If] [the king] suffers a death in his family, he does not leave the gate of his palace. And when they provide him with the funeral meal, all the people sit on the ground, while he sits on a couch.

B. 2:3 I. 1/20A IN A PLACE IN WHICH WOMEN ARE ACCUSTOMED TO GO FORTH AFTER THE BIER, THEY GO FORTH IN THAT WAY. IF THEY ARE ACCUSTOMED TO GO FORTH BEFORE THE BIER, THEY GO FORTH IN THAT MANNER.

M. 2:4 [The king] calls out [the army to wage] a war fought by choice on the instructions of a court of seventy-one. He [may exercise the right to] open a road for himself, and [others] may not stop him. The royal road has no required measure. All the people plunder and lay before him [what they have grabbed], and he takes the first portion. "He should not multiply wives to himself" (Deut. 17:17) — only eighteen. "He should not multiply horses to himself" (Deut. 17:16) — only enough for his chariot. "Neither shall he greatly multiply to himself silver and gold" (Deut. 17:16) — only enough to pay his army. "And he writes out a scroll of the Torah for himself" (Deut. 17:17). When he goes to war, he takes it out with him; when he comes back, he brings it back with him; when he is in session in court, it is with him; when he is reclining, it is before him, as it is said, "And it shall be with him, and he shall read in it all the days of his life" (Deut. 17:19).

T. 4:7 "And he writes for himself a scroll of the Torah" (Deut. 17:17) — for his own use, that he not have to make use of the one of his fathers, but rather of his own, as it is said, "And he will write for himself" — that the very writing of the scroll should be for him [in particular]. And an ordinary person has no right to read in it, as it is said, "And he will read in it" — he, and no one else. And they examine [his scroll] in the court of the priests, in the court of the Levites, and in the court of the Israelites who are of suitable genealogical character to marry into the priesthood. [When] he goes to war, it is with him, when he comes back, it is with him [cf. M. San. 2:4M]; when he goes to court it is with him; when he goes to the urinal, it waits for him [outside] at the door.

T. 4:10 They do not appoint a king outside of the Land. They appoint a king only if he was married into the priesthood. And they anoint kings only over a spring, as it is said, "And he said to them, Take with you the servants of your lord and mount Solomon, my son, upon my own mule, and bring him down to Gihon" (I Kings 1:33).

M. 2:5 [Others may] not ride on his horse, sit on his throne, handle his scepter. And [others may] not watch him while he is getting a haircut, or while he is nude, or in the bath-house, since it is said, "You shall surely set him as king over you" (Deut. 17:15) — that reverence for him will be upon you.

C. *The Procedures of the Court-System: Property Cases*

M. 3:1 Property-cases are [decided by] three [judges] [M. 1:1A]. This litigant chooses one [judge], and that litigant chooses one judge. The two judges choose one more. This party has the right to invalidate the judge chosen by that one, and that party has the right to invalidate the judge chosen by this one. Under what circumstances? When he brings evidence about them, that they are relatives or otherwise invalid. But if they are valid [judges] or court-certified experts, he has not got the power to invalidate them. This party invalidates the witnesses brought by that one, and that party invalidates the witnesses brought by this one. Under what circumstances? What he brings evidence about them, that they are relatives or otherwise invalid. But if they are valid [to serve as witnesses], he has not got the power to invalidate them.

M. 3:2 If one litigant said to the other, "I accept my father as reliable," "I accept your father as reliable," "I accept as reliable three herdsmen [to serve as judges]," he has the power to retract. [If] one owed an oath to his fellow, and his fellow said, "[Instead of an oath], take a vow to me by the life of your head," he has not got the power to retract.

M. 3:3 And these are those who are invalid [to serve as witnesses or judges]: he who plays dice; he who loans money on interest; those who race pigeons; and those who do business in the produce of the Seventh Year.

T. 5:2 He who plays dice [M. San. 3:3] — this refers to one who plays with blocks of wood. All the same are one who plays with blocks of wood, and one who plays with nut-shells or pomegranate shells — under no circumstances does such a person have the power to reform himself unless he undertakes to break his blocks of wood and to carry out a complete reformation. One who lends on interest [M. San. 3:3B2] does not have the power to reform himself unless he tears up bonds of indebtedness owing to him, and to carry out a complete reformation. He who races pigeons [M. San. 3:3B3] — this refers to one who trains pigeons. All the same are the one who trains pigeons and the one who trains any other sort of domesticated beast, wild beast, or bird — under no circumstances does such a person have the power to reform himself unless he undertakes to break those things which disqualify him and to carry out a complete reformation. Those who do business in the produce of the Seventh Year [M. San. 3:3B4] — This is one who sits idle during the other six years of the septennate. Once the Seventh Year comes, he stretches out his hands and legs and does business in produce of transgression. Under no circumstances does such a person have the power to reform himself until another year of release arrives, so one may test him and find that he has reformed himself completely.

T. 5:4 They do not judge one another, with one another, concerning one another, or in the presence of one another. [If] one had testimony concerning another when he was [the latter's] son-in-law, [if the latter's] daughter died — [if] it was while he was trading in produce of the Seventh Year and he reformed himself — [if] he was a deaf-mute and gained the power of hearing and speech — [if] he was a blind person and regained his sight — [if] he was an idiot and regained his senses — [if] he was a gentile and he converted—he [nonetheless] is invalid [as a witness]. [If the testimony concerned the other] before [the witness] had become his son-in-law, and then he became his son-in-law, and after he became his son-in-law, [the latter's] daughter died — [or] before he became a trader in the produce of the Seventh Year, and after he became a produce trader in the produce of the Seventh Year, he reformed himself — [or] he had power of hearing and speech and was made a deaf-mute and then he went and regained his powers of hearing and speech — or before he became blind, and then he became blind but regained his sight — or before he became an idiot, and then he became an idiot, and then he went and regained his sanity — it is valid. This is the governing principle: Any evidence for which one is at the outset valid and at the end valid is valid. [If] at the outset and at the end he is invalid, or at the outset he is invalid and at the end he is valid, [the evidence] is invalid.

M. 3:4 And these are relatives [prohibited from serving as one's witnesses or judges]: (1) one's father, (2) brother, (3) father's brother, (4) mother's brother, (5) sister's husband, (6) father's sister's husband, (7) mother's sister's husband, (8) mother's husband, (9) father-in-law, and (10) wife's sister's husband — they, their sons, and their sons-in-law; but the step-son only [but not the step-son's offspring]. And anyone who is related to him at that time, [If] one was a relative but ceased to be related, lo, that person is valid.

T. 5:5 [If] he had evidence concerning him in a document in his own writing and became his son-in-law, he cannot confirm the testimony in his own writing, but others may confirm the testimony in his writing. [If] he purchased from him a house or a field for a hundred maneh and knew evidence concerning him in their regard, lo, this one may not give evidence, for a person may not testify in his own behalf. They added to [the list of those who may not give testimony or serve as judges] robbers, herdsmen, extortionist, and all who are suspect in money matters. Their testimony is invalid under all circumstances. The testimony of witnesses is confirmed only if they had been in sight of one another.

M. 3:6 How do they test the witnesses? They bring them into the room and admonish them. Then they take everyone out and keep back the most important of the group. And they say to him, "Explain: How do you know that this one owes money to that one." If he said, "He told me, 'I owe him,' 'So-and-so told me that he owes him,'" he has said nothing whatsoever, unless he says, "In our presence he admitted to him that he owes him two hundred zuz." And afterward they bring in the second and test him in the same way. If their testimony checks out, they discuss the matter. [If] two [judges] say, "He is innocent," and one says, "He is guilty," he is innocent. [If] two say, "He is guilty," and one says, "He is innocent," he is guilty. [If] one says, "He is innocent," and one says, "He is guilty," — or even if two declare him innocent and two declare him guilty — but one of them says, "I don't know," they have to add judges.

M. 3:7 [When] they have completed the matter, they bring them back in. The chief judge says, "Mr. So-and-so, you are innocent," "Mr. So-and-so, you are guilty." Now how do we know that when one of the judges leave [the court], he may not say, "I think he is innocent, but my colleagues think he is guilty, so what can I do? For my colleagues have the votes!" Concerning such a person, it is said, "You shall not go up and down as a talebearer among your people" (Lev. 19:16). And it is said, "He who goes about as a talebearer and reveals secrets, [but he that is faithful conceals the matter]" (Prov. 11:13).

T. 6:1 Witnesses who stated, "We testify concerning Mr. So-and-so that his ox killed so-and-so," or "Cut down the plants of so-and-so" — and the accused says, "I don't know about it" — [the accused] is liable. "You intended to kill him," "You intended to cut them down" — everything is in accord with the complaint. "You killed my ox," "You cut down my plants" — and the accused says, "No!" as an expression of surprise, or "Yes?" as an expression of surprise — there is such a thing as a "No!" which is like a yes, and a "Yes?" which is like a no.

T. 6:2 They give judgment only standing. And they give testimony only standing. And they accept inquiry for the absolution of vows only when standing. And they raise up someone to the status of the priesthood or to the status of an Israelite only when standing. [The judges] may not show kindness to one party and impatience with another party, nor allow one to stand and the other to sit, as it is said, "In righteousness you shall judge your neighbor" (Lev. 19:15).

T. 6:3 How do they carry out a judgment? The judges seat themselves and the litigants remain standing before them. Whoever brings claim against his fellow is the one who opens the proceedings. And if there are witnesses, they bring them in and they admonish them. Then they take all of them out, and they keep back the most important one of the group [M. San. 3:6B–C]. And they hear his testimony and bring him out. And afterward they bring in both of them at the same time and this one says his testimony in the presence of the other. If [all the judges] rule that he is innocent, he is innocent. If they rule that he is guilty, he is guilty. All the same is the rule for monetary and capital cases. Monetary cases are tried by three judges. [If] two declare free of liability or liable, but one of them says, "I do not have an opinion," they add to the judges. More powerful is the decision of one who says, "He is liable," than that of the one who says, "I do not know." And how many do they add? Step by step, two at a time. When they add to the judges, if they rule, "He is innocent," he is innocent. If they rule, "He is guilty," he is guilty. [If] one says, "He is innocent," and one says, "I don't know," they add to the judges, for up to that point, the court has been evenly divided. [If] one says, "He is liable," and one says, "He is innocent," and one says, "I don't have an opinion," they add to the judges, for up to now they have added only one judge at a time.

M. 3:8 So long as [a litigant] brings proof, he may reverse the ruling. [If] they had said to him, "All the evidence which you have, bring between this date and thirty days from now," [if] he found evidence during the thirty-day-period, he may reverse the ruling. [If he found evidence] after the thirty-day-period, he may not reverse the ruling. [If] they had said to him, "Bring witnesses," and he said, "I don't have witnesses," [if] they had said, "Bring proof," and he said, "I don't have proof" and after a time he brought proof, or he found witnesses — this is of no weight whatsoever. [If] they had said to him, "Bring witnesses," and he said, "I have no witnesses," "Bring proof," and he said, "I have no proof," [If] he saw that he would be declared liable in court and said, "Let Mr. So-and-so and Mr. Such-and-such [now] come along and give evidence in my behalf," or if [on the spot] he brought proof out of his pocket — lo, this is of no weight whatsoever.

T. 6:4 Under all circumstances they continue adding judges until the court-process has been completed [cf. M. San. 3:6–N]. One may continue to bring his witnesses and his proofs to court until the trial is complete. The witnesses may not exercise the right to retract until the trial is complete. "Do you have other witnesses," and he said, "I have only these" — "Do you have other pieces of proof," and he said, "I have only these" — after a while he discovered other witnesses or other proofs — they do not accept them from him, until he brings proof that he had never known about them [until just now] [cf. M. San. 3:8F–K]. The witnesses may continue to exercise the right to retract until their testimony will have been tested in court. Once their testimony has been tested in court, they do not have the power to retract. And this is the governing principle in this matter.

T. 6:5 Witnesses who give evidence to declare something unclean or clean, to allow someone to come near or to be put off, to prohibit or to permit, to declare exempt or to declare liable — until their testimony has been tested, [if] they said, "We're just joking" — lo, these are believed. Once their testimony has been tested, if they said, "We're just joking" they most certainly are not believed.

T. 6:6 The witnesses are never declared to be perjurers before the trial is over. They are not flogged, nor do they pay compensation, nor are they put to death [on account of their perjury] until the trial is over. One witness alone is not declared a perjurer, unless the other one also is declared a perjurer. And one is not flogged, put to death, or required to pay compensation, unless both of them are required to undergo flogging, be put to death, or to pay compensation.

D. *The Procedures of the Court-System: Capital Cases*

M. 4:1 The same [laws] apply to property cases and capital cases with respect to examination and interrogation [of witnesses], as it is said, "You will have one law" (Lev. 24:22). What is the difference between property cases and capital cases? Property cases [are tried] by three [judges], and capital cases by twenty-three. In property cases they begin [argument] with the case either for acquittal or for conviction, while in capital cases they begin only with the case for acquittal, and not with the case for conviction. In property cases they decide by a majority of one, whether for acquittal or for conviction, while in capital cases they decide by a majority of one for acquittal, but only with a majority of two [judges] for conviction. In property cases they reverse the decision whether in favor of acquittal or in favor of conviction, while in capital cases they reverse the decision so as to favor acquittal, but they do not reverse the decision so as to favor conviction. In property cases all [judges and even disciples] argue either for acquittal or conviction. In capital cases all argue for acquittal, but all do not argue for conviction. In property cases one who argues for conviction may argue for acquittal, and one who argues for acquittal may also argue for conviction. In capital cases the one who argues for conviction may argue for acquittal, but the one who argues for acquittal has not got the power to retract and to argue for conviction. In property cases they try the case by day and complete it by night. In capital cases they try the case by day and

complete it [the following] day. **In property cases they come to a final decision on the same day [as the trial itself], whether it is for acquittal or conviction. In capital cases they come to a final decision for acquittal on the same day, but on the following day for conviction. (Therefore they do not judge [capital cases] either on the eve of the Sabbath or on the eve of a festival.)**

T. 7:2 They do not judge two cases in one day, even an adulterer and adulteress. But they judge the first, and afterward they judge the second. And they do not take a vote concerning two matters at once. And they do not accept an inquiry concerning two questions at once. But they take a vote concerning the first, and then they take a vote concerning the second, they accept inquiry concerning the first, and afterward they accept inquiry concerning the second. They vote only in a large place. And they vote only on the basis of a tradition which someone has heard. [If] one speaks in the name of a tradition which he has heard, and the rest of them say, "We have not heart it" — in such a case, they do not take a standing vote. But if one prohibits and one permits, one declares unclean and one declares clean, and all of them declare, "We have not heard a tradition on the matter" — in such a case they rise and take a vote. [If] one speaks in the name of two authorities, and two speak in the name of one authority, of greater weight is the one who speaks in the name of the two authorities than the two who speak in the name of the one authority. [If] ten speak in the name of one authority, all of them count as one. And in matters pertaining to questions of uncleanness or of cleanness, as to the father and his son, the master and his disciple, both of them are counted as a single vote. And he should not sit at his side, and even if he [the elder] remains silent. In cases involving the sanctification of the new month and the intercalation of the year and in property cases, they begin the vote from the oldest. In capital cases they begin from the side [with the youngest members], so that [the younger member's] opinion should not depend upon the opinion of his master. And in capital cases they begin with the defense and they do not begin with the prosecution [cf. M. San. 4:1], except in the case of one who leads [the people] astray [to idolatry].

T. 7:3 Those sentenced to go into exile — a court may bring them back [with a changed verdict] of innocent, as it is said, "You shall not take a ransom for the life of a manslaughterer who is guilty of death" (Num. 35:31), — and also: "And this is the matter of the manslaughterer... whoever kills his neighbor unaware" (Deut. 19:4). The use of the word manslaughterer in both instances established an analogy [thus invoking in the case of the one who commits homicide accidentally the rules applicable to the one who commits murder] [cf. M. San. 4:1G].

T. 7:4 A. Those who are sentenced to flogging — a court may bring them back [with a changed verdict] of innocent, as it is said, "And they shall justify the righteous and condemn the guilty... and if the guilty man be worthy to be beaten" (Deut. 25:1–2). The use of the word guilty is for purposes of establishing an analogy [thus invoking in the case of the one who is liable to flogging the rules applicable to the trial of a murderer].

T. 7:5 The eunuch and one who has never had children are suitable for judging property cases but are not suitable for judging capital cases.

T. 7:6 They do not add to the [discussion of a case] afresh [after the vote has been taken]. [If] there were two, one declaring prohibited, one declaring permitted, one declaring unclean, and one declaring clean, the one who declares prohibited and the one who declares unclean bear the burden of proof [cf. M. San 4:2A]. And whoever takes a more strict position bears the burden of proof. They are called to court only in the place in which they vote And they seat a man [on the court] only in accord with his virtues. Once the trial is done with, one is not permitted to answer [arguments made in it]. How is it that they do not add to the [discussion of a case] afresh [after the vote has been taken]? [If] one has completed what he was saying, he has not got the right to answer [others]. [If] his fellow gave him the right, he then does have the right to answer [contrary arguments]. Once the main point has been done with, what is secondary becomes the main point. One may not answer what his fellow has said more than three times, so as not to confuse him. One may argue against two, and two may argue against one. Two may argue against three, and three may argue against two. But three may not argue against three, and none in any larger numbers than these, so as not to muddle the court proceeding.

T. 7:7 In property cases they say, "The case is stale." In capitol cases they do not say, "The case is stale." The oldest judge [alone] has the right to say, "The case is stale." They do not ask questions or answer questions while standing, from high up, from a distance, or on the other side of the elders. They ask only to the point, and they answer only with regard to the event. And one may ask to the point no more than three questions of law. [If] one asks, and another [speaks but] does not ask a question, they take up the matter of the one who asks the question. And one who asks about a precedent has to say, "I am asking about a precedent." "And in the case in which there is one who asks to the point and another who asks not to the point, they answer the question of the one who asks to the point, and the one who asked not to the point has to state, 'I asked a question not to the point,'" the words of R. Meir. And sages say, "He does not have to do so. For the entire Torah is deemed a single matter." [If there is] something relevant, and something not relevant, they attend to what is relevant; a precedent and what is not a precedent — they attend to what is a precedent; a law and an exegesis — they attend to the law; an exegesis of Scripture and a tale — they attend to the exegesis of Scripture; an exegesis and an argument a fortiori — they attend to the argument a fortiori; an argument a fortiori and an analogy — they attend to the argument a fortiori; a sage and a disciple — they attend to the sage; a disciple and a common person —

they attend to the disciple; if both were sages, both disciples, both ordinary folk, both laws, both questions, both answers, both precedents — the speaker has the right from that point [to make his own choices].

M. 4:2 In cases involving questions of uncleanness and cleanness they begin [voting] from the eldest. In capital cases they begin from the side [with the youngest]. All are valid to engage in the judgment of property cases, but all are not valid to engage in the judgment of capital cases, except for priests, Levites, and Israelites who are suitable to marry into the priesthood.

M. 4:3 The Sanhedrin was [arranged in the shape of a half of a round threshing-floor [that is, as an amphitheater], so that [the judges] should see one another, And two judges' clerks stand before them, one at the right and one at the left. And they write down the arguments of those who vote to acquit and of those who vote to convict.

M. 4:4 And three rows of disciples of sages sit before them. Each and every one knows his place. [If] they found need to ordain [a disciple to serve on the court], they ordained one who was sitting in the first row. [Then] one who was sitting in the second row joins the first row, and one who was sitting in the third row moves up to the second row. And they select for themselves someone else from the crowd and set him in the third row. [The new disciple] did not take a seat in the place of the first party [who had now joined in the court] but in the place that was appropriate for him [at the end of the third row].

T. 7:8 When the patriarch enters, everyone rises and does not sit down until he says to them, "Sit down." And when the head of the court enters, they set up for him two rows, one on one side, one on the other side, through which he goes, and he sits down in his place. A sage who comes in — one rises as another sits down, until he comes in and sits down in his place. Younger sages and disciples of sages, when the public requires their services, even step over the heads of the people. And even though they have said, "It is no praise for a disciple of a sage to come in last," if he went out for need, he comes back and sits down in his place.

T. 7:9 Younger sages and disciples of sages, when they have a capacity to understand, turn toward their fathers [on the court]. [If] they do not have a capacity to understand the proceedings, they turn toward the people.

T. 7:10 A sage who enters — they do not ask his opinion immediately, [but wait] until he has settled down. And so too a disciple who came in — he has not got the right to ask a question until he has settled down. [If] he came in and found them engaged in discussion of a law, he should not jump into their discussion until he has settled down and knows what they are talking about.

T. 8:1 Any Sanhedrin in which there are two who know how to engage in argument, and in which all of them are suitable to listen, is suitable to be constituted into a Sanhedrin. If there are three, it is average, [and if there are] four, it is one of wisdom. The Sanhedrin was set in the shape of a half of a round threshing-floor so that [the judges] should be able to see one another [M. San. 4:3A]. The patriarch sits in the middle, and the elders sit on his right and left.

T. 8:2 Three rows of disciples of sages sit before them [M. San. 4:4A], the most distinguished in the first row, the ones second to them in the second row, and the ones third to them in the third row. From that point forward there was no fixed rite. But whoever got there before his fellow into a space of four cubits has acquired [the right to sit there]. The public officers, the accused, the witnesses, those present to prove them perjured, and those present to prove the ones who prove them to be perjured themselves to be perjured stand at the outer row near the people. And they did not have to ask who is the defendant, because they set him in the position second to the chief witness.

T. 8:3 Why did he say so [cf. M. San. 4:5A–C]? So that [the witnesses] should not say, "We saw him running after his fellow, with a sword in his hand. [The victim] ran in front of him into a shop, and then the other went after him into the store. We went in after them and found the victim slain on the floor, with a knife in the hand of the murderer, dripping blood." "Now lest you say, 'If not you, then who killed him'" — [you must be admonished that this is not valid evidence].

M. 4:5 How do they admonish witnesses in capital cases? They would bring them in and admonish them [as follows]: "Perhaps it is your intention to give testimony on the basis of supposition, hearsay, or of what one witness has told another; [or you may be thinking], 'We heard it from a reliable person'" Or, you may not know that in the end we are going to interrogate you with appropriate tests of interrogation and examination. You should know that the laws governing a trial for property cases are different from the laws governing a trial for capital cases. In the case of a trial for property-cases, a person pays money and achieves atonement for himself. In capital cases [the accused's] blood and the blood of all those who were destined to be born from him [who was wrongfully convicted] are held against him [who testifies falsely] to the end of time."

M. 5:1 They interrogated [the witness] with seven points of interrogation: (1) In what septennate? (2) In what year? (3) In what month? (4) On what day of the month? (5) On what day [of the week]? (6) At what time? (7) In what place? [In case of] one who worships an idol: Whom did he worship, and with what did he worship [the idol]?

M. 5:2 The more they expand the interrogation, the more is one to be praised. What is the difference between interrogation [about the date, time, and place] and examination [about the circumstances]? In the case of interrogation, [if] one witness says, "I don't know the answer," the testimony of the witness is null. [In the case of] examination, [if] one of the witnesses says, "I don't know," or even if both of them say, "We don't

know," their testimony nonetheless stands. All the same are interrogation and examination: When [the witnesses] contradict one another, their testimony is null.

M. 5:3 [If] one [of the witnesses] says, "It was on the second of the month," and one of the witnesses says, "It was on the third of the month," their testimony stands, for one of them may know about the intercalation of the month, and the other one may not know about the intercalation of the month. [if] one of them says, "On the third," and one of them says, "On the fifth," their testimony is null. [If] one of them says, "At two," and one of them says, "At three," their testimony stands. [If] one of them says, "At three," and one of them says, "At five," their testimony is null. [If] one of them says, "At five," and one of them says, "At seven," their testimony is null. For at five the sun is at the east, and at seven the sun is at the west.

T. 9:1 [If] one of the witnesses says, "It was on the second of the month," and one of the witnesses says, "It was on the third of the month," their testimony stands [M. San. 5:3A], for not everybody is an expert in the matter of intercalation [M. San. 5:3B]. If one of them says, "At two hours," and one of them says, "At three," their testimony stands [M. San. 5:3D], for not everybody is an expert in the matter of telling time. [If] one of them says, "At three," and one of them says, "At four," their testimony is null. If one of them says, "At five," and one of them says, "At seven," their testimony is null, for everybody knows that at five the sun is at the east, and at seven the sun is at the west [M. San. 5:3E–H3]. [If] their statements check out [M. San. 5:4B], the most important judge opens the argument in favor of acquittal and his fellow supports him. If they found him innocent, they sent him away. If not, they postpone judging him until the next day [M. San. 5:5A]. They come together in pairs and would not eat very much or drink wine that entire day, and they would discuss the matter all that night [M. San. 5:5B]. If he was a murderer, they discuss the passage which deals with the murderer. And if he was one who had had sexual relations with a forbidden relative, they' discuss the passage which deals with fornication. And the next day they would get up and come to court [M. San. 5:5C]. The court-officers call on each one, "[Judge] So-and-so," and "[Judge] Such and-such." [If he answered], "I held him innocent and now I hold him innocent" — they accept that statement [cf. M. San. 5:5D]. "I held him innocent and now I hold him guilty" — they do not accept that statement [M. San. 5:5F]. "I held him guilty and now I hold him innocent" — they accept that statement [M. San. 5:5F]. "I held him guilty and now I hold him guilty" [M. San. 5:5E] — they said to him, "Explain your opinion first." [If] one of those who had held him innocent made a mistake in his opinion, the scribes of the court remind him [cf. M. San. 5:5G]. [If] one of those who hold the accused guilty erred, the scribes of the judges do not remind him. But they say to him, "Explain your opinion afresh."

M. 5:4 And afterward they bring in the second witness and examine him. If their statements check out, they begin the argument in favor of acquittal. [If] one of the witnesses said, "I have something to say in favor of acquittal," or [if] one of the disciples said, "I have something to say in favor of conviction," they shut him up. [If] one of the disciples said, "I have something to say in favor of acquittal," they promote him and seat him among the [judges], and he did not go down from that position that entire day. If there is substance in what he says, they pay attention to him. And even if [the accused] said, "I have something to say in my own behalf," they pay attention to him, so long as there is substance in what he has to say.

M. 5:5 If they found him innocent, they sent him away. If not, they postpone judging him till the next day. They would go off in pairs and would not eat very much or drink wine that entire day, and they would discuss the matter all that night. And the next day they would get up and come to court. The one who favors acquittal says, "I declared him innocent [yesterday], and I stand my ground and declare him innocent today." And the one who declares him guilty says, "I declared him guilty [yesterday] and I stand my ground and declare him guilty today." The one who argues in favor of guilt may [now] argue in favor of acquittal, but the one who argues in favor of innocence may not now go and argue in favor of guilt. [If] they made an error in some matter, the two judges' clerks remind them [of what had been said]. If they now found him innocent, they sent him off. And if not, they arise for a vote. [If] twelve vote for acquittal and eleven vote for conviction, he is acquitted. [If] twelve vote for conviction and eleven vote for acquittal, and even if eleven vote for acquittal and eleven vote for conviction, but one says, "I have no opinion," and even if twenty-two vote for acquittal or vote for conviction, but one says, "I have no opinion," they add to the number of the judges. How many do they add? Two by two, until there are seventy-one. [If] thirty-six vote for acquittal and thirty-five vote for conviction, he is acquitted. [If] thirty six vote for conviction and thirty-five vote for acquittal, they debate the matter, until one of those who votes for conviction accepts the arguments of those who vote for acquittal.

T. 9:2 A. If they now found him innocent, they sent him off. And if not, they rise to a vote [M. San. 5:5H]. [If] thirty-six vote for acquittal, and thirty-five vote for conviction, he is acquitted. If thirty-six vote for conviction, and thirty-five vote for acquittal, they debate the matter [M. San. 5:5R–S], with one another, until one of those who votes for conviction says, "I accept the arguments of those who vote for acquittal."

T. 9:3 [If] one of the disciples said, "I have an argument to offer in favor of acquittal," they receive him in a friendly way, and promote him and seat him among the [judges] [M. San. 5:4D], and if there is substance in what he has to say, they dismiss [the accused], and [the disciple] did not go down from that position [M. San. 5:4D] ever. And if not, he did not go down from that position that entire day [M. San. 5:4D], so that people should not say, "His going up was his downfall."

T. 9:4 [If] the accused] said, "I have something to say in behalf of my own innocence," they pay attention to him [M. San. 5:4F]. [If he said, "I have something to say] in favor of my own conviction," they emphatically shut him up. A witness does not give an argument either for acquittal or for conviction [cf. M. San. 5:4C]. [If] twelve vote for acquittal and eleven vote for conviction, he is acquitted. If twelve vote for conviction and eleven vote for acquittal [and eleven vote for conviction, and one says, "I have no opinion," . . .] they add to the number of judges [M. San. 5:5J-P] — until there is a majority of one for acquittal or two for conviction.

Y. 5:5 I.2 In what regard do they add judges to the court? It is so that, if two of the first judges declare the accused to be innocent, and one of the second pair concurs that he is innocent, the decision may be reached by three judges [out of the five now on the court]. [The one who declares he has no opinion is treated as if he is not present. That is the case even if one of the two additional judges also declares that he has no opinion.]

ii. *The Death Penalty*

A. *Stoning*

M. 6:1 [When] the trial is over, [and the felon is convicted], they take him out to stone him. The place of stoning was well outside the court, as it is said, "Bring forth him who cursed [to a place outside the camp]" (Lev. 24:14). One person stands at the door of the courthouse, with flags in his hand, and a horseman is some distance from him, so that he is able to see him. [If] one [of the judges] said, "I have something to say in favor of acquittal," the one [at the door] waves the flags, and the horseman races off and stops [the execution]. And even if [the convicted party] says, "I have something to say in favor of my own acquittal," they bring him back, even four or five times, so long as there is substance in what he has to say. [If] they then found him innocent, they dismiss him, And if not, he goes out to be stoned. And a herald goes before him, crying out, "Mr. So-and-so, son of Mr. So-and-so, is going out to be stoned because he committed such-and-such a transgression, and Mr. So-and-so and Mr. So-and-so are the witnesses against him. Now anyone who knows grounds for acquittal — let him come and speak in his behalf!"

T. 9:4 And even if the convicted party says, "I have something to say in favor of my own acquittal," they bring him back [M. San. 6:1E], one time, two times, even three times, whether or not there is substance in what he has to say, they pay attention to him. From that point on, if there is substance in what he has to say, they pay attention to him, and if not, they do not pay attention to him.

M. 6:2 [When] he was ten cubits from the place of stoning, they say to him, "Confess," for it is usual for those about to be put to death to confess. For whoever confesses has a share in the world to come. And if he does not know how to confess, they say to him, "Say as follows: 'Let my death be atonement for all of my transgressions.'"

T. 9:5 Those who are put to death by a court have a portion in the world to come, because they confess all their sins [M. San. 6:2B].

M. 6:3 [When] he was four cubits from the place of stoning, they remove his clothes. A man is stoned naked, but a woman is not stoned naked.

M. 6:4 The place of stoning was twice the height of a man. One of the witnesses would push him over from the hips, so [hard] that he turned upward [in his fall]. He turned him over on his hips again [to see whether he had died]. [If] he had died thereby, that sufficed. If not, the second [witness] would take a stone and put it on his heart. [If] he died thereby, it sufficed. And if not, stoning him is [the duty] of all Israelites, as it is said, "The hand of the witnesses shall be first upon him to put him to death, and afterward the hand of all the people" (Deut. 17:7). Only the blasphemer and the one who worships an idol are hung. How do they hang him? They drive a post into the ground, and a beam juts out from it, and they tie together his two hands, and thus do they hang him. And they untie him forthwith. And if he is left overnight, one transgresses a negative commandment on his account, as it is said, "His body shall not remain all night on the tree, but you will surely bury him on the same day, for he who is hanged is a curse against God" (Deut. 21:23), that is to say, "On what account has this one been hung? Because he cursed the Name, so the Name of Heaven turned out to be profaned."

M. 6:6 When the flesh had rotted, they [they do] collect the bones and bury them in their appropriate place. And the relatives [of the felon] come and inquire after the welfare of the judges and of the witness. As if to say, "We have nothing against you, for you judged honestly." And they did not go into mourning. But they observe a private grief, for grief is only in the heart.

T. 9:8 The sword with which one is killed, the cloth with which he is strangled, the stone with which he is crushed, and the wood on which he is hung — all of them require immersion. But they did not bury them with him. When his flesh had rotted, agents of the court gather up the bones [M. San. 6:6A], and bury them in a sarcophagus. And even if he were a king of kings, they would not bury him in the burial grounds of his ancestors, but in the burial grounds of the court.

T. 9:9 There were two graveyards made ready for the use of the court one for those who were beheaded or strangled, and one for those who were stoned or burned [M. San. 6:5F].

B. *The Four Modes of Execution that Lie in the Power of the Court and How They Are Administered*

M. 7:1 Four modes of execution were assigned to the court, [listed in order of severity]: (**1**) stoning, (**2**) burning, (**3**) decapitation, and (**4**) strangulation.

M. 7:2 The religious requirement of burning [is carried out as follows]: They would bury him up to his armpits in manure, and put a towel of hard material inside one of soft material, and wrap it around his neck. This [witness] pulls it to him from one side, and that witness pulls it to him at the other side, until he opens up his mouth. And one kindles a wick and throws it into his mouth, and it goes down into his bowels and burns his intestines.

M. 7:3 The religious requirement of decapitation [is carried out as follows]: They would cut off his head with a sword, just as the government does. The religious requirement of strangulation [is carried out as follows:] They would bury him in manure up to his armpits, and put a towel of hard material inside one of soft material, and wrap it around his neck. This [witness] pulls it to him from one side, and that witness pulls it to him at the other side, until he perishes.

C. *Stoning*

M. 7:4 These are [the felons] who are put to death by stoning: He who has sexual relations with his mother, with the wife of his father, with his daughter-in-law, with a male, and with a cow; and the women who brings an ox on top of herself; and he who blasphemes, he who performs an act of worship for an idol, he who gives of his seed to Molech, he who is a familiar spirit, and he who is a soothsayer; he who profanes the Sabbath, he who curses his father or his mother. he who has sexual relations with a betrothed maiden, he who beguiles [entices a whole town to idolatry], a sorcerer, and a stubborn and incorrigible son. He who has sexual relations with his mother is liable on her account because of her being his mother and because of her being his father's wife [Lev. 18:6–7, 20:11]. He who has sexual relations with his father's wife is liable on her account because of her being his father's wife and because of her being a married woman, whether this is in the lifetime of his father or after the death of his father, whether she is only betrothed or already married [to the father]. He who has sexual relations with his daughter-in-law is liable on her account because of her being his daughter-in-law and because of her being another man's wife, whether this is in the lifetime of his son or after the death of his son [Lev. 20:12, whether she is only betrothed or already married [to the son]. He who has sexual relations with a male [Lev. 20:13, 15–16], or a cow, and the woman who brings an ox on top of herself. if the human being has committed a sin, what sin has the beast committed? But because a human being has offended through it, therefore the Scripture has said, "Let it be stoned." Another matter: So that the beast should not amble through the market place, with people saying, "This is the one on account of which Mr. So-and-so got himself stoned."

T. 10:2 He who has sexual relations with his mother [M. San. 7:4BI], [who also is] a widow married to a high priest, a divorcee or a woman who has undergone the rite of removal of the shoe married to an ordinary priest, or who was a woman whom the father had raped or seduced, or who was in one of any of the prohibited degrees of relationship to his father is liable. He who has sexual relations with his father's wife [M. San. 7:4B2], [who also is] a widow married to a high priest or a divorcee or a woman who has undergone the rite of removal of the shoe married to an ordinary priest, is liable. [If] she was a woman whom the father had raped or seduced, or who was in one of any of the prohibited degrees of relationship to his father, he is exempt. He who has sexual relations with his sister is liable on the count of her being his sister and on the count of her being his father's daughter. And so too: He who has sexual relations with his daughter-in-law and he who has sexual relations with a male nine years and one day old, and he who has sexual relations with a cow [M. San. 7:4B3, 4, 5], either through the vagina or through the anus, and the woman who brings an ox on top of her [M. San. 7:4C], whether through the vagina or through the anus, and he who performs an act of service to an idol — all the same are the one who performs an act of service, who actually sacrifices, who offers up incense, who pours out a libation offering, and who bows down, and the one who accepts him upon himself as a god, saying to him, "You are my god [M. San. 7:6A–C] so save me" — all of them are punished by stoning.

M. 7:5 He who blasphemes [M. 7:4D1] [Lev. 24:10] is liable only when he has fully pronounced the divine Name.

M. 7:6 He who performs an act of worship for an idol [M. 7:4D] — all the same are the one who performs an act of service, who [actually] sacrifices, who offers up incense, who pours out a

libation offering, who bows down, and the one who accepts it upon himself as a god, saying to it, "You are my god." But the one who hugs, it, kisses it, polishes it, sweeps it, and washes it, anoints it, puts clothing on it, and puts shows on it, [merely] transgresses a negative commandment [Ex. 20:5]. He who takes a vow in its name, and he who carries out a vow made in its name transgress a negative commandment [Ex. 23:13]. He who uncovers himself to Baal Peor [is stoned, for] this is how one performs an act of service to it. He who tosses a pebble at Merkolis [Hermes] [is stoned, for] this is how one performs an act of service to it.

T. 10:3 He who makes an idol, carves it, sets it up, anoints it, dries it, or scrapes it, transgresses a negative commandment [M. San. 7:6D–E]. But they are liable only on account of a matter which involves an actual deed, for example, sacrificing, burning incense, pouring out a libation, or bowing down [M. San. 7:6B–C]. But he who hugs it, kisses it, polishes it, sweeps it, washes it, anoints it, puts clothing on it, puts shoes on it, [M. San. 7:6D], or puts a cloak on it — lo, these are subject to warning.

M. 7:7 He who gives of his seed [child] to Molech [M. 7:4D] [Lev. 20:2] is liable only when he will both have given him to Molech and have passed him through fire. [If] he gave him to Molech but did not pass him through fire. passed him through fire but did not give him to Molech, he is not liable — until he will both have given him to Molech and have passed him through fire. He who has a familiar spirit [M. 7:4D4] [Lev. 20:27] — this is a ventriloquist, who speaks from his armpits; and he who is a soothsayer [M. 7:4D5] — this is one whose [spirit] speaks through his mouth — lo, these are put to death by stoning. And the one who makes inquiry of them is subject to a warning [Lev. 19:31, Deut. 18:10–11].

T. 10:4 He who gives of his seed to Molech is liable only when he will have given him to Molech and have passed him through fire. If he gave him to Molech but did not pass him through fire, passed him through fire but did not give him to Molech, he is not liable — until he will both have given him to Molech and passed him through fire [M. San. 7:7 A–E]. And he is liable only when he will have passed him through fire in the usual way. [If he passed him through fire by foot, he is exempt. And he is liable, moreover, only on account of those who are his natural children.

T. 10:5 He who passes his father, mother, or sister through fire [for Molech] is exempt. He who passes through himself is exempt. All the same is doing so for Molech and for any other idol, he is liable.

T. 10:6 He who has a familiar spirit — this is one who has a Python which speaks [M. San. 7:7F] from between his joints or from between his elbows. A soothsayer [M. San. 7:7G] — this one who has the bone of a familiar spirit in his mouth. Lo, these are put to death by stoning, and the one who makes inquiry of them is subject to a warning [M. San. 7:7H–I].

T. 10:7 He who inquires of the dead (Deut. 18:11) this is one who raises up the dead by witchcraft or one who makes inquiry of a skull. What is the difference between one who makes inquiry of a skull and one who raises up the dead by witchcraft? For the one who raises up the dead by witchcraft — the ghost does not come up in his normal way and does not come up on the Sabbath. But the one who makes inquiry of a skull — [the spirit] comes up in the normal way and comes up on the Sabbath.

M. 7:8 He who profanes the Sabbath [M. 7:4E] — in regard to a matter, on account of the deliberate doing of which they are liable to extirpation, and on account of the inadvertent doing of which they are liable to a sin-offering. He who curses his father and his mother [M. 7:4F] is liable only when he will have cursed them by the divine Name. [If] he cursed them with a euphemism, sages declare him exempt.

M. 7:9 He who has sexual relations with a betrothed maiden [M. 7:4G] [Deut. 22:23–4] is liable only if she is a virgin maiden, betrothed, while she is yet in her father's house. [If] two different men had sexual relations with her, the first one is put to death by stoning, and the second by strangulation. [The second party, B. has not had intercourse with a virgin (M. 11:1). The maiden is between twelve years and one day and twelve years six months and one day old.]

T. 10:8 A. He who has sexual relations with a betrothed maiden is liable only if she is a virgin maiden, betrothed, while she is yet in her father's house [M. San. 7:9A]. If she was a betrothed maiden but living in her husband's house, a mature maiden, betrothed, living in her father's house.

T. 10:9 A married woman, whether in the house of her father or in the house of her husband — he who has sexual relations with her — lo, this one is put to death by strangling. [If] ten men had intercourse with her, and she was yet a virgin, all of them are put to death by stoning. But if she was not a virgin, the first is put to death by stoning, and all the others by strangulation [cf. M. San. 7:9B].

T. 10:10 A. She who receives her husband while in her father's house, and even though she is a virgin — he who has sexual relations with her is put to death through strangulation [M. San. 7:9B]. A betrothed maiden who committed fornication — they stone her at the doorway of her father's house. [If] she does not have a doorway of her father's house, they stone her in the place in which she fornicated. But if it was a gentile town, they stone her at the door of the [Israelite] courthouse.

M. 7:10 He who beguiles others to idolatry [M. 7:4H] — this [refers to] an ordinary fellow who beguiles some other ordinary fellow. [If] he said to him, "There is a god in such a place, who eats thus, drinks thus, does good in one way, and harm in another" — against all those who are liable to the death penalty in the Torah they do not hide witnesses [for the purposes of entrapment] except for this one. [If] he spoke [in such a way] to two, and they serve as witnesses against him, they bring him to court and stone him. [If] he spoke [in such a way]

to [only] one person, [the latter then] says to him, "I have some friends who will want the same thing." If he was clever and not prepared to speak in [the friends'] presence, they hide witnesses on the other side of the partition, and he says to him, "Tell me what you were saying to me now that we are by ourselves." And the other party says to him [what he had said], and then this party says, "Now how are we going to abandon our God who is in Heaven and go and worship sticks and stones?" If he repents, well and good. But if he said, "This is what we are obligated to do, and this is what is good for us to do," those who stand on the other side of the partition bring him to court and stone him. [He who beguiles others is] one who says, "I am going to worship," "I shall make an offering," "I shall offer incense," "I shall go and offer incense," "Let's go and offer incense," "I shall make a libation," "I shall go and make a libation," "Let's go and make a libation," "I shall bow down," "I shall go and bow down," "Let's go and bow down." He who leads [a whole town astray] [M. 10:4H] is one who says, "Let's go and perform an act of service to an idol."

T. 10:11 Against all those who are liable to the death penalty in the Torah they do not hide witnesses, except for the one who beguiles others to idolatry [M. San. 7:10C]. How do they do it? They hand over to him two disciples of sages, [who are put] in an inside room, and he sits in an outside room. And they light a candle, so that they can see him. And they listen to what he says. They begin his trial by day and complete it even by night. They begin and complete it on the very same day, whether for acquittal or for conviction. They reach a decision on the basis of a majority of one, whether for acquittal or conviction. All have the right to argue for acquittal or conviction. He who argues for acquittal has the right to revert and to argue for conviction. A eunuch and one who has never had children may serve on the court.

T. 11:2 [If] they warn him and he was silent, or if they warn him and he nods his head even though he says, "I know" — he is exempt — unless he will say, "I know it, and it is with that very stipulation that I am doing what I am doing!"

T. 11:3 How so? [If] they saw him profaning the Sabbath, [and] said to him, "You should know that it is the Sabbath today and Scripture says, 'Those who profane it will certainly die' (Ex. 31:14)" — even though he said, "I know" — he is exempt, unless he says, "I know, and it is with that very stipulation that I am doing what I am doing!"

T. 11:4 How so? [If] they saw him killing somebody, and said to him, "You should know that that man is subject to the [divine] covenant, and it is said, 'Whoever sheds the blood of man by man shall his blood be shed' (Gen. 9:6)" — even though he said, "I know it" — he is exempt, unless he says, "I know, and it is with that very stipulation that I am doing what I am doing!"

M. 7:11 The sorcerer [M. 7:4I] — he who does a deed is liable, but not the one who merely creates an illusion.

M. 8:1 A rebellious and incorrigible son [M. 7:4J] — at what point [does a child] become liable to be declared a rebellious and incorrigible son? From the point at which he will produce two pubic hairs, until the "beard" is full — (that is the lower [pubic], not the upper [facial, beard], but the sages used euphemisms). As it is said, "If a man has a son" (Deut. 21:18) — (1) a son, not a daughter; (2) a son, not an adult man. And a minor is exempt, since he has not yet entered the scope of the commandments.

M. 8:2 At what point is he liable? Once he has eaten a tartemar of meat and drunk a half-log of Italian wine. [If] he ate in an association formed for a religious duty. [if] he ate on the occasion of the intercalation of the month, [if] in Jerusalem he ate food in the status of second tithe, [if] he ate carrion and terefah-meat, forbidden things or creeping things, [if] he ate untithed produce, first tithe, the heave-offering of which had not been removed, second tithe or consecrated food which had not been redeemed [by money], [if] he ate something which fulfilled a religious duty or whereby he committed a transgression, [if] he ate any sort of food except meat, drank any sort of liquid except wine — he is not declared a rebellious and incorrigible son — unless he eats meat and drinks wine, since it is said, "A glutton and a drunkard" (Deut. 21:20). And even though there is no clear proof for the proposition, there is at least a hint for it, for it is said, "Do not be among the wine-drinkers, among gluttonous meat-eaters" (Prov. 23:20).

M. 8:3 [If] he stole something belonging to his father but ate it in his father's domain, or something belonging to others but ate it in the domain of those others, or something belonging to others but ate it in his father's domain, he is not declared a rebellious and incorrigible son — until he steals something of his father's and eats it in the domain of others.

M. 8:4 [If] his father wanted [to put him to judgement as a rebellious and incorrigible son] but his mother did not want to do so, [if] his father did not want and his mother did want [to put him to judgment], he is not declared a rebellious and incorrigible son — until both of them want [to put him to judgment]. [If] one of them was maimed in the hand, lame, dumb, blind, or deaf, he is not declared a rebellious and incorrigible son, since it is said, "Then his father and his mother will lay hold of him" (Deut. 21:20) — so they are not maimed in their hands; "and bring them out" — so they are not lame; "and they shall say" — so they are not dumb; "This is our son" — so they are not blind; "He will not obey our voice" — so they are not deaf. They warn him before three judges and flog him. [If] he went and misbehaved again, he is judged before twenty-three judges. He is stoned only if there will be present the first three judges, since it is said, "This, our son" — this one who was flogged before you. [If] he fled before his trial was over, and afterward [while he was a fugitive,] the lower "beard" became full, he is exempt. If after his trial was done he fled, and afterward the lower beard became full, he is liable.

M. 8:5 A rebellious and incorrigible son is tried on account of [what he may] end up to be. Let him die while yet innocent, and let him not die when he is guilty. For when the evil folk die, it is a benefit to them and a benefit to the world. But [when the] righteous folk [die], it is bad for them and bad for the world. Wine and sleep for the wicked are a benefit for them and a benefit for the world. But for the righteous, they are bad for them and bad for the world. Dispersion for the evil is a benefit for them and a benefit for the world. But for the righteous, it is bad for them and bad for the world. Gathering together for the evil is bad for them and bad for the world. But for the righteous, it is a benefit for them and a benefit for the world. Tranquility for the evil is bad for them and bad for the world. But for the righteous, it is a benefit for them and a benefit for the world.

M. 8:6 He who breaks in [Ex. 22:1] is judged on account of what he may end up to be. [If] he broke in and broke a jug, if bloodguilt applies to him, he is liable. If blood-guilt does not apply, he is exempt.

T. 11:9 He who breaks in — if he came to kill someone, they save him at the cost of his life. If he came to steal money, they do not save him at the cost of his life. If it is a matter of doubt whether he came to kill or to take something, they do not save him at the cost of his life, as it is said, "If the sun has risen on him, there shall be guilt for his blood" (Ex. 22:3).

M. 8:7 And these are those who are to be saved [from doing evil] even at the cost of their lives: he who pursues after his fellow in order to kill him — after a male, or after a betrothed girl; but he who pursues a beast, he who profanes the Sabbath, he who does an act of service to an idol — they do not save them even at the cost of their lives.

T. 8:9 I:1 He who pursues after his fellow to kill him [M. 8:9B] whether at home or in the field — they save him at the cost of his life. All the same are he who pursues his fellow to kill him and all the other prohibited relationships which are listed in the Torah — they save [the one who pursues them] at the cost of his life. But if it was a widow pursued by a high priest, or a divorcée or a woman who had performed the rite of removing the shoe pursued by an ordinary priest, or a mamzeret girl or a Netinah girl pursued by an Israelite, or an Israelite girl pursued by a Netin or a mamzer, they do not save him at the cost of his life. If the deed already was done, they do not save him at the cost of his life. If there are present people able to save [the prospective victim], they do not save him at the cost of his life.

D. *Burning or Decapitation*

M. 9:1 And these are those who are put to death through burning: he who has sexual relations with both a woman and her daughter [Lev. 18:17, 20:14], and a priest's daughter who committed adultery [Lev. 21:9]. In the same category as a woman and her daughter are [the following]: his daughter, his daughter's daughter, his son's daughter, his wife's daughter, the daughter of her daughter, the daughter of her son, his mother-in-law, the mother of his mother-in-law, and the mother of his father-in-law. And these are those who are put to death through decapitation: the murderer, and the townsfolk of an apostate town. A murderer who hit his neighbor with a stone or a piece of iron [Ex. 21:18], or who pushed him under water or into fire, and [the other party] cannot get out of there and so perished, he is liable. [If] he pushed him into the water or into the fire, and he can get out of there but [nonetheless] he died, he is exempt. [If] he sicked a dog on him, or sicked a snake on him, he is exempt. [If] he made a snake bite him, sages declare him exempt. He who hits his fellow, whether with a stone or with his fist, and they diagnosed him as likely to die, but he got better than he was, and afterward he got worse and he died he is liable.

T. 12:1 And these are those who are put to death through burning: he who has sexual relations with both a woman and her daughter [Lev. 18:17, 20:14], and a priest's daughter who is bound to her husband. If he had sexual relations with the woman and afterward had sexual relations with her daughter, had sexual relations with her daughter and afterward had sexual relations with the mother, he is liable. Even though we do not derive evidence from Scripture that one who had sexual relations with the daughter of a woman whom he raped is liable to be burned, we have an indication at Lev. 20:14, "And the man who shall take a woman and her daughter — it is lewdness" — Scripture thus speaks of someone in whom he has a potential right of marriage. Scripture says, "And the daughter of a man, a priest" (Lev. 21:9) — deriving from any source, even the daughter of a woman whom he has raped.

Y 9:2 I:2 If one pushed a man in front of a horse, or if he pushed him in front of an arrow, or if he pushed him in front of a spear, if he put him out in the cold, if he gave him polluted water to drink, if he removed the roof covering from over him so that it rained on him, and in one of these ways he died, if he directed a watercourse over him and the water came along and drowned him, [all of these constitute acts of murder].

M. 9:2 [If] he intended to kill a beast and killed a man, a gentile and killed an Israelite, an untimely birth and killed an offspring that was viable, he is exempt. [If] he intended to hit him on his loins with a blow that was not sufficient to kill him when it struck his loins, but it went and hit his heart, and there was sufficient force in that blow to kill him when it struck his heart, and he died, he is exempt. [If] he intended to hit him on his heart, and there was in that blow sufficient force to kill when it struck his heart, and it went and hit him on his loins, and there was not sufficient force in that blow to kill him when it struck his loins, but he died, he is exempt. [If] he intended to hit a large person, and there was not sufficient force in that blow to kill a large person, but it went and hit a small person, and there was sufficient force in that blow to kill a small person, and he died, he is exempt. [If] he intended to hit a small person, and there was in that blow sufficient force to kill a small person, and it went and struck the large person, and there was not sufficient force in that blow to kill the large person, but he died, he is exempt. But: [if] he intended to hit him on his loins, and there was sufficient force in the blow to kill him when it struck his loins, and it went and hit him on his heart and he died, he is liable. [If] he intended to hit a large person, and there was in that blow sufficient force to kill the large person, and it went and hit a small person and he died, he is liable.

M. 9:3 A murderer who was confused with others — all of them are exempt. All those who are liable to death who were confused with one another are judged [to be punished] by the more lenient mode of execution. [If] those to be stoned were confused with those to be burned — they are adjudged [to be executed] by burning, for stoning is the more severe mode of execution of the two. Those who are to be decapitated who were confused with those who are to be strangled — they are killed by strangling.

M. 9:4 He who is declared liable to be put to death through two different modes of execution at the hands of a court is judged [to be executed] by the more severe: [if] he committed a transgression which is subject to the death penalty on two separate counts, he is judged on account of the more severe.

T. 12:5 Those who are convicted to be executed by more severe modes of execution who also were convicted to be put to death by less severe forms of they put them to death with the less severe mode of execution [vs. M.].

T. 12:6 A. [If] one has transgressed a rule which is punishable by two modes of execution, they kill him by the more severe of them [cf. M. San. 9:4B]. All those who are condemned to death which are [listed in] the Torah whom you cannot put to death with a more severe mode of execution, execute with any one of the modes of execution, whether lenient or severe, as it is said, "And you will exterminate the evil from your midst" (Deut. 17:7).

E. *Strangulation*

M. 10:1 These are the ones who are to be strangled: he who hits his father and his mother [Ex. 21:15]; he who steals an Israelite [Ex. 21:16, Deut. 24:7]; an elder who defies the decision of a court, a false prophet, a prophet who prophesies in the name of an idol; He who has sexual relations with a married woman, those who bear false witness against a priest's daughter and against one who has sexual relations with her. He who hits his father and his mother is liable only if he will make a lasting bruise on them. This rule is more strict in the case of the one who curses than the one who hits them. For the one who curses them after they have died is liable. But the one who hits them after they have died is exempt. He who steals an Israelite is liable only when he will have brought him into his own domain.

M. 10:2 An elder who defies the decision of a court [M. 10:1B] as it is said, "If there arise a matter too hard for you in judgment, between blood and blood, between plea and plea" (Deut. 17:8) — there were three courts there. One was in session at the door gate of the Temple mount, one was in session at the gate of the courtyard, and one was in session in the hewn-stone chamber. They come to the one which is at the gate of the Temple mount and say, "Thus I have explained the matter, and thus my colleagues have explained the matter." "Thus I have ruled in the matter, and thus my colleagues have ruled." If they had heard a ruling, they told it to them, and if not, they come along to that court which was at the gate of the courtyard. And he says, "Thus I have explained the matter, and thus my colleagues have explained the matter. Thus I have ruled in the matter [lit.: taught], and thus my colleagues have ruled." If they had heard a ruling, they told it to them, and if not, these and those come along to the high court which was in the hewn-stone chamber, from which Torah goes forth to all Israel, as it is said, "From that place which the Lord shall choose" (Deut. 17:12). [If] he went back to his town and again ruled just as he had ruled before, he is exempt. But if he instructed [others] to do it in that way, he is liable, as it is said, "And the man who does presumptuously" (Deut. 17:12). He is liable only if he will give instructions to people actually to carry out the deed [in accord with the now-rejected view]. A disciple of a sage who gave instruction to carry out the deed [wrongly] is exempt. It turns out that the strict ruling concerning him [that he cannot give decisions] also is a lenient ruling concerning him [that he is not punished if he does give decisions].

M. 10:3 A more strict rule applies to the teachings of scribes than to the teachings of Torah. He who, in order to transgress the teachings of the Torah, rules, "There is no requirement to wear phylacteries," is exempt. [But if,] in order to add to what the scribes have taught, [he said,] "There are five partitions [in the phylactery, instead of four], he is liable."

M. 10:5 A false prophet [M. 10:1B], one who prophesies concerning something which he has not actually heard or concerning something which was not actually said to him, is put to death by man. But he who holds back his prophesy, he who disregards the words of another prophet, or the prophet who transgresses his word words is put to death by heaven, as it is said, "I will require it of him" (Deut. 18:19).

M. 10:6 He who prophesies in the name of an idol [M. 10:1B5], and says, "Thus did such-and-such an idol say to me," even though he got the law right, declaring unclean that which in fact is unclean, and declaring clean that which in fact is clean. He who has sexual relations with a married woman [M. 10:1C1] as soon as she has entered the domain of the husband in marriage, even though she has not had sexual relations with him he who has sexual relations with her — lo, this one is put to death by strangling. And those who bear false witness against a priest's daughter and against one who has sexual relations with her [M. 10:1C2,3] — for all those who bear false witness first suffer that same mode of execution, except for those who bear false witness against a priest's daughter and her lover.

B. 10:5–6 I. 1/89A THREE [FALSE PROPHETS] ARE PUT TO DEATH BY MAN, AND THREE ARE PUT TO DEATH BY HEAVEN. HE WHO PROPHESIES CONCERNING SOMETHING WHICH HE HAS NOT ACTUALLY HEARD OR CONCERNING SOMETHING WHICH WAS NOT ACTUALLY SAID TO HIM [M. 10:5B], AND ONE WHO PROPHESIES IN THE NAME OF AN IDOL — SUCH AS THESE ARE PUT TO DEATH BY MAN. BUT HE WHO HOLDS BACK HIS PROPHECY, HE WHO DISREGARDS THE WORDS OF ANOTHER PROPHET, OR THE PROPHET WHO TRANSGRESSES HIS OWN WORDS IS NOT TO DEATH BY HEAVEN [M. 10:5D–F].

F. *Extra-Judicial Punishment*

M. 9:5 He who was flogged [and did the same deed] and was flogged again — [if he did it yet a third time] the court puts him in prison and feeds him barley until his belly explodes. He who kills a someone not before witnesses they put him in prison and feed him the bread of adversity and the water of affliction (Is. 30:20).

M. 9:6 He who stole a sacred vessel [of the cult (Num. 4:7)], and he who curses using the name of an idol, and he who has sexual relations with an Aramaean woman — zealots beat him up [on the spot (Num. 25:8, 11)]. A priest who performed the rite in a state of uncleanness — his brothers, the priests, do not bring him to court. But the young priests take him outside the courtyard and break his head with clubs. A non-priest who served in the Temple — he is put to death] at the hands of Heaven.

T. 12:7 [If they warn him and he remains silent, warn him and he nods his head, warn him once, twice, and a third time [and he repeated the same transgression], they put him into prison.

T. 12:8 Similarly: Those who are liable for flogging who were flogged and did the same deed and were flogged again [M. San. 9:5A] — and this happened once, twice, and yet a third time — they put him into prison.

T. 14:16 A non-priest, a person who has immersed on that day and awaits sunset to complete his purification, and one whose atonement rite is not yet complete, and one whose clothing [for service in the cult] is lacking in some aspect, and one whose hands and feet are not washed, and one whose head is disheveled, or who is drunk, who served in the cult — all of them are subject to the death penalty. And how are they put to death? Through the action of Heaven.

T. 14:17 All perjurers and illicit lovers go and suffer the form of death which they had brought on their victim, if by stoning, they are stoned. If it was by burning, they are burned. Under what circumstances? When they are in the same status as the victim to be subject to that same mode of execution: if the death penalty attached to the crime is stoning, the accused is stoned, and the witnesses are stoned; if it was to be burning, the victim is burned, and they are burned. But here [M. San. 11:6H], he is subject to the death penalty through burning, while the perjurers are executed through strangulation.

G. *Death At the Hands of Heaven: Denial of Eternal Life*

M. 11:1 [Mishnah = 10:1, and so throughout] All Israelites have a share in the world to come, as it is said, "your people also shall be all righteous, they shall inherit the land forever; the branch of my planting, the work of my hands, that I may be glorified" (Is. 60:21). And these are the ones who have no portion in the world to come: He who says, the resurrection of the dead is a teaching which does not derive from the Torah, and the Torah does not come from Heaven; and an Epicurean.

T. 12:9 They added to the list of those [who have no portion in the world to come] [M. San. 10:1]: he who breaks the yoke, violates the covenant, misinterprets the Torah, pronounces the Divine Name as it is spelled out [M. San. 10:1G], who have no portion in the world to come.

T. 13:5 But heretics, apostates, traitors, Epicureans, those who deny the Torah, those who separate from the ways of the community, those who deny the resurrection of the dead, and whoever both sinned and caused the public to sin and those who sent their arrows against the land of the living and stretched out their hands against the "lofty habitation" [the Temple], Gehenna is locked behind them, and they are judged therein for all generations, since it is said, "And they shall go forth and look a he corpses of the men who were transgressors against me. or their worm dies not, and heir pre is not quenched. And they shall be an abhorring unto all flesh" (Is. 66:24). Sheol will waste away, but they will not waste away, for it is written, "and their form shall cause Sheol to waste away" (Ps. 49:14). What made this happen to them? Because they stretched out their hand against the "lofty habitation," as it is said, "Because of his lofty habitation, and lofty habitation refers only to the Temple, as it is said, I have surely built you as a lofty habitation, a place for you to dwell in forever" (I Kings 8:13).

M. 11:2 Three kings and four ordinary folk have no portion in the world to come. Three kings: Jeroboam, Ahab, and Manasseh. Four ordinary folk: Balaam, Doeg, Ahitophel, and Gehazi.

M. 11:3 The generation of the flood has no share in the world to come, and they shall not stand in the judgment, since it is written, "My spirit shall not judge with man forever" (Gen. 6:3) neither judgment nor spirit. The generation of the dispersion has no share in the world to come, since it is said, "So the Lord scattered them abroad from there upon the face of the whole earth" (Gen. 11:8). "So the Lord scattered them abroad" — in this world, "and the Lord scattered them from there" — in the world to come. The men of Sodom have no portion in the world to come, since it is said, "Now the men of Sodom were wicked and sinners against the Lord exceedingly" (Gen. 13:13) "Wicked" — in this world, "And sinners" — in the world to come. But they will stand in judgment. The spies have no portion in the world to come, as it is said, "Even those men who brought up an evil report of the land died by the plague before the Lord" (Num. 14:37) "Died" — in this world. "By the plague" — in the world to come.

M. 11:4 The townsfolk of an apostate town have no portion in the world to come, as it is said, "Certain base fellows [sons of Belial] have gone out from the midst of thee and have drawn away the inhabitants of their city" (Deut. 13:14). And they are not put to death unless those who misled the [town] come from that same town and from that same tribe, and unless the majority is misled, and unless men did the misleading. [If] women or children misled them, of if a minority of the town was misled, or if those who misled the town came from outside of it, lo, they are treated as individuals [and not as a whole town], and they [thus] require [testimony against them] by two witnesses, and a statement of warning, for each and every one of them. This rule is more strict for individuals than for the community: for individuals are out to death by stoning. Therefore their property is saved. But the community is put to death by the sword, Therefore their property is lost.

T. 14:1 They do not declare three towns to be apostate towns in the Land of Israel, so as not to Wipe out settlement in the Land of Israel. But they declare one or two [to be apostate cities].

M. 11:5 "And you shall surely smite the inhabitants of the city with the edge of the sword" (Deut. 13:15). Ass-drivers, camel-drivers, and people passing from place to place — lo these have the power to save it, as, it is said, "Destroying it utterly and all that is therein and the cattle thereof, with the edge of the sword" (Deut. 13:17) On this basis they said, The property of righteous folk which happens to be located in it is lost. But that which is outside of it is saved. And as to that of evil folk, whether it is in the town or outside of it, lo, it is lost.

T. 14:2 Ass-drivers, camel-drivers, and people passing from place to place [M. San. 10:5B] who spent the night in its midst and became apostate with [the others of the town], are put to death by the sword. Their property and the town are prohibited. And if they spent thirty days in the town, they are put to death by the sword, and their property and the town are prohibited. But if they did not spend thirty days in the town, while they are put to death by the sword, their property and the town are permitted. But under all circumstances those who have incited the town to apostatize are put to death by stoning, and their property and the town are prohibited. [If] women and children enticed the townsfolk to apostatize, they are put to death by the sword, but their property and the town are permitted. [If] women enticed the population to apostatize and not men, children and not adults — is it possible that the town should be declared an apostate town? Scripture says, "The inhabitants of their town" (Deut. 13:14) — the matter is determined by the deeds of the residents of the town, and the matter is not determined by the deeds of all such sorts as these [cf. M. San. 10:4C–I].

T. 14:3 The minor children of the residents of an apostate city who apostatized with it are not put to death.

T. 14:4 The property of the righteous which is in the town is lost, but that which is outside of it is saved. And that of the wicked, whether in it or outside of it, is lost [M. San. 10:5D–E].

T. 14:5 If there were Holy Things in it, things that have been consecrated for use on the altar are left to die; things which are consecrated for the upkeep of the Temple building are to be redeemed; heave-offering left therein is allowed to rot; second tithe and sacred scrolls are hidden away.

M. 11:6 [As it is said,] "And you shall gather all the spoil of it into the midst of the wide place thereof" (Deut. 13:17). If it has no wide place, they make a wide place for it. [If] its wide place is outside of it, they bring it inside. "And you will burn with fire the city and all the spoil thereof, (ever whit, unto the Lord your God)" (Deut. 13:17). "The spoil thereof" — but not the

spoil which belongs to heaven. On this basis they have said: Things which have been consecrated which are in it are to be redeemed; heave-offering left therein is allowed to rot; second tithe and sacred scrolls are hidden away. "And there shall cleave naught of the devoted things to your hand [that the Lord may turn from the fierceness of his anger and show you mercy and have compassion upon you and multiply you]" (Deut. 13:18) for so long as evil people are in the world, fierce anger is in the world. When the evil people have perished from the world, fierce anger departs from the world.

II. Analysis: The Problematics of the Topic, Sanhedrin

Once we see whole and complete the halakhah in its classical statement, we find no difficulty in defining the problematics of the topic. The topic is sanctions for the protection of the social order, that is treated in the category-formation defined at tractate Sanhedrin. The problematic is revealed in the exposition of the topic. What captures sages' interest in the topic is a hierarchization of sins or crimes as indicated by the severity of the penalties that are imposed, matched, also, by the formality and procedural punctiliousness of the courts' process. Stated simply, we may say that sages find important in the category-formation, criminal justice, the issue, which sin is more severe than the other, and how does the penalty fit the crime in a set of hierarchized sins with matching sanctions? That is the center of the matter. Once that question is asked of this topic — the problematics of hierarchization as that pertains to criminal justice — the order of presentation is set, the sequence dictated, start to finish, with only a few flaws, for some of which I cannot account.

For tractate Sanhedrin, we move from property cases to capital cases, and, within capital cases, through the penalties for catalogued crimes from the heaviest to the lightest in context. Then, at the end, we turn to the most severe penalty of all — one that the earthly court cannot inflict but only the Heavenly court can impose. The auxiliary tractate that follows then proceeds from capital to corporal punishment. So the order of the whole is [1] the earthly court and property cases; [2] the earthly court and capital punishment; [3] the heavenly court; and, appended, [4] corporal punishment. That manner of exposition then identifies for us what is at issue when the topic at hand is addressed. Let me now spell these matters out. As we shall see, sages come to the topic of criminal justice bearing in mind a profound theological issue, which is, how God's justice is to be done in such a way as to express God's mercy — even for sinners and criminals. But that matter will emerge in full detail only when we turn to the task of interpretation and identify the religious principles that the law embodies. And in due course, we shall see, it is only through the topic at hand that sages can have made the statement concerning God's merciful justice that they wished to set forth.

The framers of the halakhah on the surface intend to set forth the design a court system. The name of the tractate that defines the category-formation promises just that. And a first glance at the definition and exposition of the category reinforces the same impression: facts of Scripture neatly organized. It is obvious that Scripture contributes many of the facts. But when we consider the layout of the halakhah viewed whole, we realize that it is the structure that imparts consequence to the facts, not the facts that accumulate to define the character of the structure. The Written Torah contributes remarkably slight information, for example, to the chapters on the organization of the court system (number of judges for cases of various classifications) and on the character of the Israelite government (king, high priest, sage). Once the category-formation in its subdivisions is fully exposed, by contrast, the Written Torah makes its full and rich endowment of information.

But the category as defined by the generative problematics is distinctive to the halakhah. Seen all together, the outline leaves no doubt whatsoever as to the focus of interest. Chapters One through Three signal that we deal with a systematic account of the government and political institutions of Israel in the Land of Israel. The intrusion of Chapter Two, with its comparison of the principal authorities, the king and the high priest, not withstanding, the account stresses the workings of the sages' courts, taken for the norm in Chapters One and Three. So the presentation of the halakhah creates the impression of a systematic account of the government, with special interest in the administration of justice.

Once we reach Chapter Four, however, we learn that that reading errs. In fact the opening three chapters provide a miscellaneous prologue to the main topic of the category, and that concerns capital cases, which form the shank of the tractate to the end. If we view Sanhedrin and Makkot as a single tractate, moreover, the focus on capital cases is still clearer, since from that angle of vision we find a match for the three episodic chapters on property cases at the outset in the three episodic chapters on flogging and banishment at the end, thus, property, capital, and corporal penalties, together with the crimes or sins that bring on those sanctions, respectively. And then the center is all the more blatant: capital crimes.

The Mishnah's presentation of the halakhah is, as usual, elegant and deft, with careful transitions masking the abrupt shifts. I.D, from M. 4:1 forward, moves us into the topic of capital cases by comparing what is coming with what has now been expounded: The same [laws] apply to property cases and capital cases with respect to examination and interrogation of witnesses. Then comes the death penalty, with which the remainder of the halakhah as set forth in the Mishnah-Tosefta and extenuated in the two Talmuds is preoccupied. Here, once more, we find a subtle transition. We are supposed to be talking about stoning, that is, the first of the four modes of inflicting death, but the law that is set forth is not particular to stoning and pertains to all forms of the death penalty. That is, those to be executed in one of the other three modes are also going to be instructed to declare, "Let my death be atonement for all of my transgressions." The upshot is, the requirement of establishing the transition to the death penalty — how administered, to whom — accounts for the duplication of the presentation of stoning, once as exemplary for the generic death penalty, the second time as particular for the species at hand. From that point forth, the point of interest is the classification of the severity of various crimes in the order of the severity of the penalties that are inflicted, from stoning downward. Here the halakhah takes as its task the comprehensive organization of the facts of Scripture. As slight an impact as is Scripture's account of ancient Israel's government upon the halakhah's provisions, that is how weighty is the burden of Scripture's facts on the death penalty. We note that the Mishnah's presentation is tightly organized, and Tosefta's responds point by point to the Mishnah's.

The organizational logic that tells us about four modes of the death penalty and that spells out those sins or crimes subject to each requires that we follow the sequence given here. That is to say, the mode of presentation of the halakhah chosen by the framers of the Bavli in putting the chapter on the world to come at the end, thus making it Chapter Eleven. That permits us to conclude the systematic exposition with strangulation, the fourth of the modes of capital punishment. But then the two modes of extra-judicial punishment the death penalty inflicted in an extraordinary manner — have to move to the end of the exposition of capital punishment. Their present position disrupts the orderly presentation of matters that dominates throughout. But the entry does form a fine bridge to the third extra-judicial penalty, the ultimate penalty inflicted by Heaven itself, denial of resurrection and eternal life at the last judgment. Ideally, M. 9:6–7 ought to introduce "And these are the ones who have no portion in the world to come," and not (as in the Mishnah's organization of matters) "These are the ones who are to be strangled." Here, therefore, the character of what is said offers no obvious solution to the problem of the ordering of the halakhah.

But the intent of the composition seen whole proves blatant. Promising an account of the courts and their procedures in adjudicating both property and capital cases, the halakhah in detail delivers a systematic exercise to show how the various sins or crimes defined by Scripture are hierarchized, leading to the climax — the worst possible penalty — of denial of a portion in the world to come. That is to say, life eternal beyond the grave. When we have considered the construction of the halakhah of Makkot, on occasions for flogging, with special reference to perjury, and for banishment, along with the procedures of both sanctions, we shall find ourselves able to identify the religious heart of the halakhah of aimed at protecting the Israelite commonwealth from sinners and criminals. Only when we turn to the religious meaning of the halakhah will the full intention and message emerge with clarity, and then we shall see in the halakhic disquisition a powerful theological statement, one that can have been made only through the exposition of the topic at hand.

5.

TRACTATE MAKKOT

I. An Outline of the Halakhah of Makkot

The penalties other than capital are set forth in tractate Makkot, covering perjury (with variable penalties), banishment, and flogging. While Scripture supplies many facts, the Oral Torah organizes and lays matters out in its own way. Where the Written Torah does not provide information that sages deem logical and necessary, they make things up for themselves. Where verses of Scripture play a role in the halakhic statement of matters, they are cited in context. The details of the organization of the court system do not derive from the Written Torah, nor are the specificities of the death penalty supplied there.

For Makkot, the only verse that is critical pertains to tractate Makkot's presentation of the penalties for perjury, Dt. 19:15–21, and for flogging, Dt. 23:1–3. The former is as follows:

> A single witness shall not prevail against a man for any crime or for any wrong in connection with any offense that he has committed; only on the evidence of two witnesses or of three witnesses shall a charge be sustained. If a malicious witness arises against any man to accuse him of wrongdoing, then both parties to the dispute shall appear before the Lord, before the priests and the judges who are in office in those days; the judge shall inquire diligently, and if the witness is a false witness and has accused his brother falsely, then you shall do to him as he had meant to do to his brother, so you shall purge the evil from the midst of you . . . your eye shall not pity; it shall be life for life, eye for eye, tooth for tooth, hand for hand, foot for foot.

The latter is as follows:

> If there is a dispute between men and they come into court and the judges decide between them, acquitting the innocent and condemning the guilty, then if the guilty man deserves to be beaten, the judge shall cause him to lie down and be beaten in his presence with a number of stripes in proportion to his offense. Forty stripes may be given him but not more; lest if one should go on to beat him with more stripes than these, your brother be degraded in your sight.

As we shall see, the exposition of the halakhah adheres closely to the program of Scripture.

i. *Penalties for Perjury*

M. 1:1 How are witnesses treated [punished] as perjurers? [If they had said,] "We testify concerning Mr. So-and-so, that he is the son of a divorcée," or, "... the son of a woman who has performed the rite of removing the shoe," [and had been proved perjurers], they do not say, "Let this one be declared the son of a divorcée," or, "Let him be declared the son of a woman who has performed the rite of removing the shoe." But he is flogged [on account of perjury] with forty stripes.... "We testify concerning Mr. So-and-so, that he is liable to exile," they do not say, "Let this one go into exile in his stead." But he is flogged with forty stripes. [If they had said,] "We testify concerning Mr. So-and-so, that he has divorced his wife and not paid off her marriage settlement," — (and is it not so that whether it is today or tomorrow, he certainly is going to pay off her marriage settlement —) they make an estimate of how much a man will be willing to pay [now] for the ownership of her marriage settlement, on the condition that, if she should be widowed or divorced, [he will take it over], but if she should die, her husband will inherit her [estate, including said marriage settlement]. [If they had said,] "We testify concerning Mr. So-and-so, that he owes his fellow a thousand zuz, on condition that he will pay him in thirty days," and the accused says, "... in the next ten years," they make an estimate of how much a man is willing to pay for the use of a thousand zuz, whether he pays them in thirty days or in ten years.

B. 1:1 I.4/2B: FOUR STATEMENTS HAVE BEEN MADE WITH REGARD TO CONSPIRATORIAL WITNESSES: THEY ARE NOT PUNISHED BY BEING DECLARED THE SON OF A DIVORCÉE OR THE SON OF A WOMAN WHO HAS PERFORMED THE RITE OF REMOVING THE SHOE IF THEY HAVE GIVEN FALSE WITNESS IN SUCH A MATTER [BUT ARE FLOGGED]. THEY ARE NOT SENT INTO EXILE TO THE CITIES OF REFUGE. THEY ARE NOT REQUIRED TO PAY RANSOM. THEY ARE NOT SOLD AS SLAVES [IF THEY ACCUSED SOMEONE OF HAVING STOLEN AND THE ACCUSED IS TO BE SOLD INTO SLAVERY TO PAY COMPENSATION FOR THE THEFT].

M. 1:2 [If they had said,] "We testify concerning Mr. So-and-so, that he owes his fellow two hundred zuz," and they turn out to be perjurers — whoever pays restitution is not flogged."

M. 1:3 [If they had said,] "We testify concerning Mr. So-and-so, that he is liable to receive flogging in the measure of forty stripes," and they turn out to be perjurers — they are flogged only forty stripes." They divide up [among the perjurers] a penalty for making restitution, but they do not divide up the penalty of flogging. How so? [If] they gave testimony about someone that he owes his fellow two hundred zuz, and they turned out to be perjurers, they divide [the two hundred zuz] among them [and make restitution of that amount]. But if they gave testimony about him that he is liable to receiving flogging in the measure of forty stripes, and they turned out to be perjurers, each one is flogged forty times.

T. 1:6 Witnesses who say, "We testify concerning Mr. So-and-so, that he has divorced his wife and not paid off her marriage-settlement," [M. Mak. 1:1] and so does the woman claim — and they turn out to be perjurers — they pay off the value of her marriage-contract to the husband. [If they say that] he has divorced his wife and has paid off her marriage-contract, and so does the husband claim — and they turn out to be perjurers — they pay off the value of her marriage-contract to her husband. [If they say] that he has divorced his wife and not paid off her marriage-contract, and lo, she is yet in his domain and serving him, and they turn out to be perjurers — they do not rule that they should pay off to her the value of her marriage-settlement, but [they pay] only the value of deriving benefit from her marriage settlement. And is there a value in deriving benefit from her marriage-settlement? Yes. They make an estimate of how much a man will be willing to pay [now] for the marriage-contract of this woman, on the condition that, if she should die in her husband's lifetime, her husband will inherit her [estate, including said marriage-settlement], but [if it is] after the death of her husband, she will inherit her marriage-settlement, and they will inherit her [M. Mak. 1:1]. In accord with that estimate they pay restitution.

M. 1:4 Witnesses are declared to be perjurers only if they [by their own testimony] incriminate themselves. How so? [If] they said, "We testify concerning Mr. So-and-so, that he killed someone," [and] they said to them, "How can you give any testimony, for lo, this one who is supposed to have been killed, or that one who is supposed to have killed, was with us on that very day and in that very place" — they are not declared perjurers. But if they said to them, "How can you give testimony, and lo, you yourselves were with us on that very day in that very place" — lo, these are declared perjurers, and they are put to death on the basis of their own testimony [against the third party].

T. 1:1 A perjured witness is not sold on account of [paying compensation for] perjury.

T. 1:2 A. Witnesses who said, "We testify concerning Mr. So-and-so that he borrowed from Mr. Such-and-such two hundred zuz on such and such a day, in such and such a place" — and others came along and said to them, "How in the world can you give evidence in this matter? For lo, the lender or the borrower was with us on that day in such-and-such a place" — these are not deemed perjured witnesses, but their testimony in any event is null. But if they had said to them, "How in the world can you give evidence in this matter? For lo, you yourself were with us in such and such a place" — lo, these are deemed perjured witnesses. And they pay restitution on the basis of the testimony of the [others]. [If] they were inscribed on the writ, "on the first of Nisan, in the year of release," and others came along and said to them, "How in the world can you have signed that writ, for lo, you were with us on that day in such and such a place" — their testimony remains valid, and the writ remains valid, for I say, "Perhaps one postdated the writ and wrote it out."

T. 1:4 The witnesses who testified "We give evidence that Mr. So-and-so blinded the eye of his slave and afterward he knocked out his tooth" — and so the master says, and who turned out to be perjurers — they pay compensation to the slave. [If they said], "... he knocked out his tooth and afterward he blinded his eye," and so the slave says, and they turned out to be perjurers — they pay to the master. [If they said], "He blinded both of them at once," or "He knocked out both of them at once," and others came and said, "Not so, but it was two of them in succession," and they turned out to be perjurers — they pay to the slave.

T. 1:5 [If they said,] "He blinded both of them one after the other, or knocked out both of them one after the other, and others came along and said, "Not so, but he did both of them at once," and they turned out to be perjurers — they pay to the master. He blinded the eye of his slave, and lo, he is yet subject to him and working for him — and they turn out to be perjurers — they pay both the value of the slave and of the blinding to the master.

M. 1:5 [If] others came and gave false testimony against them, and still others came and gave false testimony against them, even a hundred — all of them are put to death.

M. 1:6 Perjured witnesses [in a capital case] are put to death only at the conclusion of the trial.

T. 1:8 At what point are perjured witnesses liable to pay compensation? At the point at which their testimony is spelled out in court. Once it comes out that [their evidence] has caused him to be declared liable by the court, at that point the perjurer has to pay compensation.

M. 1:7 "At the mouth of two witnesses or three witnesses shall he that is to die be put to death" (Dt. 17:6). If the testimony is confirmed with two witnesses, why has the Scripture specified three? But: [the purpose is] to draw an analogy between three and two. Just as three witnesses prove two witnesses to be false, also two witnesses may prove three witnesses to be false. And how do we know that [two witnesses may prove false] even a hundred? Scripture says, "Witnesses."

M. 1:8 Just as, in the case of two [witnesses], if one of them turns out to be a relative or otherwise invalid, the testimony of both of them is null, so in the case of three, [if] one of them turns out to be a relative or otherwise invalid, the testimony of all three of them is null. How do we know that the same rule

applies even in the case of a hundred? Scripture says, "Witnesses." This is the rule when [both witnesses] warned the transgressor. But if they had not joined in warning the transgressor, what should two brothers do who saw someone commit homicide?

M. 1:9 [If] two saw the incident from one window, and two saw it from another window, and one warns [the transgressor] in the middle, when part of one group see part of another, lo, these constitute [disjoined witnesses nonetheless form] a single body of testimony [subject to the rules given above]. But if not, lo, these constitute two distinct bodies of testimony. Therefore, if one of them turns out to be perjured, [the transgressor] and those two witnesses are put to death, but the other group of witnesses is exempt.

M. 1:10 He whose trial ended and who fled and was brought back before the same court — they do not reverse the judgment concerning him [and retry him]. In any situation in which two get up and say, "We testify concerning Mr. So-and-so that his trial ended in the court of such-and-such, with Mr. So-and-so and Mr. So-and-so as the witnesses against him," lo, this one is put to death. [Trial before] a Sanhedrin applies both in the land and abroad. A Sanhedrin which imposes the death penalty once in seven years is called murderous.

ii. *The Penalty of Exile (Banishment)*

A. *Those Who are Sent into Exile*

M. 2:1 These are the ones who go into exile: he who kills someone accidentally. (1) [If] he was rolling [the roof] with a roller, and it fell down on someone and killed him, (2) [if] he was letting down a jar [from the roof], and it fell on [a man] and killed him, (3) [if] one was climbing down a ladder and fell down on someone and killed him — lo, this person goes into exile. But: (1) if he was pulling up a roller, and it fell on [a man] and killed him, (2) [if] he was drawing up a jar, and the rope broke, and [the jar] fell on a man and killed him, (3) [if] he was climbing up a ladder and fell on a man and killed him, lo, this one does not go into exile. This is the governing principle: Whatever happens en route downward — the person goes into exile. [And whatever happens] not en route downward — the person does not go into exile. [If] the iron flew from the heft and killed someone, he goes into exile. [If] it flew from the wood which is being split, he does not go into exile.

T. 2:1 These are the ones who go into exile [M. Mak. 2:1A] — [If] one intended to hit the wood and hit a man and killed him, to hit a chip and hit a man and killed him — lo, this one goes into exile.

T. 2:2 If one was letting down utensils from above to below and the rope snapped or slipped, lo, this one goes into exile. [If] he was drawing up a jug, and it hit someone on its way down, one goes into exile. [If it was] not on its way down, he does not go into exile.

T. 2:4 A butcher who was chopping meat and hit someone behind him and killed him — lo, this one goes into exile. [If] one did not know that there was a baby in the crib and he sat on it and killed it, — [if] he did not know that there was a man in the pit and he tossed a stone into it and it crushed the man and killed him — lo, this one goes into exile [cf. M. Mak. 2:3L–N].

T. 2:11 [If] the iron flipped out of its haft or out of its handle, even not as it was coming down he does not go into exile [M. Mak. 2:1M–O]. Whither does he go into exile? To the cities of refuge. And if he killed someone, this one goes into exile. When the occasion arises, rule as follows: There are two sorts of those who commit involuntary manslaughter, and two who commit homicide. [If] one has committed homicide on the testimony of two witnesses and after suitable warning, he is liable. [If] he did so not at the testimony of two witnesses and after suitable warning, he is exempt.

T. 2:12 In the case of one who committed involuntary homicide, if this was as the object was being brought down, he goes into exile. If it was not as the object was being brought down, he does not go into exile [cf. M. Mak. 2:1 K–L]. Where does he go into exile? To a city of refuge. And in the case of the wilderness, he goes into exile to the camp of the Levites. A Levite who goes into exile goes to another district. But if he goes into exile to his own district, lo, this affords him protection.

M. 2:2 He who throws a stone into the public domain and so committed manslaughter — lo, this one goes into exile. [If] he threw the stone into his own courtyard and killed him, if the victim had every right to go into there, [the other party] goes into exile. And if not, he does not go into exile, as it is said, "As when a man goes into the forest with his neighbor" (Dt. 19:5) — just as the forest is a domain in which both the victim and the one who inflicted injury have every right to enter, so the courtyard belonging to the householder is excluded [from reference], since the victim had no right to go there.

T. 2:5 A court officer who hit someone at the instance of a court [and the person died] — lo, this one goes into exile. An expert physician who administered a remedy at the instance of a court [and the patient died] — lo, this one goes into exile. He who chops up the foetus in the belly of the woman at the instance of a court and killed it — lo, this one goes into exile. He who throws a stone in the public domain and it killed someone — lo this one goes into exile.

T. 2:6 These are the ones who do not go into exile: if one was chopping wood and hit a man and killed him, chopping a chip and hit a man and killed him, lo, this one does not go into exile.

T. 2:7 A slave who went into exile to a city of refuge — his master is not liable to provide him with food. Not only so, but the fruit of his labor still belongs to his master. A woman who went into exile to a city of refuge — her husband is liable to provide her with food. But if he said, "Let the fruit of her labor to go to her in exchange for her upkeep," the right is in his hand to say just that.

T. 2:10 One who bears enmity [for the man whom he has killed] does not go into exile [M. Mak. 2:3I]. But he is not put to death except on the evidence of witnesses and after suitable warning [of the consequences of his deed].

M. 2:3 The father goes into exile because of [the death of] the son. And the son goes into exile because of the [the death of] father. All go into exile because of [the death of] an Israelite. And an Israelite goes into exile on their account, except on account of [the death of] a resident alien. A resident alien goes into exile only on account of [the death of] another resident alien. One who bears enmity [for his victim] does not go into exile.

B. *The Cities of Exile*

M. 2:4 Where do they go into exile? To the cities of refuge — to three which are in Transjordan, and to three which are in the Land of Canaan, as it is said, "You shall set aside three cities beyond Jordan and three cities you shall set aside in the Land of Canaan" (Num. 35:14). Before the three in the Land of Israel had been selected [Josh. 20:7], the three which were on the other side of the Jordan [also] did not afford refuge, as it is said, "They shall be for you six cities of refuge" — [they do not afford refuge] until all six of them afford refuge at the same time.

T. 3:1 Three cities [of refuge] did Moses set aside in Transjordan, and when they came to the Land, they set aside three more. But even so, neither these nor those afforded protection until they had conquered and divided up [the Land]. Once they had conquered and divided up the Land, and so had become liable to tithes and to the laws of the Seventh Year, both these and those began to afford protection [to the manslayer] [M. Mak. 2:4E–G].

T. 3:4 [If] one of them fell down, they build it up in the same location And how do we know that they may build it up even in some other location? Scripture says, "Six cities of refuge" (Num. 25:13). [They are to be] in that same tribe['s land]. And how do we know that one may build them up in the land Scripture says, "They will be" — that they should be lined up and should afford protection just as do the first ones.

M. 2:5 And [direct] roads [were prepared] from one to the other, as it is said, "And you shall prepare the way and divide the borders of your land" (Dt. 19:3). And they hand over to him two disciples of sages, lest [the avenger of the blood] should kill him en route. They will speak to [the avenger of the blood].

M. 2:6 All the same are [the deaths of] the high priest who is anointed with anointing oil, the one who is consecrated by being clothed in many garments, and the one who has passed from his anointment as high priest — they bring back the murderer [from the city of refuge, his term having ended]. Therefore the mothers of the priests provide food and clothing for those [who are in the cities of refuge,] so that they will not pray that their sons will die. [If] after one's trial has ended [with the sentence of exile], a high priest died, lo, this one does not go into exile. [If] it was before the trial had ended that the high priest died and another was appointed in his stead, and afterward his trial came to an end, he comes back only at the death of the next high priest.

M. 2:7 [If] (1) one's trial ended at a time at which there was no high priest, (2) he who kills a high priest, and (3) a high priest who committed involuntary manslaughter — [none of these] leaves there forever. And one does not leave [the city of refuge] either for giving testimony having to do with a religious duty, or to give testimony having to do with property, or to give testimony having to do with a capital crime. And even if the Israelites need him, and even if he is a general of the Israelite army of the quality of Joab b. Zeruiah, he may not leave there ever, as it is said, "Whither he has fled" (Num. 35:25) — there will be his dwelling, there will be his death, there will be his burial. Just as the town affords refuge, so the territory within the extended, Sabbath limit of the town affords refuge. A tree standing in the Sabbath limit, with its branches extending outside of the Sabbath limit — or standing outside of the Sabbath limit, with its branches extending within the Sabbath limit — everything follows the location of the branches. [The boundaries of the city of refuge extend to the outer limit of the branches.] [If] one has committed manslaughter in that very town he goes into exile from one neighborhood to another. And a Levite goes into exile from one town to another.

T. 3:6 And they build him a house and he lives in it, as it is said, "And he will dwell there" (Num. 35:26) — and not within its Sabbath-limit [but in the city itself]. [If] the avenger of the blood found him within the Sabbath-limit of the town [and killed him], lo, he is equivalent to anyone else, [M. Mak. 2:7K], and is liable for hitting him or for cursing him and he is liable for damages [he may do to him], whether it is a man or a woman. And if he kills him deliberately, he is put to death; [if he does so] inadvertently, he himself goes into exile to the cities of refuge.

M. 2:8 Similarly: a manslayer who went into exile into a city of refuge, whom the townsfolk wanted to honor, must say to them, "I am a manslayer." [If] they said to him, "Even so, [we still want to honor you,]" he may accept [the honor] from them, as it is said, "This is the word of the manslayer" (Dt. 19:4).

iii. *The Penalty of Flogging*

A. *Those Who Are Flogged*

M. 3:1 These are the ones who are flogged: He who has sexual relations with (1) his sister, (2) the sister of his father, (3) the sister of his mother, (4) the sister of his wife, (5) the wife of his brother, (6) the wife of the brother of his father, (7) a menstruating woman, (8) a widow in the case of a high priest, (9) a divorcée or a woman who has performed the rite of removing the shoe with an ordinary priest, (10) a mamzer girl and a (11) Netin girl with an Israelite, (12) an Israelite girl with a Netin [descendant of the caste of Temple slaves] or with a mamzer [offspring of a couple who cannot legally marry, e.g., by reason of consanguinity]. As to a widow and a divorcée, [priests] are liable in her case on two counts. In the case of a divorcée and a woman who has performed the rite of removing the shoe, [a priest) is liable in her case on only one count alone.

T. 4:9 He who has sexual relations with his sister, with the sister of his father, with the sister of his mother, with the sister of his wife, with the wife of his brother, with the wife of the brother of his father, [or] with a menstruating woman [M. Mak. 3:1B-C] — lo, this one is liable. And just as he is flogged, so she is flogged. And he transgresses on each and every count which applies to him. And if it was a widow in the case of a high priest [M. Mak. 3:1E] and a divorcee, one of impaired genealogical ancestry [whom a priest may not marry], and a whore — he is liable on each count. [If she was] a widow of five different husbands, or had been divorced by five different husbands, he should not be liable for more than a single count [cf. M. Mak. 3:1F]. He who eats a limb chopped off of a living animal, taken from a clean domestic beast, a wild beast, or fowl — in any measure at all, or taken from unclean ones — in the measure of an olive's bulk, [if] he ate an olive's bulk of a clean domestic beast, a clean wild beast, or a clean fowl while they were yet alive — they join together when they are dead. [If they were] dead, they do not join together. [But] meat from an unclean domestic beast, an unclean wild beast and an unclean bird, whether they are alive or dead, — lo, [pieces of meat from them] join together [to form the requisite volume to impose punishment by flogging].

M. 3:2 [Also subject to flogging are]: (**1**) an unclean person who ate food in the status of Holy Things: (**2**) he who enters the Temple unclean, (**3**) he who eats forbidden fat, blood, remnant of a sacrifice left overnight, meat of a sacrifice rendered invalid by the improper intention of the officiating priest, or unclean [sacrificial meat]; (**4**) he who slaughters an animal and offers it up outside of the Temple; (**5**) he who eats leaven on Passover; (**6**) and he who eats or who does an act of labor on the Day of Atonement; (**7**) he who prepares anointing oil like the anointing oil of the Temple, (**8**) he who prepares incense like the incense of the Temple, or (**9**) he who anoints himself with anointing oil; (**10**) he who eats carrion or *terefah* meat [that is, meat from a beast that was dying on its own], forbidden things, or creeping things. [If] one ate (**1**) food from which tithes had not been removed at all, (**2**) first tithe from which heave offering had not been removed, (**3**) second tithe or consecrated food which had not been redeemed, [he is liable to flogging]. How much food which had not been tithed at all does one eat so as to be liable? An olive's bulk.

T. 4:1 He who eats of the Passover-offering an olive's bulk of living flesh, an olive's bulk of raw flesh, an olive's bulk of seethed flesh, an olive's bulk of boiled flesh is liable [cf. Ex. 12:9]. [If] he took an olive's bulk of it out from one house to another, or from one association [formed for sharing a Passover-offering] to another such association [formed for sharing a Passover-offering], at the time of eating it, lo, this one is liable, since it is said, "You will not take any of the meat out of the house" (Ex. 12:46). And if one has boiled it, he is liable on its account because of the invalidation of Holy Things.

T. 4:2 He who prepares incense [like the incense of the Temple] [M. Mak. 3:2F] in its required measure is liable. But he who sniffs it is exempt. And [the latter] is liable solely by reason of having committed sacrilege alone.

T. 4.3 He who anoints himself with anointing oil [M. Mak. 3:2F] [such as that] which Moses made in the wilderness — lo, this one is liable to extirpation. [If] he put it on his head and body or on one of his limbs, even though he did not rub it in, he is liable. And how much does he rub in order to incur liability? An olive's bulk. All the same are the one who anoints himself and the one who anoints others. Under what circumstances? When both of them did so deliberately. But if both of them did so inadvertently, they are exempt. If one of them did so inadvertently and one of them did so deliberately, the one who did so inadvertently is exempt, and the one who did so deliberately is liable.

T. 4:4 He who eats food which has not been tithed [M. Mak. 3:2H] — even if all that is lacking is the great heave-offering alone, first tithe, second tithe, or even poorman's tithe — lo, this one is liable [M. Mak. 3:2H].

T. 4:7 A. He who cooks meat in milk — lo, this one is liable. And just as they are liable for cooking it, so are they liable for eating.

T. 5:2 He who offers up an olive's bulk of the bread of the Two Show Breads for an idol, or outside [of the courtyard], lo, this one is liable.

T. 5:3 All the same are the altar and the ramp for this purpose. He who offers up a piece of the meat of a sin-offering, a piece of the meat of the guilt-offering, a piece of the meat of Most Holy Things, a piece of the meat of Lesser Holy Things, a bit of the remnant of the 'omer, of the Two Loaves and the Show Bread and of the residue of meal-offerings, or of leaven or of honey — [all of these] transgress a negative commandment.

M. 3:3 [Also subject to flogging are]: (1) he who eats first fruits over which one has not made the required declaration; (2) Most Holy Things outside the Temple veils, (3) Lesser Holy Things or second tithe outside the wall [of Jerusalem]. He who breaks the bone of a Passover offering which is in a state of cleanness — lo, this one is flogged with forty stripes. But he who leaves over meat of a clean Passover offering or who breaks the bone in the case of an unclean one is not flogged with forty stripes.

T. 5:4 He who consecrates [and actually slaughters and offers] a blemished animal for the altar transgresses on five counts: because of not slaughtering, not consecrating, not tossing its blood, not burning up its fat, and not burning up even part of it, since it is said, "[When any one .... presents his offering ...., to be accepted you shall offer a male without blemish. ... You shall not offer anything that has a blemish, for it will not be acceptable. ..." (Lev. 22:18–20)] To be accepted it must be perfect; "there shall be no blemish in it" (Lev. 22:21). [If] one consecrated it but did not actually slaughter it [as an offering], he is liable on only a single count. [If] he consecrated it, slaughtered it, and tossed its blood, he is liable on each count. He who consecrates a beast which has had sexual relations with a human being and a beast upon which a human being has had sexual relations, a beast set aside for idolatry and a beast which has been used for idolatrous purposes, the hire of a harlot and the price of a dog, transgresses on all of these specified counts, and lo, these [beasts] are tantamount to blemished animals, the act of consecration of which came before their suffering a blemish. But they go forth to secular purposes only if they suffer a permanent blemish alone.

T. 5:5 He who effects an act of substitution (Lev. 27:10) in the case of animals which have been consecrated, and he who shears animals which have been consecrated, and he who does an act of labor with animals which have been consecrated, or who slaughtered them [with the improper intention of offering up the sacrificial parts or eating the meat] outside of their proper time, or who slaughtered them [with the improper intention of offering up the sacrificial parts or eating the meat] outside of their proper place transgresses a negative commandment. There is he who plucks two hairs and becomes liable on four counts, because of being a Nazirite, because of being a person afflicted with the skin ailment [Lev. 13–14], because of [doing so on] a festival day, and because of making a bald spot.

T. 5:6 He who kills a man, domestic beast, wild beast, fowl, whether fully grown or minor, whether male or female, all the same are making many injuries and making few injuries, transgresses a negative commandment, as it is said, "[But if any man hates his neighbor and lies in wait for him and attacks him] and wounds him mortally so that he died" (Deut. 18:11). All the same is the one who injures a snake or a scorpion. And he who sterilizes man, domestic beast, wild beast, fowl, whether fully grown or minor, whether male or female — lo, this one is liable.

T. 5:7 He who makes an idol, chisels it, sets it up, anoints it, dries it off, or planes it, transgresses a negative commandment.

T. 5:8 He who turns over a single stone of the hall, the sanctuary, the area between the hall and the altar, or from the altar, transgresses a negative commandment, as it is said, "[You shall surely destroy all the places where the nations whom you shall dispossess served their gods, upon the high mountains and upon the hills and under every green tree;] you shall tear down their altars and dash in pieces their pillars and burn their Asherim with fire; you shall hew down the graven images of their gods and destroy their name out of that place. You shall not do so to the Lord your God" (Deut. 12:2–4).

M. 3:4 He who removes the dam with the offspring sends the dam away, and he is not flogged. This is the governing principle, In the case of any negative commandment which involves doing a positive deed, one is not liable.

T. 5:10 He who postpones [offering] animals which have been consecrated, and he who leaves over animals which have been consecrated, and he who leaves over leaven on the Passover, and he who preserves mixed seeds in a vineyard, transgresses a negative commandment. But he is not flogged with forty stripes, for there is no concrete affirmative action involved in these things [cf. M. Mak. 3:4D]. This is the governing principle: In consequence of any transgression which involves a concrete action, one is flogged. But in consequence of any transgression which does not involve a concrete action, one is not flogged, except for the case of one who effects an act of substitution [Lev. 27:10] and one who curses his fellow with the divine name.

T. 5:16 These are those who are flogged: All those who transgress a negative commandment. As to those who have transgressed any of the negative commandments which are in the Torah which involve a concrete [affirmative] action — even though they are liable to be put to death by the hands of Heaven or extirpation by the hands of Heaven, they flog them [vs. M. Mak. 3:4D].

T. 5:17 [If they are liable to] the death penalty at the hands of a court, they do not flog them, since it is said, "Proportionate to his transgression" (Deut. 25:2). [If] he is put to death, he is not flogged. [If] he pays restitution, he is not flogged.

M. 3:5 (1) He who makes a baldness on his head [Dt. 14:1], (2) he who rounds the corners of his head and (3) mars the corners of his beard [Lev. 19:27], (4) or he who makes a single cutting for the dead [Lev. 19:28] is liable. [If] he made a single cutting

on account of five different corpses, or five cuttings on account of one corpse, he is liable for each and every one of them. For [cutting off the hair of] the head, he is liable on two counts, one for each side of the head. For cutting off the beard, he is liable on two counts for one side, two counts for the other side, and one count for the lower part. And he is liable only if he will remove it with a razor.

T. 4:10 He who dresses his fellow in diverse kinds, and he who imparts uncleanness to a Nazirite, even though the one who puts clothing deliberately, and the one who imparts uncleanness deliberately is liable, [the one to whom it is done] is exempt. [If] he put on diverse kinds deliberately or contracted uncleanness deliberately, he is liable. He who rounds the corners of his fellow's head — both of them are liable. Under what circumstances? When both of them do so deliberately. But if both of them did so inadvertently, they are exempt. If one of them did so inadvertently and one of them did so deliberately, the one who did so inadvertently is exempt, and the one who did so deliberately is liable. And he is liable in his regard on two counts, one for the top of the temple on this side, and one for the top of the temple on the other side. But he is liable only if he will go around [his head] with a razor [cf. M. Mak. 3:5H]. He who rounds the corners of the head of a woman or a minor is exempt. And he who rounds the corners of the beard of his fellow — both of them are liable. Under what circumstances? When both of them did so deliberately. But if both of them did so inadvertently, both of them are exempt. If one of them did so inadvertently and one of them did so deliberately, the one who did so inadvertently is exempt, and the one who did so deliberately is liable. And he is liable in his regard on five counts, for two on one side, for two on the other, and for one for the lower part [M. Mak. 3:5F]. If he raises up [a hair] and removes it, raises it up and removes it, he is liable for each one. But he is liable only if he will remove it with a razor [M. Mak. 3:5H]. If he removed it with scissors or with an adze, he is exempt [cf. M. Mak. 3:5I].

T. 4:11 He who makes a baldness on the head [M. Mak. 3:5A] of his fellow — both of them are liable. Under what circumstances? When both of them did so deliberately. But if both of them did so inadvertently, both of them are exempt. If one of them did so inadvertently and one of them did so deliberately, the one who did so inadvertently is exempt, and the one who did so deliberately is liable.

T. 4:12 He who makes a single bald spot on account of five different corpses is liable for each and every one of them. [If he made] five bald spots on account of one corpse, he is liable for each and every cutting. And he is liable only if he will make a bald spot on account of a corpse. And how much does he make bald so as to be liable? Enough so that one can discern the place of the bald spot.

T. 4:13 He who makes a cutting [M. Mak. 3:5A4] on the flesh of his fellow — both of them are liable. Under what circumstances? When both of them did so deliberately. But if both of them did so inadvertently, both of them are exempt. If one of them did so inadvertently and one of them did so deliberately, the one who did so inadvertently is exempt, and the one who did so deliberately is liable.

T. 4:14 He who makes a single cutting on account of five different corpses is liable for each and every one of them [M. Mak. 3:5B, D]. [If he made] five cuttings on account of a single corpse, he is liable for each and every cutting. But he is liable only if he will make a cutting on a corpse. And how much does he cut so as to be liable? Sufficient to be able to discern a single cutting.

M. 3:6 He who tattoos his skin — [If] he made a mark but did not tattoo it in, tattooed it in but did not make a mark, he is not liable — unless he makes a mark and tattoos with ink or with eye paint or with anything that makes a permanent mark.

T. 4:15 He who tattoos the skin [M. Mak. 3:6A] of his fellow — both of them are liable. Under what circumstances? When both of them did so deliberately. But if both of them did so inadvertently, both of them are exempt. [If] one of them did so inadvertently and one of them did so deliberately, the one who did so inadvertently is exempt, and the one who did so deliberately is liable. But not liable unless he makes the tattoo with ink or eye paint [M. Mak. 3:6E], for an idol. [If] he scraped him with a scalpel, he is exempt. And he who makes a mark on his slave, so that he will not run away, is exempt [so far as the prohibition of tattooing is concerned].

T. 4:16 He who cuts himself because of the dead — if he does so with his hands [e.g. fingernails], he is exempt. [If he does so] with a utensil, he is liable. [If he does so] for an idol, whether he does so by hand or with a utensil, he is liable.

M. 3:7 A Nazirite who was drinking wine all day long is liable on only one count. [If] they said to him, "Don't drink, don't drink!" yet he continued to drink, he is liable on each count.

M. 3:8 [If a Nazirite] was contracting corpse uncleanness all day long, he is liable on only one count. [If] they said to him, "Do not contract corpse uncleanness! Do not contract corpse uncleanness!" yet he continued to contract corpse uncleanness, he is liable on each count. [If] he was shaving himself all day long, he is liable on only one count. [If] they said to him, "Don't shave! don't shave!" yet he continued to shave, he is liable on each count. If someone was wearing a garment of diverse kinds [Lev. 19:19, Dt. 22:11] all day long, he is liable on only one count. [If] they said to him, "Don't put it on! don't put it on!" yet he took it off and then put it on, he is liable on each count.

M. 3:9 There is one who ploughs a single furrow and is liable on eight counts of violating a negative commandment: [specifically, it is] he who (1) ploughs with an ox and an ass [Dt. 22:10], which are [2, 3] both Holy Things, in the case of (4) [ploughing] Mixed Seeds in a vineyard [Dt. 22:9], (5) in the Seventh Year [Lev. 25:41, (6) on a festival [Lev. 23:7) and who was both

a (7) priest [Lev. 21:1] and (8) a Nazirite [Num. 6:6] [ploughing] in a graveyard.

T. 5:1 A. He who muzzles the cow [in its threshing], and he who yokes up mixed species [an ox and an ass] are exempt. You have none who is liable except the one who actually leads or drives them [cf. M. Mak. 3:9B].

B. *The Conduct of the Flogging*

M. 3:10 How many times do they flog him? Forty stripes less one, as it is said, "By number, forty" (Dt. 25:2,3) — a number near [but less than] forty. And where does the additional one fall? Between the shoulders.

M. 3:11 They make an estimate of his capacity to take the flogging [without being irreparably injured or killed] only by a number divisible by three. [If] they estimated him as able to take forty, [if] he then received part of the flogging, and they said that he cannot take all forty, he is exempt. [If] they estimated him as able to take eighteen, [and] once he has received the flogging [of eighteen], they said that he can take all forty, he [still] is exempt from the rest. [If] he committed a transgression on which he is liable on two counts of violating negative commandments, and they make a single estimate [of what he can take, covering both sets], he is flogged and exempt [from the other]. And if not, he is flogged and allowed to heal, and then goes and is flogged again.

T. 4:17 A high priest who was unkempt or disheveled, or who contracted uncleanness on account of any of his relatives — lo, this one is liable [to flogging]. This is the governing principle: [On account of] any sort of corpse uncleanness because of which a Nazir has to cut his hair, [a high priest] is flogged with forty stripes. And [on account of] any sort of corpse-uncleanness because of which a Nazir does not have to cut his hair, [a high priest] is not flogged with forty stripes. But an ordinary priest who contracts uncleanness from other corpses [than relatives'], or who goes into a graveyard, is liable. [If] he went into a field in which a grave has been lost, he is liable only when he will have traversed the entire field. [If] he went into a grave-area or to survey the territory of the land of the peoples [deemed to be unclean like a grave-area,] or if he went abroad, they flog him with a flogging by reason of rebellion. Flogging administered because of violation of the law of the Torah is forty stripes less one. They estimate the culprit [cf. M. Mak. 3:11]. If he is able to receive the flogging, he is flogged. If not, he is not flogged. But in the case of flogging administered by reason of rebellion against the law, it is not so. But they flog him until he accepts [the ruling of the court and agrees to carry it out], or until he perishes.

T. 5:12 [If] one did a transgression which is subject to two counts of violating negative prohibitions, they do not make an estimate of his capacity to take the flogging to cover both of them. But he is flogged and healed and again is flogged [M. Mak. 3:11F]. [If] they made an estimate that he can take only forty stripes, they do not add even one more stripe to that number. But they take one off that number. [If] they made an estimate that he can take only twenty, they do not add even a single one to that number. But they take off two. Therefore if the minister added even a single stripe and the man died, lo, this one is sent into exile on his account [M. Mak. 3:14C].

T. 5:13 [If] they made an estimate that he can take only three stripes, even if he is standing there and defies them [to lay on more], they do not add even a single one. Therefore if the minister added even a single stripe and the man died, lo, this one is sent into exile on his account.

M. 3:12 How do they flog him? One ties his two hands on either side of a pillar, and the minister of the community grabs his clothing — if it is torn, it is torn, and if it is ripped to pieces, it is ripped to pieces — until he bares his chest. A stone is set down behind him, on which the minister of the community stands. And a strap of cowhide is in his hand, doubled and redoubled, with two straps that rise and fall [fastened] to it.

M. 3:13 Its handle is a handbreadth long and a handbreadth wide, and its end must reach to his belly button. And he hits him with a third of the stripes in front and two-thirds behind. And he does not hit [the victim] while he is either standing or sitting, but bending low, as it is said, "And the judge will cause him to lie down" (Dt. 25:2). And he who hits him hits with one hand, with all his might.

M. 3:14 And a reader reads: "If you will not observe to do . . . the Lord will have your stripes pronounced, and the stripes of your seed" (Dt. 28:58ff.) (and he goes back to the beginning of the passage). "And you will observe the words of this covenant" (Dt. 29:9), and he finishes with, "But he is full of compassion and forgave their iniquity" (Ps. 78:38), and he goes back to the beginning of the passage. And if the victim dies under the hand of the one who does the flogging, the latter is exempt from punishment. [But if] he added even a single stripe and the victim died, lo, this one goes into exile on his account, If the victim dirtied himself, whether with excrement or urine, he is exempt [from further blows].

T. 5:14 [If] they made an estimate of him that if he is flogged, he will have loose bowels, they flog him. [If they made an estimate] that if he leaves the court, he will have loose bowels, they flog him. [If] he had loose bowels before he was flogged, they [nonetheless] flog him, as it is said, "[Then if the guilty man deserves to be beaten, the judge shall cause him to lie down and be beaten in his presence with a number of stripes in proportion to his offence. Forty stripes may be given him, but not more; lest, if one should go on to beat him with more stripes than these, your brother be degraded [in your sight]" (Deut. 25:2–3). [If] after he was flogged, he had loose bowels, they do not flog him [anymore].

T. 5:15 Flogging is done by three: one hits, one counts, and one reads [cf. M. Mak. 3:14A]. And they did not change the strap [used] on him. And it was not long but short, so that it should not touch the "bird of life" [the belly-button] and he die.

II. Analysis: The Problematics of the Topic, Makkot

The tractate concerns itself with the judicial sanctions of flogging and banishment. The order of the topical exposition is somewhat puzzling, since Chapters One and Three belong together. But I take it the compiler deemed the three chapters to be free-standing; he then began with a special case of flogging, proceeded to banishment, conventionally portrayed (who gets it, how is it done), then to flogging, described within the same pattern (who, then how). I myself would have preferred the order, banishment, flogging, then the special case of flogging for perjury (2, 3, 1). The special case is simple. When we cannot inflict upon the perjurer what he intended to bring upon his victim, as Scripture decrees, then the conspiratorial witnesses are flogged. That is what explains the treatment of perjury here, rather than in Mishnah-tractate Sanhedrin Chapters Three and Four, where laws of testimony and evidence are set forth. It further indicates that the heart and soul of Sanhedrin-Makkot is the match between the crime or sin and the penalty, not the exposition of the court system and procedures in their own terms. But that same principle of organization requires that materials better placed elsewhere, e.g., rules of perjury that have no bearing upon the penalty of flogging, be set here. The upshot is, the topic, perjury, is fully exposed, and the exposition is then situated where it is, even though the fit is awkward, because of the plan of the entire document. The sanction of banishment is then expounded in the model of the presentation of the capital penalties: who gets it, how it is inflicted. Scripture's contribution predominates, so far as I can see.

Then, from banishment we turn to flogging, once more following the model of Sanhedrin: those subjected to the penalty, the manner in which the penalty is carried out. With Chapters Two and Three closely aligned to the prior tractate, we see why Makkot is properly viewed as a continuation of Sanhedrin, and how a single problematic, as defined above, governs throughout the systematic exposition of the topic. That problematic should not be missed, even though it is familiar: how does the punishment fit the crime? Here the question is answered out of Scripture and tradition: what punishment is inflicted for what crime? But it is only in the framework of the religious statement that the halakhah proposes to make that we can fully make sense of the halakhic problematics of Sanhedrin-Makkot.

III. Interpretation: Religious Principles of Sanhedrin-Makkot

The most profound question facing Israelite thinkers concerns the fate of the Israelite at the hands of the perfectly just and profoundly merciful God. Since essential to their thought is the conviction that all creatures are answerable to their Creator, and absolutely critical to their system is the fact that at the end of days the dead are raised for eternal life, the criminal justice system encompasses deep thought on the interplay of God's justice and God's mercy: how are these reconciled in the case of the sinner or criminal?

Within Israel's social order the halakhah addresses from a theological perspective the profound question of social justice: what shall we make of the Israelite sinner or criminal? Specifically, does the sin or crime, which has estranged him from God, close the door to life eternal? If it does, then justice is implacable and perfect. If it does not, then God shows his mercy — but what of justice? We can understand the answer only if we keep in mind that the halakhah takes for granted the resurrection of the dead, the final judgment, and the life of the world to come beyond the grave. From that perspective, death becomes an event in life but not the end of life. And, it must follow, the death penalty too does not mark the utter annihilation of the person of the sinner or criminal. On the contrary, because he pays for his crime or sin in this life, he situates himself with all of the rest of supernatural Israel, ready for the final judgment. Having been judged, he will "stand in judgment," meaning, he will find his way to the life of the world to come along with everyone else. Within the dialectics formed by those two facts — punishment now, eternal life later on — we identify as the two critical passages in the halakhah of Sanhedrin-Makkot M. Sanhedrin 6:2 and 10:1: Achan pays the supreme penalty but secures his place in the world to come, all Israel, with only a few exceptions, is going to stand in judgment and enter the world to come, explicitly including all manner of criminals and sinners.

That is what defines the stakes in this critical component of sages' account of God's abode in Israel. What the halakhah wishes to explore is, how is the Israelite sinner or criminal rehabilitated, through the criminal justice system, so as to rejoin Israel in all its eternity. The answer is, the criminal or sinner remains Israelite, no matter what he does — even though he sins — and the death-penalty exacted by the earthly court. So the halakhah of Sanhedrin embodies these religious principles: [1] Israel endures for ever, encompassing (nearly) all Israelites; [2] sinners or criminals are able to retain their position within that eternal Israel by reason of the penalties that expiate the specific sins or crimes spelled out by the halakhah; [3] it is an act of merciful justice that is done when the sinner or criminal is put to death, for at that point, he is assured of eternity along with everyone else. God's justice comes to full expression in the penalty, which is instrumental and contingent; God's mercy endures forever in the forgiveness that follows expiation of guilt through the imposition of the penalty.

That explains why the governing religious principle of Sanhedrin-Makkot is the perfect, merciful justice of God, and it accounts for the detailed exposition of the correct form of the capital penalty for each capital sin or crime. The punishment must fit the crime within the context of the Torah in particular so that, at the resurrection and the judgment, the crime will have been correctly expiated. Because the halakhah rests on the premise that God is just and that God has made man in his image, after his likeness, the halakhah cannot deem sufficient that the punishment fit the crime. Rather, given its premises, the halakhah must pursue the issue, what of the sinner once he has been punished? And the entire construction of the continuous exposition of Sanhedrin-Makkot aims at making this simple statement: the criminal, in God's image, after God's likeness, pays the penalty for his crime in this world but like the rest of Israel will stand in justice and, rehabilitated, will enjoy the world to come.

Accordingly, given their conviction that all Israel possesses a share in the world to come, meaning, nearly everybody will rise from the grave, the sages took as their task the specification of how, in this world, criminals-sinners would receive appropriate punishment in a proper procedure, so that, in the world to come, they would take their place along with everyone else in the resurrection and eternal life. So the religious principle that comes to expression in Sanhedrin-Makkot concerns the meaning of man's being in God's image. That means, it is in man's nature to surpass the grave. And how, God's being just, does the sinner or criminal survive his sin or crime? It is by paying with his life in the here and now, so that at the resurrection, he may regain life, along with all Israel. That is why the climactic moment in the halakhah comes at the end of the long catalogue of those sins and crimes penalized with capital punishment. It is with ample reason that the Bavli places at the conclusion and climax of its version the ringing declaration, "all Israel has a portion in the world to come, except...." And the exceptions pointedly do not include any of those listed in the long catalogues of persons executed for sins or crimes.

The sole exceptions, indeed, pertain to persons who classify themselves entirely outside of the criminal justice system: those who deny that the resurrection of the dead is a teaching of the Torah or (worse still) that the Torah does not come from God. Now, as we realize, these classes of persons hardly belong in the company of the sinners and criminals catalogued here. Then come specified individuals or groups: Three kings and four ordinary folk have no portion in the world to come. Three kings: Jeroboam, Ahab, and Manasseh. Four ordinary folk: Balaam, Doeg, Ahitophel, and Gehazi. There follow the standard trilogy, the generation of the flood, the generation of the dispersion, the generation of Sodom and Gomorrah. We note the difference between the individual who commits an act of idolatry and the entire community, the townsfolk of the apostate town, that does so; God punishes and forgives the individual, but not an entire generation, not an entire community. That is the point at which the criminal justice system completes its work.

That the two religious principles just now specified play a critical role in the formulation and presentation of the halakhah of Sanhedrin-Makkot is made explicit in the context of legal exposition itself. The rite of stoning involves an admonition that explicitly declares the death penalty the means of atoning for all crimes and sins, leaving the criminal blameless and welcome into the kingdom of Heaven:

> A. **[When] he was ten cubits from the place of stoning, they say to him, "Confess," for it is usual for those about to be put to death to confess.**
> B. **For whoever confesses has a share in the world to come.**

C. For so we find concerning Achan, to whom Joshua said, "My son, I pray you, give glory to the Lord, the God of Israel, and confess to him, [and tell me now what you have done; hide it not from me]. And Achan answered Joshua and said, Truly have I sinned against the Lord, the God of Israel, and thus and thus I have done" (Josh. 7:19). And how do we know that his confession achieved atonement for him? For it is said, "And Joshua said, Why have you troubled us? The Lord will trouble you this day" (Josh. 7:25) — This day you will be troubled, but you will not be troubled in the world to come.

D. And if he does not know how to confess, they say to him, "Say as follows: 'Let my death be atonement for all of my transgressions.'"

M. Sanhedrin 6:2

So within the very center of the halakhic exposition comes the theological principle that the death-penalty opens the way for life eternal. It follows that at stake in the tractate Sanhedrin-Makkot is a systematic demonstration of how God mercifully imposes justice upon sinners and criminals, and also of where the limits to God's mercy are reached: rejection of the Torah, the constitution of a collectivity — an "Israel" — that stands against God. God's merciful justice then pertains to private persons. But there can be only one Israel, and that Israel is made up of all those who look forward to a portion in the world to come: who will stand in justice and transcend death. In humanity, idolaters will not stand in judgment, and entire generations who sinned collectively as well as Israelites who broke off from the body of Israel and formed their own Israel do not enjoy that merciful justice that reaches full expression in the fate of Achan: he stole from God but shared the world to come. And so will all of those who have done the dreadful deeds catalogued here.

The upshot should not be missed. It is not merely that through the halakhah at hand sages make the statement that they make. I claim much more, specifically: the religious principle expressed here — God's perfect, merciful justice, correlated with the conviction of the eternity of holy Israel — cannot have come to systematic statement in any other area of the halakhah. It is only in the present context that sages can have linked God's perfect, merciful justice to the concrete life of ordinary Israel, and it is only here that they can have invoked the certainty of eternal life to explain the workings of merciful justice.

Sages insist that without mercy, justice cannot function. Now that we have seen how, in the halakhah, that statement is made, let us explore some of the counterpart formulations of the same principle in the aggadah. God created the world with the attribute of mercy and also of justice, so that in complementary the balance, the world might endure:

Genesis Rabbah XII:XV.1

A. "The Lord God [made earth and heaven]" (Gen. 2:4):
B. The matter [of referring to the divinity by both the names, Lord, which stands for mercy, and God, which stands for justice] may be compared to the case of a king who had empty cups. The king said, "If I fill them with hot water, they will split. If I fill them with cold water, they will contract [and snap]."
C. What did the king do? He mixed hot water and cold water and put it into them, and the cups withstood the liquid.
D. So said the Holy One, blessed be he, "If I create the world in accord with the attribute of mercy, sins will multiply. If I create it in accord with the attribute of justice, the world cannot endure."
E. "Lo, I shall create it with both the attribute of justice and the attribute of mercy, and may it endure!"
F. "Thus: The Lord [standing for the attribute of mercy] God [standing for the attribute of justice] [made the earth and heavens]" (Gen. 2:4).

Just as too much justice will destroy the world, but too much mercy, ruin its coherence, so throughout, each set of traits achieving complementarity must be shown, like dancers, to move in balance one with the other. Then, and only then, are excesses avoided, stasis in motion attained. That brings about the world of justice at rest that sages deemed God to have created in the beginning, to have celebrated on the original Sabbath, and to intend to restore in the end. But notice, when the aggadah makes its statement, it speaks in generalities, and, further, it addresses the world at large. It is the halakhah that formulates the matter not only in specificities but well within the limits of holy Israel. Seeing how the halakhah and the aggadah make the same statement, we once more see the way in which the halakhah portrays the interiorities of Israelite life.

But there is more. Sages recognize that, in the setting of this life, the death penalty brings anguish, even though it assures the sinner or criminal expiation for what he has done. That matter is stated in so many words:

Mishnah-tractate Sanhedrin 6:5

A. Said R. Meir, "When a person is distressed, what words does the Presence of God say? As it were: 'My head is in pain, my arm is in pain.'"

B. "If thus is the Omnipresent distressed on account of the blood of the wicked when it is shed, how much the more so on account of the blood of the righteous!"

God is distressed at the blood of the wicked, shed in expiation for sin or crime, so too man. So while sages recognize the mercy and justice that are embodied in the sanctions they impose, they impute to God, and express in their own behalf, common sentiments and attitudes. They feel the same sentiments God does, as the exposition of the court process in Chapters Three and Four makes explicit.

That fact alerts us to the fundamental principle embodied in the halakhah: man is responsible for what he does, because man is like God. That is the basis for penalizing sins or crimes, but it also is the basis for the hope for eternal life for nearly all Israel. Like God, man is in command of, and responsible for, his own will and intentionality and consequent conduct. The very fact that God reveals himself through the Torah, which man is able to understand, there to be portrayed in terms and categories that man grasps, shows how the characteristics of God and man prove comparable. The first difference between man and God is that man sins, but the one and the just God, never; connecting "God" and "sin" yields an unintelligible result. And the second difference between creature and Creator, man and God, is that God is God.

It is not an accident that in the setting of the category-formation of Sanhedrin-Makkot, sages set forth how God's emotions correspond with man's. Like a parent faced with a recalcitrant child, he takes no pleasure in man's fall but mourns. Not only so, but even while he protects those who love him, Israel, from his, and their, enemies, he takes to heart that he made all man; he does not rejoice at the Sea when Israel is saved, because, even then, his enemies are perishing. This is said in so many words in the context of a discussion on whether God rejoices when the wicked perish:

Bavli-tractate Sanhedrin 4:5 VI.1/39b

A. Therefore man was created alone [4:5J]:

B. "And there went out a song throughout the host" (1 Kgs. 22:36) [at Ahab's death at Ramoth in Gilead].

- C. Said R. Aha b. Hanina, "'When the wicked perish, there is song' (Prov. 11:10).
- D. "When Ahab, b. Omri, perished, there was song."

Does God sing and rejoice when the wicked perish? Not at all:

- E. But does the Holy One, blessed be he, rejoice at the downfall of the wicked?
- F. Is it not written, "That they should praise as they went out before the army and say, 'Give thanks to the Lord, for his mercy endures forever' (2 Chr. 20:21),
- G. and said R. Jonathan, "On what account are the words in this psalm of praise omitted, 'Because he is good'? Because the Holy One, blessed be he, does not rejoice at the downfall of the wicked."

Now we revert to the conduct of God at the very moment of Israel's liberation, when Israel sings the Song at the Sea:

- H. For R. Samuel bar Nahman said R. Jonathan said, "What is the meaning of the verse of Scripture [that speaks of Egypt and Israel at the sea], 'And one did not come near the other all night'" (Ex. 14:20)?
- I. "At that time, the ministering angels want to recite a song [of rejoicing] before the Holy One, blessed be he".
- J. "Said to them the Holy One, blessed be he, 'The works of my hands are perishing in the sea, and do you want to sing a song before me?'"

Now the matter is resolved:

- K. Said R. Yosé bar Hanina, "He does not rejoice, but others do rejoice. Note that it is written, '[And it shall come to pass, as the Lord rejoiced over you to do good, so the Lord] will cause rejoicing over you by destroying you' (Deut. 28:63) — and not 'so will the Lord [himself] rejoice'"
- L. That proves the case.

God's emotions correspond, then, to those of a father or a mother, mourning at the downfall of their children, even though their children have rebelled against them. Even at the moment at which Israel first meets God, with God's act of liberation at the Sea, God cannot join them in their song. God and Israel then correspond, the eternal God in heaven, Israel on earth, also destined for eternal life. Israel forms on earth a society that corresponds to the retinue and court of God in heaven. The halakhah in its way, in Sanhedrin-Makkot, says no less. But it makes the statement, as we have seen, in all of the intimacy and privacy of Israel's interior existence: when (in theory at least) Israel takes responsibility for its own condition. Sanhedrin-Makkot, devoted to the exposition of crime and just punishment, turns out to form an encompassing exercise in showing God's mercy, even, or especially, for the sinner or criminal who expiates the sin or crime: that concludes the transaction, but a great deal will follow it — and from it. In the context of the Torah I cannot think of any other way of making that statement stick than through the halakhah of Sanhedrin-Makkot: this sin, this punishment — and no more.

6.

TRACTATE SHEBUOT

I. An Outline of the Halakhah of Shebuot

The halakhah of Shebuot covers two distinct topics, imparting uncleanness to the sanctuary and its Holy Things and oaths.[1] They are joined by reason of the Written Torah's formulation of matters; the focus there is on common penalties for diverse sins or crimes. Like Keritot, Shebuot sets forth penalties effected through sacrificial offerings, now the guilt-offering required at Leviticus Chapters Five and Six. It therefore finds its place within the presentation of Sanhedrin-Makkot, Horayot and Keritot on penalties for crimes or sins. A principal occasion for a guilt-offering is the violation of an oath or transgression against a bailment. Leviticus 5:1–6 set forth the oath of testimony, the case of one who in the cult touches what is unclean, and the rash oath; all bring a guilt-offering. Lev. 6:1–7 proceed to bailments in which a false oath has been taken.

The themes then are [1] oaths of adjuration; [2] imparting uncleanness to the Temple and its Holy Things; [3] the rash oath; [4] the false claim in connection with bailments. Lev. 5:1–13 are as follows:

> If any one sins in that he hears a public adjuration to testify and though he is a witness, whether he has seen or come to know the matter yet does not speak, he shall bear his iniquity. Or if any one touches an unclean thing, whether the carcass of an unclean beast or a carcass of unclean cattle or a carcass of unclean swarming things, and it is hidden from him, and he has become unclean, he shall be guilty. Or if he touches human uncleanness, of whatever sort the uncleanness may be with which one becomes unclean, and it is hidden from him, when he comes to know it he shall be guilty; or if anyone utters with his lips a rash oath to do evil to do good, any sort or rash oath that men swear, and it is hidden from him, when he comes to know it, he shall in any one of these be guilty. When a man is guilty in any of these, he shall confess the sin he has committed, and he shall bring his guilt offering

---

[1] Vows should not be confused with oaths. They represent a very different category and are dealt with in the setting of the household, in tractate Nedarim.

> to the Lord for the sin that he has committed, a female from the flock, a lamb or a goat, for a sin offering, and the priest shall make atonement for him for his sin. But if he cannot afford a lamb, then he shall bring as his guilt offering to the Lord for the sin that he has committed two turtledoves or two young pigeons, one for a sin offering and the other for a burnt offering. He shall bring them to the priest, who shall offer first the one for the sin offering; he shall wring its head from its neck, but shall not sever it, and he shall sprinkle some of the blood of the sin offering on the side of the altar; it is a sin offering. Then he shall offer the second for a burnt offering according to the ordinance; and the priest shall make atonement for him for the sin that he has committed, and he shall be forgiven. But if he cannot afford two turtledoves or two young pigeons, then he shall bring, as his offering for the sin that he has committed, a tenth of an ephah of fine flour for a sin offering; he shall put no oil upon it, and shall put no frankincense on it for it is a sin offering. And he shall bring it to the priest, and the priest shall take a handful of it as its memorial portion and burn this on the altar, upon the offerings by fire to the Lord; it is a sin offering. Thus the priest shall make atonement for the sin that he has committed in any one of these things, and he shall be forbidden, and the remainder shall be for the priest, as in the cereal offering.

Lev. 6:1–7 on bailments proceed:

> The Lord said to Moses, "If any one sins and commits a breach of faith against the Lord by deceiving his neighbor in a matter of deposit or security, or through robbery, or if he has oppressed his neighbor or has found what was lost and lied about it, swearing falsely, in any of all the things that men do and sin therein, when one has sinned and become guilty, he shall restore what he took by robbery, or what he got by oppression or the deposit that was committed to him or the lost thing that he found or anything about which he has sworn falsely; he shall restore it in full and shall add a fifth to it and give it to him to whom it belongs, on the day of his guilt offering. And he shall bring to the priest his guilt offering to the Lord, a ram without blemish out of flock, valued by you at the price for a guilt offering, and the priest shall make atonement for him before the Lord, and he shall be forgiven for any of the things that one may do and thereby become guilty."

In the exposition of the topic, uncleanness can have come at the beginning or the end, so as not to interrupt the orderly presentation of the matter of primary concerns, oaths. As it happens, uncleanness comes first, then the shank focuses upon a single, coherent account of oaths. The order of the presentation then follows Scripture's plan.

i. *The Uncleanness of the Cult and its Holy Things and the Guilt Offering*

A. *General Introduction*

M. 1:1 Oaths are of two sorts, which yield four subdivisions [on account of each of which one may be liable on one distinct count]. Awareness of [having sinned through] uncleanness is of two sorts, which yield four subdivisions [on account of each of which one may be liable on one distinct count]. Transportation [of objects from one domain to the other] on the Sabbath is of two sorts, which yield four subdivisions [on account of each of which one may be liable on one distinct count]. The symptoms of the presence of the skin disease [*Negaim*] are of two sorts, which yield four subdivisions [on account of each of which one may be liable on one distinct count].

T. 1:5 All those who are unclean, mentioned in the Torah, whether they are made unclean by a severe source of uncleanness, or whether they are made unclean by a minor source of uncleanness, are liable for making unclean the sanctuary and its Holy Things, as it is said, "Or if any one touches any unclean thing, [whether the carcass of an unclean beast or a carcass of unclean cattle or a carcass of unclean swarming things, and it is hidden from him, and he has become unclean — he shall be guilty]" (Lev. 5:2) — to include all the forms of uncleanness which are listed in the Torah.

B. *Uncleanness and the Cult*

M. 1:2 In any case in which there is awareness of uncleanness at the outset and awareness [of uncleanness] at the end but unawareness in the meantime — lo, this one is subject to bringing an offering of variable value. [If] there is awareness [of uncleanness] at the outset but no apprehension [of uncleanness] at the end, a goat which [yields blood to be sprinkled] within [in the Holy of Holies], and the Day of Atonement suspend [the punishment], until it will be made known to the person, so that he may bring an offering of variable value.

M. 1:3 [If] there is no apprehension [of uncleanness] at the outset but there is apprehension [of uncleanness] at the end, a goat which [yields blood to be sprinkled] without [on the outer altar], and the Day of Atonement effect atonement, as it is said, "Beside the sin offering of atonement" (Num. 29:11). For that which this [goat, prepared inside] makes atonement, the other [the goat prepared outside] makes atonement. Just as the goat prepared inside makes atonement only for something for which there is certain knowledge, so that which is prepared outside effects atonement only for something for which there is certain knowledge.

M. 1:6 And for a deliberate act of imparting uncleanness to the sanctuary and its Holy Things, a goat [whose blood is sprinkled] inside and the Day of Atonement effect atonement. And for all other transgressions which are in the Torah — the minor or serious, deliberate or inadvertent, those done knowingly or done unknowingly, violating a positive or a negative commandment, those punishable by extirpation and those punishable by death at the hands of a court, the goat which is sent away [Lev. 16:21] effects atonement.

M. 1:7 [It effects atonement] all the same, for Israelites, priests and the anointed priest. What is the difference between Israelites, priests, and the anointed priest? But: The blood of the bullock effects atonement for priests for imparting uncleanness to the sanctuary and its Holy Things.

M. 2:1 Awareness of uncleanness is of two sorts, which yield four subdivisions [= M. 1:1B]. (1) [If] one was made unclean and knew about it, then the uncleanness left his mind, but he knew [that the food he had eaten was] Holy Things, (2) the fact that the food he had eaten was Holy Things left his mind, but he knew about [his having contracted] uncleanness, (3) both this and that left his mind, but he ate Holy Things without knowing it and after he ate them, he realized it — lo, this one is liable to bring an offering of variable value. (1) [If] he was made unclean and knew about it, and the uncleanness left his mind, but he remembered that he was in the sanctuary; (2) the fact that he was in the sanctuary left his mind, but he remembered that he was unclean, (3) both this and that left his mind, and he entered the sanctuary without realizing it, and then when he had left the sanctuary, he realized it — lo, this one is liable to bring an offering of variable value.

M. 2:2 All the same are he who enters the courtyard and he who enters the addition to the courtyard. For [the latter is in the same classification as the former, since] they add to the city, and courtyards only on the instructions of the king and prophet, the Urim and Thummim, and the Sanhedrin of seventy-one members, with two thank offerings and singing. The court goes along with the two thank offerings behind them, and all the Israelites after them. The one offered inside is eaten, and the one offered outside is burned. And any area which is not treated wholly in this way [with the proper rites] — he who enters that area — they are not liable on its account.

M. 2:3 (1) [If] he was made unclean in the courtyard, and the uncleanness left his mind, but he remembered the sanctuary — (2) [if] the sanctuary left his mind, but he remembered the uncleanness, (3) [if] this and that left his mind, and he prostrated himself or remained there for an interval sufficient for prostrating himself, [if] he went out by the longer way, he is liable. [If he went out] by the shorter way, he is exempt. This is a positive commandment regarding the sanctuary on account of which [a court] is not liable [to a sin offering].

M. 2:4 And what is a positive commandment concerning the menstruating woman, on account of which [a court] is liable? [If] he was having sexual relations with a clean woman, and she said, "I have become unclean," [even if] he separated forthwith, he is liable, for the going out is just as much a pleasure for him as the going in.

ii. Oaths

A. Oaths in General

M. 3:1 Oaths are of two sorts, which yield four subdivisions [M. 1:1A]: (1) "I swear I shall eat," and (2) "... I shall not eat," (3) "... that I ate," and (4) "... that I didn't eat." "I swear that I won't eat," and he ate and drank — he is liable on only one count. "I swear that I won't eat and drink," and he ate and drank — he is liable on two counts.

M. 3:2 "I swear I won't eat," — and he ate a piece of bread made of wheat, a piece of bread made of barley, and a piece of bread made of spelt, he is liable on one count only. "I swear that I won't eat a piece of bread made of wheat, a piece of bread made of barley, and a piece of bread made of spelt," and he ate — he is liable on each and every count.

M. 3:3 "I swear I won't drink," and he drank many different beverages — he is liable on one count only. "I swear that I won't drink wine, oil, and honey," and he drank — he is liable on each and every count.

Y. 3:3 I:1 [If one said,] "I swear that I shall not eat a piece of bread," and he wrapped the bread in reeds or grape-leaves and ate it. he is liable on only one count [that is. that still is an act of eating the bread even though the bread was wrapped in undesirable things]. [If he said,] "I take an oath that I shall not eat a piece of bread, grape pits. grape husks and he wrapped the bread up in grape pits and grape husks, he is liable on each count [for the oath referred to all three, and even though he ate them altogether, it still counts as three separate items]. And if he was a Nazirite, he is liable on three counts [As a Nazirite he is liable for a sin-offering on the counts of consuming grape pits or husks.]

M. 3:4 "I swear I won't eat," and he ate food which is not suitable for eating, or drank liquids which are not suitable for drinking — he is exempt. "I swear that I won't eat," but he ate carrion and *terefah*-meat, abominations and creeping things — he is liable. [If] he said, "Qonam be benefit that I give to my wife, if I ate anything today" and he had eaten carrion, *terefah*-meat, abominations and creeping things — lo, his wife is prohibited [to give benefit to him].

T. 2:1 "I swear that I shall not eat," — and he ate prohibited foods, refuse, remnant, or unclean sacrificial meat — "I swear that I shall not drink," and he drank prohibited liquids, wine deriving from "uncircumcised vines," or from vines which had grown as Mixed Seeds in a vineyard — he is liable.

T. 2:2 "I swear that I shall eat," and he ate prohibited things, refuse, remnant, or unclean sacrificial meat — "I swear that I shall drink," and he drank prohibited liquids, wine deriving from "uncircumcised vines," or from vines which had grown as Mixed Seeds in a vineyard — he is exempt.

Y. 3:4 II:1 *[Referring to M. 3:4F], it is not the end of the matter that he makes such a statement without further specification, but even if he spells it out [he is liable]. And it is not the end of the matter that he treats matters within a general category, but even if he states them in detail [he is liable]. And it is not the end of the matter that what he swears applies in the future, but even if what he says applies to what has happened in the past, he is still liable. And it is not the end of the matter that he is liable in the view of rabbis, but that is the case even within the view of R. Aqiba, who specifies no minimum quantities]. And it is not the end of the matter that he is liable on account of eating carrion and terefah-meat, but even if he should eat dirt, he will be liable.*

M. 3:5 It is all the same [whether the oath pertains to] things which belong to himself, things which belong to others, things which are of substance, and things which are not of substance. How so? [If] he said, "I swear that I shall give [this] to Mr. So-and-so," "... that I shall not give ...," "... that I gave ...," "... that I did not give ...," "... that I shall go to sleep," "... that I shall not go to sleep," "... that I slept," "... that I didn't sleep," "... that I'll throw a stone into the sea," "... that I won't throw ...," "... that I threw ..." "... that I didn't throw ...," he is liable only concerning what happens in the future [which he states in the form of an oath].

M. 3:6 [If] he took an oath to nullify a commandment, but he did not nullify it, he is exempt [from penalty for violating the oath]. [And if he took an oath to] carry out [a commandment] and did not carry it out, he is exempt.

B. *The Rash Oath, the Vain Oath*

M. 3:7 "I swear that I won't eat this loaf of bread," "I swear that I won't eat it," "I swear that I won't eat it" — and he ate it — he is liable on only one count. This is a rash oath (Lev. 5:4). On account of deliberately [taking a rash oath] one is liable to flogging, and on account of inadvertently [taking a rash oath] he is liable to bring an offering of variable value. As to a vain oath, they are liable for deliberately [taking a vain oath] to flogging, and for inadvertently [doing so], they are exempt.

M. 3:8 What is the definition of a vain oath? [If] one has taken an oath to differ from what is well known to people. If he said (1) concerning a pillar of stone that it is made of gold, (2) concerning a man that he is a woman, (3) concerning a woman that she is a man — [if] one has taken an oath concerning something which is impossible — (1) "... if I did not see a camel flying in the air ...," (2) "... if I did not see a snake as thick as the beam of an olive press ...," [if] he said to witnesses, "Come and bear witness of me," [and they said to him,] "We swear that we shall not bear witness for you," [if] he took an oath to nullify a commandment — (1) not to build a *Sukkah*, (2) not to take *lulab* and (3) not to put on phylacteries — this is a vain oath, on account of the deliberate making of which one is liable for flogging, and on account of the inadvertent making of which one is exempt [from all punishment].

M. 3:9 "I swear that I shall eat this loaf of bread," "I swear that I shall not eat it," — the first statement is a rash oath, and the second is a vain oath. [If] he ate it, he has violated a vain oath. [If] he did not eat it, he has violated a rash oath.

T. 2:3 "I swear that I won't eat," and then he went and said, "I swear that I'll eat," for the latter [oaths] he is flogged immediately. For the former ones, if he ate he is liable, and if not, he did not eat, he is exempt [cf. M. Sheb. 3:9].

T. 2:4 "I swear that I shall eat," and then he went and said, "I swear that I won't eat," "... and that I won't eat," "... and that I won't eat," for the latter ones he is flogged immediately. And as to the former ones, if he ate he is exempt, and if not, he did not eat, he is liable. "I swear that I won't eat," "... and that I won't eat," "... and that I won't eat ..." and he ate — he is liable only on one count [M. Sheb. 3:7A–C], for he said the latter ones only to back up the former ones. "I swear that I didn't eat," "... and that I didn't eat," "... and that I didn't eat," he is liable for each and every one of them. This rule is more strict concerning an oath involving what already has happened than it is concerning an oath about what is going to happen in the future.

M. 3:10 [The law governing] a rash oath applies (1) to men and women, (2) to those who are not related and to those who are related, (3) to those who are suitable [to bear witness] and to those who are invalid [to bear witness], (4) before a court and not before a court. (5) [But it must be stated] by a man out of his own mouth. And they are liable for deliberately taking such an oath to flogging, and for inadvertently taking such an oath to an offering of variable value.

M. 3:11 [The law governing] a vain oath applies (1) to men and women, (2) to those who are not related and to those who are related, (3) to those who are suitable [to bear witness] and to those who are not suitable [to bear witness], (4) before a court and not before a court. (5) [But it must be stated] by a man out of his own mouth. And they are liable for deliberately taking such an oath to flogging, and for inadvertently taking such an oath, one is exempt [from all punishment]. All the same are this oath and that oath: he who was subjected to an oath by others is liable. How so? [If] one said, "I did not eat today, and I did not put on phylacteries today," [and his friend said,] "I impose an oath on you [that that is so]," and he said, "Amen," he is liable.

Y. 3:10 I:1 *"[If] any one [sins in that he hears a public adjuration to testify, whether he has seen or come to know the matter, yet does not speak, he shall bear his iniquity" (Lev. 5:1). "[If] any one [sins and commits a breach of faith against the Lord by deceiving his neighbor in a matter of deposit or security . . . or has found what was lost and lied about it, swearing falsely]" (Lev. 6:2–3). [The use of "anyone" serves to link the law governing both an oath of testimony and an oath of bailment.] Just as the use of "any one" stated with reference to an oath of testimony means that the one who has an oath imposed upon him by others is treated as equivalent to the one who imposes an oath upon himself, so in regard to the oath of bailment, the one who has an oath imposed upon him by others is treated as equivalent to the one who imposes an oath upon himself [and in either case, if the oath is false, whether imposed by others or imposed by himself, the person is liable, as at M. 3:10/I–O].*

Y. 3:10 I:2 *[With regard to the penalty of flogging for violating a false oath even though it is a negative commandment not containing an actual deed,] this is the general rule: [Violation of] any negative commandment that includes an actual deed entails the penalty of flogging, and [violation of] any negative commandment that does not contain a concrete deed does not entail the penalty of flogging. Except for [1] one who substitutes a beast for one already consecrated [saying "This beast. previously unconsecrated, is in the place of that one, already consecrated"] (Lev. 27:10); [2] the one who imposes an oath on himself; and [3] the one who curses his fellow by the Holy Name of God.*

C. The Oath of Testimony

M. 4:1 [The law governing] an oath of testimony (Lev. 5:1) applies (1) to men and not to women, (2) to those who are not related and not to those who are related, (3) to those who are suitable [to bear witness] and not to those who are not suitable [to bear witness], and it applies only to those who are suitable to bear witness, before a court and not before a court, [and it must be stated] by a man out of his own mouth.

T. 2:5 He who imposes an oath [of testimony] upon gentiles, women, children, relatives, and those invalid to give testimony — they are exempt [cf. M. Sheb. 4:1A]. For it is said, "And he is a witness" (Lev. 5:1).

Scripture speaks of a witness who is suitable to require a person to pay out money, excluding these, who are not suitable to require a person to pay out money. Testimony concerning property is confirmed on the basis of what one has seen without knowing it, or what one has known without directly seeing And what is a case of evidence based on seeing without direct knowledge? "Give me two hundred zuz which I have in your possession!" "You don't have such money in my possession!" "Did I not count out for you exactly that sum of money in the presence of Mr. So-and-so and Mr. Such-and-such?" "Let them so state, and I'll pay you" — this is evidence based on what people have seen without knowing the meaning of what they have seen. And what is a case of evidence on knowledge without one's directly seeing? "Give me the two hundred zuz which I have in your possession!" "You don't have two hundred zuz in my possession!" "Did you not admit to me in the presence of Mr. So-and-so and Mr. Such-and-such?" "Let them say so, and I'll pay it out to you" — this is evidence based on what people know without their having seen [the incident itself].

Y. 4:1 Before a court: This excludes the case of a single witness [without a corroborating witness], in a case in which they said to him, "Lo, you are acceptable to us as two witnesses." Is it possible to suppose that, in the stated case, such a one should be liable [to the oath of testimony]? Scripture has stated, "whether he has seen or come to know the matter, yet does not speak" (Lev. 5:1) — this refers to one who is suitable to give testimony valid by the law of the Torah, excluding a lone witness, who is not valid to give testimony by the law of the Torah. and not before a court: "If he does not speak, he shall bear his iniquity" (Lev. 5:1) — [the oath thus applies to] the one who reports what he has seen and pays what he owes, excluding a case outside of a court, in which even if one reports what he knows, his fellow is not going to have to pay out compensation.

M. 4:2 They are liable if they deliberately took a [false] oath or took a [false] oath in error along with deliberately denying their testimony. But they are not liable if they inadvertently denied [their testimony]. And for what are they liable on account of deliberate violation? An offering of variable value.

T. 2:6 They are liable for deliberately denying their testimony and deliberately taking a false oath, and for deliberately denying testimony along with inadvertently taking a false oath [M. Sheb. 4:2A]. But for inadvertently denying their testimony, one is exempt. And what is deliberately denying one's testimony along with deliberately taking a false oath, on account of which one is liable? [If] one knew evidence concerning another party, and also knew that whoever takes a false oath [in this circumstance] brings an offering — this is a case in which there is deliberate denying of one's testimony along with deliberately taking a false oath, on account of which one is liable. And what is a case in which there is a deliberate denying of one's having testimony along with an inadvertent taking of a false oath? If one knew evidence concerning another party but he did not know that whoever takes a false oath is liable to bring an offering — this is a case in which there is deliberate denying of one's testimony along with inadvertently taking a false oath, on account of which one is liable. And what is a case of inadvertent denying of one's testimony, on account of which one is exempt? A case in which one did not know any evidence about the man's case at all, or knew something but forgot about it at the moment at which he took the oath — for it is said, "And he took an oath falsely" (Lev. 5:1).

Y. 4:2 I:1 "[If] any one [sins in what he hears a public adjuration to testify, and though he is a witness . . . does not speak]" (Lev. 5:1). "[If] any one [sins and commits a breach of faith . . . by deceiving his neighbor in a matter of deposit or security]" (Lev. 6:2). Just as [with reference to the oath of bailment] the oath is taken on one's own initiative ["I swear"], so with reference to the oath of testimony, the oath may be taken on one's own initiative [as at M. 4:2C]. Just as with reference to the oath of testimony, the oath may be administered by others ["Do you swear . . . ?" "Amen"], so with reference to the oath of bailment the oath may be administered by others [as at M. 1:2D, thus in accord with the sages of M. 4:1].

M. 4:3 An oath of testimony — how so? [If] one said to two people, "Come and testify about me," [and they replied,] "We swear that we don't know any testimony about you" — for if they said to him, "We don't know any testimony concerning you," [and he said to them], "I impose an oath upon you," and they said to him, "Amen," — lo, these are liable [if they did have testimony to present and thus swore falsely]. [If] one imposed an oath on them five times outside of court, and then they came to court and confessed [that they did have testimony to offer, which they now are willing to offer], they are exempt. [If] they denied [that they had testimony to offer, and turned out to have violated their oaths], they are liable on each and every count. [If] he imposed an oath on them five times before the court and they denied [having testimony, and then turned out to have sworn falsely], they are liable on only one count.

T. 2:15 He who says, "May God smite you," "May he smite you thus," "May he do good for you," "May he do no good for you," "May he do such good for you," "May he do harm to you," "May he not do harm to you," "Thus may he do harm to you" — this is an adjuration which is written in the Torah (Lev. 5:1) [M. Sheb. 4:13J–K]. He is liable in the case of one who says, "May he do good for you," "May he do good for you if you come and give testimony about me," "May he not do good for you if you do not come and give testimony about me," "May he do evil to you if you do not come and give testimony about me," "May he not do good for you if you do not come and give testimony about me" [cf. M. Sheb. 4:13J–M].

M. 4:4 [If] both of them denied at the same time [that they had testimony], both of them are liable. [If they made their denials] one after the other, the first is liable, but the second is exempt. [If] one denied and one confessed, the one who denies is liable. [If] there were two groups of witnesses, [and] the first group denied [having testimony] and then the second group denied,

both of them are liable — because the testimony in any event can be confirmed by the testimony of either one of them.

M. 4:5 "I impose an oath on you that you come and testify about me, that in the hand of Mr. So-and-so there are a bailment, a loan, stolen goods, and lost property of mine," "We swear that we do not know any testimony concerning you" — they are liable on only one count, "We swear that we know nothing about your having in Mr. So-and-so's hand a bailment, a loan, stolen goods, and lost property," they are liable on each and every count. "I impose an oath on you that you come and testify about me that I have a bailment in the hand of Mr. So-and-so: wheat, barley, and spelt," "We swear that we know no testimony about you" — they are liable on only one count. "We swear that we know no testimony about you, that you have a bailment in the hand of Mr. So-and-so wheat, barley, and spelt" they are liable on each and every count.

M. 4:6 "I impose an oath on you that you come and testify about me that I have in the hand of Mr. So-and-so a claim for damages, half-damages, twofold restitution, fourfold and fivefold restitution, "and that Mr. So-and-so raped my daughter," "seduced my daughter," "and that my son hit me," "that my friend injured me," and "that he set fire to my grain on the Day of Atonement" — lo, these are liable [on any of these counts].

M. 4:7 "I impose an oath on you that you come and testify about me that I am a priest," "that I am a Levite," "that I am not the son of a divorcée," "that I am not the son of a woman who has performed the rite of removing the shoe," "that Mr. So-and-so is a priest," "that Mr. So-and-so is a Levite," "that he is not the son of a divorcée," that "he is not the son of a woman who has performed the rite of removing the shoe," "that Mr. So-and-so raped his daughter," "seduced his daughter," "that my son injured me," "that my friend injured me," "that someone set fire to my grain on the Sabbath" — lo, these are exempt.

T. 2:16 A. "You have raped and seduced my daughter" — and he says, "I did not rape and I did not seduce" — "I impose an oath on you" — and he said, "Amen" — he is liable. This is the governing principle: In any case in which there is a fine and one would have to pay it on the basis of his own evidence, [if the plaintiff said], "I impose an oath on you," and the defendant said, "Amen" — the defendant is exempt [if he has sworn falsely]. And in any case in which there is no fine, and in which one is not going to have to pay on the basis of his own testimony, and the plaintiff said, "I impose an oath on you," and the defendant said, "Amen" — he is liable. He who says, "I am subject to an oath by the Torah" is liable [If he said, "I am subject to an oath] by heaven," he is exempt.

Y. 4:6 I:1 [In connection with an oath of testimony, it is said, "If anyone [sins" (Lev. 5:1), and in connection with an oath of bailment it is said, "If] anyone [sins]"

(*Lev. 6:1*). *The purpose of using the same language is to establish grounds for a proof by analogy from one case to the other: just as "When anyone sins" in the case of a bailment speaks of a case in which there is a monetary claim actually within the claimant's domain [thus excluding M. 4:6A–B], so, "When anyone sins" in the case of an oath of testimony speaks of a case in which there is a monetary claim actually within the claimant's domain.*

M. 4:8 "I impose an oath on you that you come and testify about me that Mr. So-and-so promised to give me two hundred zuz and has not given it" — lo, [if, despite taking the oath, they fail to testify,] these are exempt, for they are liable only in the case of a monetary claim which is equivalent to a bailment.

M. 4:9 "I impose an oath on you that when you have evidence to give in my behalf, you come and testify about me" — lo, [if, despite taking the oath, they fail to testify,] these are exempt, for the oath has come before the matter about which testimony is to be given.

M. 4:10 [If] one has gotten up in the synagogue and said, "I impose an oath on you that if you know any evidence concerning me, you come and give testimony about me" — lo, [if, despite taking the oath, they fail to testify,] these are exempt, unless he address himself to [some] of them in particular.

M. 4:11 [If] he said to two people, "I impose an oath on you, Mr. So-and-so and Mr. So-and-so, that if you know evidence concerning me, you come and testify about me" — "We swear that we know no evidence about you" but they do have evidence concerning him, consisting of what they have heard from a witness [M. San. 4:5], or one of them is a relative or otherwise invalid to testify [M. 4:1] — lo, these are exempt.

M. 4:12 [If] he had sent through his slave [to impose the oath on the witnesses], or if the defendant had said to them, "I impose an oath on you, that if you know testimony concerning him, you come and give evidence concerning him," they are exempt, unless they hear [the oath] from the mouth of the plaintiff.

M. 4:13 (1) "I impose an oath on you," (2) "I command you," (3) "I bind you," — lo, these are liable. [If he used the language,] "By heaven and earth," lo, these are exempt. (1) "By [the name of] Alef-dalet [Adonai]" or (2) "Yud-he [Yahweh]," (3) "By the Almighty," (4) "By Hosts," (5) "By him who is merciful and gracious," (6) "By him who is long-suffering and abundant in mercy," or by any other euphemism — lo, these are liable. "He who curses making use of any one of these is liable," he is exempt. He who curses his father or his mother with any one of them is exempt. He who curses himself and his friend with any one of them transgresses a negative commandment. [If he said,] (1) "May God smite you," (2) "So may God smite you," this is [language for] an adjuration [conforming to] which is written in the Torah (Lev. 5:1). (3) "May he not smite you," (4) "may he bless you," (5) "may he do good to you" — he is exempt.

D. *The Oath of Bailment*

M. 5:1 An oath concerning a bailment (Lev. 6:2ff.) applies to men and to women, to relatives and to strangers, to people suitable to give testimony and to people not suitable to give testimony, before a court and not before a court, from one's own mouth. But as to one from the mouth of others, whether it is from his own mouth or from the mouth of others, once he has denied him, he is liable." [If one took a false oath,] one is liable if he deliberately took a [false] oath, or [if he took one] in error, while deliberately [denying] bailment. But one is not liable [if he] inadvertently [took a false oath in regard to a bailment]. And for what are they liable on account of deliberate violation? A guilt offering which is worth [two] shekels of silver (Lev. 5:15).

T. 2:7 They are liable for deliberately denying that one has a bailment along with deliberately taking a false oath, and for deliberately denying that one has a bailment along with inadvertently taking a false oath, but for inadvertently denying that one has a bailment, one is exempt [from liability] [cf. M. Sheb. 5:1G–H].

T. 2:8 And what is a case of deliberately denying that one has a bailment along with deliberately taking a false oath, in which case one is liable? [If] one knew that he had in hand a bailment and knew that whoever takes a false oath brings an offering — Lo, this is a case which there is a deliberate denial of the bailment along with a deliberate taking of a false oath, in which case one is liable.

T. 2:9 [If] one knew that he had in hand a bailment but did not know that whoever takes a false oath brings an offering — this is a case in which there is a deliberate denial of the bailment along with an inadvertent taking of a false oath, in which one is nonetheless liable.

T. 2:10 What is a case of a false oath concerning a bailment, in which one is exempt? In a case in which one did not know that he had in hand a bailment belonging to the other party, or in which he had known about it but forgot it at the moment at which he took the oath, and he took the oath — he is exempt, as it is said, "And he swears falsely" (Lev. 6:5).

M. 5:2 An oath concerning a bailment — how so? He said to him, "Give me my bailment which I have in your hand" "I swear that you have nothing in my hand" — or if he said to him, "You have nothing in my hand," "I impose an oath on you", and he said, "Amen" lo, this one is liable. [If] he imposed an oath on him five times, whether this is before a court or not before a court, and the other party denied it, he is liable for each count.

T. 2:11 [If] one was looking for witnesses — "Why are you coming after us? We swear that we know no testimony concerning you" — they are exempt until he will lay claim on them. But in the case of a bailment, the law is not so. But: "Why are you coming after me? I swear you have nothing in my hands" — he is liable. This rule is more strict in the case of an oath regarding a bailment than in the case of an oath regarding the giving of testimony by witnesses [cf. M. Sheb. 5:2].

T. 2:12 [If] he said to witnesses, "Come and give testimony concerning me, that I have in the hand of Mr. So-and-so two hundred zuz, deriving from the matter of a hired hand or money owing to my wife and daughters" — "We swear that we will not testify concerning you" — Lo, these are exempt, until they say, "We swear that we do not know any evidence concerning you." And so is the rule concerning a bailment: [If] he said to him, "Give me the two hundred zuz which I have in your hand, deriving from the matter of a hired hand or money owing to my wife and daughters" "I swear that I will not give a thing to you" — he is exempt, until he will say to him, "I swear that you have nothing whatsoever in my hands."

T. 2:13 [If he] said to witnesses, "Come and give testimony concerning me, that Mr. So-and-so promised to give me two hundred zuz, and he has not given it to me," "a garment in which to clothe myself, and he has not clothed me." "We swear that we know no evidence concerning you" — they are exempt, for they may claim, "He promised to give you, but it is not possible for him to give it to you." Or, "He promised to clothe you, but it is not possible to clothe you." And so is the rule for a bailment.

Y. 5:2 I:1 *"If any one [sins in that he hears a public adjuration to testify, and though he is a witness . . . does not speak]," (Lev. 5:1). "[If] any one [sins and commits a breach of faith . . . by deceiving his neighbor in a matter of deposit or security]" (Lev. 6:1). Just as [with reference to the oath of bailment] the oath is taken on one's own initiative ["I swear"], so with reference to the oath of testimony, the oath may be taken on one's own initiative [as at M. 5:2C]. Just as with reference to the oath of testimony, the oath may be administered by others ["Do you swear" "Amen"], so with reference to the oath of bailment the oath may be administered by others [as at M. 5:2D, thus in accord with the sages of M. 5:1].*

M. 5:3 [If] five people laid claim on him and said to him, "Give us the bailment which we have in your hand" — "I swear that you have nothing in my hand" — he is liable on only one count. "I swear that you have nothing in my hand, nor you, nor you" — he is liable on each and every count. "Give me my bailment, loan, stolen goods, and lost property [Lev. 6:2] which I have in your hand" — "I swear you have nothing in my hand" — he is liable on only one count. "I swear that you do not have in my hand a bailment, loan, stolen goods, or lost property" — he is liable for each and every count. "Give me the grain, barley, and spelt, which I have in your hand" — "I swear you have nothing in my hand" — he is liable on only one count. "I swear

that you have not got in my hand wheat, barley, or spelt" — he is liable for each and every count.

M. 5:4 "You raped and seduced my daughter" — and he says, "I did not rape and I did not seduce" "I impose an oath on you" — and he said, "Amen" — he is liable.

M. 5:5 "You stole my ox" — and he says, "I did not steal it" "I impose an oath on you," — and he said, "Amen" — he is liable. "I stole it, but I did not slaughter it, and I did not sell it" — "I impose an oath on you" — and he said, "Amen" — he is exempt. "Your ox killed my ox" — and he said, "It did not kill" — and he says, "I impose an oath on you" — and he said, "Amen" — he is liable. "Your ox killed my slave" — and he says, "It did not kill" — "I impose an oath on you" — and he said, "Amen," — he is exempt. [If] he said to him, "You injured me and made a wound on me," and he said, "I did not injure you and I did not make a mark on you," "I impose an oath on you" — and he said, "Amen" — he is liable. [If] his slave said to him, "You knocked out my tooth and you blinded my eye," and he said, "I did not knock out your tooth or blind your eye," and he said to him, "I impose an oath on you," — and he said to him, "Amen" — he is exempt. This is the governing principle: Whoever pays compensation on the basis of his own testimony is liable. And whoever does not pay compensation on the basis of his own testimony is exempt [in the case of these oaths].

E. *The Oath Imposed by Judges 6:1–7:8*

M. 6:1 The oath imposed by judges [is required if] the claim is [at least] two pieces of silver, and the concession [on the part of the defendant is that he owes] at least a penny's [perutah's] worth. But if the concession is not of the same kind as the claim, [the defendant] is exempt [from having to take the oath]. How so? "Two pieces of silver I have in your hand" — "You have in my hand only a perutah" — he is exempt [from having to take the oath]. "Two pieces of silver and a perutah I have in your hand" — "You have in my hand only a perutah" — he is liable. "A maneh I have in your hand" — "You have nothing at all in my hand"—he is exempt [from having to take the oath]. "I have a maneh in your hand" — "You have nothing in my hand except for fifty denars" — he is liable. "A maneh belonging to my father you have in your hand" "He has nothing in my hand but fifty denars" — he is exempt [from having to take the oath], for he is in the status of one who returns lost property.

T. 3:1 He who imposes an oath on his fellow concerning a matter which involves a value of [at least] a perutah — Lo, this one [who has sworn falsely] pays the principal and an added fifth, and also brings a guilt-offering [Lev. 6:5]. And so too: he who imposes an oath on witnesses concerning a matter which involves a value of a perutah, and they denied [having evidence to give, and it turns out that they did have such evidence] — Lo, these are liable for an offering. But they are exempt from having to pay monetary compensation, since it is said, "And he will bear his iniquity" (Lev. 5:1).

T. 5:1 The oath imposed by judges [is imposed] if the claim is [at least] two pieces of silver and a perutah, and the concession [on the part of the defendant is that he owes at least] a perutah's worth [M. Sheb. 6:1A]. And the concession is a perutah — of the same kind as the claim. And if the concession is not of the same kind as the claim, he is exempt [M. Sheb. 6:1B]. How so? "Two pieces of silver I have in your hand" — "You have in my hand only a perutah," — he is exempt. "Two pieces of silver and a perutah I have in your hand" — "You have in my hand only a perutah" — he is liable [M. Sheb. 6:1C–I].

T. 5:5 "I have a maneh in your hand" — "You have nothing in my hand" — "You had it in my hand, but I gave it back to you" — or, "I have a maneh's worth of clothing," ". . . . a maneh's worth of produce in your hand" — or if he said to him, "You have only fifty zuz in my hand, but I have fifty zuz of utensils," or "fifty zuz of produce, in your hand" — he is exempt [from the requirement of taking an oath]. But if he said to him, "I gave you back fifty zuz of them," he would have been liable. For he is subjected to an oath on the strength of his own claim.

T. 5:6 "A maneh belonging to my father is in your hand "[M. Sheb. 6:1P] — "He has nothing at all in my hand" — "He had something in my hand, but I gave it back to him" — or, "I have a maneh's worth of clothing," or "a maneh's worth of produce in his hand" — he is exempt [from the requirement of taking an oath]. Or if he had said to him, "He has only fifty zuz in my hand, and I have fifty zuz worth of produce, or "fifty zuz worth of utensils in his hand," he is exempt. But if he had said, "I gave back to him fifty zuz," he is liable . . . For lo, he is subjected to an oath on the strength of his own claim.

T. 5:7 "I have a maneh in your father's hand" — "You have nothing in his hand" — "You had something in his hand, but he gave it back to you" — or, "He has in your hand clothing worth a maneh," or, "produce worth a maneh" — he is exempt. Or if he had said to him, "You have in his hand only fifty zuz, and he has in your hand fifty zuz worth of utensils," "fifty zuz worth of produce," he is exempt. But if he had said to him, "I gave him back fifty zuz," he would have been liable. For he is subjected to an oath on the strength of his own claim.

M. 6:2 "I have a maneh in your hand" — before witnesses he said to him, "Yes" — On the next day he said to him, "Give it to me" — "I already gave it to you" — he is exempt [from having to take the oath]. "You don't have anything in my hand" — he is liable [to pay]. "I have a maneh in your hand," and he said to him, "Yes," — "Don't give it to me except before witnesses" — On the next day, he said to him, "Give it to me" — "I already

gave it to you" — he is liable [to pay], because he has to hand it over to him before witnesses.

T. 5:3 If the plaintiff was claiming a maneh in the presence of a court, and the defendant denied it, and two witnesses came and gave testimony that he owes him fifty zuz, Lo, this one pays [fifty zuz] and is exempt from the requirement of taking an oath. But if there was only a single witness who was giving evidence against him, Lo, this one takes an oath covering the whole amount.

T. 5:9 "A golden denar I have in your hand" — "You have in my hand only a silver denar, a terisit, a pondion — he is liable [M. Sheb. 6:2D–F] If he laid claim against him for wheat, and the other party conceded barley, he is exempt [from taking an oath].

M. 6:3 "I have a litra of gold in your hand" — "You have in my hand only a litra of silver" — he is exempt [from having to take the oath]. "A denar of gold I have in your hand" — "You have in my hand only a denar of silver, a terisit, a pondion, and a perutah," — he is liable, for all of them are kinds of a single coinage. "I have a kor of grain in your hand" — "You have in my hand only a letekh of pulse" — he is exempt [from having to take the oath]. "A kor of produce I have in your hand" — "You have in my hand only a letekh of pulse" — he is liable, for pulse falls into the category of produce. [If] he claimed wheat and the other admitted to having barley, he is exempt [from having to take the oath]. He who claims jars of oil from his fellow, and the other confessed to having flagons — this confession is not of the same kind as that which is subject to claim. [If] one laid claim against him for utensils and real estate, and the other party conceded the claim for utensils but denied the claim for real estate, or conceded the claim for real estate and denied the claim for utensils, he is exempt [from having to take the oath]. [If] he conceded part of the real estate, he is exempt [from having to take the oath]. [If] he conceded part of the utensils, he is liable [to take an oath]. For property for which there is no security imposes the requirement of an oath in regard to property for which there is security.

M. 6:4 They do not take an oath in the case of a claim made by a deaf — mute, an idiot, or a minor. And they do not impose an oath upon a minor. But an oath is imposed in the case of a claim against [the property of] a minor, and against property which has been consecrated.

T. 5:10 [If] one laid claim against him for produce, clothing, and utensils and the defendant conceded one of them he is liable [cf. M. Sheb. 6:3R]. And these are the ones upon whom they impose an oath, but in the case of whom they do not take an oath [cf. M. Sheb. 6:4].

M. 6:5 And what are matters on account of which an oath is not imposed? [claims involving] slaves, bonds, real estate, and consecrated property. To these also do not apply the rules of twofold restitution or fourfold or fivefold restitution. [In the case of these] an unpaid bailiff is not subjected to an oath. [In the case of these] a paid bailiff does not pay compensation.

T. 5:11 "Ten chests full of bonds I have in your hand" — "You have in my hand only one chest, and in it is one bond, as is" — "Ten slaves and on them ten garments I have in your hand" — "You have in my hand only a single slave, as is" —

T. 5:12 "Ten chests full of bonds I have in your hand" — "You have in my hand only one chest, and in it is one bond" — "Ten slaves and on them ten garments I have in your hand" — "You have in my hand only one slave, and on him is a little loin cloth," "Ten houses full of produce I have in your hand" — "You have in my hand only a single house filled with wheat" — he is exempt because he did not lay claim by reference to a particular measure.

T. 5:13 "A kor of wheat of mine is in your possession," and the other says, "You have nothing at all in my possession," the latter is exempt from taking an oath. "A large candelabrum of mine is in your possession" — "You have nothing in my possession except for a small candelabrum" — the latter is exempt from taking an oath. "A large girdle of mine is in your possession" — "You have nothing in my possession except for a small girdle" — he latter is exempt from taking an oath. But if he said to him, "A kor of wheat of mine do you have in your possession," and the other says, "You have in my possession not so much as a kor but only a letekh," he is liable. "A candelabrum of ten liters of mine is in your possession," "you have in my possession one of only five liters [in weight]," he is liable. The governing principle of the matter is this: one is liable to take an oath only in a matter involving a claim which specifies a concrete measure, weight, or number, and in which he concedes a claim which specifies a concrete measure, weight, or number.

T. 5:14 "Candelabrums I have in your hand" — "You have in my hand only a single candelabrum" — "Clothing worth ten litras I have in your hand" — "You have in my hand only a single small loin cloth" — "Produce I have in your hand" — "You have in my hand only a single kor of wheat" — he is exempt. For he did not lay claim by reference to a particular measure. "Candelabrums I have in your hand" — "You have in my hand only one candelabrum of ten litras" — "Ten garments I have in your hand" — "You have in my hand only a single small loin cloth" — "Ten kors of wheat I have in your hand" — "You have in my hand only one kor of wheat" — he is liable. For he laid claim against him by measure, and he conceded [part of the claim] to him by measure.

T. 5:16 A. "Ten candelabrums of a hundred litras I have in your hand" — and the other party claims he has no information about it — "Lo, they are before you" — he is exempt. For he did not concede [a thing] to him. "Ten cups I have in your hand" — and the other party claims he has no information about it — "Lo, they are before you" — "Ten kors of wheat I have in your hand" — and the other party claims he has no information about it — "Lo, they are before you" — he is exempt. For the other party did not concede the claim by measure.

T. 5:17 "A room full of produce I have in your hand" — "A wallet full of money I have in your hand" — "You have in my hand only half of them" or "a third of them" — he is liable. For a house constitutes a fixed measure, and a half and a third constitute fixed measures. A wallet constitutes a fixed measure, and half or a third of it constitutes a fixed measure.

T. 4:1 A strict rule applies to oaths concerning testimony which does not apply to an oath concerning a bailment, and to an oath concerning a bailment which does not apply to an oath concerning testimony. For an oath concerning testimony applies with regard to litigations about slaves, bonds, and real estate [cf. M. Sheb. 6:5]. How so? [If] one said to witnesses, "Come and give testimony about me, that I have slaves, bonds, or real estate in the hand of Mr. So-and-so," and they said to him, "We swear that we know no testimony relevant to you at all, lo, these are liable [should they turn out to have been able to give evidence m his case]. And they are liable for having done so deliberately to flogging, and for having done so inadvertently to an offering of variable value — which is not the case with regard to an oath concerning a bailment. A strict rule applies to an oath concerning a bailment. An oath concerning a bailment (Lev. 6:2ff.) applies to men and to women, to relatives and to strangers, to people suitable to give testimony and to people not suitable to give testimony, before a court and not before a court, from one's own mouth." He said to him, "Give me the bailment of mine which is in your hand" — "What are you coming to me for? I swear that you have nothing in my hand! Lo, this one is liable and pays principal and an added fifth and brings a guilt-offering worth two selas — which is not the case in the matter of an oath regarding testimony.

T. 4:2 A strict rule applies to an oath concerning testimony which does not apply to a rash oath, and to a rash oath which does not apply to an oath concerning testimony. For an oath regarding testimony applies to a matter of free choice and to a matter of religious duty, and people are liable to an offering for deliberately violating it, which is not the case in the instance of a rash oath [cf. M. Sheb. 3:6A–B]. A strict rule applies to a rash oath, for a rash oath applies to a matter of substance and to a matter of no substance [cf. M. Sheb. 3:8]. And for deliberately violating it people are liable to flogging, which is not the case in the instance of an oath concerning testimony. A strict rule applies to an oath regarding a bailment which does not apply to a rash oath, and to a rash oath which does not apply to an oath regarding bailment. For an oath regarding bailment applies to a matter of free choice and a matter of religious duty, and [he who violates it] pays the principal and an added fifth and brings a guilt-offering worth two selas, which is not the case in the instance of a rash oath.

T. 4:4 A strict rule applies to a rash oath, for a rash oath applies to a matter of substance and a matter of no substance, and for deliberately violating it people are liable to flogging, and for inadvertently violating it, to an offering of variable value, which is not the case in the instance of an oath regarding a bailment.

T. 4:5 A strict rule applies to a vain oath which does not apply to a rash oath, and to a rash oath which does not apply to a vain oath. For a vain oath applies to a matter of free choice and to a matter of religious duty, and people are liable for each and every [vain oath which they may take], which is not the case in the instance of a rash oath [cf. M. Sheb. 3:7–11]. A strict rule applies to a rash oath, for a rash oath applies to a matter which is of substance and to a matter which is of no substance, and for inadvertently violating it they are liable to an offering of variable value, which is not the case in the instance of a vain oath.

M. 6:6 "Ten fruit-laden vines I handed over to you" — and the other says, "They were only five" — Whatever is attached to the ground is classified as real property. They are forced to take an oath only in a matter involving a claim which specifies a concrete measure, weight, or number. How so? "A room full of goods I gave you," "A wallet full of money I gave to you," and this one says, "I don't know — but whatever you left is what you can take" — he is exempt [from having to take the oath]. This one says, "[I gave you a heap of produce] as high as the projection," and that one says, "It was only as high as the window," he is liable [to take an oath for denying the bailment].

M. 6:7 He who lends money to his fellow on the strength of a pledge, and the pledge got lost — [The creditor] said to him, "I lent you a sela on the strength of it, but it was worth only a shekel," and [the debtor] says to him, "Not so. But you lent me a sela on the strength of it, and it was worth a sela" — he is exempt [from having to take the oath]. "A sela I lent you on the strength of it, and it was worth a shekel, "and the other says, "Not so. But a sela you lent to me on the strength of it, and it was worth three denars" — he is liable. "A sela you lent to me on the strength of it, and it was worth two," and the other says, "Not so. But I lent you a sela on the strength of it, and it was worth a sela" — he is exempt [from having to take the oath]. "A sela you lent me on the strength of it, and it was worth two," and the other says, "Not so, but a sela I lent to you on the strength of it, and it was worth five denars" — he is liable. And upon whom is the oath imposed? Upon him with whom the bailment was left, lest this one take an oath, and the other one then produce the bailment.

M. 7:1 All those who are subjected to oaths [that are required] in the Torah take [said] oaths and do not pay [the claim against them]. And who are they who take an oath and collect [what they claim is owing to them]? (1) a hired hand, (2) the victim of a theft, (3) the victim of a beating, (4) he whose contrary litigant is not trusted [even if he takes] an oath, (5) and a shopkeeper concerning [what is written in] his account book. A hired hand — how so? [If] he said to him, "Give me my wage, which you have in your hand" — he says to him, "I already gave it to you," — and this one says, "I never got it" — he takes an oath and collects [what he claims].

T. 6:1 A. All those who are subjected to oaths which are required in the Torah take oaths and do not pay the claim against them, [M. Sheb. 7:1A] as it is said, "If a man delivers to his neighbor an ass or an ox or a sheep or any beast to keep, and it dies, or is hurt, or is driven away, without anyone seeing it, an oath by the Lord shall be between them both to see whether he has not put his hand to his neighbor's property, and the owner shall accept the oath, and he shall not make restitution" (Ex. 22:10–11). Once the owner has accepted the oath, he is exempt from having to pay compensation. A hired hand takes an oath and collects [his claim]. But if the time [in which he should have been paid] has passed, he does not take an oath and collect [his claim]. But if there are witnesses that he had laid claim against [the employer] during the specified time, even after twelve months, lo, this one still may take an oath and collect his claim. Under what circumstances? When he said to him, "I already paid you your salary," while [the worker] says, "He did not pay it to me." But if he said to him, "You hired me," and the other said, "I never hired you," "I promised you a sela," and the other says, "You promised me two" — he who lays claim against his fellow bears the burden of proof.

Y. 7:1 II:3 *If the householder claims that] he paid him his salary in advance, in such a case the worker takes an oath and collects his salary. [If the hired hand] had a pledge belonging to the employer in his possession, in such a case the hired hand collects his salary without taking the oath.*

Y. 7:1 III:2 *They superimpose an oath by reason of Torah law on an oath by reason of Torah law, an oath by reason of a remedy created by the rabbis on an oath by reason of a remedy, an oath by reason of Torah law on an oath by reason of a remedy, an oath by reason of a remedy on an oath by reason of Torah law.*

M. 7:2 The victim of a theft — how so? [If people] were giving testimony against a person that he had gone into his house to exact a pledge without permission, and [the victim of the theft] says, "You took my utensils," — and the other party says, "I never took them" — lo, this one takes an oath and collects [what he claims].

M. 7:3 The victim of a beating — how so? [If people] were giving testimony against a person that [the plaintiff] had gone into his [the defendant's] hand whole and come forth injured, and he said, "You beat me up," — and he says, "I never beat you up" — lo, this one takes an oath and collects [compensation].

T. 6:2 The victim of a beating — how so [M. Sheb. 7:3A]? [If] people were giving testimony against a person that he had gone in, his hand whole and come forth injured, and he said, "You beat me up," and he says, "I never beat you up" — Lo, this one takes an oath and collects compensation [M. Sheb. 7:3A–E]. So long as they are friends with one another, lo, they take an oath and collect what is owing. But if one of them was bitten in a place in which one cannot bite himself, he collects compensation without taking an oath. [If] after a while, this one says, "You beat me up," and that one says, "I never beat you up," lo, this one is equivalent to all other claims [and evidence is required].

M. 7:4 He whose contrary litigant is not trusted [even if he takes] an oath — how so? All the same are an oath regarding testimony, an oath regarding a bailment, and even a rash oath — [if] one of the litigants was a dice player, gave out loans on usury, [was] a pigeon racer, or a dealer in Seventh-Year produce [M. San. 3:3], the other litigant takes an oath and collects [his claim].

T. 6:3 A. He whose contrary litigant is not trusted [even if he takes] an oath — how so [M. Sheb. 7:4A]? The other party takes an oath and collects [his claim]. If both of them were suspect concerning an oath, both of them are exempt [cf. M. Sheb. 7:4E], since it is said, "An oath by the Lord shall be between them both" (Ex. 22: 10) at a time at which one of them may be suspect [concerning an oath] but not at a time at which both of them are suspect. Between them both — it does not emerge from between the two of them. If the one who takes an oath swears falsely, ultimately [the curse accompanying] the oath will come to rest on him, as it is said, "This is the curse ... and everyone who swears falsely shall be cut off henceforth according to it. I will send it forth says the Lord of hosts and it shall enter the house of the thief and the house of him who swears falsely by my name; and it shall abide in his house and consume it, both timber and stones" (Zech. 5:3). Come and see that even things which fire cannot consume a false oath burns up.

M. 7:5 A storekeeper concerning [what is written in his] account book — how so? It is not that he may say to him, "It is written in my account book that you owe me two hundred zuz." But [if the householder] said to him, "Give my son two seahs of wheat," [or] "Give my worker change for a sela," and he says, "I already gave it to him," — and they say, "We never got it" — [the storekeeper] takes an oath and collects what is owing to him, and [the workers] take an oath and collect what they claim from the householder.

M. 7:6 [If] one said to the storekeeper, "Give me produce for a denar," and he gave it to him — he said to him, "Give me the denar," — he said to him, "I already gave it to you, and you put it in the till" — let the householder take an oath. If he gave him a denar and said to him, "Give me produce" — he said to him, "I already gave it to you and you brought it home" — let the storekeeper take an oath. [If] he said to the money changer, "Give me small coins for a denar," and he gave them to him — he said to him, "Give me the denar" — he said to him, "I already gave it to you, and you put it in the till" — let the householder take an oath. If he gave him a denar and said to him, "Give me small change," he said to him, "I already gave them to you, and you tossed them into your wallet," let the money changer take an oath.

T. 6:4 A storekeeper concerning what is written in his book [M. Sheb. 7:5A] — and not what is sold on terms have they stated the rule. For if one may claim, "You have written [the debt] in this page, it has been erased from that page." But if he said, "Give my son two seahs of wheat," "Give my worker change for a sela," and he says, "I already gave it to him," and they say, "We never got it" — he takes an oath and collects what is owing to him, and they take an oath and collect what they claim [M. Sheb. 7:5C–F]. He said to the storekeeper, "Give me produce for a denar," and he gave it to him. He said to him, "Give me the denar" and he said to him, "I already gave it to you, and you put it in the let the householder take an oath [M. Sheb. 7:6A–E] or let him bring proof that he had given [the money] to him. [If] he gave him a denar and said to him, "Give me produce," and he said to him, "I already gave it to you and you brought it home," let the storekeeper take an oath [M. Sheb. 7:6F–H], or let him bring proof that he had given him [the produce].

M. 7:7 Just as they have said [M. Ket. 9:7], (1) A woman who impairs her marriage settlement collects only by taking an oath, [and] (2) [if] a single witness testifies that it has been collected, she collects it only by taking an oath; [and] (3) she collects from indentured property and from property belonging to the estate only by taking an oath; [and] (4) she who collects her marriage settlement not in her husband's presence collects it only by taking an oath, so (5) heirs of an estate collect [debts owing to the deceased] only through an oath: "(1) We swear that father gave us no instructions [in this matter], (2) father said nothing to us about it, and (3) we did not find among his bonds evidence that this bond had been paid off."

T. 6:5 A. He who impairs his bond of indebtedness may collect on the strength of it only with an oath [cf. M. Sheb. 7:7A]. How so? [If] one produced against him a bond for two hundred zuz, and he says, "I collected a maneh of that amount," he may collect [the rest of the sum indicated in the bond] only through an oath. And if to begin with the sum was only a maneh, he may collect it without an oath. An heir, the father of whom has impaired his bond, may collect without an oath [cf. M. Sheb. 7:7E–F]. In this case the power of the heir is stronger than the power of the father. [If] the father had become liable for an oath in court [in order to collect a sum owing to him] and died, the sons cannot collect [the debt at all].

M. 7:8 And these [must] take an oath even when there is no claim [laid against them]: (1) partners, (2) tenants, (3) guardians, (4) a woman who manages her household, and (5) a manager of a common legacy ("son of the household"). [If] he said to him, "What is your claim against me?" "I want you to take an oath to me" — he is liable. [Once] the partners have divided up the property, or the tenant farmers, then one cannot impose an oath upon the other. [If the requirement to take] an oath happened to come upon him from some other source [cause], they

impose upon him an oath covering the entire [enterprise]. The advent of the Sabbatical Year releases the requirement to take an oath.

F. *Oaths and Bailments 8:1–6*

M. 8:1 There are four kinds of guardians: (1) an unpaid bailiff, (2) a borrower, (3) a paid bailiff, and (4) a renter. (1) An unpaid bailiff takes an oath under all circumstances. (2) A borrower pays compensation for damages in all circumstances. (3) A paid bailiff and (4) a renter take an oath on account of a beast which is lamed, driven off, taken for ransom, or deceased, but they pay compensation for what is lost or stolen.

Y. 8:1 1:4 A borrower, to whom the Torah applied a strict rule, when the owner is present, is exempt. When the owner is not present, he is liable. A paid bailee, to whom the Torah applied a lenient rule, all the more so should be exempt when the owner is present, and liable when the owner is absent. [That is, the borrower has to pay restitution in the case of injury, ransom, or death. But if these events take place in the presence of the owner, he is exempt. The paid bailee, who is under a more lenient rule in that he is exempt in the stated instances, all the more so should be liable for theft or loss only when the owner is absent. But if the owner is present, he surely should be exempt.]

M. 8:2 [If] one said to an unpaid bailiff, "Where is my ox?" (1) he said to him, "It died," but in fact it had been lamed, driven off, stolen, or lost, (2) "It was lamed," but in fact it had died, or been driven off, stolen, or lost, (3) "It was driven off," but in fact it had died, been lamed, stolen or lost, (4) "It was stolen," but in fact it had died, or been lamed, driven off, or lost, (5) "It was lost," but in fact it had died, been lamed, driven off, or stolen, "I impose an oath on you," and he said, "Amen" — he is exempt.

M. 8:3 "Where is my ox?" (1) and the bailiff said to him, "I have no idea what you're talking about" — but in fact it had died or been lamed or driven off or stolen or lost — "I impose an oath on you," and he said to him, "Amen" — he is exempt. (2) "Where is my ox?" He said to him, "It got lost" — "I impose an oath on you" — and he said, "Amen" — and witnesses testify against him that he had eaten it — he pays him compensation for the principal. If he conceded on his own, he pays compensation for the principal, the added fifth, and a guilt offering. (3) "Where is my ox?" he said to him, "It was stolen" "I impose an oath on you" he said, "Amen" — and witnesses testify against him that he had stolen it — he pays twofold compensation. [If] he confessed on his own, he pays the principal, an added fifth, and a guilt offering [but not twofold compensation (M. 5:4)].

M. 8:4 (4) He said to someone in the market, "Where is my ox which you stole?" and he says, "I never stole it," but witnesses testify against him that he had stolen it — he pays twofold restitution. [If] he had slaughtered and sold it, he pays fourfold or fivefold restitution. [If] he saw witnesses [to what he had done] coming along and said, "I stole it, but I never slaughtered or sold it," he pays only the principal."

M. 8:5 He said to a borrower [M. 8:1A2], "Where is my ox?" (1) He said to him, "It died," but in fact it had been lamed or driven away, stolen, or lost — (2) "It was lamed," but in fact it had died or been driven off or stolen or lost — (3) "It was driven off," but it had died or been lamed or stolen or lost — (4) "It was stolen," and in fact it had died or been lamed or driven off or lost — (5) "It was lost," and in fact it had died or been lamed, driven off, or stolen — "I impose an oath on you" and he said, "Amen" — he is exempt.

M. 8:6 "Where is my ox?" — He said to him, "I have no idea what you're talking about" — and it had in fact died or been lamed or driven off or stolen or lost — "I impose an oath on you" and he said, "Amen" — he is liable. If he said to a paid bailee or a renter [M. 8:1A3,4], "Where is my ox?" (1) he said to him, "It died," but in fact it had been lamed or driven off — (2) "It has been lamed," but in fact it had died or been driven off — (3) "It has been driven off," and in fact it had died or been lamed — (4) "It has been stolen," and in fact it had been lost — (5) "It has been lost," and in fact it had been stolen — "I impose an oath on you," — and he said, "Amen" — he is exempt. "It died or was lamed or driven off," and in fact, it had been stolen or lost — "I impose an oath on you," and he said, "Amen" — he is liable. "It was lost or was stolen," but in fact it had died or been lamed or been driven off — "I impose an oath on you," and he said, "Amen" — he is exempt. This is the governing principle: Whoever [by lying] changes [his claim] from one sort of liability to another sort of liability, from one count of exemption to another count of exemption, or from a count of exemption to a reason for liability, is exempt. [If he changed his claim, by lying] from grounds for liability to a reason for exemption [from having to make restitution], he is liable. This is the governing principle: Whoever [falsely] takes an oath so as to lighten the burden on himself is liable. Whoever takes an oath so as to make more weighty the burden on himself is exempt.

T. 6:6 To an unpaid bailee apply two rules, which do not apply to the borrower. To the borrower apply two rules, which do not apply to the unpaid bailee. To the borrower who did business [with the ox which he had borrowed] apply two rules, which do not apply to the borrower. One applies to the paid bailee, There are two which do not apply to the unpaid bailee.

T. 6:7 [If one] said to an unpaid bailee, a borrower, a paid bailee, and a renter, "Where is my ox?" and he said, "I don't know," "I impose an oath on you," and he said, "Amen," and afterward he confessed that he had eaten it, he is liable. [If] he said to an unpaid bailee, "Where is my ox?" he said to him, "I don't know" 1. "I impose an oath on you" and he said, "Amen," and afterward he confessed that it had been stolen, or that it had gotten lost, he is exempt, which is not the case for a borrower. "It was stolen or lost" — "I impose an oath on you" — and he said, "Amen," and afterward he confessed that he had eaten it, he is liable, which is not the case for the [read:] unpaid bailee. [If he said to an unpaid bailee,] "Where is my ox?" and he said to him, "I don't know," and he said to him, "I impose an oath on you," and he said, "Amen," and afterward he confessed that it had been stolen or lost, he is exempt, which is not the case for the paid bailee and renter. "It was stolen or lost," "I impose an oath on you," and he said, "Amen," and afterwards he confessed that it had died or been lamed or driven away, he is exempt, which is not the case for the paid bailee and the renter. If he said to a paid bailee, "Where is my ox?" and he said to him, "I don't know" I impose an oath on you," and he said, "Amen," and afterward he confessed that it had died or been lamed or driven away, he is liable, which is not the case for the borrower. "It died, or was lamed or driven away," and afterward he confessed that it had been stolen, or that it was he is liable, which is not the case for the borrower. [If] he said to a paid bailee or renter, "Where is my ox?" and he said to him, "I don't know" "I impose an oath on you" and he said, "Amen," and afterward he confessed that it had been stolen or lost, he is exempt — which is not the rule for the unpaid bailee. "It was stolen or lost" "I impose an oath on you," and he said, "Amen," and after a while he confessed that he had eaten it, he is exempt, which is not the case for the unpaid bailee. It turns out that for a claim for which one is liable in the case of a borrower, he is exempt in the case of an unpaid bailee. [If he is] liable in the case of an unpaid bailee, he is exempt in the case of a borrower. [If he is] liable in the case of a borrower, he is exempt in the case of a paid bailee and a renter. If he is liable in the case of a paid bailee and renter, he is exempt in the case of a borrower. This is the governing principle. Whoever changes his claim] from one sort of exemption from liability to another sort of exemption of liability, or from one sort of liability to another sort of liability, or from one sort of exemption from liability to liability, is exempt. [If it is from] liability to exemption from liability, he is liable [M. Sheb. 8:6X–Y].

II. ANALYSIS: THE PROBLEMATICS OF THE TOPIC, SHEBUOT

As usual in the halakhah, a great deal of work goes into precise definitions of categories and the consequences that inhere in their law. In a rough way, we may say that the topic of our tractate is the definition of binding words and the consequence for violating commitments; the religious dimension emerges, as we shall see, when God's stake in the formulation of commitments enters into the matter. So, in all, we move from actions and their consequences — crime or sin and the penalty therefore — to the effects of saying certain words, starting with the word, God, properly formulated in context. The penalty for violating one's oath is the guilt offering. It follows that tractate Shebuot concerns itself principally with the guilt-offering, a sanction imposed for a range of specific crimes or sins having to do mainly (but not solely) with violating one's oath.

Specifically, Sanhedrin-Makkot deals with deeds that violate the law, both those of omission and those of commission. The protracted discussion of crimes of commission focuses upon the penalties for various actions. As its name declares, Shebuot centers its interest upon the intangibles of words that are spoken, their power and consequences of false speech. But what, about the law, the presentation finds important to record is noteworthy. Unlike Sanhedrin-Makkot, where the main effort goes into elaborate catalogues of various sins subject to a single penalty (stoning, burning, denial of the resurrection and the like) and only secondary energies are devoted to the definition of most of the sins or crimes that lead to capital punishment, the halakhah of Shebuot takes as its focus the systematic definition of the crime that is under discussion, the use of words to deceive, rather than the penalty and procedures required in inflicting the penalty. That is to say, while Sanhedrin-Makkot provide ample details to explain how the several penalties are inflicted and the agency that inflicts them and its procedures, Shebuot does not follow suit. Rather, the aspect of the law that is systematically explored concerns the sorts of statements that constitute false oaths.

The fact that the Written Torah deems the specified offering to effect atonement for the two classes of sins or crimes indicates that, within the theory of the Written Torah, the sins or crimes are of the same order. These we may differentiate in a rough sort of way as follows. What the guilt offering covers is sins or crimes principally affecting God, and man only contingently if at all. Capital punishment and flogging, by contrast penalize sins or crimes that principally affect man. (Denial of resurrection penalizes sins or crimes of so gross and indelible character, so profoundly repugnant to God and offensive to the Torah, as to fall into a unique category: sins or crimes beyond redemption. Sanhedrin's presentation of that penalty forms the key to all else, the criterion by which all other crimes and sins and the penalties therefor are measured.) Scripture itself classifies false oaths with other intangible matters, imposing a penalty of a single type, the guilt offering, for a variety of matters that bear the common trait of impalpability. In general, the acts of commission or omission (mostly the former) covered by Sanhedrin-Makkot involve things one does that people can witness, sequences of deeds of a tangible, palpable character, e.g., murder, idolatry, invest, and the like. And the larger number of those sins or crimes affect man directly, God only contingently. But when it comes to taking a false oath, on the one side, or imparting uncleanness to the Temple and its Holy Things, on the other, God is immediately engaged. The false oath calls on God's name to validate a statement that is false. Coming to the Temple in a condition of cultic uncleanness bears the same consequence so far as God is concerned. The principal characteristic throughout is breach of faith, whether with man in the protection of the bailment or with God in the sanctity of the Temple and its Holy Things. Confession restores the faith, the offering removes the guilt.

It is in that context that we may make sense of the formulation of the problematics of uncleanness and the cult. What the halakhah of the Oral Torah wants to investigate is the state of consciousness of uncleanness involved in the contamination of the cult. That is because the breach of faith — here, as I said, protecting the cult where God abides from sources of uncleanness — must take the form of an explicit and deliberate action, one that expresses contempt for the established obligation of the Torah. So what we want to know transcends the guilt offering. We ask about the penalties incurred when, in transit through the Temple, one was aware that he was unclean, when not. If someone knew he was unclean but went into the Temple unaware of that fact and then, en route, realized it, the act mixes deliberate and unintended action and is dealt with accordingly. A range of other patterns is explored along the same lines. So the halakhah plays itself out in a study of the effects of both knowing and not knowing one's condition in relationship to the Temple. A sequence of derivative cases formulate interstitial problems working within the established principles.

The halakhah of oaths, which fills the greater part of the tractate, then defines types of oaths and the counts on which, in the taking of an oath that turns out to be false or that is violated, one incurs culpability. The first issue, familiar from the opening presentation, involves all oaths in general. It concerns the assessment of the divisibility of a mental condition: how many counts of guilt does one incur within a single oath by multiple acts in violation thereof? The answer derives from a close reading of the language that is used; if it is partitive, treating as distinct each component of the oath ("wine, oil, and honey"), each action is culpable, forming a distinct classification. If it is inclusive, treating as a group a variety of categories ("many different beverages"), all actions fall into the same classification and are penalized under a single count.

From rules pertinent to all oaths, we proceed to the subdivision of oaths into four categories, rash, vain, testimony and bailment. A separate category of oaths, those imposed by the judges as part of a court proceeding, is taken up in due course. These four principal types obviously fall into two distinct categories as well, the former being oaths of a private character, the latter involving public policy — the courts, the protection of property. Once more we distinguish inadvertent taking of such an oath, in which case an offering suffices, from deliberately doing so, in which case the sanction is corporal. Taking the former two types of oath is itself culpable, in the latter cases, violating the oath or taking the oath under false pretenses is culpable, an important difference. The rash or vain oath takes effect as a general statement, the oath of testimony or of bailment must be particular to the case at hand. One is not penalized for taking a true oath of testimony or oath of bailment, but one is automatically subject to sanctions for taking a rash or a vain oath. That difference accounts also for the character of the rules that define the application of the law: men and women, relatives and otherwise, and the like. Oaths pertaining to the court matter only when taken by those qualified to give testimony, e.g., men not women, unrelated parties but not relatives of the litigants, and the like. That explains, also, why for these categories of oaths only taking a false oath is penalized. In these cases, too, the oath must be particular to the case, e.g., imposed on specific, named persons.

The judges investigate the case by imposing oaths. These form their own category, involving not only private persons but the agency of the community at large. The judges exercise the power to impose an oath upon contesting parties, in the certainty that Israelites will not take a false oath, involving God's name or Presence. Here the character of the claim and the concession governs. If the defendant denies that he owes anything, he is exempt from having to take an oath; if he concedes the facts but quibbles about details, he is required to do so. And once he does, he prevails and pays no more than he has conceded. That indicates the power of the oath in court. Five classes of claimant take the oath and collect what they claim. The oaths as they affect bailments are subdivided in terms of the character and quality of the guardianship promised by the bailiff, the unpaid bailiff being held to a lower standard than the paid bailiff, and so on. Here the oath proves effective where there are no witnesses as to the facts.

III. Interpretation: Religious Principles of Shebuot

If the sages wished to make the statement that man's word is comparable to God's and that, for man as for God, words form media of sanctification, they could find no more suitable occasion for doing so than in their discussion of the oath. And if, further, they wanted to say, God is everywhere present, a sentient being who pays close attention to everyone all the time, to what people say, not only to what they do, and, especially, to what they say upon the invocation of God's presence in particular — if that is what they wanted to say, then Shebuot provides not the ideal occasion but the only really appropriate one.

That is for two reasons. First, the oath by definition calls God to witness the transaction; the person who takes the oath invokes God's name and calls upon God to confirm his allegation. So the consequence of asking God to join in one's claims and certify them, the conviction that God is everywhere, all the time, when he is called upon, forms the foundation of all else. Second, the oath represents a purely verbal transaction, not ordinarily confirmed by concrete action, not commonly subjected to the supervision of all parties. It is the transaction that in the end depends upon the integrity of the person who makes the statement in God's name, "By an oath, I shall not eat," for who is going to keep watch to see that the man does not eat?

The religious premise of oath-taking accordingly involves an assessment of man's and of God's character. God oversees all things; he will know when his name has been taken in vain. Man is possessed of character and conscience; he does not need to be subjected to supervision by a this-worldly force outside of himself, when, having invoked God's name, he has subjected himself to God's oversight. So to language sages impute remarkable power, specifically the capacity to change a transaction, through intangible but powerful formulations, by the introduction of an interest on God's part into an arrangement otherwise between men alone. These religious convictions come to full expression in the halakhah at hand, stating in concrete language and norms the conviction that God responds when his name is invoked and is not to be deceived — ever. That conviction provides ample motivation for a detailed definition, in norms of speech, of the circumstances and formulas that engage God's interest and participation, respectively.

The oath represents the use of words for an inviolable and utterly dependable result: if I take an oath, I invoke God's name, and in doing so, I declare myself completely truthful — "so help me God." But God not only enforces the oath, having a personal stake therein. God himself takes oaths and binds himself thereby, Scripture being rich in divine oath-takings, e.g., Gen. 22:15, "By myself I have sworn and oath, says the Lord, because you have done this and have not withheld your son, your only son, I will indeed bless you. . . ." In formulating matters in that way, God undertakes a perpetual blessing for Abraham's heirs, the taking of the oath securing credence from Abraham and imposing an iron-clad obligation upon God. The upshot is, the oath possesses an integrity, an autonomy of power, such that God as much as man is bound. Words properly formulated therefore exert extraordinary power, and that is why, from deeds that represent sins or crimes, the halakhah now turns to words. It follows that the halakhah will carefully define the formula by which words take on the power to bind or loose, by which God himself is engaged in the transaction among men. But, as we already realize, the halakhah also focuses its attention upon the power of the oath here at home, within Israel's interior transactions, in relationships between one Israelite and another. That is not how the aggadah frames its discussion of the same matter.

The oath involves the name of God, and at the foundation of the halakhah is the fourth of the Ten Commandments, "You shall not take the name of the Lord your God in vain, for the Lord will not hold him guiltless who takes his name in vain" (Ex. 20:7). the oath figures, as noted, in the Ten Commandments, the fourth commandment being explicitly linked to not taking false oaths. The view of the Oral Torah that at issue in the fourth commandment is the inviolability of oaths is stated explicit in the following:

1. A. R. Hiyya taught, "(The statement, 'Say to all the congregation of the people of Israel' (Lev. 19:2)) teaches that the entire passage was stated on the occasion of the gathering (of the entire assembly)."
    B. "And what is the reason that it was stated on the occasion of the gathering (of the entire assembly)? Because the majority of the principles of the Torah depend upon (what is stated in this chapter of the Torah)."
    C. R. Levi said, "It is because the Ten Commandments are encompassed within its (teachings)."
    D. "'I am the Lord your God' (Ex. 20:2), and here it is written, 'I am the Lord your God' (Lev. 19:2)."
    E. "'You shall have no (other gods)' (Ex. 20:3), and here it is written, 'You shall not make for yourselves molten gods' (Lev. 19:4)."
    F. "'You shall not take (the name of the Lord your God in vain)' (Ex. 20:7), and here it is written, 'You shall not take a lying oath by my name' (Lev. 19:12)."

Leviticus Rabbah XXIV:V

The principles of the Torah may be derived from a few basic statements, which yield them all, and the Ten Commandments serve as the source for the rest. Here the way in which the oath forms a fundamental component of man's relationship to God is made explicit. In taking the oath, man is like God; God binds himself by an oath, so does man. There is one difference between God and man. God supervises man. God needs no supervision; he is truth. That is what the aggadah, building upon the facts of the Written Torah, sets forth as the theology implicit in oaths, and that is what the halakhah, organizing both the facts of the Written Torah and the facts produced by logical reflection, defines as the action-symbols, the norms expressed in concrete ways, of that same theology.

But the difference between the aggadah and the halakhah when addressing the oath is not to be missed. The aggadah speaks to the larger world of humanity, the halakhah to the inner life, the domestic transactions, of Israel at home, within its own social frontiers. The aggadah takes for granted the power and probative capacity of the oath, the halakhah, for its part, embodies that power, defining how it is invoked and exercised. The aggadah speaks of the power of the oath at large, the halakhah the concrete force of the oath in workaday transactions in Israel's inner life. The halakhah then bears the message that the language Israelites use among themselves in the engagement with God's name affects not only the intangibles of transcendent faith but the palpable results of ordinary activities: acts of faith and faithlessness, acts of honesty and dishonesty, acts of integrity and deceit — all of them measured by the criterion of truth established in what is said and in the way it is formulated. Using God's name in certain contexts brings God into the here and now, and that represents a power that language, rightly used, possesses. No wonder sages find the topic so richly engaging.

In general, the Oral Torah focuses upon the oath as God is bound by it, the halakhah always centers on the oath as man is affected by it. Here is how the aggadah of the Oral Torah expresses the conception that God is bound by the oath:

X:I.1. A. "[The Lord said to Moses,] 'Take Aaron [and his sons with him, and the garments, the anointing oil, the bull of the sin offering, the two rams, and the basket of unleavened bread, and assemble all the congregation at the door of the tent of meeting]'" (Lev. 8:1–3).
    B. (Gen. R. 39:6:) "You love righteousness and hate wickedness, [therefore God, your God, has anointed you with the oil of gladness above your fellows]" (Ps. 45:7).
    C. R. Yudan in the name of R. Azariah interpreted the verse to speak of Abraham, our father:
    D. "When [Abraham] was pleading for mercy for the people of Sodom, he said before him, 'Lord of the world! You have taken an oath that you will not bring a flood upon the world.'
    E. "That is in line with the following verse of Scripture: 'For this is like the days of Noah to me; as I swore that the waters of Noah should no more go over the earth, so I have sworn that I will not be angry with you and will not rebuke you' [Is. 54:9].
    F. "'Now [Abraham continued], it is a flood of water that you will not bring, but a flood of fire you will bring! Then you turn out to practice deception with regard to the oath.
    G. "'If so, you will not carry out the obligation of your oath.'
    H. "That is in line with the following verse: 'Far be it from you to do such a thing!' [Gen. 18:25].
    I. "He said before him, 'Far be it from you ... shall not the judge of all the earth do justly' [Gen. 18:25].
                                          Leviticus Rabbah X:I–III.1

What emerges is that the language of the oath is deemed precise and determinative, so that Abraham can read God's oath concerning the flood to be exclusionary, not a flood of water but of some other flood; that would represent an act of deception, violating the oath in spirit if not in letter.

How in the aggadah does an oath figure? It is to impose upon oneself restrictions or limitations, to strengthen one's own resolve to avoid sin. For example, these three invoked an oath so as to avoid temptation by the impulse to do evil, specifically, sexual sin:

1. A. Said R. Yosé, "There were three who were tempted by their inclination to do evil, but who strengthened themselves against it in each case by taking an oath: Joseph, David, and Boaz.
   B. "Joseph: 'How then can I do this great wickedness and sin against God' (Gen. 39:9).
   E. "David: 'And David said, "As the Lord lives, no, but the Lord shall smite him" (1 Sam. 26:10).'
   J. "Boaz: 'As the Lord lives, I will do the part of the next of kin for you. Lie down until the morning.'"

Ruth Rabbah LXXII:iii.1

To avoid sexual sin, the three principals take the oath, thus gaining fear of God as a buttress against sin. Now these are private transactions, so the oath brings God's oversight into the conduct of the named saints even when they are all by themselves. The oath here governs God's relationship to individuals, as much as the oath as taken to Abraham governs God's relationship to Abraham (and his seed). In the halakhah, by contrast, matters are otherwise; there the oath is invoked to regulate man's relationship to man, God being asked to validate the commitment therein undertaken.

Further, in the aggadic representation of the world, the nations are adjured as much as Israelites, and in the same transaction. By an oath, God imposes the arrangement that the gentiles must not rule Israel so harshly that Israel will rebel, and Israel must not rebel against the gentiles but must accept their government as punishment for sin:

1. A. R. Yosé b. R. Hanina said, "The two oaths [Song 2:7: 'I adjure you, O daughters of Jerusalem,' and Song 3:5, 'I adjure you, O daughters of Jerusalem, by the gazelles or the hinds of the field'] apply, one to Israel, the other to the nations of the world.
   B. "The oath is imposed upon Israel that they not rebel against the yoke of the kingdoms.
   C. "And the oath is imposed upon the kingdoms that they not make the yoke too hard for Israel.
   D. "For if they make the yoke too hard on Israel, they will force the end to come before its appointed time."

Song of Songs Rabbah XXIV:ii.1

The upshot is simple. The aggadic representation of the oath in no way prepares us for the issues that will predominate in the halakhic treatment of the same topic. In the aggadah the setting for the oath proves either entirely private and personal or public and political. It affects an individual's relationship with God and Israel's collective relationship with the gentiles. The intermediate ground, between Israelites all by themselves and Israel's outer frontiers with the nations, is taken up by the halakhah.

In the aggadah the oath figures as a medium of securing a stable relationship between God and man, a mode of setting and maintaining the rules that will govern. God binds himself and imposes bonds upon man, all through the medium of words. When man takes an oath, for his part, the concern is an equivalent transaction of power. Nothing in the aggadah prepares us for what is at stake in the halakhah, which is trustworthy relationships, effected through verbal formulas, between man and man. The upshot is, God's relationship with man, defined and regulated by the use of language to impose an oath, forms the model of man's relationship to man. If God is bound by the oath that he takes by his own name, man all the more so is bound by the oath that he takes in God's name; man is like God, and man's words matter just as God's words matter; the same formulas pertain. To that principle of theological anthropology the laws in detail attest, even though the principle itself remains implicit, being articulated only in the aggadic setting.

What then is at stake in the four types of oath that people impose upon themselves, the rash, the vain, the oath of testimony, the oath of bailment? The rash oath attracts attention because it is one that in the end is going to be violated willy-nilly: the oath not to do something that one is highly likely to do. The vain oath is one that is contrary to fact or condition, e.g., an oath that one has seen what is impossible, or an oath not to do what one is commanded to do. These oaths misuse, abuse language; they represent the utilization of the formula of the oath in inappropriate ways, asking by an oath that people believe one will do the impossible or believe the implausible. In the context of the halakhah, we require two things: a definition of the sin or crime, and a specification of the penalty for deliberate and for inadvertent commission of the sin or crime. The halakhah then identifies those whose oaths bear consequences. In the present instance anyone may take such an oath, anyone may be affected by it: men and women, persons not related and those related, and the like. But what distinguishes the classification is that the oath represents an act of one's own volition.

The other two types of oath — oath of testimony, oath of bailment — by contrast may be imposed by the court or by the law, but pertain only to those who to begin with are able to give testimony. Men, not related to the parties to the conflict, suitable to bear witness, are subject to the oath of testimony. Gentiles, women, children, and others invalid to testify in a court of Judaism are not. The oath of testimony then serves the process of the courts in the administration of law, imposing the requirement to testify upon reluctant witnesses. The oath of testimony is particular to the person on whom it is imposed; it cannot form a generalized imprecation applicable to all who hear it. The transaction moreover takes a highly personal form, the oath being imposed by the party that requires the testimony upon the party that is supposed to know pertinent facts. The oath of bailment has no bearing upon court transactions, so anyone may take it. It must pertain to something of value. Its terms and consequences are defined by the diverse definitions of responsibilities for bailments. The oath imposed by the judges, finally, embodies Scripture's disposition of the conflicting claims to property, e.g., the claim of an undischarged debt in specie or in kind, but one that is tangible and not personal or theoretical (ownership of land), e.g., to money but not slaves, to movables but not real estate.

How, then, do oaths figure in the halakhah? They represent media for the resolution of conflict, the more important cases all involving competing claims of one kind or another. The oath of the judges, the oath of testimony, and the oath of bailment all serve to introduce the criterion of truth and to exclude the exercise of force. The claimant seeks a just restoration of his property or compensation for his loss, the defendant insists upon a fair adjudication of the matter. For that purpose, words backed up not by deeds but by divine supervision serves. But contention precipitates also the taking of the vain and rash oath. The rash oath involves securing credence for a preposterous allegation — one that others deny. The vain oath asks people to believe one will carry out an implausible resolve, again bearing within itself the implicit motive to secure credibility where there is none. So one way or another, the oath serves, within the Israelite polity, to engage God's participation within the transactions of man, to involve God in Israel's points of inner conflict, to ask God to impart certainty to the points of stress and strain.

So in the end my claim of the religious meaning of Shebuot proves, if anything, insufficient. The power imputed to the oath, the context in which the oath exercises its controlling authority, the cogency of the details of the types of oaths — all work together to say in concrete and detailed ways precisely what the sages wish to express, God's intimate, eternal, and on-going engagement with what Israelites say to one another within Israel's interior social order. If sages wanted to say, God listens carefully to what people say and pays attention to the details of what they do, God knows what you promise and observes how you carry out your promise, God oversees what no man witnesses, God lives among us and abides with us — if sages wished to underscore the perpetual presence of God within Israel's everyday life, they could have accomplished their goal no more effectively than by setting forth the laws of Shebuot in the way that they have. And, as we have seen in our brief consideration of the oath in the aggadah, it is in particular through the interior spaces given structure by the halakhah that they have framed for themselves.

Once more two conclusions emerge. First, it is through the halakhah, and only through the halakhah, that sages found it possible to state their doctrines concerning God's presence within Israel's inner being. Second, it is through the particular halakhah at hand, and in no other native category of the halakhah, that the specific doctrine identified as fundamental to the matter before us can have been set forth. In the union of the two parts of the Torah, the written and the oral, sages discerned the facts of God's presence in Israel, but only in the halakhah did sages explain how that perpetual presence secured for Israel — severally and jointly — a life of truth and equity. The oath — taken or merely potential — animated all transactions within Israel. And the rest followed: an Israel able to live with controversy, such as is natural to the human condition, an Israel able to trust itself even midst conflict and contention, an Israel at peace.

7.

TRACTATE KERITOT

I. An Outline of the Halakhah of Keritot

Sinners and criminals have to answer not only to man but also to God. Man's penalties are spelled out in Sanhedrin-Makkot, and those inflicted by, or involving engagement with, God, are worked out in Keritot. Like Sanhedrin and Makkot, Keritot concerns atonement for sin or punishment for crime. But here, instead of fines, capital punishment, or flogging, what is required is either a sin-offering or a suspensive guilt offering or extirpation. What is the difference between the sin-offering and extirpation? Man bears responsibility for what he does, and the halakhah provides the opportunity to atone for doing what God has commanded is not to be done. The Written Torah explicitly imputes guilt even for actions committed inadvertently and not with the intention of violating the Torah. It follows that the halakhah has to provide for penalties to expiate sin or crime, whether deliberate or otherwise. Here making its statement concerning the taxonomic power of intentionality, the halakhah distinguishes deliberate from inadvertent sin or crime. A sin-offering is required in the case of an action, the deliberate commission of which is penalized by extirpation (early death, before the age of 60), and a suspensive guilt offering in the case of doubt. The principal interest then is in animal-offerings that expiate sin. The Written Torah contributes to the topic the following statement, at Lev. 5:17–19:

> If any one sins, doing any of the things that the Lord has commanded not to be done, though he does not know it, yet he is guilty and shall bear his iniquity. He shall bring to the priest a ram without blemish out of the flock, valued by you at the price for a guilt offering, and the priest shall make atonement for him for the error that he committed unwittingly, and he shall be forgiven. It is a guilt offering; he is guilty before the Lord

Three divisions make up the topical presentation, occasions on which the sin-offering or extirpation, as the case may be, is required, a single sin-offering and multiple sins, and the suspensive guilt-offering, required where one inadvertently may or may not have committed a sin. The order is logically necessary, since the suspensive guilt-offering cannot come before the sin- or guilt-offering for what one is certain he has done.

i. *The Sin-Offering*

A. *Classes of Transgressions that are Subject to Extirpation or the Sin-Offering*

M. 1:1 Thirty-six [classes of] transgressions set forth in the Torah are subject to extirpation: he who has sexual relations with (1) his mother, and (2) with his father's wife, and (3) with his daughter-in-law; he who has sexual relations (4) with a male, and (5) with a beast; and (6) the woman who has sexual relations with a beast; he who has sexual relations (7) with a woman and with her daughter, and (8) with a married woman; he who has sexual relations (9) with his sister, and (10) with his father's sister, and (11) with his mother's sister, and (12) with his wife's sister, and (13) with his brother's wife, and (14) with his father's brother's wife, and (15) with a menstruating woman (Lev. 18:6ff.); (16) he who blasphemes (Num. 15:30), and (17) he who performs an act of blasphemous worship (Num. 15:31), and (18) he who gives his seed to Molekh (Lev. 18:21), and (19) one who has a familiar spirit (Lev. 20:6); (20) he who profanes the Sabbath day (Ex. 31:14); and (21) an unclean person who ate a Holy Thing (Lev. 22:3), and (22) he who comes to the sanctuary when unclean (Num. 19:20); he who eats (23) forbidden fat (Lev. 7:25), and (24) blood (Lev. 17:14), and (25) remnant (Lev. 19:6–8), and (26) refuse (Lev. 19:7–8); he who (27) slaughters and who (28) offers up [a sacrifice] outside [the Temple court] (Lev. 17:9); (29) he who eats leaven on Passover (Ex. 12:19); and he who (30) eats and he who (31) works on the Day of Atonement (Lev. 23:29–30); he who (32) compounds anointing oil [like that made in the Temple (Ex. 30:23–33)], and he who (33) compounds incense [like that made in the Temple], and he who (34) anoints himself with anointing oil (Ex. 30–32); [he who transgresses the laws of] (35) Passover (Num. 9:13) and (36) circumcision (Gen. 17:14), among the positive commandments.

T. 1:1 He who anoints [himself] with the oil of anointing [like] that which Moses made in the wilderness, lo, this one is liable to extirpation. Passover and circumcision, even though [people] are liable to extirpation for deliberate transgression thereof [M. Ker. 1:1P], are not subject to an offering, because they are [commandments] which require affirmative action ["they are subject to, 'Arise and do'"].

T. 1:2 An unclean person who ate Holy Things, and he who comes to the sanctuary while unclean [M. Ker. 1:1 K], even though they are liable for deliberately doing so to extirpation and for accidentally doing so to a sin-offering are not subject to a suspensive guilt-offering, because they are subject to a sliding-scale-offering.

T. 1:3 He who curses his father and his mother, he who says to his fellow, "Go and carry out an act of liturgy to idolatry," he who incites and he who leads [Israel] astray, false prophets, and conspiring witnesses, even though they are liable to be put to death at the hands of a court, are not subject to bring an offering, because their [transgressions] do not contain a concrete action [M. Ker. 1:2F].

T. 1:6 This is the general principle: [For violation of] any negative commandment containing within itself a concrete deed do [violators] receive the penalty of forty stripes. And for the violation of any which does not contain within itself a concrete deed they do not receive the penalty of forty stripes. And as to all other negative commandments in the Torah, lo, these are subject to warning. He who transgresses them violates the decree of the King.

T. 1:19 There are five guilt-offerings: a guilt-offering for theft, a guilt-offering for sacrilege, a guilt-offering brought for having sexual relations with a betrothed handmaiden, a guilt-offering of a Nazirite, and a guilt-offering of a mesora'.

B. 1:1 VI.1/6A HE WHO COMPOUNDS INCENSE IN ORDER TO LEARN ABOUT IT OR IN ORDER TO HAND IT OVER TO THE COMMUNITY IS EXEMPT. BUT IF HE DOES SO IN ORDER TO SNIFF IT, HE IS LIABLE. BUT HE WHO ACTUALLY SNIFFS IT IS EXEMPT FROM LIABILITY, EVEN THOUGH HE HAS COMMITTED AN ACT OF SACRILEGE.

B. 1:1 VII:1/6B HE WHO POURS ANOINTING OIL ON CATTLE OR UTENSILS IS EXEMPT FROM LIABILITY; IF HE DOES SO OVER GENTILES OR CORPSES, HE IS EXEMPT FROM LIABILITY.

M. 1:2 For those [thirty-six classes of transgressions] are people liable, for deliberately doing them, to the punishment of extirpation, and for accidentally doing them, to the bringing of a sin offering, and for not being certain of whether or not one has done them, to a suspensive guilt offering [Lev. 5:17] — [except for] the one who blasphemes, as it is said, "You shall have one law for him that does anything unwittingly" (Num. 15:29) — excluding the blasphemer, who does no concrete deed.

T. 1:4 He who hits his father and his mother, he who kidnaps an Israelite, an elder who rebels against a court ruling, a wicked and incorrigible son, and a murderer, even though [their transgressions] involve a deed and even though they are subject to be put to death by a court, are not subject to an offering, because they are punished by extirpation.

T. 1:5 These are those [transgressions] punishable by death: he who eats untithed food, a non-priest who ate clean heave-offering, an unclean priest who ate clean heave-offering, and a non-priest, one who had immersed that self-same day, one who lacked proper garments, one who lacked proper completion of rites of purification, one with unkempt hair, one who was drunk, [any of whom] served at the altar — all of them are subject to the death penalty. But the uncircumcised [priest], the priest in mourning, and the priest who [performed the rite while he] was sitting down, lo, these are subject to warning.

T. 1:20 A drunkard is unfit for the sacred service, and [if he carries out an act of service in the cult] he is liable to the death penalty. What is a drunkard? Any one who has drunk a quarter-log of wine forty days old or older than that. [If] he drank [wine fresh] from his press in a volume of more than a quarter-log, he is exempt. [If] he drank less than a quarter-log of wine four or five years old, he Whether he mixed it and drank it, or drank it in little sips, he is liable.

M. 2:6 In all forbidden sexual relationships, [if] one is an adult and one is a minor, the minor is exempt. [If] one is awake and one is asleep, the one asleep is exempt. [If] one does the act inadvertently and one deliberately, the one who does it inadvertently is liable to bring a sin offering, and the one who does it deliberately is subject to extirpation [M. 1:2A].

T. 1:16 These are the points of difference between [intercourse with] the betrothed bondwoman and all other forbidden sexual relationships: All other forbidden sexual relationships which are stated in the Torah — lo, these [others] are liable, in the case of deliberate transgression, to extirpation, and in the case of inadvertent transgression, to a sin-offering, and in a case of uncertain transgression, to a suspensive guilt-offering [M. Ker. 1:2], which is not the case for the one who has intercourse with a betrothed handmaiden [M. Ker. 2:4, M, 2:6D]. All [other] forbidden sexual relationships in the Torah treat the one who does the act under constraint as equivalent to the one who does it willingly, the one who does it unintentionally as equivalent to the one who does it intentionally, [M. Ker. 2:4M], the one who begins the act only as equivalent to the one who actually completes it [M. Ker. 2:4K], the one who is sleeping as equivalent to the one who is awake [M. Ker. 2:6C], the one who does it in the normal way as equivalent to the one who does it not in the normal way, [and the law] imposes a liability for each and every act of sexual intercourse [M. Ker. 2:3C/I], which is not the case with the betrothed handmaiden. In the case of all other forbidden sexual relationships, [the law] has treated a minor as equivalent to an adult, to impose the liability solely on the adult [M. Ker. 2:6B]. But in the case of a handmaiden, if he [the male who had sexual relations] was a minor, lo, these are exempt from liability. In the case of all other forbidden sexual relationships, both of the participants receive stripes. But in the case of a handmaiden, she receives stripes but he does not receive stripes. In the case of all other forbidden sexual relationships, both parties bring an offering. But in the case of a handmaiden, he brings, but she does not bring [an offering]. In the case of all other forbidden sexual relationships, the penalty is a sin-offering. But in the case of a handmaiden, the penalty is a guilt-offering. In the case of all other forbidden sexual relationships, one brings a female [sin-offering]. But in the case of a handmaiden, one brings a male [guilt-offering] [M. Ker. 2:4G–H]. In the case of all other forbidden sexual relationships, one is liable for each and every act of sexual intercourse. But in the case of a handmaiden, one brings a single offering for many acts of sexual intercourse [M. Ker. 2:3C/I]. In the case of all other forbidden sexual relationships which are stated in the Torah, a court is liable to give instruction in their regard, which not the case for the betrothed handmaiden. In the case of all other forbidden sexual relationships, an anointed priest who gave instruction and did the deed is liable. In the case of the handmaiden, if he did the deed, even though he did not give instruction, he brings a guilt-offering on account of a confirmed case.

T. 1:18 He who has sexual relations with any one of all those who are prohibited by the Torah — he in a single spell of inadvertence, but she in five spells of inadvertence — he brings a single sin-offering. But she brings five sin-offerings. [If] she does so in a single spell of inadvertence, but he does so in five spells of inadvertence, she brings one sin-offering and he brings five sin-offerings. In respect to all prohibited relationships, [if] one is an adult and one is a minor, the minor is exempt. [If] one is awake and one asleep, the one asleep is exempt. [If] one does it inadvertently and the one does it intentionally: the one who does it inadvertently is liable to bring a sin-offering, and [he one who does it intentionally is subject to extirpation [M. Ker. 2:6].

B. *The Sin-Offering*

M. 1:3 (1) There are women who bring a [sin] offering [after childbirth], and it is eaten [by the priests], (2) and there are women who bring an offering, and it is not eaten, (3) and there are women who do not bring [an offering]. These [women after childbirth] bring an offering, and it is eaten: She who aborts (1) a sandal or (2) an afterbirth or (3) a fully fashioned foetus or (4) an offspring which is cut up [during delivery]. And so a slave-girl who gives birth brings an offering, and it is eaten.

M. 1:4 These bring [an offering], but it is not eaten: (1) She who aborts, and it is not known what it is that she has aborted; and so: two women who aborted, one [producing] something which is exempt [from the requirement of bringing an offering], and one [producing] something which is liable [to an offering].

T. 1:7 She who aborts after the completion of the days of purifying and she who aborts an eight-month-old foetus, alive or dead, or a child past term and a proselyte who converted while circumcised, and a deaf-mute, an imbecile, and a minor who lacked the completion of atonement rites bring an offering and it is eaten.

T. 1:8 [If] a woman is subject to doubt whether or not she gave birth to anything at all, or [if] she is subject to doubt that it is viable or not viable or [if] she is in doubt that the foetus does or does not bear human appearance, she brings an offering, but it is not eaten.

T. 1:10 A woman who is liable for the offering for giving birth and for yet another offering for giving birth, or an offering for flux and for yet another offering for flux brings a single offering. [If she is subject to an offering for] giving birth and an offering for suffering flux, she brings two offerings. [If she is subject to an offering] for possibly having given birth and [to an offering for] certainly having given birth, [to an offering for] possibly suffering a flux and [to an offering for] certainly having suffered a flux, she brings an offering for each obligation to which she is certainly subject among them [and] has fulfilled her obligation.

M. 1:5 These are those who do not bring [an offering at all]: She who aborts a foetus (1) filled with water, (2) filled with blood, (3) filled with variegated matter; she who aborts something shaped like (1) fish, (2) locusts, (3) abominable things, or (4) creeping things; she who aborts on the fortieth day. And [she who produces] that which comes forth from the side.

T. 1:12 All those who owe pairs of bird-sacrifices stated in the Torah — half of them [the sacrifices] are a sin-offering, and half of them are burnt-offerings, except for the bird-offering of a proselyte, for even though they are an obligation, both of them were burnt-offerings. [If] he wanted to offer beasts for those which are required, he may offer them [as he wishes]. [If] he offered beasts as burnt-offerings for atonement, he has fulfilled his obligation. [If he did so with] meal-offerings and drink-offerings, he has not fulfilled his obligation. They spoke of a pair of birds only to lighten the burden for him. [If] he brought one sort of offering for his purification from cereal, let him go and bring the same for his atonement-offering. [If he brought one sort of offering] for his Nazirite-offering, let him go and bring the same for his atonement-offering.

M. 2:1 [There are] four whose atonement is not complete [until they bring an offering]. And four bring [an offering] for [a transgression done] deliberately as they do for [one done] inadvertently. These are those whose atonement is not complete [until they bring an offering]: (1) The male-Zab [afflicted with flux in terms of Lev. 15], and (2) the female-Zabah, and (3) the woman who has given birth, and (4) the mesora [afflicted with the skin disease discussed at Lev. 13–14].

B. 2:1 II.2/8B A PROSELYTE IS PREVENTED FROM EATING HOLY THINGS UNTIL HE HAS OFFERED HIS PAIR OF BIRDS. IF HE HAS PRESENTED ONE BIRD IN THE MORNING RITE, HE MAY EAT HOLY THINGS IN THE EVENING [THOUGH HE STILL OWES THE OTHER]. ALL OF THE PAIRS OF BIRDS THAT ARE LISTED IN THE TORAH ARE DESIGNATED, ONE FOR A SIN OFFERING AND ONE FOR A BURNT OFFERING, BUT HERE BOTH OF THEM ARE BURNT OFFERINGS. IF HE HAS BROUGHT HIS OBLIGATORY OFFERING IN THE FORM OF CATTLE [THIS COVERS TWO BIRDS], AND HE HAS CARRIED OUT HIS OBLIGATION. IF HE

OFFERED A BURNT OFFERING AND A PEACE OFFERING, HE HAS CARRIED OUT HIS OBLIGATION. IF HE OFFERED A MEAL-OFFERING AND A PEACE-OFFERING, HE HAS NOT CARRIED OUT HIS OBLIGATION. THE PROVISION THAT HE MAY BRING A PAIR OF BIRDS HAS BEEN STATED ONLY AS A LENIENT RULING [TO MAKE THE PROCESS EASIER FOR THE PROSELYTE].

M. 2:2 These bring [an offering for a transgression done] deliberately as for [one done] inadvertently: (1) He who has sexual relations with a bondwoman; and (2) a Nazirite who was made unclean; and (3) for [him who utters a false] oath of testimony, and (4) for [him who utters a false] deposit oath.

ii. *Multiple Sin-Offerings*

A. *The Single Sin-Offering and Multiple Sins*

M. 1:7 The woman who is subject to a doubt concerning [the appearance of] five fluxes, or the one who is subject to a doubt concerning five miscarriages brings a single offering. And she [then is deemed clean so that she] eats animal sacrifices. And the remainder [of the offerings] are not an obligation for her. [If she is subject to] five confirmed miscarriages, or five confirmed fluxes, she brings a single offering. And she eats animal sacrifices. But the rest [of the offerings, the other four] remain as an obligation for her [to bring at some later time].

M. 2:3 Five bring a single offering for many transgressions. And five bring a sliding scale offering. These bring a single offering for many transgressions: (1) He who has sexual relations with a bondwoman many times, and (2) a Nazirite who is made unclean many times. (3) he who suspects his wife of adultery with many men, and (4) a mesora who was afflicted by nega'im many times. [If] he brought his birds and [then] was afflicted with a nega [the skin ailment discussed at Lev. 13–14], they [the birds] do not go to his credit until he brings his sin offering.

T. 1:13 Four sorts of transgressor bring [an offering] in [the case of deliberate transgression] as in the case of inadvertent [transgression. In the case of all of them, if they are under constraint, they are exempt [from liability] except for the Nazir. Five bring a sliding-scale-offering [M. Ker. 2:3A]. There are among them poor-and-rich, there are among them the poorest of the poor. A mesora and one who has given birth [M. Ker. 2:4E4–5] are poor and rich, bringing one for one. One who contaminates the sanctuary [M. Ker. 2:4E3] is the poorest of the poor, bringing two offerings for one infringement.

T. 1:21 He who has sexual relations with his mother is liable on two counts. He who has sexual relations with his father's sister is liable on two counts.

M. 2:4 A woman suffered many miscarriages — (1) she aborted a female during eighty days, and went and aborted another female during eighty days following, and (2) she who bore a multiple of abortions ["twins" — each in the period of purifying of the foregoing].

M. 3:2 [If] he ate [forbidden] fat and [again ate] fat in a single spell of inadvertence, he is liable only for a single sin offering, [If] he ate forbidden fat and blood and remnant and refuse [of an offering] in a single spell of inadvertence, he is liable for each and every one of them. This rule is more strict in the case of many kinds [of forbidden food] than of one kind. And more strict is the rule in [the case of] one kind than in many kinds: For if he ate a half-olive's bulk and went and ate a half-olive's bulk of a single kind, he is liable [since they are deemed to join together to form the requisite volume for incurring guilt]. [But if he ate two half-olive's bulks] of two [different] kinds, he is exempt.

T. 2:1 [If] one witness says, "He ate forbidden fat," and one witness says, "he ate permitted fat," [or if] one witness says, "He ate forbidden fat," and a woman says, "He ate permitted fat," [or if] one woman says, "He ate forbidden fat," and one woman says, "He ate permitted fat," he brings a suspensive guilt-offering. [If] one witness says to him, "You ate forbidden fat," and he says, "I ate permitted fat," he is exempt.

T. 2:2 All the same are he who eats and he who dissolves [produce into a liquid] and drinks it and one who anoints [with it] — if he ate and went and ate again and went and ate again — if there is from the beginning of the first act of eating to the end of the last act of eating sufficient time for the eating of a half-loaf of bread, the several acts of eating join together. And if not, they do not join together [M. Ker. 3:2E]. [If] he drank and went and drank again and went and drank again, if there is from the beginning of the first act of drinking to the end of the last act of drinking sufficient time for the drinking of a quarter-log, the several acts of drinking join together [to form the requisite volume to render him unclean or culpable]. And if not, they do not join together.

M. 3:3 And how much should he who eats them tarry? [He is not liable] unless he tarries from beginning to end for sufficient time to eat a half-loaf [of bread]. [If] one ate unclean foods [or] drank unclean liquids, drank a quarter-*log* of wine, and entered the sanctuary and tarried there, [the measure of time between entering the Temple having eaten unclean food or drunk wine is] sufficient time to eat a half-loaf [of bread].

M. 3:4 There is he who carries out a single act of eating and is liable on its account for four sin offerings and one guilt offering: An unclean [lay] person who ate (1) forbidden fat, and it was (2) remnant, (3) of Holy Things, and (4) it was on the Day of Atonement.

M. 3:5 There is he who carries out a single act of sexual intercourse and becomes liable on its account for six sin offerings: He who has intercourse with his daughter is liable on her account because of violating the prohibition against having intercourse with (1) his daughter, and (2) his sister, and (3) his brother's wife, and (4) his brother's father's wife, and (5) a married woman, and (6) a menstruating woman. And who has intercourse with his daughter's daughter is liable on her account because of violating the prohibitions against having intercourse with (1) his daughter's daughter, and (2) his daughter-in-law, and (3) his wife's sister, and (4) his brother's wife, and (5) his brother's father's wife, and (6) a married woman, and (7) a menstruating woman.

M. 3:6 He who has sexual relations with his mother-in-law may turn out to be liable on her account because of the prohibitions against having sexual relations with (1) his mother-in-law, and (2) his daughter-in-law, and (3) his wife's sister, and (4) his brother's wife, and (5) his father's brother's wife, and (6) a married woman and (7) a menstruating woman. And so is the case for him who has sexual relations with the mother of his mother-in-law and with the mother of his father-in-law.

B. *The Offering of Variable Value*

M. 2:4 These bring an offering of variable value: (1) for [oaths such as are involved in] refusing to give evidence ["for hearing the voice" (Lev. 5:1)]; and (2) for an expression of the lips [a rash oath]; and (3) for contaminating the sanctuary and its Holy Things; and (4) the woman who has given birth, and (5) the *mesora*. And what is the difference between the bondwoman and other forbidden sexual relationships (Lev. 18), that they are not alike (1) either in punishment or (2) in the offering [required for the transgression]? For all [other] forbidden sexual relations [are expiated] with a sin offering, but forbidden sexual relations with a bondwoman, with a guilt offering. All other sexual relations [are atoned] with a female animal, but the bondwoman, with a male animal. In respect to all other sexual relations, all the same are the man and the woman. They are equivalent as to flogging and as to an offering. But in respect to the bondwoman, the man is not treated as equivalent to the woman in regard to flogging, and the woman is not regarded as equivalent to the man in respect to an offering. In respect to all other forbidden sexual relations Scripture has treated him who begins the act as culpable as him who completes it, and he is liable for each and every act of sexual relations [which is not the case here, M. 2:3C1]. But this strict rule does the law stringently impose in the case of the bondwoman: that it treats in her regard the man who does the act intentionally as equivalent to the one who does it inadvertently.

B. 2:4D–E I.1/10B THERE ARE SOME WHO BRING THE OFFERING THAT IS REQUIRED BOTH IN POVERTY [BIRD] AND IN WEALTH [LAMB], SOME WHO BRING THE OFFERING REQUIRED ONLY IN POVERTY, SOME WHO BRING THE OFFERING REQUIRED OF THE POOREST OF THE POOR [A MEAL OFFERING]. A WOMAN WHO HAS GIVEN BIRTH PRESENTS THE OFFERING THAT IS REQUIRED OF THE POOR AND OF THE RICH [A DOVE, A LAMB]; A MESORA BRINGS THE OFFERING REQUIRED OF THE POOR [THE PAIR OF BIRDS]; AND THOSE CULPABLE FOR REFUSING TO GIVE EVIDENCE ["FOR HEARING THE VOICE" (LEV. 5:1)]; AND (2) FOR AN EXPRESSION OF THE LIPS [A RASH OATH]; AND (3) FOR CONTAMINATING THE SANCTUARY AND ITS HOLY THINGS BRING THE OFFERING REQUIRED IN POVERTY OR OF THE POOREST OF THE POOR [A MEAL OFFERING]. SOMETIMES ONE BRINGS ONE OFFERING IN PLACE OF ONE [IN THE CASE OF POVERTY], TWO IN PLACE OF TWO, TWO IN PLACE OF ONE, AND ONE IN PLACE OF TWO — ON THIS BASIS YOU DERIVE THE LESSON THAT THE TENTH EPHAH MUST BE WORTH A PENNY. THE WOMAN WHO HAS GIVEN BIRTH ONE BRINGS ONE OFFERING IN PLACE OF ONE — THE PIGEON THAT SHE OWED ANYHOW AS A SIN OFFERING PLUS ONE BIRD IN PLACE OF A LAMB; A *MESORA* BRINGS TWO IN PLACE OF TWO — TWO BIRDS IN PLACE OF TWO LAMBS; THOSE CULPABLE FOR REFUSING TO GIVE EVIDENCE ["FOR HEARING THE VOICE" (LEV. 5:1)]; AND (2) FOR AN EXPRESSION OF THE LIPS [A RASH OATH]; AND (3) FOR CONTAMINATING THE SANCTUARY AND ITS HOLY THINGS BRING TWO BIRDS IN PLACE OF ONE LAMB; AND THE POOREST OF THE POOR BRING ONE TENTH OF AN EPHAH IN PLACE OF TWO BIRDS.

iii. *The Suspensive Guilt-Offering*

A. *Cases of Doubt in which the Suspensive Guilt-Offering is Required*

M. 3:1 [If] they said to him, "You have eaten forbidden fat," he brings a sin offering. [If] one witness says, "He ate," and one witness says, "He did not eat" — [of if] a woman says, "He ate," and a woman says, "He did not eat," he brings a suspensive guilt offering. [If] a witness says, "He ate," and he says, "I did not eat" — he is exempt [from bringing an offering]. [If] two say, "He ate," and he says, "I did not eat" — he is exempt.

M. 4:1 It is a matter of doubt whether or not one has eaten forbidden fat, And even if he ate it, it is a matter of doubt whether or not it contains the requisite volume — Forbidden fat and permitted fat are before him, he ate one of them but is not certain which one of them he ate — His wife and his sister are with him in the house — he inadvertently transgressed with one of them and is not certain with which of them he transgressed — The Sabbath and an ordinary day — he did an act of labor on one of them and is not certain on which of them he did it — [in all the foregoing circumstances] he brings a suspensive guilt offering.

M. 4:2 Just as, if he ate forbidden fat and [again ate] forbidden fat in a single spell of inadvertence, he is liable for only a single sin offering [M. 3:2A], so in connection with a situation of uncertainty involving them, he is liable to bring only a single guilt offering. If there was clarification [of the facts of the matter] in the meantime, just as he brings a single sin offering for each and every transgression, so he brings a suspensive guilt offering for each and every [possible] transgression. Just as, if he ate forbidden fat, and blood, and remnant, and refuse, in a single spell of inadvertence, he is liable for each and every one [M. 3:2B], so in connection with a situation of uncertainty involving them, he brings a suspensive guilt offering for each and every one.

T. 2:4 [If] it is a matter of doubt whether or not one has sinned, he brings a suspensive guilt-offering [M. Ker. 4:1, 2A–B]. [If] he has sinned, but is not certain what particular sin he has committed, he brings a sin-offering. [If] he has sinned and is informed of the character of his sin but he as or gotten what sin he has committed, Lo, this one brings a sin-offering [M. Ker. 4:2C–D], and it is slaughtered for the sake of whichever [sin he has committed] and it is eaten. Then he goes and brings a sin-offering for that sin of which he is informed, and It is slaughtered for the sake of whatever [particular sin he has done] and it [too] is eaten.

T. 2:5 He who brings one sin-offering for two distinct sins — it is set out to pasture until it is disfigured, then sold. And [the man] brings with half of its proceeds one for this sin, and with half of its proceeds one for that sin. Two sin-offerings designated for a single sin — let the man offer whichever one of them he prefers. The second then is put out to pasture until it is blemished, and then it is sold, and its proceeds fall [to the Temple-treasury] as a freewill-offering. Two sin-offerings for two sins — this one is slaughtered for one of them, and that one is slaughtered for one of them.

T. 2:10 [If] one forgot the Torah and committed many transgressions, he is liable to bring a sin-offering for each and every one of them. How so? [If] he knew that there is such a thing as forbidden fat but said, "This is not the sort of forbidden fat for which we have been declared liable" — [if] he knew that there is such a thing as [the prohibition of] blood but said, "This is not the sort of blood for which we have been declared liable" — he is liable for each and every violation of the law.

T. 2:11 He who eats an olive's bulk of forbidden fat, an olive's bulk of refuse, an olive's bulk of remnant, and an olive's bulk of that which is unclean in one spell of inadvertence brings [one] sin-offering [M. Ker. 4:2E].

M. 5:1 If one ate the blood of slaughtering in the case of cattle, wild beast, and fowl, whether [said animals are] unclean or clean, the blood [shed in the case of] stabbing, and the blood [shed in the case] of tearing [the windpipe or gullet], and the blood let in bloodletting, by which the lifeblood flows out — they are liable on its account. Blood from the spleen, blood from the heart, the blood from the eggs [or testicles], the blood of fish, the blood of locusts, blood which is squeezed out [that is, blood which oozes out of the arteries after the lifeblood flows out] — they are not liable on their account.

T. 2:18 He who eats an olive's bulk of blood of a clean beast, wild animal or fowl brings a sin-offering. [If] it is a matter of doubt whether or not he ate [it], he brings a suspensive guilt-offering. But he is liable only for the blood of slaughtering alone

T. 2:19 The blood shed in the case of stabbing, blood shed in the case of tearing the windpipe or the gullet, and blood let in blood-letting, by which the life-blood flows out — they are liable on its account [M. Ker. 5:1C]. Blood from the spleen, blood from the heart, blood from the kidneys, blood from the limbs — lo, these are subject to a negative commandment. Blood of those who go on two feet, blood of eggs [testicles], blood of creeping things is prohibited. But they are not liable on their account. Blood of fish and blood of locusts, lo, this is permitted.

T. 2:20 He who mashes forbidden fat and swallowed it, he who coagulates [forbidden] blood and ate it, if it is of the volume of an olive's bulk, is liable. [If] it was mixed up with others, if it is of the volume of an olive's bulk, lo, this one is liable. [If] it was cooked with others, lo, this is prohibited if it is of sufficient quantity to impart a flavor to the whole mixture. [If] one ate a half olive's bulk or drank a half olive's bulk of a single sort [of prohibited fat or blood], lo, this one is liable.

M. 5:3 A woman [after giving birth] who brought a sin offering of fowl in a case of doubt [as to the character or viability of the foetus], if before the neck was severed, it became known to her that she had certainly brought forth [a viable foetus] — let her make it into an unconditional offering [for certainty]. For the kind of animal that she brings in the case of uncertainty she brings in the case of certainty.

T. 2:22 The woman who brought a sin-offering of fowl in a case of doubt as to whether or not she has given birth to a viable offspring and learns that she has indeed not given birth [M. Ker. 5:3D–G], Lo, this [bird] is unconsecrated. She should give it to her girl-friend [who requires it]. And the one who discovers that she has certainly given birth — let her make it into an unconditional offering [M. Ker. 5:3F]. For the sort of animal which she brings in a case of uncertainty she brings in a case of certainty [M. Ker. 5:3G].

M. 5:4 A piece of meat of unconsecrated food and a piece of meat of Holy Things — [if] one ate one of them, and it is not known which of them he ate — he is exempt. [If] he ate the second, he brings an unconditional guilt offering.

T. 3:1 A piece of meat of forbidden fat of Holy Things and a piece of meat, of unconsecrated food — [if] one ate one of them and does not know which of them he ate he brings [delete: a sin-offering and] a suspensive guilt-offering. [If] he ate the second, he brings a sin-offering and an unconditional guilt-offering.

T. 3:2 A piece of meat of Holy Things and a piece of meat of unconsecrated food [M. Ker. 5:4A] — [if] one ate the first and then went and ate the second in a single spell of inadvertence he brings a sin-offering and an unconditional guilt-offering. [If] he ate them in two spells of inadvertence, he brings two sin-offerings and one unconditional guilt-offering.

T. 3:3 A piece of meat [of forbidden fat] of refuse and a piece of meat of [if] one ate one of them and does not know which of them he ate, he brings a suspensive guilt-offering.

T. 3:4 A piece of meat of forbidden fat which is refuse and a piece of meat [of forbidden fat which is] of unconsecrated food — [if] one ate one of them and does not know which of them he ate he brings two suspensive guilt-offerings. [If] he ate the second, he brings two sin-offerings.

T. 3:5 A piece of meat of forbidden fat which is refuse and a piece of meat which is remnant — [if] one ate one of them and does not know which of them he ate he brings two suspensive guilt-offerings.

M. 5:5 A piece of meat of unconsecrated food and a piece of meat consisting of forbidden fat — [if] one ate one of them, and it is not known which of them he ate — he brings a suspensive guilt offering. [If] he ate the second, he brings a sin offering. [If] one person ate the first, and another came along and ate the second, this one brings a suspensive guilt offering and that one brings a suspensive guilt offering.

M. 5:6 A piece of meat consisting of forbidden fat and a piece of meat of Holy Things — [if] one ate one of them, and it is not known which of them he ate — he brings a suspensive guilt offering. [If] he ate the second, he brings a sin offering and an unconditional guilt offering. [If] one person ate the first, and another came along and ate the second, this one brings a suspensive guilt offering, and that one brings a suspensive guilt offering.

M. 5:7 A piece of meat consisting of forbidden fat and a piece of meat consisting of forbidden fat of Holy Things — [if] one ate one of them, and it is not known which of them he ate — he brings a sin offering. [If] he ate the second, he brings two sin offerings and an unconditional guilt offering. If one person ate the first, and another came along and ate the second, this one brings a sin offering and that one brings a sin offering.

M. 5:8 A piece of meat consisting of forbidden fat and a piece of meat consisting of forbidden fat which is remnant — [if] one ate one of them, and it is not known which of them he ate — he brings a sin offering and a suspensive guilt offering. [If] he ate the second, he brings three sin offerings. [If] one person

ate the first, and someone else came along and ate the second, **this one brings a sin offering and a suspensive guilt offering, and that one brings a sin offering and a suspensive guilt offering.**

T. 4:1 He who eats five pieces of meat from a single animal-sacrifice in five dishes in a single spell of inadvertence brings only a single sin-offering. And in a matter of doubt concerning them he brings only a single suspensive guilt-offering. [But if he does so] in five spells of inadvertence, he brings five sin-offerings. And in a matter of doubt concerning them he brings five suspensive guilt-offerings. This is the general principle: Whoever brings a sin-offering for a matter of certainty, brings a suspensive guilt-offering for a matter of uncertainty. And whoever does not bring a sin-offering for a matter of certainty does not bring a guilt-offering for a matter of uncertainty. But if he ate five pieces of meat from a single animal-sacrifice before the sprinkling of the blood, even in a single spell of inadvertence, he brings a sin-offering for each and every piece [which he ate].

B. *When the Animal Designated for the Suspensive Guilt Offering May Not be Required*

M. 6:1 He who brings a suspensive guilt offering, and is informed that he did not commit a sin — if this was before it was slaughtered, it [the animal] is set out to pasture until it is blemished, then it is sold, and its proceeds fall [to the Temple treasury] as a freewill offering. If after it was slaughtered he is [so] informed, the blood is to be poured out. And the meat goes forth to the place of burning. [If the man is informed after] the blood is [properly] tossed, the meat is to be eaten.

M. 6:2 An unconditional guilt offering is not subject to the foregoing rule. If [the man is so informed] before it is slaughtered, it goes forth and pastures in the flock. [If the man is so informed] after it has been slaughtered, lo, this is to be buried. [If the man is so informed after] the blood has been tossed, the meat goes out to the place of the burning. The ox which is stoned is not subject to the foregoing rule. If [it turns out that the ox has not killed a man] before it is stoned, it goes forth and pastures in the flock. [If it turns out that the ox has not killed a man] after it is stoned, it is available for benefit. The heifer whose neck is broken is not subject to the foregoing rule. If [the murderer is found] before its neck is broken, it goes forth and pastures in the flock. [If the murderer is found] after its neck is broken, it is buried in its place. For on account of a matter of doubt did it come in the first place. It has made atonement for its matter of doubt and goes its way [having served its purpose].

T. 2:6 Two people whose sin-offerings were mixed up in respect to two sins — it is set out to pasture until it is blemished and then sold. And let him bring with the proceeds of half of it a sin-offering for this one, and with the proceeds of half of it a sin-offering for that one. Two sin-offerings for a single sin — let the man offer whichever one of them he prefers. The second is put out to pasture until it is blemished, then it is sold, and its proceeds fall [to the Temple-treasury] as a freewill-offering. Two sin-offerings for two sins — this one is slaughtered for the sake of one of them, and that one is slaughtered for the sake of one of them.

T. 2:7 Two whose sin-offerings were confused — the sin-offering of an individual and the sin-offering of an individual, [or] the sin-offering of the community and the sin-offering of the community, [or] the sin-offering of an individual and the sin-offering of the community — even if they are two distinct sorts — this one is slaughtered for the sake of one of them, and that one is slaughtered for the sake of one of them.

T. 2:8 He who brings his sin-offering and slaughtered it — it is a matter of doubt whether or not its blood was [properly] tossed —, he has carried out his obligation. If he was lacking the completion of his atonement, it is a matter of doubt whether or not it has gotten dark [so that the blood was tossed by night] — Lo, this one brings the sin-offering of fowl as a matter of doubt.

T. 2:17 The Day of Atonement which coincides with the Sabbath and he did an act of labor, whether before it or afterward, he is exempt from the requirement of bringing a suspensive guilt — For the entire day effects atonement.

T. 2:23 In the case of her the neck of whose bird is broken, and who [then] is informed [that she certainly has given birth] — let its [the bird's] blood be drained out. [Its blood] has effected atonement. It is prohibited as to eating. [If this takes place] after its blood has been drained out [its blood] has effected atonement. is prohibited for enjoyment. For to begin with it is brought on account of doubt. It has effected atonement for its matter of doubt and gone its way [M. Ker. 6:2K].

T. 4:2 He who brings a sin-offering or a guilt-offering for a sin and is informed that he did not commit a sin — [if [this is] before it is slaughtered, it goes forth and pastures in the flock [M. Ker. 6:2B. [If this is] after it is slaughtered, its appearance is allowed to rot, and it is taken forth to the place of burning.

T. 4:3 A beast which is to be stoned, [if] the witnesses against it turn out to be conspirators, is available for benefit. A heifer whose neck is to be broken, [if] the witnesses against it turn out to be conspirators, is available for benefit. Those who owe a heifer whose neck is to be broken, for whom the Day of Atonement passed, are liable to bring it after the Day of Atonement. [If] one found the murderer, one way or the other, they slay him, since it is said, "You shall not thus pollute the land in which you live, for blood pollutes the land, and no expiation can be made for the land, for the blood that is shed in it, except by the blood of him who shed it" (Num. 35:33).

M. 6:4 Those who owe sin offerings and unconditional guilt offerings for whom the Day of Atonement passed [without their making

those offerings] are liable to bring [the offerings] after the Day of Atonement. Those who owe suspensive guilt offerings are exempt. [The Day of Atonement has atoned for those transgressions that may or may not have taken place.] He who is subject to a doubt as to whether or not he has committed a transgression on the Day of Atonement, even at twilight, is exempt. For the entire day effects atonement.

M. 6:5 A woman who owes a bird offering as a matter of doubt, for whom the Day of Atonement passed [without her making said bird offering] is liable to bring it after the Day of Atonement. For it renders her fit for eating animal sacrifices [and is not expiatory in character]. A sin offering of fowl which is brought on account of doubt, if after its neck is pinched it is known [that the woman has not actually sinned at all], lo, this is to be buried.

M. 6:6 He who sets aside two selas [Lev. 5:15] for a guilt offering and purchased with them two rams [at one sela each] for a guilt offering — if one of them [went up in value so that it now] is worth two selas, let it be offered for his guilt offering. And the second, [which is no longer required, the proper value having been attained in the first of the two,] is set out to pasture until it is blemished, then sold, and its proceeds fall [to the Temple treasury] as a freewill offering [M. Tem. 3:3: that is, in the class of a guilt offering, the owners of which have effected atonement]. [If] he [who sets aside two selas for a guilt offering] purchased with them two rams for unconsecrated use, one worth two selas and one worth ten zuz — the one worth two selas is offered for his guilt offering [incurred through the act of sacrilege]. And the second is for restitution for his sacrilege. [If] one was for a guilt offering and one was for unconsecrated purposes, if the one for the guilt offering was worth two selas it is offered for his guilt offering. And the second is for restitution for his sacrilege. And let him bring with it a sela and its added fifth.

T. 4:5 A guilt-offering for thievery, a guilt-offering for sacrilege, a guilt-offering for sexual relations with a betrothed handmaiden, which [offering] one brought at an age of less than thirteen months and one day, not worth [two] silver sheqels, are invalid. [If] one brought them at an age of more than thirteen months and one day, even if they are superannuated, they are valid.

T. 4:6 A guilt-offering of a Nazir and a guilt-offering of a mesora' which one brought at an age of more than twelve months are invalid. [If] one brought them at an age of less than twelve months, even on the eighth day [of their life], they are valid. [If] one brought them at the value of a sela, [if] one brought them at the value of a sheqel, [if] one brought them at the value of five denars, they are valid.

T. 4:7 A. He who separates two selas for a guilt-offering [and] purchased

[M. Ker. 6:6A] with one of them a ram for a guilt-offering — if it was worth two selas, it is to be offered as his guilt-offering. And the [funds for the] second fall to [to the Temple-treasury] as a freewill-offering. If not, let it be put out to pasture until it is blemished and then be and let him bring with its proceeds a guilt-offering. worth two selas And as to the second, let it[s proceeds] fall [to the Temple-treasury] [If] he purchased with them [the two selas] two rams for a guilt-offering. If one of them was worth two selas, it is to be offered as his guilt-offering. And the second is to be put out to pasture until it is blemished then is to be sold, and its proceeds are to fall to the Temple-treasury as a freewill offering [M. Ker. 6:6A–D]. If not, then both of them are to be put out to pasture until they are blemished, then they are to be sold, and let him bring with them a guilt-offering worth two selas. And the rest [of the proceeds] fall [to the Temple-treasury] as a freewill-offering.

T. 4:8 [If] he purchased with them two rams for unconsecrated use, one of them worth two selas and one of them worth ten zuz the one which is worth two selas is to be offered as his guilt-offering. And the second is his restitution for sacrilege. [If] one was for guilt-offering and one for unconsecrated purposes, if the one purchased as a guilt-offering is worth two selas, it is to be offered as his guilt-offering. And the second is for the restitution for sacrilege. Let him [further] bring a sela and its added fifth form his own property [M. Ker. 6:6E–L].

T. 4:9 [If] he purchased one ram for a sela and fattened it up, so that, lo, it is worth two, it is valid. Let him [however] bring a sela from his own property.

T. 4:10 [If] he separated one ram from his flock, worth, at the time of its being separated, a sela, and at the time of its being offered up, two, it is valid. [If] it was worth two selas at the time of its separation and at the time of its being offered up, one sela, it is invalid.

M. 6:7 He who sets aside his sin offering and dies — his son should not bring it after him [for a sin the son has committed (M. Tem. 4:1)]. Nor should one bring for one sin [a beast set aside in expiation] for another — even [a beast set aside as a sin offering] for forbidden fat which he ate last night should he not bring [as a sin offering] for forbidden fat which he ate today, since it is said, "His offering for his sin" (Lev. 4:28) — that his offering should be for the sake of his [particular] sin.

T. 4:11 A. He who brings a suspensive guilt-offering for a matter of doubt concerning forbidden fat or for a matter of doubt concerning blood, and is informed that he did not commit a sin, [if this happened] before it was slaughtered, it goes forth to pasture in the flock. If this happened] after it was slaughtered, its appearance is allowed to rot and it goes forth to the place of burning.

M. 6:8 [With funds] consecrated [for the purchase of] a female lamb [as a sin offering], they purchase a female goat. [With funds] consecrated [for the purchase of] a female goat [as a sin offering], [they bring] a lamb. [With funds] consecrated [for

the purchase of] a female lamb and a female goat [they purchase] turtledoves or young pigeons (Lev. 5:7). [With funds] consecrated [for the purchase of]turtle doves or young pigeons [they purchase] a tenth of an ephah [of fine flour, for a meal offering]. How so? [If] one set aside [funds] for the purchase of a female lamb or a female goat and then grew poor, he may bring a bird. [If] he grew still poorer, he may bring a tenth of an ephah [of flour]. [If] he set aside funds for a tenth of an ephah [of flour] and got rich, he may bring a bird. [If] he got still richer, he may bring a female lamb or a female goat. [If] he set aside a female lamb or a female goat and they were disfigured, if he wants, he may bring a bird with their proceeds. [If] he set aside a bird and it was disfigured, he should not bring a tenth of an ephah with its proceeds, for a bird is not subject to redemption.

T. 4:14 [If] he separated coins for the tenth of an ephah or fine flour and got rich — let him add to them [the coins] and purchase with it [the money] turtle-doves or pigeons. [If] he separated turtle-doves or pigeons and got rich, [if they have] not been expressly designated, let them be left to die, for fowl is not subject to redemption [M. Ker. 6:8L]. [If they have been] expressly designated, that which is the sin-offering is left to die. But that which has been designated as a burnt-offering is offered as a burnt-offering. [If] he set aside coins for turtle-doves and pigeons and got rich, let him add and purchase with them [the whole sum] a female lamb and a female goat [M. Ker. 6:8].

II. Analysis: The Problematics of the Topic, Keritot

The tractate carries forward the investigation of sin and the penalty thereof, now with special attention to the use of animal offerings to expiate sins committed inadvertently. At issue to begin with is the penalty of extirpation, inflicted by Heaven for deliberately doing the sins specified above, matched by the sin-offering, required when said sins are inadvertent. These fall into three main categories: incest and other forms of improper sexual relationships, blasphemy, and violations of specified negative commandments (not to impart uncleanness to the Temple, not to eat Holy Things and the like). We note that the earthly court penalizes some of these same actions through flogging, as Chapter Three of Makkot indicates. So what we see here is how God's court not only, or in addition to, the earthly court, takes its part in removing the consequences of sin or crime. The tri-partite system of penalties — in the hands of, respectively,

God, what we should call civil authorities (sages, king), and priests — functions to express the interests of the three components of the politics of holy Israel, the three agencies that legitimately inflict violence, God, king through sages, and priests.

But in Keritot we deal only with God's role in the process of saving people from the effects of their crime or sin, in Sanhedrin-Makkot having taken up man's role in the same process, in some instances even in sanctions for one and the same action. God's intervention takes two forms, extirpation for what is done deliberately, an offering in expiation for what is not. If someone deliberately performs these actions, his life is cut short, meaning, he dies before the age of sixty. If he inadvertently does any of them, when he finds out, he offers a sin-offering. It follows that at issue here as in Shebuot and Sanhedrin-Makkot is the discovery of the appropriate penalty to expiate the correct sin or crime, the premise throughout being that set forth in Sanhedrin-Makkot. As in the kindred tractates, so here too, the halakhah focuses on two matters: the catalogue of sins, the disposition of the offering presented in expiation thereof. The secondary development at unit two — the case of multiple sin offerings, whether a single sin-offering for many sinful actions, or several sin-offerings for a single, complex one — represents a familiar inquiry, one that characterizes the Mishnah's reading of many halakhic topics.

The second penalty for inadvertent sin is the offering of variable value, and once more, we list those who are required to present such an offering, and special situations in that regard. The third is the suspensive guilt-offering, presented when one has some reason to suppose that he has carried out a sin but lacks adequate, positive grounds for confessing inadvertent commission of a sin. That once more carries us to address cases of doubt and how these are to be resolved.

Since we are concerned to match the sin or crime with the correct penalty, we cannot find surprising the halakhic principle that for an animal to serve in expiation of a given sin, it must be correctly designated for that purpose and only for that purpose. That is a point that we meet many times in the halakhah, e.g., in the presentation of animal and meal offerings. Not only must the punishment fit the crime or sin, but the particular punishment must match the particular criminal or sinner. What that means is that the beast that the inadvertent sinner or criminal designates for the particular sin or crime that he has committed must be offered by the priest for that particular man and (it goes without saying) that sin or crime and no other. The animal designated as a suspensive guilt offering turns out not to be needed, the man having found out he did not commit the act he thought he might have done. That animal can serve some other purpose, since the designation turns out to have been in error; the proceeds of the beast are available for a freewill offering. A different rule responds to the mis-designation of the unconditional guilt offering. Here there was no doubt, at the moment the beast was designated, that the offering was required. It is, then, an act of sanctification carried out in error and is null.

The affect of the Day of Atonement comes under consideration. It functions as does a suspensive guilt offering, that is, to make atonement in cases where whether the sin has been committed is in doubt. That accounts for the role of the Day of Atonement in the atonement process; it has no bearing on the requirement of sin- or unconditional guilt-offerings; these must be paid for the specified deed.

III. Interpretation: Religious Principles of Keritot

What question pertinent to sin and atonement, crime and punishment, does the halakhah of Keritot address that no other component of the larger halakhic treatment of the general theme takes up? Sanhedrin-Makkot inflict penalties for sins that have certainly been committed and that have been adjudicated by a court, so too Shebuot, so the answer is obvious. Here we want to make the distinction, critical to the halakhic system overall, between an act that is deliberate and one that is inadvertent. In its principal divisions — the sin-offering as against extirpation, the suspensive guilt-offering as against the unconditional guilt-offering — the halakhah treats in concrete terms the distinction between deliberate, intentional sin and unintentional law-violation. Nowhere else in the halakhah do we find so sharp a line distinguishing the unintentional sin, penalized by an offering, and the intentional one, penalized by extirpation. The reason that that critical distinction concerns us in the particular halakhah at hand is self-evident. Here is where God intervenes, and it is God above all who knows what is in man's heart and can differentiate intentional from unintentional actions. And it also is God who has the heaviest stake in the matter of intentional sin, for intentional sin represents rebellion against the Torah and God's rule through the Torah.

Offerings expiate those sins that are not committed as an act of rebellion against God. These God accepts, graciously, as an appropriate act of atonement for an act for which one bears responsibility but which was not meant as defiance of God. The ones that embody an attitude of rebellion, by contrast, can be expiated not through the surrogate, the blood of the beast, but through the sinner himself, who is put to death by the court here on earth or is flogged by the court's agents or is cut off in the prime of life. So the religious principle that pervades Keritot is simple: God sees into man's heart. That is why the same act produces diverse consequences, based upon the intentionality with which the act is done. Indeed, in its own way that same conception animates the exercises on how many sin-offerings are owing for a single action or how many actions may be subsumed under, and expiated by, a single sin-offering. Beyond Keritot, the matter is expressed best in the halakhah of Shabbat. There it is made explicit: A sin is atoned for by a sin-offering only when the act is inadvertent. A deliberate action is not covered, so M. Shab. 11:6J–K: "This is the general principle: All those who may be liable to sin offerings in fact are not liable unless at the beginning and the end, their sin is done inadvertently. But if the beginning of their sin is inadvertent and the end is deliberate, or the beginning deliberate and the end inadvertent, they are exempt — unless at the beginning and at the end their sin is inadvertent."

Now the issue of intentionality on its own pervades the aggadic discourses. But what does the halakhah, in particular, contribute to the exposition of the principle that God responds to man's attitude? To answer that question, let us survey some of the main meanings imputed to intentionality in the aggadic counterparts to the halakhah.

Intentionality, or expression of an attitude, governs the action's classification, e.g., as to effect or lack of effect, as to acceptability or lack of acceptability, e.g., in recitation of prayer. While a single word, *kavvanah*, corresponds, the category, intentionality, is shown by context to pertain even where that particular word does not appear. Intentionality classifies actions, so that with one intention an action is cursed, but with the opposite, it is blessed, so T. Bik. 2:15: He who sells a Torah scroll never sees a sign of blessing. Scribes who copy Torah scrolls, tefillin-parchments, and mezuzah-parchments — they and their dealers who buy these items from scribes, and their dealers' dealers who buy them from other merchants, and all those who deal in sacred objects for the sake of making a profit will never see a sign of blessing. But if they were dealing with these objects for the sake of Heaven, lo, they shall be blessed. Dealing in holy objects for the sake of a profit is not acceptable, for the sake of Heaven is.

One's intention affects the assessment of one's deed, whether it is for good or ill. Miriam criticized Moses and was punished, but her intention was honorable; had it been dishonorable, the punishment would have been greater, so Sif. Num. XCIX:II.2: Now it is an argument *a fortiori*: if Miriam, who intended to speak against her brother not to his detriment but to his credit, and not to lessen procreation but to increase it, and who spoke only in private, yet she was punished, if someone intends to speak ill of his fellow and not in praise, to diminish and not to increase procreation, and speaks not in private but among others — how much the more so will such a one be punished! Now it is an argument *a fortiori*: if Uzziah the king, who had no intention of arrogating greatness to himself for his own honor but for the honor of his creator, was punished as he was, one who arrogates greatness to himself for his own honor and not for the honor of his creator — how much the more so will such a one be punished!

Concrete actions take on consequence only by reference to the intention with which they are carried out. For example, what matters in the offerings is intentionality; the size of the offering makes no difference, only the intent of the person who presents it, so b. Men. 13:11 I.2/110a: "It is said of the burnt offering of a beast, 'An offering by fire, a smell of sweet savor' (Lev. 1:9) and of the bird offering, 'An offering by fire, a smell of sweet savor' (Lev. 1:17) and even of the meal offering, 'An offering by fire, a smell of sweet savor' (Lev. 2:9) — to teach that all the same are the one who offers much and the one who offers little, on condition that a man will direct his intention to Heaven. Now might you say, 'Then it is because God needs the food,' Scripture states, 'If I were hungry, I would not tell you, for the world is mine and the fullness thereof' (Ps. 50:12); 'For every beast of the forest is mine and the cattle upon a thousand hills; I know all the fowl of the mountains and wild beasts of the field are mine; do I eat the meat of bulls or drink the blood of goats' (Ps. 50:10, 11, 13). I did not order you to make sacrifices so you might say, 'I will do what he wants so he will do what I wants.' You do not make sacrifices for my sake but for your sake: 'you shall sacrifice at your own volition' (Lev. 19:5)."

Intentionality forms a critical theological category, since it is the actor's intention to which God responds in his evaluation of an action, its consequence, and his — God's — response. The correct attitude in serving God is on account of reverence or fear, not as an entirely votive action, out of love, e.g., M. Sot. 5:5: On that day did R. Joshua b. Hurqanos expound as follows: "Job served the Holy One, blessed be He, only out of love, since it is said, Though he slay me, yet will I wait for him (Job 13:15). But still the matter is in doubt as to whether it means, 'I will wait for him,' or 'I will not wait for him.' Scripture states, Until I die I will not put away mine integrity from me (Job. 27:5). This teaches that he did what he did out of love." Said R. Joshua, "Who will remove the dirt from your eyes, Rabban Yohanan b. Zakkai? For you used to expound for your entire life that Job served the Omnipresent only out of awe, since it is said, The man was perfect and upright and one who feared God and avoided evil (Job. 1:8). And now has not Joshua, the disciple of your disciple, taught that he did what he did out of love."

One is permitted to fear God alone, and that is the sole correct source of intentionality, as the following story indicates (Y. B.M. 2:4 I.2): Samuel bar Suseretai went to Rome. The queen had lost her jewelry. He found it. A proclamation went forth through the city: "Whoever returns her jewelry in thirty days will receive thus and so. If he returns it after thirty days, his head will be cut off." He did not return the jewelry within thirty days. After thirty days, he returned it to her. She said to him, "Weren't you in town?" He said to her, "Yes I was here." She said to him, "And didn't you hear the proclamation?" He said to her, "Yes I heard it." She said to him, "And what did it say?" He said to her. that it said, "Whoever returns her jewelry in thirty days will receive thus-and-so. If he returns it after thirty days. his head will be cut off." She said to him, "And why didn't you return it within thirty days?" "So that people should not say, 'It was because I was afraid of you that I did so.' But it was because I fear the All-Merciful." She said to him. "Blessed be the God of the Jews."

The correct intentionality involves submission to God's will, and that is what governs under all conditions, so M. Rosh Hashanah 3:8: Now it happened that when Moses held up his hand, Israel prevailed, and when he let his hand fall, Amalek prevailed (Ex. 17:11). Now do Moses's hands make war or stop it? But the purpose is to say this to you: So long as the Israelites would set their eyes upward and submit their hearts to their Father in heaven, they would grow stronger. And if not, they fell. God plays a role by responding to

Man's intentionality, thus: As regards a good intention — the Omnipresent, blessed be He, refines it so that it produces a corresponding deed. As for an evil intention — the Omnipresent does not refine it, so that it does not produce a corresponding deed (T. Peah 1:4).

Intentionality is critical in doing one's religious duties; one must not utilize the Torah and the commandments for an inappropriate purpose, so B. Ned. 8:3–4 II.8–9/62a: "That you may love the Lord your God and that you may obey his voice and that you may cleave to him" (Deut. 30:20): This means that someone shouldn't say, "I shall study Scripture, so as to be called a sage, I shall repeat Mishnah teachings, so as to be called 'my lord.' I shall reason critically, so that I may be an elder and take a seat at the session. Rather: Learn out of love, and honor will come on its own: "Bind them on your fingers, write them on the table of your heart" (Prov. 7:3); "Her ways are ways of pleasantness" (Prov. 3:17); "She is a tree of life to those that hold onto her, and happy is everyone who keeps her" (Prov. 3:18). R. Eliezer b. R. Sadoq says, "Do things for the sake of the One who has made them and speak of them for their own sake, and don't turn them into a crown for self-glorification or make them into a spade with which to dig. It derives from an argument a fortiori in the case of Belshazzar, namely, if Belshazzar — who used the holy utensils that were removed from their status of sanctification, in line with the statement, 'for the robbers shall enter into it and profane it' (Ezek. 7:22), since they had broken in, the utensils were profaned — was removed from the world — 'in that night was Belshazzar slain' (Dan. 5:30) — one who makes selfish use of the crown of the Torah, which lives and endures forever, all the more so will be uprooted from this world!"

The correct intentionality is to carry out the requirements of the Torah for their own sake, not for the sake of a reward, so Sif. Dt. CCCVI:XXII.1: "May my discourse come down as the rain, my speech distill as the dew, like showers on young growths, like droplets on the grass. For the name of the Lord I proclaim": R. Benaiah would say, "If you carry out the teachings of the Torah for their own sake, the teachings of the Torah will live for you. For it is said, 'For they are life to those that find them' (Prov. 4:22). But if you do not carry out teachings of the Torah for their own sake, they will kill you. For it is said, "My doctrine shall drop as the rain.' And the word for 'drop' yields the sense of 'killing,' in line with its usage in the following verse: 'And he shall break the heifer's neck there in the valley' (Dt. 21:4). 'For she has cast down many wounded, yes, a mighty host are all those she has slain' (Prov. 7:26)."

What governs the relationship between intentionality and action? The intention to carry out one's obligation must accompany the act that effects that obligation; otherwise, the act bears no effect, so M. Ber. 2:1A–C: One who was reading the verses of the *Shema* in the Torah and the time for the recitation of the *Shema* arrived: If he directed his heart towards fulfilling the obligation to recite the *Shema*, he fulfilled his obligation to recite. And if he did not direct his heart, he did not fulfill his obligation. Whether or not the recitation of the Prayer of supplication requires intentionality is subject to discussion, e.g., M. Ber. 4:4 A. R. Eliezer says, "One who makes his prayers a fixed task — his prayers are not valid supplications of God." Intentionality may take precedence over actual activity, as at M. Ber. 4:5A–C: If he was riding on an ass, he should dismount to recite the Prayer. But if he cannot dismount, he should turn his face toward the east. And if he cannot turn his face, he should direct his heart toward the Chamber of the Holy of Holies. When one prays, he is to direct his heart to God, e.g., M. Ber. 5:1A–E: One may stand to pray only in a solemn frame of mind. The early pious ones used to tarry one hour before they would pray, so that they could direct their hearts to the Omnipresent. While one is praying even if the king greets him, he may not respond. And even if a serpent is entwined around his heel, he may not interrupt his prayer. Intentionality governs the effect of all rites, so M. Rosh Hashanah 3:7D–J: He who was going along behind a synagogue, or whose house was near a synagogue, and who heard the sound of the Shofar or the sound of the reading of the Scroll of Esther, if he paid attention thereby intending to carry out his obligation, he has fulfilled his obligation. But if not, he has not fulfilled his obligation. That is the rule even if this one heard and that one heard, for this one paid attention, and that one did not pay attention to what he heard.

Now in light of these examples of the role of intentionality in aggadic discourse, we return to the halakhah of Keritot and ask, does the statement made by that halakhah recapitulate what we already know? The answer is yes and no. In general terms, Keritot underscores the decisive taxonomic power of intentionality — a commonplace in the Oral Torah. But in specific terms, when we wish to discover how intentionality differentiates among the penalties that sanction a given sin or crime, nothing in the aggadah states what so powerfully emerges in the halakhah: that at that very point at which man does what God has said is not to be done, the penalty fits the crime only when intentionality is taken into account. The aggadah addresses issues of intentionality in prayer, in moral relationships and transactions, in affirmative actions in fulfillment of God's wishes. But when it comes to the negative side to matters, there we turn principally to Keritot and its powerful exposition of the concrete results, in particular penalties, of doing an action willfully as against doing it without meaning to. If we wish to know the difference between rebelling against God and merely erring in innocently doing what is not to be done, we must turn to this category of halakhah and particularly here. That is, as I said, because here the penalties are exacted by God in particular: extirpation (rather than denial of eternal life), a sin-offering (to right the balance).

That is not to suggest the halakhah only in connection with penalties or sanctions inflicted by man or by God makes the distinction between intention and inadvertence. That is not true. Let me give two pertinent instances. The first involves law-violation. The intentional violation of the law always invalidates the consequent action. What is done in violation of the law but not by intention, by contrast, may well be accepted, since it was not an act of rebellion against the Torah, e.g., M. Ter. 2:3: One who immerses unclean utensils on the Sabbath — if he does so unintentionally, he may use them; but if he does so intentionally, he may not use them. One who tithes his produce, or who cooks on the Sabbath — if he does so unintentionally, he may eat the food he has prepared; but if he does so intentionally, he may not eat the food. One who plants a tree on the Sabbath — if he does so unintentionally, he may leave it to grow; but if he does so intentionally, he must uproot it. But in the Seventh Year of the Sabbatical cycle, whether he has planted the tree unintentionally or intentionally, he must uproot it. Along these same lines, intentionality forms the principal criterion for effecting atonement through repentance. If one manifests the inappropriate intentionality, then the rite is null, thus M. Yoma 8:9 A. He who says, "I shall sin and repent, sin and repent" — they give him no chance to do repentance. "I will sin and the Day of Atonement will atone," — the Day of Atonement does not atone. So too the law distinguishes inadvertence from deliberation in action, with appropriately diverse penalties, T. Shab. 2:17–18: He who slaughters an animal on the Sabbath — if he did so inadvertently — it may be eaten at the end of the Sabbath. If he did so deliberately, it may not be eaten. Produce which one gathered on the Sabbath — if he did so inadvertently, it may be eaten at the end of the Sabbath. If he did so deliberately, it may not be eaten.

The second shows that intentionality overrides action. Thus, for example, a mere accident of speech is not binding; one must say exactly what he intended to say for the act of speech to be binding, whether in regard to oaths or offerings. Thus M. Ter. 3:8: (1) One who in designating agricultural gifts intends to say, "heave offering," but says, "tithe," "tithe," but says "heave offering," (2) or who, in designating a sacrifice, intends to say, "burnt offering," but says, "peace offering," "peace offering," but says, "burnt offering"; (3) or who, in making a vow, intends to say, "that I will not enter this house," but says, "that house," "that I will not derive benefit from this one," but says, "from that one," has not said anything, until his mouth and heart agree. Along these same lines, to incur guilt, one must intend the action that one has carried out. If he acted in a manner different from his intended action, he is not culpable as he would have been had he accomplished his purpose, so M. San. 9:4: If he intended to kill a beast and killed a man, an untimely birth and killed an offspring that was viable, he is exempt. If he intended to hit him on his loins with a blow that was not sufficient to kill him when it struck his loins, but it went and hit his heart, and there was sufficient force in that blow to kill him when it struck his heart, and he died, he is exempt. If he intended to hit him on his heart, and there was in that blow sufficient force to kill when it struck his heart, and it went and hit him on his loins, and there was not sufficient force in that blow to kill him when it struck his loins, but he died, he is exempt. These and numerous available counterparts show that the distinction between deliberate sin and inadvertent law-violation permeates the halakhah. But when it comes to the specification of the penalty for sin or crime, Keritot remains the principal point at which the halakhah makes its statement of the prevailing distinction.

Why here in particular? Because of the sanction for inadvertent sin, which is an offering. Hence, in the present context, it is in the Temple, God's abode, that man meets God; there the offering is brought that expiates inadvertent sins or crimes. God is party to the transaction, for reasons already spelled out. And, corresponding to the Temple, it is in the course of the Israelite's life that God intervenes, shortening the years of the deliberate sinner in response to the offense against life represented by deliberate sin or crime of the specified character. And that brings us back to the classes of transgressions that God punishes and man does not punish: sins involving sex, the Temple, and the violation of negative commandments (e.g., not to eat forbidden fat, not to work on the Day of Atonement and the like). None of these represents a social sin, and none endangers the social order. All involve God and principally God, and none encompasses a victim other than God.

So where else, if not in the activities subject to extirpation or the sin-offering (and so too with the other offerings treated here) will God's power to know precisely what man intends be better brought to bear? Sins or crimes that affect the social order, that endanger the health of the commonwealth, come to trial in the court conducted by sages and are penalized in palpable and material ways: death, flogging, and the like. Here God does not intervene, because man bears responsibility for this-worldly transactions. But just as man shortens the life of the criminal or sinner in the matters specified in Sanhedrin and exacts physical penalty in the matters covered by Makkot (not to mention Shebuot, where specified), so God shortens the life of the criminal or sinner in matters of particular concern to God. These are matters that, strictly speaking, concern only God and not the Israelite commonwealth at large: sex, food, the Temple and its cult, the laws of proper conduct on specified occasions. Where the community does not and cannot supervise, God takes over. Israel does Israel's business, God does God's. For both the upshot is the same: sin or crime is not indelible. An act of rebellion is expiated through life's breath, an act of inadvertent transgression through the blood of the sacrificial beast, with the same result: all Israel, however they have conducted themselves in their span of time on earth, will enjoy a portion in the world to come: all but the specified handful, enter to eternal life beyond the grave.

8.

TRACTATE HORAYOT

I. An Outline of the Halakhah of Horayot

The sequence of tractates — Sanhedrin, Makkot, Shebuot, Keritot — that spell out how the sinner or criminal restores a right relationship to God through undergoing the penalty for the sin or crime he has carried out concludes with Horayot. Each organizes itself around types of penalties associated with particular crimes and the definition of how those penalties are inflicted and by whom or by what agency that is done. But Horayot takes up a problem of social organization not addressed in its companions devoted to Israel's social order. Up until this point in our survey of the halakhah of the interiority of Israel's public life we have met crimes or sins involving individuals, differentiating among them in accord with the penalty, the institution that imposes it, and the type of penalty that is inflicted. Now we turn to crime or sin committed by the community as a whole. Here too, the governing distinctions — intentional and deliberate versus inadvertent and unintended — come to bear. But we learn new things as well.

Companion of tractate Shebuot, which centers on Leviticus Chapters Five and Six, Horayot deals with collective sin and its atonement and fits well into the sequence, Sanhedrin-Makkot, Keritot, and Shebuot, all of them on sanctions for sin or crime, intentional or otherwise. Here we deal with erroneous decisions made by instruments of government, as distinct from individuals or self-constituted collectivities (the town that goes astray through idolatry). Scripture makes provision for collective expiation of guilt incurred on account of collective action effected through public institutions of government or instruction. The Written Torah refers to a sin committed in error. A court instructs the community to do something that should not be done, thus the erroneous instruction to which the halakhah pertains. Lev. 5:1–5, 13:21, 22:26, and Num. 15:22–26, deal with that situation. Cultic penalties for official instruction — that of the anointed priest — in error and the consequent sin are specified at Lev. 4:1–5:

And the Lord said to Moses, Say to the people of Israel, If anyone sins unwittingly [in any of the things that the Lord has commanded not to be done and does any one of them, if it is the anointed priest who sins, thus bringing guilt on the people, then let him offer for the sin that he has committed a young bull without blemish to the Lord for a sin offering. He shall bring the bull to the door of the tent of meeting before the Lord, and lay his hand on the head of the bull, and kill the bull before the Lord. And the anointed priest shall take some of the blood of the bull and bring it to the tent of meeting, and the priest shall dip his finger in the blood and sprinkle part of the blood even times before the Lord in front of the veil of the sanctuary.

Now we deal with the entire congregation's doing so, Lev. 4:13–21:

If the whole congregation of Israel commits a sin unwittingly and the thing is hidden from the eyes of the assembly, and they do anyone of the things that the Lord has commanded not to be done and are guilty, when the sin that they have committed becomes known, the assembly shall offer a young bull for a sin offering and bring it before the tent of meeting; and the elders of the congregation shall lay their hands upon the head of the bull before the Lord, and the bull shall be killed before the Lord. Then the anointed priest shall bring some of the blood of the bull to the tent of meeting, and the priest shall dip his finger in the blood and sprinkle it seven times before the Lord in front of the veil. And he shall put some of the blood on the horns of the altar that is in the tent of meeting before the Lord, and the rest of the blood he shall pour out at the base of the altar of burnt offering that is at the door of the tent of meeting. And all its fat he shall take from it and burn upon the altar. Thus shall he do with the bull, as he did with the bull of the sin offering, so shall he do with this; and the priest shall make atonement for them, and they shall be forgiven. And he shall carry forth the bull outside the camp and burn it as he burned the first bull; it is the sin offering of the assembly.

Lev. 4:22–26 move on to the ruler:

When the ruler sins, doing unwittingly any one of all the things that the Lord his God has commanded not to be done and is guilty, if the sin that he has committed is made known to him, he shall bring as his offering a goat, a male without blemish, and shall lay his hand upon the head of the goat and kill it in the place where they kill the burnt offering before the Lord; it is a sin offering. Then the priest shall take some blood of the sin offering with his finger and put it on the horns of the altar of burnt offering and pour out the rest of its blood at the base of the altar of burnt offering. And all its fat he shall burn on the altar, like the fat of the sacrifice of peace offerings; so the priest shall make atonement for him for his sin and he shall be forgiven.

Finally, at Num. 15:22–29, the unwitting sin of the entire community is addressed (the deliberate sin of the entire community, in the case of idolatry, already having been taken up elsewhere):

> But if you err [as a community] and do not observe all these commandments that the Lord has spoken to Moses, all that the Lord has commanded you by Moses, from the day that the Lord gave commandment and onward throughout your generations, then if it was done unwittingly, without the knowledge of the congregation, all the congregation shall offer one young bull for a burnt offering, a pleasing odor to the Lord, with its cereal offering and its drink offering according to the ordinance, and one male goat for a sin offering. And the priest shall make atonement for all the congregation of the people of Israel and they shall be forgiven; because it was an error, and they have brought their offering, an offering by fire to the Lord, and their sin offering before the Lord, for their error. And all the congregation of the people of Israel shall be forgiven, and the stranger who sojourns among them, because the whole population was involved in the error.

So whether the ruler, the high priest, or the people, all are subject to the sanction invoked by the erroneous ruling of the court, which has caused this unwitting sin. Interstitial issues — did the court and the public act together, did the court issue the ruling while the public carried it out, and the like — are addressed in the Oral Torah's contribution to the halakhah. The court, the ruler, and the high priest embody the community at large, the body of political institutions that, each in its own realm, bears responsibility for the whole. This tripartite division of political power dictates the organization of the halakhic exposition before us. As usual, the center of interest is divided between the crime and its penalty. In the present instance of inadvertent crime penalized by a particular offering, the careful specification of which sort of beast matches which condition of inadvertent sin demands close attention. Sages clearly knew the code of animal offerings, understanding why a given situation demanded a particular type of beast, and how to decipher that code is to be reconstructed out of the facts at hand.

i. *The Offering Brought Because of an Erroneous Decision by a Court*

M. 1:1 [If] the court gave a decision to transgress any or all of the commandments which are stated in the Torah, and an individual went and acted in accord with their instructions, [so

transgressing] inadvertently, (1) whether they carried out what they said and he carried out what they said right along with them, (2) or whether they carried out what they said and he carried out what they said after they did, (3) whether they did not carry out what they said, but he carried out what they said — he is exempt, since he relied on the court. [If] the court gave a decision, and one of them knew that they had erred, or a disciple who is worthy to give instruction, and he [who knew of the error] went and carried out what they said, (1) whether they carried out what they said and he carried out what they said right along with them, (2) whether they carried out what they said and he carried out what they said after they did, (3) whether they did not carry out what they said, but he carried out what they said — lo, this one is liable, since he [who knew the law] did not in point of fact rely upon the court. This is the governing principle: He who relies on himself is liable, and he who relies on the court is exempt.

T. 1:1 [If] the court gave a decision, and one of them knew that they had erred [M. Hor. 1:1H], or if one of the experienced disciples was sitting before them and worthy of giving a decision, like Simeon b. Azzai, and he went and carried out what they had said Lo, this one is liable, since he did not [in point of fact] rely upon the court [M. Hor. 1:1J, N–O]. [If] the court gave a decision, and the entire community, or the majority of the community, carried out their decision, when their decision is the decision of a court, they are exempt. And those who carry out their decision bring a sheep and a goat.

M. 1:3 [If] a court gave a decision to uproot the whole principle [of the Torah] — [for example,] (1) [if] they said, "[The prohibition against having intercourse with] a menstruating woman is not in the Torah [Lev. 15:19]." (2) "[The prohibition of labor on] the Sabbath is not in the Torah." (3) "[The prohibition against] idolatry is not in the Torah." Lo, these are exempt [from the requirement of Lev. 4:14]. [If] they gave instruction to nullify part and to carry out part [of a rule of the Torah], lo, they are liable. How so? (1) [If] they said, "The principle of prohibition of sexual relationships with a menstruating woman indeed is in the Torah, but he who has sexual relations with a woman awaiting day against day is exempt." (2) "The principle of not working on the Sabbath is in the Torah, but he who takes out something from private domain to public domain is exempt." (3) "The principle of not worshipping idols is in the Torah but he who bows down [to an idol] is exempt." — lo, these are liable, since it is said, "If something be hidden" (Lev. 4:13) — something and not everything.

T. 1:7 A. [If] a court gave a decision to uproot the whole principle [of the Torah] [M. Hor. I:3A] — [if] they said, "The prohibition of blood is not in the Torah," and, "The prohibition of forbidden fat is not in the Torah," and, "The prohibition of refuse [sacrificial meat] is not in the Torah," Lo, these are exempt. [If] they gave instruction to nullify part and to carry out part, lo, they are liable [M. Hor. 1:3F]. How so? [If they decided,] "There is blood prohibited in the Torah, but they are not liable on account of blood which is offered as peace-offerings" — "There is the prohibition of refuse in the Torah, but people are liable only in regard to refuse deriving from peace-offerings" — Lo, these are liable, as it is said, "The word of the Lord" (Deut. 17:8). Word is said here, and word is said below. Just as word stated later on refers to part of a word but not the whole of it, so word stated in this context means part of a word but not the whole of it. You maintain that word refers to part but not the whole of it. But perhaps it refers only to the whole of it. Scripture says, "Between blood and blood" (Deut. 17:8) — and not all types of blood. "Between judgment and judgment" — and not the whole of a judgment. Between nega' and nega' — and not the whole nega'. Lo, one need not state matters in accord with the latter version but only in accord with the former version. It is stated here, word, and later on, word also is stated. Just as word which is stated later on refers to part of it but not the whole of it, so word which is stated here refers to part of it and not the whole of it.

M. 1:4 (1) [If] the court gave a decision, and one of the members of the court realized that they had erred and said to them, "You are in error," or (2) if the head of the court was not there, or (3) if one of them was a proselyte, a mamzer, a Netin, or an elder who did not have children — lo, these are exempt [from a public offering under the provisions of Lev. 4:14], since "Congregation" is said here [Lev. 4:13], and "Congregation" is said later on [Num. 15:24]. Just as "congregation" later on applies only in the case in which all of them are suitable for making a decision, so "congregation" stated here refers to a case in which all of them are suitable for making a decision. [If] the court gave an incorrect decision inadvertently, and the entire community followed their instruction [and did the thing in error] inadvertently, they bring a bullock. [If the court gave an incorrect decision] deliberately, but the community, following their instruction, did the thing in error] inadvertently, they bring a lamb or a goat (Lev. 4:32, 27). [If the court gave incorrect instruction] inadvertently, and [the community followed their instruction and did the thing in error] deliberately, lo, these are exempt [under the provisions of Lev. 4:4].

T. 1:2 [If] the court gave an [erroneous] decision, and two or three tribes, or the majority of two or three tribes, carried out their instructions, when their decision is the decision of a court, they are exempt [cf. M. Hor. 1:5Q-R] ... And those who carry out their decision bring a bullock ... [If] their instruction is not the instruction of a court, they are liable. And those who carry out their instructions bring a sheep and a goat [cf. M. Hor. 1:41–K]. [If] they carried out their own decision, they are exempt. [If they carried out] the decision of an anointed priest, they are liable [cf. M. Hor. 2:1]. [If] the court gave an [erroneous] decision, and one of them was not there, they are exempt.

T. 1:3 A strict rule applies to the making of a wrong decision which does not apply in a capital case, and a strict rule applies in a capital case which does not apply to the making of a wrong decision [on the part of a court]. For in the case of the making of a wrong decision, [they are culpable] only when all of them will join in the [false] decision [M. Hor. 1:4A]. But in capital cases they follow the majority.

T. 1:4 A. In the case of the making of a wrong decision, [they are liable] only when the court in the hewn-stone chamber will have made the wrong decision [M. Hor. 1:5Q-R], while in capital cases courts are set up in every place. An individual who gave an [erroneous] decision on his own testimony and carried it out — Lo, this one is liable, as it is said, "But the person who does anything with a high hand [whether he is native or a sojourner, reviles the Lord, and that person shall be cut off from among his people. Because he has despised the word or the Lord" (Num. 15:30).

1:6 [If] a court gave a decision that it was after the Sabbath [the sun having set], and afterward the sun shone — this is not a decision but merely an error.

ii. *The Offering Brought by the High Priest Who Has Unwittingly Done What is Contrary to the Commandments of the Torah. The Ruler*

M. 2:1 [If] an anointed [high] priest made a decision for himself [in violation of any of the commandments of the Torah], doing so inadvertently, and carrying out [his decision] inadvertently, he brings a bullock (Lev. 4:3). [If] he [made an erroneous decision] inadvertently, and deliberately carried it out, deliberately [made an erroneous decision] and inadvertently carried it out, he is exempt. For an [erroneous] decision of an anointed [high] priest for himself is tantamount to an [erroneous] decision of a court for the entire community.

Y. 2:1 I:1 *["If any one sins unwittingly in any of the things which the Lord has commanded not to be done and does any one of them, if it is the anointed priest who sins, thus bringing guilt on the people, then let him offer for the sin which he has committed a young bull" (Lev. 4:2–3).] "Anyone...," "if it is the high-priest...," — lo, [the Scripture would seem to imply that] the high priest is tantamount to an individual. [In this case, Scripture's purpose is to say:] Just as an individual, if he ate [something prohibited] at the instruction of a court is exempt, so this one [subject to court authority], if he ate something at the instruction of the court, is exempt. Just as an individual, if he ate [something prohibited] without the instruction of a court is liable, so this one, if he ate something not at the instruction of a court, is liable. [To encounter that possible interpretation] Scripture states, "Thus bringing guilt on*

the people," [meaning] lo, [the high anointed priest's] guilt is tantamount to the guilt of the entire people [just as M. 2:1F states]. Just as the people are not guilty unless they gave instruction [Lev. 4:13], so this one is not guilty unless he gave instruction.
Y. 2:1 I:3 An anointed high priest who ate [forbidden food] at the instruction of a court [thus inadvertently sinning] is exempt. [If he did so] at the instruction of another anointed high priest [and inadvertently sinned], he is liable. [If he did so] at the instruction of a court, he is exempt [from bringing a bullock, but covered by the bullock they will bring], because the instruction of others as compared to the instruction of [a court] is null. [If he did so] at the instruction of another anointed high priest, he is liable.

M. 2:2 [If] he made an [erroneous] decision by himself and carried it out by himself, he effects atonement for himself by himself. [If] he made [an erroneous] decision with the community and carried it out with the community, he effects atonement for himself with the community. For a court is not liable until it will give an erroneous decision to nullify part and to carry out part [of the teachings of the Torah], and so is the rule for an anointed [high priest] [M. 1:3]. And [they] are not [liable] in the case of idolatry [subject to an erroneous decision] unless they give a decision to nullify in part and to sustain in part [the requirements of the Torah] [M. 1:3].

M. 2:3 They are liable only on account of something's being hidden (Lev. 4:13) along with an act [of transgression] which is performed inadvertently, and so in the case of the anointed [high priest]. And [they are] not [liable] in the case of idolatry except in the case of something's being hidden along with an act [of transgression] which is performed inadvertently. The court is liable only if they will give an erroneous decision in a matter, the deliberate commission of which is punishable by extirpation, and the inadvertent commission of which is punishable by a sin offering, and so in the case of the anointed [high priest], and [they are] not [liable] in the case of idolatry, except in the case in which they gave instruction in a matter the deliberate commission of which is punishable by extirpation, and the inadvertent commission of which is punishable by a sin offering.

M. 2:4 They are not liable on account of [a decision inadvertently violating] a positive commandment or a negative commandment concerning the sanctuary. And they do not bring a suspensive guilt offering on account of [violation of] a positive commandment or a negative commandment concerning the sanctuary. But they are liable for [violating] a positive commandment or a negative commandment involving a menstruating woman. And they do bring a suspensive guilt offering on account of [violation of] a positive commandment or a negative commandment concerning a menstruating woman. What is a positive commandment concerning a menstruating woman?

To keep separate from a menstruating woman. And what is a negative commandment? Not to have sexual relations with a menstruating woman.

T. 1:9 They are not liable on account of [a decision inadvertently violating] a positive commandment or a negative commandment concerning the sanctuary. They do not bring a suspensive guilt offering on account of [violation of a positive commandment or a negative commandment concerning the sanctuary [M. Hor. 2:4A–B].

iii. *The Individual. The Anointed Priest. The Community*

M. 2:6 In the case of all the commandments in the Torah, on account of which they are liable for deliberate violation to extirpation, and on account of inadvertent violation to a sin offering, an individual brings a female lamb or a female goat [Lev. 4:28, 32] a ruler brings a male goat [Lev. 4:23], and an anointed [high priest] and a court bring a bullock [M. 1:5, 2:1]. But in the case of idolatry, the individual, ruler, and anointed [high priest] bring a female goat [Num. 15:27]. And the court brings a bullock and a goat [M. 1:5], a bullock for a whole offering and a goat for a sin offering.

M. 2:7 As to a suspensive guilt offering, an individual and a ruler may become liable, but the anointed [high priest] and court do not become liable. As to an unconditional guilt offering, an individual, a ruler, and an anointed [high priest] may become liable, but a court is exempt. On account of hearing the voice of adjuration, a rash oath, and imparting uncleanness to the sanctuary and its Holy Things, a court is exempt, but an individual, a ruler, and an anointed [high priest] are liable.

M. 3:1 An anointed [high] priest who sinned and afterward passed from his office as anointed high priest, and so a ruler who sinned and afterward passed from his position of greatness — the anointed [high] priest brings a bullock, and the patriarch brings a goat [M. 2:6].

Y. 3:1 I:2 *[If a person] ate half an olive's bulk [of forbidden fat] before he was appointed to high office and half an olive's bulk afterward [thus completing the minimum volume of an olive's bulk to become culpable], even in a single spell of inadvertence, he is exempt [from obligation to bring an offering. The half-olive's bulk eaten while the person was an ordinary man does not join together with the half-olive's bulk he ate after he rose to high office, since the offering required for the commission of such a sin differs in accord with the change in the person's status]. [If it is] a matter of doubt whether a person ate a half-olive's bulk [of forbidden fat] before he was appointed to high office, and it is a matter of doubt whether he ate a half-olive's bulk [of forbidden fat] after he was appointed to high office, he brings a suspensive guilt-offering.*

Y. 3:1 I:3 *[If a man] ate an olive's bulk of forbidden fat before he was appointed to high office, and an olive's bulk of forbidden fat after he was appointed to high office, in a single spell of inadvertence, he is liable only for a single [sin-offering, in line with [If] it is a matter of doubt whether he ate an olive's bulk before he was appointed, and a matter of doubt whether he ate an olive's bulk after he was appointed, in a single spell of inadvertence, he is liable for only a single suspensive guilt-offering. [If he did so] in two distinct spells of inadvertence, he is liable for two suspensive guilt-offerings.*

M. 3:2 An anointed [high] priest who passed from his office as anointed high priest and then sinned, and so a ruler who passed from his position of greatness and then sinned — a high priest brings a bullock. But a ruler is like any ordinary person [and brings an offering appropriate to a commoner].

M. 3:3 [If] they sinned before they were appointed, and then they were appointed, [when expiating the action committed prior to elevation to office,] lo, they are in the status of any ordinary person. (1) And who is a ruler? This is the king, as it is said, And does any one of all the things which the Lord his God has commanded not to be done (Lev. 4:22) — a ruler who has none above him except the Lord his God.

M. 3:4 (2) Who is the anointed [high priest]? It is the one who is anointed with the anointing oil, not the one who is dedicated by many garments. There is no difference between the high priest who is anointed with anointing oil, and the one who is dedicated with many garments, except for [the latter's obligation to bring] the bullock which is brought because of the [violation] of any of the commandments. There is no difference between a [high] priest presently in service and a priest [who served] in the past except for the [bringing of] the bullock of the Day of Atonement and the tenth of an ephah. (1) This one and that one are equivalent in regard to the service on the Day of Atonement. (2) And they are commanded concerning [marrying] a virgin. And they are forbidden to [marry] a widow. (3) And they are not to contract corpse uncleanness on account of the death of their close relatives. (4) Nor do they mess up their hair. (5) Nor do they tear their clothes [on the occasion of a death in the family]. (6) And [on account of their death] they bring back a manslayer.

T. 2:1 These are the differences between a high priest and an ordinary priest: the bullock that is brought on account of violation of any of the commandments, the bullock that is brought on the Day of Atonement, and the tenth of an ephah. He does not mess up his hair nor does he tear his clothes on the occasion of the death of a close relative [M. Hor. 3:4H–I]. But a high priest tears his garment below, and an ordinary one above [M. Hor. 3:5A]. He does not contract corpse uncleanness on the death of relatives [M. 3:4G]. He is commanded concerning marrying a virgin and he is warned against marrying a widow [M. 3:4E]. And on the occasion of his death, the manslayer who has gone into exile is brought back home [M. Hor. 3:4J]. And a high priest makes an offering while he is in the status of one who has yet to bury his dead, though he may not eat the priestly portion while in that status [M. Ho 3:5B]. He makes an offering of a portion of the sacrificial animal at the head of the other priests, and he takes a portion of the sacrificial animal given over to the priests at the head of the other priests. And he serves in the eight garments. And all acts of worship on the Day of Atonement are valid only if done by him. And he is exempt on account of imparting uncleanness to the sanctuary and its Holy Things [M. 2:4]. And all the stated rules apply to the anointed high priest who has passed from office, except for those pertaining to the Day of Atonement and the tenth of an ephah of fine flour [M. Hor. 3:4C]. And all of the stated rules apply to the high priest consecrated through many garments who has passed from office except for the requirement to bring a bullock on account of violating any of the commandments [M. Hor. 3:4A]. And none of them applies to the anointed for battle, except for the five rules that Scripture itself has explicitly spelled out in the relevant passage: he does not mess up his hair or contract corpse-uncleanness because of the death of close relatives, and he is commanded to marry a virgin and admonished against marrying a widow [T. Hor. 2:1A–Q].

M. 3:5 A high priest [on the death of a close relative] tears his garment below, and an ordinary one, above. A high priest makes an offering while he is in the status of one who has yet to bury his dead, but he may not eat [the priestly portion]. And an ordinary priest neither makes the offering nor eats [the priestly portion].

M. 3:6 [When the priest faces a choice on tending to two or more animals that have been designated as offerings, then:] Whatever is offered more regularly than its fellow takes precedence over its fellow, and whatever is more holy than its fellow takes precedence over its fellow. [If] a bullock of an anointed priest and a bullock of the congregation [M. 1:5] are standing [awaiting sacrifice] — the bullock of the anointed [high priest] takes precedence over the bullock of the congregation in all rites pertaining to it.

T. 2:4 [If] a bullock of an anointed priest and a bullock of the congregation are standing [awaiting sacrifice], the bullock of the anointed [high priest] takes precedence over the bullock of the congregation in all rites pertaining to it [M. Hor. 3:6B–C], because the anointed [high priest] effects atonement, while for the congregation, atonement is effected. It is better that that which effects atonement should take precedence over that for which atonement is effected, as it is said, "And it will atone for him, for his house, and for all the congregation of Israel" (Lev. 16:17). A bullock which is offered on account of [violation of] any of the commandments takes precedence over the bullock and goat offered on account of idolatry. And the bullock brought on account of idolatry takes precedence over the goat brought on account of idolatry. And the goat offered on account of idolatry takes precedence over the goat brought for the ruler. And the goat brought for the ruler takes precedence over the goat and lambs. The offering of the sheaf of first grain ['omer] takes precedence over the lamb which is offered with it. This is the operative principle: that which is offered on account of the day takes precedence over that which is offered on account of the bread.

M. 3:7 The man takes precedence over the woman in the matter of the saving of life and in the matter of returning lost property [M. B.M. 2:11]. But a woman takes precedence over a man in the matter of [providing] clothing and redemption from captivity. When both of them are standing in danger of defilement, the man takes precedence over the woman.

T. 2:5 He, his father, and his master are standing in captivity [and awaiting ransom]: he takes precedence over his master, and his master takes precedence over his father. But [ransoming] his mother takes precedence over all other people.

B. 3:7 I:1/13A IF HE, HIS FATHER, AND HIS MASTER ARE STANDING IN CAPTIVITY [AND AWAITING RANSOM]. HE TAKES PRECEDENCE OVER HIS MASTER, AND HIS MASTER TAKES PRECEDENCE OVER HIS FATHER. HIS MOTHER TAKES PRECEDENCE OVER ALL OF THEM [T. HOR. 2:5]. A SAGE TAKES PRECEDENCE OVER A KING. [FOR IF] A SAGE DIES, WE HAVE NONE WHO IS LIKE HIM, WHILE [IF] A KING DIES, ANY ISRAELITE IS SUITABLE TO MOUNT THE THRONE [T. HOR. 2:8]. A KING TAKES PRECEDENCE OVER A HIGH PRIEST, AS IT IS SAID, "AND THE KING SAID TO THEM, TAKE WITH YOU THE SERVANTS OF YOUR LORD, AND CAUSE SOLOMON MY SON TO RIDE ON MY OWN MULE, AND BRING HIM DOWN TO GIHON." AND THE HIGH PRIEST TAKES PRECEDENCE OVER THE PROPHET, AS IT IS SAID, "AND LET ZADOK THE PRIEST AND NATHAN THE PROPHET THERE ANOINT HIM KING OVER ISRAEL" (1 KGS 1:33–34). [DAVID] GAVE PRECEDENCE TO ZADOK OVER NATHAN. AND [SCRIPTURE FURTHER] SAYS, "HEAR NOW, O JOSHUA THE HIGH PRIEST, YOU AND YOUR FRIENDS WHO SIT BEFORE YOU, FOR THEY ARE MEN OF GOOD OMEN" (ZECH. 3:8). IS IT POSSIBLE THAT HE SPEAKS OF ORDINARY MEN? SCRIPTURE SAYS, "FOR THEY ARE MEN OF GOOD OMEN," AND "OMEN" REFERS ONLY TO PROPHECY, AS IT IS SAID, "AND HE GIVES YOU A SIGN OR AN OMEN" (DT. 13:2) [T. HOR. 2:9]. A HIGH PRIEST ANOINTED WITH OIL TAKES PRECEDENCE OVER ONE DEDICATED THROUGH MANY GARMENTS. A HIGH PRIEST DEDICATED THROUGH MANY GARMENTS TAKES PRECEDENCE OVER THE ANOINTED HIGH PRIEST WHO GAVE UP OFFICE BY REASON OF AN INVOLUNTARY DISCHARGE OF SEMEN. THE ANOINTED HIGH PRIEST WHO GAVE UP OFFICE BY REASON OF AN INVOLUNTARY DISCHARGE OF SEMEN TAKES PRECEDENCE OVER ONE WHO IS BLEMISHED. THE PRIEST WHO IS BLEMISHED TAKES PRECEDENCE OVER THE PRIEST ANOINTED FOR BATTLE. AND THE HEAD OF THE COURT TAKES PRECEDENCE OVER THE AUDITOR [SUPERINTENDENT OVER THE CASHIERS (AMARKAL)]. AND THE AUDITOR [SUPERINTENDENT OVER THE CASHIERS] TAKES PRECEDENCE OVER THE TREASURER, AND THE TREASURER TAKES PRECEDENCE OVER THE HEAD OF THE WEEKLY COURSE [OF THE PRIESTS, WHO TAKE CARE

OF THE CULT IN A GIVEN WEEK]. AND THE HEAD OF THE PRIESTLY COURSE TAKES PRECEDENCE OVER THE HEAD OF THE COURT. THE HEAD OF THE COURT TAKES PRECEDENCE OVER AN ORDINARY PRIEST. AND AN ORDINARY PRIEST TAKES PRECEDENCE OVER A LEVITE. AND A LEVITE TAKES PRECEDENCE OVER AN ISRAELITE. AND AN ISRAELITE TAKES PRECEDENCE OVER A MAMZER. AND A MAMZER TAKES PRECEDENCE OVER A NETIN. AND A NETIN TAKES PRECEDENCE OVER A PROSELYTE. AND A PROSELYTE TAKES PRECEDENCE OVER A FREED SLAVE.

M. 3:8 A priest takes precedence over a Levite, a Levite over an Israelite, an Israelite over a mamzer [a person whose parents may not legally ever marry, e.g., brother and sister], a mamzer over a Netin [a descendant of the cast of Temple servants], a Netin over a proselyte, a proselyte over a freed slave. Under what circumstances? When all of them are equivalent. But if the mamzer was a disciple of a sage and a high priest was an 'am ha'ares [in context: ignorant of the Torah], the mamzer who is a disciple of a sage takes precedence over a high priest who is an 'am ha'ares.

T. 2:10 A high priest anointed with oil takes precedence over one dedicated through many garments, and the one dedicated through many garments takes precedence over the priest anointed for battle, and the priest anointed for battle takes precedence over the prefect, and the prefect takes precedence over the head of the weekly course [of the priests, who take care of the cult in a given week], and the head of the priestly course takes precedence over the head of the court. And the head of the court takes precedence over the auditor [superintendent over the cashiers (amarkal)], and the auditor [superintendent over the cashiers] takes precedence over the treasurer, And the treasurer takes precedence over an ordinary priest. And an ordinary priest takes precedence over a Levite. And a Levite takes precedence over an Israelite. And an Israelite takes precedence over a mamzer. And a mamzer takes precedence over a Netin. And a Netin takes precedence over a proselyte. And a proselyte takes precedence over a freed slave. Under what circumstances? When all are equivalent [in other respects]. But if the mamzer was a disciple of a sage and a high priest was an *'am ha'ares*, the mamzer who is a disciple of a sage takes precedence over a high priest who is an *'am ha'ares* [M. Hor. 3:8]. For it is said, "She is more precious than jewels" (Prov. 3:15) — that is, [more precious] than a high priest who enters into the innermost chamber of the sanctuary.

II. Analysis: The Problematics of the Topic, Horayot

What links the individual to the community, so assigning to the collectivity the consequence of private behavior? Here we turn to the matter of where and how the public bears responsibility for private, individual conduct — collective guilt for individual action. The individual is subsumed within the community when his action results from a common misconception fostered by the community's representative agencies. What triggers the application of the collective penalty provided by the halakhah of Horayot is reliance upon the community's court. He who relies on himself is liable, and he who relies on the court is exempt. Here is a case, then, in which "he told me to do it" represents a valid claim; the case is carefully restricted. The halakhah ordinarily does not accept such a claim, as we noted in the explicit statement that ordinarily no one can blame a third party for damages that he does, with the allegation that so-and-so told me to do it:

> Even though [the defendant] pays off [the plaintiff], he is not forgiven until he seeks [forgiveness] from [the plaintiff]. He who says, "Blind my eye," "Cut off my hand," "Break my leg" — [the one who does so] is liable. [If he added,] "... on condition of being exempt," [the one who does so] is liable [anyhow]. "Tear my cloak," "Break my jar," [the one who does so] is liable. [If he added,] "... on condition of being exempt," [the one who does so] is exempt. "Do it to Mr. So-and-so, on condition of being exempt," he [who does so] is liable, whether this is to his person or to his property.
>
> M. B.Q. 8:7

When, then, does the person who does a deed validly assign guilt to a third party?

It is when the court speaks in the name of the Torah — erroneously; but even here, the conditions under which such a claim may register are narrowly defined. The only case in which the community at large does not deliberately violate the Torah and incur the penalty of death now and the loss of eternity at the last judgment involves erroneous instruction on the part of the court. Then, when an individual sins in ignorance, he is exempt from penalty, having relied on the court. Even though an individual knows the law, if he relies upon the court, he is exempt. The court is liable. But the error of the court must pertain to details, not to the basic rule, which the court is expected to know. The individual, as much as the community, bears responsibility to know the Torah's explicit laws. Inadvertent errors in detail based on court instruction alone allow the individual to assign guilt to the community at large. And then Scripture then provides for a means of expiating the collective sin. But inadvertence affects both the community and the court, so a range of possibilities comes under consideration, e.g., if the court gave an incorrect decision inadvertently, and the entire community followed their instruction and did the thing in error, if the court gave an incorrect decision deliberately, but the community, following their instruction, did the thing in error inadvertently, if the court gave incorrect instruction inadvertently, and the community followed their instruction and did the thing in error deliberately, and so on. So much for the court and community.

What about unwitting sin carried out by the two other institutions of politics and public policy, the high priest and the ruler? These two also fall into the class of the community at large. Here too, inadvertent sin is wiped away by an appropriate offering, the bullock in the present case. Then the issue concerns whether the priest or ruler erroneously decided and acted by himself or did so with the community. Then the same rules that govern a mistaken decision taken by the court come into play. As to the ruler or high priest, a sequence of situations is worked out: what offering pertains to an anointed priest who sinned upon leaving office, so too a ruler; what do we do with one who sinned before appointment and then were appointed?

The specification of the beasts that are required clearly takes for granted a code that links animals of a given type to deeds of a specified classification, thus: an individual brings a female lamb or a female goat [Lev. 4:28, 32] a ruler brings a male goat [Lev. 4:23], and an anointed [high priest] and a court bring a bullock [M. 1:5, 2:1]. But in the case of idolatry, the individual, ruler, and anointed [high priest] bring a female goat [Num. 15:27]. And the court brings a bullock and a goat.

III. Interpretation: Religious Principles of Horayot

What we address, therefore, is the problem of the individual and the community, private sin and collective guilt. To understand the particular problem solved in the halakhah of Horayot, we must step back and consider the context in which the legal texts at hand find their place, that is to say, where and how Israelites individually atone for sin or crime so as to regain that relationship with God that will lead to resurrection beyond the grave and to eternal life. Here the halakhah legislates for the radically-isolated individual, that is to say, the individual who bears whole and sole responsibility for what he has done. The purpose of the halakhah then is to secure for that individual eternal life through the expiation of guilt or sin incurred in this life. That motive is made explicit as follows:

> [When] he was ten cubits from the place of stoning, they say to him, "Confess," for it is usual for those about to be put to death to confess. For whoever confesses has a share in the world to come. For so we find concerning Achan, to whom Joshua said, "My son, I pray you, give glory to the Lord, the God of Israel, and confess to him, [and tell me now what you have done; hide it not from me.] And Achan answered Joshua and said, Truly have I sinned against the Lord, the God of Israel, and thus and thus I have done" (Josh. 7:19). And how do we know that his confession achieved atonement for him? For it is said, "And Joshua said, Why have you troubled us? The Lord will trouble you this day" (Josh. 7:25) — This day you will be troubled, but you will not be troubled in the world to come. And if he does not know how to confess, they say to him, "Say as follows: 'Let my death be atonement for all of my transgressions.'"
>
> M. Sanhedrin 6:2A–D

The case of Achan suffices to make the point: paying the penalty in this age secures resurrection, judgment, and the life of the world to come in the age that will follow.

Accordingly we focus on the individual and his crime, punishment, and rehabilitation before God. Oft-times the court, sometimes the Temple, and occasionally God all collaborate to secure expiation of sin in this life, so that the individual will rise from the grave and stand in judgment and enter the eternal life. The system moreover works out the distinction between deliberate and inadvertent sin or crime, so a complete picture of the process by which rebellion against God is punished in its way, inadvertent sin in its manner. When it comes to the community at large, deliberate sin is dealt with, as I shall point out in a moment. But what of the interstices between public and personal sin or crime? There, as we shall now see, the aggadah remains remarkably silent, but the halakhah sets forth a systematic and cogent statement, entirely coherent with the larger systemic message.

Let us first consider how the system deals with individual and collective sin, encompassing private persons and all Israel. Only then the lacuna filled by the halakhah before us will come into view. The distinction between the private person and the public entity emerges in the doctrine of last things. The two principal components of the Oral Torah's eschatology — [1] resurrection and judgment, [2] the world to come and eternal life — are laid out in sequence, first involving the individual, then community. First comes the resurrection of individuals, and, with it, judgment of individuals one by one. Then, those chosen for life having been identified, "the world to come" takes place, and that final restoration of perfection, involving all Israel in place of Adam, lasts forever. Israel forms the cohort of those chosen for life, and Israelites are restored to life in the Land of Israel. That sequence suggests a single, uninterrupted narrative of last things, while in general, passages that concern themselves with resurrection do not ordinarily join together with composites that deal with the world to come. While mutually complementary, each of the two components of eschatology in the Oral Torah defines its distinctive focus.

The basic logic of the system requires the doctrine of personal resurrection, so that the life of this world may go onward to the next. We have already seen how the entire system of criminal justice, involving corporal and capital punishment, revolves around the conception of life beyond the grave, which justifies punishing sinners or criminals in this world so that they may be fully at one with God at the resurrection and the last judgment. Indeed, without the conception of life beyond the grave the system as a whole yields a mass of contradictions and anomalies: injustice to the righteous, prosperity to the wicked, never recompensed. Without resurrection and judgment, the system cannot account for the very being of the private person. That explains why at one point after another, the path to the future passes through, and beyond, the grave and the judgment that, for all Israel with few exceptions, leads to eternity. The principal continues and yields interest, or punishment may take place in this world, while eternal punishment goes onward as well, especially for the trilogy of absolute sins, idolatry, incest (or fornication) and murder, capped by gossip. But how all of this squares with the conception of "all Israel" that transcends individual Israelites remains to be seen.

A simple approach may address the logical relationship of the two components, the personal (Israel) and the public (Israelite). "Israel," sometimes refers to the entire community, the holy people, and other times speaks of the individual Israelite. But each component requires articulation within its own framework. When "Israel" in a composition stands for the individual Israelite, "Israel" as the holy people rarely intervenes. But when a passage clearly refers to the entirety of "Israel," the people, the individual Israelite (except for saints such as Abraham) rarely plays a role. So too, sin characterizes the attitude of all Israel and of individual Israelites, and while sin bears a single meaning in both settings, rebellion, its specific valence requires articulation and definition particular to each. That fact is demonstrated by the diverse penalties — different animal offerings — assigned to each category. So too, when we examine the principal components of the doctrine of eschatology, which means, the account of the ultimate restoration of creation to its initial perfection, we deal [1] with Israel meaning the Israelite and then [2] with Israel meaning the people. The identification of "Israel" as the Israelite as the focus of resurrection and judgment proves equally logical. "Israel" the holy people, by contrast, never dies. It is an enduring component of humanity, the part of humanity that knows God through God's own self-manifestation in the Torah the sector of mankind that accepts the law of the Torah as the will of God. This Israel, integral to the perfection of creation, cannot die any more than God can. Then to Israel the people, resurrection categorically does not pertain.

True, judgment does. But for Israel the people judgment is not left to the end of days, when the dead will rise from their graves. For holy Israel judgment takes place in this world and in this age. The Written Torah laid down the principle that Israel suffers for its sins, and everything that has happened since the closure of the Written Torah only confirms that principle. The very continuation of Scripture beyond the Pentateuch and the account of the inheritance of the Land makes that point, as we noted earlier. Not only so, but the very heart of the doctrine of paradigm against historical time — the explanation of Israel's subjugation to the gentiles and their idolatry — carries within itself a profound statement about Israel's identity, its enduring presence, from this age to the world to come, without interruption. Israel is judged and suffers its punishment in the here and now. That conviction animates the entire theological system before us. Then that same Israel, the never-dying people, emerges in the world to come fully at one with God. Indeed, that is the meaning of the advent of the world to come: "today if all Israel will it," "today if all Israel keeps a single Sabbath." To Israel the holy people, the resurrection of the dead therefore bears no categorical relevance. The advent of the world to come and eternal life bears its own meaning for Israel the holy people. To Israel the Israelite, the resurrection of the dead forms the beginning of the restoration of Eden, now meaning, the restoration of Israel to the Land of Israel, as we have noted many times.

As it happens, the documents of the Oral Torah tend to sustain the distinction just now set forth. The sources that deal with resurrection rarely refer to the world to come, except as an ordinal consequence of resurrection. And when it comes to speak of resurrection, the Oral Torah rarely speaks of Holy Israel, but nearly always addresses Israel the Israelite. Along these same lines, gentiles occur only as a collectivity, non-Israel, and rarely as individuals, except in a special case of a gentile who had a special relationship with Israel, such as Balaam. Nearly all proofs in the Talmud, for example, for the facticity of resurrection invoke the metaphor of individual, not collective life; even with the opportunity near at hand, in the very hermeneutics of the discourse, not a single one in the sizable exercise in Bavli-tractate Sanhedrin Chapter Eleven points to the eternity of holy Israel as evidence, in Scripture, for the resurrection of the dead. Most cases, most analogies, most arguments appeal to the private person. And, concomitantly, the sources that address the world to come ordinarily refer to all Israel, speaking of the Israelite only in the setting of the beginning of the age that will not end. The Israelite is subsumed within, though never obliterated by, all Israel. To be sure, we shall note that the promise of "the life of the world to come" addresses individual Israelites, whose conduct dictates their ultimate destination; but there, implicit is the intervention of the last judgment, which assures the correct reward or punishment.

The logic of the halakhah dictates that Israel, not only individual Israelites, answer for sins or crimes committed by the holy people as a whole. That logic is expressed in the key-statement, "All Israel has a portion in the world to come," so that being part of holy Israel carries the promise of resurrection and eternal life. Individuals secure their position in Israel by atoning for sin, paying the penalties that are specified in Sanhedrin-Makkot, Shebuot, and Keritot. As we now realize, having paid those penalties, the sinner or criminal enjoys the certainty of rising from the grave, standing in judgment, and entering the world to come. But when the halakhah thinks of Israel, it addresses not only individuals but the entirety of the community: Israel, not merely Israelites, form that community that God called to Sinai to form the kingdom of priests and the holy people. And all Israel is subject to judgment.

The Written Torah leaves no doubt about the penalties inflicted upon deliberately-sinful Israel: loss of the Land and exile. The narrative from Genesis through Kings — the Authorized History — fully spells out the meaning of national sin and exile. To that set of facts, the Oral Torah, for its part, contributes a separate consideration: the disposition of a sinful (idolatrous) community. The law calls that collectivity to judgment before the court of seventy-one members such entities that sin collectively as the community formed by a sinful town, one that goes over to idolatry:

> (1) They judge a tribe, a false prophet [Deut. 18:20], and a high priest, only on the instructions of a court of seventy-one members. (2) They bring forth [the army] to wage a war fought by choice only on the instructions of a court of seventy-one. (3) They make additions to the city [of Jerusalem] and to the courtyards [of the Temple] only on the instructions of a court of seventy-one. (4) They set up sanhedrins for the tribes only on the instructions of a court of seventy-one. (5) They declare a city to be "an apostate City" [Deut. 13:12ff.] only on the instructions of a court of seventy-one.
>
> Mishnah-tractate Sanhedrin 1:5

Deliberately committed sins by the community at large — a tribe, a town — provoke judgment by the great Sanhedrin, and the penalty for articulate rebellion against God, e.g., through idolatry, is the destruction of the entire community, which, furthermore, loses its portion in the world to come:

> The townsfolk of an apostate town have no portion in the world to come, as it is said, "Certain base fellows [sons of Belial] have gone out from the midst of thee and have drawn away the inhabitants of their city" (Deut. 13:14). And they are not put to death unless those who misled the [town] come from that same town and from that same tribe, and unless the majority is misled, and unless men did the misleading. [If] women or children misled them, of if a minority of the town was misled, or if those who misled the town came from outside of it, lo, they are treated as individuals [and not as a whole town], and they [thus] require [testimony against them] by two witnesses, and a statement of warning, for each and every one of them. This rule is more strict for individuals than for the community: for individuals are out to death by stoning. Therefore their property is saved. But the community is put to death by the sword, Therefore their property is lost.
>
> M. Sanhedrin 11:4

So much for the sanctions imposed for collective guilt that is deliberately incurred, e.g., by an entire tribe that willfully and knowingly violates the law or a city that all together opts for idolatry. But how about the other classification of collective sin, namely, sin collectively committed that is inadvertent, not deliberate? That is the subject of Horayot, which defines the occasion for inadvertent sin on the part of the entire community and specifies the appropriate penalty, which, as with Keritot, takes the form of an offering.

What is at stake in the halakhah of Horayot, it is not so much the distinction between the community and the individual as the interrelationship of the Israelite with the embodiment of Israel in the high priest or the ruler or the court, the three foci of politics that serve to govern Israel and inflict the this-worldly sanctions that pertain. When the halakhah deals with the deliberate sin or crime of the individual, it inflicts capital or corporal punishment, as the case requires. When the halakhah deals with the deliberate sin or crime of the individual or of the community, it for the most part falls silent: God intervenes, and we have little halakhah that spells out the rules for divine intervention: we know who is subject to extirpation but not how extirpation is imposed upon the individual, and only a handful of rules pertain to how extermination or exile is imposed upon the community.

Since the halakhah addresses the inner life of Israel and the aggadah its public and manifest affairs, we may make sense of the presentation at hand. In Horayot the halakhah fills a gap left by the aggadah in its presentation of man's fate in relationship to the community's collective destiny. The aggadah provides a full account of what happens to the individual at the end of days, the resurrection of the dead and the last judgment constituting the focus of discussion. The aggadah further offers a fine and detailed picture of what happens to the Israel that collectively enters the world to come, all those who pass judgment, having accepted the Lord as the one God. But what about the interplay between the individual and the community as represented by its embodiments in the court, monarch, and priesthood? There in the aggadah I find nothing, in the halakhah, everything.

What sages wished to say through the halakhah of Horayot is, when it comes to deeds performed in good faith by the individual at the instance of the community and its authorities, the community, not the individual, bears collective guilt, and the individual is atoned for within the offerings of the community at large. And, since that is the distinctive message of the present halakhah, once more, we realize, it is only through the halakhah before us that the sages can have made the statement that their system demanded: inadvertent error by court, priest, and ruler, representing and implicating the community at large, is to be expiated by offerings appropriately specific to the circumstance. Horayot in its way bears all of the messages that Sanhedrin-Makkot or Keritot, respectively, delivers in its manner: an exact match between inadvertent sin or crime, whether personal or public, and the animal offering that expiates the sin or crime, accomplishes Israel's atonement. On that basis, eternal life must come to (nearly) all Israel, one by one and all together.

9.

TRACTATE ABODAH ZARAH

I. An Outline of the Halakhah of Abodah Zarah

We turn from the halakhah governing Israel's inner social order to the halakhah that mediates between Israel and the world beyond. That world, by the definition of the halakhah of the Oral Torah, forms an undifferentiated realm of idolatry, and the halakhah takes as its task the negotiation between Israelites and the pagan world in which they live: how are they to conduct themselves in accord with the Torah so that at no point and in no way do they give support to idolatry and so betray the one and only God, him who made himself known in the Torah. In its basic exposition of the theme of idolatry, the halakhah rests squarely on the foundations of Scripture, supplying rules and regulations that carry out the fundamental Scriptural commandments about destroying idols and everything that has to do with idolatry. But the halakhah so formulates matters as to transform the entire topic of idolatry into an essay on Israel's relationships with the gentiles, who, as I said, are idolaters by definition. Here too, as we shall see, the halakhah addresses the condition of individuals, the ordinary life of common folk, rather than concentrating on the situation of all Israel, viewed as a collective entity. The halakhah therefore tends to find its problem in the condition of the private person and in the interiorities of his life in the Israelite community.

For the Written Torah the community at large forms the focus of the law, and idolatry is not to be negotiated with by the collectivity of holy Israel. In its Land Israel is to wipe out idolatry, even as a memory. Scripture is clear that Israel is to obliterate all mention of idols (Ex. 23:13), not bow down to gentiles' gods or serve them but overthrow them and break them into pieces (Ex. 23:24): "You shall break down their altars and dash in pieces their pillars and hew down their Asherim and burn their graven images with fire" (Dt. 7:5). Israelites are commanded along these same lines:

> The graven images of their gods you shall burn with fire; you shall not covet the silver or the gold that is on them or take it for yourselves, lest you be ensnared by it; for it is an abomination to the Lord your God. And you shall not bring an abominable thing into your house and become accused like it (Dt. 7:25–26).
>
> You shall surely destroy all the places where the nations whom you shall dispossess served their gods, upon the high mountains and upon the hills and under every green tree; you shall tear down their altars and dash in pieces their pillars and burn their Asherim with fire; you shall hew down the graven images of their gods and destroy their name out of that place (Dt. 12:2–3).

Accordingly, so far as the Written Torah supplies the foundations for the treatment of the matter by the Oral Torah, the focus of discourse concerning the gentiles is idolatry. Scripture's halakhah does not contemplate Israel's co-existing, in the land, with gentiles and their idolatry.

But the halakhah speaks to a world that is not so simple. The Land belongs to Israel, but gentiles live there too — and run things. And Israel no longer forms a coherent collectivity but a realm made up of individuals, with their distinctive and particular interests. The halakhah of the Oral Torah commences its treatment of the same subject with the opposite premise: gentiles live side by side (whether or not in the Land of Israel) with Israelites, and Israelites have to sort out the complex problems of co-existence with idolatry. And that co-existence involves not whole communities, the People, Israel, and the peoples, whoever they may be, but individuals, this Israelite living side by side with that gentile.

Not only so, but the Oral Torah uses the occasion of idolatry to contemplate a condition entirely beyond the imagination of Scripture, which is the hegemony of idolatrous nations and the subjugation of holy Israel. The Oral Torah, fully considered, makes of the discussion of idolatry the occasion for the discussion of Israel's place among the nations of the world and of Israel's relationships with gentiles. Furthermore, the Oral Torah's theory of who Israel is finds its context in the contrast with the gentiles. The meeting point with the Written Torah is defined by the indicative trait of the gentiles, which is their idolatry; that is all that matters about them. But, as we shall now see, while the halakhah of the Oral Torah expounds the local details of everyday relationships with gentiles, the aggadah of the same Oral Torah vastly expands the range of thought and takes up the more profound issues of gentile dominance in this age, Israel's subjugated position, the power of the idolaters, and the like. So once more, we shall observe, the aggadah deals with the world at large, the halakhah, the world at home.

Specifically, the halakhah of the Oral Torah deals first with commercial relationships, second, matters pertaining to idols, and finally to the particular prohibition of wine part of which has served as a libation to an idol. The whole is regularized and ordered. There are relationships with gentiles that are absolutely prohibited, particularly occasions of idol-worship; as we shall see, the halakhah recognizes that these are major commercial events. When it comes to commerce with idolaters Israelites may not sell or in any way benefit from certain things, may sell but may not utilize certain others, and may sell and utilize yet others. Here, we see immediately, the complex and systematic mode of thought that governs the Oral Torah's treatment of the topic vastly transcends the rather simple conception that animates Scripture's discussion of the same matter. There are these unstated premises within the halakhah: [1] what a gentile is not likely to use for the worship of an idol is not prohibited; [2] what may serve not as part of an idol but as an appurtenance thereto is prohibited for Israelite use but permitted for Israelite commerce; [3] what serves idolatry is prohibited for use and for benefit. In reflecting upon relationships with the gentiles, meaning, idolaters, the Oral Torah moreover takes for granted a number of facts. These turn out to yield a single generalization: gentiles are assumed routinely to practice bestiality, murder, and fornication. Further negative stereotypes concerning idolaters occur. The picture of the halakhah finds its context in the larger theory of idolatry and its ephemeral hegemony that the aggadah sets forth, as we shall note in the concluding unit of this chapter.

i. *Commercial Relationships with Gentiles*

A. *Festivals and Fairs*

M. 1:1 Before the festivals of gentiles for three days it is forbidden to do business with them. (1) To lend anything to them or to borrow anything from them. (2) To lend money to them or to borrow money from them. (3) To repay them or to be repaid by them.

T. 1:1 Under what circumstances [M. A.Z. 1:1A]? In the case of recurrent festivals, but in the case of festivals which do not recur, prohibited is only that day alone. And even though they have said, It is forbidden to do business with them [M. A.Z. 1:1A] — under what circumstances? In the case of something which lasts. But in the case of something which does not last, it is permitted. And even in the case of something which lasts, [if] one bought or sold it, lo, this is permitted.

T. 1:2 A person should not do business with a gentile on the day of his festival, nor should one talk frivolously, nor should one ask after his welfare in a situation which is taken into account. But if one happened to come across him in a routine way, he asks after his welfare with all due respect.

T. 1:3 They ask after the welfare of gentiles on their festivals for the sake of peace. Israelite workmen who were working with a gentile — in the case of an Israelite's household, it is permitted. In the case of a gentile's household, it is prohibited. And even though one has finished work on his utensils before his festival, he should not deliver them to him on the day of his festival, because this increases his rejoicing [on his festival].

M. 1:2 Before their festivals it is prohibited, but after their festivals it is permitted

M. 1:3 (1) On the day on which [a gentile] shaves off his beard and lock of hair, (2) on the day on which he came up safely from an ocean voyage, (3) on the day on which he got out of prison. And a gentile who made a banquet for his son — it is prohibited for only that day, and in regard to only that individual alone [to enter into business relationships of any sort, as listed at M. 1:1].

T. 1:4 [If] one town celebrates, and another town does not celebrate, one people celebrates, and another people does not celebrate, one family celebrates, and another family does not celebrate — those who celebrate are subject to the stated prohibitions, and those who do not celebrate are permitted in regard to them. As to *Calendae*, even though everyone observes the festival, it is permitted only with regard to the actual rite of sacrifice itself. *Saturnalia is* the day on which they took power. *Kratesis is* the day of the anniversary of the emperors [cf. M. A.Z. I:3B–C]. The day of each and every emperor — lo, it is tantamount to a public festival.

M. 1:4 A city in which there is an idol — [in the area] outside of it — it is permitted [to do business]. [If] an idol was outside of it, [in the area] inside it is permitted. What is the rule as to going to that place? When the road is set aside for going to that place only, it is prohibited. But if one is able to take that same road to some other place, it is permitted. A town in which there is an idol, and there were in it shops which were adorned and shops which were not adorned — those which are adorned are prohibited, but those which are not adorned are permitted.

T. 1:6 [If] there is a fair in the town, into the town it is prohibited [to go], but outside of the town it is permitted. And if it is outside of the town, outside of the town it is forbidden [to go], but into the town it is permitted [M. A.Z. 1:4A–C]. And shops which are decorated under any circumstances, lo, these are forbidden [M. A.Z. 1:4I]. [If] a person is passing in a caravan from one place to another, and enters a town in which a fair is going on, he need not scruple that he may appear to be going to the fair [M. A.Z. I:4E–F].

T. 1:7 A fair which the empire held, or which a province held, or which the leaders of a province held, is permitted. Prohibited is only a fair honoring an idol alone.

T. 1:8 They go to a gentiles' fair and accept healing from them — healing involving property, but not healing involving the person. And they do (not) purchase from them fields, vineyards, boy-slaves, and girl-slaves, because he is as one who rescues these from their power. And one writes and deposits [a deed] in an archive. A priest contracts uncleanness [in connection with redemption of land] to give testimony and to engage in a law-suit against them abroad. And just as he contracts uncleanness in connection with affairs abroad, so he surely contracts uncleanness in a graveyard [in the same matter]. And [a priest] contracts uncleanness [if it is] to study Torah or to marry a woman.

T. 1:9 Merchants who pushed up the day of a fair or who pushed back the day of a fair — it is permitted. Prohibited is only the time of the fair alone.

T. 1:15 Israelites who are going to a fair — it is permitted to do business with them. And on [their] return, it is [likewise] permitted. Gentiles who are going to their debauchery — it is forbidden to do business with them. And on [their] return, it is permitted. For [the fair] is tantamount to idolatry, which [on their return trip] its worshippers have abandoned. And as to an Israelite, whether it is on the way there or on the way back, it is prohibited.

T. 1:16A. One should not travel with a caravan [en route to an idolatrous fair], even to go out, even to go before it, even to be with it when it gets dark, even if one is fearful because of gentiles, thugs, or an evil spirit, since it is said, "You shall not go after other gods" (Deut. 6:14).

B. 1:4AA–F/12A IF WHILE SOMEONE IS IN FRONT OF AN IDOL, HE GOT A SPLINT IN HIS FOOT, HE SHOULD NOT BEND OVER TO REMOVE IT, BECAUSE HE LOOKS AS THOUGH HE IS BOWING DOWN TO THE IDOL. BUT IF IT DOES NOT LOOK THAT WAY, HE IS PERMITTED TO DO SO. IF HIS MONEY GOT SCATTERED IN FRONT OF AN IDOL, HE SHOULD NOT BOW DOWN TO PICK IT UP, BECAUSE HE LOOKS AS THOUGH HE IS BOWING DOWN TO THE IDOL. BUT IF IT DOES NOT LOOK THAT WAY, HE IS PERMITTED TO DO SO. IF A SPRING FLOWS IN FRONT OF AN IDOL, ONE SHOULD NOT BEND DOWN TO DRINK, BECAUSE HE LOOKS AS THOUGH HE IS BOWING DOWN TO THE IDOL. BUT IF IT DOES NOT LOOK THAT WAY, HE IS PERMITTED TO DO SO. ONE SHOULD NOT PUT HIS MOUTH ON THE MOUTH OF HUMAN FIGURES WHICH SERVE AS FOUNTAINS IN TOWNS IN ORDER TO DRINK WATER, BECAUSE HE MAY APPEAR TO BE KISSING THE IDOL.

B. *Objects Prohibited Even in Commerce*

M. 1:5 What are the things that are forbidden to sell to gentiles? (1) fir cones, (2) white figs, (3) and their stalks, (4) frankincense, and (5) a white cock. And as to everything else, [if] they are left without specification [as to their proposed use], it is permitted, but [if] they are specified [for use for idolatry], it is prohibited.

T. 1:21 One sells [the stated substances] to a merchant, but does not sell [them] to a householder [M. A.Z. 1:5A]. But if the merchant was suspect [of idolatrous practices], it is prohibited to sell [them] to him. One sells them pigs and does not scruple that he might offer them up to an idol. One sells him wine and does not scruple that he might offer it as a libation to an idol. But if he explicitly stated to him [that his intent was to make use of what he was buying for idolatry], it is prohibited to sell him even water, even salt [M. A.Z. 1:5F].

T. 2:1A. They purchase a beast from them for a trial and return it to them that entire day. And just as they purchase from them a beast for a trial and return it to them that entire day so they purchase from them (a beast) slave-boys and slave-girls for a trial and return them to them that entire day. So long as you have the right to return [what is purchased] to an Israelite, you have the right to return [the same thing] to a gentile. [If] you have not got the right to return [what is purchased] to an Israelite, you have not got the right to return [the same thing] to a gentile. An Israelite sells his beast to a gentile on the stipulation that the latter slaughter it, with an Israelite supervising him while the gentile slaughters the beast [so as to make sure it is not turned into a sacrifice to an idol]. They purchase from [gentiles] cattle for an offering, and need not scruple on the count of [the gentile's having practiced] bestiality or suffered bestiality, or having set aside the beast for idolatrous worship, or having actually worshipped [the beast].

M. 1:6 In a place in which they are accustomed to sell small cattle to gentiles, they sell them. In a place in which they are accustomed not to sell [small cattle] to them, they do not sell them. And in every locale they do not sell them large cattle, calves, or foals, whether whole or lame.

T. 2:2 And just as they do not sell them a large domesticated beast, so they do not sell them a large wild beast [M. A.Z. 1:6B]. And also in a situation in which they do not sell them a small domesticated beast, they do not sell them a small wild beast.

Y. 1:6 III. 2 [If] one transgressed [the law in a locale in which it is prohibited to sell such beasts to gentiles] and sold [such a beast to a gentile], do they impose a fine upon him [so depriving the Israelite of the use of the proceeds]? Just as the sages impose such a penalty on the Israelite in the case of the violation of a law [e.g., deliberately blemishing a firstling so that the priest has no claim to it], so they impose a penalty on him for the violation of a custom [operative in a given locale].

M. 1:7 They do not sell them (1) bears or (2) lions, or (3) anything which is a public danger. They do not build with them (1) a

basilica, (2) scaffold, (3) stadium, or (4) judges' tribunal. But they build with them (5) public bathhouses or (6) private ones. [Once] they reach the vaulting on which they set up an idol, it is forbidden [to help build any longer].

T. 2:3 And just as they do not sell [the listed animals] to them, they also do not exchange them with them, either bad ones for good ones, or good ones for bad ones; either lame ones for healthy ones, or healthy ones for lame ones.

M. 1:8 And they do not make ornaments for an idol: (1) necklaces, (2) earrings, or (3) finger rings. They do not sell them produce as yet unplucked. But one may sell it once it has been harvested.

T. 2:4 They do not sell them either a sword or the paraphernalia for a sword. And they do not polish a sword for them. And they do not sell them stocks, neck-chains, ropes, or iron chains, scrolls, phylacteries, or *mezuzot*. All the same are the gentile and the Samaritan. They sell them fodder which has been cut down, grain which has been harvested, and trees which have been picked.

T. 2:7 He who goes up into gentiles' amphitheaters, if he was going about on account of the service of the state's requirements, lo, this is permitted. If one takes account [of what is happening therein], lo, this is for bidden. He who sits in an amphitheater [e.g., where gladiators are fighting], lo, this one is guilty of bloodshed. They may go to stadiums because [an Israelite] will cry out in order to save the life of the loser, and to the performance in a camp on account of the task of preserving order in the province. But if one takes account of what is happening [in the entertainment], lo, this is forbidden.

M. 1:9 Even in the situation concerning which they have ruled [that they may] rent, it is not for use as a residence that they ruled that it is permitted, because he brings an idol into it, as it is said, "You shall not bring an abomination into your house" (Deut. 7:26). And in no place may one rent him a bathhouse, since it would be called by his [the Israelite's] name [and its use on the Sabbath will be attributed to the Israelite].

T. 2:8 They do not rent to them houses, fields, or vineyards. And they do not provide for them fields on the basis of sharecropping [a variable or fixed proportion of the crop, respectively] or of contracting to raise beasts. All the same are a gentile and a Samaritan.

T. 2:9 Here and there an Israelite should not rent out his house to a gentile, because it is certain that the latter will bring an idol into it [M. A.Z. 1:9A–C]. But they may rent out to them stables, storehouses, and inns, even though it is certain that the gentile will bring into it an idol.

M. 2:1 They do not leave cattle in gentiles' inns, because they are suspect in regard to bestiality. And a woman should not be alone with them, because they are suspect in regard to fornication. And a man should not be alone with them, because they are suspect in regard to bloodshed. An Israelite girl should not serve as a midwife to a gentile woman, because she serves to

bring forth a child for the service of idolatry. But a gentile woman may serve as a midwife to an Israelite girl. An Israelite girl should not give suck to the child of a gentile woman. But a gentile woman may give suck to the child of an Israelite girl, when it is by permission.

T. 3:1 They leave cattle in Samaritans' inns, even male [cattle] with women, and female [cattle] with men, and female [cattle] with women. And they hand over cattle to their shepherds, and they hand over a child to him to teach him reading and to teach him a craft, and to be alone with him. An Israelite girl serves as a midwife and gives suck to the child of a Samaritan woman. And a Samaritan woman serves as midwife and gives suck to an Israelite child.

T. 3:2 They do not leave cattle in gentiles' inns [M. A.Z. 2:1A], even male cattle with men, and female cattle with women, because a male may bring a male [beast] over him, and a female may do the same with a female beast, and it goes without saying, males with women, and females with men. And they do not hand over cattle to their shepherds. And they do not hand a child over to him to teach him reading, to teach him a craft, or to be alone with him.

T. 3:3 An Israelite girl should not give suck to the child of a gentile woman [M. A.Z. 2:1J], because she raises a child for the service of idolatry [cf. M. A.Z. 2:1H]. But a gentile woman may give suck to the child of an Israelite girl, when it is by permission [M. A.Z. 2:1K]. An Israelite girl should not serve as a midwife to a gentile woman, because she serves to bring forth a child for the service of idolatry [M. A.Z. 2:1G–H].

M. 2:2 They accept from them healing for property, but not healing for the person.

T. 3:4 They accept from them healing as to matters of property, but not healing as to matters of the person [M. A.Z. 2:2A–B]. A gentile woman should not be called upon to cut out the foetus in the womb of an Israelite girl. And she should not give her a cup of bitters to drink, for they are suspect as to the taking of life. And an Israelite should not be alone with a gentile either in a bathhouse or in a urinal. [When] an Israelite goes along with a gentile, he puts him at his right hand, and he does not put him at his left hand.

T. 3:5 An Israelite who is getting a haircut from a gentile watches in the mirror [cf. M. A.Z. 2:2C–E]. [If it is] from a Samaritan, he does not watch in the mirror. They permitted the house of Rabban Gamaliel to look at themselves in the mirror, for they are close to the government.

T. 3:6 An Israelite who is giving a haircut to a gentile, when he has reached the forelock, removes his hands [from the hair and does not cut it off]. They purchase from a gentile scrolls, phylacteries, and mezuzot, so long as they are written properly.

T. 3:16 He who sells his slave to gentiles — [the slave] has gone forth free. And he requires a writ of emancipation from his first master. Whether he sold him to him or gave him to him as a gift, he has gone forth free.

And if not, he has not gone forth free, lest he has gone forth to a domain which is not a domain. He borrows money from a gentile on the strength of him. If the gentile did what the law requires [making acquisition], he has gone forth free. And if not, he has not gone forth free. [If] he took him in compensation for his debt, or if he fell to him under the law of the usurper, he has gone forth free. [If] one has inherited slaves from gentiles, before they have actually entered his domain, he is permitted to sell them to gentiles. Once they have actually entered his domain, he is prohibited from selling them to gentiles. And so you say in the case of wine which has served for a libation, which one has inherited: before it has come into one's domain, money received for it is permitted. Once it has come into one's domain, money received for it is prohibited.

T. 3:17 An Israelite and a gentile who made a purchase in partnership and went and made another purchase — he may not say to him, "You take the things which are in such-and-such a place in lieu of the first purchase, and I shall take the things which are in such-and-such a place in lieu of the second purchase." But he says to him, "You take the things which are in such-and-such a place, and I shall take the things which are in such-and-such a place." "In lieu of the first purchase, you take the things which are in such-and-such a place, and I shall take the things which are in such-and-such a place in lieu of the second purchase."

T. 3:18 He who sells his slave abroad — he has gone forth free. And he needs a writ of emancipation from his second master.

T. 3:19 He who sells his slave to a gentile fair — the money received for him is prohibited, and one must take it to the Salt Sea. And they force his master to redeem him, even at a hundred times the price received for him, and then he puts him out to freedom. You turn out to rule: He who does business at a gentile fair — in the case of a beast, it is to be hamstrung. In the case of clothing and utensils, they are left to rot. In the case of money and metal utensils, they are to be taken off to the Salt Sea. As to produce, that which is usually poured out is to be poured out. That which is usually burned is to be burned. That which is usually buried is to be buried.

M. 2:3 These things belonging to gentiles are prohibited, and the prohibition affecting them extends to deriving any benefit from them at all: (1) wine, (2) vinegar of gentiles which to begin with was wine, (3) Hadrianic earthenware, and (4) hides pierced at the heart. With those who are going to an idolatrous pilgrimage — it is prohibited to do business. With those that are coming back it is permitted.

T. 4:7 What are hides pierced at the heart [M. A.Z. 2:3B]? Any which is perforated at the heart [of the beast], and made into a kind of peephole. But if it is straight, it is permitted [M. A.Z. 2:3C].

T. 4:8 A. Pickled and stewed vegetables of gentiles, into which it is customary to put wine and vinegar, and Hadrianic earthenware [cf. M. A.Z. 2:3B, 2:6D] — the prohibition affecting them is a prohibition extending to deriving any benefit from them whatsoever. Sodden olives which are sold at the doors of bathhouses are prohibited for eating, but permitted so far as deriving benefit.

Y. 2:3 I. 2Gff. There are three types of wine [so far as the prohibition of gentiles' wine on the count of libation to idolatry is concerned]: [There is wine] that [an Israelite] assuredly saw a gentile offer up as a libation to an idol. This sort of wine imparts uncleanness of a severe sort, like a dead creeping thing. [There is] ordinary wine [of a gentile]. It is prohibited [for Israelite use or benefit]. But it does not impart uncleanness. [If an Israelite] deposited [wine] with [a gentile], sealed by a single seal, it is prohibited for drinking, but permitted for [other sorts of] gain [e.g., sale].

C. *Objects Prohibited For Use but Permitted in Commerce*

M. 2:4 Skins of gentiles and their jars, with Israelite wine collected in them — the prohibition affecting them does not extend to deriving benefit from them. Grape pits and grape skins belonging to gentiles if they are moist, they are forbidden. If they are dry, they are permitted. Fish brine and Bithynian cheese belonging to gentiles — the prohibition of them does not extend to deriving benefit from them.

T. 4:9 A water tank on wheels and a leather-bottle belonging to gentiles, with Israelite wine collected in them — [the wine] is prohibited for drinking, but available for other benefit [cf. M. A.Z. 2:4A, C].

T. 4:10 Skins belonging to gentiles which are scraped are permitted. Those which are sealed or covered with pitch are prohibited. [If] a gentile works it and pitches it, while an Israelite supervises him, one may collect wine or oil in it without scruple. Jars belonging to gentiles — new ones are permitted. Old ones which are old and rubbed are prohibited. And one in which a gentile collected water — [if] an Israelite filled out, an Israelite is permitted also to put wine or oil into it. And if a gentile collected wine in it, an Israelite fills it with water for three whole days, seventy-two hours. [Then] he may collect wine in it without scruple. And in one in which a gentile collected Israelite wine, pickling brine, or brine an Israelite is permitted to collect wine.

Y. 2:4 II:3 [If] a gentile has collected water in [jars], an Israelite [who wishes to make use of the same jars] puts water into them and then goes and puts wine into them and need not scruple. [If] a gentile collected brine or fish-brine in them, an Israelite may put wine into those same jars. [If] a gentile collected wine in them, an Israelite may put into them brine or fish-brine and then go and put wine into them, and he need not scruple.

M. 2:6 And what are things of gentiles which are prohibited, but the prohibition of which does not extend to deriving benefit from them? (1) milk drawn by a gentile without an Israelite's watching him; (2) their bread; and (3) their oil — (4) stewed and pickled [vegetables] into which it is customary to put wine and

vinegar; (5) minced fish; (6) brine without kilkit fish floating in it; (7) hileq fish, (8) drops of asafoetida, and (9) sal-conditum — lo, these are prohibited, but the prohibition affecting them does not extend to deriving benefit from them.

M. 2:7 These are things which [to begin with] are permitted for [Israelite] consumption. (1) milk which a gentile drew, with an Israelite watching him; (2) honey; (3) grape clusters, (even though they drip with moisture, they are not subject to the rule of imparting susceptibility to uncleanness as liquid); (4) pickled vegetables into which it is not customary to put wine or vinegar; (5) unminced fish; (6) brine containing fish; (7) a [whole] leaf of asafoetida, and (8) pickled olive cakes. Locusts which come form [the shopkeeper's] basket are forbidden. Those which come from the stock [of his shop] are permitted. And so is the rule for heave-offering.

T. 4:11 They purchase from gentiles grain, pulse, dried figs, garlic, and onions, under all circumstances, and they do not scruple on account of uncleanness. As to red berry of sumac, under all circumstances it is deemed unclean. As to cedar, under all circumstances it is deemed clean. A hunter is believed to testify, "This bird is unclean," "This bird is clean." An 'am ha'ares is believed to testify, "These pickled vegetables did I pickle in a state of cleanness, and I did not sprinkle liquids [capable of imparting susceptibility to uncleanness] upon them." But he is not believed to testify, "These fish I caught in a state of cleanness, and I did not shake the net over them." Their caper-fruit, leeks, liverwort, boiled water and parched corn [prepared by gentiles] are permitted. An egg roasted by them is prohibited. A loaf of bread which a gentile baked, not in the presence of an Israelite, and cheese which a gentile curdled, not in the presence of an Israelite, are prohibited. A loaf of bread which an Israelite baked, even though the gentile kneaded the dough, and cheese which an Israelite curdled, even though a gentile works it — lo, this is permitted. An Israelite may sit at the other side of his corral, and a gentile may milk the cows and bring the milk to him, and one does not scruple. What is unminced fish [M. A.Z. 2:7E]? Any in which the backbone and head are discernible. What is brine containing fish [M. A.Z. 2:7F]? Any in which one or two kilbit-fish are floating. A piece of meat on which there is a recognizable sign, whether it is on the whole of it or only part of it, and even if it is on only one out of a hundred — lo, this is permitted. Brine made by an expert, lo, this is permitted.

T. 4:12 Boiled wine and aromatic water — lo, these are prohibited because they begin as wine. Aromatic water in its natural condition — lo, this is permitted. Apple-wine which comes from storage, the storehouse, or a ship — lo, this is permitted. But if it is sold over the counter in the market, lo, this is prohibited, because it may be adulterated [with gentile wine or vinegar]. Locusts and pieces of meat which come from storage or from the storehouse or from a ship — lo, these are permitted. But if they are sold in a basket in front of a store, lo, they are prohibited, because they sprinkle them with wine so as to improve their appearance [M. A.Z. 2:7F–H].

T. 4:13 They purchase Bithynian cheese only from an expert. But seethed [cheese] is purchased from any source. They purchase drops of asafoetida only from an expert. But a leaf is purchased from any source [cf. M. A.Z. 2:6D8, 2:7D7]. They purchase wine in Syria only from an expert. And they purchase brine only from an expert, and a piece of meat lacking any mark only from an expert. But any of these may be eaten in the home of one who is not an expert, and one need not scruple on that account.

ii. *Idols*

A. *General Principles*

M. 3:1 Images are prohibited that have in its hand a staff, bird, or sphere.

M. 3:2 He who finds the shards of images — lo, these are permitted. [If] one found [a fragment] shaped like a hand or a foot, lo, these are prohibited, because objects similar to them are worshipped.

M. 3:3 He who finds utensils upon which is the figure of the sun, moon, or dragon, should bring them to the Salt Sea. One breaks them into pieces and throws the powder to the wind or drops them into the sea. Also: they may be made into manure, as it is said, "And there will cleave nothing of a devoted thing to your hand" (Dt. 13:18).

T. 5:2 A. A ring on which there is an idol — when it projects, it is prohibited for benefit. But if it does not project [outward from the ring], it is permitted for benefit. And one way or the other, it is prohibited to make a seal with it. And one on which there is no idol is permitted for benefit and permitted for use as a seal. A ring on which there is a seal is permitted for use as a seal. A ring, the seal of which is incised, is prohibited for use as a seal, because with it an image which projects is made. But it is permitted to put it on one's hand. And one, the seal of which projects, is permitted for use as a seal, because the seal which it makes is embedded [in the clay and does not project]. And it is forbidden to put it on one's hand. A ring on which there is a figure is permitted for use as a seal. The reptile-shaped gem which is made in the figure of a dragon is prohibited, and one on which a dragon is suspended — [if] one takes it off and throws it out, as to the rest [of the object], lo, this is permitted.

M. 3:5 Gentiles who worship hills and valleys — these [hills or valleys] are permitted, but what is on them is forbidden [for Israelite use], as it is said, "You shall not covet the silver or

gold that is upon them not take it." On what account is an *asherah* prohibited? Because it has been subject to manual labor, and whatever has been subject to manual labor is prohibited.

M. 3:6 He [the wall of] whose house was adjacent to [and also served as the wall of the temple of] an idol, and [whose house] fell down — it is forbidden to rebuild it. What should he then do? He pulls back within four cubits inside his own property and then rebuilds his house. [If there was a wall belonging] both to him and to [the temple of an] idol, it is judged to be divided half and half. The stones, wood, and mortar deriving from it impart uncleanness in the status of a dead creeping thing, for it is said, "You will utterly detest it" (Deut. 7:26).

T. 6:2 He who designates his house for an idol — the whole of it imparts uncleanness upon entry [to one who comes in]. And he who stands in it, it is as if he is standing in a temple of idolatry. If the public way cuts through it, however, unclean is only that path alone. He who sets up his house near a temple — the whole of it imparts uncleanness upon entry. [If someone else] set up [a temple] near his house, the whole of it does not impart uncleanness upon entry. But that wall [which is nearest to the idol] is deemed to be divided half and half [M. A.Z. 3:6E]. [If the house] fell down, however, it is permitted to rebuild it [If] one has rebuilt it, it has returned to its original condition. [If other people] rebuilt it, not the whole of it imparts uncleanness upon entry, but only that wall alone. It is deemed to be divided half and half. He who sells his house to an idol — the proceeds received for it are forbidden, and one has to bring them to the Salt Sea. But gentiles who forced someone and took over his house and set up an idol in it — the proceeds received for it are permitted. And one may write a deed in that regard and deposit it in the archives.

B. *The Asherah*

M. 3:7 There are three sorts of houses [so far as use as a shrine for idolatry is concerned]: (1) a house which was built to begin with for the purposes of idolatry — lo, this is prohibited. (2) [If] one stuccoed and decorated it for idolatry and renovated it, one removes the renovations. (3) [If] one brought an idol into it and took it out — lo, this is permitted. There are three sorts of stones: (1) a stone which one hewed to begin with for a pedestal — lo, this is forbidden. (2) [If] he set up an idol on [an existing] stone and then took it off, lo, this is permitted. There are three kinds of *asherahs*: (1) A tree which one planted to begin with for idolatry — lo, this is prohibited. (2) [If] he chopped it and trimmed it for idolatry, and it sprouted afresh, he may remove that which sprouted afresh. (3) [If] he set up an idol under it and then annulled it, lo, this is permitted.

T. 6:3 He who pokes his head and the greater part of his body into a temple containing an idol is unclean. A clay utensil, the contained airspace of which one has poked into a temple containing an idol, is unclean. Benches and chairs, the greater part of which one has poked into a temple containing an idol, are unclean.

M. 3:8 One should not sit in [an *asherah's*] shade, but if he sat in its shade, he is clean. And he should not pass underneath it, but if he passed underneath it, he is unclean. If it was overshadowing public domain, taking away property from public use, and one passed beneath it, he is clean. And they sow seeds underneath it in the rainy season, but not in the dry season. But as to lettuce, neither in the dry season nor in the rainy season [may one plant it there].

T. 6:8 Gentiles who worship hills and valleys [M. A.Z. 3:5A] — even though they [hills and valleys] are permitted, those who worship them are put to death by stoning. A man who is worshipped — even though he is permitted, those who worship him are put to death through stoning. And what is an asherah [M. A.Z. 3:7N]? It is any tree which gentiles worship and guard, and the produce of which they do not eat. They sow seeds underneath it in the rainy season, but not in the dry season. But as to lettuce. neither in the dry season nor in the rainy season [may one plant it there] [M. A.Z. 3:8C–E]. He who comes under it is as if he came into a temple of idolatry. But if the public way passed through it, lo, this is permitted [cf. M. A.Z. 3:8C].

M. 3:9 [If] one has taken pieces of wood from [an *asherah*], they are prohibited for benefit. [If] he lit a fire in the oven with them, if it is a new oven, it is to be overturned. If it is an old oven, it must be allowed to cool down. [If] he baked a loaf of bread in [the oven heated by the wood of an *asherah*], it is prohibited for benefit. [If] the loaf of bread was mixed up with other loaves of bread, all of them are prohibited as to benefit. [If] one took a piece of wood for a shuttle, it is forbidden for benefit. [If] he wove a garment with the shuttle, the garment is forbidden for benefit. [If] it was mixed up with other garments, and other garments with still others, all of them are forbidden for benefit.

M. 3:8 How does one desecrate [an *asherah*]? [If] one trimmed it or pruned it, took from it a branch or twig, even a leaf — lo, this constitutes desecration. [If] one has trimmed it for the good of [the tree], it remains forbidden. [If he trimmed it] not for the good of the tree, it is permitted.

T. 6:9 A. An Israelite who trimmed an asherah, whether it was for the good of the tree, or whether it was for his own good — it is prohibited. A gentile who trimmed an asherah — if it was for the good of the tree, the tree is prohibited, but he is permitted. If it was for his own good, one way or the other, it is prohibited [cf. M. A.Z. 3:10].

C. *The Merkolis*

M. 4:1 Three stones, one beside the other, beside a Merkolis statue, — those which appear to belong to it are forbidden, and those which do not appear to belong to it as permitted.

Y. 4:1 I:1 *[If an Israelite] put on the second stone [thus not completing the idol, and also slaughtered a beast before the incomplete idol, and the beast was the dam of an offspring that had been slaughtered on that day, or the offspring of a dam that had been slaughtered on that day, so that there are two transgressions in view, one, building an idol, the other, slaughtering a dam and its offspring on the same day], and they had warned [the Israelite] concerning violation of the law against slaughtering the dam and its offspring on the same day, [the Israelite] is given a flogging [on the count of violating the prohibition against slaughtering the dam and its offspring on the same day], [but on the count of idolatry he is not stoned to death.]*

M. 4:2 [If] one found on its head coins, clothing, or utensils, lo, these are permitted. [If one found] bunches of grapes, garlands of corn, jugs of wine or oil, or fine flour or anything the like of which is offered on the altar — it is forbidden.

T. 6:10 One should not climb up to the top of a pedestal, even to disfigure it, even to defile it, as it is said, "Nothing of what is dedicated shall cleave to your hand" (Deut. 13:18).

T. 6:11 One should not say to his fellow, "Wait for me by the idol of so and so," or, "I'll wait for you by the idol of such-and-such," as it is said, "You will not make mention of the name of any other god" (Ex. 23:13).

T. 6:12 An idol and everything on it — lo, this is forbidden. [If] one found on it jugs of wine, oil, or fine flour, or anything the like of which is offered on the altar [M. A.Z. 4:2C], it is forbidden. [If he found on it] utensils which are used for it and for its body, they are forbidden. [If they are] not [used] for its body, they are permitted. Also as to utensils which are used for them and for its body, [if] priests of idolatry stole and sold them — lo, they are permitted.

T. 6:13 A. One Scripture says, "You shall not covet the silver or the gold that is on them or take it for yourself" (Deut. 7:25). And one Scripture says, "And you have seen their detestable things, their idols of wood and stone, of silver and gold, which were among them" (Deut. 29:17). How is it possible to carry out both of these verses? On them — whether its body is clothed in them or not clothed in them, they are forbidden. Among them — Those, the body of which is clothed in them, are forbidden, and those, the body of which is not clothed in them, are permitted. And also clothing in which the body [of the idol] is clothed [if] they have sold them, lo, these are permitted. A Merkolis and whatever is on it is forbidden. [If] one found on it jugs of wine, oil, or fine flour, or anything, the like of which is offered on the altar, it is forbidden. [If one found on it] coins or utensils, they are permitted.

T. 6:14 Stones which dropped away from a Merkolis, if they appeared to belong with it, they are forbidden, and if not, they are permitted [M. A.Z. 4:1C]. An Israelite who brought stones from a Merkolis — lo, they are forbidden, for they have been forbidden by the idol. A gentile who brought stones from a Merkolis — lo they are permitted, for they are in the status of an idol where worshippers have abandoned it. And a Merkolis which was ripped up from its place is permitted for benefit [for Israelites].

D. *Nullifying an Idol*

M. 4:3 An idol which had a garden or a bathhouse — they derive benefit from them [when it is] not to the advantage [of the temple], but they do not derive benefit from them [when it is] to the advantage [of the temple]. If it belonged both to the idol and to outsiders, they derive benefit from them whether or not it is to the advantage [of the temple].

T. 6:1 A cow which one fattened using vetches belonging to an idol — [or if such a cow] went down to pasture in a garden which one has manured with a manure belonging to an idol — [the field] must be left fallow. A garden which one ploughed with [a plough made of] pieces of wood of an asherah — [the field] must be left fallow. Kelilan-wool which one stamped with wood belonging to an idol — one must burn it. Others say, "One assigns to it the more stringent ruling until its appearance will return to what it was." [If] there were bagpipes belonging to an idol, one is prohibited from making a lamentation with them. If they were rented from the state, even though they were made for the use of an idol, it is permitted to make a lamentation using them. Ships belonging to an idol — it is prohibited to rent [space] in them. But if they were rented from the state, even though they were made for the use of an idol, it is permitted to rent them. Charity collectors for a temple of idolatry — it is prohibited to give anything to them. But if they were paid by the state, even though they are working for the welfare of an idol, it is permitted to give a contribution to them [cf. M. A.Z. 4:3].

T. 6:4 All places which are called by names complimentary to idolatry does one rename with euphemisms insulting to idolatry. A place which they call, "The face of god," do they call, "The face of the dog." "A spring for all" ('YN KL) do they call "A spring of a thorn" ('YN QOS) "Good fortune (GDGYA)" do they call "A mound (GLYA)." He whose coins were scattered in the direction of an idol should not bend over before it to pick them up, because it looks as if he is bowing down to an idol. But he turns his back on the idol and collects the coins [with his behind toward the idol]. And in a place in which he is not seen, it is all right [to do it the other way].

T. 6:5 A spring which flows out of an idol — one should not bend down before it and drink, because he appears to bow down before an idol. But he turns his back and drinks. And in a place in which he is not seen, it is all right.

T. 6:6 Figures which spout out water in towns — one should not place his mouth on the mouth of the figurine and drink, because it appears that he is kissing the idol. But he collects the water in his hand and drinks it.

Y. 4:3 I:1 As to bagpipes belonging to an idol, it is forbidden to sell them [to make a lamentation with them]. If they were rented from the state, even though they were made for use of an idol, it is permitted to make lamentation using them. Shops belonging to an idol's [temple} it is prohibited to rent space in them. But if they provided a rental for the state, even though they were built for the use of an idol['s temple], it is permitted to rent them. Charity collectors for a temple of idolatry — it is prohibited to give anything to them. But if they provided funds to the state, even though they are working for the welfare of an idol — it is permitted to give a contribution to them [as at M. A.Z. 4:3D].

M. 4:4 An idol belonging to a gentile is prohibited forthwith [when it is made]. And one belonging to an Israelite is prohibited only after it will have been worshipped. A gentile has the power to nullify an idol belonging either to himself or his fellow gentile. But an Israelite has not got the power to nullify an idol belonging to a gentile. He who nullifies an idol has nullified its appurtenances. [If] he nullified [only] its appurtenances, its appurtenances are permitted, but the idol itself [remains] prohibited.

T. 5:3 He who purchases metal filings from gentiles and found an idol therein takes it and tosses it away, and the rest — lo, this is permitted. An Israelite who found an idol before it has come into his domain may tell a gentile to nullify it. For a gentile has the power to nullify an idol, whether it belongs to him or to his fellow [M. A.Z. 4:4C], whether it is an idol which has been worshipped or whether it is one which has not been worshipped, whether it is inadvertent or deliberate, whether it is under constraint or willingly. But an Israelite who made an idol — it is prohibited, even though he has not worshipped it [vs. M. A.Z. 4–4B] Therefore he has not got the power to nullify it.

T. 5:4A. A gentile who made an idol — it is permitted until it has been worshipped [vs. M. A.Z. 4:4A]. Therefore he has the power to nullify it.

T. 5:5 A gentile who sold an idol to people who worship it — it is prohibited. If he sold it to people who do not worship it, it is permitted. One may lend money on the strength of it [as a pledge]. [If] a wreck fell on it, if a river swept it away, or thugs grabbed it — as in the case of the war of Joshua — if the owner is going to go looking for it, it is forbidden. If not, it is permitted.

T. 5:6 The pedestals which gentiles set up during the persecution [by Hadrian] — even though the time of persecution is over — Lo, these are forbidden. Is it possible that an idol which a gentile nullified — is it possible that it should be deemed prohibited? Scripture says, "The graven images of their gods you shall burn with fire" (Deut. 7:25). That which he treats as a god is prohibited. And that which he does not treat as a god is permitted. Is it then possible that an idol which a gentile nullified should be deemed permitted? Scripture says, The graven images of their gods . . . — Whether he treats it as a god or does not treat it as a god, it is forbidden.

T. 5:7 How does one nullify [an idol]? A gentile nullifies an idol belonging to himself or to an Israelite. But an Israelite does not nullify an idol belonging to a gentile [cf. M. A.Z. 4:4C–D].

T. 5:9 At what point is it called "set aside [for idolatrous purposes]"? Once some concrete deed has been done to it [for that purpose]

T. 5:10 What is one which has been worshipped? Any one which people worship — whether inadvertently or deliberately. What is one which has been set aside? Any which has been set aside for idolatry. But if one has said, "This ox is for idolatry," "This house is for idolatry," he has said nothing whatsoever. For there is no such thing as an act of consecration for idolatry.

M. 4:5 How does one nullify it? [If] he has cut off the tip of its ear, the tip of its nose, the tip of its finger, [if] he battered it, even though he did not break off [any part of] it, he has nullified it. [If] he spit in its face, urinated in front of it, scraped it, threw shit at it, lo, this does not constitute an act of nullification.

T. 5:8 A pedestal, the greater part of which was damaged — lo, this is permitted. One the whole of which was damaged is prohibited until one will restore it. That belonging to him is permitted, and that belonging to his fellow is prohibited. Before it has been sanctified, it is prohibited. After it has been sanctified, it is permitted.

M. 4:6 An idol, the worshippers of which have abandoned it in time of peace, is permitted. [If they abandoned it] in time of war, it is forbidden. Idol pedestals set up for kings — lo, these are permitted, since they set [images up on them only] at the time kings go by.

iii. *Libation Wine*

M. 4:8 They purchase from gentiles [the contents of] a wine press which has already been trodden out, even though [the gentile] takes [the grapes] in hand and puts them on the heap ["apple"], for it is not made into wine used for libations until it drips down into the vat. [And if wine has] dripped into the vat, what is in the cistern is prohibited, while the rest is permitted.

T. 7:1 At first they ruled, They do not gather grapes with a gentile. And they do not press grapes with an Israelite who prepares his wine in a state of uncleanness [cf. M. A.Z. 4:9C–D]. Truly they gather grapes with a gentile All the same are new and old ones: they assist him until he passes out of sight. Once he has passed out of sight, he may turn the wine into libation wine [but Israelites are not responsible for the fact].

T. 7:3 An Israelite who works with a gentile at the winepress — Lo, this one brings up the 'bread' [that is, the mass of wine-pulp] to the "apple" [the heap to be pressed], and brings down the wine from the "apple." Even though the wine flows over his hands, it is permitted. For it is not their custom to make a libation under such circumstances [M. A.Z. 4:8 A–C]. A gentile who works with an Israelite at the winepress — Lo, this one brings up the "bread" to the "apple," and brings down the "bread" from the "apple." Even though the wine flows over his hands, it is permitted. For it is not their custom to make a libation under such circumstances.

Y. 4:8 I:2 A winepress that a gentile stopped up [filling in the cracks] — [if he stopped up the vat from] the inside, [the wine] is forbidden, [and if he stopped up the vat] from the outside, it is permitted. [The basis for this distinction is that] it is not possible that there was not there a single moist drop [of wine in one of the cracks], which the gentile will touch and offer as a libation, thus rendering into libation wine whatever thereafter flows into the cistern.

M. 4:9 [Israelites] tread a wine press with a gentile [in the gentile's vat]. But they do not gather grapes with him. An Israelite who prepares [his wine] in a state of uncleanness — they do not trample or cut grapes with him. But they do take jars with him to the wine press, and they bring them with him from the wine press. A baker who prepares bread in a state of uncleanness — they do not knead or cut out dough with him. But they may take bread with him to the dealer.

M. 4:10 A gentile who is found standing beside a cistern of wine — if he had a lien on the vat, it is prohibited. [If] he had no lien on it, it is permitted. [If] he fell into the vat and climbed out, or (2) [if gentiles] measured it with a reed — or (3) [if] he flicked out a hornet with a reed, or [if] (4) he patted down the froth on the mouth of a jar — in regard to each of these there was a case let it be sold. [If] (5) he took a jar and threw it in a fit of temper into the vat — this was a case, and they declared it valid.

T. 7:4 He who weighs out grapes on a scale — even though the wine flows over his hands, it is permitted, for it is not their custom to make a libation [under such circumstances]. He who presses wine into a jar, even though the wine flows over his hands — it is permitted. For it is not their custom to make a libation under such circumstances. [If a gentile] fell into the cistern and even a single drop of wine of any amount touched him, it is forbidden [M. A.Z. 4:10D]. [If] he went down to draw the grape-skins and the grape pits out of the cistern — this was a case, and they asked sages. And they ruled, "Let the whole of it be sold to gentiles."

T. 7:5 A gentile who was bringing up grapes in baskets and barrels at the winepress, even though one has beaten them in the winepress, and the wine has spurted onto the grapes — it is permitted. For it is not their custom to make a libation under such circumstances. He who bought pressed grapes from a gentile, and found under it little holes [containing wine] — it is prohibited.

M. 4:11 He who in a condition of cleanness prepares the wine belonging to a gentile, and leaves it in his domain, in a house which is open to the public domain, in a town in which there are both gentiles and Israelites — [the wine] is permitted. [If it is] in a town in which all the residents are gentiles, [the wine] is prohibited, unless he sets up a guard. And the guard need not sit there and watch [the room all the time]. Even though he comes in and goes out, [the wine] is permitted.

T. 7:7 An Israelite who put wine into the domain of a gentile — if there is a lock or a seal on [the jug of wine], it is permitted. And if not, it is forbidden [cf. M. A.Z. 4:12A–B]. [If] one borrowed money on the strength of it from a gentile, even though there is on it a lock or a seal, it is forbidden [cf. M. A.Z. 4:12C–D]. But if the storehouse was open to the public domain, it is permitted. In a town, all the residents of which are gentiles, it is forbidden, unless one sits down and guards it [cf. M. A.Z. 4:11].

T. 7:9 An Israelite who prepared the wine of a gentile in a condition of cleanness, and put it in two courtyards or in two towns, even though [the Israelite] comes out and goes in from this courtyard to that courtyard, or from this town to that town — it is permitted. For it is in the assumption of being guarded [cf. M. A.Z. 4:11F–G]. But if it is taken for granted that [the Israelite] spends the night in some one place, it is forbidden [since the gentile may then make a libation of that which he assumes the Israelite will not see].

M. 4:12 He who prepares the wine of a gentile in a condition of cleanness and leaves it in his domain, and the latter wrote for [the Israelite a receipt, saying], "I received its price from you" — it is permitted. But if an Israelite wants then to remove the wine, and [the gentile] would not let him do so unless he paid the price of the wine — this was a case in Bet Shean, and sages declared [the wine] forbidden.

T. 7:8 An Israelite who prepared the wine of a gentile in a condition of cleanness, and the latter wrote for him a quittance, saying, "I received its price from you" [M. A.Z. 4:12A–B] ... [if the gentile will not let him remove the wine unless he paid the price of the wine — this was a case, and they came and asked R. Simeon b. Eleazar, who ruled, "Whatever was in the domain of a gentile is subject to the same law" [M. A.Z. 4:11H].

M. 5:1 A [gentile] who hires an [Israelite] worker to work with him in the preparation of libation wine — [the Israelite's] salary is forbidden. [If] he hired him to do some other kind of work, even though he said to him, "Move a jar of libation wine from one place to another," his salary is permitted. He who hires an ass to bring libation wine on it — its fee is forbidden. [If] he hired it to ride on it, even though the gentile [also] put a flagon [of libation wine] on it, its fee is permitted.

T. 7:10 A market into which an Israelite and a gentile bring wine, even though the jars are open, and the gentile is sitting nearby — it is permitted. Because it is assumed to be guarded. He who hires a worker to work with him for half a day in that [wine] which was subject to a prohibition, and half a day in that [wine] which was subject to permission, and one put all [the wine which had been prepared] in a single town — Lo, these [both] are forbidden. [If] these are kept by themselves and those are kept by themselves, the first ones are forbidden, and the second ones are permitted. [A gentile] who hires a worker to do work with him toward evening, and said to him, "Bring this flagon to that place," even though an Israelite is not permitted to do so — his wages are permitted. A person may say to his ass drivers and his workers, "Go and get yourselves some food with this denar," "Go and get yourselves some wine with this denar" and he does not scruple because of tithes, violation of the rules governing the seventh year, or the prohibition of wine used for libations. But if he had said to them, "Go and eat a loaf of bread, and you pay for it," lo, this one then must take account of the matter of tithes, produce of the seventh year, and use of libation-wine."

T. 8:1 He who pours out wine from one utensil to another [M. A.Z. 5:7H] [if he places] the spout against the lips of the jar and below — Lo, this is prohibited. The vat, ladle, and siphon of gentiles — sages prohibit. And on what account are these prohibited and those permitted? These are made for holding liquid, and those are not made for holding liquid. As to those of wood and of stone, one has to dry them off [M. A.Z. 5:1A–E]. If they were of pitch, he has to scale them.

M. 5:2 Libation wine which fell on grapes — one may rinse them off, and they are permitted. But if [the grapes] were split, they are prohibited. [If] it fell on figs or dates, if there is sufficient [libation wine absorbed] to impart a flavor [to them], they are forbidden. This is the governing principle: anything which bestows benefit through imparting a flavor is forbidden, and anything which does not bestow benefit through imparting a flavor is permitted — for example, vinegar [from libation wine] which falls on crushed beans.

M. 5:3 A gentile who with an Israelite was moving jars of wine from place to place — if [the wine] was assumed to be watched, it is permitted. If [the Israelite] informed him that he was going away [the wine is prohibited if he was gone] for a time sufficient to bore a hole [in a jug of wine] and stop it up and [for the clay] to dry.

M. 5:4 He who leaves his wine on a wagon or in a boat and went along by a shortcut, entered into a town and bathed — it is permitted. But if he informed [others] that he was going away, [the wine is prohibited if he was gone] for a time sufficient to bore a hole and sop it up and for the clay to dry. He who leaves a gentile in a store, even though he is going out and coming in all the time — it is permitted. But if he informed him that he was going away, [the wine is prohibited if he was gone] for a time sufficient to bore a hole and stop it up and for the clay to dry.

T. 7:12 He who leaves his wine in a store and went into a town, even though he remained there for a considerable time, Lo, this [wine] is permitted. But if he informed him or locked the store, it is forbidden.

T. 7:13 He who leaves his wine on a boat and entered town, even though he remained there for a considerable time, it is permitted. But if he informed him that he was going away, or if the boat cast anchor, Lo, this is forbidden [cf. M. A.Z. 5:4A–C].

M. 5:5 [If an Israelite] was eating with [a gentile] at the same time, and he put a flagon [of wine] on the table and a flagon on a side table, and he left it and went out — what is on the table is forbidden. But what is on the side table is permitted. And if he had said to him, "You mix and drink [wine]," even that which is on the side table is forbidden. Jars which are open are forbidden. And those which are sealed [are forbidden if he was gone] for a time sufficient to bore a hole and stop it up and for the clay to dry.

T. 7:14 He who sends a jug of wine with a Samaritan, or one of juice, vinegar, brine, oil, or honey, with a gentile — if he recognizes his seal, which stopped it up, it is permitted. And if not, it is forbidden. Wine with a gentile which is sealed is forbidden on the count of libation-wine. But as to juice, brine, oil, and honey, if he saw a gentile who offered them up as a libation, they are forbidden. If not, they are permitted.

T. 7:15 An Israelite who is suspect — they drink from his wine-cellar, but they do not drink from his flask. If he was suspect of [opening the jars and] sealing them, even wine from his wine-cellar is prohibited.

M. 5:6 A band of gentile [raiders] which entered a town in peace-time — open jars are forbidden, closed ones, permitted. [If it was] wartime, these and those are permitted. because there is no time for making a libation.

M. 5:7 Israelite craftsmen, to whom a gentile sent a jar of libation wine as their salary, are permitted to say to him, "Give us its value." But if it has already entered their possession, it is prohibited. He who sells his wine to a gentile [and] agreed on a price before he had measured it out — proceeds paid for it are permitted. [If] he had measured it out before he had fixed its price, proceeds paid for it are prohibited. [If] he took the funnel and measured it out into the flask of the gentile and then went and measured wine into the flask of an Israelite, if there remained [in the funnel] a drop of wine [from what had been poured into the gentile's flask, then what is in the Israelite's flask] is forbidden. He who pours [wine] from one utensil to another — that from which is emptied [the wine] is permitted. But that into which he emptied [the wine] is forbidden.

T. 7:16 A gentile who owed [money] to an Israelite, even though he sold libation-wine and brought him the proceeds, [or sold] an idol and brought him the proceeds, it is permitted [cf. M. A.Z. 5:7A]. But if not [that is, the gentile did not sell the wine or idol, but delivered the wine or idol to him directly], it is forbidden. But if he said to him, "Wait until I sell my libation-wine [or my] idol and I'll bring you the proceeds," it is forbidden.

T. 7:17 He who makes an agreement to sell wine to a gentile, and agreed on the price and measured out the wine — even though he is going to dry out the siphons and the measures, it is permitted [cf. M. A.Z. 5:7 C–D]. And a storekeeper, one way or the other, is permitted, for each drop as it comes becomes an obligation upon [the gentile] [M. A.Z. 5:7C–D]. A gentile who sent a flagon to an Israelite, and a drop of wine is in it — Lo, this one fills up the flagon and takes from him the value of the whole of it and does not scruple [about libation-wine which may be in it].

M. 5:8 Libation wine is forbidden and imparts a prohibition [to wine with which it is mixed] in any measure at all. [If it is] wine [poured] into wine, or [libation] water [poured] into water, in any quantity whatever [it is forbidden]. [If it is] wine [poured] into water or water [poured] into wine, [it is forbidden] if it imparts flavor. This is the governing principle: [If it is] one species [poured] into its own species [B], [it is forbidden] in any measure at all. [If it is] not [poured] into its own species [C], it is forbidden if it imparts flavor.

M. 5:9 These are forbidden and impose a prohibition in any measure at all: (1) libation wine, (2) an idol, (3) hides with a hole at the heart, (4) an ox which is to be stoned, (5) a heifer, the neck of which is to be broken, (6) birds belonging to a *mesora'*, (7) the hair cut off a Nazir (Num. 6:18), (8) the [unredeemed] firstborn of an ass (Ex. 13:13), (9) meat in milk, (10) the goat which is to be sent forth, (11) unconsecrated beasts which have been slaughtered in the Temple courtyard — lo, these are forbidden and impose a prohibition in any measure at all.

M. 5:10 Libation wine that fell into a vat — the whole of [the vat] is forbidden for benefit.

M. 5:11 A stone wine press which a gentile covered with pitch — one scours it, and it is clean. And one of wood — let him scale off the pitch. And one of earthenware — even though one has scaled off the pitch, lo, this is forbidden.

M. 5:12 He who purchases utensils [for use with food] from a gentile — that which is usually immersed one must immerse. That which is usually scalded one must scald. That which is usually heated to a white-hot flame one must heat to a white-hot flame. A spit or gridiron one must heat to a white-hot flame. A knife one must polish, and it is clean.

T. 8:2 He who purchases utensils from gentiles [M. A.Z. 5:12A] — in the case of things which one knows have not been used, one immerses them and they are clean. In the case of things which one knows have been used, in the instance of cups and flasks, one rinses them in cold water [M. A.Z. 5:12B]. [If they were] pitchers, water-kettles, frying pans, or kettles, one rinses them in boiling water [M. A.Z. 5:12C]. In the case of knives, spits, and grid-irons, one heats them to a white heat, and they are clean [M. A.Z. 5:12D]. In the case of all of them which have been used before they have been polished, if one has scalded, immersed, or heated them to white heat, (and) lo, this is permitted.

T. 8:3 He whose wine-vats and olive-presses were unclean and who wants to clean them — the boards and the two posts supporting the beams of the press and the troughs does he dry, and they are clean. The cylinders of twigs and of hemp does he dry. As to those of bast and of reeds, he leaves them unused.

II. Analysis: The Problematics of the Topic, Abodah Zarah

While the Written Torah concerns itself with the disposition of idolatry — destroying idols and tearing down altars and the like — the Oral Torah has taken as its problem the relationship of the Israelite to the gentile, who is assumed to practice idolatry. And, as I shall suggest in a moment, the Oral Torah takes as the problematics of the halakhah the way in which the Israelite can interact with the idol-worshipping gentile in such a manner as to be uncorrupted by his idolatry. So the treatment of the halakhah of Abodah Zarah not only shifts the focus but vastly broadens the treatment of it, providing a handbook for the conduct of foreign relations between Israel and the gentiles. (In this regard Bavli-tractate Abodah-Zarah commences with a massive and compelling essay on how Israel and the gentiles relate and why God has rejected the gentiles in favor of Israel, the Torah supplying the center of the discussion.)[1] The relationship between the two components of the Torah may be simply stated: the Written Torah provides instruction on destroying idolatry, in the premise that Israel has the opportunity to do so. The halakhah of the Oral Torah explains how to co-exist with idolatry, recognizing that Israel has no choice but to do so.

How, exactly, is the Israelite supposed to live in a world dominated by idolatry, and how is Israel subjugated to pagan nations to conduct its life with God? The question is not one that concerns the morale of holy Israel, let alone its theological apologetics. Rather, at issue is the conduct of everyday life — a fine instance of what I mean when I claim that the halakhah takes up issues of the interiority of Israel's life, the inner structure and architectonics of its everyday life. In the present case, the problematics finds its definition in

---

[1] *The Theology of the Oral Torah: Revealing the Justice of God.* Kingston and Montreal, 1998: McGill and Queens University Press spells out the larger theory of Israelite/gentile relationships as defined by the Torah. But it is not mainly a halakhic exposition, though it is easy to see how the halakhah embodies the theology set forth in the aggadah addressed in that work. In the next section I return to this matter.

differentiating what is absolutely forbidden for all purposes, what is forbidden for Israelite use but permitted for Israelite trade, and what is wholly permitted for both trade and utilization. The problematics of the tractate focuses upon commercial transactions; personal relationships are not at the center of the exposition and do not precipitate the more protracted exegeses of the topic.

The tractate signals its problematics when it opens with rules on how to deal with gentiles before and after festivals. The issue bears heavy consequence, and the presentation of the halakhah accords the position of prominence to what must be deemed the most fundamental question the halakhah must address: may Israelites participate in the principal trading occasions of the life of commerce, which are permeated with idolatrous celebrations? Since the festival defined a principal occasion for holding a market, and since it was celebrated with idolatrous rites, the mixture of festival and fair formed a considerable problem for the Israelite merchant. Sages, with their focus upon the householder,[2] by definition an enlandised component of the social order, identified the principal unit of (agricultural) production with the main building block of Israelite society, and they gave nothing to the Israelite traders. Indeed, they so legislated as to close off a major channel of commerce. In connection with gentile festivals, which were celebrated with fairs, Israelites — meaning, traders, commercial players of all kinds — could not enter into business relationships with gentile counterparts (let alone themselves participate); cutting off all contractual ties, lending or borrowing in any form, meant the Israelite traders in no way could participate in a principal medium of trade. That principle is announced at the outset, and, as we see, the Tosefta amplifies and supplies many details to instantiate the main point. The Mishnah's prohibition of all commercial relationships is simply repeated by the Tosefta's, "A person should not do business with a gentile on the day of his festival."

But the sages differentiate between actual commercial relationships on the occasion of festivals and fairs, on the one side, and transactions of a normal, humane character, on the other. They do not require Israelites to act out Scripture's commandments utterly to destroy idolatry; they permit them to maintain normal social amenities with their neighbors, within some broad limits. First, while the general

---

[2] See my *Soviet Views of Talmudic Judaism. Five Papers by Yu. A. Solodukho*. Leiden, 1973: Brill.

prohibition covers all gentiles on the occasion of fairs and festivals, it pertains to individuals' celebrations in a limited way. All gentiles are not subjected to a prohibition for all purposes and at all times, and that is the main principle that the extension and the amplification of the law instantiates in many concrete cases. The effect is to reshape Scripture's implacable and extreme rulings into a construction more fitting for an Israel that cannot complete the task of destroying idolatry but is not free to desist from trying.

The problematics of the halakhah encompasses, also, relationships other than commercial ones. The basic theory of gentiles, all of them assumed to be idolaters, is, first, gentiles always and everywhere and under any circumstance are going to perform an act of worship for one or another of their gods. Second, gentiles are represented as thoroughly depraved (not being regenerated by the Torah), so they will murder, fornicate, or steal any chance they get; they routinely commit bestiality, incest, and various other forbidden acts of sexual congress. Within that datum, the halakhah will be worked out, and the problematics then precipitates thought on how Israel is to protect itself in a world populated by utterly immoral persons, wholly outside of the framework of the Torah and its government. Basically, the halakhah embodies the same principle of compromise where possible but rigid conformity to the principles of the Torah under all circumstances, at whatever cost, that governed commercial transactions. Just as Israel must give up all possibility of normal trading relationships with gentiles, depriving itself of the most lucrative transactions, those involving fairs, so Israel must avoid more than routine courtesies and necessary exchanges with idolaters.

That involves the principle that one must avoid entering into situations of danger, e.g., allowing for opportunities for gentiles to carry out their natural instincts of murder, bestiality, and the like. Cattle are not to be left in their inns, a woman may not be left alone with gentiles, nor a man, the former by reason of probable fornication, the latter, murder, on the part of the gentile. Their physicians are not to be trusted, though when it comes to using them for beasts, that is all right. One also must avoid appearing to conduct oneself as if he were an idolater, even if he is not actually doing so, thus if while someone is in front of an idol, he got a splint in his foot, he should not bend over to remove it, because he looks as though he is bowing down to the idol. But if it does not look that way, he is permitted to do so. But there are objects that are assumed to be destined for idolatrous worship, and these under all circumstances are forbidden for Israelite trade. Israelites simply may not sell to gentiles anything that gentiles are likely to use, or that they explicitly say they are intending to use, for idolatry. That includes wine and the like. Whatever gentiles have used for idolatry may not be utilized afterward by Israelites, and that extends to what is left over from an offering, e.g., of meat or wine. Israelites also may not sell to gentiles anything they are going to use in an immoral way, e.g., wild animals for the arena, materials for the construction of places in which gentile immorality or injustice will occur, ornaments for an idol, and the like.

Israelites may, however, derive benefit from, that is, conduct trade in, what has not been directly used for idolatrous purposes. The appurtenances of wine, e.g., skins or tanks, may be traded, but not used for their own needs by Israelites. In the case of jars that have served for water, Israelites may use the jars and put wine into them; gentiles are not assumed to offer water to their idols, so too brine or fish-brine. Gentile milk, bread, oil, and the like, may be traded by Israelites. When it comes to milk Israelites have supervised, or honey, and the like, Israelites may purchase and eat such commodities. When gentiles never use for idolatry is acceptable.

When the halakhah comes to treat idols themselves, we find no surprises and few problems that require much subtle analysis. Idols are to be destroyed and disposed of — no surprises there. The Written Torah has provided the bulk of the halakhah, and the Oral Torah contributes only a recapitulation of the main points, with some attention to interstitial problems of merely exegetical interest. When it comes to the asherah, the Merkolis, and the nullification of an idol, the halakhah presents no surprises. Here the Oral Torah shows itself derivative of, and dependent upon, the Written, introducing no unfamiliar problems, executing no generative problematics that I can discern. When it comes to libation wine, the issue is equally unremarkable. But the details here show that same concern that we noticed in connection with trade.

That is, how is the Israelite to live side by side with the gentile-idolater in the Land? Here sages find space for the householder-farmer to conduct his enterprise, that is, gentile workers may be employed, gentile produce may be utilized. The contrast with the blanket prohibition against participating in trade-fairs proves striking; here sages find grounds for making possible a kind of joint venture that, when it comes to the trade-fair, they implacably prohibit. Thus they recognize that the gentiles do not deem as wine suitable for libation the grapes in various stages of preparation. Gentile grapes may be purchased, even those that have been trodden. Gentile workers may participate to a certain point as well. Israelite workers may accept employment with gentiles in the winepress. The basic point is not particular to wine-making; the halakhah recognizes that faithful Israelites may work with other Israelites, meaning, those who do not keep the halakhah as sages define it, subject to limitations that where there is clear violation of the law, the Israelite may not participate in that part of the venture. The halakhah generally treats the gentile as likely to perform his rites whenever he can, but also as responsive to Israelite instructions wherever it is to the gentile's advantage or Israelite supervision is firm.

III. Interpretation: Religious Principles of Abodah Zarah

Gentiles are idolaters, and Israelites worship the one, true God, who has made himself known in the Torah. In the Oral Torah, that is the difference — the only consequential distinction — between Israel and the gentiles.[3] But the halakhah takes as its religious problem the concretization of that distinction, the demonstration of where and how the distinction in theory makes a huge difference in the practice, the conduct, of everyday affairs. What is at stake is that Israel stands for life, the gentiles like their idols for death. An asherah-tree, like a corpse, conveys uncleanness to those who pass underneath it, as we noted at M. 3:8: "And he should not pass underneath it, but if he passed underneath it, he is unclean." Before proceeding, let us consider a clear statement of why idolatry defines the boundary between Israel and everybody else. The reason is that idolatry — rebellious arrogance against God — encompasses the entire Torah.

---

[3] For the formative age the halakhah does not take account of monotheism resting on Scripture, other than the Judaism of the dual Torah, hence Christianity, monotheist but not "Israel" in the way in which the dual Torah's Israel defines itself, does not form a category (or, more likely, a sub-category, e.g., of Israel or of gentiles). Nor in this period does Christianity take an interstitial position. A few episodic references to people who knew the truth but abandoned it provide whatever we have as a Rabbinic theory of Christianity for late antiquity. In terms set forth here, there is life or death, but nothing in-between.

The religious duty to avoid idolatry is primary; if one violates the religious duties, he breaks the yoke of commandments, and if he violates that single religious duty, he violates the entire Torah. Violating the prohibition against idolatry is equivalent to transgressing all Ten Commandments.

The halakhah treats gentiles as undifferentiated, but as individuals. The aggadah treats gentiles as "the nations" and takes no interest in individuals or in transactions between private persons. In the theology of the Oral Torah, the category, the gentiles or the nations, without elaborate differentiation, encompasses all who are not-Israelites, that is, who do not belong to Israel and therefore do not know and serve God. That category takes on meaning only as complement and opposite to its generative counterpart, having no standing — self-defining characteristics — on its own. That is, since Israel encompasses the sector of humanity that knows and serves God by reason of God's self-manifestation in the Torah, the gentiles are comprised by everybody else: those placed by their own intention and active decision beyond the limits of God's revelation. Guided by the Torah Israel worships God, without its illumination gentiles worship idols. At the outset, therefore, the main point registers: by "gentiles" sages understand, God's enemies, and by "Israel" sages understand, those who know God as God has made himself known, which is, through the Torah. In no way do we deal with secular categories, but with theological ones.

The halakhah then serves as the means for the translation of theological conviction into social policy. Gentiles are assumed to be ready to murder any Israelite they can get their hands on, rape any Israelite women, commit bestiality with any Israelite cow. The Oral Torah cites few cases to indicate that that conviction responds to ordinary, everyday events; the hostility to gentiles flows from a theory of idolatry, not the facts of everyday social intercourse, which, as we have seen, sages recognize is full of neighborly cordiality. Then why take for granted gentiles routinely commit the mortal sins of not merely idolatry but bestiality, fornication, and murder? That is because the halakhah takes as its task the realization of the theological principle that those who hate Israel hate God, those who hate God hate Israel, and God will ultimately vanquish Israel's enemies as his own — just as God too was redeemed from Egypt. So the theory of idolatry, involving alienation from God, accounts for the wicked conduct imputed to idolaters, without regard to whether, in fact, that is how idolaters conduct themselves. That matter of logic is stated in so many words:

> Sifré to Numbers LXXXIV:IV:
> 1. D. "... and let them that hate you flee before you:"
>   B. And do those who hate [come before] him who spoke and brought the world into being?
>   C. The purpose of the verse at hand is to say that whoever hates Israel is as if he hates him who spoke and by his word brought the world into being.

The same proposition is reworked. God can have no adversaries, but gentile enemies of Israel act as though they were his enemies:

> D. Along these same lines: "In the greatness of your majesty you overthrow your adversaries" (Ex. 15:7).
> E. And are there really adversaries before him who spoke and by his word brought the world into being? But Scripture thus indicates that whoever rose up against Israel is as if he rose up against the Omnipresent.
> F. Along these same lines: "Do not forget the clamor of your foes, the uproar of your adversaries, which goes up continually" (Ps. 74:23).
> G. "For lo, your enemies, O Lord" (Ps. 92:10).
> H. "For those who are far from you shall perish, you put an end to those who are false to you" (Ps. 73:27).
> I. "For lo, your enemies are in tumult, those who hate you have raised their heads" (Ps. 83:2). On what account? "They lay crafty plans against your people, they consult together against your protected ones" (Ps. 83:3).

Israel hates God's enemies, and Israel is hated because of its loyalty to God (a matter to which we shall return presently):

> J. "Do I not hate those who hate you, O Lord? And do I not loathe them that rise up against you? I hate them with perfect hatred, I count them my enemies" (Ps. 139:21–22).
> K. And so too Scripture says, "For whoever lays hands on you is as if he lays hands on the apple of his eye" (Zech. 2:12).
> L. R. Judah says, "What is written is not, 'the apple of an eye' but 'the apple of *his* eye,' it is as if Scripture speaks of him above, but Scripture has used an euphemism."

Now the consequences of these propositions are drawn:

> V. And whoever gives help to Israel is as if he gives help to him who spoke and by his word brought the world into being, as it is said, "Curse Meroz, says the angel of the Lord, curse bitterly its inhabitants, because they came not to the help of the Lord, to the help of the Lord against the mighty" (Judges 5:23).

W. R. Simeon b. Eleazar says, "You have no more prized part of the body than the eye and Israel has been compared to it. A further comparison: if a man is hit on his head, only his eyes feel it. Accordingly, you have no more prized part of the body than the eye, and Israel has been compared to it."

X. So Scripture says, "What, my son, what, son of my womb? what, son of my vows" (Prov. 31:2).

Y. And it says, "When I was a son with my father, tender, the only one in the sight of my mother, he taught me and said to me, 'Let your heart hold fast my words'" (Prov. 4:3–4).

The proposition announced at the outset is fully articulated — those who hate Israel hate God, those who are enemies of Israel are enemies of God, those who help Israel help God — and then systematically instantiated by facts set forth in Scripture. The systematic proof extends beyond verses of Scripture, with a catalogue of the archetypal enemies assembled: Pharaoh, Sisera, Sennacherib, Nebuchadnezzar, Haman. So the paradigm reinforces the initial allegation and repertoire of texts. The context then of all thought on Israel and the gentiles finds definition in supernatural issues and context in theology. In the Oral Torah sages at no point deem as merely secular the category, the gentiles.

Now let us see how the gentiles are characterized in this-worldly terms, as we have noted how "being Israel" is assumed to mean a given set of virtues will mark the Israelite individual. When God blesses gentile nations, they do not acknowledge him but blaspheme, but when he blesses Israel, they glorify him and bless him; these judgments elaborate the basic principle that the gentiles do not know God, and Israel does. But what emerges here is that even when the gentiles ought to recognize God's hand in their affairs, even when God blesses them, they still deny him, turning ignorance into willfulness. What is striking is the exact balance of three gentiles as against three Israelites, all of the status of world-rulers, the common cluster, Pharaoh, Sennacherib, Nebuchadnezzar, vs. the standard cluster, David, Solomon, and Daniel:

Pesiqta deRab Kahana XXVIII:I.1

A. "On the eighth day you shall have a solemn assembly. [You shall do no laborious work, but you shall offer a burnt-offering, an offering by fire, a pleasing odor to the Lord... These you shall offer to the Lord at your appointed feasts in addition to your votive-offerings and your freewill-offerings, for your burnt-offerings and for your cereal-offerings and for your drink-offerings and for your peace-offerings]" (Numbers 29:35–9):

B. But you have increased the nation, "O Lord, you have increased the nation; [you are glorified; you have enlarged all the borders of the land]" (Is. 17:25):

The proposition having been stated, the composer proceeds to amass evidence for the two contrasting propositions, first gentile rulers:

C. You gave security to the wicked Pharaoh. Did he then call you "Lord"? Was it not with blasphemies and curses that he said, "Who is the Lord, that I should listen to his voice" (Ex. 5:2)!
D. You gave security to the wicked Sennacherib. Did he then call you "Lord"? Was it not with blasphemies and curses that he said, "Who is there among all the gods of the lands." (2 Kgs. 18:35).
E. You gave security to the wicked Nebuchadnezzar. Did he then call you "Lord"? Was it not with blasphemies and curses that he said, "And who is God to save you from my power" (Dan. 3:15).

Now, nicely balanced, come Israelite counterparts:

F. "... you have increased the nation; you are glorified:"
G. You gave security to David and so he blessed you: "David blessed the Lord before all the congregation" (1 Chr. 29:10).
H. You gave security to his son, Solomon, and so he blessed you: "Blessed is the Lord who has given rest to his people Israel" (1 Kgs. 8:56).
I. You gave security to Daniel and so he blessed you: "Daniel answered and said, Blessed be the name of God" (Dan. 2:20).

Here is another set of opposites — three enemies, three saints, a fair match. In each case, the Israelite responded to God's favor with blessings, and the gentile with blasphemy. In this way the gentiles show the price they pay for not knowing God but serving no-gods instead. Like philosophers, sages in the documents of the Oral Torah appeal to a single cause to account for diverse phenomena; the same factor that explains Israel has also to account for the opposite, that is, the gentiles; what Israel has, gentiles lack, and that common point has made all the difference. Idolatry is what angers God and turns him against the gentiles, stated in so many words at b. A.Z. 1:1 I. 23/4b: "That time at which God gets angry comes when the kings put on their crowns on their heads and prostrate themselves to the sun. Forthwith the Holy One, blessed be He, grows angry." That is why it is absolutely forbidden to conduct any sort of commerce with gentiles in connection with occasions of idolatrous worship, e.g., festivals and the like.

When we come to the halakhah's treatment of the same topic, our first question must be, Why do sages define a principal category of the halakhah in this wise? It is because sages must devote a considerable account to the challenge to that justice represented by gentile power and prosperity, Israel's subordination and penury. For if the story of the moral order tells about justice that encompasses all creation, the chapter of gentile rule vastly disrupts the account. Gentile rule forms the point of tension, the source of conflict, attracting attention and demanding explanation. For the critical problematic inherent in the category, Israel, is that its anti-category, the gentiles, dominate. So what rationality of a world ordered through justice accounts for the world ruled by gentiles represents the urgent question to which the system must respond. And that explains why the systemic problematic focuses upon the question, how can justice be thought to order the world if the gentiles rule? That formulation furthermore forms the public counterpart to the private perplexity: how is it that the wicked prosper and the righteous suffer? The two challenges to the conviction of the rule of moral rationality — gentile hegemony, matched by the prosperity of wicked persons — match.

Yet here the halakhah turns out to make its own point, one that we ought not to miss. The halakhah presupposes not gentile hegemony but only gentile power; and it further takes for granted that Israelites may make choices, may specifically refrain from trading in what gentiles value in the service of their gods, and may hold back from gentiles what gentiles require for that service. In this regard the halakhah parts company from the aggadah, the picture gained by looking inward not corresponding to the outward-facing perspective. Focused upon interiorities that prove real and tangible, not matters of theological theory at all, the halakhah of Abodah Zarah legislates for a world in which Israelites, while subordinate in some ways, control their own conduct and govern their own destiny. Israelites may live in a world governed by gentiles, but they form intentions and carry them out. They may decide what to sell and what not to sell, whom to hire for what particular act of labor and to whom not to sell their own labor, and, above all, Israelite traders may determine to give up opportunities denied them by the circumstance of gentile idolatry. The halakhah therefore makes a formidable statement of Israel's freedom to make choices, its opportunity within the context of everyday life to preserve a territory free of idolatrous contamination, must as Israel in entering the Land was to create a territory free of the worship of idols and their presence. In the setting of world order Israel may find itself subject to the will of others, but in the house of Israel, Israelites can and should establish a realm for God's rule and presence, free of idolatry. And if to establish a domain for God, Israelites must practice self-abnegation, refrain from actions of considerable weight and consequence, well, much of the Torah concerns itself with what people are not supposed to do, and God's rule comes to realization in acts of restraint.

Accordingly, the religious problem of the halakhah therefore focuses on the inner world of Israel in command of itself. The religious problem of the aggadah, by contrast, explains, rationalizes as best it can, gentile hegemony such as the halakhah takes for granted gentiles simply do not exercise. The halakhah sees that world within Israel's dominion for which Israel bears responsibility; there sages legislate. The aggadah forms a perspective upon the world subject to gentile rule, that is, the world beyond the limits of Israel's own power. The halakhah speaks of Israel at the heart of matters, the aggadah, of Israel within humanity.

To see the contrast between the halakhah and the aggadah on gentiles, let me briefly reprise the aggadic account of the matter. Who, speaking categorically not historically, indeed are these "non-Israelites," called gentiles ("the nations," "the peoples," and the like)? The answer is dictated by the form of the question: who exactly is a "non-Israelite"? Then the answer concerning the signified is always relative to its signifier, Israel? Within humanity-other-than-Israel, differentiation articulates itself along gross, political lines, always in relationship to Israel. If humanity is differentiated politically, then, it is a differentiation imposed by what has happened between a differentiated portion of humanity and Israel. It is, then, that segment of humanity that under given circumstances has interacted with Israel: [1] Israel arising at the end and climax of the class of world empires, Babylonia, Media, Greece, Rome; or [2] Israel against Egypt; or [3] Israel against Canaan. That is the point at which Babylonia, Media, Greece, Rome, Egypt, or Canaan take a place in the narrative, become actors for the moment, but never givens, never enduring native categories. Then, when politics does not impose its structure of power-relationships, then humanity is divided between Israel and everyone else.

In the story of the moral plan for creation, the nations find their proportionate position in relationship to Israel. If the nations acquire importance by reason of their dealings with Israel, the monarchies that enjoy prominence benefit because they ruled Israel:

Mekhilta Attributed to R. Ishmael XX:II.5–7

5. A. "... the mind of Pharaoh and his servants was changed toward the people:"
   B. This indicates that when the Israelites went out of Egypt, the monarchy of the Egyptians came to an end,
   C. as it is said, "Who are our servants?"
6. A. "[and they said, 'What is this that we have done, that we have let Israel go] from serving us?'"
   B. "Who are our servants?"] They said, "Now all the nations of the world will be chiming in against us like a bell, saying, 'Now these, who were in their domain, they let go to leave them, how!'"
   C. "Now how are we going to send to Aram Naharim and Aram Soba officers and task-masters to bring us slave-boys and slave girls?"
   D. This indicates that Pharaoh ruled from one end of the world to the other, having governors from one end of the world to the other.
   E. This was for the sake of the honor of Israel.
   F. Of Pharaoh it is said, "The king sent and loosed him, even the ruler of peoples, and set him free" (Ps. 105:20).

We now recapitulate the matter, moving through the sequence, Assyria, then the recurring cluster of four, Babylonia, Media, Greece, and Rome, the last four standing for the world-empires to that time, the first six centuries C.E., so far as sages' memories reconstructed history:

7. A. And so you find that every nation and language that subjugated Israel ruled from one end of the world to the other, for the sake of the honor of Israel.
   B. What does Scripture say in connection with Assyria? "And my hand has found as a nest the riches of the peoples, and as one gathers lost eggs have I gathered all the earth, and there was none that moved the wing or opened the mouth or chirped" (Is. 10:14).
   C. What does Scripture say of Babylonia? "And it shall come to pass that the nation and kingdom that will not serve this same Nebuchadnezzar, king of Babylonia" (Jer. 27:8).
   D. What does Scripture say of Media? "Then king Darius wrote to all the peoples" (Dan. 6:26).
   E. What does Scripture say of Greece? "The beast had also four heads and dominion was given to it" (Dan. 7:6).
   F. What does Scripture say of the fourth kingdom [Rome]? "And shall devour the whole earth and shall tread it down and break it in pieces" (Dan. 7:23).
   G. So you learn that every nation and language that subjugated Israel ruled from one end of the world to the other, for the sake of the honor of Israel.

A nation is distinguished by its interaction with Israel, and that interaction brings about the magnification of the name of that nation. It would be difficult to express with greater power the proposition that Israel then forms the center and heart of humanity, and the gentiles circle in their orbits round about. Little in the halakhic repertoire recapitulates these convictions, which the halakhah in no way acknowledges. For the halakhah matters are very different, as we have seen.

What then is the difference between the gentile and the Israelite, individually and collectively (there being no distinction between the private person and the public, social and political entity)? A picture in cartographic form of the theological anthropology of the Oral Torah, would portray a many-colored Israel at the center of the circle, with the perimeter comprised by all-white gentiles, since, in the *halakhah*, gentiles like their idols, as we have seen, are a source of uncleanness of the same virulence as corpse-uncleanness, the perimeter would be an undifferentiated white, the color of death. The law of uncleanness bears its theological counterpart in the lore of death and resurrection, a single theology animating both. Gentile-idolaters and Israelite worshippers of the one and only God part company at death. For the moment Israelites die but rise from the grave, gentiles die and remain there. The roads intersect at the grave, each component of humanity taking its own path beyond. Israelites — meaning, those possessed of right conviction — will rise from the grave, stand in judgment, but then enter upon eternal life, to which no one else will enjoy access. So, in substance, humanity viewed whole is divided between those who get a share in the world to come — Israel — and who will stand when subject to divine judgment and those who will not.

Clearly, the moral ordering of the world encompasses all humanity. But God does not neglect the gentiles or fail to exercise dominion over them. For even now, gentiles are subject to a number of commandments or religious obligations. God cares for gentiles as for Israel, he wants gentiles as much as Israel to enter the kingdom of Heaven, and he assigns to gentiles opportunities to evince their acceptance of his rule. One of these commandments is not to curse God's name, so b. San. 7:5 I. 2/56a: "Any man who curses his God shall bear his sin" (Lev. 24:15): It would have been clear had the text simply said, "A man." Why does it specify, "Any"? It serves to encompass idolaters, who are admonished not to curse the Name, just as Israelites are so admonished. Not cursing God, even while worshipping idols, seems a minimal expectation.

But, in fact there are seven such religious obligations that apply to the children of Noah. It is not surprising — indeed, it is predictable — that the definition of the matter should find its place in the halakhah of Abodah Zarah:

> Tosefta-tractate Abodah Zarah 8:4–6
> T. 8:4A. Concerning seven religious requirements were the children of Noah admonished:
> B. setting up courts of justice, idolatry, blasphemy [cursing the Name of God], fornication, bloodshed, and thievery.

We now proceed to show how each of these religious obligations is represented as applying to gentiles as much as to Israelites:

> C. Concerning setting up courts of justice — how so [how does Scripture or reason validate the claim that gentiles are to set up courts of justice]?
> D. Just as Israelites are commanded to call into session in their towns courts of justice.
> E. Concerning idolatry and blasphemy — how so? ...
> F. Concerning fornication — how so?
> G. "On account of any form of prohibited sexual relationship on account of which an Israelite court inflicts the death-penalty, the children of Noah are subject to warning," the words of R. Meir.
> H. And sages say, "There are many prohibited relationships, on account of which an Israelite court does not inflict the death-penalty and the children of Noah are [not] warned. In regard to these forbidden relationships the nations are judged in accord with the laws governing the nations.
> I. "And you have only the prohibitions of sexual relations with a betrothed maiden alone."

The systemization of Scripture's evidence for the stated proposition continues:

> T. 8:5A. For bloodshed — how so?
> B. A gentile [who kills] a gentile and a gentile who kills an Israelite are liable. An Israelite [who kills] a gentile is exempt.
> C. Concerning thievery?
> D. [If] one has stolen, or robbed, and so too in the case of finding a beautiful captive [woman], and in similar cases:
> E. a gentile in regard to a gentile, or a gentile in regard to an Israelite — it is prohibited. And an Israelite in regard to a gentile — it is permitted.
> T. 8:6A. Concerning a limb cut from a living beast — how so?
> B. A dangling limb on a beast, [which] is not [so connected] as to bring about healing,
> C. is forbidden for use by the children of Noah, and, it goes without saying, for Israelites.
> D. But if there is [in the connecting flesh] sufficient [blood supply] to bring about healing,

E. it is permitted to Israelites, and, it goes without saying, to the children of Noah.

As in the case of Israelites, so the death penalty applies to a Noahide, so b. San. 7:5 I. 4–5/57a: "On account of violating three religious duties are children of Noah put to death: on account of adultery, murder, and blasphemy." R. Huna, R. Judah, and all the disciples of Rab say, "On account of seven commandments a son of Noah is put to death. The All-Merciful revealed that fact of one of them, and the same rule applies to all of them." But just as Israelites, educated in the Torah, are assumed to exhibit certain uniform virtues, e.g., forbearance, so gentiles, lacking that same education, are assumed to conform to a different model.

Gentiles, by reason of their condition outside of the Torah, are characterized by certain traits natural to their situation, and these are worldly. Not only so, but the sages' theology of gentiles shapes the normative law in how to relate to them. If an Israelite is by nature forbearing and forgiving, the gentile by nature is ferocious. That explains why in the halakhah as much as in the aggadah gentiles are always suspect of the cardinal sins, bestiality, fornication, and bloodshed, as well as constant idolatry. That view of matters is embodied in normative law, as we have seen. The law of the Mishnah corresponds to the lore of scriptural exegesis; the theory of the gentiles governs in both. Beyond the Torah there not only is no salvation from death, there is not even the possibility of a common decency. The Torah makes all the difference. The upshot may be stated very simply. Israel and the gentiles form the two divisions of humanity. The one will die but rise from the grave to eternal life with God. When the other dies, it perishes; that is the end. Moses said it very well: Choose life. The gentiles sustain comparison and contrast with Israel, the point of ultimate division being death for the one, eternal life for the other.

If Israel and the gentiles are deemed comparable, the gentiles do not acknowledge or know God, therefore, while they are like Israelites in sharing a common humanity by reason of mythic genealogy — deriving from Noah — the gentiles do not receive in a meritorious manner the blessings that God bestows upon them. So much for the points of stress of the aggadah. When it comes to the halakhah, as we have seen, the religious problematics focuses not upon the gentiles but upon Israel: what, given the world as it is, can Israel do in the dominion subject to Israel's own will and intention? That is the question that, as we now see, the halakhah fully answers. For the halakhah constructs, indeed defines, the interiority of an Israel sustaining God's service in a world of idolatry: life against death in the two concrete and tangible dimensions by which life is sustained: trade and the production of food, the foci of the halakhah. No wonder Israel must refrain from engaging with idolatry on days of the festivals for idols that the great fairs embody — then especially. The presentation of the halakhah commences with the single most important, comprehensive point — as usual.

GENERAL INDEX

Aaron 267
Abraham 267, 268, 316
Achan 314
Adam 315
adultery 278
Aggadah xiv, 162, 167, 231, 266-269, 271, 292, 296, 314, 319, 323, 344, 353, 354, 358
altar 37, 205, 220, 221, 301, 335, 344
 invalidity for use on the 16, 17, 35
Amalek 294
apostatize 205
asherah(-tree) 333, 334, 336, 347
Asherim 321, 322
atonement (*see also* reconciliation) 177, 187, 191, 203, 208, 229, 230, 236, 238, 261, 272, 276, 267, 285-287, 291, 292, 297, 300-302, 306, 309, 313, 314, 317, 320

Baal Peor 194
Baba Mesia 162
Baba Qamma 162-164, 167
Babylonia 354, 355
bailee 17, 35, 61, 101, 107, 132, 160, 170
 paid 26, 36, 40, 66, 79, 80, *83-86*, 252, 258-260, 264
 unpaid 26, 61, 63, 66, 79, 80, *83-86*, 252, 258-260, 264
bailment 36, 60-62, 79, *83-86*, 101, 104, 107, 121, 131, 132, 160, 235, 244-248, 253, 254, 256, 264
Balaam 317
banishment *see* exile
Belshazzar 295
benefit 2, 4-6, 16, 18, 37, 155, 212, 285, 323, 329, 330, 332, 336, 341, 355
bestiality 175, 327
birthright 144
blasphemy 191-193, 273, 274, 289, 352, 357
blemish 286-288, 301, 326
blessing 352
Boaz 268
bonds 251, 252, 253, 257
 – of indebtedness 180

borrowing 62, 83-86, 97, 103, 147, 151, 152, 154, 212, 245, 248, 258, 259, 260, 323, 329, 345

cattle 114, 125, 126, 130, 135, 136, 274, 275, 277, 283, 293, 326-328, 346
chattels 1, 45, 159-161, 165
circumcision 273, 274
city of refuge 211, *215-218*
cleanness 27, 183, 184, 186, 202, 218, 220, 278, 283
commandments 305-308
compensation *2-51*, 59, 61, 62, 79, 85, 164, 165, 174, 183, 213, 243, 249, 251, 252, 255, 256, 258, 270
conflagration 2, 29
consecration 175, 205, 206, 217, 219, 220, 221, 242, 251
 – for idolatry 338
court 173, 319
 court system *174-190*
covenant 196, 203, 225
creation 162, 316
criminal justice 206
crop 27, 143
crop-destroying beast 2, *21-22*, 29, 46, 49

damages 1-9, 78, 83, 91, 93, 159, 160, 164-166, 168-171, 174, 245, 258, 312
danger attested – *2-20*, 47, 49, 51, 165, 169
 public – 326
Daniel 351, 352
David 268, 310, 351, 352
Day of Atonement *see* festivals
deaf-mute 3, 14-16, 20-22, 31, 32, 165, 180, 251, 276
death penalty 15, 16, 30, 33, 173, 174, 176, 183, *190-206*, 208, 210, 214, 221, 227, 228, 230, 231, 238, 261, 272, 275, 299, 305, 312, 315, 319
 burning 192, 199, 200, 261
 decapitation 192, 199, 200
 stoning 175, 176, 190, 192, 193, 196, 198, 200, 204, 205, 208, 228, 261, 314, 334

strangulation 192, 200-203
Divine Name 203, 221, 242

Eden 167-172, 317
elder *see* firstborn
Elijah
   until – comes 54, 59, 62
employee *see* worker
employer 52, *75-77, 96,* 104
Encyclopedic account
Epicureans 203
eschatology 316
eunuch 185, 196
exile 171, 173, 177, 184, 208-210, 211, *214-218,* 225, 226, 309, 318, 319
   exilic communities 175
extirpation 272-276, 289-291, 297, 299, 307, 319

festivals 184, 220, 223, 324, 345
   Day of Atonement 12, 24, 31, 219, 237, 238, 245, 273, 279, 287, 291, 297, 299, 308, 309
   Passover 35, 88, 134, 219, 220, 221, 273
   Pentecost 134
   Tabernacles 88, 113, 134
fire 2, 3, 10, 11, *22-23,* 41, 46, 49
firstborn 144, 147
flogging 173, 174, 183-185, 202, 203, 208-212, *218-226,* 240-242, 253, 261, 274, 275, 280, 289, 299, 335
fraud 65-67, 102

gentiles (*see also* the nations) 14, 15, 34, 38, 61, 71, 72, 82, 89, 139, 180, 195, 200, 242, 268-270, 274, 316, 317, *321-359*
   –' fair 325
   – woman 327, 328
gift 141, 142, 147, 148, 157, 158
God
   –'s justice 207, 227, 228, 230, 231
   –'s mercy 207, 227, 228, 230, 231, 233, 234
   as Creator 227, 228, 231, 233
   names of – 246
   penalties by – 290, 299
Greece 354, 355
guardian 15, 16, 143
guilt
   collective – 319

Hadrian 337
Halakhah 156-159, 161, 162, 165-168, 170-173, 206-211, 227-233, 235, 260, 262, 265, 266-272, 290-292, 296-298, 300, 302, 312, 313, 317, 319, 321-323, 344, 346-349, 352-354, 356, 358, 359
Haman 351
heirs 141, 142, 146, 204, 257
   Abraham's – 265
holy days *see* festivals
holy objects 293
Holy of Holies 237
   Chamber of – 296
Holy Things 205, 219, 223, 235, 237, 238, 262, 273, 277, 279, 283
   Lesser – 220
   Most – 220
homocide *see* murder

idolatry 191-195, 220, 229, 262, 272, 302, 303, 306, 307, 309, 313, 315-318, 321-323, 326, 328-330, *333-338,* 344-349, 353, 354, 357-359
   idols 198, 201, 202, 223, 342, 343
   idolaters 230
incest 315, 346
income   loss of 29-31, 47
indignity 29-32, 47
inheritance 69, 110, 114, 120, *138-150,* 156-158, 160, 172, 211
   – of the land 203
injured party 1, 10
   domain of 4
injury 3, 8-10, 17, 23, 28, 30-33, 47, 48, 165, 168, 169, 221, 224, 245, 249, 255, 258
insane person 3, 14-16, 20-22, 31, 32, 165, 180, 251, 276
intentionality *293-298*
intercalation
   – of the year 174, 184
   – of the month 197
interest 67, 70-72, 75, 103, 180
Israel xvi, 159, 161, 162, 164, 169, 171, 172, 201, 207, 228, 232, 234, 265, 266, 268, 269, 299, 302, 315, 316, 321, 344, 346, 351, 352, 354, 355
   holy Israel 163, 230, 321
   the Land Israel 151, 165, 168, 169, 171, 172, 179, 205, 207, 216, 316, 317, 321, 353

GENERAL INDEX

loss of – 318
Israelite government 173
Israelite polity 270
Israelite social order *158-161*, 167, 170, 171, 271, 299, 300, 321, 345
Israelite society 167
Israelite civil society 158, 162, 163
Israelite 71, 72, 114, 127, 158, 164, 167-169, 178, 179, 181, 186, 198, 200, 201, 203, 216-218, 228, 238, 263, 265, 266, 268, 271, 274, 294, 298, 310, 311, 322, 327, 329, 330, 335, 337, 340-342, 344, 353, 354, 356, 358
girl 139, 327, 328
workmen 324

joint holding of property *98-100*, 106, 110, 146, 155, 157
Joseph 268
Joshua 114, 176, 310, 314, 337

king 173, 176-178, 207, 238, 274, 296, 301, 302, 307, 308, 310, 313, 319, 338
usurper 329

land 27, 43, 53, 68, 76, 77, 82, 87, 90-95, 100, 111, 112, 114, 115, 118, 120, 122-124, 127, 129, 130, 135-138, 140, 143, 145, 147-149, 157, 181, 198, 325
landlord 52, *88-95*, 104, 105
Law
  of Sacrilege 3
  of Robbery 8
Levites 178, 179, 186, 215, 217, 245, 311
  levirate bond 175
  levirate marriage 177, 178
liability *2-51*, 55, 56, 58, 59, 63, 65, 72-74, 77-79, 83, 84, 86, 88, 90, 92, 97, 100, 107, 132, 134, 135, 164, 165, 169, 176, 181-183, 192-198, 200-203, 211-212, 215-217, 219-224, 237-251, 253, 254, 257-260, 274-276, 278, 280, 282, 292, 303-306, 312
lost objects *52-61*, 84, 101, 108, 245, 248, 249, 258-260, 310
lulab 241

mamzer 218, 304, 311
manure 100, 111, 115, 117, 123, 129, 192, 332, 36

marriage
  marriage-contract 149, 150, 154
  marriage settlement 33, 54, 140, 144, 146, 148, 151, 211, 212, 257
Media 354, 355
medical costs 28-31, 47
Merkolis 194, 335, 336, 347
mesora' 274, 277, 278, 280, 281, 287, 343
Messiah 172
mezuzah 89, 292, 327, 328
midwife 141
minor 3, 14, 15, 20-22, 31, 32, 38, 42, 54, 63, 143-146, 157, 165, 197, 205, 220, 222, 251, 275, 276
Miriam 293
miscarriage 19, 50, 282
Mishnah 156, 169
misrepresentation *64-67*
mixed
  – seeds 223, 240
  – species 223, 224
Molech 192, 194
monotheism 348
Moses xiv, 216, 218, 257, 293, 294, 302
movables 122, 155, 158, 175, 270
movables *125-131*
murder 173, 177, 184, 185, 188, 198, 200, 214, 215, 217, 262, 274, 285, 308, 315, 323, 346, 349, 358

Nathan 310
nations *see* gentiles
Nazirite 60, 220, 222-224, 239, 274, 277, 278, 343
Nebuchadnezzar 351, 352
Netin 218, 304, 311
Noah 267, 356, 357

oaths 235, 239, 242, *250- 259*, 262, 263, 264, *266-269*, 271
  – of adjuration 235
  – of bailment 269, 270, 278
  – of testimony 253, 256, 263, 269, 270, 278
  false – 235, *242-244*, 247, 254, *262-266*
  rash – 235, 240, 241, 253, 256, 263, 269, 270, 280, 281, 307
  vain – 241, *253, 254*, 263, 269, 270

offering 219, 220, 221, 241, 243, 253, 261, 263, 290, 292, 301, 326, 347
— of variable value 290
animal – 289
burnt – 277, 289, 298, 351
cereal – 351
drink – 351
freewill – 351
guilt – 235, 237, 247, 249, 253, 258, 260, 262, 272-275, 279, 285, 287, 288
suspensive – *282-288*, 290, 291, 307, 308
unconditional – 283, 284, 291, 307
peace – 351
sin – 236, 237, 239, *272-279*, 282-289, 292, 297, 299, 301, 307
— after childbirth 276, 280, 281, 283
votive – 351
orphans 16, 143
overcharge *64-67*
ox *2-18*, 20, 23, 25-27, 29, 31, 35, 46, 47, 49, 50, 58, 60, 82, 101, 128, 130, 169, 175, 176, 181, 255, 258-260, 285, 343

pain 28-31, 47
Passover *see* festivals
penalty 1, 7, 23, 32, 46, 206, 226, 228, 235, 237, 260, 262, 269, 290, 312
extrajudicial 173
Pentateuch (*see* Torah) 316
perjury 6, 24, 25, 32, 123, 183, 187, 210-213, 226
perjury 66, 173, 203, 209
Pharaoh 351, 352, 35
phylactery 202, 241, 242, 327, 328
pit 2, 3, *19-21*, 29, 46, 47, 49
pledge 97, 105, 175, 254, 255, 337
possession (*see also* property) 8, 34, 53, 90, 97, 107, 108, 111, 127, 128, 131, 135, 139, 141-143, 149, 160
prayer 292, 297
precedence *310-311*
priesthood 179, 181
high priest 176, 177, 193, 198, 217, 218, 224, 302, 305-311, 313, 318
priests xiv, 27, 37, 60, 130, 141, 153, 163, 173, 175, 178, 179, 186, 193, 198, 199, 201, 203, 207, 217, 218, 224, 236, 238, 245, 276, 290, 300, 301, 305, 311, 317
profanation of the Divine Name 38, 133, 191
property 1-4, 10, 34, 39, 41, 53, 82, 109, 111, 122, 124, 125, 141-143, 146, 148-150, 154-159, 161, 165, 174, 175, 179, 183, 184, 185, 205, 217, 243, 251, 254, 257, 263, 270, 325, 328
property rights *117-120*
movables *see* movables
real estate *see* real estate
prophets 113, 202, 238, 310
false – 176, 201, 202, 274, 318
proselyte 12, 15, 16, 25, 37, 66, 121, 127, 139, 276-278, 304, 311
protection 216
public domain 2, 4, 8, 9, 19, 47, 56, 60, 118, 120, 124, 125, 131, 165, 215, 303, 334, 339, 340
punishment 22, 23, 65, 173, 202, 206, 208, 211, 225, 227, 234, 238, 241, 242, 272, 290, 293, 315
extra-judicial – 208
purification 203
Python 194

R.
Aha b. Hanina 233
Aqiba 240
Azaria 267
Benaiah Eliezer b. R. Sadoq 295
Gamaliel (Rabban) 328
Hiyya 266
Huna 358
Ishmael Jonathan 233
Joshua 294
Joshua b. Hurqanos 294
Judah the Patriarch (*see also* Rabbi) Judah 55, 350, 358
Levi 266
Meir 55, 185, 232, 357
Samuel bar Nahman 233
Simeon b. Azzai 303
Simeon b. Eleazar 340, 351
Yohanan b. Zakkai (Rabban) 294
Yosé bar Hanina 233, 268
Yudan 267
Rabbi *see* R. Judah the Patriarch
rape 174, 193, 199, 245, 249, 349
real estate *87-100*, 102, 104, *110-130*,

GENERAL INDEX

122, *125-131*, 135, 143, 146, 155, 160, 172, 175, 251, 253, 270
reconciliation *see* atonement
redemption 175, 261, 289, 329
– from captivity 310
– of land 325
rental 62, *77-79*, 91, 93, 104, 109, 122, 131, 132, 153, 160, 260, 336, 337
repentance 297
ressurection 203, 227, 229, 313-317, 319
denial of – 209, 261
restitution 174
Rome 354, 355

Sabbath 11, 24, 25, 32, 33, 58, 65, 80, 113, 116, 184, 192, 195, 196, 198, 231, 237, 245, 273, 282, 297, 298, 303, 305, 316, 327
Sabbath limit 217
Sabbatical Year 97, 147, 258
Sacred Scriptures 115
sacrifice *see* offering
sacrilege 274, 287, 288
sage 61, 100, 103, 106, 140, 157, 162, 163, 165, 168, 185-187, 195-197, 199, 201, 206, 207, 210, 217, 228, 230, 231, 232, 244, 264, 265, 267, 271, 290, 295, 299, 302, 304, 310, 311, 319, 326, 339-341, 345, 347-349, 352, 357, 358
sale 55, 87, 112, *125-131*, 132, 137, 138, 152, 155, 158, 257, 337, 347, 353
Salomon 351, 352
Salt Sea 331-333
Samaritan 327, 328, 342
sanctification 127, 130, 184, 264, 290
sanctuary 14, 16, 95, 136, 221, 239, 273, 278, 279, 301, 307, 311
Sanhedrin 176, 177, 186, 187, 214, 238
scribes 202, 292
Scripture xii,1-3, 7, 20, 44, 48, 51, 58, 100, 103, 104, 106, 155-157, 161, 163, 165, 173, 185, 193, 196, 199, 205, 207-211, 214, 216, 226, 227, 236, 243, 262, 265, 267, 270, 280, 293, 294, 300, 304, 305, 309, 310, 312, 316, 317, 321-323, 335, 337, 345, 348, 350, 351, 357
scroll(s) 59, 113, 143, 178, 327, 328
– of Esther 296
sacred – 205, 206
Sennacherib 351, 352

Seventh Year 175, 179, 180, 187, 216, 223, 256, 297, 341
sexual relationships 278, 289
forbidden – 188, 192, 193 ,199, 201-203, 274-276, 278, 280, 303, 307, 346, 358
share-cropping 55, 68, *90-95*, 121, 152
Shema 296
shepherd 121
Shofar 296
sin 170, 176, 191, 204, 206-209, 226-232, 234-236, 242, 244, 245, 248, 260, 262, 265, 268, 269, 272, 273, 285, 288, 290-292, 296-301, 308, 312-317, 320
collective – 300, 302, 319
Sisera 351
slave 11, 12, 15, 20, 21, 25, 29, 31-33, 38, 42, 43, 53, 54, 66, 87, 102, 107, 120, 122, 128, 139, 141, 142, 145, 149, 152, 153, 213, 216, 217, 223, 246, 249, 251-253, 270, 328
boy – 129, 142, 325, 326
freed – 15, 16, 25, 139, 141, 143, 311, 328, 329
writ of emancipation 328, 329
girl – 128, 142
sorcerers 197
stoning *see* death penalty
Sukkah 241
synagogue 113, 143, 246, 296

Talmud 317
Temple xiv, 17, 24, 35, 89, 130, 176, 201, 203-205, 219, 220, 262, 273, 279, 298, 299, 314, 318, 343
– slaves 218
– treasury 282, 286-288
Ten Commandments 265, 266, 349
tenant 52, *88-95*, 104
theft 1, *23-27*, *33-41*, 50, 51, 52, 60-63, 66, 79, 83, 84, 101, 129, 159, 174, 245, 248, 254-256, 258, 259, 274, 346, 357
tithes 65, 66, 68, 81-83, 143, 175, 197, 205, 206, 216, 219, 297, 298, 341
first tithe 219
second tithe 219, 220
Torah xv, 19, 80-84, 103, 105, 108, 113, 139, 140, 143, 147, 156, 158, 163-165, 167, 169-172, 178, 185, 195, 196, 198, 200-203, 224, 228-230, 232,

234, 235, 237, 238, 243-245, 247, 254, 255, 258, 261, 266, 273-277, 282, 291, 295-297, 303, 305, 306, 312, 316, 318, 321, 346, 348, 354, 356, 358
    Oral Torah xi, xvi, 1, 44, 48, 51, 156, 158, 161, 162, 168, 173, 210, 262, 266, 267, 296, 302, 314, 317, 318, 321-323, 344, 347-349, 351, 352
    Written Torah xi, xii, xvi, 44, 48, 106, 163, 168, 173, 174, 207, 210, 235, 272, 300, 316, 317, 322, 344, 347
    Torah of Moses xi
    dual Torah 348
    – scroll 292
tractate
    Horayot 235, 300, 312, 313, 319, 320
    Keritot 235, 272, 290, 291, 292, 296, 297, 298, 300, 317, 319, 320
    Makkot 173, 209, 210, 227-230, 232-235, 261, 262, 272, 290, 291, 299, 300, 317, 320
    Sanhedrin 173, 206, 226-230, 232-235, 261, 262, 272, 290, 291, 299, 300, 317, 320
    Shabbat 292 Shebuot 235, 261, 264, 270, 271, 290, 291, 299, 300, 317

uncleanness 183, 184, 186, 202, 203, 218, 219, 222-224, 236, 237, 240, 273, 274, 278, 279, 282, 283, 297, 325, 330, 331, 333, 338, 339, 348
    corpse uncleanness 60, 225, 308, 309, 356
        imparting – to the sanctuary 235, 237, 238, 262, 274, 280, 281, 289, 307, 309
usucaption 120-124, 155, 157
usufruct 121-123, 141, 143, 146
usury 52, *67-75*, 102-104, 107, 108, 147, 160, 256
Uzziah 293

wages *95-98*
wills 110, *138-150*, 156, 160, 172
wine
    libation – *338-344*
witnesses 3, 6, 7, 25, 33, 53, 55, 71, 75, 84, 96, 122, 123, 142, 143, 149, 150, 151, 153, 154, 173, 179-183, 187-191, 195, 196, 202, 204, 211-215, 226, 241-244, 246, 248, 250, 251, 255, 257-259, 262, 264, 274, 279, 281
    false – 201, 202, 213, 274
    –; refusal to give evidence 280, 281, 307
women 21, 25, 31, 33, 42, 43, 54, 61, 65, 78, 83, 120, 121, 125, 146, 151, 152, 168, 169, 175, 178, 198, 204, 205, 211, 216-28, 222, 241, 245, 247, 253, 257, 263, 269, 273, 276, 277, 346
    daughters 145, 197
    mother 156
    possession by – 16
    testimony by – 242, 270
    virgin 308 wife 135, 138, 140, 144, 147, 148, 150, 154, 177, 178, 212, 248
    widow 308
worker 9, 22, 43, 52, 69, *75-77*, *80-83*, 95, 104, 113, 114, 160, 172, 255, 341
world to come 171, 172, 187, 191, 203, 204, 209, 227, 228, 230, 232, 233, 297, 299, *313-315*, 317, 320, 356, 358
    loss of – 312
writ of debt *150-154*, 157
    of divorce 152

Zab
    female – 277
    male – 277
Zadok 310
zealots 203

INDEX OF TEXTUAL REFERENCES

1. *Hebrew Bible*

Genesis
3:11-13   168
6:3   204
9:6   196
11:8   204
13:13   204
17:14   273
20:7   34
22:15   265

Exodus
7:15ff   102
12:9   219
12:19   273
12:46   219
13:13   343
17:11   294
19:12   20
20:5   194
20:7   265
20:10   20
21:15   201
21:16   201
21:18   199
21:18-19 50
21:20   33
21:22   31, 32
21:22-25 50
21:26-27 32
21:28   16
21:28-32 50
21:31   15
21:32   15
21:33   2, 49
21:35   14, 174
21:35-36 2, 49
21:37   174
22:1   23, 198
22:1-3   50
22:3   174, 198
22:4   2
22:5   2, 33, 49
22:6   49
22:7   20, 50, 64
22:9   83
22:10   256
22:10-11 255
22:13   85
22:14   85
22:15-16 174
22:20   66
22:25   67, 75
22:25-27 105
23:4   20
23:4   60
23:13   194, 321, 335
23:24   321
23:34-35 60
23:51   20
29:38-46 xi
30-32   273
30:23-33 273
31:14   196, 273

Leviticus
1:9   293
1:17   293
2:9   293
4:1-5   301
4:2-3   305
4:3   305
4:4   304
4:13   303, 304, 306
4:13-21   301
4:14   303, 304
4:22-26   301
4:22   308
4:23   307, 313
4:27   304
4:28   288, 307, 313
4:32   304, 313
5-6   235, 300
5:1   242-245, 247, 248, 250, 280, 281
5:1-5   300
5:1-6   235
5:1-13   235
5:2   237

5:4	240	21:10-12	173
5:7	289	22:3	273
5:15	247, 287	22:18-20	220
5:17	274	22:21	220
5:17-19	272	22:26	300
5:20-24	51	23:7	223
6:1	248	23:29-30	273
6:1-7	235, 236	24:10	193
6:2	244, 248	24:14	190
6:2-3	242	24:15	356
6:2ff	247, 253	24:22	183
6:5	247, 250	25:35-37	103
7:25	273	25:36	75
9:13	105	25:37	75
13-14	220, 277, 278	27:10	220, 221, 242
13:21	300		
15	277	Numbers	
16:17	309	4:7	202
16:21	238	6:6	224
17:9	273	6:18	343
17:14	273	9:13	273
18	280	11:16	176
18:6-7	192	14:27	176
18:6ff	273	14:37	204
18:17	199	15:22-26	300
18:21	273	15:22-29	302
19:4	75	15:24	304
19:5	293	15:27	307, 313
19:6-8	273	15:29	274
19:7-8	273	15:30	273, 305
19:13	96	15:31	273
19:15	182	19:20	273
19:16	181	25:8	203
19:19	20, 223	25:11	203
19:23-26	175	25:13	216
19:24	83	27:8	139
19:27	221	27:8-11	156
19:28	221	29:11	237
19:31	194	35:9ff	177
19:35-36	156	35:14	216
20:6	273	35:24,25	176
20:11	192	35:25	217
20:12	193	35:26	217
20:13	193	35:30	173
20:14	199	35:31	184
20:15	175	35:33	286
20:15-16	193		
20:16	175	Deuteronomy	
20:27	194	5:14	20
21:1	224	6:14	325
21:9	199	7:5	321
21:10	177	7:25	335, 337
		7:25-26	322

INDEX OF TEXTUAL REFERENCES

7:26	327, 333	24:10-13	105
12:2-3	322	24:11	97
12:2-4	221	24:14	96
13:2	310	24:14-15	105
13:12-18	173	24:15	96
13:12ff	176	24:17-18	105
13:14	204, 205	24:27	97
13:15	205	25:1-2	185
13:17	205	25:2	221, 224
13:18	206, 332, 335	25:2-3	174, 224, 225
14:22-26	175	25:13ff	156
16:18-20	173	25:4	20
17:6	213	25:7-9	175, 177
17:6-7	173	25:16	133
17:7	191	28:58ff	225
17:8	201, 304	29:9	225
17:8-13	173	29:17	335
17:12	201	30:20	295
17:14-20	173	32:28-29	174
17:15	179		
17:16	178	Joshua	
17:17	178, 191	7:19	230, 314
17:19	178	7:25	230, 314
18-19	202	20:7	216
18:1	195		
18:11	221	Judges	
18:20	176	6:1-7:8	249
19:3	217		
19:4	184, 218	2 Samuel	
19:5	215	20:3	178
19:15-21	210		
19:19	7, 25, 123	1 Kings	
21:4	296	1:33	133
21:18	197	1:33-34	310
21:18-21	173	6:17	136
21:20	197	8:13	204
21:22-23	173		
21:23	191	Isaiah	
22:1	59	30:20	202
22:1-3	58	60:21	203
22:1-4	101	66:24	204
22:3	20		
22:9	223	Ezekiel	
22:10	20, 223	7:22	295
22:11	223		
23:1-3	210	Zechariah	
23:20-21	103	3:8	310
23:23-24	195	5:3	256
23:25-26	104	Psalms	
24:6	97, 98, 105	49:14	204
24:7	201	50:10	293
24:10-11	97	50:11	293
		50:12	293
		50:13	293
		78:38	225

Job			3:18	295
1:8	294		4:22	295
13:15	294		7:3	295
27:5	294		7:26	296
27:16-17	72		11:13	181
27:17	38		23:20	197
Proverbs			Daniel	
3:15	311		5:30	295
3:17	295			

2. Rabbinic Literature

a. *Mishnah*

Ber.
2:1 A-C   296
4:4   296
4:5 A-C   296
5:1 A-E   296

B.Q.
8:7   312

R.H.
3:7 D-J   296
3:8   294

San.
1:5   318
2:1ff   173
4:5   2446
6:2   227, 230, 314
6:5   232
9:4   298
9:7   257
10:1   227
11:4   318

Shab.
11:6J-K   292

Sot.
5:5   294

Tem.
3:3   287
4:1   288

Ter.
2:3   297
3:8   298

Yoma
8:9   297

b. *Tosefta*

A.Z.
8:4-6   357

Bik.
2:15   292

Mak.
1:4-5   32

Peah
1:4   295

Shab.
2:17-18   297

c. *Yerushalmi*

B.M.
2:4 I.2   294

d. *Bavli*

A.Z.
1:1 I.23/4b   352

Men.
13:11 I.2/110a 293

Ned.
8:3-4 II8-9/62a 295

San.
4:5 VI.1/39b   232
7:5 I.2/56a   356
7:5 I.4-5/57a 358
11   317

e. *Halakhic Midrashim*

Genesis Rabbah
XII:XV.1   231

Leviticus Rabbah
XXXIV:V   266
X:1-III.1   267

Mekhilta Attributed to R. Ishmael
XX:II.5-7   355

Pesiqta deRab Kahana
XXVIII:I.1   351

Ruth Rabbah
LXXII:iii.1   268

Sifré to Numbers
LXXXIV:IV   350
XCIX:II.2   293

Sifré to Deuteronomy
CCCVI:XXII.1 295

Song of Songs Rabbah
XXIV:ii.1   268

WITHDRAWN